CRITICAL SURVEY OF
Poetry
Fourth Edition

European Poets

CRITICAL SURVEY OF
Poetry
Fourth Edition

European Poets

Volume 3
Jacques Prévert—Stefan Zweig
Resources
Indexes

Editor, Fourth Edition
Rosemary M. Canfield Reisman
Charleston Southern University

SALEM PRESS
Pasadena, California
Hackensack, New Jersey

Editor in Chief: Dawn P. Dawson

Editorial Director: Christina J. Moose

Development Editor: Tracy Irons-Georges

Project Editor: Rowena Wildin

Manuscript Editor: Desiree Dreeuws

Acquisitions Editor: Mark Rehn

Editorial Assistant: Brett S. Weisberg

Research Supervisor: Jeffry Jensen

Research Assistant: Keli Trousdale

Production Editor: Andrea E. Miller

Page Design: James Hutson

Layout: Mary Overell

Photo Editor: Cynthia Breslin Beres

Cover photo: Breyten Breytenbach (Ulf Andersen/Getty Images)

Some of the essays in this work, which have been updated, originally appeared in the following Salem Press publications, *Critical Survey of Poetry, English Language Series* (1983), *Critical Survey of Poetry: Foreign Language Series* (1984), *Critical Survey of Poetry, Supplement* (1987), *Critical Survey of Poetry, English Language Series, Revised Edition*, (1992; preceding volumes edited by Frank N. Magill), *Critical Survey of Poetry, Second Revised Edition* (2003; edited by Philip K. Jason).

∞ The paper used in these volumes conforms to the American National Standard for Permanence of Paper for Printed Library Materials, X39.48-1992 (R1997).

Library of Congress Cataloging-in-Publication Data

Critical survey of poetry. — 4th ed. / editor, Rosemary M. Canfield Reisman.

    v. cm.

Includes bibliographical references and index.

    ISBN 978-1-58765-582-1 (set : alk. paper) — ISBN 978-1-58765-756-6 (set : European poets : alk. paper) — ISBN 978-1-58765-757-3 (v. 1 : European poets : alk. paper) — ISBN 978-1-58765-758-0 (v. 2 : European poets : alk. paper) — ISBN 978-1-58765-759-7 (v. 3 : European poets : alk. paper)

1. Poetry—History and criticism—Dictionaries. 2. Poetry—Bio-bibliography. 3. Poets—Biography—Dictionaries. I. Reisman, Rosemary M. Canfield.

    PN1021.C7 2011

    809.1'003--dc22

2010045095

First Printing

PRINTED IN THE UNITED STATES OF AMERICA

CONTENTS

COMPLETE LIST OF CONTENTS

Volume 1

VOLUME 2

Contents

VOLUME 3

Contents

RESOURCES

INDEXES

PRONUNCIATION KEY

To help users of the *Critical Survey of Poetry* pronounce unfamiliar names of profiled poets correctly, phonetic spellings using the character symbols listed below appear in parentheses immediately after the first mention of the poet's name in the narrative text. Stressed syllables are indicated in capital letters, and syllables are separated by hyphens.

VOWEL SOUNDS

Symbol	Spelled (Pronounced)
a	answer (AN-suhr), laugh (laf), sample (SAM-puhl), that (that)
ah	father (FAH-thur), hospital (HAHS-pih-tuhl)
aw	awful (AW-fuhl), caught (kawt)
ay	blaze (blayz), fade (fayd), waiter (WAYT-ur), weigh (way)
eh	bed (behd), head (hehd), said (sehd)
ee	believe (bee-LEEV), cedar (SEE-dur), leader (LEED-ur), liter (LEE-tur)
ew	boot (bewt), lose (lewz)
i	buy (bi), height (hit), lie (li), surprise (sur-PRIZ)
ih	bitter (BIH-tur), pill (pihl)
o	cotton (KO-tuhn), hot (hot)
oh	below (bee-LOH), coat (koht), note (noht), wholesome (HOHL-suhm)
oo	good (good), look (look)
ow	couch (kowch), how (how)
oy	boy (boy), coin (koyn)
uh	about (uh-BOWT), butter (BUH-tuhr), enough (ee-NUHF), other (UH-thur)

CONSONANT SOUNDS

Symbol	Spelled (Pronounced)
ch	beach (beech), chimp (chihmp)
g	beg (behg), disguise (dihs-GIZ), get (geht)
j	digit (DIH-juht), edge (ehj), jet (jeht)
k	cat (kat), kitten (KIH-tuhn), hex (hehks)
s	cellar (SEHL-ur), save (sayv), scent (sehnt)
sh	champagne (sham-PAYN), issue (IH-shew), shop (shop)
ur	birth (burth), disturb (dihs-TURB), earth (urth), letter (LEH-tur)
y	useful (YEWS-fuhl), young (yuhng)
z	business (BIHZ-nehs), zest (zehst)
zh	vision (VIH-zhuhn)

CRITICAL SURVEY OF

Poetry

Fourth Edition

European Poets

JACQUES PRÉVERT

Born: Neuilly-sur-Seine, France; February 4, 1900
Died: Omonville-la-Petite, France; April 11, 1977

PRINCIPAL POETRY

Paroles, 1945
Histoires, 1946 (with André Verdet)
Poèmes, 1946
Contes pour enfants pas sages, 1947
La Pluie et le beau temps, 1955
Selections from "Paroles," 1958 (Lawrence
      Ferlinghetti, translator)
Carmina burana, 1965 (translation)
Fatras, 1966
Prévert, 1967
Arbres, 1976
Words for All Seasons, 1979
Soleil de nuit, 1980
*Blood and Feathers: Selected Poems of Jacques
      Prévert*, 1988 (includes selections from *Paroles*,
      Spectacle, *Soleil de nuit*, and more)

OTHER LITERARY FORMS

Outside France, Jacques Prévert (pray-VEHR) is best
known as a screenwriter; among his credits are a number of films that have become classics of the French
cinema. His first screenplay was written for his brother,
Pierre Prévert, the director of *L'Affaire est dans le sac*
(1932). The success of his dialogue in Jean Renoir's *Le
Crime de Monsieur Lange* (1935) led to more such
scripts, marked by Prévert's sparkling wit and poetic
repartee. His long collaboration with director Marcel
Carné produced eight major films by 1950, including
such masterpieces as *Jenny* (1936), *Drôle de drame*
(1937), and *Les Enfants du paradis* (1945; *Children of
Paradise*, 1968). Many film historians credit Carné's
success to Prévert's scripts, although it must be pointed
out that the highly successful *Le Jour se lève* (1939)
was simply adapted by Prévert from an existing script,
and that Prévert also adapted the unsuccessful 1956
version of *Notre Dame de Paris*. Carné regards Prévert
as "the one and only poet of the French cinema," one
whose contribution "reflects the soul of the people."

Prévert's cabaret-style songs and stage pieces for
the group Octobre are often overlooked in his oeuvre.
Although they predate his major film successes and
seem minor in comparison, these verses contain the
seeds of both Prévert's screen dialogue and his later poetry. Most screenwriters of Prévert's time came to the
new art burdened with preconceptions from the theater
or literature, but Prévert simply wrote scenarios that
he thought would appeal to moviegoers, and he succeeded. Many of his scripts have been published and
today provide texts for students writing screenplays

Prévert also produced several charming books for
children, including *Le Petit Lion* (1947; the little lion)
and *Des bêtes . . .* (1950; the beasts . . .). In 1953, he
wrote lyrics for Christiane Verger's *Tour de chant* and
L'Opéra de la lune. His translation into French of the
medieval *Carmina burana*, set to the music of Carl
Orff, was published in 1965 and achieved high critical
esteem. In the United States, Prévert is known as the
lyricist of such popular songs as "Les Feuilles mortes"
("Autumn Leaves") and "Ne me quitte pas" ("Don't
Leave Me").

ACHIEVEMENTS

Despite his sweeping success, Jacques Prévert received no major literary awards. For his work as a film-
maker, he received the Grand Prix from Société des
Auteurs et Compositeurs Dramatiques in 1973 and the
Grand Prix National from *Cinéma* in 1975.

The appellation "the most popular poet" (in this
case, of postwar France) carries a stigma in the world of
poetry, where popularity is not usually a mark of quality. The French writer Guy Jacob good-naturedly referred to Prévert's "easy-going muse," who had "lent
him in place of a lyre a barrel-organ." His apparent simplicity of expression, his concern with the emotions and
things of everyday life, and his singsong rhythms and
insistent rhymes combined to create a poetry at once
accessible and self-explanatory. Prévert restored the
popular validity of poetry to a literature that had been
rarefied and intellectualized by movements such as
Surrealism, Dadaism, and Symbolism. He refused to
permit poetry to remain the means of expression of the
privileged, helping himself freely to the argot of the
streets for his verses.

Free of allegiance to any literary clique, Prévert reinforced the very idea of individuality at a time when the historical and political developments of World War II had necessitated conformity. A Marxist without theoretical pretensions and an anarchist at heart, he mocked pomposity and unmasked exploitation wherever he found them, all the while maintaining an aloof attitude toward partisan politics. His poetry demonstrates the charm, wit, and humanistic goals of popular poetry as well as its limitations.

BIOGRAPHY

The son of working-class parents, Jacques Prévert was born February 4, 1900, in Neuilly-sur-Seine. At the age of fifteen, having completed his primary education—a process he obviously did not enjoy—he left school and began to earn his living. He once, in a radio interview, confessed that, had the label "juvenile delinquent" been part of the vocabulary of the early twentieth century, it would have been applied to him.

Despite his distaste for school, Prévert read a great deal and was particularly interested in the authors of the

Jacques Prévert

Enlightenment and their ideas about the natural rights of humankind, as well as such distinctions as natural evil as opposed to human evil. Nevertheless, he quickly developed a distrust of great intellectual constructs and philosophical debate. His friendship with the Surrealist painter Yves Tanguy began in the regiment in which they both served in 1920, as part of the occupation army of Thessaloníki, Greece. There he also made the acquaintance of Marcel Duhamel, who would later become a film director. The three young men went to Paris upon their demobilization and established what they jokingly called a phalanstery (after the Fourierist communes known by that name) in the no longer extant rue de Château. Raymond Queneau, who thirty years later would write critical works on Prévert, soon joined them, and their house became a gathering point for the young writers and artists of the Surrealist movement.

A shared passion for the cinema prompted them to attend films daily, sometimes three or four in a single day. Prévert and his friends, including his brother, Pierre, later attested the significant impact of these cinematic experiences upon their later work. Prévert fondly recalled long walks in the middle of the night through the streets of Paris, from which he returned to the rue de Château full of life and impatient with the intellectual turmoil of the Surrealists. His disdainful attitude toward the dogmatism of the movement ultimately led to his being excluded by its leader, André Breton.

Prévert circulated his poems in handwritten form, a habit that led to the existence of numerous textual variations. Between 1930 and 1936, three long poems appeared in reviews. "Souvenirs de famille, ou l'Ange garde-chiourme" (family souvenirs or the Martinet angel), published in *Bifur* in 1930, appealed to an extremely refined literary audience. In 1931, the magazine *Commerce* at first hesitated to publish "Tentative de description d'un diner de têtes à Paris-France" ("An Endeavor to Describe a Dinner of Heads at Paris, France"), but it conceded at the insistence of Saint-John Perse. The third poem, "La Crosse en l'air" (the crook in the air), appeared in *Soutes* in 1936, a communist tract more dedicated to politics than to literature. Such beginnings reflect the diversity of Prévert's appeal as well as his difficulty in getting his poetry published.

In 1933, with the theater group Octobre, Prévert visited Moscow to perform on the occasion of the International Olympiad of Theater. In 1938, he spent a year in the United States, returning home in time to be called up in the French mobilization in 1939. An attack of appendicitis prevented his military service in the war.

After the war, the Hungarian-born composer Joseph Kosma, who had worked on films with the Prévert-Carné team, began to set Prévert's verses to music, and the songs were every bit as popular as Prévert's volumes of poetry, which had also begun to appear after the war. Prévert carried his celebrity quite modestly and was regarded as a man of the people. He was, for example, a figure of interest for the most popular magazines in France, which celebrated him in interviews and profiles.

Other artistic inclinations found expression in Prévert's collages. He enjoyed two exhibitions, one in Paris in 1957 and one in 1963 in Antibes on the Riviera. In 1977, Prévert died after a long illness and was buried in a quiet, simple ceremony in his village of Omonville-la-Petite near the English Channel.

ANALYSIS

The poetry of Jacques Prévert is pervaded by an innocence that allows him to cultivate a world in which animals, plants, and objects speak or are metamorphosed at will. There is in his verse no development of a self-contained world of fable or faerie with symbolic weight; rather, the Surrealist influence manifests itself in vignettes or episodes within individual poems. Prévert brought an unaccustomedly cheerful mien to Surrealism, employing its devices not to frighten or to dwell on the victimization of people but to portray the imagination as an escape route from the dreariness of life's minor burdens.

In his less childlike or innocent verses, Prévert expresses outraged indignation at social and political injustice and is capable of piercing the affectations of those whom he considers unworthy of respect. There is a remarkable consistency of tone and outlook throughout Prévert's work, and whether one draws examples from early volumes or later ones, one finds an unchanging *Weltanschauung*. In part, this consistency can be attributed to Prévert's comparatively late success at a time when stylistic experiment was behind him.

POEMS ABOUT CHILDREN

From Prévert's poems about children to his antiwar utterances, there persists a naïveté that seems to challenge the values of the adult world and its rationalizations of people's inhumane acts toward others. Children, according to Prévert, are blessed with an innocence and a capacity to dream that can be corrupted only by growing up. One of his oft-cited poems, "Page d'écriture" (page of writing), from *Paroles* (words), depicts a math lesson during which a child, seeing a lyrebird fly by, asks it for help. The bird's help is forthcoming but causes something of an insurrection in the classroom before the entire scenario is metamorphosed in the final lines into a scene from nature.

In "En sortant de l'école" (upon leaving school), from *Histoires* (stories), Prévert portrays the gentle fantasies of a group of children, who, upon coming out of school, discover a train with a gilded wagon to take them through the world, where the sea promenades with all her seashells. From the same volume comes "Jour de fête" (day of the party), a heartfelt expression of the disappointment of a child who wants to celebrate a holiday dedicated to the frog, an animal that is not only a friend but that also sings to him nightly. The adults, who cannot comprehend this liaison, will not let the child go out in the rain. In the opening line, Prévert captures the parents' inhibiting concern: "Ou va-tu mon enfant avec ces fleurs/ Sous la pluie/ Il pleut il mouille/ Aujourd'hui c'est la fête à la grenouille" ("Where are you going my child with these flowers/ in the rain/ it's raining it's pouring/ Today is a holiday in honor of the frog"). The difference between the child's world and the world of adults is expressed in another way in "Arbres" (trees, from *Arbres*), in which a child understands when trees "speak tree"; only later, when he learns to speak "arboriculture," does he not understand the voice of the trees, the song of the wind. The dreamworld of the child is that of the poet. In "Dehors" (outside of), from *La Pluie et le beau temps* (rain and nice weather), Prévert describes a child who, dreaming, follows his dream smiling, for the dream is hilarious and almost alive. In "Encore une fois sur le fleuve" (along the river once more, from *Histoires*), Prévert advises: "alors fais comme moi . . ./ parle seulement des choses heureuses/ des choses merveilleuses rêvées et arrivées . . ." ("Then do as I . . ./ speak only of happy things/ of marvelous things dreamed and come to pass . . .").

ANIMALS

Some of Prévert's most charming poems are addressed, in fact, to children by way of amusing descriptions of animals. *Contes pour enfants pas sages* (tales for misbehaving children) contains a dialogue between Tom Thumb and an ostrich who rescues him; the latter complains that the child's mother sports ostrich feathers in her hat and that his father, upon seeing an ostrich egg, thinks: "That would make a great omelette!" Another dialogue, "L'Opéra des girafes" (the giraffe's opera), is written as an opera. A dromedary, antelopes, elephants, a horse on an island, a young lion in a cage, and a good-natured donkey are all subjects of brief fables, unburdened by any higher mythology. Throughout, Prévert's sympathies lie with the beasts, who are maltreated or misunderstood by humans.

The bird achieves a special status in Prévert's poems—sometimes representing liberation, as in "Quartier libre" ("Free Sector," from *Paroles*), sometimes as a symbol of sorrow, as in "Les Oiseaux du souci" ("Birds of Sorrow"), where the first line, "Pluie des plumes, plume de pluie" ("Rain of feathers, feather of rain"), reflects the indifference of the lonely poet in an atmosphere of despair and boredom to some birds who are trying to console him. One of Prévert's best-known poems, featuring a consummate demonstration of his technique of repetition, is "Chanson de l'oiseleur" (the birdcatcher's song), a poem of thirteen brief lines, the first twelve of which begin with the words "L'Oiseau," followed by descriptive characteristics. In the thirteenth and final line, the bird becomes a woman's heart beating its wings pathetically in her hard, white breast.

In "Au hasard des oiseaux" (the randomness of birds, from *Paroles*), the poet opens by regretting that he learned to love the birds too late, then continues with a diatribe against a certain Monsieur Glacis, who is ironically portrayed as having fought courageously in the war against young Paul, a character described as poor, handsome, and decent, who later becomes old Paul, rich, aged, honorable, and stingy but masquerading as philanthropic and pious. Prévert adds that Paul had a servant who led an exemplary life, because she never quarreled with her master or mentioned the unmentionable question of wages. The poem concludes by contrasting again the bestial nature of humans with the humane nature of the birds: "La lumière des oiseaux" (the light of the birds), in the final line, carries the implication of enlightenment.

JUSTICE AND PACIFISM

Prévert's sense of justice finds metaphoric expression in "Les Prodiges de la liberté" (the wonders of life, from *Histoires*), which opens with the pathetic picture of the paw of a white fox caught in the teeth of a trap in the snow. The fox holds between its teeth a rabbit, still alive. Prévert seems to be able to reconcile himself to the natural order but continually objects to the evil that originates with humankind. For example, in the poem "La Pêche à la baleine" ("Whaling," from *Paroles*), a father is astounded that his son does not want to go whaling with him. "Why," asks the son, "should I hunt a beast who has done nothing to me, Papa?"

Prévert's antiwar sentiments were perhaps best formulated in "Barbara" (*Paroles*), in which a tender and tragic tone is established in his comparison between the fate of a young girl and that of the city of Brest. The individual experiences pain in the loss of life, love, hope, and happiness, while the collective loss is shown in the destruction of the town, the ruins, and the fire raining down on one and all.

In 1952, Prévert took up his pen against the colonial war in "Entendez-vous gens du Viet-Nam" (do you hear people of Vietnam, from *La Pluie et le beau temps*), in which he denounces the French use of sophisticated tactics against the unarmed peasants. He notes that with the arrival of Admiral Thierry d'Argenlieu came a recrudescence of terror and suffering.

"FAMILIALE"

One of Prévert's best-known pacifist poems is "Familiale" (family, from *Paroles*), which is characteristic of his ability to paint in a brief scene a moral dilemma:

> La mère fait du tricot
> Le fils fait la guerre
> Elle trouveça tout naturel la mère
> Et le père qu'est-ce qu'il fait le père?
> Il fait des affaires. . . .

(A mother makes a sweater,
a son makes war,
which she finds quite natural,
but the father—what is he doing?
Business.)

The rhymes and the singsong rhythm lend the poem the aspect of a children's chant, but the content grows grim after the innocent opening of a mother knitting. The reduction of each life to its most typical activity shows the isolation in which people play out their roles, unconscious of the interdependence of their activities.

LOVE

Prévert championed love as passionately as he railed against war. Human happiness recognizes its most profound expression in love, and Prévert's contribution to erotic poetry has the simplicity of the classical Greek lyric poets. "Fiesta" (*Histoires*) describes a seduction over empty glasses and a shattered bottle; the bed is wide open and the door closed; the poet is drunk and his lover is likewise drunk but lively and naked in his arms. The image of a woman "naked from head to toe" occurs frequently in Prévert's poems, but his physical descriptions rarely go further. In "Les Chiens ont soif" (the dogs are thirsty, from *Fatras*), the poet describes two lovers he has seen naked and entwined; he then assumes the point of view of the man: "He looks at her and knows without saying it that there is nothing more . . . indispensable, more simple and more inexplicable than love on a bed, than love on this earth."

The lighter side or more ephemeral aspect of love does not escape Prévert's wit. A character in *Fatras* exclaims how happy she is because her lover has said that he loves her, but she is even happier because she is still free, since he did not say he would love her forever. The lover in "Les Chansons les plus courtes . . ." (the shortest songs, from *Histoires*) complains of the bird in his head repeating the refrain "I love you" so insistently that he will have to kill him the next morning. In "Le Lézard" (the lizard, from *Histoires*), the poet declares: "The lizard of love has fled once again and left his tail between my fingers and that's all right/ I wanted to keep something for myself."

Many critics find the mechanics of Prévert's poetry too obtrusive, arguing that his rhymes and his wordplay,

the adroit twists with which he frequently concluded his poems, lack the depth and resonance of great poetry. That he was a genuinely popular poet, however, is denied by none. The natural quality of his verse had an appeal that revived the spirit of France after World War II, and his can be called a poetry of recovery.

OTHER MAJOR WORKS

SCREENPLAYS: *L'Affaire est dans le sac*, 1932; *Le Crime de Monsieur Lange*, 1935; *Jenny*, 1936; *Drôle de drame*, 1937 (with Marcel Carné); *Le Jour se lève*, 1939; *Les Visiteurs du soir*, 1942 (with Carné and Pierre Laroche); *Les Enfants du paradis*, 1945 (with Carné; *Children of Paradise*, 1968); *Notre Dame de Paris*, 1956.

TRANSLATION: *Carmina burana*, 1965.

CHILDREN'S LITERATURE: *Le Petit Lion*, 1947; *Des bêtes . . .* , 1950; *Bim, le petit âne*, 1952 (*Bim, the Little Donkey*, 1973).

MISCELLANEOUS: *Spectacle*, 1949, 1951 (includes poetry, plays, and prose); *L'Opéra de la lune*, 1953 (song lyrics); *Tour de chant*, 1953 (songs for piano and voice).

BIBLIOGRAPHY

Baker, William E. *Jacques Prévert*. New York: Twayne, 1967. An overview that is fair and balanced in its assessment and limited only by its date. Prévert's work is discussed as antipoetry, as the poetry of plain talk, and as an expression of both romanticism and stark political views. A good annotated bibliography in both French and English is included.

Bishop, Michael. *Jacques Prévert: From Film and Theater to Poetry, Art, and Song*. New York: Rodopi, 2002. Examines Prévert's life and the many genres in which he worked, including poetry.

_____. *Jacques Prévert Revisited*. New York: Twayne, 2000. A general biography of Prévert that looks at his life and works.

Blakeway, Claire. *Jacques Prévert: Popular French Theatre and Cinema*. Cranbury, N.J.: Associated University Presses, 1990. Although the focus is on Prévert's work in cinema and theater, especially his collaborations with Marcel Carné, the discussions of politics and Surrealism apply to the poetry as well. Of special interest are the abundant black-and-white photographs.

Greet, Anne. *Jacques Prévert's Word Games*. Berkeley: University of California Press, 1968. A brief examination of Prévert's wordplay. Includes bibliographical footnotes.

Karen Jaehne

SEXTUS PROPERTIUS

Born: Asisium (now Assisi, Umbria, Italy); c. 57-48 B.C.E.
Died: Rome (now in Italy); c. 16 B.C.E.-2 C.E.

PRINCIPAL POETRY

Monobiblos, wr. c. 30 or 29 B.C.E.

Elegies, c. 24 C.E.-after 16 B.C.E. (first printed version, 1472; English translation, 1854)

Propertius Elegies: Book I, 1961 (*Book II*, 1967, *Book III*, 1966, *Book IV*, 1965; W. A. Camps, editor)

OTHER LITERARY FORMS

Sextus Propertius (proh-PUR-shee-uhs) is known primarily for his poetry.

ACHIEVEMENTS

An extremely popular poet in Augustan Rome, Sextus Propertius brought to perfection the love elegy form which flourished briefly in Rome in the late first century B.C.E. Clearly influenced by the poetry of Catullus and the elegies of such contemporary poets as Calvus and Gallus, whose works are now lost, Propertius claimed in his poetry to have imitated the style of the Alexandrian poets Callimachus and Philetas. Like the other Latin love elegists whose works have survived, Propertius made the elegiac meter, previously used especially for epigrams and reflective themes, into a meter of love. The Latin love elegist focuses his poetry on his devotion to a single woman and depicts the love affair in its various stages but not necessarily chronologically. Propertius's poetry, centered

on a woman he called Cynthia, reveals his ability to handle well the conventional themes and forms of the genre, including the theme of the *exclusus amator*, or "locked-out lover," and forms such as the birthday poem, the ecphrastic poem, which describes a piece of artwork, and the love letter (elegy 3 in the fourth book may have provided the model for Ovid's *Heroides*, before 8 C.E.; English translation, 1567). Preeminently, however, Propertius is admired for his ability to combine the personal love theme with a whole range of elements from Greek mythology and Roman religion and politics in a sophisticated and original way.

Propertius's influence on Ovid is evident especially from book 4, elegy 3, and book 4, elegy 5. Propertius was mentioned favorably or imitated by later Latin writers, including Lucan, Juvenal, and Martial. In the late Silver Age, a revival of interest in Propertius was evident, especially in the poetry of Claudian (late fourth century C.E.). Propertius was known but not popular in the Middle Ages, during which period his fellow elegist, Ovid, was preferred. Petrarch was the first Renaissance humanist to show an interest in Propertius and even imitated the Roman elegist in his sonnets. In the eighteenth century, Johann Wolfgang von Goethe's *Römische Elegien* (1793; *Roman Elegies*, 1876) was also influenced by Propertius. It has been in the twentieth century, however, that Propertius has made the strongest impact, especially on the poetry of Ezra Pound, whose *Homage to Sextus Propertius* (1934) is partly free translation and partly poetic creation in its own right, and whose *Literary Essays* (1954) provide a significant modern interpretation of the Latin elegist.

BIOGRAPHY

Sextus Propertius wrote in the period just after the tumultuous series of civil wars that followed the assassination of Julius Caesar in 44 B.C.E. Both Propertius's life and his poetry were deeply affected by the social and political changes which resulted from the near anarchy lasting from 44 B.C.E. until the defeat of Marc Antony by Octavian, the future Augustus, at Actium in 31 B.C.E. In the early years of the Pax Augustana, Octavian's near-paranoid dread of opposition to his autocratic rule, as well as a general fear of the return of civil war, encouraged intensely propagandistic literature, evident in the poetry of both Vergil and Horace. It was a period of contradictions when Augustus strove vainly, through legislation, to encourage a return to old Roman values and virtues centered on marriage and the family, while, at the same time, Roman society experienced major social upheavals resulting from the political rise of the equestrian class and from the emancipation of women. The major themes of Latin love elegy, including allusions to contemporary political events and a yearning for the Golden Age of Rome's past, were clearly the result of the prevailing social and political mood, and the women about whom the Latin love elegists wrote, such as Propertius's Cynthia, were examples of the new breed of Roman women, socially independent and politically powerful.

What little is known about Propertius's life is derived from references in his own poetry, especially book 1, elegy 22, and book 4, elegy 1. There are almost no independent ancient references to the poet, and what information can be inferred from his poetry is often unreliable because of the difficulty in distinguishing between the historical Propertius and the persona projected in the poetry. Propertius was writing love elegies, not autobiography, and was therefore not bound by historical accuracy, even in references to his own life. Consequently, there is almost no aspect of his biography that is not disputed today.

Propertius was born sometime in the decade 57-48 B.C.E. into a well-to-do equestrian family of Umbria, in North Italy. Traditionally, he is said to have been from Assisi, but this is uncertain. Propertius's pride in his native Umbria and its Etruscan heritage is evident in his poetry (book 1, elegy 22; book 4, elegy 1; and book 4, elegy 2). His family supported the wrong side in the war between Octavian and Anthony, and their property was almost certainly confiscated by Octavian in 41-40 B.C.E. to pay his troops. While Propertius was still a child, his father died, and the boy was reared by his mother. Book 4, elegy 1, line 134, implies that Propertius was sent by his mother to study in Rome for a career as a lawyer; the many rhetorical features of Propertius's poetry, such as his fondness for methodically enumerating instances as proof, support such an inference.

While in Rome, Propertius apparently met the woman who so strongly affected his life and made him into a poet instead of a lawyer. She is called Cynthia in his poetry, but this is clearly a pseudonym in the tradition of ancient love poetry; Catullus's Lesbia was really named Clodia. Cynthia's pseudonym is poetically appropriate because of its associations with Apollo, the Greek god of inspiration, and with his sister Diana, the Roman goddess of the moon. Ancient sources say that Cynthia's real name was Hostia, but Propertius's poetic reference to Hostius, an epic poet of the late second century B.C.E., as Hostia's grandfather, is generally discounted today as poetic license. The image of Cynthia developed in Propertius's poetry is of a well-educated freedwoman, probably a high-class *meretrix*, or prostitute (although some still argue today that Cynthia was actually a respectable married woman). Propertius developed a relationship with Cynthia in his poetry that appears to have lasted, on and off, for approximately five years. Based on the evidence of book 4, elegy 7, Cynthia probably died in poverty about 18 B.C.E. and was buried at Tibur. Experts generally agree today that the poetic relationship between Propertius and Cynthia was based loosely upon actual events, although facts cannot be distinguished from poetic distortion in the *Elegies*.

J. P. Sullivan, in his book on Propertius, has used these meager biographical details concerning Propertius, as well as the attitude of the poet toward Cynthia in his *Elegies*, to advance the theory that Propertius's relationship with Cynthia can be explained by Sigmund Freud's theory of *Dirnenliebe*, or prostitute love. Propertius's loss of his father at an early age and his maternal upbringing suggest the Freudian description of men who are unable to dissociate their lofty maternal image from the general female image and are thus able to develop a passionate relationship only with a female who is the opposite of the maternal image, such as a prostitute. The general pattern of this passion exactly fits Propertius's relationship with Cynthia: the presence of an injured third party, either a husband or another lover; the love of a woman who is neither faithful nor chaste; a contradictory overestimation of the beloved, despite her sexual shortcomings; a false ideal of the lover's own fidelity; intense jealousy toward potential rivals; and the desire to "rescue" the beloved from her degradations. The close similarity between Propertius's feelings for Cynthia and Freud's theory of *Dirnenliebe* sheds great light on Propertius's characterization of his relationship with Cynthia and strongly suggests a kernel of personal experience and feeling lying behind the poetic screen.

It is generally assumed that after the appearance of his first book of *Elegies*, Propertius was invited to join the poetic circle of Maecenas, who was the patron of Vergil and Horace and the intimate friend of Augustus. Certainly, Maecenas is presented in book 2, elegy 1, and book 3, elegy 9, as suggesting historical/epic themes for Propertius, which the poet rejects in favor of love elegy. The unsuitability of elegiac themes to the political and social program of Augustus is something of which Propertius is acutely conscious in his poetry. Book 4, published after 16 B.C.E. and conspicuously different from the earlier books with its prominent aetiological poems and praise of Actium, is usually said to mark Propertius's final conversion to the propaganda poetry advocated by Maecenas and Augustus and demonstrated by Horace and Vergil; Sullivan, however, has argued convincingly that this is not the case at all, that the poems of book 4 are not sincere but rather deliberate parodies of propaganda poetry. Whatever the actual relationship between Propertius and Maecenas, it is clear that the poet moved in Maecenas's circle, at least after 30 B.C.E. Propertius gives evidence of his good relations with the imperial family in book 3, elegy 18, and book 4, elegy 11. He knew Vergil and appears to have been greatly influenced in book 3 by Horace's *Odes* (23 B.C.E., 13 B.C.E.; English translation, 1621). There is a strong suggestion in their poetry, however, that Horace and Propertius disliked each other, at least professionally. Curiously, Propertius and Tibullus, another contemporary love elegist, appear to have worked independently, with no allusions to each other's works. Ovid, however, shows a deep regard for Propertius and frequently imitates Propertius's work.

The later part of Propertius's life lies completely in shadows. The last datable reference to contemporary events in his poetry, the funeral of Cornelia, took place in 16 B.C.E. From a reference in Ovid's *Remedia amoris* (before 8 C.E.; *Cure for Love*, 1600), it is certain that Propertius was dead by 2 C.E. Some critics argue that Propertius's poetic silence after 16 B.C.E. was caused by early death; others, by the dangerous political climate that led eventually to Ovid's banishment in 8 C.E. Some ancient evidence exists to suggest that Propertius married and produced an heir before his death. Propertius's trip to Greece about 20 B.C.E., mentioned by some critics, is completely hypothetical.

The personality of Propertius projected through his poetry is that of a young man whose unhappy childhood, scarred by the death of his father and the loss of his family farm, led to an only slightly veiled disillusionment with the totalitarian rule of Augustus, whose conception of poetry as a political tool Propertius rejected. Indeed, Propertius's infatuation with the love theme and with the creation of poetry for its own sake was clearly antithetical to Augustan tastes and may help to explain his poetic silence after 16 B.C.E.

ANALYSIS

The genre of Latin love elegy in which Sextus Propertius wrote was a rich amalgam of the early Greek lyric tradition of Archilochus and Sappho; of the intensely learned and form-conscious poetry of Hellenistic writers, especially Callimachus; and of the distinctly Roman contributions of the lyric poet Catullus and of the elegiac writers, such as Propertius himself. From the Greek lyricists, the Roman elegist inherited the "lyric," first-person voice which permits the vivid expression of moods and personal feelings, including love, for which the elegist is noted. Especially from the Hellenistic poets, the love elegy derived a fondness for mythic and geographical allusions, as well as a particular concern for artificial poetic expression, in selection of both form and word, of which Propertius became a master. To this Greek tradition, which provided the Roman poet with a well-established list of conventional themes and poetic forms, were added indigenous Latin themes, such as references to Roman institutions and to the Golden Age of Rome's past. In particular, the Romans brought to lyric and elegy a marked tendency toward autobiographical expression and a habit of writing poetry as if it were addressed to friends, which is not common in Greek. It is this autobiographical mode, permitting the poet to unify his poems around the real or imagined history of a love affair, which is the distinctive characteristic of the Latin love elegy.

ELEGIES

Propertius's poetry starts from this autobiographical form of expression and from the conventions of the Greek tradition but exhibits some particularly Propertian themes and characteristics. The *Elegies* of Propertius are distinctive especially for a unity of structure and theme not achieved by earlier love and elegiac poets; the poet shows, in the arrangement of his poems within each book, a new concern for balance and contrast of mood and structure between particular poems that intensify the overall unity based upon the love theme. Even within individual elegies, the poet is noted for his ability to combine sudden changes of mood and thought and complex structures to create an especially intense and unified poem (a feature unfortunately not always recognized by many editors, who, overly conscious of Propertius's poor manuscript tradition, often tend to interpret a change of mood as a new poem).

Propertius was a poet of the city, of Rome, rather than of the bucolic landscape, like Tibullus. He was particularly fond of incorporating Roman religious themes into his elegies, especially metaphorically—for example, depicting the poet as priest and the love relationship between himself and Cynthia as a marriage rite. This Roman emphasis is extended, however, only indirectly to themes, especially military ones, from the glorious Roman past or from contemporary events. Despite apparently intense pressure from the Augustan political establishment to write poetry more acceptable to the regime, Propertius generally introduced such historical themes only in the form of a *recusatio*, the refusal to write on themes that the author finds unsuitable; in Propertius's case, *recusatio* is the love elegist's refusal to write on more historical subjects in lofty genres such as epic or tragedy. It has, in fact, been argued by Sullivan that in book 4, Propertius used the *recusatio*, perhaps more ironically and subtly, as a final rejection of approved Augustan themes in favor of love poetry. Finally, Propertius's conscious efforts to be a Roman Callimachus not only made him employ mythic allusions more than earlier love elegists but also made him a particularly skilled master of language who could control the multiple meanings of words rather than be controlled by them. This ability to manipulate words and their meanings, which Pound called *logopoeia*, lies at the core of Propertius's poetry and, perhaps, constitutes its crux, since it has often led to confusion and ambiguity in the reading of his *Elegies*.

BOOK 1, ELEGY 19

Book 1, elegy 19, is part of a series dealing with different aspects of separation from the beloved, either by geographic distance or by death. The conversational tone of book 1, elegy 19, contrasts with the soliloquy structure of book 1, elegy 17 and elegy 18; as book 1, elegy 19, begins, Propertius is in the middle of a discussion with Cynthia about death. In a colloquial tone marked by phrases such as "now I don't" and "but least perhaps," the poet begins to develop a reflection on death which is not unusual in Latin love elegy but which Propertius expresses in his distinctive style. Sudden thought transitions and mood changes are particularly noteworthy in this poem. Propertius moves in thought, from his undying love for Cynthia even after his own death, to his continued love for Cynthia after her death, to his fear that she will not be true and, finally, to the plea that they love each other while both are still alive. This rambling train of thought is unified not only by the themes of the poet's fidelity and Cynthia's faithlessness, which are basic to the relationship as developed in Propertius's *Elegies*, but also by a sequence of mood changes, which draws the poem together in a ring structure.

The poet's initial colloquial mood is maintained through the first six lines but changes in the center of the poem into a more formal tone marked by a combination of mythological allusions and the triple anaphora of "there." The solemn reference to the story of Protesilaus's love for Laodamia beyond the grave shows Propertius's tendency to incorporate mythological *exempla* of his love for Cynthia and "the chorus of beautiful heroines," possibly derived from traditional catalogs of dead mythological beauties such as in the *Aeneid* (c. 29-19 B.C.E.; English translation, 1553), and further develops Propertius's love for Cynthia in a formal and hyperbolic way. In the last section of the poem, the poet returns to the colloquial tone of the beginning with the use of a parenthetical statement and exclamation. The poem thus begins and ends on an informal note, in marked contrast to its grave subject matter and formal central section. This contrast is furthered on the level of vocabulary, where Propertius juxtaposes concrete and abstract terms throughout the poem, such as "fate" and "pyre" in the second line and "dust" and "love" in line 6 (repeated in line 22). The vivid concrete words, such as "pyre" and "dust," invoke the Roman burial rite of cremation and provide further reinforcement of the formal, solemn tone of the poem. At the same time, Propertius's manipulation of words, his *logopoeia*, can be noted in the use of "dust" in lines 6 and 22 to refer not only to the physical remains of Propertius after death and to the Roman funeral rite, but also, metaphorically, to the psychological condition of Propertius when his love for Cynthia is forgotten (*oblito . . . amore*) and when Cynthia forgets the dead Propertius in line 22. In either case, "dust" is an appropriate term to describe Propertius both physically and emotionally.

BOOK 2, ELEGY 6

The tight control of tone, structure, and vocabulary that Propertius demonstrates in book 1, elegy 19, can also be seen in book 2, elegy 6. Together with elegy 5 from the same book, elegy 6 is an exhortation to Cynthia to be true to Propertius, but, while the tone of book 2, elegy 5, is threatening and critical of Cynthia and is modeled, perhaps, on the harsh invective of Catullus in a similar situation, book 2, elegy 6, is a formal and polite warning to Cynthia against the dangers of promiscuity. The formality is established at the very beginning of the poem by the use of the favorite Hellenistic convention of the catalog. In lines 1 through 6, Propertius presents a list of prostitutes culled from Greek comedy and implies a contrast with Cynthia by the words "thus," "so great," and "so." This contrast is only indirect and polite because the specific reference to Cynthia that the comparatives "thus," "so great," and "so" demand is not made by Propertius.

The catalog structure is continued in lines 7 through 14, where Propertius lists all people whose closeness to Cynthia makes him jealous. The formal tone of both catalogs is tempered by the use of references from Greek comedy for humorous effect as well as by the exaggerated jealousy of Propertius for infants whom Cynthia kisses. In lines 15 through 26, Propertius turns

to a third catalog, this one mythological, where Cynthia is given mythic examples of the dangers of masculine lust. Humor is added here, too, by the reference to the Centaurs breaking their wine jugs over Perithous's head. In the final exemplum, a reference to the rape of the Sabine women, the humorous tone is completely lost as Propertius's train of thought moves from the mild warnings to Cynthia against lust to a new theme of the deterioration of Roman morals that dominates the rest of the poem.

A reference to the long-past Golden Age of Roman virtue leads the poet into a tirade against contemporary painters, whose obscene works corrupt Roman morals. Perhaps the reader is meant to imagine the setting of the elegy to be Cynthia's own house, where such paintings may be seen. The word order reinforces the contrast in morals with the juxtaposition of "chaste"/"base" and "ingenuous"/"corrupt." This passage on the painters' contribution to the baseness of contemporary Roman morals is framed by two references to a parallel deterioration of Roman religious sentiment in lines 25 to 26 and 35 to 36. The second reference, describing empty Roman temples veiled with spiderwebs, is another example of Propertius's *logopoeia*, his conscious use of words in unusual contexts. "Veiled" suggests the Roman custom of worshiping with the head covered, but this pious act is distorted in context by the fact that the veil is a spiderweb. The veil becomes a vivid metaphoric statement of Rome's lost religious zeal. The yearnings that the poet expresses in these lines for a return to old Roman virtues and piety appear to agree with Augustan policy, but the solemnity and formality of this appeal for virtue is deliberately undermined in the following ways: Not only does the next elegy joyfully celebrate the repeal of one of the very marriage laws that Augustus had passed to improved Roman morals, but also book 2, elegy 6, lines 38 through 43, shows that for Propertius the desire for virtue does not go beyond his own illicit relationship with Cynthia. The poet wants Cynthia to be faithful to him and lists two of love poetry's traditional impediments to love, a "guard" and the "closed door," which are useless barriers if the girl wishes otherwise.

Propertius's plea for Cynthia's exclusive love is climaxed in the last elegiac couplet of the poem with a promise of his own fidelity. This contrast between Propertius's and Cynthia's attitudes toward their relationship was also noted in book 1, elegy 19, and is a unifying theme of the *Elegies*. In lines 41 and 42, Propertius promises to have no "wife" and no "girlfriend" except Cynthia. The application of the term "wife" to Cynthia is a final example of Propertius's *logopoeia* in this poem. The poet's earlier call for a return to Roman virtue, including a respect for marriage, is debased by his own reference to his mistress as his wife. Propertius does here to the Roman vocabulary of marriage what the obscene painter in the poem did to the innocent walls of Roman houses. However, "wife" at the same time implies a sanctity of the marriage bond which Propertius is metaphorically and ironically applying with great effect to his relationship with Cynthia. For Propertius, Cynthia is both wife and religion.

BOOK 3, ELEGY 4

Both book 1, elegy 19, and book 2, elegy 6, were written as private conversations with Cynthia. Book 3, elegy 4, must be read in the context of the elegies that surround it, especially book 3, elegies 1 through 5, all of which are considered appropriate subject matter for Propertius's poetry. As a group, these five elegies firmly argue that Propertius can be nothing but a poet of love, specifically a poet-priest (*sacerdos*) who gets his inspiration from the Greek poets Callimachus and Philetas and from Cynthia herself. In book 3, elegy 4, too, Propertius sings as a priest-prophet who prays for and predicts the success of Augustus's campaign to avenge the defeat of Crassus by the Parthians. The disaster of Carrhae in 53 B.C.E., in which Crassus perished, haunted Augustan politics and poetry until the Roman military standards were quietly restored by the Parthians in 20 B.C.E. Book 3, elegy 4, begins with a patriotic fervor vividly at odds with the normally private tone of the Latin love elegy. In lines 1 through 6, Propertius anticipates the actual victory and describes Parthia as already a Roman province; lines 7 through 10 constitute an exhortation to the armed forces to avenge Crassus's defeat; and lines 11 through 22 consist of a prayer to the gods that Augustus will celebrate a triumph in Rome for his defeat of Parthia and that Propertius will live to see it. The formal and public prayer form is here suddenly made quite personal, with

the poet's reference to his own death and his eyewitness account of the future triumph.

The reader's attention to the public success of Augustus is distracted by the poet himself, who watches the triumphal procession while reclining on his lady's breast, and the poem ends with a significant *recusatio*, Propertius's rejection of personal military glory. The poet is content, rather, to cheer the victor from the sidelines. The love elegist's distaste for military success is particularly strong in Propertius, and the juxtaposition of public and private themes in book 3, elegy 4, shows that, for Propertius, the public world intrudes into his poetry only by way of contrast with his private world. This contrast, however, is a fertile one semantically, for, on another level of interpretation, Propertius is not rejecting the military world and its vocabulary but appropriating them for his own amorous theme. Is the victor in this poem Augustus on his chariot or Propertius in the arms of his mistress? Does the poet cheer in the last line because the Parthians have been defeated or because Cynthia has been won? Propertius has transformed a public poem into a very personal statement and has demonstrated once again his control over structure, tone, and diction.

The *Elegies* of Propertius thus function in a carefully delineated and controlled world centered on the poet's relationship with his mistress Cynthia. The love theme is not strong in every elegy; for example, the aetiological and historical poems of book 4 are usually said to represent Propertius's attempts to reconcile the elegiac form with Augustan demands for more acceptable themes. As Sullivan has shown, however, even these poems cannot be separated from the personal love tone that pervades the corpus and can be seen to operate in an ironic mode as the poet's ultimate *recusatio* of the public world in favor of the private world. Propertius's desire to apply Callimachean poetic principles to the love elegy made his poetry particularly dependent on careful manipulation of structure and tone within and between elegies and on a striking attempt to employ vocabulary in violently different semantic contexts.

BIBLIOGRAPHY

Arkins, Brian. *An Interpretation of the Poetry of Propertius (50-15 B.C.)*. Studies in Classics 30. Lewiston, N.Y.: Edwin Mellen Press, 2005. A general guide to understanding the poetry of Propertius and the culture in which he lived.

Cairns, Francis. *Sextus Propertius: The Augustan Elegist*. New York: Cambridge University Press, 2006. This work examines the sources of the elegies as it traces Propertius's career and looks at his relationship with his patrons.

Debrohun, Jeri Blair. *Roman Propertius and the Reinvention of Elegy*. Ann Arbor: University of Michigan Press, 2003. In her assessment of book 4 of *Elegies*, Debrohun finds the themes to be polarized, with some describing love and others topics of national significance.

Greene, Ellen. *The Erotics of Domination: Male Desire and the Mistress in Latin Love Poetry*. Baltimore: Johns Hopkins University Press, 1998. Chapter 3 is a feminist critique of gender roles and ideology in the *Monobiblos*. Greene sees Cynthia not as a true subject but rather as being reduced to *materia*, an object of Propertius's male fantasy.

Günther, Hans Christian. *Quaestiones Propertianae*. New York: Brill, 1997. A comprehensive study dealing with the major critical problems of one of the most difficult authors of Latin literature. A systematic examination of the two major factors which have been assumed to be responsible for the state of the transmitted text of Propertius: dislocation and interpolation. Günther covers a large number of cases of verbal corruption and discusses problems of the manuscript tradition on the basis of the most recent research.

Heyworth, S. J. *Cynthia: A Companion to the Text of Propertius*. 2007. Reprint. New York: Oxford University Press, 2009. This scholarly work examines the *Monobiblos*. Heyworth has extensively researched each poem and its variants to determine the most "correct" version and to provide the best interpretation.

Janan, Micaela Wakil. *The Politics of Desire: Propertius IV*. Berkeley: University of California Press, 2000. Reassesses Propertius's last elegies using psychoanalytic theory. Includes bibliography and index.

Johnson, W. R. *A Latin Lover in Ancient Rome: Readings in Propertius and His Genre*. Columbus: Ohio State University Press, 2009. This examination of Propertius focuses on the genre of the love elegy and how the poet used it.

Keith, Alison. *Propertius: Poet of Love and Leisure*. London: Duckworth, 2008. Part of the Classical Literature and Society series, this work examines the life of Propertius, discussing his works and the culture that surrounded him.

Thomas J. Sienkewicz

Q

SALVATORE QUASIMODO

Born: Modica, Sicily, Italy; August 20, 1901
Died: Naples, Italy; June 14, 1968

PRINCIPAL POETRY

Acque e terre, 1930
Oboe sommerso, 1932
Odore di eucalyptus, ed altri versi, 1933
Erato e Apollion, 1936
Poesie, 1938
Ed è subito sera, 1942
Con il piede straniero sopra il cuore, 1946
Giorno dopo giorno, 1947
La vita non è sogno, 1949
Il falso e vero verde, 1954
La terra impareggiabile, 1958, 1962
Tutte le poesie, 1960
Noeve poesie, 1963
Dare e avere, 1959-1965, 1966 (*To Give and to Have, and Other Poems*, 1969; also known as *Debit and Credit*, 1972)
Complete Poems, 1983
Day After Day: Selected Poems, 2002
The Night Fountain = La fontana notturna: Selected Early Poems, 2008 (bilingual text)

OTHER LITERARY FORMS

Outside his native country, the reputation of Salvatore Quasimodo (kwoz-ee-MUH-doh) rests primarily on his poetry, but in Italy, he achieved prominence for his many other literary activities as well. He wrote a number of important critical studies, and his librettos have been performed in opera theaters as well known as those of Venice and Palermo. More important, however, is his work as a translator. One of the finest literary translators of his time, Quasimodo ranged from Homer to the twentieth century: His translations include classical Greek and Latin poetry, the Gospel of John, and writers as varied as William Shakespeare, Molière, Pablo Neruda, E. E. Cummings, Conrad Aiken, Tudor Arghezi, Yves Lecomte, and Paul Éluard.

ACHIEVEMENTS

Together with Giuseppe Ungaretti and Eugenio Montale, Salvatore Quasimodo unquestionably belongs to the select circle of world-renowned modern Italian poets. Of the three, however, Quasimodo was the first to win wide acclaim, perhaps because he was able to express most lucidly the anguish and the doubts of a poet in a time when the irrational seemed to gain steadily at the expense of the rational, when poetry had gradually turned inward, divorcing itself from its tormented historical and social context. In 1959, Quasimodo received the Nobel Prize in Literature. His other awards include the San Babila Prize (1950), the Etna-Taormina International Poetry Prize (1953, shared with Dylan Thomas), and the Viareggio Prize (1958).

BIOGRAPHY

Born in Modica, Sicily, the second of four children born to Gaetano Quasimodo and Clotilde Ragusa, Salvatore Quasimodo spent the first years of his life following his father, a humble stationmaster, as the family moved from one small Sicilian railroad station to another. In 1908, his father settled in Gela, where Quasimodo was able to attend grade school. In 1909, he again followed his father, this time to Messina, the Sicilian town that, along with Reggio Calabria, had just been hit by the terribly destructive earthquake of 1908. In 1916, after a few years spent near Palermo, Quasimodo returned with his family to Messina, where he and his older brother were enrolled in the local trade school.

At this time, Quasimodo's poetic vocation, nurtured by careful reading of the classics as well as the major contemporary Russian and French writers, began to surface. He published his first two lyrics, one in the journal *Humanitas* and the other, a Futurist poem, in *Italia futurista*. In 1917, together with his lifelong friends Giorgio La Pira and Salvatore Pugliatti, Quasimodo founded the *Nuovo giornale letterario*, which was in print from March to November of that year.

In 1919, Quasimodo left Messina for Rome to attend the engineering school of that city's university. He soon dropped out, however, and spent the next few years working at odd jobs and leading a rather bohemian life. In 1926, he succeeded in obtaining a position as a land surveyor with the government's Civil Engineering Department at Reggio Calabria and thus was able once again to meet regularly with his friends among the Sicilian literati. At this point, he began to write seriously; some of the poems included in *Acque e terre* (waters and lands) date from this period.

The year 1929 was a decisive one in Quasimodo's life. He was invited by his brother-in-law Elio Vittorini (later to become one of the leading literary figures of contemporary Italy) to go to Florence. There, he was introduced to an influential group of writers and poets, among them Montale, and in 1930, he published his first collection of poems, *Acque e terre*, which met with favorable critical reviews. For work-related reasons, he

Salvatore Quasimodo (©The Nobel Foundation)

was sent to Liguria in 1931, where he published the widely acclaimed *Oboe sommerso* (the sunken oboe) in 1932. That same year, he was awarded the Florentine Prize of the Antico Fattore, which had been given the year before to Montale. Sent in 1934 to Valtellina (Lombardy) after a short stay in Sardinia, Quasimodo entered the Milanese intellectual milieu, and in 1935, his daughter, Orietta, was born out of wedlock.

In Milan in 1936, Quasimodo published another book, *Erato e Apollion* (Aerato and Apollyon), and in 1938, he finally quit his job as a land surveyor to begin working as an editor and assistant to Cesare Zavattini, then the editor of several Mondadori periodicals. In 1939, Quasimodo was made literary editor of the weekly magazine *Il tempo*. The same year, his son, Alessandro, was born. In 1940, Quasimodo published his controversial translation *Lirici greci* (Greek lyric poets), notable for its aggressively modern idiom, and the following year, he was appointed professor of Italian literature at the Giuseppe Verdi Conservatory in Milan. In 1942, he published the most successful of his works: *Ed è subito sera* (and suddenly it is evening), the volume that marked his shift from the Hermetic style of his early verse.

During the war years, without being overtly involved in the antifascist resistance movement, Quasimodo nevertheless took a firm stand against fascism, and in 1945, soon after the war, he joined the Italian Communist Party. That same year, he published his masterful translations of Sophocles and the Gospel of John. Belonging also to this period are a number of critical essays and two collections of socially and ideologically oriented poems: *Con il piede straniero sopra il cuore* (with an invader's foot on your heart), published in 1946, and *Giorno dopo giorno* (day after day), published the following year. In 1948, following the death of his first wife, Bice Donetti, he married Maria Cumani, the mother of his son, Alessandro; he then began his career as a theater editor for the journal *Omnibus* and in the same capacity, shortly after, for the weekly *Il tempo*, while continuing to publish translations and another collection of poems titled *La vita non è un sogno* (life is not a dream), which appeared in 1949.

In 1950, Quasimodo received the San Babila Prize

and, in 1953, with Dylan Thomas, the Etna-Taormina International Poetry Prize. In 1954, *Il falso e vero verde* (the true and the false green) was published; it was republished two years later with added translations and the famous speech, "Discorso sulla poesia" (speech on poetry), in which Quasimodo maintained the necessity for the true poet to express in his verses his ideological and social commitment. In 1958, after the publication of several other translations, he published yet another collection of poems, *La terra impareggiabile* (the incomparable land), but during a trip to Russia in that same year, he had a heart attack, which forced him to remain there until the spring of 1959. His hospital expenses were covered by a subscription organized by Russian writers on his behalf. In 1959, Quasimodo attained world recognition on receiving the Nobel Prize in Literature "for his lyric poetry, which expresses with classic fire the tragic experience of life in our time." In Italy, however, this award prompted a negative reaction from critics who thought that Ungaretti and Montale were both more deserving of the honor.

Shortly after receiving the Nobel Prize, Quasimodo began to travel throughout Europe and the United States. In 1960, he separated from his second wife and published a collection of essays titled *Il poeta e il politico e altri saggi* (*The Poet and the Politician, and Other Essays*, 1964), which includes the acceptance speech he had read in Stockholm. He was thereafter the recipient of several other honors and awards. In 1966, he published his last collection of poems, *To Give and to Have, and Other Poems*, which is virtually a balance sheet of his life, strongly overshadowed by the presentiment of death. In 1967, Oxford University bestowed an honorary degree on him. He died in Naples the following year as a result of a cerebral hemorrhage suffered in Amalfi, where he had been invited to preside over a poetry competition.

ANALYSIS

Salvatore Quasimodo lived and worked in a period that harbored innumerable contrasting poetic voices. His courageous attempt to extricate himself from the arid, desolate sphere of an excessively introspective style pointed the way to a new poetry—a poetry that,

without losing its lyric essence, aspires to a modern aesthetic in which civil ethics and poetic vision can coexist.

Unlike the poetry of his two great contemporaries, Quasimodo's poetic works can be divided into two sharply distinct periods. In his first phase, before World War II, Quasimodo wrote Hermetic poetry characterized by highly compressed images, allusive language, and a pervasive existential anguish. In his second phase, Quasimodo became convinced that Hermetic poetry had exhausted itself in excessively self-absorbed, contorted, and abstract imagery. He came to believe that the poet's moral duty was to be socially committed and to express the collective despair, sorrow, and frustration of his time, a position first made clear in the collection *Ed è subito sera*.

This second phase of Quasimodo's poetry characterized by a more discursive style, the use of a plainer language, and, above all, a strong ideological and social content—need not be interpreted, however, as an unequivocal rejection of his Hermetic past, but may rather be seen as an evolution (dictated, perhaps, by the historical situation) toward new themes and a more decisive social, political, and moral commitment. In his evolution from modernist Hermeticism to a poetry of engagement, Quasimodo was able to capture and express with rare insight and sensitivity not only his own feelings and aspirations but also those of his era.

ACQUE E TERRE

Echoes of many poetic traditions, particularly of such poets as Pascoli, D'Annunzio, Filippo Tommaso Marinetti, and Sergio Corazzini, are clearly detectable in Quasimodo's first book of verses, *Acque e terre*. The gravitational presence of Ungaretti and Montale is even more noticeable in this volume. The recurrent theme of the poet's youth, evoked through the rediscovery of the ancient myths of Sicily, is a constant in Quasimodo's work. Quasimodo further intertwines an incisive imagery, boldly carved, and a personal use of antithesis employed on a conceptual as well as on a semantic level. It is through the analysis of opposites such as life/death and joy/sorrow that the reader gradually penetrates the existential inner world of the poet and the quasi-metaphysical anguish of the moral and historical wasteland of his age.

IDEOLOGY AND SOCIAL ENGAGEMENT

World War II brought about the externalization of the poet's feelings, a sort of psychological denouement along with a measure of objectivity induced by the mercilessly all-encompassing war years. Beginning with the poems of *Giorno dopo giorno*, Quasimodo made a conscious and coherent effort to overcome early unresolved dissonances and to present the reader with his own historical experience defined within the framework of a choral poetic. As Quasimodo moved toward a poetry of ideological and social engagement, he gradually rejected the poetics of memory, seen as a negation of life as exemplified in "Quasi un madrigale" ("Almost a Madrigal") from *La vita non è un sogno*: "I have no more memories, I do not want to remember;/ memory stems from death,/ life is endless." The final assimilation of opposites was dialectically assured by Quasimodo's realization of the necessity for a new ethical dimension; he was forced to abandon once and for all his poetic monologue in favor of a socially committed dialogue with his fellow humans. In "Epitaffio per Bice Donetti" ("Epitaph for Bice Donetti"), from *La vita non è un sogno*, life and death are no longer antithetical and their synthesis is suggested by his discovery of a shared destiny: He is "one of many others" and thus finds his roots in the sorrowful plight common to all humankind.

ED È SUBITO SERA

The collected verses of *Ed è subito sera* were the result of painstaking revision and selection of poems from Quasimodo's previous collections, from *Acque e terre* and *Oboe sommerso* to *Erato e Apollion*. With the addition of a number of new poems, *Ed è subito sera* constituted both the definitive statement of his past work and the assertion of a new aesthetic vision. With the new poems that concluded the collection, Quasimodo turned to longer, more discursive verse forms (especially the hendecasyllable) and to a less cryptic use of language. While these changes reflected to a certain extent the vogue for neorealism, Quasimodo's stylistic evolution was also influenced significantly by two other factors: first, the stylistic models that he encountered in translating the classics, and second, the urgency of speaking out against the ills of fascism and war, which necessitated the establishment of a new relationship with his readers.

FROM "I" TO "WE"

The twenty poems of *Con il piede straniero sopra il cuore*, eighteen of which were to be included the following year in *Giorno dopo giorno*, dramatically reaffirm the new poetic phase initiated in *Ed è subito sera*. Quasimodo's Hermetic phase, with its inward focus on the self and on memory, is typified by the careful choice of a few nouns and adjectives in the poem "L'eucalyptus" ("The Eucalyptus") from *Oboe sommerso*: "In me un albero oscilla/ da assonnata riva,/ alata aria/ amare fronde esala" ("Within me sways a tree/ from sleeping shores/ winged air exhales/ my bitter fronds"). By contrast, in "Alle fronde dei salici"—published in 1947 in *Giorno dopo giorno* but written three years earlier, in the winter of 1944, during the harshest period of the German Occupation—Quasimodo is painfully aware that the time has come to break away from his Hermetic past in order to speak with a new voice and of new themes: "E come potevamo noi contare/ con il piede straniero sopra il cuore,/ fra i morti abbandonati nelle piazze/ . . . Alle fronde dei salici, per voto/ anche le nostre cetre erano appese" ("And how could we sing/ with an invader's foot on your heart/ among the dead abandoned in the squares/ . . . To the branches of the willow, as a vow/ also our lyres were hung up"). The language is no longer rarefied and impenetrable; it is almost epic in tone, and the poet has switched from "I" to the choral "we." As Quasimodo himself said in a speech in 1953,

> something happened in the field of poetry about 1945, a dramatic destruction of the content inherited from an indifferent idealism and the poetic language flourishing up to that time. . . . All of a sudden the poet found himself thrust out of his own internal history; in war his individual intelligence was worth no more than the collective intelligence of the people. . . . The private (lyric) discourse . . . became choral.

Quasimodo continued to develop in this direction; in *La vita non è un sogno*, certain poems are unusually long, and throughout the volume, the poet actively seeks dialogue with his readers. *Il falso e vero verde* comprises fourteen poems and translations covering a wide variety of themes and levels of experience, moving from the medieval Lauds (honoring a fallen Resistance fighter) to a quasi-surrealistic search for roots. A progression of moods and subjects, from the Athenian Acropolis to Sputnik, also prevails in the twenty-five poems of *La terra impareggiabile*. A dominant theme, however, is clearly identifiable in the first poem of the collection, "Visibile, Invisibile" ("Visible, Invisible"): The search for the great divide of time, for a dividing line between the present (visible) and the past or future (invisible), bears witness to Quasimodo's unrelenting quest for a poetic and ideological fusion of form and content.

TO GIVE AND TO HAVE

The final stage, the "synthesis" of Quasimodo's dialectical probing into the self while reaching for universal truths, is contained in the twenty-three poems of *To Give and to Have* (also published under the title *Debit and Credit*). In this last book of poems—to which are appended the text of the libretto *Billy Budd* (1949), as well as translations from Homer's *Iliad* (c. 750 B.C.E.; English translation, 1611), from Giovanni Boccaccio's *Buccolicum carmen* (c. 1351-1366; *Boccaccio's Olympia*, 1913) and from the Romanian poet Tudor Arghezi—Quasimodo makes his final statement on life and death, an absorbed and reflective pulling together of the threads of his total poetic experience. As the title implies, *To Give and to Have* is a sort of balance sheet of the poet's life, a summation, of his dialectic search.

Somberly reviewing his life and world, the poet softens the tones of his social and ideological commitment, looking again within the self, pondering his human adventure and his passage through time. The presentiment of death is everywhere, but in conjunction with calm acceptance: "I am not fearful before death/ just as I was not timid before life," he writes while lying in his hospital bed in Russia ("Varvàra Alexandrovna"). Acceptance, if not detachment, is again pervasive in "Il silenzio non m'inganna" ("The Silence Does Not Deceive Me"): "I write down words, analogies, and try/ to trace a possible link/ between my life and death. The present is outside."

Quasimodo's language, too, seems to have gained a new equilibrium in which meditative expression predominates. More accessible than his obscure and often strident early style, it is, at the same time, less discursive and more controlled than the language of the war

years. The poet has taken stock of himself and appears reconciled to the idea of impending death, which he acknowledges in a kind of spiritual testament to his fellow humans, devoid of anguish and metaphysical anxieties.

OTHER MAJOR WORKS

NONFICTION: *Petrarca e il sentimento della solitudine*, 1945; *Il poeta e il politico e altri saggi*, 1960 (*The Poet and the Politician, and Other Essays*, 1964); *Scritti sul teatro*, 1961; *Leonida di Taranto*, 1968.

EDITED TEXTS: *Lirica d'amore italiana, dalle origini ai nostri giorni*, 1957; *Poesia italiana del dopoguerra*, 1958.

TRANSLATIONS: *Lirici greci*, 1940 (of Greek lyric poets); *Il fiore della Georgiche*, 1944 (of Vergil's *Georgics*); *Dall'Odissea*, 1945 (of Homer's *Odyssey*); *Veronensis Carmina*, 1945 (of Catullus); *Edipo re*, 1946 (of Sophocles' play); *La Bibbia di Amiens*, 1946 (of John Ruskin); *Romeo e Giulietta*, 1948 (of William Shakespeare's play); *Le Coefore*, 1949 (of Aeschylus's play *Choēphoroi*); *Il Vangelo secondo Giovanni*, 1950 (of the Book of John); *Macbeth*, 1952 (of Shakespeare's play); *Poesie*, 1952 (of Pablo Neruda); *Riccardo III*, 1952 (of Shakespeare's play); *Elettra*, 1954 (of Sophocles' play); *Canti*, 1955 (of Catullus); *La tempesta*, 1956 (of Shakespeare's play); *Il Tartufo*, 1957 (of Molière's play); *Poesie scelte*, 1958 (of E. E. Cummings); *Dalle Metamorfosi*, 1959 (of Ovid); *Otello*, 1959 (of Shakespeare's play); *Ecuba*, 1962 (of Euripedes' play); *Mutevoli pensieri*, 1963 (of Conrad Aiken); *Antonio e Cleopatra*, 1966 (of Shakespeare's play); *Eracle*, 1966 (of Euripides' play); *Poesie*, 1966 (of Tudor Arghezi); *Chemin de Croix*, 1967 (of Pericle Patocchi); *Dall'Iliade*, 1968 (translation from Homer's *Iliad*); *Leonida di Taranto*, 1969 (of Leonidas); *Donner à voir*, 1970 (translation of Paul Éluard's book of the same title).

MISCELLANEOUS: *The Selected Writings of Salvatore Quasimodo*, 1960.

BIBLIOGRAPHY

Condini, Ned, ed. *An Anthology of Modern Italian Poetry in English Translation, with Italian Text*. New York: Modern Language Association of America, 2009. Contains a section featuring the Hermeticists, including Quasimodo. Introduction to the bilingual text provides information on Quasimodo and places him in context.

Cro, Stelio. "Salvatore Quasimodo." In *Twentieth Century Italian Poets, First Series*, edited by Giovanna De Satasio. Vol. 114 in *Dictionary of Literary Biography*. Detroit: Gale, 1992. A full biographical treatment in English. Traces the development of Quasimodo's poetry and translation from his early explorations of Hermeticism to his more political (and less successful) poetry after World War II.

Hays, Gregory. "Le morte stagioni: Intertextuality in Quasimodo's *Lirici greci*." *Forum Italicum* 29, no. 1 (Spring, 1995): 26-43. A critical study of Quasimodo's translations of ancient Greek poetry.

Jones, F. J. "The Poetry of Salvatore Quasimodo." *Italian Studies* 16 (1961): 60-77. An overview of the poet's major themes and genres.

Loriggio, Francesco. "Modernity and the Ambiguities of Exile: On the Poetry of Salvatore Quasimodo." *Rivista di studi italiani* 12, no. 1 (June, 1994): 101-120. Loriggio examines Quasimodo's poetry on the theme of exile and shows how it was this theme that caused Quasimodo's popularity to decline in the middle of the twentieth century and to be rekindled at century's end. Loriggio's analysis is clear and readable but unfortunately the passages of poetry he examines closely are rendered in the original Italian.

McKendrick, Jamie, ed. *The Faber Book of Twentieth-Century Italian Poems*. London: Faber and Faber, 2004. Presents translations of the major Italian poets of the twentieth century, including Quasimodo. Introduction places the poet among his contemporaries.

Roberto Severino

R

MIKLÓS RADNÓTI
Miklós Glatter

Born: Budapest, Austro-Hungarian Empire (now in Hungary); May 5, 1909
Died: Near Abda, Hungary; November 8(?), 1944

PRINCIPAL POETRY

Pogány köszöntő, 1930 (*Pagan Salute*, 1980)
Újmódi pásztorok éneke, 1931 (*Song of Modern Shepherds*, 1980)
Lábadozó szél, 1933 (*Convalescent Wind*, 1980)
Újhold, 1935 (*New Moon*, 1980)
Járkálj csak, halálraítélt!, 1936 (*Walk On, Condemned!*, 1980)
Meredek út, 1938 (*Steep Road*, 1980)
Naptár, 1942 (*Calendar*, 1980)
Tajtékos ég, 1946 (*Sky with Clouds*, 1980)
Bori notesz, 1970 (*Camp Notebook*, 2000)
Subway Stops, 1977
The Witness: Selected Poems by Miklós Radnóti, 1977
Radnóti Miklós müvei, 1978
Forced March, 1979
The Complete Poetry, 1980
Last Poems of Miklós Radnóti, 1994

OTHER LITERARY FORMS

Miklós Radnóti (RAWD-not-ee) excelled as a translator of classical and modern poetry from a number of Western languages into Hungarian. A collection of his translations appeared in 1943 under the title *Orpheus nyomában* (in the footsteps of Orpheus). Of his prose, *Ikrek hava* (1939; *The Month of Gemini*, 1979), a quasi autobiography, is most significant; also noteworthy is his doctoral dissertation on the Hungarian novelist and poet Margit Kaffka, *Kaffka Margit művészi fejlődése* (1934; the artistic development of Margit Kaffka).

ACHIEVEMENTS

Miklós Radnóti received his doctoral degree in 1934 and was awarded the prestigious Baumgarten Prize only four years later. From this auspicious beginning, he began building his readership, so that by the height of his career few modern Hungarian poets had a wider reading public than Radnóti. Radnóti's forte was his ability to fuse elements from diverse poetic traditions, filling traditional forms with new, unexpected messages, especially the terrifying experiences resulting from the Nazi Occupation of Central and Eastern Europe. While young, he boldly experimented with free verse, but his mature poetry is devoid of flamboyance, characterized instead by classical simplicity and dignity. His major contribution to Hungarian letters is that he served as an artistic and a moral example for several generations of Hungarian artists by speaking for his nation and representing his country's best humanist traditions amid war, privation, and persecution.

BIOGRAPHY

Miklós Radnóti (born Miklós Glatter) lived for only thirty-five years, and even his birth was darkened by tragedy in that his mother and twin brother both died. Radnóti's father soon remarried; Radnóti deeply loved his stepmother and the daughter born of the second marriage, yet grief and guilt feelings concerning the double tragedy of his birth influenced his entire creative life. The figure of his mother is a recurring image in Radnóti's poetry and prose.

Radnóti completed his elementary and high school education in Budapest. Then, following the suggestion of his guardian (his father, too, had died), he spent 1927 and 1928 in Liberec, Czechoslovakia (now Czech Republic), studying textile technology and working in an office. In the fall of 1930, he enrolled at Szeged University, majoring in Hungarian and French. By the time he received his doctorate in 1934, he had several volumes of poetry in print. It was during this period that he assumed the name "Radnóti," after Radnót, the town in northeastern Hungary where his father had been born.

During the late 1920's and at the beginning of the 1930's, Radnóti became involved with youth organizations that were culturally nurtured by ideas from the

Left. During this period, he wrote "engaged" poetry, using a deliberately nonpoetical language meant to identify him with the working class. Since that identification lacked the reality of experience, it exhausted itself in language and remained unconvincing. During his first trip to Paris in 1931, Radnóti met a number of French writers and artists, who introduced him to the poetry of Guillaume Apollinaire, Blaise Cendrars, Paul Valéry, and Valery Larbaud. The progressive nature of this poetry liberated Radnóti from the confines of narrow social protest, and with his Storm and Stress period behind him, he began to develop his mature style.

In 1935, Radnóti married his childhood sweetheart, Fanni Gyarmati, hoping to secure a teaching position in the Hungarian high school system. When this did not work out, he took temporary jobs, chiefly private tutoring, and accepted partial support from his wife's family.

As Hungary's political climate turned increasingly fascist, Radnóti shared the fate of those who had been persecuted for their Jewish origins. With the exception of brief periods of respite, he spent the years from 1940 until his death in various forced-labor camps, first in Hungary and later, after Hungary's occupation by the Nazis (March 19, 1944), working a copper mine in Bor, Yugoslavia (now Serbia). In the course of the Nazi retreat, Radnóti's company was also returned to Hungary, then moved west in the direction of the German (Austrian) border. Radnóti, however, died while still in Hungary, murdered by the soldiers guarding his group. He was among those who were shot after being forced to dig their own graves.

When Radnóti's body was exhumed on June 23, 1946, nearly two years after his death, a small, black notebook was found in which Radnóti had written ten poems. (These poems appear in the volume *Sky with Clouds*.) It is a measure of Radnóti's current standing in Hungarian poetry that a scholarly facsimile edition of this notebook, *Camp Notebook*, originally issued in 1970, had gone into multiple printings.

ANALYSIS

At the beginning of his career, Miklós Radnóti saw himself as a representative of a new literature, different in language and style from that of the previous genera-

tion of Hungarian poets. Together with fellow rebels, he attacked what he regarded as the tepid traditions of the past, boldly declaring himself one of the "modern shepherds." The title of his first volume, *Pagan Salute*, suggests the rebellious spirit of Radnóti's early work. The narrator of this first collection rejects the pacifying teachings of church and state and sings about the freedom of love and his desire for a natural life. The Romantic image of the shepherd placed in a pastoral landscape is one of the few happy, carefree images in all of Radnóti's work.

"LAW"

Radnóti's youthful poems are characterized by social commentary, often obliquely expressed by means of images from nature. In "Law," for example, an allegory about the illegal Socialist movement after the Nazi victories of 1933, Radnóti advances his political views in the guise of a "nature poem." The wind "drops" passwords and whistles the secret signals of the conspirators. The political freeze is described as winter, and the new grass bares not the expected "blade" but a "dagger." The laws of nature are translated by Radnóti into the law of revolution, and in the last stanzas, the poet confirms his ties with the underground movement and calls on others to follow his example. A tree dropping a "leaf," which by this point in the poem can be interpreted only as a political "leaflet" or flier, compels the reader to respond; thus, the poem becomes its own political leaflet.

LOVE POEMS

Radnóti's early work is also characterized by a strong erotic charge, although it is often unclear whether this represents a genuine expression of sexual desire or is merely another manifestation of the poet's urge to revolt against social conventions. Between 1933 and 1935, when he married Fanni Gyarmati, however, Radnóti's erotic/political poems changed dramatically. A new gravity and a mood approaching resignation accompanied his awareness of impending war; his manner became calmer and more controlled. His language, too, was simplified, so that a more personal, lyric voice could emerge.

The erotic flame of the sexual poems was replaced by a lyric glow, and the violent sexual images by intimate, tender descriptions of lovers. Radnóti became protective of married love, remaining silent about sexual relations. Indeed, Radnoti's love poems to Fanni recall in their classical simplicity the great love lyrics of Mihály Vörösmarty and Sándor Petőfi, the preeminent Hungarian poets of the nineteenth century.

"LIKE A BULL"

Finally, the transition from Radnóti's youthful, rebellious stance to his mature style can be traced in the poet's changing self-image. In "Like a Bull," written in 1933, the poet is represented by a young bull, a pointedly strong and masculine image chosen to reflect an unsentimental view of the cruelties of the world during troubled times. In other poems of this period, the narrators are young men who do not attempt to hide from their fate and who openly condemn the perpetrators of evil.

"WAR DIARY"

Gradually, however, there is a transformation in the poet's self-image: He is reduced, as it were, to his pure function as a poet. This transformation begins with the cycle "War Diary," in which the poet envisions himself both as a corpse and as a disembodied spirit. The entire cycle of four poems is marked by a sense of distance, as if the poet had already died and was now observing life from the other side. The effect is not one of detachment but rather of extraordinary poignancy: The poet has stripped himself of all that is inessential, but not of his humanity. This cycle anticipates the poems that Radnóti wrote in Serbian concentration camps during the final days of his life; in one of these last poems, "Root," the poet writes: "I am now a root myself—/ it's with worms I make my home,/ there, I am building this poem." This image is a far cry from the bold, patriotic, young songster of Radnóti's early verse.

"I CANNOT KNOW . . ."

Among Radnóti's images, a few run throughout his oeuvre as recurring metaphors and symbols. He uses the figure of the pilot, for example, as an embodiment of the amorality chillingly evident in the war. The pilot becomes a symbol of all willing instruments in the service of inhumanity; his actions derive from a worldview in which separation leads to indifference. When sufficient distance is created between malefactor and victim, the wrongdoer ceases to feel any guilt concerning his crime. In the poem "I Cannot Know . . ."

(written in 1944), Radnóti pits the humanist's values against those of the pilot. It is a poem about Hungary as seen, on one hand, by a native son, the poet, and, on the other hand, by a pilot of a bomber from another country. The poet sees his "tiny land" on a human scale: "when a bush kneels, once in a while,/ at my feet, I know its name and can name its blossom;/ I know where people are headed on the road, as I know them." To the man in the plane, however, "it's a map, this country,/ he could not point to the home of Mihály Vörösmarty." The pilot sees only military targets—"army posts, factories" while the poet sees "grasshoppers, oxen, towers, farms, gentle fields."

"SECOND ECLOGUE"

Radnóti treats the symbolic figure of the pilot with greater complexity in his "Second Eclogue," a poem in dialogue form that opens with the bragging of a dashing pilot. The pilot concludes his speech, the first of the poem's four parts, by asking the poet, "Have you written since yesterday?" The poet answers, "I have," and while he retains a touch of a child's wonder at the miracle of people being able to fly, he goes on to identify the differences between his permanent role as a humanitarian and the pilot's temporary role in social change. Listening to each other, they begin to perceive themselves better. The poet recognizes the strengths of his own position by measuring his moral courage against the daring stunts of the pilot. As the poet discovers with surprise his own courage, so in his second speech the pilot admits his fears. Indeed, he goes beyond this admission to acknowledge a far more troubling truth: He, who "lived like a man once," has become something inhuman, living only to destroy. Who will understand, he asks, that he was once human? Thus, he closes his second speech with a plea to the poet: "Will you write about me?" The poet's answer, which concludes the dialogue, is brief: "If I live. And there's anyone around to read it."

In this poem, written in 1941, Radnóti anticipated the conclusions drawn by survivors of the Holocaust: He penetrated and understood the psyche of the offender. He does not forgive. Rather, he draws a circle to connect the murderer and his victim, by which a sort of intimacy is established: In a terrible, absurd way, they alone share the crime.

"Song" and "A Little Duck Bathes"

Radnóti employed recurring images such as that of the pilot to add resonance to his verse, to create a rich texture of associations and layers of meaning. The same impulse lies behind his "quotation" of poetic forms and themes from a great diversity of sources, varying from Vergil to Hungarian folk culture, in which he establishes a fruitful tension with his models. "A Little Duck Bathes," for example, is based on one of the most popular Hungarian nursery rhymes. By reversing the structure of the first sentence, Radnóti establishes the dialectical tension by which the entire poem is structured: The unabashed eroticism of the text is counterpointed by the original meter of the nursery rhyme. The energy of the new poem derives from its conflict with its model. Similarly, Radnóti's poem "Song" is modeled on the "outlaw song," a readily identifiable type of Hungarian folk song. Dealing with the misery of the homeless refugee, the poor exile, and the defeated patriot, the outlaw song (derived in turn from the *kuruc* song) provides Radnóti with a vehicle for calling attention to historical precedents for the exile of poets within their homeland.

Radnóti's technique of complex "quotation" is supremely exemplified in his eclogues. Radnóti's eight poems written in this classical form constitute his literary testament. In them, he describes and responds to the devastating events of his time, deliberately choosing this traditionally bucolic genre to convey his tragic vision.

"Eighth Eclogue"

Radnóti's eclogues achieve their greatest evocative power precisely from this conflict between form and content, which forces the reader to assume a critical distance, to reflect on the implications of this violation of genre. In these poems, Radnóti meditates on the nature of poetry and on the poet's commitment to a better world. For Radnóti, to live meant to create, and even amid filth, indignities, and the fear of death, the concept of home appears in a literary metaphor, a land in which it is known what a hexameter is. The "Eighth Eclogue," the last of the series, combines biblical and classical traditions. Here, the poet conducts a dialogue with the biblical Nahum, a true prophet; Nahum encourages the poet by telling him that prophets and poets are closely related, suggesting that they should "take to the road" together. Thus, in his "Eighth Eclogue," Radnóti revived the messianic conception of the poet that was at the heart of the Romantic movement in Hungary.

Long before the actual forced march that ended in his death, Radnóti spiritually set out on the lonely road leading to the grave. By 1940, his imminent death had become a recurring image in his poems, frequently appearing in concluding lines. Here, Fanni alone can offer him comfort; her bodily closeness is his only haven. Her presence quiets his fears following nightmares about death ("Your Right Hand on My Nape"), and only her embrace can make the moment of death pass as if it were a dream ("In Your Arms").

"Forced March"

Although he had long been prepared for death, Radnóti paradoxically regained a hope for survival during the last bitter weeks of his life. The wish to live, to return to Fanni, to tell about the horrors, and to wait for a "wiser, handsome death" permeates several of the poems so aptly called the "hymns from Bor." Well aware that this hope was flimsy at best, based on desire more than on truth, Radnóti expressed its elusiveness in "Forced March."

The poem begins with a judgmental view of the poet, observed in the third person. His unreasonable behavior is exposed, his foolish agreement to his own torture is condemned. He is called upon to explain his decision to walk on, and his answer is shown up as a naïve, self-deceiving daydream. Halfway through the poem, however, a sudden transformation occurs, a shift from the third person to the first. Judgment turns into a confession of hope, the war-torn landscape is transmuted into an idyll of bygone days, dogged resistance into a cosmic, optimistic message. In a world from which reason has disappeared, anything, including superstition and magic, can serve as crutches. Thus, by the end of the poem, the two halves of the lyric ego merge, and harmony is reestablished—a new harmony in which primordial beliefs are accepted as truth, befitting a world devoid of civilization.

Each line of "Forced March" is broken by a caesura, marked by a blank space, so that the poem is divided into two jagged columns. The pounding rhythm of the verse re-creates the sound of the heavy footsteps with which the exhausted men dragged themselves on the road—a beautiful example of form functioning as message. "Forced March" impresses and moves the reader with its spontaneity, its simple vocabulary and familiar imagery, its emotional directness, and yet—characteristically of Radnóti—the texture of the poem is more complex than might at first appear, for woven into it are allusions to a medieval masterpiece, Walther von der Vogelweide's "Ouwe war sint verswunden alliu miniu jar?" ("Where Have All My Years Disappeared?")—a poem that Radnóti had translated. There, too, home can never again be what it once was; the people are gone, the farmhouse has collapsed, and what was once joyous has disappeared.

"Forced March" has a special place in Radnóti's oeuvre: It represents hope's triumph over despair. Above all, it shows the artist's triumph over his own fate. It proves that even during the last weeks of his tormented life, Radnóti was able to compose with precise poetic principles in mind, that he was in control of his material, playing secretly with literary and existential relationships and creating out of all this an enduring testament.

"RAZGLEDNICAS"

Radnóti's last poems were four short pieces that chart his final steps toward death and, at the same time, signal his withdrawal from participation in life. These poems are collectively titled "Razglednicas," a word of Serbo-Croatian origin meaning picture postcards, and indeed they provide a terrifyingly precise pictorial description of the horrors that the poet experienced in the last month of his life. Separate as they stand in their unique message, the "Razglednicas" are by no means unrelated to the rest of Radnóti's poetry. They have a particularly close emotive and textual contact with his longer poems (such as "Forced March" and "Letter to My Wife") written during the same period, and together they render a final panorama of Radnóti's surroundings, depicting the devastation that humans and nature suffer in a ravaging war.

OTHER MAJOR WORKS

NONFICTION: *Kaffka Margit művészi fejlődése*, 1934; *Ikrek hava*, 1939 (*The Month of Gemini*, 1979).

TRANSLATION: *Orpheus nyomában*, 1943.

BIBLIOGRAPHY

Birnbaum, Marianna D. *Miklós Radnóti: A Biography of His Poetry*. Munich: Finnish-Ugric Seminar, University of Munich, 1983. Connects Radnóti's poems to events in his life. Useful as an introduction to both.

George, Emery. *The Poetry of Miklós Radnóti: A Comparative Study*. New York: Karz-Cohl, 1986. The best scholarly analysis of Radnóti's poetry by his leading translator.

Gömöri, George, and Clive Wilmer, eds. *The Life and Poetry of Miklós Radnóti: Essays*. Boulder, Colo.: East European Monographs, 1999. A good collection of critical essays on various, often highly esoteric, themes in Radnóti's poetry.

Ozsváth, Zsuzsanna. *In the Footsteps of Orpheus: The Life and Times of Miklós Radnóti*. Bloomington. Indiana University Press, 2000. A very readable biography of the poet.

M. D. Birnbaum

PIERRE REVERDY

Born: Narbonne, France; September 13, 1889
Died: Solesmes, France; June 17, 1960

PRINCIPAL POETRY
Poèmes en prose, 1915 (*Prose Poems*, 2007)
La Lucarne ovale, 1916
Quelques poèmes, 1916
Les Ardoises du toit, 1918 (*Roof Slates*, 1981)
Les Jockeys camouflés, 1918
La Guitare endormie, 1919
Cœur de chêne, 1921
Étoiles peintes, 1921
Cravates de chanvre, 1922
Grande Nature, 1925
La Balle au bond, 1928
Sources du vent, 1929
Pierres blanches, 1930
Ferraille, 1937
Plein verre, 1940

Plupart du temps, 1945 (collected volume, 1913-
    1922)
Le Chant des morts, 1948
Main d'œuvre: Poèmes, 1913-1949, 1949
Pierre Reverdy: Selected Poems, 1969
Roof Slates, and Other Poems of Pierre Reverdy,
    1981
Selected Poems, 1991

OTHER LITERARY FORMS

Pierre Reverdy (ruh-VEHR-dee) worked extensively in other forms besides poetry. He wrote two novels and many stories and published collections of prose
poems. Most of these are in a Surrealist vein, mixing
experimentation in language with personal and unconscious reflection. As an editor of an avant-garde review, Reverdy also contributed important theoretical
statements on cubism and avant-garde literary practice.
Later in his career, he published several volumes of
reminiscences, including sensitive reevaluations of the
work of his near contemporaries, including Guillaume
Apollinaire.

Pierre Reverdy

ACHIEVEMENTS

Pierre Reverdy is one of the most central and influential writers in the tradition of twentieth century
avant-garde poetry. Already well established in terms
of both his work and his theoretical stance by the mid-
1910's, Reverdy exerted considerable influence over
the Dada and Surrealist movements, with which he was
both officially and informally affiliated.

Reverdy's firm conviction was in a nonmimetic, non-
traditional form of artistic expression. The art he championed and practiced would create a reality of its own
rather than mirror a preexisting reality. In this way, the
language of poetry would be cut loose from restraining
conventions of meter, syntax, and punctuation in order
to be able to explore the emotion generated by the poetic image.

In connection with the avant-garde artists of cubism, Dada, and Surrealism, Reverdy's formulations
helped to break down the traditional models of artistic
creation that then held firm sway in France. Reverdy's
firm conviction was that artistic creation precedes aesthetic theory. All the concrete means at an artist's disposal constitute his aesthetic formation.

Along with Apollinaire, his slightly older contemporary, Reverdy became a central figure and example for a whole generation of French poets generally
grouped under the Surrealist heading. His having been
translated into English by a range of American poets
from Kenneth Rexroth to John Ashbery shows the importance of his work to the modern American tradition
as well.

BIOGRAPHY

Pierre Reverdy was born on September 13, 1889, in
Narbonne, France, a city in the Languedoc region. The
son and grandson of sculptors and artisans in wood
carving, he grew up with this practical skill in addition
to his formal studies. The Languedoc region at the turn
of the century was an especially volatile region, witnessing the last major peasant uprising in modern
French history.

After completing his schooling in Narbonne and
nearby Toulouse, Reverdy moved to Paris in 1910,
where he lived on and off for the rest of his life. Although exempted from military service, he volunteered

at the outbreak of World War I, saw combat service, and was discharged in 1916. By profession a typesetter, Reverdy also worked as the director of the review *Nord-Sud*, which he founded in 1917.

From 1910 to 1926, Reverdy worked in close contact with almost all the important artists of his time. He had especially close relationships with Pablo Picasso and Juan Gris, both of whom contributed illustrations to collections of his verse. As the editor of an influential review, he had close contact with and strong influence on the writers who were to form the Dada and Surrealist movements. Already an avant-garde poet and theorist of some prominence by the late 1910's, Reverdy was often invoked along with Apollinaire as one of the precursors of Surrealism. He collaborated with the early Surrealist efforts and continued his loose affiliation even after a formal break in 1926.

That year saw Reverdy's conversion to a mystic Catholicism. From then until his death in 1960, his life became more detached from the quotidian, and he spent much of his time at the Abbey of Solesmes, where he died.

ANALYSIS

In an early statement on cubism, Pierre Reverdy declaimed that a new epoch was beginning, one in which "one creates works that, by detaching themselves from life, enter back into it because they have an existence of their own." In addition to attacking mimetic standards of reproduction, or representation of reality, he also called for a renunciation of punctuation and a freeing of syntax in the writing of poetry. Rather than being something fixed according to rules, for Reverdy, syntax was "a medium of literary creation." Changing the rules of literary expression carried with it a change in ideas of representation. For Reverdy, the poetic image was solely responsible to the discovery of emotional truth.

From 1915 to 1922, Reverdy produced many volumes of poetry. The avant-garde called for an overturning of literary conventions, and Reverdy contributed with his own explosion of creative activity. In addition to editing the influential review *Nord-Sud*, he used his experience as an engraver and typesetter to publish books, including his own. The list of artists who con-

tributed the illustrations to these volumes of poetry by Reverdy reads like a Who's Who of the art world of the time: Gris, Picasso, André Derain, Henri Matisse, Georges Braque, among others. Reverdy's work, along with that of Apollinaire, was cited as the guiding force for Surrealism by André Breton in his *Manifestes du surréalisme* (1962; *Manifestoes of Surrealism*, 1969).

Reverdy's early work achieves an extreme detachment from mimetic standards and literary conventions that allows for the images to stand forth as though seen shockingly for the first time. The last two lines from "Sur le Talus" (on the talus), published in 1918, show this extreme detachment: "L'eau monte comme une poussière/ Le silence ferme la nuit" (The water rises like dust/ Silence shuts the night). There can be no question here of establishing a realistic context for these images. Rather, one is cast back on the weight of emotion that they carry and that must thus guide their interpretation. Reflections off water may appear to rise in various settings, though perhaps particularly at twilight. The dust points to a particular kind of aridity that may be primarily an emotional state. The sudden transition from an (implied) twilight to an abrupt nightfall undercuts any kind of conventional emotional presentation. The quick cut is a measure perhaps of the individual's lack of control over external phenomena and, by extension, inner feelings as well.

"CARREFOUR"

Much of Reverdy's early work is based on just such an imagistic depiction of interior states, with a strong element of detachment from reality and a certain resulting confusion or overlapping. The force of emotion is clearly there, but to pin it down to a particular situation or persona proves difficult because any such certainty is constantly being undercut by the quick transitions between images. The complete suppression of punctuation as well as a certain freedom of syntax as one moves from line to line are clearly tools that Reverdy developed to increase the level of logical disjunction in his poetry. At times, however, this disjunction in the logical progression of word and image gives way to a resolution. The short poem "Carrefour" (crossroad) sets up a surreal image sequence:

De l'air
De la lumière
Un rayon sur le bord du verre
Ma main déçue n'attrape rien

Air
Light
A ray on the edge of the glass
My disappointed hand holds nothing

Here the elements are invoked, and then two images, one of an inanimate object and one the hand of the speaker. From this atmosphere of mystery and disjunction, the poem's conclusion moves to a fairly well-defined emotional statement:

Enfin tout seul j'aurai vécu
Jusqu'au dernier matin
Sans qu'un mot m'indiquât quel fut le bon chemin

After all I will have lived all alone
Until the last morning
Without a single word that might have shown me
which was the right way

Here, as in many of Reverdy's poems, the emotion evoked is a kind of diffused sadness. The solitary individual is probably meant to stand for an aspect of the human condition, alone in a confrontation with an unknown destiny.

It was Reverdy's fate to see actual military duty during World War I, and it may well be that the magnitude of human tragedy he witnessed at the front lines served to mute the youthful enthusiasm that pervades his earliest works. It may also be the case that Reverdy, while espousing radical measures in literary practice, still was caught in the kind of bittersweet ethos that characterizes fin de siècle writers generally.

"Guerre"

Whatever the case may be, there is no question that Reverdy wrote some of the most affecting war poems in the French language. One of the most direct is titled simply "Guerre" (war). Running through a series of disjointed, if coherent, images, Reverdy toward the end of the poem approaches direct statement, when the speaker says:

Et la figure attristée
Visage des visages
La mort passe sur le chemin

And the saddened figure
Visage of visages
Death passes along the road

Close to a medieval allegorizing of death, this figure also incorporates a fascination with the effect of the gaze. One's face is revealing of one's emotion because of the way one looks—the distillation of the phenomenon into a general characteristic is a strong term to describe death. If this image is strong, the poem's ending is more forceful still:

Mais quel autre poids que celui de ton corps
as-tu jeté dans la balance
Tout froid dans le fossé
Il dort sans plus rêver

But what other weight than that of your body
have you thrown in the balance
All cold in the ditch
He sleeps no longer to dream

Philosophers have questioned whether the idea of death is properly an idea, since strictly speaking, it has no content. Caught between viewing another's death from the outside and facing one's own death, which one can never know, death is a supreme mystery of human existence. Reverdy in these lines seems to cross the line between the exterior, objective view of another's death and the unknowable, subjective experience of the individual. This is what he means by the emotion communicated through the poetic image.

Despite a continued tendency toward the surreal image in Reverdy's work, these poems in *Sources du vent* (sources of the wind) also represent the first major collection of poems after Reverdy's conversion to a mystic Catholicism in 1926. Increasingly, his poetry of the postconversion period tends toward an introjection of the conflicts raised through the poetic image. While a tone of lingering sadness had always been present from the earliest work, in these poems, the atmosphere of sadness and loss moves to the center of the poet's concerns. Unlike the conservative Christian poets Charles-Pierre Péguy and Paul Claudel, the content of the poems is never directly religious. Rather, a mood of quietism seems to become more prominent in the collections of poems after the conversion. A concurrent falling off in the level of production also takes place. After 1930, Reverdy publishes only two more individual collections of verse, along with two collected volumes and works in other forms. After 1949, for the last twelve years of his life, the heretofore prolific Reverdy apparently ceased to write altogether.

"MÉMOIRE"

The poem "Mémoire" (memory) from *Pierres blanches* (white stones), shows this mood of increasing resignation in the face of worldly events. The poem invokes a "she," someone who has left or is going to leave, but then, in apparent reference to the title, says there will still be someone:

> Quand nous serons partis là-bas derrière
> Il y aura encore ici quelqu'un
> Pour nous attendre
> Et nous entendre
>
> When we will have gone over there behind
> There will still be someone
> To wait for us
> And to understand us

The positive mood of these lines, however, is undercut by the poem's ending: "Un seul ami/ L'ombre que nous avons laissée sous l'arbre et qui s'ennuie" ("A single friend/ The shadow we have left beneath a tree and who's getting bored"). The impersonality tending toward a universal statement that was present in Reverdy's early work here seems to work toward an effacement of the individual personality. If memory can be imaged as a bored shadow left beneath a tree, the significance of the individual seems tenuous at best. The emotion generated through the poetic image here seems to be one of sadness and extreme resignation.

The interpretation of a poet's work through biography must always be a hazy enterprise, all the more so in a poet such as Reverdy, whose life directly enters into his work not at all. In a general sense, then, the course of his poetic life and production might be said to mirror the course of French literary life generally. The enthusiasm of the avant-garde literary and artistic move-

ments in Europe generally in the early years of the twentieth century saw a reaction in the post-World War I years toward an art that questioned societal assumptions. Dada and Surrealism can be seen in terms of this large movement, and Reverdy's work as an example. The coherence of the Surrealist movement in turn breaks down in the late 1920's and early 1930's with the split coming over what political allegiance the Surrealist artists should take, according to its leaders. Reverdy's personal religious convictions cause him to cease active involvement with the movement altogether. It is a measure of his status as a strong precursor to the movement that he is not attacked directly by the more politically motivated leaders of Surrealism.

"MAIN-MORTE"

With the extreme politicization of the Surrealist movement in the late 1930's, even some of the most dedicated younger adherents to Surrealism cut their formal ties with the movement. René Char is an example. The young Yves Bonnefoy is an example of a poet with early leanings toward Surrealism who in the late 1940's moved more in the direction of a poetry expressive of essential philosophical and human truths. It might be possible, in like manner, to trace Reverdy's increasing distance from Surrealism as a movement to some kind of similar feelings that have been more openly expressed by his younger contemporaries. His collection *Plein Verre* (full glass) does indeed move more toward the mode of longer, contemplative poems, still in the atmosphere of sadness and resignation to life. The end of "Main-Morte" (dead-hand) shows this well:

> Entre l'aveu confus et le lien du mystère
> Les mots silencieux qui tendent leur filet
> Dans tous les coins de cette chambre noire
> Où ton ombre ni moi n'aurons jamais dormi
>
> Between the confused vow and the tie of mystery
> The silent words which offer their net
> In every corner of this black room
> Where your shadow nor I will have ever slept

Even the highly suggestive early lyrics do not contain quite the level of hovering mystery and intricate emotional states offered in these lines. One may well wonder if the "you" invoked here even refers to a person or whether it might be a quasi-human interior presence such as that invoked in the later poems of Wallace Stevens (such as "Final Soliloquy of the Interior Paramour"). The weight of the images in the direction of silence lends to this whole utterance an aura of high seriousness.

"ENFIN"

The last poem in *Plein Verre*, titled "Enfin" (at last), also ends with a statement hinting at a highly serious attitude. The speaker states:

> À travers la poitrine nue
> Là
> Ma clarière
> Avec tout ce qui descend du ciel
> Devenir un autre
> À ras de terre
>
> By means of the naked breast
> There
> My clearing
> Along with all that descends from the sky
> To become an other
> At earth level

More and more in the later poems, a level of ethical statement seems to emerge. Whereas the early poems introduce strange and startling images in an apparently almost random fashion, the images here seem to be coordinated by an overall hierarchy of values, personal and religious. The naked breast at the beginning of this passage thus could refer to the lone individual, perhaps alone with his or her conscience. This is in contrast to something which descends from the sky, an almost unavoidably religious image. The wish "To become an other/ At earth level" might then be interpreted as the fervent desire of an extremely devoted individual to attain a higher level of piety here on earth.

LE CHANT DES MORTS

The extended sequence, *Le Chant des morts* (the song of the dead), composed in 1944-1948 and published in 1948 as part of the collected volume *Main d'œuvre* (work made by hand), presents an extended meditation on the emotional inner scene of war-devastated France. In this sequence, as in his earlier poems on World War I that drew on his direct experience of the horrors of war, Reverdy uses a diction stripped bare of rhetoric, preferring instead the direct, poignant images of death and suffering. Death in these poems is both inescapable and horrible, or as he calls it: "la mort entêtée/ La mort vorace" ("stubborn death/ Voracious death"). As a strong countermovement to the implacable march of death, there is also a tenacious clinging to life. As the poet says: "C'est la faim/ C'est l'ardeur de vivre qui dirigent/ La peur de perdre" ("It is hunger/ It is the ardor to live that guide/ The fear of losing"). The poet of the inner conscience in these poems confronts the essential subject of his deepest meditations: the conscious adoption of his authentic attitude toward death.

The ultimate renunciation of poetry that characterizes the last years of Reverdy's life is preceded by an exploration of the subject most suited to representing death (remembering Sigmund Freud)—that is, silence.

"ET MAINTENANT"

The poem that Reverdy seems to have chosen to come at the end of his collected poems, titled "Et Maintenant" (and now), ends with a poignant image of silence: "Tous les fils dénoués au delà des saisons reprennent leur tour et leur ton sur le fond sombre du silence" ("All the unknotted threads beyond the seasons regain their trace and their tone against the somber background of silence"). Reverdy here seems to hint at what lies beyond poetic expression in several senses. His entire ethos of poetic creation has been consistently based on an act of communication with the reader. Thus, the threads he refers to here could well represent the threads of intention and emotion that his readers follow in his poetry to achieve an experience of that emotion themselves, or to discover an analogous emotional experience in their own memory or personal background. He might also be hinting at those threads of intention and emotion that led beyond the limitations of individual life in a reunification with a divine creator. In the former interpretation, the background of silence would be that silence which precedes the poetic utterance or act of communication, as well as the silence after the act of communication or once the poet has ceased to write. In the religious interpretation, the background of silence would be that nothingness or nonbeing out of which the divine creation takes place and which, in turn, has the capability of incorporating silence or nonbeing into self, a religious attitude of a return to the creator even in the face of one's own personal death.

LEGACY

Reverdy is a complex and fascinating figure in the history of French poetry in the first half of the twentieth century. He was a committed avant-garde artist in the years directly preceding, during, and following World War I; his outpouring of poetry and aesthetic statements made him one of the most significant precursors to the movements of Dada and Surrealism. Though his formal affiliation with the Surrealist movement was of brief duration, his example of using the poetic image to communicate emotion is central to everything for which Surrealism stood. The extreme respect shown to his work by other poets and artists confirms his importance as a creative innovator. Reverdy, in turn, paid respectful homage to his poet and artist contemporaries a stance that shows his ongoing intellectual commitment to the importance of art and literature in human terms, despite his personal isolation and quietism toward the end of his life. The poems from the end of his career that bear the weight of a continued meditation on death are a moving commentary on that from which language emerges and into which it returns: silence.

OTHER MAJOR WORKS

LONG FICTION: *Le Voleur de Talan*, 1917; *La Peau de l'homme*, 1926.

SHORT FICTION: *Risques et périls*, 1930.

NONFICTION: *Self Defence*, 1919; *Le Gant de crin*, 1927; *Le Livre de mon bord*, 1948; *Cette émotion appellée poésie: Écrits sur la poésie, 1932-1960*, 1975; *Nord-Sud, Self Defence, et autres écrits sur l'art et la poésie*, 1975; *Note éternelle du présent*, 1975.

BIBLIOGRAPHY

Greene, Robert W. *The Poetic Theory of Pierre Reverdy*. 1967. Reprint. San Bernardino, Calif.: Borgo Press, 1990. An analysis of Reverdy's work in poetic theory.

Pap, Jennifer. "Transforming the Horizon: Reverdy's World War I." *Modern Language Review* 101, no. 4 (October, 2006): 966-978. Pap examines the theme of war in Reverdy's works, noting that although he favored an art that followed its own aims, he did treat the war in his poetry.

Rizzuto, Anthony. *Style and Theme in Reverdy's "Les Ardoises du toit."* Tuscaloosa: University of Alabama Press, 1971. Rizzuto's critical study of one of Reverdy's poetic works. Includes bibliographic references.

Rothwell, Andrew. *Textual Spaces: The Poetry of Pierre Reverdy*. Atlanta: Rodopi, 1989. A critical analysis of Reverdy's works. Includes bibliographic references.

Schroeder, Jean. *Pierre Reverdy*. Boston: Twayne, 1981. An introductory biography and critical study of selected works by Reverdy. Includes an index and bibliographic references.

Sweet, David LeHardy. *Savage Sight/Constructed Noise: Poetic Adaptations of Painterly Techniques in the French and American Avant-gardes*. Chapel Hill: Department of Romance Languages, University of North Carolina, 2003. The poetry of experimental poets Reverdy, Guillaume Apollinaire, André Breton, Frank O'Hara, and John Ashbery is examined for the poets' use of painterly techniques.

Peter Baker

RAINER MARIA RILKE

Born: Prague, Bohemia, Austro-Hungarian Empire; December 4, 1875

Died: Valmont, Switzerland; December 29, 1926

PRINCIPAL POETRY

Leben und Lieder, 1894

Larenopfer, 1896

Wegwarten, 1896

Traumgekrönt, 1897

Advent, 1898

Mir zur Feier, 1899

Das Buch der Bilder, 1902, 1906 (*The Book of Images*, 1994)

Das Stundenbuch, 1905 (*Poems from the Book of Hours*, 1941)

Neue Gedichte, 1907-1908 (2 volumes; *New Poems*, 1964)

Die frühen Gedichte, 1909

Requiem, 1909 (*Requiem, and Other Poems*, 1935)

Das Marienleben, 1913 (*The Life of the Virgin Mary*, 1951)

Duineser Elegien, 1923 (*Duinese Elegies*, 1931; better known as *Duino Elegies*)

Die Sonette an Orpheus, 1923 (*Sonnets to Orpheus*, 1936)

Vergers, suivi des Quatrains Valaisans, 1926 (*Orchards*, 1982)

Gesammelte Werke, 1927

Les Fenêtres, 1927 ("The Windows" in *The Roses and the Windows*, 1979)

Les Roses, 1927 ("The Roses" in *The Roses and the Windows*, 1979)

Verse und Prosa aus dem Nachlass, 1929

Späte Gedichte, 1934 (*Late Poems*, 1938)

Poèmes français, 1935

Aus dem Nachlass des Grafen C. W.: Ein Gedichtkreis, 1950

Christus—Visionen, pb. 1950 (wr. 1896-1898)

Poems, 1906 to 1926, 1957

Poems, 1965

Uncollected Poems, 1996

OTHER LITERARY FORMS

The rich symbolic content and specific themes that characterize the famous lyrics of Rainer Maria Rilke (RIHL-kuh) also inform his narrative prose. Recollections of his boyhood and youth are given romantic, fairy-tale coloring in *Vom lieben Gott und Anderes* (1900; republished as *Geschichten vom lieben Gott*, 1904; *Stories of God*, 1931, 1963), a cycle of short tales that replace traditional Christian perceptions of God with depictions of a finically careful artist. *Die Weise von Liebe und Tod des Cornets Christoph Rilke* (1906; *The Tale of the Love and Death of Cornet Christoph Rilke*, 1932), a terse yet beautifully written story, is more like an epic poem than a prose work, especially in its emphasis on the power of the individual word and its intensely rhythmic language. The psychologically intricate novel *Die Aufzeichnungen des Malte Laurids Brigge* (1910; *The Notebooks of Malte Laurids Brigge*,

1930; also known as *The Journal of My Other Self*) is one of Rilke's most profound creations. Written from the point of view of a young Danish nobleman living in exile in Paris, it offers in random sketches a peculiar summation of the central concerns of the author's literary art.

Between 1894 and 1904, Rilke wrote more than twenty plays, many of which were lost and never published. The most important of his remaining theatrical works are either pessimistically Naturalistic or intense dramas of the soul. *Jetzt und in der Stunde unseres Absterbens* (pr., pb. 1896; *Now and in the Hour of Our Death*, 1979) and *Im Frühfrost* (pr., pb. 1897; *Early Frost*, 1979) reflect the influence of Rudolf Christoph Jenny in their materialistic determinism, while later pieces such as *Höhenluft* (pr. 1969; *Air at High Altitude*, 1979) and *Ohne Gegenwart* (pb. 1898; *Not Present*, 1979) document a development in the direction of Symbolism, motivated especially by the dramatic theories of Maurice Maeterlinck. Rilke's best-remembered play is *Die weisse Fürstin* (pb. 1929; *The White Princess*, 1979), which in its lyric depth and power illustrates his view that drama and poetry have similar goals.

Apart from his writings in other genres, Rilke also produced a few works of nonfiction. Most notable among these are the biographical study *Auguste Rodin* (1903; English translation, 1919) and the descriptive lyric essays of *Worpswede* (1903). Much of his extensive correspondence has been collected and published. Especially important for what they reveal of his artistic personality and poetic process are volumes of letters exchanged with Lou Andreas-Salomé and Princess Marie von Thurn und Taxis.

ACHIEVEMENTS

Commonly ranked alongside Hugo von Hofmannsthal and Stefan George as a giant of twentieth century German poetry, Rainer Maria Rilke is perhaps the most controversial of the three in point of critical and popular reception of his works. Although his substantial collections published soon after the turn of the century, especially *The Book of Hours* and *New Poems*, were greeted with uniformly favorable recognition, there is wide disagreement among critics concerning the literary value of both his early poems and those of his final, major creative period. A significant key to the divided viewpoints is his boldly daring, uniquely creative use of language in strange new relationships, his peculiar departures from traditional grammar and syntax, and his unusual forms of subjective and objective expression. The pure individuality of his poetic utterances often makes them difficult to understand and repels the reader who approaches Rilke's art with anything less than full and active concentration. As a result, the most problematic of Rilke's mature poems, especially the *Duino Elegies*, are regarded by some scholars as the most important German lyric creations of the first half of the twentieth century, whereas others dismiss them as lacking substance. Regardless of these disagreements, Rilke's influence on the development of German verse is unrivaled by that of any other German-language poet of his time. His most lasting and important contribution remains the concept of the *Dinggedicht* (thing poem) introduced in *New Poems*.

BIOGRAPHY

The life of René Karl Wilhelm Johann Josef Maria Rilke can be described in its entirety as a productive, if not always successful, search for fulfillment in reaction to an inhibiting, psychologically destructive childhood. Critical elements of Rilke's early experience contributed to his development as a hypersensitive individual unsuited to the demands of practical existence. They include the rapid failure of his parents' marriage; the rape of his personality by a mother who dressed him in feminine clothing and reared him for a time as a replacement for a lost daughter; a partial education in military academies and a school of commerce to which he could never adapt; and a brief exposure to the university world in Prague. The young Rilke responded to a continuing feeling of being out of place by trying diligently to become part of active cultural and artistic circles. While still a student, he published his first lyric anthology, composed naturalistic plays, contributed literary reviews to newspapers and journals, and founded his own periodical. He also participated in cultural organizations, lec-

ture presentations, readings of drama and poetry, and similar activities.

When Rilke left the university in 1896, he went to Munich. An incurable restlessness dictated his lifestyle from that time forward. His serious evolution as a writer began under the influence of significant figures whom he encountered in Munich; friendships with Jacob Wassermann and Wilhelm von Scholz were especially productive. Wassermann acquainted him with the writings of Jens Peter Jacobsen, which Rilke soon learned to treasure. Still more important was the relationship that he formed with Andreas-Salomé, whom he met in 1897. It was she who persuaded him to change his name from René to Rainer. After she became his mistress, she exposed him to contemporary philosophical trends and the ideas of the Italian Renaissance. He quickly followed her to Berlin and later traveled with her and her husband twice to Russia, where he was introduced to Leo Tolstoy and other authors. The vast Russian landscape and the Russian people impressed him as examples of original, elemental nature.

Rainer Maria Rilke (Hulton Archive/Getty Images)

From them, he drew ideas and perceptions that informed his verse long afterward.

Rilke's only attempt to establish a permanent family situation ended in failure. In 1902, he dissolved his household in the Worpswede artists' colony, left his wife, the sculptress Clara Westhoff, and their daughter, and moved to Paris, where he intended to write a book about Auguste Rodin. His friendship with the famous sculptor was extremely significant for the direction of his poetic development in the years between 1902 and the beginning of World War I. Rodin provided Rilke with an example of strict artistic discipline that had profound impact on his maturation as a poet.

Even more critical to his literary growth during this time was Rilke's association with Impressionist painter Paul Cézanne, whose painting technique contributed much to the evolving visual orientation of Rilke's verse. Not only special individuals but also Paris itself, the French people, and even the French language indelibly marked Rilke's subsequent creations, giving them substance and eventually, during his final years, their very medium of expression.

The atmosphere of two other locales gave peculiar flavor to Rilke's most powerful, most complex masterworks. The first was Duino Castle near Trieste; the second, the Château de Muzot in Valais. After visiting North Africa and Egypt in 1910 and 1911, he went to Duino Castle at the invitation of Princess Marie von Thurn und Taxis. There, he wrote the first two of the *Duino Elegies* before moving on to Spain and then back to Germany. The war years, which he spent primarily in Munich, constituted an unproductive interlude that was inwardly devastating to him. He found it exceedingly difficult to begin writing again when hostilities ceased. Only after moving to Switzerland and his secluded refuge at the Château de Muzot did he find inner peace sufficient to complete his finest lyric cycles. He spent most of the remainder of his life in the Rhône Valley, where he died of leukemia.

ANALYSIS

During the course of his development as a poet, the creative task became for Rainer Maria Rilke a process of objectification and externalization of his own inner world. Couched in language that is notable for its musi-

cality and its frequently playful moods are the peculiarities of a unique spiritual life that emerged from special responses to outside stimuli. The melody of lyrics rich in alliteration, assonance, consonance, and rhyme provides a naturally flowing framework for the presentation of the poet's feelings and reflections. Especially typical components of his verse are encounters with sorrow and pain, powerful absorption in specific objects, a strange blending of the experiences of death and love, and an overwhelming sense of isolation.

The landscape of these revelations of self is transformed and varied in direct relationship to new outward contacts with people, things, and places. Russia, Paris, Duino, and Valais provide for different works, shaping influence and substance, timeless symbols and concrete reality, worldview and microcosmic conception. Taken in sequence, Rilke's cycles and poems document his endeavors to purify the portrayal of the scenes within him, to clarify obscurities and nail down uncertainties. By its very nature, this act of poetic refinement was deeply religious, reflecting a sincere humility in the face of creation's vast mysteries. Rilke's entire oeuvre proclaims a consciousness of an artistic calling that had its basis in an existential anxiety that was translated into joyful, almost rapturous affirmation of mortality.

EARLY POEMS

Rilke's earliest published poems, which appeared in the collections *Leben und Lieder* (life and songs), *Larenopfer* (offering to the household gods), *Wegwarten* (watch posts), and *Traumgekrönt* (dream-crowned), are marked by a naïve simplicity and a degree of sentimentality that are absent from his more mature writings. Under the influence of Jens Peter Jacobsen, he created particularly sensitive lyrics centered on nature, as well as penetrating psychological portraits of people. Among his favorite subjects were women and children. Even in these youthful creations, there is already a strong emphasis on visual imagery, although the artistic focus of attention is frequently not the object that is described, but rather the spiritual stirrings that occur within the poet because of what he sees.

MIR ZUR FEIER

In *Mir zur Feier* (celebrating me), Rilke began to move from the lyric forms and approaches of his student years, adopting in the transition techniques that he later perfected in his first broadly successful cycle, *The Book of Hours*. The poems of *Mir zur Feier* present in precise detail their creator's innermost personal concerns, describing in tones of religious fervor his yearnings, prayers, and self-perceptions. Framed in language that is rich in texture yet soft in tone, the poems glorify things that cannot be comprehended through human volition. These verse productions represent a calculated justification of the poet's art as a means of celebrating that which can be revealed in its essence and fullness in no other manner.

THE BOOK OF IMAGES

The Book of Images, a collection written at about the same time as *The Book of Hours*, is in some respects poetically stronger. Under the influence of Rodin, Rilke made the transition from a poetry informed by blurred feeling to precise, objective, carefully formed verse characterized by the complete sacrifice of the poet's immanence to an emphasis upon things in themselves. The creations of *The Book of Images* reveal the writer's progress toward the establishment of a literary integration of visual impressions with sight-oriented components of language. The artistic process becomes a perfecting of the act of seeing, in which the poet organizes the elements of the visual image through subjective cognition of his external world. Although these lyrics do not attain to the plastic monumentality of Rilke's later writings, they are forerunners of the *Dinggedichte* that are collectively the most important product of Rilke's years in Paris.

THE BOOK OF HOURS

The commemoration of self is a significant aspect of *The Book of Hours*, divided into three sections that were the product of diverse influences and experiences: Rilke's impressions of Russia and Paris, his love affair with Andreas-Salomé, the dramatic writings of Maurice Maeterlinck and Henrik Ibsen, Friedrich Nietzsche's philosophical ideas, and the cultural legacy of the Italian Renaissance. The work as a whole portrays the author's movement toward an internalization of external phenomena in a poetic act of preservation and redemption. There is evident within the individual poems a new kind of friendly relationship between the poet and God's handiwork that surrounds him. Neverthe-

less, what is presented is definitely not a traditional Christian attitude toward life. These lyrics are the product of an aggressively demanding mind; in them, a strongly individual interpretation of the religious dimension of experience is advanced without equivocation. The thrust of *The Book of Hours* is to refine the notion that God is not static, a complete and perfect being, but rather a continually evolving artistic creation. Rilke insists that the reader accept this idea on faith, equating his poetic message with spiritual revelation. The result is a celebration of "this world" that the poet continued to elaborate and modify until his death.

The three parts of *The Book of Hours* are discrete sets of deeply intimate confessions that arose out of special relationships and encounters that shaped Rilke's artistic outlook. "Das Buch vom mönchischen Leben" ("Of the Monastic Life"), written in 1899, reflects the strong influence of the poet's attachment to Andreas-Salomé and the cultural, historical, and philosophical ideas to which she introduced him. His ecstatic love for Andreas-Salomé and their visits to Russia are the key elements that give "Das Buch von der Pilgerschaft" ("Of Pilgrimage") its specific flavor, while "Das Buch von der Armut und vom Tod" ("Of Poverty and Death") was a product of Rilke's impressions during his first year in Paris. The individual poems of the three cycles are experiments in which Rilke tested various symbols and metaphors, metric and rhythmic possibilities, and rhyme schemes in documenting a deep worship of life as a sacred motivating force.

"Of the Monastic Life" is a series of prayerful outpourings of the spirit in which a young monk addresses God. In this context, prayer is an elemental religious act with two goals: self-discovery in the process of establishing and expanding personal modes of expression, and the "creation" of God and the growth of a sense of brotherhood with him in one's relationship to nature. The fictive prayer situations provide the setting for a portrayal of the innermost stirrings of the soul in an endless reaching outward to illuminate the divine. Melodic language and strength of visual image are brought together with rich imagination to reveal the lyricist's almost Franciscan sympathy with the world.

Specific items of the cycle "Of Pilgrimage" attain peaks of religious rapture in the glorification of the mystical union between man and woman, offered in newly intensified homage to Andreas-Salomé. Thematically, however, this portion of *The Book of Hours* focuses primarily on key aspects of the poet's Russian experience. It emphasizes especially the idea that the pious Russian people are the embodiment of humility and spirituality within a topographical frame that is the archetype of God's creation. Spatial relationships are particularly important as the vastness of the Russian countryside melts into the author's inner landscape. A few of the lyrics reveal an inclination toward things that need humans, presenting them in impressionistic trappings that show a predilection for that which is most immediate and intricate.

"Of Poverty and Death," the final segment of *The Book of Hours*, anticipates the negative, sometimes melancholy tone of Rilke's later collections. Its substance is human misery presented in variations that expose in stark coloration the world of the homeless, the infirm, the abandoned, and the afraid. Christian motifs and themes are employed to accentuate Rilke's rejection of the Christian God, while rich images establish a substantial tie to "Of the Monastic Life" in the affirmation of God as an original poetic creation.

DINGGEDICHTE

Rilke's most lasting legacy and most important contribution to German poesy is the *Dinggedicht*, an originally conceived interpretation of inner experience generated in response to encounters with external objects and phenomena that the poet transformed into symbols for the elements of human life. With *New Poems*, in which he perfected this particular form, Rilke made a breakthrough that was immeasurably far-reaching in its implications for the expansion of German poetry's expressive domain.

A reflection of Rilke's attention to impulses from Rodin's sculpture and Cézanne's paintings, the *Dinggedicht* is the product of disciplined and thorough scrutinization of its model. Outwardly, it seeks to offer the character and intrinsic constitution of an object that is described for its own sake in painstakingly refined language. On another level, however, it documents the acquisition of external things for the poet's inner domain, thereby transforming the physical phenomenon into a precise and specifically calculated symbol for a

portion of his re-creation of the world for himself. Some of the poems analyze people, buildings, natural and artificial scenes, plants, animals, and even motifs from mythology and the Bible; others are lyric translations of statues and paintings. Each provides a segment of Rilke's new interpretation and clarification of existence. Unlike the earlier forms, the *Dinggedicht* renounces the commitment to melodic sound relationships and connected imagery chains. The exacting identification of the poem's external object and its reduction to its fundamental nature permitted the poet to place it into an absolute domain of pure symbol.

NEW POEMS

Rilke achieved his most representative mastery of the *Dinggedicht* in *New Poems*, a collection in which heavy stress is placed on negative moods in the explication of the view that God is the direction and not the object of love. In their extreme subtlety and refinement of language, their worldly elegance, and their moral and emotional engagement, the most representative poems of Rilke's Paris period form the center of his work as a whole. The *Dinggedichte* of *New Poems* are a detailed reflection of his view that his poetic task was the interpretation and clarification of existence for the purpose of healing the world. By accepting, recognizing, and loving things for themselves, the poet places himself in a position to trace animals, plants, works of art, human figures, and other objects back to their true nature and substance. Precise seeing and artistic transformation enable him to project in symbols the content and meaning both of his surroundings and of that which is within him.

Divided into two loosely chronological parts, the poems in *New Poems* examine in objectively plastic, precisely disciplined structures representative manifestations and individuals that belong to the world of nature and to humanity's most important cultural attainments, from the Bible to classical antiquity, from the Middle Ages to the Renaissance. Mystical inwardness is projected in carefully defined symbols that objectively externalize the events within the poet that are stimulated by the process of seeing. Gloom, absurdity, and disintegration are common moods in poems that question the possibility for everything, including humanity, to exist and thereby to become the subject of literature.

"THE PANTHER"

The symbolic portraits of *New Poems* focus on a broad variety of models. Among the most successful are those based on impressions from the Jardin des Plantes. "Der Panther" ("The Panther"), the earliest and most famous of the *Dinggedichte*, transforms its object into a symbol of heroic existence. By the very power of its seeing, the panther, like the poet, is able to create its own inner landscape, absorbing the visual impressions of external objects into itself, where it may modify, penetrate, or even destroy them. One of Rilke's most vivid depictions of rapport with an object, achieved in the act of intense observation, is given in "Archaïscher Torso Apollos" ("Archaic Torso of Apollo"), the first work in the second volume of *New Poems*. The headless statue becomes a kind of spiritual mirror that directs the onlooker's gaze back into the self, enabling him to recognize the need for change in his own life.

DUINO ELEGIES AND SONNETS TO ORPHEUS

An important consequence of Rilke's Paris experience was a reevaluation of his literary existence that led ultimately to a significant turning point in his career. The problem of an irreconcilable conflict between the demands of practicality and art was compounded by a philosophical crisis involving the tensions that he felt in his need to make a definitive break with Christianity and in his loathing of modern technology. Against this background, an encounter with Søren Kierkegaard's existential philosophy led eventually to Rilke's production of the mythologically exaggerated *Duino Elegies* and *Sonnets to Orpheus* as the peak of his literary endeavor. In these mature lyrics, the creative attitudes and symbolic devices of *New Poems* were refined and perfected. Rilke responded to many different stimuli—World War I, the works of Friedrich Gottlieb Klopstock, Johann Wolfgang von Goethe, and Heinrich von Kleist, Sigmund Freud's psychology, among others—in creating a culminating synthesis of his own poetic view of human life and destiny. Dactylic and iambic meters, free rhythms, questions, and exclamations provide the frame for bold images that pinpoint once again the fundamental directions of Rilke's work as a whole.

Between 1912 and 1922, Rilke created the ten Duino elegies in monumental celebration of humanity as the final, most extreme possibility of existence. The ultimate refinement of the delineation of his own calling focuses no longer on the artist as interpreter and clarifier of his surroundings, but rather ordains the poet as a prophet and savior whose task is to preserve everything that has being. He thus becomes the protagonist and representative of humanity in a new religion of life that is an expression of unchecked aestheticism. By saving the world from a collapse that seems unavoidable, the poet engages in an act of self-purification and follows the only possible course of personal redemption.

Taken together, the elegies offer a mural of Rilke's inner landscape. Internalization of travel experiences, the lonely scenery at Duino Castle, the flight of birds, mythological constructs, and other phenomena create a background of timeless "inner space" against which the author projects his coming to grips with the existential polarities of life and death. Progressing from lament to profound affirmation of mortality, the poems glorify the fulfillment of humanity's promise to maintain all things of value through a process of transformation that rescues external nature by placing it in the protected realm of the spirit. The power by which this is accomplished is love, supremely manifested by lovers, people who die young, heroes, children, and animals. By bringing together earth and space, life and death, all dimensions of reality and time into a single inward hierarchical unity, Rilke sought to ensure the continuation of humanity's outward existence.

In the first elegy, the poet states his view of the human condition: imperfection, the questionable status of humanity, the experience of transience, the pain of love. On this basis, he builds a new mythology of life. Its center is the non-Christian angel who appears in the second elegy as a symbol for the absolute and unattainable, the norm from which humans in their limitations deviate. In a valid transformation of psychoanalysis into images, Rilke pinpoints the threat that exists within the human self in the power of natural drives. Illumination of the brokenness, ambiguity, superficiality, and mechanical senselessness of human pursuits is followed in the sixth elegy by identification of the hero as a symbolic concept that contrasts with average life. The seventh poem of the cycle breaks away from the lament of human insufficiency, suddenly glorifying the here and now in hymnic language that moves to a confessional peak. Renewed expression of the idea that the difference between humans and the natural creature cannot be resolved is followed by an attempt to show that life must be accepted and made fruitful despite its limitations. The culminating elegy creates a balance between mourning and celebration that unites the antithetical problems in a grand, affirmative vision of pain and death as the destiny of humanity and the only true evidence of his existence.

LATE POEMS IN FRENCH

The verse written in French after *Duino Elegies* and *Sonnets to Orpheus* was anticlimactic for Rilke's career. It lacks the depth and profundity of earlier works, although individual poems achieve lightness and sparkle in their reflection of a new rejoicing in mortal existence.

OTHER MAJOR WORKS

LONG FICTION: *Am Leben hin*, 1889; *Die Letzten*, 1902; *Die Weise von Liebe und Tod des Cornets Christoph Rilke*, 1906 (*The Tale of the Love and Death of Cornet Christopher Rilke*, 1932); *Die Aufzeichnungen des Malte Laurids Brigge*, 1910 (*The Notebooks of Malte Laurids Brigge*, 1930; also known as *The Journal of My Other Self*).

SHORT FICTION: *Zwei Prager Geschichten*, 1899 (*Two Stories of Prague*, 1994); *Vom lieben Gott und Anderes*, 1900 (republished as *Geschichten vom lieben Gott*, 1904; *Stories of God*, 1931, 1963); *Erzählungen und Skizzen aus der Frühzeit*, 1928.

PLAYS: *Murillo*, pb. 1895 (English translation, 1979); *Jetzt und in der Stunde unseres Absterbens*, pr., pb. 1896 (*Now and in the Hour of Our Death*, 1979); *Im Frühfrost*, pr., pb. 1897 (*Early Frost*, 1979); *Vigilien*, wr. 1897 (*Vigils*, 1979); *Ohne Gegenwart*, pb. 1898 (*Not Present*, 1979); *Das tägliche Leben*, pr. 1901 (*Everyday Life*, 1979); *Waisenkinder*, pb. 1901 (*Orphans*, 1979); *Die weisse Fürstin*, pb. 1929 (*The White Princess*, 1979); *Höhenluft*, pr. 1969 (wr. 1897; *Air at High Altitude*, 1979); *Nine Plays*, 1979.

NONFICTION: *Auguste Rodin*, 1903 (English translation, 1919); *Worpswede*, 1903; *Briefe an einen jungen Dichter*, 1929 (*Letters to a Young Poet*, 1934); *Wartime Letters of Rainer Maria Rilke, 1914-1921*, 1940;

Tagebücher aus der Frühzeit, 1942 (*Diaries of a Young Poet*, 1997); *Letters of Rainer Maria Rilke*, 1945-1948 (2 volumes); *Selected Letters of Rainer Maria Rilke, 1902-1926*, 1947; *Briefwechsel [zwischen] Rainer Maria Rilke und Marie von Thurn und Taxis*, 1951 (*The Letters of Rainer Maria Rilke and Princess Marie von Thurn und Taxis*, 1958); *Rainer Maria Rilke, Lou Andreas-Salomé: Briefwechsel*, 1952; *Rainer Maria Rilke and Lou Andreas-Salomé: The Correspondence*, 2006.

MISCELLANEOUS: *The Poet's Guide to Life: The Wisdom of Rilke*, 2005 (Ulrich Baer, editor).

BIBLIOGRAPHY

Andreas-Salomé, Lou. *You Alone Are Real to Me: Remembering Rainer Maria Rilke*. Translated by Angela von der Lippe. New York: BOA Editions, 2003. In her memoir, Andreas-Salomé describes her relationship with Rilke.

Bernstein, Michael André. *Five Portraits: Modernity and the Imagination in Twentieth-Century German Writing*. Edited by Gary Saul Morson. Evanston, Ill.: Northwestern University Press, 2000. Presents Rilke's poetry in the context of the shift among German writers from Romanticism and aestheticism to twentieth century modernism.

Freedman, Ralph. *Life of a Poet: Rainer Maria Rilke*. New York: Farrar, Straus and Giroux, 1996. A helpful complement to Donald Prater's definitive biography, this work draws extensive parallels between Rilke's life and the content of his poetry. Also contains several photographs of Rilke and his family.

Kleinbard, David. *The Beginning of Terror: A Psychological Study of Rainer Maria Rilke's Life and Work*. New York: New York University Press, 1993. A critical rather than comprehensive biography, attempting a psychoanalysis of Rilke and his published writing. Examines issues such as Rilke's childhood, his relationships with his parents (both biological and surrogate), and his debilitating blood disorder and its effect on his work.

Prater, Donald. *A Ringing Glass: The Life of Rainer Maria Rilke*. New York: Clarendon Press, 1993. A definitive biography of Rilke that concentrates on his European travels and correspondence with friends. Also, the bibliography is highly helpful for those who need a comprehensive, expert guide to Rilke criticism. Illustrated.

Ryan, Judith. *Rilke, Modernism, and Poetic Tradition.* New York: Cambridge University Press, 1999. Although Rilke saw himself as a more or less self-created writer, who needed extended periods of solitude in which to work, Ryan shows him in his relationship to other writers and even painters in the European culture of his day. Traces his movement from the art-for-art's-sake school of writing into modernism.

Schoolfield, George C. *Young Rilke and His Time.* Rochester, N.Y.: Camden House, 2009. A biography of Rilke that focuses on the writer as a youth and how the circumstances of his youth affected his writing.

Lowell A. Bangerter

ARTHUR RIMBAUD

Born: Charleville, France; October 20, 1854
Died: Marseilles, France; November 10, 1891

PRINCIPAL POETRY

Une Saison en enfer, 1873 (*A Season in Hell*, 1932)
Les Illuminations, 1886 (*Illuminations*, 1932)

OTHER LITERARY FORMS

The impact of Arthur Rimbaud (ram-BOH) on the literary world stems entirely from his poetry.

ACHIEVEMENTS

Arthur Rimbaud's meteoric career has forever earned for him a place as the brilliant *enfant terrible* of French verse. Since his death, he has attracted more critical attention than any French poet save Stéphane Mallarmé. A revolutionary both in his life and in his art, Rimbaud exerted a radical influence on the scope and direction of French poetry. He has been credited with introducing *vers libre* (free verse), which would come to dominate modern poetry, and his systematic cultivation of

dreams, hallucinations, and madness anticipated modern interest in the irrational side of the human mind. He became, for a time, the patron saint of André Breton and the Surrealists. Rimbaud's conception of the poetical "I" as "other" ("Je est un autre") has been acclaimed as an intuitive perception of the unconscious that predated its mapping by Sigmund Freud. Finally, Rimbaud was the first French literary figure to sound a distinctly feminist note in his writings, condemning the cultural repression of women and looking forward to a future day of liberation when they would assume their rightful place in society and art. Faithful to his own precept, "Il faut être absolument moderne" ("We must be absolutely modern"), he prefigured key trends in modern art and thought.

BIOGRAPHY

Jean-Nicolas-Arthur Rimbaud was born in the provincial town of Charleville on the Franco-Prussian border. His mother, Vitalie Cuif, was of peasant stock and a devout Jansenist; his father, Captain Frédéric Rimbaud, was an itinerant army officer who abandoned the family when Rimbaud was only six years old. A brilliant student, Rimbaud completed nine years of schooling in eight, earning numerous literary prizes in the course of his studies. His earliest attempts at verse were in Latin, followed by his first poem in French, "Les Étrennes des orphelins" ("The Orphans' New Year's Day Gifts"), published in January, 1870. Encouraged by his teacher, Georges Izambard, Rimbaud sent off three poems to the Parnassian poet Théodore de Banville, who, however, failed to express any interest.

The outbreak of the Franco-Prussian War in July, 1870, put an end to Rimbaud's formal schooling. Alienated by the hypocrisy of provincial society, which he satirized in various poems composed in the early months of 1870, he ran away from home three times: first to Paris, then to Belgium, and again to Paris. He was back in Charleville when the Paris Commune was declared on March 18, 1871. Although much critical attention has been devoted to Rimbaud's possible ties with the Commune, there is no clear evidence that he ever left Charleville during the crucial period of the Paris uprising. On May 15, Rimbaud composed his celebrated "Lettre du voyant" ("Seer Letter"), addressed to a friend, Paul Demeny. Rimbaud's break with traditional poetry was by this time already complete, and on August 15, he again wrote to Banville, enclosing a new poem, "Ce qu'on dit au poète à propos de fleurs" ("What One Says to the Poet in Regard to Flowers"), a vitriolic attack on Parnassian poetics. Shortly thereafter, Rimbaud also sent off eight new poems, in two installments, to Paul Verlaine, who responded with the famous phrase "Venez, chère grande âme, on vous appelle, on vous attend" ("Come, dear great soul, we call to you, we await you").

Rimbaud arrived in the capital with a copy of his newly composed poem, "Le Bateau ivre" ("The Drunken Boat"), which brought him some notoriety among the Parisian literary crowd. The young poet's obnoxious behavior soon alienated him, however, both from Verlaine's family and his fellow artists, and March, 1872,

found him back in Charleville. Rimbaud returned to Paris in May and there began a series of escapades with Verlaine that some have characterized as simply youthful exuberance and others as an unhappy love affair. The pair fled first to Brussels, then to London, where a quarrel erupted. Verlaine returned to Brussels, where he was soon followed by Rimbaud.

In Brussels, events soon took a tragic turn. In a moment of drunken rage, Verlaine fired on Rimbaud, wounding him slightly in the hand. The incident might have ended there, but Verlaine later accosted Rimbaud in the street, and the frightened youth sought help from a passing police officer. The authorities intervened, and Verlaine was sentenced to two years in prison. Rimbaud returned to his mother's family farm at Roche, where he completed *A Season in Hell*, begun in April. In late 1873, Rimbaud again visited Paris, where he made the acquaintance of the young poet Germain Nouveau, with whom he traveled to London in the early months of 1874. Almost nothing is known of this second friendship beyond the fact that it ended with Nouveau's abrupt return to Paris in June of that year.

In 1875, Rimbaud embarked on a new series of travels that led him to Stuttgart, across the Swiss Alps on foot into Italy, and back to Charleville via Paris. After visiting Vienna in April, 1876, he enlisted in the Dutch colonial army on May 19 and set sail for Java. He deserted ship in Batavia (modern Djakarta) and returned to Charleville. In May, 1877, Rimbaud was in Bremen, where he attempted (in vain) to enlist in the American Marines. Subsequent travels the same year took him to Stockholm, Copenhagen, Marseilles, Rome, and back to Charleville. In early 1878, he visited Hamburg, returning during the summer to work on the family farm at Roche. In October, he again traversed Switzerland on foot, crossing the Alps into Italy. There he took the train to Genoa and embarked for Alexandria, later departing for Cyprus, where he worked as a foreman in a marble quarry. Stricken with typhoid, he returned to Charleville in May, 1879, once again spending the summer at Roche. In

Arthur Rimbaud (Library of Congress)

March, 1880, he was back in Cyprus, where he found work as a construction foreman. An intemperate climate and a salary dispute soon forced him to resign his position and to seek employment elsewhere.

Rimbaud spent the remaining eleven years of his life as the business agent of a French colonial trading company in the remote wilds of Abyssinia (modern-day Ethiopia) and Aden. At the end of this time, he had amassed, through agonizing labor and in the face of constant adversity, the modest sum of 150,000 francs (approximately 30,000 dollars). In February, 1891, intense pain in his right knee forced him to return to France for medical treatment. Doctors in Marseilles diagnosed his illness as cancer and ordered the immediate amputation of the infected right leg. The cancer proved too widespread to check, however, and Rimbaud died in a state of delirium on November 10, 1891. According to a tradition spawned by his devout sister, Isabelle, who was with the poet in his final moments, Rimbaud returned to Catholicism on his deathbed. Since Isabelle is, however, known to have tampered with her brother's personal letters, critics have given little credence to her testimony.

ANALYSIS

Arthur Rimbaud's early verse (of which he published only three short pieces in various academic bulletins) falls into two general categories. First, there is his satiric verse, exemplified by such poems as "Les Premières Communions" ("First Communions") and "Les Assis" ("The Seated Ones"), which attacks religious hypocrisy and the sterility of bourgeois society. Second, there is his erotic verse, typified by such poems as "Vénus anadyomène" ("Venus Emerging from the Waves") and "Le Coeur volé" ("The Stolen Heart"), which speaks of the trauma of sexual coming-of-age. A pastiche of traditional styles and forms, these initial works nevertheless evidence a brilliant gift for verbal expression and announce the theme of revolt which informs all Rimbaud's writings.

"SEER LETTER"

On May 15, 1871, Rimbaud declared his emancipation from traditional poetics in his celebrated "Seer Letter," addressed to his friend Paul Demeny. This letter, Rimbaud's *ars poetica*, begins with a contemptuous denunciation of all previous poetry as nothing more than rhymed prose. Only Charles Baudelaire, "un vrai dieu" ("a true god"), is spared and, even then, only partially—he frequented a self-consciously artistic milieu, and he failed to find new forms of expression. Rimbaud then calls for a radically new conception of the poet's mission: "Car je est un autre" ("For I is an other"). It is the essential task of the poet to give voice to the repressed, unconscious "other" that lies concealed behind the mask of the rational, Cartesian "I"—the "other" that societal restrictions have condemned to silence. This can be accomplished only by "un long, immense et raisonné dérèglement de tous les sens" ("a long, immense and reasoned derangement of all the senses"). Unlike his Romantic predecessors and such Symbolist contemporaries as Mallarmé, who passively awaited the return of the muse, Rimbaud insists on the active role the poet must take: "Le Poète se fait voyant" ("The poet makes himself a seer"). The poet must actively cultivate dreams, hallucinations, and madness. In so doing, he becomes the great liberator of humanity, a Prometheus who steals fire from the gods, the spokesperson for all those whom society has ostracized: "Il devient entre tous le grand malade, le grand criminel, le grand maudit—et le grand Savant!" ("He becomes, more than anyone, the great sick one, the great criminal, the great accursed one—and the great Learned One!"). Such a poet will be "un multiplicateur de progrès" whose genius, unrestrained by societal taboos and the limitations of rational thought, will lead humankind into a new golden age.

Throughout the remaining months of 1871 and the following year, Rimbaud endeavored to give form to this poetic vision in a new series of songs and verse that are best exemplified by two poems that critics have universally acclaimed as masterpieces: "Le Bateau ivre" ("The Drunken Boat") and "Voyelles" ("Vowels").

"THE DRUNKEN BOAT"

Perhaps the best known of Rimbaud's works, "The Drunken Boat" was composed during the summer of 1871 and presented to Verlaine in September of that same year. Although the work borrows from a wide variety of sources (Victor Hugo, Baudelaire, Jules Verne, and Vicomte Chateaubriand, to name but a few), it remains a stunning and original tour de force—particularly for a young poet of sixteen. The poem, composed of twenty-five quatrains in classical Alexandrines and narrated in the first person, is a symbolic drama in three acts. In the first act (quatrains 1 through 4), set on a vast river in the New World, the boat recounts its escape from its haulers, who are massacred by screaming natives, and its subsequent descent toward the sea. There follows a brief, transitional interlude (quatrain 5) in which the boat passes through a ritual purification: Its wooden shell is permeated by the seawater that cleanses it of wine stains and vomit and bears off the boat's rudder and anchor.

The second and central act (quatrains 6 through 22) tells of the boat's intoxicating maritime adventures and its fantastic, hallucinatory vision of a transcendental reality that ordinary mortals have only glimpsed in passing. Yet, the boat's long and frenetic voyage of discovery ultimately begins to turn sour. After braving whirlpools, hurricanes, raging seas, and Leviathans from the deep, the boat unexpectedly declares its nostalgia for the ancient parapets of Europe.

In the third and final act (quatrains 23 through 25), the boat's delirious optimism turns to anguished despair. Its quest for the absolute has at length proved futile, and the boat now seeks dissolution in death. If it desires a return to European waters, it is to the cold, black puddle into which a sad, impoverished child releases a boat as frail as a May butterfly. At the same time, the boat realizes the impossibility of any turning back to its previous mode of existence. It can no longer follow in the wake of the merchant ships, nor bear the haughty pride of the military gunboats, nor swim beneath the horrible eyes of the prison ships that lie at anchor in the harbor.

"The Drunken Boat" reflects both Rimbaud's new conception of the poet as "seer" and the influence of the French Symbolists, such as Verlaine and Baudelaire, who sought to replace the effusive, personalized verse of the Romantics with a symbolic, impersonal mode of expression. Critics have generally equated the work's "protagonist," the boat, with the poet himself, reading the poem as a symbolic account of Rimbaud's own efforts to transcend reality through language. Most critics are also agreed that the poem's final two stanzas, while they suggest the advent of a new self-awareness, evince a disillusionment with the "seer" experiment and prefigure Rimbaud's later renunciation of poetry.

"VOWELS"

Rimbaud's celebrated sonnet "Vowels," written in decasyllabic verse, dates from the same period as "The Drunken Boat" and was similarly presented to Verlaine in September, 1871. Another of Rimbaud's "seer" poems, the work postulates a mystic correspondence between vowels and colors: "A noir, E blanc, I rouge, U vert, O bleu" ("A black, E white, I red, U green, O blue"). The poem has its literary source in Baudelaire's famous sonnet "Correspondences," which had asserted an underlying connection between sounds, perfumes, and colors and had popularized the concept of synesthesia. Another probable source for the work has been found in an illustrated alphabet primer that Rimbaud may have read as a child and that has served to elucidate some of the sonnet's enigmatic imagery.

Perhaps the most ingenious interpretation of the poem is that of the critic Lucien Sausy, who argued that the work exploits correspondences not between sound and color (there are, in fact, few traces of such matching within the phonetic content of the poem) but rather between the visual form of the vowels themselves and the images to which the latter are linked: *A*, if inverted, thus suggests the delta-shaped body of a fly; *E* (written as a Greek epsilon in the manuscript), if turned on its side, suggests vapors, tents, and glaciers; and so on. (Sausy's interpretation, first advanced in *Les Nouvelles Littéraires*, September 2, 1933, is available in the notes to the Pléiade edition of Rimbaud's works.) As a counterbalance, however, one might mention Verlaine's explanation of the sonnet: "Rimbaud saw things that way and that's all there is to it."

A SEASON IN HELL

By his own account, Rimbaud composed *A Season in Hell* during the period from April to August of 1873. Rimbaud supervised the book's publication, and it was printed in Brussels in the fall of 1873 in an edition of five hundred copies. Rimbaud was unable, however, to pay the printing costs, and this first edition, save for six author's copies that circulated among his friends, remained in the attic of a Brussels publishing house until discovered in 1901 by a Belgian bibliophile, who did not make his discovery public until 1914.

The text, which Rimbaud had originally intended to entitle "Livre païen" (pagan book) or "Livre nègre" (Negro book—the French adjective is pejorative), consists of nine prose poems and seven poems in verse, the latter all contained within the section "Délires II" ("Deliria II"). The work has been variously acclaimed by critics for its original and stunning verbal display, its fantastic, visionary imagery, and its prophetic pronouncements concerning Rimbaud's own future. As the title indicates, *A Season in Hell* is Rimbaud's poetic attempt to come to grips with his recent "dark night of the soul"—his unhappy adventure with Verlaine and his anguished experience as "seer." Viewed from the perspective of Rimbaud's own metaphysical dictum— "I is an other"—the work, narrated in the first person, recounts a confrontation between the rational, conscious "I" and the irrational, unconscious "other" which the poet had systematically worked to cultivate.

The text opens with a brief introductory section (untitled) in which the poet evokes with longing his lost state of childhood innocence. He recalls his frenzied flight from reason, his revolt against traditional concepts of beauty and morality, his pursuit of crime, and his cultivation of madness. He momentarily dreams of regaining his former state of innocence through a return to Christian charity but immediately rejects the latter as an empty illusion. Inescapably condemned to death and damnation, he dedicates his opus not to the traditional poetic Muse but rather to Satan. This introductory segment serves to announce the key themes that the body of the work will subsequently develop: the abandonment of the "seer" experiment, the nostalgia for the comfort afforded by traditional Christian values, and the attainment of a new self-awareness that, however, prevents any naïve return to the past.

"BAD BLOOD"

In the following prose poem, "Mauvais Sang" ("Bad Blood"), the poet attributes his failure to transcend the vulgar world or reality to some inherited defect that now condemns him to a life of manual toil. Nor does he envision any hope in the progress promised by Cartesian rationalism and the advent of science. The world may yet be headed toward total destruction. Disillusioned with Western civilization, he seeks imaginative shelter in what he perceives as the savage freedom

of black African society. His amoral utopia is, however, destroyed by the arrival of the white colonialists, who impose their debilitating Christian ethics by force of arms. Momentarily seduced by Christianity, the poet ultimately rejects it as an infringement on human freedom and refuses to embark on a honeymoon with Jesus Christ as father-in-law. Rather than remain enslaved, he hurls himself to his death beneath the horses of the conquering Europeans.

"NIGHT IN HELL"

The conflict between Christianity and paganism is further developed in "Nuit de l'enfer" ("Night in Hell"). Here, the poet is engulfed in the fires of Hell, to which his parents have condemned him through baptism and catechism lessons. His suffering derives from his inability to choose between the absolute but terrible freedom offered by Satan and the serene but limited freedom promised by the Christian God. Hell, in short, is a state of eternal and lucid alienation.

"DELIRIA I"

"Délires I" ("Deliria I") introduces a "Vièrge folle" ("Foolish Virgin") who recounts her difficult life with "l'Époux infernal" ("The Infernal Spouse") who seduced her with the false promise of an amoral and transcendent Paradise. Numerous critics have found in this passage a mythic retelling of Verlaine's intellectual and erotic seduction by Rimbaud; other critics have preferred to read the passage as emblematic of the seduction of the poet's rational and moral self by his own irrational and amoral unconscious. In either case, the poem is a bitter indictment of Rimbaud's failed efforts to transform reality.

"DELIRIA II"

In "Délires II" ("Deliria II"), subtitled "L'Alchimie du verbe" ("Verbal Alchemy"), the poet looks back on what he now views as an act of folly: his attempt to transcend reality through the systematic cultivation of the irrational and the invention of a new language that would draw in all the human senses and give voice to everything in humans that had previously been barred from expression. He gives as tangible examples of this enterprise six verse poems, the visionary imagery of which speaks symbolically of his hunger and thirst for the absolute, his frustration with past theology and future technology, and his fervent conviction that he has indeed found the mystic line of juncture between sea and sky, body and soul, the known and unknown. This metaphysical quest has ultimately failed, the poet says, for he has been damned by the rainbow—an ironic allusion to the rainbow sent by God to Noah as a sign of future redemption. As his dream-filled night draws to a close, and morning approaches, the poet awakes to hear the strains of the hymn "Christus venit" (Christ has come) resounding through the somber cities of the world. His career as "seer" has ended with the bleak dawn of reality.

"THE IMPOSSIBLE," "LIGHTNING," "MORNING," AND "FAREWELL"

The four remaining prose poems, all of them brief, further expand on major themes in the work. In "L'Impossible" ("The Impossible"), the poet tells of his futile efforts to reconcile Christianity and Eastern mysticism and his ultimate rejection of both. In "Éclair" ("Lightning"), the poet finds momentary comfort in the dignity of work but cannot avoid perceiving the vanity of all human efforts in the face of death and dissolution. "Matin" ("Morning") announces the end of the poet's night in Hell. In spite of the limitations imposed by the human condition, he chooses life over death. Although all men are slaves, they should not curse life. In the final passage, "Adieu" ("Farewell"), the poet renounces his unsuccessful career as "seer" in favor of a newfound divine clarity, the anguished self-knowledge that his experience has brought him. There will be no turning back to the past for solace, nor any attempt to seek oblivion in the love of a woman. Humans must be absolutely modern, the poet declares; for himself, he is content to possess the truth that humans are both body and soul.

ILLUMINATIONS

Illuminations was published in 1886, without Rimbaud's knowledge. Some years earlier, he had left a manuscript of the work with Verlaine, whence it passed through several hands before it was published in the Symbolist periodical *La Vogue*, appearing in book form (edited and with a preface by Verlaine) later in the same year.

Although a century has passed since the first appearance of *Illuminations*, a number of fundamental questions concerning the collection remain to be resolved and perhaps will never be definitely resolved.

First there is the matter of the title. The manuscript itself is untitled, and the only evidence for the title by which the collection is known is the statement of Paul Verlaine, a notoriously unreliable witness. In a letter written in 1878 to his brother-in-law, Charles de Sivry, Verlaine says: "Have re-read *Illuminations* (painted plates). . . ." Later, in the preface to the first edition of *Illuminations*, he adds that "the word [that is, "illuminations"] is English and means *gravures coloriées*, colored plates," claiming that this was the subtitle that Rimbaud had chosen for the work.

The question of the title and subtitle may seem a mere scholarly quibble, but it is more than that, for at issue is the significance that Rimbaud himself attached to the title and, by extension, the spirit in which he intended the work to be read. Some critics, accepting Verlaine's testimony without qualification, suggest that by "painted plates" or "colored plates," Rimbaud meant the cheap colored prints that had recently become widely available. The tone of the title, then, would be highly ironic. Other critics suggest that Verlaine garbled Rimbaud's meaning—that Rimbaud had in mind the illuminated manuscripts of the Middle Ages. Still others reject Verlaine's testimony on this matter as another of his fabrications, arguing that by "illuminations" Rimbaud meant moments of spiritual insight; some readers have seen in the title a reference to the occult doctrines of Illuminism.

Another important debate concerns the date of composition. It was long believed that *Illuminations* preceded *A Season in Hell*, but later this assumption was seriously challenged. Again, the question of dating may appear to be of interest only to specialists, but such is not the case. The conclusion to *A Season in Hell* has been widely regarded as Rimbaud's farewell to poetry. If, in fact, he wrote *Illuminations* after *A Season in Hell*, many existing critical interpretations are invalid or in need of substantial revision.

This argument for dating *Illuminations* after *A Season in Hell* is primarily based on the pioneering research of Henri de Bouillane de Lacoste. Bouillane de Lacoste's graphological analysis of the manuscript, in conjunction with other, more subjective, arguments, has persuaded many scholars to accept Verlaine's once-rejected assertion that the work was written during the period from 1873 to 1875 in the course of Rimbaud's European travels. On the other hand, there are a number of reputable Rimbaud scholars who find Bouillane de Lacoste's analysis inconclusive at best and who thus retain the old chronology. In any case, one cannot know with certainty the date of composition of the individual poems themselves, nor is there any clear indication of the final order in which Rimbaud intended them to appear. The reason for Rimbaud's prolongation of his poetic career beyond his abdication from poetry in *A Season in Hell* seems destined to remain a mystery.

Illuminations is regarded by many critics as Rimbaud's most original work and his consummate contribution to French poetry. Although it represents a continuation of the "seer" experiment conducted in his earlier verse, it also marks a radical departure from the narrative, anecdotal, and descriptive modes of expression to be found in his previous poetry and in that of his contemporaries. The poems in *Illuminations* are strikingly modern in that each forms a self-contained, self-referential unit that stands independent of the collection as a whole and remains detached from any clear point of reference in the world of reality. They do not purport to convey any didactic, moral, or philosophical message to the reader. Ephemeral and dreamlike, each emerges from the void as a spontaneous flow of images generated by free association. They are works in which the rational "I" allows the unconscious "other" to speak. As manifestations of the unconscious, they reveal an almost infinitely rich condensation of meaning that defies any linear attempts at interpretation. They thus elucidate Rimbaud's earlier remark in *A Season in Hell* that he "reserved all translation rights." They are, again in the poet's own words, "accessible to all meanings." If they are coherent, it is in the way dreams are coherent, and like dreams, they speak from the hidden recesses of the mind. Hermetic in form, they lead down a different path from that charted by the Symbolist verse of Rimbaud's contemporary, Mallarmé: They reflect not an aesthetic obsession with the problematics of language but a perpetual striving to give voice to all that reason and social mores have condemned to silence.

Although *Illuminations* consists of a discontinuous series of pieces devoid of any central narrative plot,

critics have drawn attention to a number of major recurring themes to be found within the text. Given the work's dreamlike qualities and its close affinity with the unconscious, it is not surprising that the theme most often cited by critics is that of childhood. Numerous passages in the work evoke the blissful innocence of childhood, Rimbaud's "paradise lost," irrevocably destroyed by the advent of civilization and Christianity. The theme is developed at particular length in the two prose poems "Enfance" ("Childhood") and "Après le déluge" ("After the Deluge"). In the first, the child-poet tells of his Satanic fall from a state of divine omniscience and absolute freedom into a subterranean prison, where he is condemned to silence. In the second, which ironically alludes to the biblical story of the Flood and the promise of divine redemption, the poet sees the natural innocence of childhood as being progressively corrupted by the rise of civilization, and he ends by conjuring up new floods that will sweep away the repressive work of society.

A second and related major theme, exemplified by such prose poems as "Villes I" ("Cities I"), "Villes II" ("Cities II"), and "Métropolitain" ("Metropolitan"), is that of the city. Although modeled in part on the Paris and London of Rimbaud's own time, the cities in *Illuminations* are phantasmagoric, shimmering cities of the future that present a vision of technological wonder and bleak sterility. Promised utopias, they repeatedly and rapidly degenerate into vast urban wastelands that devour their pitiful human prey. In the end, they are bitterly renounced by their creator and verbally banished back to the void from which they emerged.

A third major theme is that of metamorphosis—a theme that is a logical outgrowth of Rimbaud's own assertion that "I is an other." For Rimbaud, as his "Seer Letter" makes clear, the seemingly stable Cartesian I is merely an illusion that masks the presence of a multiplicity of repressed others. Humans have no central, defining essence. In *Illuminations*, the poet thus undergoes a continual series of metamorphoses. In "Parade," he appears as a procession of itinerant comedians; in "Antique," as the son of the pagan god Pan, at once animal, man, and woman; in "Bottom," as the character in William Shakespeare's *A Midsummer Night's Dream* (pr. c. 1595-1596) who seeks to appropriate all the other characters' roles; and finally, in "Being Beauteous," as the incarnation of beauty itself. There are no limits to humanity's being, Rimbaud suggests, if people will only realize the vast potential within them.

OTHER MAJOR WORKS

MISCELLANEOUS: *Œuvres complètes*, 1948 (*Complete Works, Selected Letters*, 1966); *Rimbaud Complete*, 2002-2003 (2 volumes; Wyatt Mason, editor).

BIBLIOGRAPHY

Ahearn, Edward J. *Rimbaud: Visions and Habitations.* Berkeley: University of California Press, 1983. Discusses the influence of Rimbaud's early life and surroundings on his brief poetic career, including the anticlerical and anticonventional guidance he received during his teen years, when he began writing poetry. Points out links between Rimbaud's poetic images and his actual physical environment.

Cohn, Robert Greer. *The Poetry of Rimbaud.* 1973. Reprint. Columbia: University of South Carolina Press, 1999. A critical analysis of the poetry that Rimbaud wrote during his short life.

Hackett, Cecil Arthur. *Rimbaud: A Critical Introduction.* New York: Cambridge University Press, 1981. A good introduction for those beginning to explore Rimbaud's poetry. Contains much poem-by-poem explication, as well as analyses of Rimbaud's overall poetic achievement and cultural influence.

Lawler, James R. *Rimbaud's Theatre of the Self.* Cambridge, Mass.: Harvard University Press, 1992. A unique book that translates Rimbaud's work into a theatrical progression, explaining why the poet stopped writing to explore the dark side of his personality.

Oxenhandler, Neal. *Rimbaud: The Cost of Genius.* Columbus: Ohio State University Press, 2009. An examination of the life of Rimbaud that argues that his talent had a destructive side to it.

Perloff, Marjorie. *The Poetics of Indeterminacy: Rimbaud to Cage.* Evanston, Ill.: Northwestern University Press, 2000. This work contains only one chapter on Rimbaud but is highly useful in placing him within his historical context. Discusses his influence on modernist poets such as Gertrude Stein, Ezra Pound, and William Carlos Williams, as a transitional force between Symbolism and modernism.

Robb, Graham. *Rimbaud: A Biography.* New York: W. W. Norton, 2000. Presents a "reconstruction of Rimbaud's life"; discusses the revolutionary impact his poetry had on twentieth century writers and artists, especially since Rimbaud's admirers primarily arose after his early death. Examines the influence of Rimbaud's early family life, in particular his stormy relationship with his mother, and presents thoroughly his checkered career after his abandonment of poetry at the age of twenty-one.

Steinmetz, Jean-Luc. *Arthur Rimbaud: Presence of an Enigma.* Translated by Jon Graham. New York: Welcome Rain, 2001. A comprehensive biography, this work focuses on Rimbaud's numerous self-contradictions and extremes of behavior, particularly in his stormy relationship with the older poet Paul Verlaine. The author analyzes Rimbaud's poetry primarily in its relation to the poet's life.

James John Baran

YANNIS RITSOS

Born: Monemvasia, Greece; May 14, 1909
Died: Athens, Greece; November 11, 1990

PRINCIPAL POETRY

Trakter, 1934
Pyramides, 1935
Epitaphios, 1936
To tragoudi tes adelphes mou, 1937
Dokimasia, 1943
Agrypnia, 1954
Romiosyne, 1954 (*Romiossini: The Story of the Greeks*, 1969)
E sonata tou selenophotos, 1956 (*The Moonlight Sonata*, 1975)
Poiemata A', 1961
Poiemata B', 1961
To nekro spiti, 1962 (*The Dead House*, 1974)
Martyries, A' seira, 1963

Poiemata G', 1964

Philoktetes, 1965 (English translation, 1975)

Martyries, B' seira, 1966

Orestes, 1966

Gestures, and Other Poems, 1971

Cheironomies, 1972

E Elene, 1972

Petres, epanalepseis, kigklidoma, 1972

Tetarte diastase, 1972 (*The Fourth Dimension*, 1993)

Chartina, 1974

Selected Poems, 1974

E Kyra ton Ampelion, 1975 (*The Lady of the Vineyards*, 1978)

Poiemata D', 1975

Ta epikairika, 1975

Chronicle of Exile, 1977

The Fourth Dimension: Selected Poems of Yannis Ritsos, 1977

Gignesthai, 1977

To Makrino, 1977

Monemvasiotisses, 1978 (*The Women of Monemvasia*, 1987)

Phaidra, 1978

Ritsos in Parentheses, 1979

Scripture of the Blind, 1979

Diaphaneia, 1980

Monochorda, 1980 (*Monochords*, 2007)

Oneiro kalokairinou mesemeriou, 1980

Subterranean Horses, 1980

Erotika, 1981 (*Erotica*, 1982)

Monovasia, 1982 (English translation, 1987)

Selected Poems, 1983

Exile and Return: Selected Poems, 1967-1974, 1985

Antapokriseis, 1987

Yannis Ritsos: Selected Poems, 1938-1988, 1989

Yannis Ritsos: Repetitions, Testimonies, Parentheses, 1991

Arga, poly arga mesa ste nychta, 1992 (*Late into the Night: The Last Poems of Yannis Ritsos*, 1995)

Yannis Ritsos: A Voice of Resilience and Hope in a World of Turmoil and Suffering, Selected Poems, 1938-1989, 2001

OTHER LITERARY FORMS

Although known almost exclusively as a poet, Yannis Ritsos (REETS-ohs) published prolifically as a journalist and translator, and less prolifically as a critic and dramatist. His collected criticism, available in *Meletemata* (1974; studies), includes, in addition to essays on Vladimir Mayakovsky, Nazim Hikmet, Ilya Ehrenburg, and Paul Éluard, two invaluable commentaries on Ritsos's own work. Among his translations are Aleksandr Blok's *Dvenadtsat* (1918; *The Twelve*, 1920), anthologies of Romanian, Czech, and Slovak poetry, and selected poems by Mayakovsky, Hikmet, and Ehrenburg.

ACHIEVEMENTS

Ignored or banned for decades by the establishment, Yannis Ritsos gradually became recognized, and was nominated for the Nobel Prize three times, although, unlike his compatriots George Seferis and Odysseus Elytis, he never received that honor. He received many others, however, including the International Dimitrov Prize (Bulgaria, 1974), an honorary doctorate from the University of Thessaloníki (1975), the Alfred de Vigny Poctry Prize (France, 1975), two of Italy's International Prizes for Poetry (1976), the Lenin Peace Prize (1977), Italy's Mondello Prize (1978), and honorary doctorates from Greece's Salonica University (1975) and the University of Birmingham, England (1978). In addition to his prolific output (nearly one hundred volumes of poetry), Ritsos continues to enjoy a growing reputation as more of his work is translated into English; were he not a poet of modern Greek, a minority language, his work would be as important a part of the comparative literature curriculum in Anglo-American colleges as is that of his more thoroughly translated and celebrated compatriots, such as Seferis, Elytis, Constantine Cavafy, and Nikos Kazantzakis.

Perhaps more important than such recognition is the contribution Ritsos made to his homeland: More thoroughly than any other Greek writer, Ritsos amalgamated the two ideologies that divided his country, the communist and the bourgeois. Though he espoused Marxist Leninism early in his career and remained faithful to the party to the end, he nevertheless borrowed from Western literary movements, especially

Surrealism, and struggled frankly with the Western attractions of individualism and subjectivism. All in all, because he presents a communist orientation expressed through techniques that have evolved in ways typical of noncommunist authors, he speaks for and to the entire Greek nation.

Ritsos proved himself a virtuoso in technique. His range was enormous: from the tiniest lyric to huge narrative compositions, from impenetrable surrealistic puzzles to occasional verse promulgating blunt political messages, from poetry of almost embarrassing sensuality to rarefied philosophical meditations. He is also greatly esteemed because of his personal integrity, demonstrated over years of persecution, exile, and imprisonment. As he said in 1970 when interrogated by the ruling junta: "A poet is the first citizen of his country and for this very reason it is the duty of the poet to be concerned about the politics of his country."

BIOGRAPHY

Yannis Ritsos was born into a wealthy landowning family of Monemvasia, but he did not have a happy

Yannis Ritsos (Greek Press and Information Service)

childhood. His father's fortunes declined because of the land reforms under Eleftherios Venizelos in the early 1900's, and their wealth was obliterated by the Asia Minor campaigns between 1919 and 1922, when labor was unavailable for the harvests. In addition, Ritsos's father gambled compulsively, accelerating the family's decline. As if this were not enough, Ritsos's older brother and his mother died of tuberculosis when Ritsos was only twelve—a prelude to the hardships and suffering that would mark his adult life.

Upon his graduation from high school in the town of Gythion, Ritsos moved to Athens; the year was 1925, a time when that city was desperately trying to assimilate a million and a half refugees from Asia Minor. He managed to find work as a typist and then as a copyist of legal documents, but in 1926, he returned to Monemvasia after coughing blood. There he devoted himself to painting, music, and poetry, completing a group of poems that he called "Sto paleo mas spiti" (in our old house). He returned to Athens in 1927, but a new crisis in his health confined him to a tuberculosis sanatorium for three years, during which, while continuing to write poems, he also began to study Marxism. By 1930, he had committed himself to the communist cause. Transferred to a sanatorium in Crete, he found conditions there so abominable that he exposed the facility's managers in a series of newspaper articles; this led to the removal of all the patients, including Ritsos, to a better facility, where his disease came under temporary control.

Back in Athens, Ritsos directed the artistic activities of the Workers' Club, appearing in in-house theatricals and also on the stage of the Labor Union Theater. Meanwhile, his father was confined to an insane asylum. While eking out a living as actor, dancer, copy editor, and journalist, Ritsos published his first two collections, *Trakter* (tractor) and *Pyramides* (pyramids). His career took a leap forward when, in May of 1936, he composed his *Epitaphios* immediately after the slaughter of twelve tobacco workers by Thessaloníki police during a strike. Issued in ten thousand copies, this became the first of Ritsos's poems to be banned. The dictatorship of Yannis Metaxas, when it began in August, publicly burned the 250 unsold copies at the Temple of Olympian Zeus.

In this same year, Ritsos composed *To tragoudi tes adelphes mou* (the song of my sister), after his sister

Loula was committed to the same asylum that housed their father. This private dirge, balancing the public one for the slain strikers, so impressed Kostis Palamas, Greece's most influential poet at the time, that he hailed the young poet as his own successor. Ritsos suffered a brief recurrence of his tuberculosis, requiring another period in a sanatorium, after which he worked again as an actor, all the while publishing new collections of verse.

During the period of the Albanian Campaign, the German invasion, and the Axis Occupation of Greece (1940-1944), Ritsos—now confined to bed almost continuously—wrote without respite but was unable to publish freely. Among the works produced was a long novel burned during the second round of the Civil War (December, 1944) and another prose composition, never published, titled "Ariostos o prosechtikos aphegeitai stigmes tou biou tou kai tou ypnou tou" (careful Ariostos narrates moments from his life and his sleep).

After the second round of the Civil War, Ritsos fled to northern Greece with the defeated communist forces. While in Kozani, he wrote plays for the People's Theater of Macedonia. The Varkiza Accord (February 12, 1945) enabled him to return to Athens, where he regularly contributed poems, prose pieces, translations, and dance criticism to the periodical *Elefthera grammata*, as well as collaborating with the artistic branch of the communist youth movement. It was at this time that he began to write *Romiossini* and *The Lady of the Vineyards*, his twin tributes to the Greek Resistance.

In 1948, Ritsos was arrested because of his political activities and sent to various concentration camps on Greek islands. Under the worst of conditions, he nevertheless wrote about his privations, burying manuscripts and notes in bottles to hide them from the guards. Naturally, his work was banned. An international protest by figures such as Pablo Picasso, Louis Aragon, and Pablo Neruda led to his release in August, 1952. Free again in Athens, he joined the newly founded party, the EDA (United Democratic Left), wrote for the left-wing newspaper *Avgi*, married Falitsa Georgiadis in 1954, and became the father of a daughter in 1955. The following year, he visited the Soviet Union, traveling outside Greece for the first time. *Epitaphios* was reissued in a twentieth-anniversary edition, and *The Moonlight*

Sonata brought him his first public recognition since Palamas's early enthusiasm, in the form of the State Prize for Poetry. This, in turn, led to international acclaim when Aragon published *The Moonlight Sonata* in *Les Lettres françaises*, accompanied by a flattering notice. In Greece, the publishing firm Kedros began to bring out all the work that could not be published earlier and planned for a multivolume collection of Ritsos's poems.

In 1960, the popular composer Mikis Theodorakis set eight sections of *Epitaphios* to music, making Ritsos a household name in Greece. In 1962, Ritsos traveled again, this time to Romania, Czechoslovakia, and East Germany, as a result of which he became acquainted with the Turkish poet Hikmet and his anthologies of Balkan poets. Despite a relapse of his tuberculosis, Ritsos composed prolifically during this period. In May, 1963, he journeyed to Thessaloníki to participate in the vigil for the parliamentary deputy Gregory Lambrakis, who had been mortally wounded by right-wing thugs. The following year, Ritsos himself stood for parliament as an EDA candidate. In 1966, he traveled to Cuba. Theodorakis set *Romiossini* to music, again with immense popular success.

On April 21, 1967, the day of the Colonels' Coup, Ritsos was arrested and again sent into exile on various islands, his works once more under ban. Protests poured in from around the world, leading to his transfer to house arrest in his wife's home in Samos. A group of seventy-five members of the French Academy and other writers, including several Nobel laureates, nominated him for the Nobel Prize. Translations of his poetry multiplied, especially in France.

Offered a passport by the junta to attend a poetry festival in England in 1970—on the condition that he refrain from all criticism of the regime—Ritsos refused, but later in the same year, owing to his health, he was allowed to return to Athens to undergo an operation and to remain there. In 1971, he joined others in publishing in *Ta nea keimena* in defiance of the regime. After the relaxation of censorship in 1972, Ritsos's works written in exile came out in a flood of publication that increased after the junta's fall in 1974. Thereafter, Ritsos continued to write poetry, but largely of a different sort; in the absence of a police state and finally out of prison, his concerns turned to more lyric and personal works. He produced some of his best work in this mode—attesting to the difficulty of pigeonholing him as a political poet.

He died in Athens, Greece, on November 11, 1990, fatefully on Armistice Day as well as the eve of the Soviet Union's dissolution. Despite his communist politics, Greece's president Constantine Mitsotakis announced that this nationally mourned poet would be buried with full state honors.

ANALYSIS

Greece produced at least three world-class poets in the mid-twentieth century: Seferis, Elytis, and Yannis Ritsos. The first two received the Nobel Prize and are bourgeois; Ritsos received the Lenin Prize and was a communist. However, it would be entirely wrong to call him Greece's leading leftist poet or even a political poet. His range is so immense, his career so diverse, the traditions from which he draws so eclectic that these or any other labels distort his contribution. Though the leftist element is clearly present in Ritsos's work, he shares with bourgeois poets an interest in nature, in personal anguish, even in Christianity, and he participates as fully as they do in pan-European movements such as Surrealism and folklorism. In sum, Ritsos speaks not only to one camp but also to all humanity.

EPITAPHIOS

It is clear, however, that Ritsos found his first voice only because he had aligned himself with the political Left. It was communism that transformed him, in the decade 1926-1936, from an imitator of others in content and style to a unique singer of revolution. *Epitaphios* provided the breakthrough. A dirge gasped out by a simple mother over the body of her son, slain by police in a labor dispute, this poem modulates from the dirge itself to the mother's thirst for revenge and finally to her solidarity with the oppressed working class. Every aspect of the poem—not merely its content—is intended by the author to make it accessible to the common people and not just about them. Thus, it exploits diverse elements from their cultural storehouse, primarily their Greek Orthodox liturgy and their folk songs, melding a call to revolution with the Christian hope for Resurrection, and voicing all this through the

tone, metrics, and imagery of the demotic ballads that were produced by anonymous folk poets throughout the centuries of Turkish rule. Ritsos did not do this self-consciously to erect a bulwark of tradition that would fortify national identity, but almost naïvely; the liturgy and the demotic ballads were friends with which he had grown up as a child. What he sought to avoid, and conversely to accomplish, is best expressed by his estimation of Hikmet in *Meletemata*: "His poetry is not just . . . 'folkloristic' (that is, extremely . . . 'aesthetic' on a so-called popular plane—hence nonpopular) . . . but essentially *popular* because of participation . . . in popular forces, which it expresses not in their static, standardized forms . . . but . . . in their dynamic motion."

TO TRAGOUDI TES ADELPHES MOU

It is characteristic of Ritsos's own dynamic motion that the mode of *Epitaphios* was never to be repeated. The poet broadened his range immediately—owing to the external circumstances of Metaxas's censorship, which confined Ritsos to nonpolitical subjects. However, even when he returned to political poetry after the dictator's death early in 1941, Ritsos did so in a different way, if only because he had liberated his technique in the meantime from the constraints of rhyme and strict stanzaic form. *To tragoudi tes adelphes mou* is the chief fruit of the Metaxas period. The first of many extended elegies about family members or others, chiefly women, overcome by misfortune, it matches *Epitaphios* in that it shows how pain can lead to illumination, here the lamenting poet's conviction that poetry itself—the very act of singing of his sister's insanity—will save both him and her:

> The poem has subdued me.
> The poem has granted me the victory. . . .
> I who could not
> save you from life
> will save you from death.

Poetry thus joins revolution as a wonder-working power for Ritsos, who in his espousal of an "aesthetic solution" joined hands with his bourgeois colleagues throughout Europe.

"ENGRAVING"

In the many short poems written during this same period, Ritsos learned to escape the stridency still present in both *Epitaphios* and *To tragoudi tes adelphes mou*; he learned to distance himself from his material, to be laconic, to have poems "be," not merely "say." This he achieved chiefly through a painterly technique whereby motion, time, and sound were transfixed into immobility, space, and sight. Consider these lines:

> Lone chimes speak silence,
> memories in groups beneath the trees,
> cows sad in the dusk.
> Behind the young shepherds a cloud was bleating
>   at the sunset.

In this Keatsian, cold pastoral, sound is frozen into a composition, time is spatialized. It is no wonder that the poem is titled "Engraving."

"THE BURIAL OF ORGAZ"

Similar techniques are more difficult to apply to longer works, which cannot help but evolve in time. One of Ritsos's most successful works is an extended political poem written in September and October, 1942. Titled "The Burial of Orgaz," it employs El Greco's celebrated painting *Burial of the Conde de Orgaz* (1586-1588) as a static, two-tiered composition, holding in place the extraordinarily varied figures of the poet's political vision: on the earthly level, mutilated veterans of Albania, resisters executed by the Germans, innocent Athenians dying from famine; on the heavenly, in place of El Greco's John the Baptist kneeling at Christ's feet, robust workers building a new road—a Marxist paradise. Because of the painterly technique, the emotions are frozen into beauty; life is transformed into art. Later in his career—as in *Philoktetes*, for example—Ritsos was to achieve the same control over the mad flow of life's images by superimposing them on a myth rather than on a painting.

"The Burial of Orgaz" treats war tragically. It is ironic that Ritsos could treat it exultantly only after his side had met defeat in the second round of the Civil War and had then begun to suffer systematic persecution. Mortified at the discrediting of the Resistance by the Greek Right, he determined to apotheosize the heroes (communist or not) who had opposed the Axis throughout the Occupation period and to insist on their patriotism. In *Romiossini*, written between 1945 and 1947 but obviously not publishable until much later, he

therefore amalgamated his twentieth century heroes with the historical freedom fighters in the Greek War of Independence and the legendary stalwarts who had harassed the Turks in preceding centuries. Ending as it does with the hope of a peaceful, loving tomorrow, the resulting ode combines visionary transcendentalism, realism, and epic exaggeration into a blend that energetically celebrates—along with *The Lady of the Vineyards*, written at the same time—Greece's most difficult years.

IN THE INTERNMENT CAMPS

The exultant tone disappeared from Ritsos's poetry during the four years (1948-1952) that he spent once more in internment camps. His aim was no longer either epic or transcendental; it was merely to encourage his fellow prisoners with simple verses that they could understand. There is an entire collection of these poems written in 1949 while he was on the infamous island of Makronesos, the "Makronesiotika," available in *Ta epikairika*.

Many more were composed on Agios Efstratios (Ai-Strati), the most celebrated being the "Letter to Joliot-Curie" of November, 1950, which was smuggled out of Greece at the time. It begins:

> Dear Joliot, I'm writing you from AiStrati.
> We're about three thousand here,
> simple people . . .
> with an onion, five olives and a stale crust of light in
> our sacks
> . . . people who have no other crime to their account
> except that we, like you, love
> freedom and peace.

To his credit, Ritsos later realized that the comrades did have other crimes to their account, but the circumstances of imprisonment made such self-criticism inappropriate for the moment. What is remarkable, as Pandeles Prevelakes remarks, is that Ritsos "not only maintained his intellectual identity, but also prodded his sensibility to adjust to the conditions of exile."

More important is the tender poem titled "Peace," written soon after Ritsos's release. Here, the title word is no longer a political slogan; it expresses the poet's genuine sense of tranquillity after four years of terror:

Peace is the evening meal's aroma,
when a car stopping outside in the street isn't fear,
when a knock on the door means a friend. . . .

THE PEACEFUL DECADE

The years 1956 to 1966 were Ritsos's most remarkable decade of artistic productivity and growth. The great outpouring of this period surely derived in part from unaccustomed happiness—this was the first outwardly peaceful decade of his life—but also, paradoxically, from a new, disagreeable condition to which his sensibility (along with that of all communists) had to adjust. Soviet premier Nikita Khrushchev denounced dictator Joseph Stalin in 1956, whereupon the Greek Communist Party immediately denounced its Stalinist leader, Nikos Zachariades. Later in the same year, the Soviet Union—presumably a lover of freedom and peace—invaded Hungary. Ritsos, who had sung hymns to both Stalin and Zachariades, was forced to step back from his previous commitments and certainties, to view them with doubt or irony. "The first cries of admiration," he wrote in his introduction to his criticism on Mayakovsky, "have given way to a more silent self-communing. . . . We have learned how difficult it is not to abuse the power entrusted to us in the name of the supreme ideal, liberty. . . ." This new understanding, he continued, has led modern poets to a self-examination which is at the same time self-effacing and hesitant. Elsewhere, he spoke of his growing consciousness of all that is "vague, complicated, incomprehensible, inexplicable and directionless in life."

THE MOONLIGHT SONATA

The first fruit of this new awareness of the complexity of life was *The Moonlight Sonata*, a nonpolitical poem constituting for Ritsos a breakthrough fully as significant as the one achieved precisely twenty years earlier by the quintessentially political *Epitaphios*. The 1956 poem, though once again a kind of elegy for a suffering woman, avoids all stridency and authorial assertion by hiding its tragic elements behind a mask of ironic impassivity. At the same time, however, it allows the woman's anguished emotions to stir the reader's emotions. Ritsos accomplishes this by making the major voice not his own but the woman's and then by framing her dramatic monologue inside yet another

nonauthorial voice, a narrator's, which questions and neutralizes the emotions of the first voice. As a result, the reader is never quite sure how to feel about the poem or how to interpret it; instead, both emotionally and mentally, the reader is ushered into all that is "vague, complicated, incomprehensible. . . ."

PHILOKTETES

Philoktetes carries this process still further. It retains the technique of dramatic monologue inside a narrative frame but adds to it an all-encompassing myth that fulfills the same kind of "painterly" purpose served earlier by El Greco's *Burial of the Conde de Orgaz*. At the same time, the myth connects Ritsos's version of the Philoctetes story and hence the Greek Civil War (which is clearly suggested) not only with Homer's Achaeans and Trojans but also with the Peloponnesian War, clearly suggested in Sophocles' version. If one notes as well that the poem employs the surrealistic and expressionistic techniques that Ritsos had been perfecting in short poems dating from the same period (collected as *Martyries, A' seira*; testimonies), it becomes clear that a work of such complexity is deliberately meant to make the reader feel uncomfortably suspended above nothing. That, in turn, is a perfect technical equivalent for the thrust of the poem, which dismisses every justification for Philoctetes' collaboration in the Trojan War yet affirms his need to stand by his comrades even though he knows their perfidy. The poem thus examines Ritsos's own dilemma as a Stalinist betrayed by Stalin, determined to bring his understanding and indulgence to the cause instead of merely defecting. It is a self-examination which is at the same time self-effacing and hesitant.

JUNTA YEARS: 1967-1974

The poet's new stance was soon put to the test by imprisonment under the Colonels. Despite this provocation, Ritsos did not revert to the optimistic assurance displayed during earlier privations; the new poems of exile are exasperated, sardonic, even sometimes despairing. Bitten (like Philoctetes) by the snake of wisdom, he could never return to the propagandistic verse produced on Agios Efstratios. On the contrary, he felt the need to reaffirm the predominance of mystery. "The Disjunctive Conjunction 'Or,'" written in exile on June 18, 1969, says this loud and clear: "O that 'or,'" cries the poet, that "equivocal smile of an incommunicable . . . wisdom/ which . . ./ [knows] full well that precision/ . . . does not exist (which is why the pompous style of certainty is so unforgivable . . .)./ Disjunctive 'or' . . ./ with you we manage the troubles of life and dream,/ the numerous shades and interpretations. . . ."

LATER POEMS

With the demise of the Colonels' dictatorship in the mid-1970's, Ritsos's poetry understandably began to retreat from the subjects so compelling during his days in prisons and a police state. Still, he continued to grapple with mystery, asking basic questions but realizing that answers do not always follow:

> So many dead
> without death
> so many living corpses.
> You sit in a chair
> counting your buttons.
> Where do you belong?
> What are you?
> What are you doing?

The sardonic element is still present, but so is a certain spirit of indulgence or clemency—precisely what Philoctetes brought to Troy. Furthermore, a parodistic flavor entered many of Ritsos's poems, a kind of macabre humor that neutralizes the worst that life can offer. Ritsos thus stood above all that his compatriots had done to him, playing with his experience, turning it round beneath his philosophic gaze—a gaze annealed by hardship into resilience.

He also began to compose domestic, amatory, or occasional lyrics; some of best love poems appear in 1981's *Erotica*, for example. The epic, mythic, poems that mined Greece's past to question its national present receded. It was not until near the end of his life that Ritsos returned to myth, and then the expression was intensely personal. As one of his chief translators, Peter Green, notes:

> Ritsos saw 'the black double-oared boat with its dark boatman drawing near.' . . . Ritsos paid more, over a long lifetime, than most writers are ever called upon to do, but the legacy that he left is imperishable.

OTHER MAJOR WORKS

PLAYS: *Pera ap ton iskio ton kyparission*, pb. 1958; *Mia gynaika plai sti thalassa*, pr., pb. 1959.

NONFICTION: *Meletemata*, 1974.

BIBLIOGRAPHY

Green, Peter. Review of *Yannis Ritsos: Repetitions, Testimonies, Parentheses*. *The New Republic* 205, no. 16 (October 14, 1991). This lengthy essay reviews not only Ritsos's late work but also his entire career. An excellent resource in English. Green is one of Ritsos's primary translators.

Keeley, Edmund. *Inventing Paradise: The Greek Journey, 1937-47*. New York: Farrar, Straus and Giroux, 1999. The eminent translator of modern Greek literature—including Ritsos's poetry—provides a discussion that casts light on the context for much Greek poetry during the turbulent middle of the twentieth century. Bibliography.

_____. *On Translation: Reflections and Conversations*. Amsterdam: Harwood Academic, 2000. Keeley's comments in this brief monograph of just over one hundred pages offers non-Greek readers some insights into translations from modern Greek, important to any full understanding of Ritsos's poetry.

Pilitsis, George. Introduction to *Yannis Ritsos: A Voice of Resilience and Hope in a World of Turmoil and Suffering—Selected Poems (1938-1989)*. Brookline, Mass.: Hellenic College Press, 2001. Pilitsis provides biographical background and critical analysis in his introduction to translations of poems by Ritsos.

Savvas, Minas. "Remembering Yannis Ritsos." *Literary Review* 36, no. 2 (Winter, 1993): 238-247. Savvas, who translated several of Ritsos's works, recalls an early meeting with the poet and other aspects of their relationship.

Peter Bien
Updated by Christina J. Moose

PIERRE DE RONSARD

Born: Castle of la Possonnière, near Couture,
Vendômois, France; September 11, 1524
Died: Saint-Cosme, near Tours, France; December
27, 1585

PRINCIPAL POETRY

L'Hymne de France, 1549
Odes, 1550
Les Amours, 1552
Cinquième Livre des odes, 1552
Le Bocage, 1554
Continuation des amours, 1555
Les Hymnes, 1555-1556
Nouvelle Continuation des amours, 1556
Discours des misères de ce temps, 1562
*Résponce aux injures et calomnies de je ne sçay
quels prédicans et ministres de Genève*, 1563
La Franciade, 1572
Les Amours sur la mort de Marie, 1578
Sonnets pour Hélène, 1578 (*Sonnets for Helen*,
1932)
Les Derniers Vers, 1586
Songs and Sonnets, 1903
Salute to Ronsard, 1960
Poems of Pierre de Ronsard, 1979 (Nicholas
Kilmer, editor)
Selected Poems, 2002

OTHER LITERARY FORMS

In 1565, Pierre de Ronsard (rohn-SAHR) published
his *Abbregé de l'art poëtique français* (brief treatise on
French poetics), a theoretical work written in prose. In
addition, he wrote a number of prose prefaces to his poetry (notably to the first volume of odes), and political
or religious tracts.

ACHIEVEMENTS

Pierre de Ronsard, the Prince of Poets, was both a
great writer and a writer fully aware of his greatness.
Although he and the poets around him did not, as they
may have thought, create something out of nothing,
they clearly did create new and often brilliant poetry.

They demonstrate a fresh and sometimes naïve exhila-
ration in their poetic mission and boundless pride in
their accomplishments.

Fascinated with classical culture, with the possibilities of the French language, and with his own abilities,
Ronsard set out to emulate and to rival the Greek and
Latin poets. At times, his pursuit of that goal led him
into pedantry, with conspicuous and often heavy-
handed references to classical antiquity and myth. When
he was at his best, however, such references were a poetic means, not an end; they were a way of translating
his vision into accessible form. Moreover, at his best
(particularly in his love lyrics), he used such material
judiciously, occasionally dispensing with it altogether
in order to let his persona speak in a direct poetic voice.

Ronsard himself published only a minor treatise on
poetic art, but he almost certainly played a major role in
formulating the theory propounded in Joachim Du
Bellay's *La Défense et illustration de la langue
française* (1549; *The Defence and Illustration of the
French Language*, 1939), the principal manifesto and
manual of Ronsard's poetic circle. Moreover, implicit
in his poetry itself, there is a fully developed theory of
poetic inspiration and composition. His contribution to
the development of the French language and of French
letters was considerable, as he put into practice many of
the specific precepts of du Bellay's work. Ronsard
sought the creation of new and compound words, the
acceptance of regional, technical, and archaic forms,
and the Gallicizing of foreign words. Ironically, these
very practices—his liberties with, and expansions of,
the language—led in part to Ronsard's disfavor among
the writers and theorists of the following two centuries,
when he was most often considered a pedant and a
corrupter of the language. Partly for those same reasons
as well, but primarily because he is a great poet, he was
rediscovered during the nineteenth century, and he has
since been accorded a fair measure of the favor he had
attained in his own day.

Ronsard was a remarkably prolific poet, the preeminent poet of his age, and one of the primary creators of
French lyrics. If he was mistaken in his impression that
France produced no notable lyric poets before his century, that error in no way diminishes his own achievement. Anthologists have unfortunately created for many

modern readers a "homogenized" Ronsard, by ignoring much of his work and by repeatedly reproducing a few well-known love poems. His poetry is in fact extremely varied; it can be whimsical or introspective, lyrical or vigorous, occasionally even vicious. His vision, his command of tone and style, his realization and exploitation of the full poetic potential of the French language all give persuasive evidence that his designation as Prince of Poets, while not undisputed, is far more than idle praise.

BIOGRAPHY

Pierre de Ronsard was born of a noble family in the Vendômois region of France in 1524. At the age of twelve, he became a page for the dauphin François, only to have his master die a mere three days later. He then began to serve Madeleine de France (the new wife of James Stuart and daughter of François I). Ronsard accompanied her to Scotland, where she died almost immediately, in 1537. Three years later, a disease left Ronsard partially deaf and apparently destroyed his hopes for a diplomatic or other public career. It may have been this condition, as much as his exposure to the arts (an exposure provided both by his father and by his association with other Humanists and poets), that pushed him toward a career in letters.

Whatever the reason, Ronsard threw himself into Humanistic studies and into his early poetic efforts with single-minded energy and ambition. In 1547, he and the poet du Bellay entered the College of Coqueret to study with the Humanist Jean Dorat. Along with others, Ronsard and du Bellay constituted a poetic group designated as the Brigade, which (later, and with some changes in membership) was to be known as the Pléiade. In 1549, du Bellay published *The Defence and Illustration of the French Language*; this composition, to which Ronsard certainly contributed, was an important manifesto that provided both a theoretical foundation for poetry in the vernacular and practical advice for the development of its resources. A year later, Ronsard published his *Odes*.

Ronsard's poetic beginnings immediately earned for him large numbers of admirers—but also a good many detractors, who in general criticized him for pedantry. Subsequently, he moved gradually toward sim-

pler, more direct, and more accessible poetry. This movement is evident already in *Les Amours*. Within several years, his poetry and his success had silenced most of his critics, and he had earned not only praise and respect, but also the honor and financial benefits that accompanied royal approval: after the death of Mellin de Saint-Gellais in 1558, Ronsard became court poet to Charles IX.

In addition to being a court poet, Ronsard soon became a pamphleteer and polemicist as well, using his pen as a potent weapon in the wars of religion and frequently interspersing his diatribes against the Protestants with attacks against his own political or literary enemies. The year 1572 saw the publication—and failure—of Ronsard's epic, *La Franciade*. His disappointment and his loss of favor with the new king, Henri III (who preferred the poetry of Philippe Desportes), led Ronsard to retire from court life. In 1578, he published the remarkable *Sonnets for Helen*, and throughout this period he continued to write, as well as revising and ed-

Pierre de Ronsard (Hulton Archive/Getty Images)

iting his complete works. His health had deteriorated significantly, and he suffered from recurrent attacks of gout and a variety of other ailments. In 1585, he died at Saint-Cosme, at the age of sixty-one.

ANALYSIS

More than any other single theme or idea, it is Pierre de Ronsard's awareness of the role of the poet and of his own mission and immortality that defines his literary production. The true poet, he says, is the recipient of divine inspiration, and the implication (or, frequently, the explicit contention) is that the preeminent example of the true poet was Ronsard. He boasts of raising poetry in France to the level of a sublime art; indeed, he was known as the first French lyric writer. These are themes that recur with a striking degree of regularity throughout his work, interrupted only once, in the early 1560's, when he briefly doubted his creative powers and referred to himself as "half a poet." His confidence and pride quickly returned, however, and in his *Résponce aux injures et calomnies de je ne sçay quels prédicans et ministres de Genève* (response to the insults and calumnies of certain pastors and ministers of Geneva), he likened himself to a poetic fountain, while other poets are mere streams who have their source in his work and his "grandeur." Others plagiarize him (he noted), and with good cause, since his work rivals Latin and Greek poetry.

For a poet who at every turn boasts of his originality, Ronsard may at times impress modern readers as strikingly derivative, as he mines classical myth and letters for images. He provides an explanation of his method, however, noting that myth hides truths—that is, clothes them in presentable literary form. Myth is for him a key to truth, and one approaches that truth by a kind of allegorical method, extrapolating from heroes and mythic events to contemporary characters and occurrences.

Ronsard would doubtless suggest that his method is far from being as mechanical as these remarks suggest; he is free to use or ignore myth or any other material; he can exploit it to reveal truth or simply to adorn his verse. In any case (he would insist), poetic inspiration obeys its own laws, which are independent of habitual or logical practices. The autonomy of poetic inspiration becomes, in fact, a major theme of Ronsard's theoreti-

cal and polemical work, and it is his inspiration, he says, that raises him above others. In the preface to the first book of *Odes*, he informs his rivals: "I follow an unknown path to arrive at immortality."

LOVE POEMS AND PETRARCHISM

For most readers, Ronsard's reputation rests most solidly on the sonnets, songs, and other lyrics expressing the poet's love for Cassandre, Marie, Hélène, and others. Occasionally obscure or pedantic in these compositions (and especially in the earliest ones), he is more often direct, accessible, and lyrical. However, even within the collections of love poems themselves, there is a considerable amount of diversity, and from one of them to the next, Ronsard's evolution is obvious. He himself acknowledges that evolution (in the preface to the second book of love poems), noting that his style is not as elevated as it had earlier been. He has come to believe that love is best expressed not by cultivated high seriousness, but by an appealing lower style. He adds that he "want[s] to follow a gentler Muse . . ." and concludes that he is now writing to please no one but his lady.

The love lyrics are strongly influenced by Petrarchan images and conventions. The poet—or at least his persona—loves his lady, finds himself constantly fascinated and inspired by her, and also suffers from the love. His suffering, however, is suspect. He asserts that, with her unpitying heart, she makes him languish; his spirit is heavy and sad, and he suffers great pain with only brief respite. There is a curious absence of passion, however, in most of these assertions; one has the impression that he makes them because the conventions he is following require it. One more readily accepts as accurate the poet's image of a "sweet venom," and in general, he seems to derive far more pleasure than pain from his love. If this is a somewhat atypical expression of Petrarchism, one soon finds an explicit rejection of one aspect of it. In the prologue to the Marie poems, Ronsard insists that Petrarch has no authority to impose rules on him. Of course, there is good reason for him to reject Petrarch's influence. The French poet is after all defending himself against a possible accusation of poetic infidelity, since, after devoting more than two hundred poems to Cassandre, he is now turning his attention and affection to Marie. In the process, he questions certain assumptions about Petrarch himself: "Either he received pleasure from his Laura, or else he was a fool to go on loving with nothing in return." Ronsard goes on to suggest, uncharitably, that women are frequently the reason for men's inconstancy: If a woman is cold and unyielding, it is not merely natural, but even advisable, for a man to turn elsewhere.

Ronsard's lyrics at this point in his career offer a very curious version of Petrarchism: Its demands include neither permanent fidelity to one woman nor excessive anguish or melancholy on the part of the lover. One can see in these departures from Petrarchan conventions not only a particular conception of love, but also an attempt by Ronsard to affirm his own poetic originality and to avoid being seen as a mere imitation or reflection of the renowned Italian writer.

In any event, the reader often has the impression that love and the lady are being "used" by the poet, for they permit him to experience and express inspiration and beauty more intensely. Petrarchism is, in a sense, turned on its head, the lady becoming a means rather than an end; in fact, there is something of a Neoplatonist substructure in Ronsard's work, as love becomes the means of apprehending truth.

In the first sonnet for Hélène, composed late in his life, Ronsard seems once again self-conscious about transferring his allegiance and love to a different woman, and he swears to Hélène that she alone pleases him and that she will be his last love. In the process, the poet insists that he chose to love her and is not doing so lightly. Ronsard appears to be deliberately rejecting the Petrarchan notion of fate and suggesting instead that love is more to be valued if the man freely chooses the object of his love, rather than having her chosen for him by fate or chance.

In the later poems, at any rate, Ronsard's suffering is either more deeply felt or at least more effectively expressed. Of the many poems that might be discussed in this regard, none is more remarkable than "Quand vous serez bien vieille" ("When You Are Old"). Ronsard pictures an aged Hélène, sitting in her room; he marvels at the fact that he immortalized her when she was still young and beautiful. This is in many ways a key poem; it describes a woman who owes her fame not simply to her beauty, but specifically to the poet whom her beauty

inspired. Moreover, the woman is portrayed long after time has stolen that beauty, and Ronsard is uncompromising to the point of brutality when he contrasts himself, famous and at rest in death, with the lady, of whom he says: "You will be an old woman hunched over the hearth."

"DARLING, LET US GO"

This text recalls many of Ronsard's earlier poems (in the exploitation, for example, of the carpe diem topos), but the technique and tone are entirely new. This poem, like earlier ones, urges the woman to live for the moment: "Gather now the roses of life." The rose, one of Ronsard's ubiquitous images, sometimes evokes the season of love or the color of a lady's cheek; more frequently (as here), it symbolizes either the pleasures of love or youth and beauty itself. In one of his best-known poems, "Mignonne, allons voir si la rose" ("Darling, Let Us Go," a poem for Cassandre), he had earlier written: "Let us go and see if the rose which bloomed just this morning has not already lost its beauty," and he concludes with an insistent plea for her to live fully, before age tarnishes her beauty, as it has so quickly for the rose.

Certainly the poems resemble each other in the rose imagery, but in spite of the similarities, there is a striking contrast between the earlier and the later poem. In works such as "Darling, Let Us Go," the threat of lost youth is blunted by a profusion of warmly lyrical rhythms, rich rhymes, and rounded back vowels, all creating an impression of beauty and lushness rather than desperation. The emphasis is on the present rather than the future, on pleasure rather than on pain and old age. In "When You Are Old," on the other hand, the tenses project the lady into a future that holds no promise for her except old age and an autumnal melancholy relieved only by recollections of the way Ronsard had presented her. The vocabulary and sound system effectively translate her bleak future into realistic terms. The word *accroupie* (hunched over, or squatting), for example, is surprising and effective, both because of its meaning and because of its sound (in contrast to *Rose, déclose*, and other sonorous words in the earlier poem).

As this brief discussion suggests, Ronsard's later work retains many of his early themes and images, but there is a distinct evolution toward realism, urgency, and a measure of resignation. He has clearly entered a new stage of his poetic (and personal) life, characterized by his continuing belief in his own poetic destiny, but especially by a new emphasis on aging, death, and the passing of beauty and sensual love.

"HYMN TO DEATH" AND "WHEN YOU ARE OLD"

In "When You Are Old," the woman is the victim of passing time, but Ronsard reserves his most realistic details for his own aging. Noting in one of his final poems that "I am nothing but bones, a virtual skeleton," he asserts: "I cannot look at my own arms without trembling in fear." As confident as he may remain about his enduring fame, he is, quite simply, terrified of aging, physical change, and death. This is in striking contrast with his views in 1555, when he had composed "Hymne de la mort" ("Hymn to Death"). There he had emphasized, quite dispassionately, that all men must die, and he had looked with some scorn upon those who, forgetting that they are children of God, fear death. His conclusion: Death is not to be feared, because after death the body feels nothing. However, thirty years later, in a radical but quite understandable change of attitude, he recoils in horror at the sight of his own emaciated body. Near the end of his life, biological inevitability comes to occupy more and more of the poet's attention, profoundly coloring his late poetry and his views of life and love.

POLEMICS

Ronsard is most often thought of as the poet of love, as a poet who sang of beauty, youth, springtime, and pleasure. In addition, however, he was both an author of occasional verse and a polemical writer. A mark of literary success was the approval of the court, and currying favor with a prince or lesser noble was a far more respectable literary enterprise in the sixteenth century than it would be considered today. Ronsard, apparently, was something of a master of the art of soliciting royal patronage. Modern readers are, however, more likely to be impressed by his polemical writings.

When religious tensions began to develop in France, Ronsard entered the debate, speaking at first in moderate tones, but as these tensions erupted into open conflict, he became as engagé—and at times as brutal—as any of his Protestant adversaries. He endured virulent abuse, and he responded in kind in his *Discours des misères de ce temps* and in various other works. Throughout these exchanges of diatribes, political and religious discussions were often mixed with violent personal attacks.

RÉSPONCE AUX INJURES ET CALOMNIES DE JE NE SÇAY QUELS PRÉDICANS ET MINISTRES DE GENÈVE

Résponce aux injures et calomnies de je ne sçay quels prédicans et ministres de Genève is Ronsard's answer to those who accused him of being an atheist, a priest, a syphilitic, and a poet of limited talent. Ronsard was stung by all these charges, but the last one must have been particularly painful for him. He defends himself against all four in masterly fashion, and some of his most eloquent passages are reserved for his proud, almost arrogant, assessment of his own poetic abilities and accomplishments and of his opponents' limitations. He asserts the primacy of inspiration and the freedom of the true poet to choose his path and set his own rules.

Thus, even when defending his faith and himself, even when he is engaged in an exchange of vicious diatribes (or perhaps especially at these times), Ronsard remains fully conscious of his poetic destiny. His awareness of his status is, indeed, one of the few constants in his work. A creature of the Renaissance and one of its prime creators, Ronsard exhibits all its characteristic energy, its confidence, and (until late in his life) its optimism. He indisputably represents an important step in the development of French poetry, as he and his circle expanded and polished its resources and advanced it through precept and example. Inevitably, he experienced poetic failures and personal reverses, but he had far more successes and satisfactions; on balance, his glory is well-deserved. Through it all, he, like many of his colleagues and contemporaries, entertained no doubt about the identity of the Prince of Poets.

OTHER MAJOR WORKS

NONFICTION: *Abbregé de l'art poëtique français*, 1565.

MISCELLANEOUS: *Œuvres complètes*, 1914-1975 (20 volumes).

BIBLIOGRAPHY

Campo, Roberto. *Ronsard's Contentious Sisters: The Paragone Between Poetry and Painting in the Works of Pierre de Ronsard.* Chapel Hill: University of North Carolina Press, 1998. Continues previous studies of the relationship of poetry and painting as expressed in Ronsard's poetry, especially of words to pictorial images in both narrative and portraits.

Cave, Terence, ed. *Ronsard the Poet.* London: Methuen, 1973. A thorough biography of the poet with a bibliography and index.

Fallon, Jean M. *Voice and Vision in Ronsard's "Les Sonnets pour Hélène."* New York: Peter Lang, 1993. A historical and critical study of Ronsard's love poetry. Includes bibliographical references and index.

Ford, Philip. *Ronsard's Hymnes: A Literary and Iconographical Study.* Tempe, Ariz.: MRTS, 1997. An examination of the parallels between methods and form in Ronsard's hymns.

Gumpert, Matthew. "Supplementarity and the Sonnet: A Reading of Ronsard's *Les Amours* 'Diverses 45.'" *French Forum* 30, no. 3 (Fall, 2005): 17-43. The "Diverses 45" has not been regarded highly by critics because it is obscene. However, Gumpert argues that it is an "exemplary piece of writing."

Jones, Kenneth R. W. *Pierre de Ronsard.* New York: Twayne, 1970. A brief overview of Ronsard's life and the major collections of his work, offering a descriptive rather than critical analysis.

Scott, Virginia, and Sara Sturm-Maddox. *Performance, Poetry, and Politics on the Queen's Day: Catherine de Médicis and Pierre de Ronsard at Fontainebleau.* Burlington, Vt.: Ashgate, 2007. In February, 1564, the queen and Ronsard organized a day of theater and other amusements at the Festival of Fontainebleau. This work examines the resulting mix of politics and literature.

Silver, Isidore. *The Intellectual Evolution of Ronsard.* 3 vols. St. Louis, Mo.: Washington University Press, 1969-1973; Geneva: Droz, 1992. A massive study of the traditions and literary influences that shaped Ronsard's poetic works. Volume 1 covers the formative influences, volume 2 Ronsard's general theory of poetry, and volume 3 Ronsard's philosophic thought. Bibliographical references, indexes.

_____. *Ronsard and the Hellenic Renaissance in France.* 3 vols. Geneva: Droz, 1981-1987. Places Ronsard's poetry in the context of the main currents in the French Renaissance, especially Greek philology and cultural studies. Examines such topics as Ronsard and the Greek epic and the Grecian lyre.

Sturm-Maddox, Sara. *Ronsard, Petrarch, and the Amours.* Gainesville: University Press of Florida, 1999. A critical analysis of *Les Amours* and the influence of Petrarch on this and other poems by Ronsard. Includes bibliographical references and an index.

Norris J. Lacy

TADEUSZ RÓŻEWICZ

Born: Radomsko, Poland; October 9, 1921

PRINCIPAL POETRY

Niepokój, 1947 (*Unease,* 1980)
Czerwona rękawiczka, 1948
Pięc poematów, 1950
Czas który idzie, 1951
Wiersze i obrazy, 1952
Równina, 1954
Srebrny kłos, 1955
Uśmiechy, 1955
Poemat otwarty, 1956
Poezje zebrane, 1957
Formy, 1958
Przerwany egzamin, 1960
Rozmowa z księciem, 1960
Głos anonima, 1961
Zielona róża, 1961 (*Green Rose,* 1982)
Nic w płaszczu Prospera, 1962
Niepokój: Wybór wierszy, 1945-1961, 1963
Twarz, 1964
Poezje wybrane, 1967
Wiersze i poematy, 1967
Twarz trzecia, 1968
Faces of Anxiety, 1969
Regio, 1969

Plaskorzezba, 1970

Poezje zebrane, 1971

Wiersze, 1974

Selected Poems, 1976

"The Survivor," and Other Poems, 1976

"Conversation with the Prince," and Other Poems, 1982

Napowierzchni poematu i w środku, 1983

Poezje, 1987

Poezja, 1988 (2 volumes)

Tadeusz Różewicz's Bas-Relief, and Other Poems, 1991

They Came to See a Poet, 1991 (originally as *Conversation with the Prince*)

Opowiadania, 1994

Slowo po slowie, 1994

Niepokój: Wybór wierszy z lat, 1944-1994, 1995

Selected Poems, 1995

"Zawsze Fragment" and "Recycling," 1996

Nozyk profesora, 2001

Recycling, 2001

New Poems, 2007

OTHER LITERARY FORMS

Tadeusz Różewicz (REWZH-veech) is known as a playwright as well as a poet, a leading figure in postwar absurdist theater. He has also published both short fiction and novels, as well as essays.

ACHIEVEMENTS

After World War II, Tadeusz Różewicz became a spokesperson for his generation, and the Polish people responded quickly to his work. In 1955, he received the government's Art Award First Category for *Równina* (the plain), and in 1959, the city of Kraków gave him its literary award. In 1962, the Polish Ministry of Culture and Art gave him its First Category Award, and in 1966, he again received the government's Art Award First Category, in recognition of his entire oeuvre. In 1970, he received a special prize from the magazine *Odra*. He received the Prize of the Minister of Foreign Affairs (Poland), 1974 and 1987; the Austrian National Prize for European Literature, 1982; the Gold Wreath Prize for Poetry (Yugoslavia), 1987; the Władysław Reymont Literary Prize, 1999. He was awarded other honors as well: the Home Army Cross (London) in 1956; the Alfred Jurzykowski Foundation Award (New York), 1966; the Medal of the Thirtieth Anniversary of the People's Poland, 1974; the Order of Banner of Labour, Second Class, 1977; and the Great Cross of Order Polonia Restituta, 1996. In 2000, he was awarded Poland's prestigious Nike Award for his book *Matka odchodzi* (1999; mother departs).

BIOGRAPHY

Tadeusz Różewicz's father, Władysław Różewicz, worked as a clerk in the courthouse in Radomsko, a town in central Poland. His mother, Stefania Różewicz, came from the village of Gelbardów. They had three sons, Tadeusz being the middle child, born on October 9, 1921. The poet began his schooling in Radomsko, where he wrote his first works for school publications. When the Germans occupied Poland, they forbade all but the most primitive education for Poles; Różewicz worked as a manual laborer and as a messenger for the city government while continuing his education in a special underground school.

In 1943 and 1944, Różewicz fought against the German occupation forces as a member of the Home Army (the underground forces directed by the Polish government-in-exile, in London). His own brother was murdered by the Gestapo in 1944. In an interview with James Hopkins for *The Guardian*'s May 19, 2001, issue, he recalled: "I saw people who were brought through the streets on carts . . . dead bodies, naked bodies." After the war, he passed a special examination and entered Jagellonian University in Kraków, where he studied art history. Faced with the horrors inflicted by the Germans during the war, Różewicz determined that he must find a way to "create [Polish] poetry after Auschwitz," since the innocent Romanticism of the nation's prewar poetry seemed incompatible with postwar realities.

Because of the special circumstances of his youth, Różewicz knew comparatively little of the world outside Radomsko when he entered the university. He first saw the mountains of southern Poland, for example, when he was twenty-five years old. His first journey outside the country took place in 1948, when he went to Hungary, a trip that he subsequently described in a travelogue. His later journeys have included visits to

China, Germany, and Italy, but his work, even when it concerns foreign places, retains its unique Polish perspective.

In 1949, Różewicz married and moved to Gliwice, where his son Kamil was born in 1950. A second son, Jan, was born in 1953. He made trips abroad, including to the United States. In 1968, Różewicz moved to Wrocław, which would become his home for more than three decades. In his interview with Hopkins, the eighty-year-old Różewicz commented sardonically:

I don't like bad journalists, bad poets, bad painters, bad singers, and bad politicians; the latter inflict most harm. Next to the Germans.

Różewicz does not forget the past.

ANALYSIS

The horrific events experienced by Tadeusz Różewicz during World War II have led to his terse poetics that seek the voices of common people, often through quotations, anecdotes, news reportage: an "art of collage," as Różewicz put it. As a result, his tone is a populist, democratic one—humane and never grandiose.

Accordingly, sparseness characterizes Różewicz's poems, if not his poetic output. Many of his poems are exceedingly short, and even his longer works are often marked by short lines and short stanzas. Różewicz is a master of the dramatic break in the line and between stanzas. He uses the broad, blank margins of the page for dramatic impact, as if he were forcing the words out into the surrounding silence, as if he did not fully trust the power of words to convey his meaning. The effect is that of a speaker who broods as he speaks, choosing his words with extreme care and, after they have been said, relapsing into a brooding silence. "I See the Mad" presents a complex drama in ten lines arranged into four stanzas. An English translation contains a total of only thirty-nine words, but the Polish original is even more concise: It has a mere twenty-nine.

Różewicz speaks in straightforward sentences with straightforward words. Ordinary, even mundane, verbs and nouns abound, sometimes in lists, as if the poet were insisting to himself that the words actually correspond to the reality he sees before him. When one considers that he spent his youth subjected to the terrors of

the Nazi occupation, one can understand his sense of wonder that the ordinary objects of daily life do indeed exist before him, that an ordinary existence is still possible.

Though the speaker of a Różewicz poem may participate in the action or even cause it, his most important role is almost always that of an observer: He witnesses the events of the poem. When he comments upon them, he often does so with terse, sardonic irony. The speaker confronts the reader, causing him to ask himself how a normal life can be possible after such horrifying experiences and even causing him to question what constitutes a normal life.

"I SEE THE MAD"

Różewicz presents his work to the reader in a double dramatic context: the drama that he describes in the work, and the drama reinforced by Różewicz's sparseness, of the poet speaking or writing his words. Many of his poems may be seen as miniature plays, the characters acting out various roles. In "I See the Mad," for example, he presents himself at sea in a small boat—a traditional metaphor for life as a journey, especially a journey through obstacles. These obstacles give the poem its unique Różewicz stamp. They consist of crazy people who believe they can walk on water; instead, they have fallen into it. As the poet sails through their struggling bodies, they try to save themselves by grasping his boat. To keep his craft afloat, he is forced to knock their hands away from the boat. In effect, he must condemn them to death by drowning.

Who are these people floundering about in the water? One thinks immediately of Christ walking across the water to his disciples and of Peter attempting to walk on the water to meet him and sinking. Are those in the poem Christians who think that the laws of physics will be suspended for them? Or are they arrogant people who think that they can perform miracles, claiming for themselves the power of God? The poet does not say. He cannot know, for he has no time, in his role of besieged traveler, for philosophical inquiries. He must keep pushing the frantic hands off his boat.

In the second stanza, the poet states: "even now they tilt/ my uncertain boat." At first reading, the words "even now" might seem superfluous, but they put the poem in a strange, new perspective. The poem is written in the present tense: "I see," not "I saw." When the poet shows himself in his boat in the first stanza, he also stands, in a sense, outside the boat, reliving the experience as he writes or thinks about it. Thus, the two actions, writing or speaking the poem and knocking away the hands that threaten the poet's safety, merge into one, just as the two narrators and the two times, past and present, also merge. In the first stanza, the poet plays a leading role in the drama. In the second, he effectively stands outside the proscenium arch, commenting on the action—only to be pulled dramatically back into the experience.

In the third stanza, the poet is again trying to keep his little boat steady. As he pushes the hands off, he notes that they are stiff, perhaps a natural result of being in cold water. With the word "stiff," the poet jumps forward in time, as if he already sees the hands as stiff and dead because of his actions. Nevertheless, he has no choice. The poem ends with the poet continuing his journey into the future: "I knock off their stiff hands/ knock them off/ year in year out."

The poem may be seen as a surrealistic nightmare, the poet sailing through a sea of the dead and dying. It contains also, with an ironic twist, the Darwinian concept of the survival of the fittest: The poet, the survivor, describes himself as "cruelly alive," and the word "cruelly" vibrates in this context. In one sense, he must be cruel to push off the desperate hands that threaten to capsize his little boat. In another sense, he is "cruelly alive" because his own life force sustains him at a time when it would be easier for him to give up the struggle and simply let his boat be overturned.

The poet remains afloat because he knows a human being cannot walk on the water. He sees the world as it is, and this concept of recognizing the nature of reality plays a central role in Rózewicz's work. One who knows the nature of the world is not guaranteed a happy or beautiful life, but at least the person has a chance to survive.

Central, too, is the function of the speaker, who acts on at least four levels: Rózewicz himself, in his personal life; Rózewicz as a Polish Everyman, responding to the situations a Pole finds in the contemporary world; Rózewicz as a twentieth century Everyman, witnessing and responding to the events of the twentieth century; and Rózewicz as a universal Everyman, witnessing and responding to the problems humanity has faced throughout its history.

"I Screamed in the Night"

In "I Screamed in the Night," the dead confront the poet. They may be people he knew as a young fighter in the Polish underground army. (In one of his short stories, Rózewicz tells of having to pass a trash can every day, into which were stuffed bodies of Polish partisans for whom the Nazis had forbidden burial.) In addition, Rózewicz, speaking as a generic Pole, refers to the many Polish dead who fought against the Germans and the Russians. He may also be thinking of the Poles killed during the time of Joseph Stalin. The poem, however, has even broader meanings. It also refers to all the dead in World War II and, indeed, to all people killed in all wars. History haunts the poet. He screams in the literal night, perhaps in dreams or nightmares, but the darkness also becomes symbolic, a moral darkness: "cold and dead/ a blade from the darkness/ went into my body." The poem seems to offer no consolation, no solution.

"The Prodigal Son"

Sometimes Rózewicz gains even greater dramatic impact and depth of narration by speaking through a persona. In "The Prodigal Son," the poet questions the routines of daily life from the point of view of an outsider. In the biblical story, the prodigal son leaves home and wastes his inheritance in riotous living. Reduced to beggary, he returns home to ask for a position as one of his father's servants. His father, however, embraces him, clothes him, kisses him, and tells his servants, "Bring out the fatted calf and kill it, and let us eat and make merry; because this my son was dead, and has come to life again; he was lost, and is found." Rózewicz adds still another dimension by basing his poem on a painting that depicts the biblical story—a painting by Hieronymus Bosch, a Flemish painter of the late Gothic period who is noted for his grotesque and amusing caricatures of people in strange situations.

The prodigal son appears first at the inn from which he set out on his travels. There, he broods on the experiences he has undergone since the door of the establishment closed behind him. In the poem, the door seems to act on its own, as if its closing and opening were a natural process. When the symbolic door of his childhood home closes behind him, the young man must go out into the world. He finds that the world is filled with incredibly cruel and grotesque monsters. Senseless suffering abounds. Thus, the late medieval world of Bosch, with its grotesque characters, overlaps the contemporary world caught in the convulsions of World War II:

> I saw life
> with a wolf's jaw
> a pig's snout
> under the hood
> of a monk
> the open guts of the world
> I saw war
> on earth and in heaven
> crucified people
> who redeemed nothing

When Różewicz's prodigal son returns, he finds no father to welcome him, clothe him, or feed him. His former friends at the inn do not even recognize him. When he pays for a beer at the inn, the waitress looks suspiciously at the money, which she suspects may be counterfeit. Then she studies his face, as if it, too, were somehow suspect. She may be the same pretty Maggie who closed the door after he went out, but so many years have passed that they do not recognize each other. Perhaps, as she studies his face, she thinks she may have seen him someplace before. Another former friend sits in a corner with his back turned.

The prodigal son then thinks of how, out in the world, he was sustained by illusions, by thoughts of the joyful reception awaiting him when he returned home. "I thought every house/ would extend a glad hand," he states, "every branch bird and stone/ come to my reception." Having come to recognize the reality of the outside world, he returns home to recognize reality there also, and he decides not to go to his father's house. Instead, without revealing his identity, he goes out the door of the inn once again, vowing this time never to return.

Here again, the speaker functions on four levels. Różewicz speaks about his personal experience of growing up and going out into the world. On a national level, the prodigal son may be seen as one of the Polish soldiers, many of whom fought as members of the Brit-

ish and French forces, returning home to Poland after the fall of Germany to find the terror of the Stalinist period. The prodigal son may also be a twentieth century person, who finds it impossible to return to the comfortable beliefs of previous centuries. Finally, he represents the universal experience of a young person coming of age to find both the world and his home different from what he has always imagined.

The poem is not, however, entirely pessimistic. The prodigal son comes to know the true nature of both the outside world and the home he left behind, and for Różewicz, such knowledge is the first step toward wisdom. Stripped of illusions, the prodigal son returns to the world with a strange, bitter sense of personal freedom, and his decision may be seen as a mark of moral growth.

"FALLING"

Much of Różewicz's art concerns such moral development, although he seldom lectures the reader as he does in "Falling," in which he laments the absence of standards in contemporary life. One might expect such a moralistic poem to focus on the absence of God and Heaven in the modern world, but instead it focuses on the absence of Hell, of lower depths to which a person might sink and from which he might rise. Różewicz looks back ironically to the good old days when there were such phenomena as fallen women and bankrupt businessmen. He quotes the *Confessiones* (397-401; *Confessions*, 1620) of Saint Augustine but laments that such distinctions between good and evil now seem possible only in literature, in such works as Albert Camus's *La Chute* (1956; *The Fall*, 1957). Stavrogin, "the monster"—and Różewicz's use of quotation marks illustrates his point about modern moral judgments—asks in Fyodor Dostoevski's *Prestapleniye i nakazaniye* (1866; *Crime and Punishment*, 1886) if faith can really move mountains. His question cannot be answered in the affirmative.

More typical of contemporary literature, Różewicz observes, is Françoise Sagan's *Bonjour tristesse* (1954; English translation, 1955), in which moral heights and moral depths do not exist, the entrance to Hell having been changed to the entrance to the vagina. Różewicz cites the Italian film *Mondo Cane* (1961) as giving an unforgettably grotesque but true moral picture of contemporary life, while the Vatican Council, which should be concerned with setting standards, tables a motion to debate the relationship between the faithful and the laity because it cannot define the term "the faithful." He concludes that contemporary human beings, like Adam, are morally fallen, but because of the lack of standards, they do not fall down but fall in all directions at once. Indeed, he says that "falling" is the wrong word.

"To the Heart"

If, however, traditional religious and social norms no longer apply, an individual may still make moral progress personally by recognizing the world as it is. In this sense, even such a short, brutal drama as "To the Heart" may be read in a moral context. The poem begins with two words that might serve as a motto for all Rόżewicz's poetry, "I saw." The poet witnesses and reports the action. In this case, he sees a specialist—a cook—killing a sheep, and by placing the cook in the broader category of specialist, he gives the cook's actions wider application. He watches as the cook places his hand in the sheep's mouth, pushes it down through the animal's throat, grasps the beating heart, and tears it out. At the end, the poet comments tersely, "Yes sir/ that was/ a specialist."

Here, a human obviously violates the natural world, but the implications go deeper. The cook, after all, does his job, putting meat on the table of those who employ him. Would it make any difference if he killed a chicken or a cow? It certainly would to the poet, for because of their nature, sheep have become important symbols. They stand for meek people. Christ, the Good Shepherd, spoke of people as sheep, and he charged Peter to care for them. If on one level the poem may be read as an allegory of humanity's violation of nature, it may be seen on another as humanity's violation of fellow humans. The cook may be compared to the man in the boat of "I See the Mad" who must beat off the hands of drowning people to stay afloat. The brutal cook, however, seems to have none of the compassion of the man in the boat. Nevertheless, the poet, viewing the action, retains his sensibility. In fact, he develops a kind of X-ray vision and supersensitive touch. He sees inside the sheep. As the cook touches the animal's heart, the poet feels it beating. He sees the cook close his fist on it and feels the heart torn out.

The title "To the Heart" has two meanings: It implies the direction of the cook's arm as he shoves it down the sheep's throat, as well as the direction of the poem, which becomes a short moral lesson directed to the heart of the poet and the heart of the reader. The "heart" of the title, therefore, comes to stand not only for the sheep's heart but also for the organ that is the traditional symbol of human kindness and love. Kindness and love that do not take into account the brutalities of life will surely lead to disaster, however, as perhaps they did for those naïve souls who believed they could walk on water.

"I Am a Realist"

Once a person sees the world as it is, can there be further progress? Is the brutal, material world the only reality? In several poems, Rόżewicz hints at a spiritual world, one that can be discovered only through recognizing all the ills of the material one. In his poem "I Am a Realist," he enumerates details of daily life: His young son plays with a ladybug, his wife makes coffee and complains that her hair is falling out, while the poet takes an apple from the table and goes to work writing realistic poetry. The poem, however, takes a strange twist at the end. The poet, tired of his realistic details, complains: "I am a realist and a materialist/ only sometimes I'm tired/ I close my eyes."

"Remembrance from a Dream in 1963"

In "Remembrance from a Dream in 1963," the poet shows what can happen when his eyes are closed. He dreams of Leo Tolstoy lying in a bed, his face pulsing with light. Suddenly, the scene becomes dark, and the poet asks Tolstoy what should be done. Tolstoy answers, "Nothing." Then he begins to glow again, even to burn like the sun: "a gigantic radiant smile/ burst into flame."

Here, Rόżewicz receives his revelation, such as it is, from a noted realistic writer, Tolstoy. When the blazing light around the novelist goes out just before he speaks, the poet notices that Tolstoy's skin is rough and broken, "like the bark of an oak." (Even in recounting dreams and mystic revelations, Rόżewicz remains a realist, noting such specific details.) When the poet asks what should be done, the reader is tempted to ask in return, "About what?" Both Rόżewicz and Tolstoy, however, understand the question, which appears on the surface to concern the temporary darkness. Darkness, however, serves as a traditional symbol of loss of faith. Różewicz's question concerns eternal verities, truth and love, and their place in the universe. He may also be asking what should be done about his own doubts about the purpose of life.

Tolstoy's answer, coming as it does with a huge smile, might seem to be a kind of cruel joke. Nevertheless, Tolstoy shares Różewicz's concerns, whereas the "specialists" of the world do not. The answer he gives comes in two ways: in his words and in his actions. He may well be counseling Różewicz that one person's actions cannot change the nature of things and that Różewicz, having done what he can, must accept that fact. To a writer who performs his task well, there may come a kind of mystical peace, even an unexplained joy in life. (Indeed, despite the gloom in his life and in his art, Różewicz in person can be at times uncommonly cheerful.)

"ALPHA"

In this way, the writer's craft itself becomes an important symbol in Różewicz's work. In "Alpha," he pictures himself as a medieval monk illuminating a manuscript that recounts a particularly brutal history:

> my left hand
> illuminates
> a manuscript
> of the murdered the blinded the burned

Why the left hand? The poet may be left-handed, but "left," signifying unlucky or awkward, is much more important. The ancient Greek augurs believed that omens seen over the left shoulder predicted evil. The Roman soothsayers divided the heavens vertically into two segments. If the omen appeared in the left side, it was considered unfavorable. In the Polish language, moreover, as in English, to say that someone did something "left-handedly" means that it was done suddenly, without much consideration, and probably badly. A student who has written an assignment poorly may be said to have done it with his left hand. Thus, Różewicz presents himself both as a prophet of ill tidings and as a rather awkward writer—implying not necessarily that his writing is inferior to that of others, but rather that it cannot equal his vision of the world. Even song, he

says, did not "escape whole," a phrase that could have two meanings: Even song did not escape untouched from the ravages of history, or even song did not escape his clumsy, left-handed efforts.

Nevertheless, despite what he considers the clumsiness of his words and the terrible message they convey, in the very act of writing, he stumbles on a kind of revelation that another world exists after all, a world of the spirit which he can but suggest in his work.

> my left hand
> paints
> white as a unicorn
> an unreal letter
> from the other world

Różewicz, in spite of the brutalities and injustices of history, which he insists on confronting head-on, retains a consistently moral stance in his work. Humans must, he insists, recognize life as it actually is, not as they would like it to be. Reflecting on his own life, on the tragic history of his nation, on the convulsions of the twentieth century, and on the history of the world, he retains his sensibility, his ability to feel as a human being in the midst of uncaring and unfeeling people. His persistence is rewarded when he catches glimpses from time to time of a possible world beyond the one in which he lives—glimpses that on rare occasions afford him inklings of joy.

RECYCLING

As he entered his eighth decade, Różewicz's concerns extended into his first English collection of the new millennium, *Recycling*. The subject matter is topical, but the themes are the enduring ones in Różewicz's poems: Man's inhumanity to man and the horrors of war. Here they are juxtaposed to the trivialities of late twentieth century Western culture. In the title poem, three sections counterpose aspects of the war to modern life: In "Fashion (1944-1994)" the fashion industry is contrasted with Nazi brutality against women; in "Gold"—a reference to Nazi gold and its inhumane origins—Różewicz satirizes revisionists who argue that the Holocaust is a fiction; and "Meat," using a collage of news clippings, plays off the 1990's fear of mad cow disease, at times through the use of lurid humor ("a cow in a shed started singing"). Recycling into the present, the past appears throughout this collection—as both threat and admonition.

OTHER MAJOR WORKS

LONG FICTION: *Śmierć w starych dekoracjach*, 1970; *Echa leśne*, 1985.

SHORT FICTION: *Opadły liście z drzew*, 1955; *Przerwany egzamin*, 1960; *Wycieczka do muzeum*, 1966; *Opowiadania wybrane*, 1968; *Opowiadania*, 1994.

PLAYS: *Kartoteka*, pr., pb. 1960 (*The Card Index*, 1961); *Grupa Laokoona*, pb. 1961; *Świadkowie albo nasza mała stabilizacja*, pb. 1962 (in German; pr. 1964, in Polish; *The Witnesses*, 1970); *Akt przerywany*, pb. 1964 (in German; pr. 1970, in Polish; *The Interrupted Act*, 1969); *Śmieszny staruszek*, pb. 1964 (*The Funny Old Man*, 1970); *Spaghetti i miecz*, pb. 1964; *Wyszedł z domu*, pb. 1964 (*Gone Out*, 1969); *Przyrost naturalny: Biografia sztuki teatralnej*, pb. 1968 (*Birth Rate: The Biography of a Play for the Theatre*, 1977); *Stara kobieta wysiaduje*, pb. 1968 (*The Old Woman Broods*, 1970); *The Card Index, and Other Plays*, 1970; *Teatr niekonsekwencji*, pb. 1970; *The Witnesses, and Other Plays*, 1970; *Na czworakach*, pb. 1971; *Pogrzeb po polsku*, pr. 1971; *Sztuki teatralne*, pb. 1972; *Białe małże stwo*, pb. 1974 (*White Marriage*, 1977; also known as *Marriage Blanc*); *Odejscie Głodomora*, pb. 1976 (*The Hunger Artist Departs*, 1977; based on Franz Kafka's story "The Hunger Artist"); *Do piachu*, pr., pb. 1979 (wr. 1955-1972); *Pulapka*, pb. 1982 (*The Trap*, 1997); *Teatr*, pb. 1988; *Dramaty wybrane*, pb. 1994.

NONFICTION: *Przygotowanie do wieczoru autorskiego*, 1971; *Nasz starszy brat*, 1992; *Forms in Relief, and Other Works*, 1994; *Matka odchodzi*, 1999.

EDITED TEXT: *Kto jest ten dziwny nieznajomy*, 1964.

MISCELLANEOUS: *Poezja, dramat, proza*, 1973; *Proza*, 1973; *Proza*, 1990 (2 volumes); *Reading the Apocalypse in Bed: Selected Plays and Short Pieces*, 1998; *Kup kota w worku: Work in Progress*, 2008 (includes poems and essays).

BIBLIOGRAPHY

Barańczak, Stanislaw, and Clare Cavanagh, eds. and trans. *Polish Poetry of the Last Two Decades of Communist Rule: Spoiling Cannibals' Fun*. Foreword by Helen Vendler. Evanston, Ill.: Northwestern University Press, 1991. Barańczak's masterful translations offer a sampling of Cold-War-era poems from an oppressed people. Bibliography, index.

Contoski, Victor. Introduction to *Unease*, by Tadeusz Różewicz. St. Paul, Minn.: New Rivers Press, 1980. Contoski's introduction provides some biographical and historical background.

Czerniawski, Adam, ed. *The Mature Laurel: Essays on Modern Polish Poetry*. Chester Springs, Pa.: Dufour Editions, 1991. More than three hundred pages address contemporary Polish poetry, placing Różewicz's work in context. Bibliography, index.

Filipowicz, Halina. *A Laboratory of Impure Forms: The Plays of Tadeusz Różewicz*. New York: Greenwood Press, 1991. Although it focuses on his drama, this monograph offers important context for understanding Różewicz's writing in general. Bibliographical references, index.

Gömöri, Georg. *Magnetic Poles: Essays on Modern Polish and Comparative Literature*. London: Polish Cultural Foundation, 2000. A brief (163-page) overview of Polish literature today and its foundations. Bibliography, index of names.

Hirsch, Edward. "After the End of the World." *American Poetry Review* 26, no. 2 (March/April, 1997): 9-12. Focusing on the works of Polish poets Zbigniew Herbert, Tadeusz Różewicz and Wisława Szymborska, Hirsch reveals how their post-World War II poetry is similarly haunted by guilt. He has found that the major poets of postwar Poland share a distrust of rhetoric, of false sentiments and words.

Sokoloski, Richard. Introduction to *Forms in Relief and Other Works: A Bilingual Edition*, by Różewicz Ottawa, Ont.: Legas, 1994. Offers useful insights into Różewicz's poetics.

_____. "Modern Polish Verse Structures: Reemergence of the Line in the Poetry of Tadeusz Różewicz." *Canadian Slavonic Papers* 37, nos. 3/4 (September, 1995): 431-453. The general evolution of verse forms in modern Polish poetry is reexamined in order to distinguish certain modifications formulated by Różewicz.

Victor Contoski
Updated by Christina J. Moose

S

UMBERTO SABA

Born: Trieste, Austro-Hungarian Empire (now in
   Italy); March 9, 1883
Died: Gorizia, Italy; August 25, 1957

PRINCIPAL POETRY

Poesie, 1911 (originally pb. as *Il mio primo libro di
   poesie*, 1903)

Coi miei occhi: Il mio secondo libro di versi, 1912

Il canzoniere, 1900-1921, 1921

Figure e canti, 1926

Tre composizioni, 1933

Parole, 1934

Ultime cose, 1944

Il canzoniere, 1900-1945, 1945

Il Mediterranee, 1946

Il canzoniere, 1900-1947, 1948

Uccelli, 1950

Quasi un racconto, 1951

Il canzoniere, 1961, 1965

Umberto Saba: Thirty-one Poems, 1978

*The Dark of the Sun: Selected Poems of Umberto
   Saba*, 1994

Songbook: Selected Poems from the "Canzoniere,"
   1998

Songbook: The Selected Poems of Umberto Saba,
   2008

OTHER LITERARY FORMS

Although remembered primarily for his poetry, particularly as assembled in the monumental editions of *Il
canzoniere*, Umberto Saba (SAH-bah) also wrote several significant prose works, most of which were collected by Saba's daughter Linuccia in *Prose* (1964).
Scorciatoie e raccontini (1946; shortcuts and vignettes) consists mainly of terse reflections on poetry
and meditations on politics and postwar society. The
collection *Ricordi-racconti, 1910-1947* (1956; remem-

brances, stories) contains stories and sketches, some directly autobiographical. Saba's prose style is usually
rich and complex, though not particularly experimental. Like his poems, the prose works are reflective
and benefit from a careful rereading. The pieces in
Scorciatoie e raccontini are "shortcuts" because they
cut through the twisting paths of conventional, logical
thought to arrive at a conclusion which is often startling
in its revelation and insight. In *Storia e cronistoria del
"Canzoniere"* (1948; *History and Chronicle of "The
Songbook,"* 1998), Saba turns his critical eye to his
own works, explaining the biographical background of
the poems in *Il canzoniere* and giving interpretations.
This self-criticism not only recalls the commentary of
Dante on his own poems in *La vita nuova* (c. 1292; *Vita
Nuova*, 1861; better known as *The New Life*) but also
exemplifies the influence of Sigmund Freud and psychoanalysis on Saba's thought and technique. The incomplete novel *Ernesto*, published posthumously in
1975, is on the surface Saba's least typical work; set in
Trieste and vividly capturing the dialect of that Mediterranean city, *Ernesto* depicts the love of a young boy
for an older man. Still, while more realistic and explicit
than Saba's other works, *Ernesto* develops the same
themes—art, love, change, and loss—with an equal
complexity and subtlety.

ACHIEVEMENTS

Often considered one of the three great Italian poets
of the twentieth century, along with Giuseppe Ungaretti
and Eugenio Montale, Umberto Saba is also one of
the most important poets to combine traditional verse
forms with a modern restraint and to treat universal
themes with an analytical and self-conscious approach
typical of the twentieth century.

The clarity and reflectiveness of Saba's earlier poems reveal the influence of the nineteenth century poet
Giacomo Leopardi, and the calm, melancholy atmosphere of many of Saba's poems has its roots in the poetry of the *crepuscolari* (twilight) poets such as Guido
Gozzano and Sergio Corazzini, who described everyday objects and settings with a wistful nostalgia. Saba's
later poems break more definitely with traditional meter and line length, reflecting the terse, ragged rhythms
of Ungaretti.

Saba won several prizes and honors, including the Premio Viareggio in 1946 for *Scorciatoie e raccontini*, the Premio dell'Accademia dei Lincei in 1951, and the honorary degree in letters from the University of Rome in 1953; critics have generally appreciated Saba's works, particularly since the 1960's. While Saba's poetical works have been generally well received and studied in Italy, however, his place in modern world literature has not yet been established, perhaps in large part because of a scarcity of translations. As critics continue to construct an account of Saba's biography and his rich inner life, his significance should become increasingly apparent.

BIOGRAPHY

The life of Umberto Saba is reflected throughout his work, and this relationship is most evident in Saba's structuring of *Il canzoniere* around the three periods of his development—youth, maturity, and old age. For Saba, all literature is in a sense autobiographical. Still, the richness and complexity of the poems and prose works give no indication of the relatively simple life of the poet.

Saba was born Umberto Poli on March 9, 1883, in Trieste, then part of the Austro-Hungarian Empire. His father, Ugo Edoardo Poli, was the son of the contessa Teresa Arrivabene; Saba's mother, Felicita Rachele Coen, was the daughter of Jewish parents who had a fairly successful business in the ghetto of Trieste. The marriage did not last long, and Ugo Poli, who had converted to Judaism, abandoned his wife as soon as Umberto was born. Saba refers to his parental background in sonnets 2 and 3 from the chapter "Autobiografia" in *Il canzoniere*. In the second, "Quando nacqui mia madre ne piangeva" (when I was born my mother cried), Saba describes both his and his mother's sorrow at being abandoned by his father. The speaker's happy memories of his relatives in the ghetto shopping for him and his mother are tempered by his loneliness: "But I soon became an expert at melancholy;/ the only son with a distant father." The third sonnet, "Mio Padre è stato per me 'l'assassino'" (my father has been for me "the assassin"), recounts the meeting between Saba and his father when Saba was twenty, a meeting that surprises the speaker, for he realizes that he has much in common with his father, the man whom he had hated for so long: "His face had my azure stare,/ a smile, amid suffering, sweet and sly." The speaker remembers his mother's warning not to be like his father and then understands for himself what she meant, that "they were two races in an ancient strife." With this awareness, the poet also sees in himself the unreconciled opposition of two forces, Jewish and Christian, old and new, victim and assassin.

As a boy, Saba was sent to stay with a nursemaid, Giuseppina Sabaz, from whom he derived his pseudonym and whom he recalls as Peppa in the chapter "Il piccolo Berto" (little Berto) in *Il canzoniere*. In "Il figlio della Peppa" (the son of Peppa), Saba remembers the paradise of his stay with Peppa, who had found in Berto a replacement for her dead son. The speaker sees this time with his Catholic nurse as lighter and happier than the time with his mother; after three years, as Saba remembers, his mother took him away from Peppa.

Saba had formal schooling beyond high school, attending the Ginnasio Dante Alighieri in Trieste. Wanting to be a sailor, he took courses at a nautical academy but did not graduate, for his mother made him take a position as a clerk in a commercial firm. In 1902, he left this job, traveling in northern Italy and reading widely such poets as Leopardi, Giosuè Carducci, and Giovanni Pascoli, major influences on Saba's first volume of poetry, which was originally published in a private edition as *Il mio primo libro di poesie* (my first book of poetry) in 1903 and republished in 1911 as *Poesie*.

In 1908, Saba was drafted into the infantry and was stationed at Salerno, an experience that he depicts in *Il canzoniere* in "Versi militari" (military verses) and an experience that gave him for the first time a sense of comradeship with others. The same year, after finishing his service, he married the seamstress Carolina Wölfler, the "Lina" of his love poetry, whom he had met in 1907. The couple settled near Trieste and had a daughter, Linuccia. Saba returned to the army during World War I as an airfield inspector but did not see combat. After the war, Saba opened an antiquarian bookstore in Trieste, which served as his chief source of income and acted as a meeting place for numerous writers and artists; from his bookstore, Saba published the first edition of *Il canzoniere* in 1921.

Much of the rest of Saba's life was relatively un-eventful, and he published little between the years 1934 and 1945. Just before World War II, the growing anti-Semitic atmosphere pressured Saba into fleeing to France; later, he returned to Italy, staying incognito in Rome and in Florence. After the Liberation, Saba returned to Trieste and published in 1944 the volume *Ultime cose* (last things). The title is somewhat misleading, though, for in 1945, Saba published the first definitive gathering and reworking of his poems in *Il canzoniere*. After this edition, Saba continued writing poetry and prose, including some of his most famous works, such as "Ulisse" ("Ulysses"). In 1956, Saba was confined to a clinic in Gorizia; his wife died in November, and nine months later, on August 25, 1957, Saba himself died.

ANALYSIS

Although overshadowed by the monumental achievements of Ungaretti and Montale, Umberto Saba has, since just before his death in 1957, begun to acquire the critical acclaim that his life's work in poetry and prose deserves. As critics begin to evaluate the subtle innovations of Saba's style and the depth of his thematic development, Saba's position as a major early modern poet should become increasingly secure.

IL CANZONIERE

The connection between Saba's life and his poetry is nowhere more evident than in his organization of the 1945 edition of *Il canzoniere*, the collection and revision of all his previous poems. *Il canzoniere* consists of chronologically arranged chapters (some of which had been published separately) and is divided into three sections or volumes, each of which corresponds to a phase of Saba's life—adolescence and youth (from 1900 to 1920), maturity (from 1921 to 1932), and old age (in the 1961 edition, this includes additional poems from 1933 to 1954). These three sections also correspond to stages of Saba's poetic development, although certain themes and techniques persist throughout his career. The most salient characteristics of Saba's poetry are his preoccupation with retrospection, his treatment of modern themes in traditional meter and form but with concrete, everyday language, and his development of the theme of love as a unifying force in a chaotic world.

Umberto Saba

The first section of *Il canzoniere* contains some very early verse, much of which is less interesting and innovative than later poems, but the section also contains several of Saba's best-known lyrics, including "A mia moglie" ("To My Wife") and "La capra" ("The Goat"). This section contains the chapters "Versi militari" (written during Saba's experience as an infantryman in 1908) and "Casa e campagna" (home and countryside), from which come "To My Wife" and "The Goat," "Trieste e una donna" (Trieste and a lady), which treats Saba's love for his wife and for his native city, and "L'amorosa spina" (the amorous thorn), thirteen poems that analyze Saba's passion for Chiarretta, a young assistant in his bookstore.

The second volume of *Il canzoniere* begins with a group of poems based on the failed love for Chiarretta, "Preludio e canzonette" (prelude and songs), but these poems, written a year or two after the affair, are more sober and reflective. In fact, the majority of the second volume is retrospective, including the fifteen sonnets that make up "Autobiografia"—poems describing events and perceptions from the poet's birth to the opening of his bookstore and the development of his poetic career. The last section, "Il piccolo Berto," is dedicated to Edoardo Weiss, an Italian psychoanalyst who introduced Saba to Freudian psychology and to an analysis of Saba's past. These poems concentrate on Saba's relationship with his mother and the various mother figures of his childhood.

The third volume begins with "Parole" ("Words"), which, written after Saba's experience with psychoanalysis, marks a new direction in his poetic diction and form. The dense, often elliptical poems in this chapter recall the Hermetic style of Montale, but Saba's sparse style often suggests a richness of emotion rather than a dryness; the purifying of language and avoidance of traditional forms and rhymes, as well as the minimalization of narrative, allow the reader to concentrate on and appreciate anew the sharpness of the images and the resonance of the sounds. The chapter "Mediterranee" (Mediterranean) contains Saba's most famous poem and perhaps his most successful synthesis of form and content—the poem "Ulysses," which parallels the wandering of the Greek hero with the poet's sense of his own age and homelessness.

The evolution of a poetic idiom should not obscure the unchanging features of Saba's artistry. Since *Il canzoniere* itself is not only a collection but also a reworking of previous poems, this anthology presents the reader with a consistent, retrospective view of the poet's career. This retrospection is clear, for example, in the inclusion of the autobiographical poems of "Il piccolo Berto" in the second volume—the volume of Saba's middle age; these poems of childhood reflect not so much the child's perspective as that of the adult looking backward and seeking to understand or assimilate the past.

TRITE RHYMES AND EVERYDAY WORDS

To an extent, the poet's use of traditional versification parallels his concern for the past. The poem "Amai" ("I Loved"), from "Mediterranee," shows that Saba views poetic tradition not as a series of principles to be slavishly venerated or as a confining set of prescriptions but as a source of inspiration for innovation: "I loved the trite words that no one/ dared to use. I was enchanted by the rhyme 'flower—love' [*fiore-amore*],/ the oldest and most difficult in the world." The trite

rhymes and everyday words are the most difficult because they have been used for so long, and yet, the poet implies, these words and forms have a beauty and a truthfulness that endures. The innovative use of tradition provides the poet with a common ground for communicating truth to the reader, and at the same time, it requires that the poet find a new and personal way of perceiving and shaping this truth.

SUFFERING AND LOVE

For Saba, in fact, the role of the poet is to perceive the world—the world of the everyday—as it is, not as custom or habit deforms it, and to convey this childlike rediscovery to the reader. Since, however, the poet is also aware of the individual's ability to overlook or forget this primal joy and to fall prey to despair, he does not represent this rediscovery as a panacea for human suffering. This suffering, in fact, becomes as integral a part of the poem as is the joy, and in many of Saba's poems, the speaker's confrontation with pain is more significant than his apprehension of happiness. This awareness links the speaker with others who have suffered; it is the highest form of love. The poem "The Goat" illustrates this perception. At first, the speaker is intrigued by a tethered goat, as if for a joke, but then the speaker hears in the goat's bleating the eternal nature of suffering and sees in the goat's Semitic face "the complaint of every other being at every other evil."

This love—the yearning that binds all living beings—is perhaps the central theme of Saba's poetry. Love may be erotic, as in the love poems to Lina; or it may be filial, as in the poem "A mia figlia" ("To My Daughter"); it may be a love of one's city or society, as in "Città vecchia" ("Old Town") and other poems in "Trieste e una donna," or the poem "Ulysses"; or it may be a longing for the past, whether the past of childhood or the tradition of poetry.

One of Saba's most frequent attempts to make contact through love is to find a sense of community with his fellow humans. In "Old Town," the speaker discovers in the humblest, most squalid section of Trieste a kinship, a feeling of belonging, since in this section, one finds the most characteristically human people (the most human because they suffer most). Still, as the poem "Il borgo" (the hamlet) shows, Saba does not expect this love to bring universal happiness or harmony.

The poet laments the fact that his goal to become one with the ordinary people can never be fully realized, since the poet, in his very yearning to unite with the people, places himself on a higher level, an unchanging intellectual unable to become part of a changing society.

The poet finds more success in his amatory relationships, especially that with Lina. The poem "La brama" (hunger, desire) reveals the influence of Freudian psychoanalysis. Desire, or the libido, impels people, often with painful or destructive results, yet it is still a positive and necessary force in the world; in fact, *eros* is the quintessential motive for human beings.

Another source of inspiration for Saba is the animal world, as in the poem "The Goat." In his most famous love poem, "To My Wife," Saba combines both the erotic and the animal, comparing his wife to various animals—a hen, a heifer, a dog, a rabbit, a swallow, an ant. The simple joy that Lina gives Saba parallels the beauty and contentment of the domestic and wild animals; unlike poets in the courtly love tradition, elevating the beloved above the physical world, the poet elevates the potential for human love by appreciating fully the bond between the animal and the human world. In an earlier poem to his wife, "A Lina" ("To Lina"), Saba describes how the hooting of an owl reminds him of his sorrows with Lina, sorrows that he had wanted to forget. The animal world, then, often acts as a stimulus, a reminder of the need to go beyond one's narrow view of the world.

The experience of fatherhood, described in "To My Daughter," provided Saba with another opportunity for going outside himself, as well as a way of understanding the natural process of growth and change: "I don't love you because you bloom again from my stock,/ but because you are so vulnerable/ and love has given you to me.

"ASHES" AND "WINTER NOON"

In his later poetry, Saba contemplates the processes of change and aging with a sense of resignation, but not with despair or cynicism. The early poem "Mezzogiorno d'inverno" ("Winter Noon"), published in 1920, hints at such a mood. The speaker describes a sudden fit of sadness amid a great happiness. The source of this melancholy is not a beautiful girl passing by but a tur-

quoise balloon floating in the azure sky, the loss of which must be causing a boy to grieve. The boy's pain is in contrast, however, to the beauty of the balloon, subtly contrasted against the sky, passing gracefully over the city of Trieste. In the later poem "Ceneri" ("Ashes"), from "Words," the poet strips away all unessential adornment and rhetoric from his description of an approaching death: "your bright/ flames engulf me as/ from care to care I near the sill/ of sleep." The speaker feels no anxiety, but instead sees death as a natural stage: "And to sleep,/ with those impassioned and tender bonds/ that bind the baby and the mother, and with you, ashes, I merge." The tone is reserved but not pessimistic: "Mute/ I leave the shadows for the immense empire."

"ULYSSES"

The poem that sums up Saba's poetic development is his "Ulysses," a compendium of his themes and a hallmark of the use of restrained, concrete language to convey a deep understanding of the eternal themes of isolation and community, love and loss. Actually, the second poem of this title, the "Ulysses" of "Mediterranee," conveys the poet's sense of age and decline, his feeling of displacement from his society, his love for his home, and his sadness after the events of World War II. Assuming the persona of the wanderer Ulysses (as many have noted, the Ulysses of canto 26 of Dante's *Inferno* (in *La divina commedia*, c. 1320; *The Divine Comedy*, 1802), the Ulysses who, imprisoned in Hell, had left behind home and family to sail in search of further knowledge of the world), Saba describes vividly and with nostalgia his past experiences and his present loneliness and sorrow. "In my youth I sailed/ along the Dalmatian coast. Islets/ emerged from the waves' surface, where rarely/ a bird intent on prey alit,/ algae-covered, skidding, sparkling in the sun like emeralds." The speaker recalls his present exile, in an allusion to Ulysses' tricking of Polyphemus: "Today my kingdom/ is No-man's land." In his old age, the speaker has become a no-man, cut off from the comforts of home; the harbor lights are for others now. "Again to the open sea/ I am impelled by my unconquered spirit/ and the sorrowful love of life." The journey of Ulysses and his indomitable spirit echo Saba's lifelong devotion to his artistry, his sense of never reaching a final destination, of never making a human contact free of pain, of feeling more sharply the sense of isolation caused by the very wish to know others, and yet at the same time of feeling the joy in recapturing through memory and poetry the bright images of the world.

OTHER MAJOR WORKS

LONG FICTION: *Ernesto*, 1975.

NONFICTION: *Scorciatoie e raccontini*, 1946; *Storia e cronistoria del "Canzoniere,"* 1948 (*History and Chronicle of "The Songbook,"* 1998); *Prose*, 1964.

MISCELLANEOUS: *Ricordi-racconti, 1910-1947*, 1956; *The Stories and Recollections of Umberto Saba*, 1993; *Poetry and Prose*, 2004.

BIBLIOGRAPHY

Cary, Joseph. *Three Modern Italian Poets: Saba, Ungaretti, Montale*. 2d ed. Chicago: University of Chicago Press, 1993. Focusing on Saba, Giuseppe Ungaretti, and Eugenio Montale, Cary presents striking biographical portraits as he facilitates understanding of their poetry and guides readers through the first decades of twentieth century Italy.

Parussa, Sergio. *Writing as Freedom, Writing as Testimony: Four Italian Writers and Judaism*. Syracuse, N.Y.: Syracuse University Press, 2008. Parussa looks at Saba, Natalia Ginzburg, Giorgio Bassani, and Primo Levi. His chapter on Saba is called "The Maternal Borders of the Soul: Identity, Judaism, and Writing in the Works of Umberto Saba."

Renzi, Lorenzo. "A Reading of Saba's 'A mia moglie.'" *Modern Language Review* 68 (1973): 77-83. A critical reading of one of Saba's poems.

Saba, Umberto. *Songbook: The Selected Poems of Umberto Saba*. Translated by George Hochfield and Leonard Nathan. New Haven, Conn.: Yale University Press, 2008. Hochfield provides an informative introduction, notes, and commentary for his joint parallel-text translation of poetry by Saba. Contains a translation of an early Saba essay, "What Remains for Poets to Do?"

Singh, G. "The Poetry of Umberto Saba." *Italian Studies* 23 (1968): 114-137. A critical analysis of Saba's poetic works.

Steven L. Hale

NELLY SACHS

Born: Berlin, Germany; December 10, 1891
Died: Stockholm, Sweden; May 12, 1970

PRINCIPAL POETRY

In den Wohnungen des Todes, 1946
Sternverdunkelung, 1949
Und niemand weiss weiter, 1957
Flucht und Verwandlung, 1959
Fahrt ins Staublose, 1961
Noch feiert Tod das Leben, 1961
Glühende Rätsel, 1964 (parts 1 and 2; 1965, part 3 in *Späte Gedichte*; 1966, part 4 in the annual *Jahresring*)
Späte Gedichte, 1965
Die Suchende, 1966
O the Chimneys, 1967
The Seeker, and Other Poems, 1970
Teile dich Nacht, 1971

OTHER LITERARY FORMS

Nelly Sachs (saks) published the short play, or "scenic poem," *Eli: Ein Mysterienspiel vom Leiden Israels* (pb. 1951; *Eli: A Mystery Play of the Sufferings of Israel*, 1967). Her fiction is collected in *Legenden und Erzählungen* (1921) and her correspondence with Paul Celan in *Paul Celan, Nelly Sachs: Correspondence* (1995).

ACHIEVEMENTS

Nelly Sachs arrived at her characteristic poetic style late in life. She was heavily influenced by the German Romantic poets and did not consider her lyric poetry of the years prior to 1943 to be representative of her mature work, excluding those poems from the collection of 1961. Her first published book, a small volume of legends and tales published in 1921, was heavily indebted in style and content to the Swedish novelist Selma Lagerlöf. In the 1920's and 1930's, Sachs published lyric poetry in such respected newspapers and journals as the *Vossische Zeitung* of Berlin, the *Berliner Tageblatt*, and *Der Morgen*, the journal of the Jewish cultural federation.

Sachs's stylistic breakthrough came with the traumatic experience of her flight from Germany and exile in Sweden. The play *Eli* was written in 1943 but published privately in Sweden in 1951. It was first broadcast on Süddeutsche Rundfunk (South German Radio) in 1958 and had its theater premiere in 1962 in Dortmund. Acceptance of her poetry in West Germany was equally slow, partly because her main theme (Jewish suffering during World War II) stirred painful memories. In the late 1950's and 1960's, however, she was hailed as modern Germany's greatest woman poet and received numerous literary prizes. She was accepted for membership in several academies. In 1958, she received the poetry prize of the Swedish broadcasting system and, in 1959, the Kulturpreis der Deutschen Industrie. The town of Meersburg in West Germany awarded her the Annette Droste Prize for female poets in 1960, and the city of Dortmund founded the Nelly Sachs Prize in 1961 and presented her with its first award. In the same year, friends and admirers published the first volume of a Festschrift, followed by the second volume, *Nelly Sachs zu Ehren*, on the occasion of her seventy-fifth birthday in 1966. On October 17, 1965, she received the Peace Prize of the German Book Trade Association, and on December 10, 1966, she was awarded the Nobel Prize in Literature. Berlin, the city where she was born and in which she had lived for nearly half a century, made her an honorary citizen in 1967. The city of Dortmund, Germany, and the Royal Library in Stockholm, Sweden, have valuable collections of her letters and transcriptions of her early poems in their Nelly Sachs Archive.

BIOGRAPHY

Nelly Leonie Sachs was born Leonie Sachs in Berlin on December 10, 1891, the only child of William Sachs, an inventor, technical engineer, and manufacturer, and his wife, Margarete (Karger) Sachs. The family lived in very comfortable financial circumstances, and Nelly Sachs was educated in accordance with the custom for daughters of the upper-middle class. Although both of her parents were of Jewish ancestry, her family had few ties with the Jewish community and did not practice their religion. Sachs attended public schools from 1897 to 1900, but because of poor health,

she was removed and received private instruction until 1903. She then attended a private secondary school for daughters of wealthy and titled families and finished her education in 1908 without any formal professional training. In the summer of that year, she fell in love with a man whose name she never revealed. That experience, which ended unhappily, escalated into a crisis, making Sachs consider suicide. The man was later killed in one of Germany's concentration camps.

For the next twenty-five years, even after the death of her father in 1930, Sachs led a sheltered and not particularly noteworthy existence. She produced some poetry, read extensively, and did watercolors, some of which have been preserved in the Nelly Sachs Archive in Stockholm. In 1906, Sachs received Lagerlöf's novel *Gösta Berling* (1891) as a birthday present. Her admiration for the writer resulted in a correspondence between the two, and Sachs sent Lagerlöf many of her own literary experiments. Through the intervention of

Nelly Sachs (©The Nobel Foundation)

Lagerlöf and the brother of the reigning Swedish king, Sachs and her mother received permission to emigrate to Sweden in 1939. Shortly after Lagerlöf's death in 1940, Sachs received orders from German authorities to appear for deportation to a work camp. Leaving all their possessions behind, Sachs and her mother fled Germany, arriving in Stockholm on May 16, 1940. They took up residence in a small apartment in the industrial harbor area, where Sachs remained until her death in 1970.

The imagery in Sachs's later lyric poetry draws to a large extent on influences from her youth. Her father's extensive collection of rocks, gems, and fossils was a source of inspiration to her, and she continued his hobby with a collection of her own in Stockholm; not unexpectedly, the use of the stones as a cipher is very prevalent in her work "Chor der Steine" ("Chorus of the Stones"). From her father's library, she was also familiar with the work of Maria Sibylla Merian, a seventeenth century entomologist and graphic artist who specialized in the study of butterflies. Sachs's poem "Schmetterling" ("Butterfly") exemplifies her metaphoric use of this and other insects in her work. In 1959, Sachs wrote that of all childhood influences on her later works, her father's musical talent was paramount. When he played the piano during evenings after work, she frequently danced for hours to the strains of his music. In addition to her early lyric poems, which she characterized as "dance and music poems," the motif of the dance is also important in her later work.

In 1960, Sachs returned to Germany for the first time since her exile to receive the Annette Droste Prize. Not wishing to spend a night in Germany, she stayed instead in Zurich, traveling the short distance to Meersburg only to accept the honor. Hearing the German language spoken again proved to be so traumatic, however, that she experienced a "memory trip to hell." In Zurich, she met Paul Celan, another exiled poet, who invited her to his home in Paris. The meeting resulted in a continuing correspondence, but Celan was in the midst of a personal crisis as well, and the relationship may have contributed to Sachs's difficulties. After her return to Stockholm, Sachs suffered a mental breakdown and was hospitalized with severe delusions of persecution. Although she worked feverishly during the next decade, she continued to suffer periodic attacks in which she imagined herself persecuted and threatened with death. Her cycle *Noch feiert Tod das Leben* (death still celebrates life) was written while she recovered in the hospital. Celan attempted to aid her recovery through an intensive, supportive correspondence that was also, however, an attempt at self-healing, inasmuch as he suffered from a similar ailment. Their poetry, beginning with Sachs's *Noch feiert Tod das Leben* and Celan's *Die Niemandsrose* (1963), shows their continuing "dialogue in poems." In the spring of 1970, Sachs became mortally ill and thus was not informed when Celan was reported missing early in April of that year. He was later found—an apparent suicide by drowning; his funeral services took place in the Cimetière Parisien near Orly, France, on the same day in May on which Sachs died in a Stockholm hospital.

ANALYSIS

It is difficult to speak of development in Nelly Sachs's poetic works, inasmuch as she was well beyond fifty years old when she produced her first significant poems. It is true that she had published lyric poetry before the 1940's, but this early work has little in common with that of her mature years. Most of the poems from the 1920's and 1930's are thematically quite distinct from the later work, devoted to musicians such as Johann Sebastian Bach, Wolfgang Amadeus Mozart, Jean-Philippe Rameau, and Luigi Boccherini or dealing poetically with certain animals, such as deer, lambs, and nightingales. The Nelly Sachs archives in Dortmund and in Stockholm have copies of a substantial number of these early efforts.

IN DEN WOHNUNGEN DES TODES

In contrast, the work of Sachs's last twenty-five years concerns itself largely with existential problems, particularly with topics related to the Holocaust and rooted in personal experiences of flight, exile, and the death of friends. Her first collection of poems, *In den Wohnungen des Todes* (in the habitations of death), refers in its title to the Nazi death camps and is dedicated to those who perished there. It is a mistake, however, to perceive her work solely in the context of these historical events. Her topic is on a larger scale, the cycle of life itself—birth, death, rebirth—and Sachs develops various metaphors and ciphers to express the agony and the hope of this cycle.

STERNVERDUNKELUNG

Although it is desirable to interpret Sachs's work separately from the context of specific historical events, it is almost impossible to analyze an individual poem without relying on information gained from a broader knowledge of her work. This difficulty is the result of her frequent use of ciphers, poetic images that can be "decoded" only by reference to other poems in which the same images occur. Such a cipher in Sachs's work is the stone. Its properties are chiefly those of inert matter: lack of emotion, or lifelessness. The cipher may depict human callousness, death, or desolation in different contexts, and it is related to similar poetic images such as sand and dust—decayed rock—which signify the mortal human condition.

The poem "Sinai," from the collection *Sternverdunkelung* (eclipse of the stars), contains entirely negative images of the stone. Sachs compares the ancient times of Moses, in which humanity was still in intimate contact with the divine and thus vibrantly alive, with the present state of lifelessness; there are only "petrified eyes of the lovers" with "their putrefied happiness." Recounting Moses's descent from Mount Sinai, Sachs asks: "Where is still a descendent/ from those who trembled? Oh, may he glow/ in the crowd of amnesiacs/ of the petrified!" The eyes of the lovers turned to stone signify the death both of sensibility and of sensuousness, and the inability to re-create or reproduce. It is ultimately a death of humankind. The call is for one perhaps still alive among the multitude of those dead in mind and body.

In "Chassidische Schriften" ("Hasidic Scriptures"), from *Sternverdunkelung*, Sachs writes: "And the heart of stones,/ filled with drifting sand,/ is the place where midnights are stored." "Drifting sand" is sand blown skyward by the wind; thus, while it is inert matter, it has lost this inertia momentarily on the wings of the wind. The dead has come to life. Midnight, on the other hand, represents the end of one day and the dawning of the next, a time of rebirth. Sachs contends that the stone, dead as it is, is imbued with the desire for rebirth and transubstantiation. Another possibility for the stone to attain a semblance of life is offered in "Golem Tod!"

("Golem Death!"), from *Sternverdunkelung*. There, "The stone sleeps itself green with moss." The suggestion that the stone is merely sleeping, not dead, and that it is capable of producing living matter (moss) is also an affirmation of the possibility of renewal of life after death.

"CHORUS OF THE STONES" AND "MELUSINE, IF YOUR WELL HAD NOT"

Scarcely less negative is the stone cipher in the poem "Wenn nicht dein Brunnen, Melusine" ("Melusine, If Your Well Had Not"), from *Und niemand weiss weiter*. If it were not for the possibility of transformation and escape, "we should long have passed away/ in the petrified resurrection/ of an Easter Island." Easter Island's petrified statues are merely reminders of an extinct civilization, not a resurrection from the dead. Still, the poem indicates that transformation is possible (the symbol for it is Melusine). In the poem "Chorus of the Stones," from *In den Wohnungen des Todes*, stones are, like the statues of Easter Island, venerable objects depicting the history of humankind. The stone is symbolic of all that has died, but it carries memories within it and thus is not entirely devoid of life. The last lines of the poem even offer the hope that the stone is only "sleeping," that it may come to life again: "Our conglomeration is transfused by breath./ It solidified in secret/ but may awaken at a kiss."

Three ideas in "Chorus of the Stones" suggest that death is not the final answer to life: The lifeless entity (the stone) contains memories; it is imbued with breath, a necessary element of life; and it may be awakened by an act of love. Transformation, resurrection, and transfiguration are therefore within the realm of possibility. Such a flight from lifelessness to a new beginning is nevertheless fraught with difficulties.

"HALLELUJA"

The most dramatic depiction of the rebirth of the dead is to be found in Sachs's poem "Halleluja" ("Hallelujah"), from the volume *Flucht und Verwandlung* (flight and metamorphosis). The poem describes a mountain rising from the sea by volcanic action. The rock is portrayed as a beloved child, the crowning glory of its mother, the ocean, as it thrusts forth from the womb to the light of day. While still embedded in the sea, the rock showed signs of sustaining life. As in "Golem Death!" with its stone covered with moss, this rock has been nurturing life. For the sea algae, birth of the rock means death, which the "winged longing" of the rock will bring about; although one form of life dies, another takes its place. These poems therefore encompass the cycle of life and death of living and inert matter on Earth.

"BUTTERFLY" AND "FLEEING"

In tracing the cipher of the stone, it is evident that the nihilism of the earlier cycles has given way to a guarded optimism in the later ones. A more traditional image of transfiguration is that of the butterfly. Its life cycle includes the apparent death of the homely caterpillar and its re-emergence from the cocoon as a beautiful winged creature, and thus it is readily adaptable as a symbol of the soul's resurrection after physical death. Sachs uses the image of the butterfly within this tradition. The poem "In der Flucht" ("Fleeing"), from *Flucht und Verwandlung*, compares the flight of the Jews from their persecutors with the never-ending process of transformation, mutation, and metamorphosis. There is no rest and no end (no "Amen") for that which is considered mortal (sand, dust), for it experiences endless metamorphoses. The butterfly, itself a symbol of metamorphosis, will reenter the life-giving element at its death and complete the cycle of life.

In "Butterfly," from *Sternverdunkelung*, the butterfly is depicted as a mortal creature (one made of "dust") which nevertheless mirrors the beauty of a world beyond: "What lovely hereafter/ is painted in your dust." The butterfly is a messenger of hope for those who are dying, because it is aware through its own metamorphosis that death is only sleep. The butterfly is the symbol of farewell, just as it was the symbol of the last greeting before sleep.

"DANCER" AND "SHE DANCES"

More obscure than the image of the butterfly are Sachs's ciphers of music and dance. The dancer appears to be able to defy gravity in graceful and effortless leaps and spins. A new image of man is created in the dance—that of emancipation from earthly limitations and acceptance into the sphere of the incorporeal. On this premise, Sachs bases her depiction of the dancer as a re-creator, savior, and emancipator from material limitations. In the poem "Sie tanzt" ("She

Dances"), from *Noch feiert Tod das Leben*, the dancer rescues her lover from the dead. This act of rescue is not meant to save him from physical death, for he is no longer alive; metamorphosis is her aim. This she achieves, paradoxically, by her own death: "Aber plötzlich/ am Genick/ Schlaf beünt Sie hinüber" ("But suddenly/ at the neck/ sleep bends her over"). In German, the word "over" (*hinüber*) signifies "to the other side" and thus clearly suggests death; this connotation is underscored by the image of her bending at the neck (hanging) and by the word "sleep," which Sachs frequently uses as a synonym for physical, but not spiritual, death. In the act of dancing, the dancer has liberated both the dead lover and herself. The metamorphosis has released her from life and has rescued him from death. They are united in the spiritual realm. In *Flucht und Verwandlung*, a somewhat different form of creation is discussed in the poem "Tänzerin" ("Dancer"). Here the dancer becomes the vessel for the hope of the future, and Sachs depicts with physiological clarity the birth canal for a messianic prophecy: "In the branches of your limbs/ the premonitions/ build their twittering nests." The dancer's body becomes the maternal, life-giving promise of the future.

In the poem "She Dances," the beginning and the end of life are shown to coincide at the point of metamorphosis, the dancer being the agent. The medium for transfiguration is music. The poem "O-A-O-A," in *Glühende Rätsel* (glowing enigmas), describes the rhythmic "sea of vowels" as the Alpha and Omega. Music is the means of metamorphosis: "Du aber die Tasten niederdrücktest/ in ihre Gräber aus Musik/ und Tanz die verlorene Sternschnuppe/ einen Flügel erfand für dein Leiden" ("But you pressed down the keys/ into their graves of music/ and dance the lost meteor/ invented a wing for your anguish"). The English word "keys" is ambiguous, but the German *Tasten* refers solely to the keys of a piano in this context. The graves are made of music, the transforming factor, and are being played like the keys of a piano, while dance provides the wings for the flight from the corporeal.

"IN THE BLUE DISTANCE"

Finally, in the poem "In der blauen Ferne" ("In the Blue Distance"), from *Und niemand weiss weiter*, the pregnant last lines combine the ciphers of stone, dust, dance, and music in the depiction of metamorphosis: "the stone transforms its dust/ dancing into music." The lifeless element needs no mediator here but performs the ritual of transubstantiation into music (release from corporeal existence) by "dancing" as "dust"—an action functionally identical to that of the drifting sand in the poem "Hasidic Scriptures."

It has frequently been assumed that Sachs is chiefly a chronicler of Jewish destiny during World War II, a recorder of death and despair. This narrow view does not do justice to her work. Sachs's poetry has many aspects of faith, hope, and love, and need not be relegated to a specific historical event or ethnic orientation. Sachs writes about the concerns of every human being— birth, life, love, spiritual renewal, and the possibility of an existence beyond physical death. To diminish the scope of her appeal is to misunderstand her message and to misinterpret her work.

OTHER MAJOR WORKS

SHORT FICTION: *Legenden und Erzählungen*, 1921.

PLAYS: *Eli: Ein Mysterienspiel vom Leiden Israels*, pb. 1951 (*Eli: A Mystery Play of the Sufferings of Israel*, 1967); *Zeichen im Sand: Die szenischen Dichtungen*, pb. 1962.

NONFICTION: *Paul Celan, Nelly Sachs: Correspondence*, 1995.

BIBLIOGRAPHY

Bahti, Timothy, and Marilyn Sibley Fries, eds. *Jewish Writers, German Literature: The Uneasy Examples of Nelly Sachs and Walter Benjamin*. Ann Arbor: University of Michigan Press, 1995. Biographical and critical essays of Sachs's and Benjamin's lives and works. Includes bibliographical references and an index.

Bosmajian, Hamida. *Metaphors of Evil: Contemporary German Literature and the Shadow of Nazism*. Iowa City: University of Iowa Press, 1979. A historical and critical study of responses to the Holocaust in poetry and prose. Includes bibliographical references and index.

Bower, Kathrin M. *Ethics and Remembrance in the Poetry of Nelly Sachs and Rose Ausländer*. Rochester, N.Y.: Camden House, 2000. Critical interpretation of the works of Sachs and Ausländer with particular attention to their recollections of the Holocaust. Includes bibliographical references and index.

Garloff, Katja. *Words from Abroad: Trauma and Displacement in Postwar German Jewish Writers*. Detroit: Wayne State University Press, 2005. This work on German Jewish writers contains a chapter on Sachs as well as one on her friend Celan.

Langer, Lawrence L. *Versions of Survival: The Holocaust and the Human Spirit*. Albany: State University of New York Press, 1982. Brilliantly illuminates the paradoxes in Sachs's verse.

Roth, John K., ed. *Holocaust Literature*. Pasadena, Calif.: Salem Press, 2008. Contains a chapter that analyzes Sachs's "In the Blue Distance."

Rudnick, Ursula. *Post-Shoa Religious Metaphors: The Image of God in the Poetry of Nelly Sachs*. New York: Peter Lang, 1995. A biography of the poet and an in-depth interpretation of seven poems. Rudnick traces the biblical and mystical Jewish tradition that grounds Sachs's work. Includes bibliographical references.

Sachs, Nelly. *Paul Celan, Nelly Sachs: Correspondence*. Translated by Christopher Clark. Edited by Barbara Wiedemann. Riverdale-on-Hudson, N.Y.: Sheep Meadow Press, 1995. A collection of letters by two poets living outside Germany and tormented by guilt that they had escaped the Holocaust. Includes bibliographical references and index.

Soltes, Ori Z. *The Ashen Rainbow: Essays on the Arts and the Holocaust*. Washington, D.C.: Eshel Books, 2007. This work on art and the Holocaust contains a chapter that discusses Sachs.

Helene M. Kastinger Riley

PEDRO SALINAS

Born: Madrid, Spain; November 27, 1891
Died: Boston, Massachusetts; December 4,
    1951

PRINCIPAL POETRY

Presagios, 1923
Seguro azar, 1929 (*Certain Chance*, 2000)
Fábula y signo, 1931
La voz a tí debida, 1933 (*My Voice Because of You*,
    1976)
Razón de amor, 1936
Largo lamento, 1936-1938
Lost Angel, and Other Poems, 1938
Truth of Two, and Other Poems, 1940
El contemplado, 1946 (*The Sea of San Juan: A
    Contemplation*, 1950)
Todo más claro, y otra poemas, 1949
Confianza, 1955
Poesías completas, 1971
To Love in Pronouns, 1974

OTHER LITERARY FORMS

Although the reputation of Pedro Salinas (sah-LEE-nahz) is based primarily on his poetry, which forms the bulk of his work, he also wrote literary criticism, essays, translations, short stories, a novel, and plays. Through his literary criticism and essays, he contributed significantly to an understanding of the process of literary creation and to the appreciation of particular Spanish authors. His critical masterpiece, *Reality and the Poet in Spanish Poetry* (1940), contains six essays which focus on six different Spanish poets from medieval times to the nineteenth century. Salinas attempts to capture and comprehend the main theme of each author's work by assessing his attitudes toward reality. The variety and scope of Salinas's interpretations are also evident in his celebrated studies of the *Modernista* poet Rubén Darío and the medieval poet Jorge Manrique, and in the two published collections of his articles: *Literatura española: Siglo XX* (1941, 1949; twentieth century Spanish literature) and *Ensayos de literatura hispánica: Del "Cantar de mío Cid" a Gar-*

cía Lorca (1958; essays in Hispanic literature: from "Poem of the Cid" to García Lorca).

In contrast to his poetry and literary criticism, which he wrote and published throughout his creative years, Salinas's narrative prose represents the work of two distinct periods: his early beginnings as a writer and his final years. The early works are extremely lyric and impressionistic, almost like poems in prose, and they contain the same themes ever prominent in his poetry: love, illusion, fate, and the poet. The later short stories represent a marked development in Salinas's narrative art. Each possesses a complex plot in which he combines lyricism, mystery, irony, humor, and criticism of the modern world. Salinas's only novel, *La bomba increíble* (1950; the incredible bomb), develops his concern about the ominous contemporary possibility: the destruction of the world by the atomic bomb. This allegorical satire of modern life ends, however, with the triumph of love.

Salinas's plays (two three-act plays and twelve one-act plays) are the fruit of his mature years. With respect to their content, they, like the narratives, are for the most part an extension of his poetic work. Of particular significance are the themes of communication, love, brotherhood, illusion versus reality, human happiness, the poetic imagination, and the dehumanization of modern humankind.

ACHIEVEMENTS

Pedro Salinas, the eldest member of the celebrated Generation of '27, was a leader in its vigorous revival of Spain's poetic past. He and his contemporaries successfully renewed appreciation of Spain's lyric tradition and fused this wealthy heritage with contemporary literary trends: The result was a second golden age of poetry in Spain. Although the Spanish Civil War (1936-1939) led to the disruption and displacement of the Generation of '27, Salinas flourished in exile and continued to stimulate interest in Spanish literature—not only as a poet but also as a teacher and critic.

BIOGRAPHY

Jorge Guillén, poet, critic, and intimate friend of Pedro Salinas y Serrano, divided Salinas's sixty years into thirty years of preparation and thirty years of production. The early years Salinas spent in Madrid, obtaining his primary education from the Colegio Hispano-Francés, his secondary education at the Instituto San Isidro, and his licentiate degree in romance philology from the University of Madrid (1913). He then left for Paris and the Sorbonne, where from 1914 to 1917, he taught Spanish literature and completed his doctoral dissertation on the illustrators of Miguel de Cervantes's *El ingenioso hidalgo don Quixote de la Mancha* (1605, 1615; *The History of the Valorous and Wittie Knight-Errant, Don Quixote of the Mancha*, 1612-1620; better known as *Don Quixote de la Mancha*). While in Paris, he married Margarita Bonmatí; they later had two children. During the years in Paris, Salinas came into contact with many of the prominent writers and literary trends of the time. These modern influences, in combination with an attachment to the Spanish literary tradition, are evident in his poetry and in that of the other members of the Generation of '27.

Salinas was the oldest of this group of poets, whose prominent members include Rafael Alberti, Vicente Aleixandre, Dámaso Alonso, Manuel Altolaguirre, Luis Cernuda, Jorge Guillén, Federico García Lorca, and Emilio Prados. The Generation of '27 (1927 was the three-hundredth anniversary of the death of Golden Age poet Luis de Góngora y Argote) was responsible for rehabilitating the reputation of Góngora, for many years considered a writer of mostly obscure and frivolously ornate poetry. The revival of Góngora was indicative of the renewed appreciation of Spain's literary past, which, fused with a variety of vanguardist currents—Symbolism, *Modernismo*, Creationism, pure poetry, and Surrealism—characterized the works of Salinas and his contemporaries.

After his return from Paris, Salinas accepted a post as professor of Spanish literature at the University of Seville, where he taught for eight years. During that time, he published his first volume of verse, *Presagios*, translated Marcel Proust's *Á la recherche du temps perdu* (1913-1927; *Remembrance of Things Past*, 1922-1931), contributed to numerous magazines, and published two critical editions and his early prose sketches. Also, he spent one year as a lecturer on Spanish literature at Cambridge University.

Salinas then moved to Madrid and worked as a

Pedro Salinas

researcher in Spain's Center for Historical Studies. There, in the country's literary center, he thrived on closer associations with his contemporaries. He taught at the University of Madrid and in 1933 founded the International Summer University of Santander. All the while, his reputation as a poet was growing. By 1936, he had published his famous love poetry along with numerous scholarly studies.

In 1936, after the outbreak of the Spanish Civil War, Salinas taught at Wellesley College as a visiting professor. Thus began his permanent exile from his native land and the period of his most prolific creative output. During the last fifteen years of his life, Salinas produced two more volumes of poetry, his finest literary criticism, his plays, a novel, and short stories. In 1940, he was appointed Turnbull Professor of Hispanic Literature at The Johns Hopkins University in Baltimore, Maryland, a position he held until his death. He spent summers at Middlebury College in Vermont and lectured at universities throughout the United States and South America.

Salinas was a very cosmopolitan man, stimulated by

all sorts of intellectual currents. At the same time, he felt an attachment to classical tradition and culture and, in his later years, a strong nostalgia for his native Spain. He was an extremely cordial man, who was devoted to his family, loved by his students, and involved in close friendships, yet he was also a profoundly private person, who attempted to penetrate the varied experiences of life through literary creation. A deeply spiritual orientation is evident in all his works, but particularly in his poetry, the most profound expression of his concern with the nature of reality, the creative process, love, and existence in the modern world.

ANALYSIS

Pedro Salinas's nine volumes of poetry can be divided into three groups, with each group representing a stage in his poetic development. In *Presagios* (presages), *Certain Chance*, and *Fábula y signo* (fable and sign), the poet reflects seriously on his inner and outer world, preoccupied with the creative process and with the deceptive nature of reality. The second period is his love cycle, for which he is best known: *My Voice Because of You*, *Razón de amor* (love's reason), and *Largo lamento*. The final three volumes make up the poetic production of Salinas in exile. *The Sea of San Juan*, composed during the two especially happy years he spent in Puerto Rico, is a love-filled portrayal of the Caribbean Sea. *Todo más claro, y otros poemas* (all more clear and other poems) combines the poet's positive reflections on the art of poetry with his anguish over the ravages of war, uncontrolled technology, and other aspects of modern life. *Confianza* (confidences) continues these themes, but here Salinas also communicates his hope and confidence in the future. Although differences of style and focus can be seen in the three phases, they overlap considerably, and there is no doubt that the poetry of Salinas forms an integral whole, in a voice that intensifies from *Presagios* to *Confianza*.

The poems of the first stage show Salinas's early attempts to come to terms with the act of creating poetry. The poet must face material reality, internalize it, and somehow transform it into a purer, more external reality. In the poem "Suelo" ("Soil"), for example, the soil or ground represents external reality. In a simple chain

of connections, Salinas links it with artistic creation and with a newer, more permanent vision: "on the soil the feet are planted," "on the feet the body erect," "on the body the head firm," "in the lee of the forehead, pure idea," "in the pure idea, the tomorrow, the key—tomorrow—eternal." However, the process is far from simple. Faced with the blank page, the poet finds it difficult to incorporate into a lyric experience his interior harmony and that which he perceives around him. The poem "Cuartilla" ("Sheet of Paper") illustrates this difficulty and also provides a representative example of Salinas's early style.

"SHEET OF PAPER"

In "Sheet of Paper," Salinas likens the writing down of one's first word to a battle. The pen is the "point of steel," "against the white." In addition to this most obvious metaphor, the poem contains a wealth of other metaphors and images that suggest whiteness and conflict and reveal the mixture of traditional and modern influences that inspired Salinas and his generation. The vocabulary is very much that of *Modernismo*, with its many indications of coldness, whiteness, flight, and opulence: "winter," "marble," "snows," "feathers," "tall columns," "flights of doves," "wings," "snowflakes," "ermines." The intertwining of metaphors and images, of paradoxical and opposing elements is reminiscent of Baroque poetry: "Light as feathers, illusive tall columns uphold roofs of white clouds"; "The snowflakes begin sudden attacks, noiseless skirmishes, snows, ermines, opposed." The "doves" are the thoughts of the poet, who stands on a border between his inner and outer worlds: "Flights of doves uncertain between white above and below, hesitant, withhold the whiteness of their wings." Finally, the pen conquers, and the word emerges, likened to "sun and dawn." The poet is engaged in a constant pursuit of clarity; the goal of poetry is to penetrate, harmonize, and illuminate internal and external reality.

"HERE"

In the course of his pursuit, the poet sometimes rejoices in his discoveries. The poem "Aquí" ("Here") communicates his acceptance, exaltation, and idealization of external reality and manifests themes that will dominate his later poetry: love and the sea. The poet is completely content: "I would remain in all/ as I am, where I am;/ calm in the calm water,/ silent, deeply submerged/ in love without light." Here, he claims to require no illumination, and never to need to retreat inward: "Never shall I go from you/ in a ship with wind singing/ at the sail." Nevertheless, the poet does withdraw, because so often he beholds the illusive and deceptive nature of reality. In the poem "Pregunta más allá" ("Further Question"), the love theme is again present, and the poet questions both his loved one and himself: "Why do I ask where you are,/ if I am not blind,/ if you are not absent?" He is afraid to trust appearances, and his comparison of her body, which terminates in a voice, with a flame that rises in smoke, "in the air, impalpable," is ultimately a metaphor for what he fears will be the fate of their relationship. The skepticism, the dialogue form, the simple, almost conversational language, the images of smoke and fire, and similar opposing elements—light/shadow, clear sky/ mist—reappear with intensified force in the final two stages of Salinas's poetic production.

THE LOVE CYCLE

Salinas's love trilogy is generally considered to be his best poetry. *My Voice Because of You* traces the history of a love relationship from its first stages to fulfillment, to separation, to a recovery of the experience by means of the poet's internalization of his past happiness. In *Razón de amor*, the poet continues to reflect on past love. In his emotional meditations, he resolves the conflicts concerning love's illusive nature and proclaims love a permanent, redemptive reality for human existence. In *Largo lamento*, as the title suggests, some of the poet's bitterness returns. The poems of this volume foreshadow the disenchantment and preoccupation with the fragility of life that Salinas expresses in *Todo más claro, y otros poemas*. Each poem of the love cycle forms an independent unit and at the same time is a part of the trilogy in its entirety.

Critics disagree on whether the poems are addressed to a real or an imaginary woman. She is never named, and all information about her is conveyed through the poet's internal consciousness. She remains quite vague, but the experiences of the poet in the love relationship are extremely vivid and deeply moving.

MY VOICE BECAUSE OF YOU

One of the most beautiful poems in *My Voice Because of You* is "¡Sí, todo con exceso!" ("Yes, Too Much of Everything"), in which the poet communicates his ecstasy in the plenitude of love. A central metaphor and its numerous variations give the poem its structure: love compared with numbers. Salinas's predilection for paradox is evident in his juxtaposition of the "oneness" of love with love's infinity and freedom from all limits. There are images of ascension—"to mount up," "our slender joys . . . aloft to their height"— yet the lovers surrender "to a great uncertain depth" from which the culminating expression of love's infinity emerges: "This is nothing yet./ Look deeply at yourselves. There's more." The language is simple, often prosaic, antipoetic: "from dozens to hundreds," "from hundreds to thousands," "writing tablets, pens, machines," "ciphers," "calculations." Nevertheless, the result is poetry: "everything to multiply/ caress by caress/ embrace by wild passion." "Light" and "sea" are again present in this immeasurable experience—"too much light, life and sea/ Everything in plural,/ plural lights, lives and seas"—but gone are the more complicated metaphors and imagery of his earlier works. Salinas employs more wordplay, internal rhythm, and short phrases, but his work still possesses elegance and still makes use of traditional Spanish meters in varied combinations, in unrhymed verses, that echo Spanish Golden Age poets.

In "No quiero que te vayas" ("Sorrow, I Do Not Wish You"), the poet engages in a dialogue with his pain and desires to hold onto it as the "last form of loving." A profoundly emotional piece, the poem describes how the poet tries to cope with separation from his beloved. There are no metaphors in this poem; its tension and profundity are bound in clear, conceptual speech containing opposing elements. The poet's sorrow is the proof that his beloved once loved him: "Your truth assures me/ that nothing was untrue." He can thus live in "that crumbled reality which/ hides itself and insists/ that it never existed." In later poems, he no longer feels such anguish, but he clings to the sorrow. For example, in "¿Serás, amor?" ("Will You Be, Love?"), Salinas writes, "From the beginning, to live is to separate." He asks that love be "a long good-bye which never ends," because, for him, love is the most authentic reality: "And that the most certain, the sure is good-bye."

Eventually, the poet-protagonist reestablishes harmony in his soul. In "Pensar en ti esta noche" ("To Think of You Tonight"), he feels love rooted not only within him but also in all nature. The poem begins with his characteristic use of paradox: "To think of you tonight/ was not to think of you." Love in this poem relates to his earlier themes: It serves as a link between inner and outer reality ("An agreement of world and being"), and as a lyric inspiration ("the canticle singing for you in my heart"). The poet beholds love everywhere and believes that its omnipresence transcends even death (". . . in a love changed to stars, to quest, to the world,/ saved now from the fear/ of the corpse which remains if we forget"). This optimism prevails in the final stage of Salinas's poetic and spiritual development.

THE SEA OF SAN JUAN

Salinas's last three volumes of poetry are quite different from one another in tone and content, but all reveal the poet's continued probing of the relationships between his inner and outer worlds. In *The Sea of San Juan*, Salinas speaks to the sea in what amounts to one long dialogue. The initial poem is labeled "El contempledo: Tema" ("Theme"), and it is followed by fourteen "Variaciones" ("Variations"). The poet rejoices in his beloved sea. Just as he finds spiritual harmony and permanence in love, so, too, he discovers the sea to be a symbol of everlasting beauty, life, and inspiration. The language and style are much like that found in his love poetry.

One of the central metaphors of this volume is that of the sea as the poet's light. In the fifth variation, "Pareja muy desigual" ("Pair So Unequal"), he completely surrenders to the sea's radiance "as a blindman to the hand" of his guide. The sea gives more to the poet than the poet can ever return with his glance. If the poet can hold its clarity in his eyes, "the past will never vanish." Through the sea, however, the poet recognizes his own temporality. In the fourteenth variation, "Salvación por la luz" ("Salvation Through the Light"), the poet writes, "Now, here, facing you, . . ./ I learn what I am: I am but a moment/ of that long gaze which eyes you." This does not disturb the poet, because he feels a bond with his "former brothers . . . blinded by death," who once contemplated the sea as he does now. He believes himself to be renewing their sight. Contempla-

tion brings salvation: "perhaps your eternity,/ turned to light, will enter us through our eyes."

TODO MÁS CLARO, Y OTROS POEMAS

The eyes of contemporary man, however, are focused elsewhere. In many of the poems of *Todo más claro, y otros poemas*, Salinas denounces the destructive and dehumanizing aspects of modern life. One of the strongest expressions of Salinas's horror is his 1944 "Cero" ("Zero"), in which he prophetically envisioned nuclear holocaust (which occurred just months later in Hiroshima). This, his longest poem, depicts the annihilation of a city by a bomb dropped from a plane. The eyes of the poet overflow with tears: "Invitation to weeping. This is a plaintive cry,/ eyes, crying endlessly." With bitter irony, he narrates how the insensitive pilot, upon seeing the white clouds of destruction, is reminded of tufts of wool, of his playful childhood romps with little lambs in fields of clover. Salinas goes on to contrast what might have flowered had it not been for the tragic effects of misguided technology. His images are haunting, and they display the poet's high level of culture and continued immersion in literary tradition. After the nothingness, or "zero," falls upon everything, the poet gropes in the rubble for his dead. He finds "total shipwreck" in the sea of destruction. The desolation is overwhelming, but the poet keeps on searching. Even in this darkest of visions, the poet, in the closing stanza, finds a glimmer of hope: "I am the shadow searching the rubbish dump."

CONFIANZA

Salinas's final volume of verse, *Confianza*, is a reaffirmation of his faith in life. His serenity returns; in "La nube que trae un viento" ("The Cloud That Bears Wind"), for example, he sings to a harmony he believes must exist: "The cloud that bears wind, the words that bring pain,/ other words cleanse those, another wind carries away." He finds this harmony in nature as seen in poems "Pájaro y radio" ("Bird and Radio"), "Nube en la mano" ("Cloud in Hand"), "¿Qué pájaros?" ("What Birds?"), and "En un trino" ("In the Trill of a Bird"). He also finds harmony in love with "Presente simple" ("Simple Present"), in art with "La estatua" ("The Statue"), and in his creation of poetry with "Ver lo que veo" ("Seeing What I See") and "Confianza" ("Confidence").

REALITY AND THE POET

Critics have followed Salinas's own guidance in *Reality and the Poet in Spanish Poetry* and have tried to determine the author's vision of the world by establishing his basic attitude toward reality. Their opinions differ greatly. He has been viewed as one who wavers between acceptance of reality and nothingness, as an escapist, a romantic idealist in search of the absolute, a kind of Neoplatonist, and a mystic. Those critics who point to Salinas's varying perspectives on reality are probably more correct. His works represent a synthesis of several possible attitudes toward reality: exaltation, idealization, escape, revolt, and acceptance. However, if one attitude can be said to prevail, it is Salinas's basic acceptance of reality. Although certain volumes convey the desire of the poet to look beyond his circumstances from a variety of perspectives, a fundamental acceptance of life is the ground note of Salinas's oeuvre.

OTHER MAJOR WORKS

LONG FICTION: *La bomba increíble*, 1950.

NONFICTION: *Reality and the Poet in Spanish Poetry*, 1940; *Literatura española: Siglo XX*, 1941, 1949; *Jorge Manrique: O Tradición y originalidad*, 1947; *La poesía de Rubén Darío*, 1948; *Ensayos de literatura hispánica: Del "Cantar de mío Cid" a García Lorca*, 1958.

BIBLIOGRAPHY

Allen, Rupert C. *Symbolic Experience: A Study of Poems by Pedro Salinas*. Tuscaloosa: University of Alabama Press, 1982. A critical interpretation of selected poems by Salinas. Includes an index and bibliography.

Crispin, John. *Pedro Salinas*. New York: Twayne, 1974. An introductory biography and critical study of selected works by Salinas. Includes bibliographic references.

Hartfield-Méndex, Vialla. *Woman and the Infinite: Epiphanic Moments in Pedro Salinas's Art*. Cranbury, N.J.: Associated University Presses, 1996. Examines the role of women in Salinas's works.

Newman, Jean Cross. *Pedro Salinas and His Circumstance*. San Juan, P.R.: Inter American University Press, 1983. A biography of Salinas offering a historical and cultural background of his life and works.

Shaughnessy, Lorna. *The Developing Poetic Philosophy of Pedro Salinas: A Study in Twentieth Century Spanish Poetry*. Lewiston, N.Y.: Edwin Mellen Press, 1995. A critical analysis of the philosophy evident in Salinas's poetry. Includes bibliographical references and an index.

Stixrude, David. *The Early Poetry of Pedro Salinas*. 1967. Reprint. Princeton, N.J.: Princeton University Press, 1975. A critical study of Salinas's early works. Includes bibliographic references.

Susan G. Polansky

SAPPHO

Born: Eresus, Lesbos, Asia Minor (now in Greece); c. 630 B.C.E.

Died: Mytilene, Lesbos, Asia Minor (now in Greece); c. 580 B.C.E.

Also known as: Psappho

PRINCIPAL POETRY

Poetarum Lesbiorum Fragmenta, 1955

Lyra Graeca, 1958 (volume 1)

Sappho: A New Translation, 1958

Sappho: Poems and Fragments, 1965

The Poems of Sappho, 1966

The Sappho Companion, 2000 (Margaret Reynolds, editor)

If Not, Winter: Fragments of Sappho, 2002 (Anne Carson, editor)

OTHER LITERARY FORMS

Sappho (SAF-oh) is known only for her poetry.

ACHIEVEMENTS

One of the most admired poets of the ancient world, Sappho was widely popular not only during her lifetime but also for centuries after. Although she wrote nine books of poetry, very little of the corpus remains. Except for a very few phrases on vase paintings or papyri, Sappho's poetry has been preserved primarily in small bits that happened to be quoted by other writers. Some 170 of these fragments are extant, and although there may be among them one or two complete poems, most of the fragments consist of only a few lines or a few words. For Sappho's poem fragments, the numerical system of Edgar Lobel and Denys Page, *Poetarum Lesbiorum Fragmenta*, is used.

These fragments indicate that Sappho's poems were largely lyrical, intended to be sung and accompanied by music and perhaps dance. Although her poetry was thus traditional in form, it differed significantly in content from the larger body of Greek verse, which was written primarily by men. Whereas other Greek poets were mainly concerned with larger and more public issues and with such traditional masculine concerns as war and heroism, Sappho's poems are personal, concerned with the emotions and individual experiences of herself and her friends. In exploring and describing the world of passion, in particular, Sappho departed from conventional poetic themes. Perhaps that is one of the reasons that her poetry was so popular in the ancient world.

Sappho's work has continued to be popular, however, not only because of the timelessness of her subject matter but also because of the exactness of her imagery and the intensity of her expression. Although her style is simple, direct, and conversational, her poems are powerful in creating an impression or evoking an emotion. Her world is therefore not the larger world of politics or warfare, but the smaller world of personal feeling; nevertheless, in depicting the outer limits of that world—the extremes of jealousy as well as tenderness, the depths of sorrow as well as the heights of ecstasy—Sappho's poetry sets a standard to which all later writers of lyrics must aspire.

In addition to being well known for her subject matter, Sappho has come to be associated with a particular metrical form. Although she was probably not the inventor of Sapphic meter, it has been so named because of her frequent use of it. In Sapphic meter, the stanza consists of three lines, each of which contains five feet—two trochees, a dactyl, and two more trochees—with a concluding fourth line of one dactyl and one trochee. The first line of the "Ode to Aphrodite" in the

original Greek illustrates this meter. This ode is thought to have been accompanied by music written in the Mixolydian mode, a musical mode with which Sappho is also associated. Plutarch, in fact, claims that this mode, which is said to arouse the passions more than any other, was invented by Sappho.

Sappho's enduring reputation is based, however, on the fragments of her poetry that remain. Although those fragments themselves indicate her poetry's worth, there is in addition the testimony of other writers regarding the greatness of her accomplishment. She was praised and revered by a long line of ancients, including Solon, Plato, Aristotle, Horace, Catullus, Ovid, and Plutarch. Proving that imitation is the highest form of praise, some later poets actually incorporated her verse into their own compositions; Catullus's Poem 51, for example, is a slight reworking of a poem by Sappho. Plutarch, who, like Catullus, admired this particular ode, described it as being "mixed with fire," a metaphor that could accurately be applied to the entire body of Sappho's remaining poetry.

BIOGRAPHY

There are few details about Sappho's life that can be stated with certainty; the only evidence is what other writers said about her, and there is no way of knowing whether what they said is true. She is thought to have been of an aristocratic family of the island of Lesbos and to have had three brothers and a daughter named Cleis; dates of her birth and death, however, are not known. Athenaeus, writing around 200 C.E., claimed that Sappho was a contemporary of Alyattes, who reigned in Lydia from 610 to 560 B.C.E.; Eusebius of Caesarea, who was writing in the late third and early fourth centuries C.E., refers to Sappho (also known as Psappho) in his chronicle for the year 604 B.C.E. Other writers indicate that Sappho lived at the time of another poet, Alcaeus of Lesbos, who seems to have been born around 620 B.C.E. It seems safe, therefore, to conclude that Sappho was born sometime during the last quarter of the seventh century and lived into the first half of the sixth century B.C.E.

Sometime between 604 and 592 B.C.E., Sappho seems to have been sent into exile in Sicily by Pittacus, who was then a democratic ruler of Mytilene on Lesbos;

an inscription on the Parian marbles of the third century B.C.E. provides confirmation. Although it seems likely that such an exile would have been for political reasons, there are no clear references in any of the fragments of Sappho's poems to indicate that she was specifically concerned with political matters; in fact, based on those fragments, her poetry appears to have been very much apolitical.

Whether Sappho was married is also uncertain; some say that she had a husband named Cercylas, but others believe this report to be a creation of the Greek comic poets. More suspect is the story that Sappho committed suicide by leaping from the Leucadian Cliff when rejected by a sailor named Phaon. To begin with, this story did not surface until more than two hundred years after her death, but more significant is the fact that Phaon has been found to be a vegetable deity associated with Aphrodite, and a god to whom Sappho wrote hymns. These hymns are thought to have provided the basis for this apocryphal account of her death.

There are, however, some assumptions that can be drawn from Sappho's own words. Her poetry indicates that she was the leader of a group of young women who appear to have studied music, poetry, and dance and who seem to have worshiped Aphrodite and the Muses. As the daughter of an aristocratic family, Sappho would probably not have conducted a formal school, but was more likely the informal leader of a circle of girls and young women. Scholars know from other references in her poetry that there were several such groups on Lesbos, with leaders who were rivals of Sappho.

Many of Sappho's poems also concern her romantic relationships with various women of her group, a fact that has evoked various responses throughout history, ranging from vilification to denial. Her reputation seems to have been first darkened in the fourth century B.C.E., long after her death, when she was the subject of a number of comic and burlesque plays; it is believed that many of the unsavory stories that came to be associated with Sappho were generated during this period. A serious and most unfortunate effect of this created and perhaps inaccurate reputation was that much of Sappho's work was later deliberately destroyed, particularly by Christians whose moral sensibilities were offended by some of the stories that circulated in the second, fourth,

Sappho

and eleventh centuries C.E. Sappho's reputation was also reworked by later scholars who admired her poetry but who were discomfited by her love for women; among their efforts to dissociate Sappho from her sexuality was the widely circulated story that there were in fact two Sapphos, one the licentious and immoral woman to whom all the unsavory tales applied, and the other a faultless and asexual woman who wrote sublime poetry. Most scholars today believe that there was only one Sappho, but they also believe that most of the stories told about her were untrue.

Thus, because of the legendary tales that have come to be associated with Sappho, and because of the lack of reliable historical evidence, there is little knowledge about her life that is certain. It seems reasonable to assume that she lived on Lesbos, that she was a poet, and that she valued personal relationships, about which she wrote. Both during her lifetime and after, she was much admired; statues were erected in her honor, coins were minted bearing her likeness, and she is said to have been given a heroine's funeral. Beyond these small pieces of information, scholars must turn to the fragments of her poetry for knowledge and understanding.

ANALYSIS

Since Sappho's poetry is largely personal, it concerns her immediate world: her dedication to Aphrodite, her love of nature and art, and her relationships with lovers, friends, and family. Her poetry reflects her enjoyment of beauty in the natural world and the close connection that existed between that world and the lives of herself and her friends. Their worship of Aphrodite, their festive songs and dances, are all celebrated with flowers from the fields and with branches from the trees. Her poetry also reflects her love of art, whether in the form of poetry, the music of the lyre, or the graceful movement of a maiden in a dance. Since these interests are, however, always presented through the perspective of a personal response, a chief defining characteristic of Sappho's poetry is that it is highly emotional.

"ODE TO APHRODITE"

Most of the extant fragments of Sappho's poetry were quoted by later writers to illustrate some point of dialect, rhetoric, grammar, or poetic style, and those writers usually quoted only that portion of Sappho's poem that was pertinent to their point. It is fortunate, then, that Dionysius of Halicarnassus, a Greek writer of treatises who lived in Rome around 30 B.C.E., quoted in its entirety Sappho's "Ode to Aphrodite," to illustrate "the smooth mode of composition." This poem, the longest of several by Sappho honoring Aphrodite, appears to be the most substantial complete work of Sappho that remains.

The ode contains the usual components of a celebration prayer to Aphrodite: the Invocation, the Sanction, and the Entreaty. The Invocation to the goddess consists of a series of epithets, "Dapple-throned Aphrodite,/ eternal daughter of God,/ snare-knitter"; the Sanction asks the goddess's generosity and assistance and reminds her of past favors she has granted; and the Entreaty urgently appeals to the goddess for aid in the present situation. Sappho employs this traditional form in a fresh way, however, not only by her use of vivid metaphors and lyrical language, but also by using the Sanction to reveal something of the goddess's character as well as something of Sappho's own psychology.

As Sappho employs it, the Sanction is a narrative passage within which both she and the goddess move back and forth in time. After describing a past occasion when the goddess came to Earth in a carriage pulled by sparrows, Sappho then recounts the goddess's questioning of her at that time. Using in her narrative the past tense and the indirect question, Sappho recalls the goddess's remarks: "You asked, What ailed me now that/ made me call you again?" Abruptly, then, Sappho places the goddess's gentle chiding within the present context; the poem shifts to direct discourse as the goddess questions Sappho directly: "Whom has/ Persuasion to bring round now/ to your love? Who, Sappho, is/ unfair to you?" This mix of the two temporal perspectives links and blends the present with the past, not only emphasizing Sappho's recurring states of anxiety over new love but also illuminating the special and friendly relationship between the poet and the goddess: Aphrodite has obviously assisted Sappho before in similar matters of the heart. Continuing to reveal Sappho's character, the goddess reminds her that they are beginning a now-familiar pattern: A bemused Aphrodite recalls, "If she [the desired lover] won't accept gifts, she/ will one day give them; and if/ she won't love you—she soon will/love." Sappho, manipulating the tradition of the Sanction for new purposes of self-mockery and character revelation, thus discloses her love for the courting period, as well as the shift in attitudes that will inevitably occur between her and her new lover. After the goddess's assurance that the sought-after lover will very shortly be seeking Sappho, the reader is then returned to the poem's outer frame, the prayer, as Sappho begs the goddess to help at once, to "Come now! Relieve this intolerable pain!"

Within the form of a traditional prayer honoring Aphrodite, the poem thus presents a delightful variety of tone. It discloses not only the intensity of Sappho's passion for the desired lover, but also her wry recognition that this intensity will be limited by time and by her own nature. The poem similarly indicates not only the immensity of the goddess's power but also her gentle amusement at the joys and woes of her followers; although Sappho's present sufferings in love will soon be in the past, a pattern underscored by the poem's movement between present and past time, there is every reason to believe that the goddess will assist Sappho once again in achieving the lover who will end her present suffering. In revealing not only something of the character of Aphrodite but also something of the character of Sappho, the poem thus transcends the limitations of its genre: It is a prayer, to be sure, and a narrative, but it is also a charmingly refreshing analysis of the poet's own psychology.

"ODE TO ANACTORIA"

Although there are a few other fragments of poems honoring Aphrodite, the largest number of Sappho's fragments which remain are concerned with love, a subject that occupied much of Sappho's attention. One love poem that may, like the "Ode to Aphrodite," be nearly complete, is the large fragment sometimes called the "Ode to Anactoria," although the poem may have been written for Atthis or even for some other woman whom Sappho loved. An unknown writer who has been labeled "Longinus," in a Greek work believed to date from the first or second century C.E., quoted this fragment to illustrate Sappho's mastery in depicting physical sensations. Extraordinary in its exquisitely precise delineation of the extremes of passion, the poem is also notable for the contrast between the control of its first section and the revealed intensity of its latter section, with the resulting alternations in tone as the speaker sits in the presence of two people, the woman she loves and the man who is evidently enjoying that woman's attentions.

Concisely and with control, the poem beings:

> He is a god in my eyes—
> the man who is allowed
> to sit beside you—he
> who listens intimately
> to the sweet murmur of
> your voice, the enticing
> laughter that makes my own
> heart beat fast.

This calm and steady beginning establishes an outer mood of control, an atmosphere of containment and casual social interplay; the poem turns, however, on the word "laughter," and the rest of the fragment describes, rapidly and with great intensity, the physical symptoms of the poet's great passion. All her senses are affected: Her "tongue is broken," and she sees nothing; she hears only her "own ears drumming" as she drips with sweat; and, as "trembling shakes" her body, she turns "paler than dry grass." In one of Sappho's most superb lines, she declares that "a thin flame runs under/ my skin." Then, ending this rapid and graphic description of the physical results of intense emotion, the poet remarks, in a powerfully reserved manner, that "At such times/ death isn't far from me."

Scholars have long debated the cause of Sappho's passion, arguing whether it is love or jealousy or both; scholars have also quarreled over the identity of the woman and the relationship between the woman and the man who sits beside her. Such discussions are, however, ultimately irrelevant; the poet's salient point is her own overpowering feeling for the woman to whom she is listening, a feeling that prevents Sappho from exercising over her body any control; it is the physical manifestations of that feeling, the effects on the body of great passion, which Sappho is recording. Within the poem, the effects of that passion are heightened by the contrast that turns on the word "laughter"; just as the poem is divided between the controlled description of the outer situation and the blaze of feelings within the poet, so Sappho and the man are divided in their response to the woman's laughter; he "listens intimately," calmly, while Sappho experiences a whole cascade of violent physical and emotional reactions.

Sappho's description in this poem of the effects of passion has not been surpassed, although a number of later poets, including Catullus, have imitated, translated, or adopted her ideas. None, however, has been able to convey such intensity of feeling with the economy and precision of Sappho. It seems safe to say that there are few who would dispute Longinus's claim that this poem illustrates "the perfection of the Sublime in poetry."

16 L.-P.

In addition to considering the physical effects of love on the individual, Sappho also analyzes love's nature and power. One such poem, 16 L.-P., which refers directly to Anactoria, appears on a papyrus of the second century. The poem begins with a paratactic trope, a common device that presents the theme as the culmination of a series of comparisons:

Some say a cavalry corps,
some infantry, some, again,
will maintain that the swift cars
of our fleet are the finest
sight on dark earth; but I say
that whatever one loves, is.

More than illustrating normal differences of opinion, this means of introducing the theme establishes, as well, a decided difference between male and female values: Sappho seems clearly to imply that while men would see the ideal of beauty to be things having to do with war, she sees the ideal of beauty to be the thing beloved—in this case, the absent Anactoria.

Sappho then reinforces her contention that the beloved is the world's most beautiful sight by a reference to Helen, who had her pick of the world's men; in contrast to what one would expect, however, Helen was obliged, because of love, to choose "one who laid Troy's honor in ruin," one who "warped" her "to his will," one who caused her even to forget the "love due her own blood, her own/ child." Sappho uses the story of Helen to illustrate love's power to make insignificant all ordinary considerations and constraints. Yet Sappho clearly intends no judgment against Helen; the purpose of her allusion is simply to demonstrate the power of love and, by analogy, Sappho's love for her beloved.

Only then, after establishing by example and comparisons the supremacy and strength of love, does Sappho reveal in an apostrophe the name of her beloved. Addressing Anactoria and expressing her fear that Anactoria will forget her, Sappho confesses that the sound of her footstep, or the sight of her bright face, would be dearer "than glitter/ of Lydian horse or armoured/ tread of mainland infantry." In an intricate linking of end and beginning by means of metaphor and comparisons, the poem thus moves full circle, back to its starting place; the final sentence of the fragment reinforces the idea contained in the opening sentence as it simultaneously contrasts the tread of the infantry with the delightful sound of Anactoria's footstep, and the glitter of armor with the bright shine of Anactoria's face. In such ways, Sappho clearly exposes the conflicting value systems that underlie her poems and those of her male contemporaries.

Several other fragments of varying size also treat the power of love, among them a particularly felicitous line quoted by Maximus of Tyre around 150 C.E.: "As a whirlwind/ swoops on an oak/ Love shakes my heart." An overpowering natural phenomenon, love is presented here as an elemental force that completely overcomes the lover, both physically and emotionally. As the wind physically surrounds the oak, so does love overpower the lover physically as well as emotionally. Love, a force that cannot be denied, is thus depicted as a violent physical and emotional assault, to which one may well respond with mixed feelings.

Sappho explores the ambiguity of the lover's response to love's violent assault in another fragment, quoted by Hephaestion around 150 C.E.: "Irresistible/ and bittersweet/ that loosener/ of limbs, Love/ reptile-like/ strikes me down." Again, love is depicted as an absolute power and as a violent force—in this instance as a reptile that, attacking a passive victim, creates in her a weakened state. That state is not, however, altogether unpleasant, as is indicated by the exquisite sensuality of the adjectival phrase describing love as "that loosener of limbs." Love's duality—its violence and its sweetness—and the lover's ambiguity of response—as the victim of assault and as reveler in love's sensuality—are further underscored by the oxymoronic adjective "bittersweet," an epithet for love that Sappho may have been the first to use.

94 L.-P.

In addition to analyzing the nature and effects of love, Sappho writes of love's termination, of separation, loss, and grief. One such fragment, 94 L.-P., found in a seventh century manuscript in very poor condition, contains many lacunae and uncertain readings. Nevertheless, enough of the poem remains to prove that Sappho was defining the state of bereavement and the effectiveness of memory in alleviating that state. In the course of exploring these themes, however, the poem presents an enchanting account of the life led by Sappho and the members of her group as they worshiped Aphrodite, celebrated the beauty of nature, and gloried in one another.

Like the "Ode to Aphrodite," the poem uses a frame of present time to contain an account of past time; in this poem, however, the past time frames an even earlier period, so that three time periods are represented. Beginning in her present situation, Sappho, alone, reveals her emotional state at the loss of her beloved: "Frankly I wish I were dead." Attempting then to console herself, Sappho recalls the occasion of their parting; at that time, in contrast to the present situation, Sappho controlled her grief to comfort her lover, who was overcome by weeping. On that occasion, Sappho urged her beloved to remember their former happiness and to comfort herself with the memory of their love. At this point in the past, the poem then removes to its third temporal setting, that idyllic period when the two were actually together. In a passage of great lyrical beauty, Sappho recalls the details of their life:

> think
> of our gifts of Aphrodite
> and all the loveliness that we shared
> all the violet tiaras
> braided rosebuds, dill and
> crocus twined around your young neck
> myrrh poured on your head
> and on soft mats girls with
> all that they most wished for beside them
> while no voices changed
> choruses without ours
> no woodlot bloomed in spring without song.

In re-creating, at the moment of their farewell, this earlier time of delight in love, nature, and each other, Sappho consoles her beloved by reminding her that the joys they shared are preserved in memories and that those memories can provide solace. At the same time, from her position in the outer frame of the poem—the present context—Sappho attempts to comfort herself by the same means.

Although the poem, on one hand, asserts the consolation that memory can offer, it testifies as well to memory's limitations. Even though Sappho has shared the joyful events of which she reminds her beloved, the poem indicates all too clearly that memory's ability to ease grief is restricted. As Sappho tersely and flatly demonstrates by her opening statement, in no way can memory truly compensate for the beloved's absence. Still, the enchantment of those memories remains, and even though they cannot totally eliminate the pain of parting, they can provide some surcease by powerfully evoking the time when the lovers' joy in nature and in their love created for them an existence truly idyllic.

In addition to these personal poems, private accounts of her own and her friends' feelings and activities, Sappho also wrote some poems of a more public nature. Notable among these "public" poems are a number of fragments from her epithalamiums, or wedding songs. Some of these are congratulatory pieces honoring bride or groom, some appear to have been part of good-humored songs of mockery or wedding jest, and some seem to have been serious considerations of what marriage meant, especially for a woman. Of the latter, particularly worthy of comment are two fragments thought by some to be part of a single poem concerning the loss of maidenhood. As is true of other poems by Sappho, opinion is divided as to the poem's ultimate meaning, some believing that it alludes to an ungentle lover who does not properly appreciate the maiden whose virginity he destroys, and others believing that the poem refers generally to the destruction of innocence and the loss of girlhood joys that marriage necessitates.

The fragments employ two similes, the first comparing the blushing girl to

> a quince-apple
> ripening on a top
> branch in a tree top
> not once noticed by
> harvesters or if
> not unnoticed, not reached.

The location of the apple high in the tree permits it to ripen without disturbance, perhaps as a girl's careful upbringing or superior social standing might shield her from importunate suitors. The second fragment compares the loss of the virginal state to

> a hyacinth in
> the mountains, trampled by shepherds until
> only a purple stain
> remains on the ground.

Through the powerful image of the delicate hyacinth roughly trod into the earth, the poem clearly delineates the destructive power of love and marriage.

112 L.-P.

That image is countered, however, in another fragment from an epithalamium, 112 L.-P., which rejoices in marriage and celebrates the groom's winning of the girl he desires. The bride is described as "charming to look at,/ with eyes as soft as/ honey, and a face/ that Love has lighted/ with his own beauty." Sappho, clearly indicating her own opinion as to which is the lucky partner in the marriage, reminds the groom, "Aphrodite has surely/ outdone herself in/ doing honor to you!" Such songs were thought to have been written for the weddings of Sappho's friends, and would have been accompanied by music and dance.

Sappho's legacy is meager in size, consisting of one or two poems that may be complete, together with a number of shorter fragments that tantalize by their incompleteness even as they enchant with what they do provide. These few pieces clearly manifest the enormous poetic talent that Sappho possessed: a genius for capturing a mood, for portraying an experience, and for depicting an emotion. Although her poetry is personal in dealing with her own responses to life, it is, paradoxically, also universal; the feelings she describes, even though they are her own, are shared by all human beings who ever love, lose, or grieve, or who experience jealousy, anger, or regret. One of the first poets to explore the range and depth of the human heart, Sappho well deserves Plato's epithet for her, "the tenth Muse."

Bibliography

Bowra, C. Maurice. *Greek Lyric Poetry: From Alcman to Simonides*. 2d ed. Oxford, England: Clarendon Press, 1961. A classic review of seven Greek lyric poets stressing their historical development and critiquing important works. Offers groundbreaking theories of the poets as a group and as individual writers. Views Sappho as the leader of a society of girls that excluded men and worshiped the Muses and Aphrodite.

Burnett, Anne Pippin. *Three Archaic Poets: Archilochus, Alcaeus, Sappho*. Cambridge, Mass.: Harvard University Press, 1983. Rejects theories of ancient Greek lyrics as either passionate outpourings or occasional verse. Describes Sappho's aristocratic circle and critiques six major poems.

DuBois, Page. *Sappho Is Burning*. Chicago: University of Chicago Press, 1995. The title is taken from part of David A. Campbell's translation of Sappho's fragment 48, in which the poet's heart is "burning with desire." DuBois assumes and examines an aesthetics of fragmentation and veers to a strained "postmodern" appreciation of the poet.

Greene, Ellen, ed. *Reading Sappho* and *Re-reading Sappho*. Berkeley: University of California Press, 1996. A two-volume collection of essays and articles (by writers such as Mary Lefkowitz, Holt N. Parker, and Jack Winkler) important in elucidating Sappho's poetry.

Jenkyns, Richard. *Three Classical Poets: Sappho, Catullus, and Juvenal*. Cambridge, Mass.: Harvard University Press, 1982. Stresses the relativistic view that no one theory can elucidate ancient poetry. Detailed analysis of Sappho's principal poems and fragments, concluding that she is a major poet.

McEvilley, Thomas. *Sappho*. Putnam, Conn.: Spring, 2008. A biography of Sappho that explores her life and works.

Prins, Yopie. *Victorian Sappho*. Princeton, N.J.: Princeton University Press, 1999. Superb study of the presentations of Sappho in nineteenth century English literature. Exposes the imperfections of editions by Dr. Henry Wharton and Michael Field (pseudonym of Katherine Bradley and Edith Cooper). Cogent chapter on Sappho and Swinburne in "Swinburne's Sapphic Sublime."

Rayor, Diane. *Sappho's Lyre: Archaic Lyric and Women Poets of Ancient Greece*. Berkeley: University of California Press, 1991. In most respects, this is the best available translation of Sappho. Includes fragments of nine women poets besides Sappho, along with poems and fragments of seven male lyric poets.

Reynolds, Margaret, ed. *The Sappho Companion*. New York: Palgrave, 2001. Contains narratives of the way societies in different times have accepted or rejected Sappho's works. Includes an introduction as well as translations of the fragments of the poems, a bibliography, and an index.

Snyder, Jane McIntosh. *The Woman and the Lyre: Women Writers in Classical Greece and Rome*. Carbondale: Southern Illinois University Press, 1989. Informative introduction to Sappho and eight female lyric poets of classical antiquity, with representative translations.

Snyder, Jane McIntosh, and Camille-Yvette Welsch. *Sappho*. Philadelphia: Chelsea House, 2005. A woman-centered perspective on Sappho that looks at whether Sappho was a lesbian and how she related to other women.

Yatromanolakis, Dimitrios. *Sappho in the Making: The Early Reception*. Washington, D.C.: Center for Hellenic Studies, Trustees for Harvard University, 2007. An examination of Sappho and the world around her, examining how it shaped her poetry and how poetry was viewed.

Evelyn S. Newlyn

FRIEDRICH SCHILLER

Born: Marbach, Württemberg (now in Germany); November 10, 1759

Died: Weimar, Saxe-Weimar (now in Germany); May 9, 1805

PRINCIPAL POETRY

Anthologie auf das Jahr 1782, 1782

Xenien, 1796 (with Johann Wolfgang von Goethe)

Gedichte, 1800, 1803

The Poems of Schiller, 1851

The Ballads and Shorter Poems of Fredrick V. Schiller, 1901

OTHER LITERARY FORMS

Although Friedrich Schiller (SHIHL-ur) wrote poetry throughout most of his life, the bulk of his oeuvre belongs to other genres. He became especially famous for his powerful dramatic works. Among the most important of his ten major plays are *Die Räuber* (pb. 1781; *The Robbers*, 1792), *Don Carlos, Infant von Spanien* (pr., pb. 1787; *Don Carlos, Infante of Spain*, 1798), *Maria Stuart* (pr. 1800; *Mary Stuart*, 1801), and *Wilhelm Tell* (pr., pb. 1804; *William Tell*, 1841). During the early part of his career, his writings brought him little income, and poverty forced him to turn to fiction for a broader audience. *Der Verbrecher aus verlorener Ehre* (1786; *The Criminal in Consequence of Lost Reputation*, 1841) and the serialized novel *Der Geisterseher* (1789; *The Ghost-Seer: Or, The Apparitionist*, 1795) were among the most successful of these endeavors. While a professor of history at the University of Jena, Schiller wrote a number of historical books and essays, and during the early 1790's, he published a variety of theoretical and philosophical studies on aesthetics, ethics, and literature. His "Uber die ästhetische Erziehung des Menschen" ("On the Aesthetic Education of Man") and "Über naive und sentimentalische Dichtung" ("On Naïve and Sentimental Poetry") are among the most significant treatises on literature and art written in Germany during the second half of the eighteenth century. His extensive correspondence with Johann Wolfgang von Goethe is the high point in the several volumes of his letters that have been collected and published since his death.

ACHIEVEMENTS

Although most of Friedrich Schiller's verse was written for a highly intellectual audience, it also enjoyed popular success. His "thought poems" laid the groundwork for the ensuing development of the poetry of ideas and brought him rightful recognition as Germany's most important eighteenth century composer of philosophical lyrics. On the other hand, his didactic purpose and his capacity for evoking moods akin to those of folk literature, especially in his ballads, made Schiller also a poet of the common people.

Schiller's poems and other writings were quickly recognized for their quality by the German literary establishment and were published in the significant periodicals of the time. Supported by Christoph Martin Wieland and Johann Gottfried Herder, Schiller became an important force among the artistic giants in Weimar, even before his friendship with Goethe. During the decade of their poetic collaboration, Schiller joined Goethe in shaping literary attitudes, approaches, and forms that influenced German poets and determined the nature of German letters from that time onward.

Even in his own time, however, some of Schiller's

Friedrich Schiller (Library of Congress)

poetic works were highly controversial. The so-called Epigram War that he and Goethe waged against their critics was evidence that his works were not universally well received. After his death, Schiller's reputation in critical circles waned in direct relationship to the increased advocacy of realism and, eventually, naturalism. Near the turn of the century, a Schiller renaissance began on two levels. Writers such as Stefan George and Hugo von Hofmannsthal, who advocated a return to classical literary values, praised Schiller for his poetic models of idealism and beauty. Among the common people, such poems as "Das Lied von der Glocke" ("The Song of the Bell") were memorized in school, exposing a new generation of German youth to Schiller's thought. Although he was overshadowed by Goethe in pure poetic endowment, Schiller's impact on the whole of German literature is such that the renowned Thomas Mann called his works the "apotheosis of art."

BIOGRAPHY

The early life of Johann Christoph Friedrich von Schiller was shaped by two powerful influences: the

Swabian Pietism of his origins, and the "benevolent" despotism of Karl Eugen, duke of Württemberg. After serving as a lieutenant in Bavarian, French, and Swabian regiments, Schiller's father was rewarded with an appointment as superintendent of the duke's gardens and plantations. Although Schiller's parents had planned for him to enter the ministry, those intentions were frustrated when the duke insisted that he be enrolled in a military academy at Stuttgart in 1773. After a brief and inconclusive period of legal studies at the academy, Schiller left the institution to become a medical officer in Karl Eugen's army. His dislike of the school's restrictions contributed substantially to the attacks on tyranny prevalent in his early writings.

Schiller's first poem was published in a Swabian literary magazine in 1776, and others appeared there and elsewhere during the remainder of his school years. Two months after his graduation, he rented a room from a widow, Luise Vischer, whom critics long regarded as the model for his Laura odes. While still in Stuttgart, Schiller wrote his first play, *The Robbers*. It premiered in Mannheim in January, 1782, and Schiller traveled, without the duke's permission, to attend the opening performance. Following Schiller's second secret theater visit to Mannheim, Karl Eugen placed him under two weeks' arrest and forbade him to write. The arrival of the Russian czar in Stuttgart took Karl Eugen's attention away from Schiller, and the latter fled to Mannheim.

Existence in Mannheim was a constant struggle for the young Schiller. His literary efforts brought him little monetary profit, and he survived only through the help of his friends. When the manager of the Mannheim theater refused to renew his contract as house dramatist, Schiller published a literary journal in an effort to straighten out his fiscal affairs. The emotional strain caused by his precarious economic condition and his unsuccessful encounters with women during those years is reflected in the poetry that he wrote after leaving Stuttgart. Not until he was rescued from financial disaster by Gottfried Körner and other admirers in 1784 did Schiller's personal life gain stability sufficient to foster the harmonious mastery of thought and form that typifies his more mature lyric creations. The friendship with Körner was a direct stimulus for the famous poem

"An die Freude" ("Ode to Joy"), which Beethoven used for the choral movement of his Ninth Symphony.

A major turning point in Schiller's life came in 1787, after he had spent two relatively carefree years in Körner's household in Dresden. Disappointed by an unrewarding relationship with Henriette von Arnim, Schiller left Dresden for Weimar. There, he renewed an acquaintance with Charlotte von Kalb, the unhappy wife of an army major. Her friendship had created emotional problems for him in Mannheim, but she now introduced him into philosophical circles in Jena that influenced his life for years. In Weimar, he also made contact with Wieland and Herder, whose favor gave him access to the court.

In 1788, Schiller met Johann Wolfgang von Goethe for the first time. Although no close relationship developed at the time, Goethe soon recommended him for a professorship in history at the University of Jena. The stable situation provided by an annual income allowed Schiller to marry Charlotte von Lengefeld in 1790. His professional involvement in the years that followed reduced his poetic activity but moved him to concern himself more extensively with the philosophy of Immanuel Kant. His philosophical studies ultimately had a major impact on his creative work. In Jena, during the winter of 1790-1791, Schiller experienced the first attacks of the tuberculosis that eventually caused his death.

The most artistically productive period of Schiller's life began in the summer of 1794 when Goethe agreed to collaborate with him in the editing of a new journal. The intimate friendship that arose between the two authors provided them with mutual stimulus and gave rise to timeless masterworks of poetry and drama. Friendly competition between them in 1797 and 1798 yielded some of the most famous ballads in German literature. Also in 1797, the last of Schiller's historical writings was completed, winning for him membership in the Swedish Academy of Sciences. During the final years of his life, Schiller was feverishly active, writing the best of his mature plays, adapting works by William Shakespeare, Louis Picard, Gotthold Ephraim Lessing, and Goethe, traveling, and gathering new dramatic materials in defiance of the malady that slowly destroyed him. Newly completed lines for "Demetrius," an unfin-

ished play that might have become his greatest masterpiece, were found lying on his desk on the day he died.

ANALYSIS

In his essay "On Naïve and Sentimental Poetry," written soon after he began collaborating with Goethe, Friedrich Schiller outlined and clarified the characteristics of two kinds of poetic art, attempting to defend his own creative approach in the careful justification of "sentimental" literature. In contrast to the naïve poet, whose work is an expression of nature, Schiller's modern lyricist is a reflective creator who seeks to regain in his poetry a natural state that has been lost. The naïve poet moves the reader through an artistic presentation of sensual reality, while the sentimental poet achieves his effect in the successful development of ideas. Throughout Schiller's literary career, the conceptual tension between "naïve" and "sentimental," couched variously in the polarities of nature and culture, real and ideal, ancient and modern, and substance and form, remained the key to his poetic endeavor. Each new poem represented a concerted effort to create through art a harmonious resolution of the perpetual conflict between these fundamental aspects of humanity's existence.

ANTHOLOGIE AUF DAS JAHR 1782

The poetry of Schiller's youth is especially interesting for its clear illumination of the broad spectrum of eighteenth century literary forces that molded his attitudes. In the *Anthologie auf das Jahr 1782*, which was published to counteract what Schiller saw as the smarmy bent of other Swabian collections of the time, there are poems that reflect such diverse influences as the pathos of Friedrich Klopstock's odes, the Anacreontic tendencies of the early Enlightenment, Gottfried August Bürger's massive realism, Albrecht von Haller's philosophical lyrics, the political tendentiousness of Christian Friedrich Daniel Schubart, Christoph Wieland's Rococo style, and the purposeful tastelessness of Storm and Stress. Although personal encounters provided immediate stimuli for some of the works, the calculated refinement of perceptions through the process of reflection sets the philosophical tone of Schiller's verse from the outset.

The naïve/sentimental dichotomy is visible in two characteristic forms in Schiller's early poetry. "Der

Eroberer" ("The Conqueror") exemplifies Schiller's juxtaposition of political and divine order in the concept of the "noble criminal," an almost mythical figure who goes beyond the limits of conventional morality. The conquering tyrant emerges as the adversary of God and the destroyer of moral order. In the Laura odes, however, which are central to the lyrics of Schiller's youth, the focus of poetic tension is the tortuous conflict between love's physical and spiritual dimensions. By 1780, in direct response to the writings of Adam Ferguson and under the mediated influence of Francis Hutcheson and the philosopher Anthony Ashley-Cooper, the third earl of Shaftesbury, Schiller had developed a personal metaphysics in which love is the binding force that holds the world together. The Laura odes and poems such as "Der Triumph der Liebe" ("The Triumph of Love") constitute the major literary treatments of those ideas.

A TRANSITIONAL PERIOD

The years immediately following the publication of the *Anthologie auf das Jahr 1782* were a transitional period in Schiller's growth as a lyric poet. In the lines of "Der Kampf" ("The Struggle") and "Resignation," the poet broadened the basic themes of his earlier works. While exploring in depth the conflict between humanity's right to joy and the reality of a tear-filled existence, he questioned the validity of God's justice in forcing humans to choose between earthly pleasure and spiritual peace. Some of the lyrics written between 1782 and 1788 examine the possibility of achieving a harmony between the polar forces that act on humans; other poems conclude with terrible finality that the only alternatives, pleasure in this world or hope of peace in the world to come, are mutually exclusive. Only the famous "Ode to Joy," which praises the harmony between God and a glorified world in a profound affirmation of earthly existence, forms a distinct anomaly in the otherwise troubled reflection that typifies the verse produced during this period of Schiller's life.

The major poetic works of Schiller's mature years, beginning with the first version of "Die Götter Griechenlands" ("The Gods of Greece"), written in 1788, and ending with "Das Siegesfest" ("The Victory Celebration"), composed in 1803, offer a more calmly ordered, evenly balanced, and formally perfected presentation of the fundamental Schillerian dichotomies than can be found in the emotionally charged poems of the early 1780's. With increasing emphasis on natural order as an answer to the problems of civilized society, Schiller attempts to resolve the tension between the ideal and the real. Instead of seeking to establish an internal harmony between the spiritual and physical elements of humanity, he tries in the later poems to move his reader to accept an external creation of the desired metaphysical unity in art. The appropriate models for the new synthesis were to be found in the artistic and literary legacy of the ancients. Schiller's most powerful philosophical poems present the search for a golden age of accord between rational humans and nature and the need to regain that state through reflection.

FROM EPIGRAM TO BALLAD TO THOUGHT POEM

It is important to understand that these writings are not simply versified philosophy. In Schiller's eyes, the poet differs from the philosopher in not being required to prove his assertions. Instead, the poet employs a variety of devices to convey his message on several levels of perception, at once teaching and moving the reader through his own personal enthusiasm. To achieve his purpose, Schiller masterfully cultivated a variety of poetic forms, ranging from the epigram to the ballad to the highly stylized "thought poem."

As a consciously developed form, the epigram is a special phenomenon of the collaboration between Schiller and Goethe. It is a particularly powerful genre for Schiller. His epigrams are basically of two kinds: satirical and purely philosophical. The sharply barbed satirical poems focus on poets, thinkers, and critics of his time, especially those who attacked Schiller and Goethe, as well as the literary movements and specific currents of thought that they represented. Epigrams in the other group, primarily the "Votivtafeln" ("Votive Inscriptions"), are more general in focus and didactic in purpose.

Schiller's ballads, which are also important documents of his friendship with Goethe, represent more clearly than the epigrams the general tendency of classical German poetry to seek and establish the harmony between the ideal and the real. In that regard, they are especially clear illustrations of Schiller's aesthetics. Many of them follow a pattern established in 1795 in

"Das verschleierte Bild zu Sais" ("The Veiled Image at Sais") and are best described as lyrically narrated parables that resolve the poet's metaphysical conflicts by appealing to the natural nobility of the human soul. A second type of ballad, exemplified by "Die Kraniche des Ibykus" ("The Cranes of Ibycus"), addresses itself to art's ethical and moral purposes, employing the elements of legend to achieve its goals. The ballads are the most readable of Schiller's lyric works, simply because they benefit from his mastery of drama.

Among the poems of Schiller's final creative period are some of the most extraordinarily beautiful "thought poems" in German. While stressing the inherent interdependency of ethics and aesthetics, Schiller dealt with basic existential questions such as suffering, death, transience, the quest for truth, and the perception of the absolute. In poems such as the lovely "Nänie" ("Nenia"), written in 1796, he arrived at a final answer to questions posed in his early lyrics, replacing hopelessness and resignation with the achievement in art of a timeless unity of humanity's real and ideal dimensions.

THE LAURA ODES

In 1781, Schiller published "Die Entzückung an Laura" ("Rapture, to Laura") in Gotthold Stäudlin's *Schwäbischer Musenalmanach auf das Jahr 1782* (Swabian almanac of the muses for the year 1782). It was the first of six poems that have since become known as the Laura odes. The other five—"Phantasie an Laura" ("Fantasy, to Laura"), "Laura am Klavier" ("Laura at the Piano"), "Vorwurf an Laura" ("Reproach, to Laura"), "Das Geheimnis der Reminiscenz" ("The Mystery of Reminiscence"), and "Melancholie an Laura" ("Melancholy, to Laura")—appeared for the first time in Schiller's *Anthologie auf das Jahr 1782*. As a group, these poems present Schiller's metaphysics of love. They are a product of creative reflection rather than intimate experience. When Schiller left the military academy, he had in fact had few encounters with women, and all his early works reveal a lack of realistic perception of the opposite sex.

"Rapture, to Laura" sets the tone for the odes in its portrayal of love as a force that links the real world with the cosmic realm of absolutes. Schiller employs well-developed images of sight and sound as the outward manifestations of love, with visual contacts playing an especially important role in the communication of feeling. The gaze and what the poet can see in the eyes of his imagined Laura transform him, granting him the ability to move from his own reality into the ideal domain symbolized by the young woman. The last stanza of the poem defines her glances and the love that they represent as a clearly comprehended creative influence that has the power to vivify even inanimate stone.

The external tension between the physical and the spiritual receives special emphasis in the lyric structure of "Fantasy, to Laura," in which bodily and mental activities are juxtaposed in alternate stanzas and lines. As in all the Laura odes, the two realms are bonded together through the force of love, without which the world would disintegrate into mechanical chaos. This poem, however, emphasizes the unresolved parallelism between sexual love, presented in the literary formulations of Storm and Stress, and the philosophical love of Enlightenment thought, causing the concept of love as such to remain somewhat ambiguous.

In "Laura at the Piano," Schiller developed a more precise representation of love as a metaphysical phenomenon. Consistent with his ultimate goal of natural harmony, love appears not so much as a personal experience with the feminine, but as a manifestation of the creative power of the masculine through which man masters all the cosmos. The dual character of love thus comes to symbolize the opposed forces of chaos and creation that mold the universe. A key to Schiller's message in "Laura at the Piano" lies once more in Laura's ability, through her very presence, to move her lover into a unified transcendent realm. The scope of this act is divine, and her being emerges as a subtle "proof" for the existence of God.

The notion of conflicting polarities is so basic to the Laura poems that even love has its own antagonist: death. Schiller's manner of coming to grips with the latter accords the odes a distinct kinship with his early elegies, including "Elegie auf den Tod eines Jünglings" ("Elegy to the Death of a Young Man") and "Trauer-Ode" ("Ode of Mourning"). In "Melancholy, to Laura," the death motif receives its most powerful illumination in the baroque imagery of the beloved's decay. Laura is presented here as a symbol for the entirety of earthly existence, which rests on "mouldering bones." Even her beauty is not immune to the ravages of death. In the struggle between the optimism of love and the finality of death, death triumphs, devaluating mortality as it ends all human striving for happiness. This conclusion anticipates the pessimistic mood of the famous poem "Resignation." Although not specifically dedicated to Laura, "Resignation" may be regarded as the thematic culmination of the ideas presented in the odes, a culmination that is encapsulated in a single stanza of the lengthy poem. There, in harshly vivid imagery, the poet tears his Laura bleeding from his heart and gives her to the relentless judge, eternity, in payment for the hope of peace beyond the grave.

Perhaps the most interesting symbol of death in "Resignation" appears in the poem's second stanza in the silent god who extinguishes the poet's torch. He is a precursor of more carefully refined images that Schiller based on models from Greek and Roman antiquity and employed in the powerful philosophical lyrics of his classical period. This personification of death signals a transition that occurred in the poet's creative orientation during the mid-1780's. By the time the first version of "The Gods of Greece" was printed in Wieland's periodical *Der teutsche Merkur*, Schiller had abandoned his metaphysics of love in favor of a poetic search for humankind's lost golden age. The characteristics of this new approach are a juxtapostion of the ancient and modern worlds, renewal of classical aesthetic and ethical values, and an appeal for the creation of a unity of sensual and spiritual experience in art.

"THE GODS OF GREECE"

The two variants of "The Gods of Greece," published in 1788 and 1793, respectively, have in common their focus on the concept of beauty. In the first version, Schiller presented a justification of sensual beauty, couching his arguments in a defense of ancient polytheism against modern monotheism and rationalism. The Christian God in his roles of avenger, judge, and rational defender of truth is too strict for the natural world. For that reason, Schiller advocated return to an order of existence based on feeling. From the notion that the Greek gods symbolize divine perfection in things earthly, a kind of theophany informs the world created by the poem, although the second rendering places heavier emphasis on the timelessness of beauty.

The carefully nurtured inner tension of "The Gods of Greece" derives from its dual nature. It is at once a lament for the loss of humankind's earlier existence in nature and a song of praise for the potential immanence of the ideal within the real. In the past for which the poet longs, a closer harmony existed between the physical and spiritual realms, because the gods were more human and humans more divine. When the old gods were driven away by reason, however, they took with them everything of beauty and majesty, leaving the world colorless, empty, and devoid of spirit. The final lines of the respective versions offer two different resolutions of the problem. In the first, the poet issues a simple plea for the return of the mild goddess, beauty. The final form of the poem places the responsibility for beauty's timeless preservation squarely in the lap of the creative artist. Next to Goethe's drama *Iphigenie auf Tauris* (pr. 1779; *Iphigenia in Tauris*, 1793), "The Gods of Greece" in its two versions is the most important document of Germanized Greek mythology in classical German literature.

BALLADS

Most of Schiller's poems reflect the instructional orientation of his literary work as a whole. Early in his career, Schiller forcefully acknowledged the author's responsibility to move his reader toward personal, moral, and ethical improvement. The ballads that he wrote after 1795 are among the most successful didactic lyrics in all German literature. They are masterful combinations of simplicity and clarity with vivid, engaging sensual imagery. The parabolic ballads, among them "Der Taucher" ("The Diver"), "Der Handschuh" ("The Glove"), "Der Kampf mit dem Drachen" ("The Battle with the Dragon"), and "Die Bürgschaft" ("The Pledge"), reveal the inherent nobility of the human soul when tested in circumstances that threaten life itself. Each presents a variation on the problem of the individual's response to extraordinary challenge or temptation, laying bare the inner motivations for action and glorifying the deed that is based on ideal and principle rather than on material gain. In "The Diver," the implications and consequences of free will are central to the story of a young man who retrieves from the sea a golden chalice, its own reward for the daredevil act, then perishes in a second venture, when the prize is the king's lovely daughter. "The Battle with the Dragon" explores the dilemma of choice between noble intent and obedience. A heroic knight defies the command of his order's leader and slays a terrible monster that has ravaged the countryside. He then meekly accepts expulsion from the order as the penalty for disobedience, thereby redeeming himself. Friendship as a moral force is the primary focus of "The Pledge," Schiller's rendering of the famous Greek legend of Damon and Pythias.

Typically, the verse parables have a two-part structure that pairs an obviously rash, foolish, and dangerous act with a reasoned deed of noble sacrifice through which the central figure ascends to a higher moral plane. In the popular ballad "The Glove," the Knight Delorges is asked by Kunigunde to retrieve her glove from the arena, where she has purposely dropped it among bloodthirsty beasts of prey. Delorges demonstrates his stature as a man, not when he faces the tiger to obtain the glove, but when he subsequently rejects Kunigunde's favors. It is not physical courage but the spiritual act of overcoming self that provides the measure of personal worth in this and similar ballads.

"THE CRANES OF IBYCUS"

Like the parable poems, "The Cranes of Ibycus" is a dramatic, didactic short story in verse form. Its orientation, however, differs markedly from that of the works that stress the importance of heroic self-mastery. In its examination and defense of art as an active moral force in society, "The Cranes of Ibycus" forms a bridge between the ballads and Schiller's more abstract philosophical lyrics, while providing a concise vindication of his own approach to the drama. The ballad describes the murder of Ibycus by two men. A flock of cranes flying overhead witnesses the crime and later reappears over an outdoor theater where the criminals sit watching a play. Caught up in the mood of the drama, the criminals forget themselves and respond to the sight of the cranes, thereby revealing themselves to the crowd. More than a simple examination of problems of guilt and atonement, the lyric work juxtaposes audience reaction to stage events with the behavior of the villain-spectators to shatter the border between theater and reality. The scene is transformed into a tribunal that has the power to bring criminals to justice, thereby influencing events in the external world.

"THE SONG OF THE BELL"

Schiller's most famous ballad, "The Song of the Bell," is also the most ambitious of his poetic works. In some 425 lines of verse, the poet projects the broad spectrum of humankind's mortal existence against the background of the magnificent bell's creation. Alternating stanzas of varying length parallel the process of casting the bell with characteristic events of life. Birth and death, joy and tragedy, accomplishment and destruction—all find their symbolic counterparts in the steps taken by the artisans to produce a flawless artifact. The imagery is vividly real, earthy, and natural, presenting the everyday world in a practical frame with which the reader readily identifies. At the same time, the stylized presentation successfully underscores the possibility of harmony between humans' physical environment and the ideal domain of the mind.

In many respects, "The Song of the Bell" represents the culmination of Schiller's poetic art. The effective integration of the poem's two threads of description and discussion is a clear realization of the creative unity that he sought to achieve in all his literary works. In his classical ballads, Schiller at last achieved the resolution of tensions caused by the opposing forces that play on humans as they search for personal meaning. Like "The Cranes of Ibycus," "The Song of the Bell" assigns to art an ultimate responsibility for humans' attainment of peace through productive interactions between their absolute and their temporal essence. The finished bell's very name, Concordia, symbolizes the final accord of material and spiritual values that was for Schiller the goal of both literature and life.

OTHER MAJOR WORKS

LONG FICTION: *Der Verbrecher aus verlorener Ehre*, 1786 (also pb. as *Der Verbrecher aus Infamie*; *The Criminal, in Consequence of Lost Reputation*, 1841); *Der Geisterseher*, 1789 (*The Ghost-Seer: Or, The Apparitionist*, 1795).

PLAYS: *Die Räuber*, pb. 1781 (*The Robbers*, 1792); *Die Verschwörung des Fiesko zu Genua*, pr., pb. 1783 (*Fiesco: Or, The Genoese Conspiracy*, 1796); *Kabale und Liebe*, pr., pb. 1784 (*Cabal and Love*, 1795); *Don Carlos, Infant von Spanien*, pr., pb. 1787 (*Don Carlos, Infante of Spain*, 1798); *Wallensteins Lager*, pr. 1798

(*The Camp of Wallenstein*, 1846); *Die Piccolomini*, pr. 1799 (*The Piccolominis*, 1800); *Wallenstein*, pr. 1799 (trilogy includes *The Camp of Wallenstein*, *The Piccolominis*, and *The Death of Wallenstein*); *Wallensteins Tod*, pr. 1799 (*The Death of Wallenstein*, 1800); *Maria Stuart*, pr. 1800 (*Mary Stuart*, 1801); *Die Jungfrau von Orleans*, pr. 1801 (*The Maid of Orleans*, 1835); *Die Braut von Messina: Oder, Die feindlichen Brüder*, pr., pb. 1803 (*The Bride of Messina*, 1837); *Wilhelm Tell*, pr., pb. 1804 (*William Tell*, 1841); *Historical Dramas*, 1847; *Early Dramas and Romances*, 1849; *Dramatic Works*, 1851.

NONFICTION: *Die Schaubühne als eine moralische Anstalt betrachtet*, 1784 (*The Theater as a Moral Institution*, 1845); *Historischer Kalender für Damen*, 1790, 1791; *Geschichte des dreissigjährigen Krieges*, 1791-1793 (3 volumes; *History of the Thirty Years War*, 1799); *Über den Grund des Vergnügens an tragischen Gegenständen*, 1792 (*On the Pleasure in Tragic Subjects*, 1845); *Über Anmut und Würde*, 1793 (*On Grace and Dignity*, 1845); *Über das Pathetische*, 1793 (*On the Pathetic*, 1845); *Briefe über die ästhetische Erziehung des Menschen*, 1795 (*On the Aesthetic Education of Man*, 1845); *Über naïve und sentimentalische Dichtung*, 1795-1796 (*On Naïve and Sentimental Poetry*, 1845); *Über das Erhabene*, 1801 (*On the Sublime*, 1845); *Briefwechsel Zwischen Schiller und Goethe*, 1829 (*The Correspondence Between Schiller and Goethe*, 1845); *Aesthetical and Philosophical Essays*, 1845; *Schillers Briefwechsel mit Körner von 1784 bis zum Tode Schillers*, 1847 (*Schiller's Correspondence with Körner*, 1849).

MISCELLANEOUS: *Sämmtliche Werke*, 1812-1815 (12 volumes; *Complete Works in English*, 1870).

BIBLIOGRAPHY

Carlyle, Thomas. *The Life of Friedrich Schiller*. 1825. Reprint. Columbia, S.C.: Camden House, 1992. A biography of Schiller by a contemporary historian and essayist. An excellent resource on Schiller's life and work. Includes bibliographical references and index. With new introduction by Jeffrey L. Sammons.

Goethe, Johann Wolfgang von. *Correspondence Between Goethe and Schiller (1794-1805)*. Translated by Liselotte Dieckmann. New York: Peter Lang, 1994. A collection of letters that offers insight into the lives and works of Schiller and Goethe. Includes bibliographical references and index.

Kerry, Paul E., ed. *Friedrich Schiller: Playwright, Poet, Philosopher, Historian*. New York: Peter Lang, 2007. This collection contains essays examining Schiller's poetry and its effect on later German poets.

Kostka, Edmund. *Schiller in Italy: Schiller's Reception in Italy—Nineteenth and Twentieth Centuries*. New York: Peter Lang, 1997. Kostka's comprehensive study expands and deepens the understanding of the German-Italian relationship during the past two centuries. The impact of Schiller's work on Italian poets, critics, musicians, and conspirators is evaluated against the history of the military upheaval in Europe.

Martinson, Steven D. *A Companion to the Works of Friedrich Schiller*. Rochester, N.Y.: Camden House, 2005. This collection of essays about Schiller includes in-depth discussions about his literary works as well as the impact he had on twentieth century Germany.

_____. *Harmonious Tensions: The Writings of Friedrich Schiller*. Newark: University of Delaware Press, 1996. A critical interpretation of selected writing by Schiller. Includes bibliographical references and index.

Pilling, Claudia. *Schiller (Life and Times)*. London: Haus Books, 2005. A biography of Schiller that uses his correspondence, along with modern records, to place him in late eighteenth century Germany, confronting a changing middle class. Includes several color and black-and-white illustrations throughout.

Reed, T. J. *Schiller*. New York: Oxford University Press, 1991. A biography of the German writer that sheds light on his writing of dramas. Bibliography and index.

Sharpe, Lesley. *Friedrich Schiller: Drama, Thought, and Politics*. New York: Cambridge University Press, 1991. Part of the Cambridge Studies in German series, this scholarly study looks at Schiller's views and how they infused his drama and other works. Bibliography and index.

Lowell A. Bangerter

GEORGE SEFERIS
Giorgos Stylianou Seferiades

Born: Smyrna, Ottoman Empire (now İzmir,
   Turkey); March 13, 1900 (old style, February 29,
   1900)
Died: Athens, Greece; September 20, 1971

PRINCIPAL POETRY

Strophe, 1931 (*Turning Point*, 1967)
E sterna, 1932 (*The Cistern*, 1967)
Mythistorema, 1935 (English translation, 1960)
Gymnopaidia, 1936 (English translation, 1967)
Emerologio katastromatos I, 1940 (*Logbook I*,
   1960)
Tetradio gymnasmaton, 1940 (*Book of Exercises*,
   1967)
Emerologio katastromatos II, 1944 (*Logbook II*,
   1960)
Kichle, 1947 (*Thrush*, 1967)
Emerologio katastromatos III, 1955 (*Logbook III*,
   1960)
Poems, 1960 (includes *Mythistorema*, *Logbook I, II*,
   and *III*)
Tria krypha poiemata, 1966 (*Three Secret Poems*,
   1969)
Collected Poems, 1967, 1981, 1995 (includes
   Turning Point, *The Cistern*, *Gymnopaidia*, *Book
   of Exercises*, *Thrush*, and others)

OTHER LITERARY FORMS

George Seferis (seh-FEHR-ees) earned distinction
as a literary critic and translator in addition to his
achievements as a poet. His collection of essays, *Dokimes* (1947), is regarded as one of the finest volumes
of modern Greek literary criticism. His other principal
prose works include *Treis meres sta monasteria tes
Kappadokias* (1953; three days in the monasteries of
Cappadocia), *Delphi* (1962; English translation, 1963),
Discours de Stockholm (1964), and *'E glossa stèn
poiésé mas* (1965). A selection of his essays was published in English as *On the Greek Style: Selected Essays in Poetry and Hellenism* (1966). Seferis translated
T. S. Eliot's *The Waste Land* (1922) and *Murder in the*

Cathedral (1935; as *Phoniko stèn ekklesia*) into Greek,
an achievement called "brilliant." Following Eliot's
death in 1965, Seferis published a brief commemorative diary of their friendship. Seferis also "transcribed,"
as he put it, the biblical Song of Songs and the Revelation of Saint John the Divine into modern language. Finally, Seferis's *A Poet's Journal: Days of 1945-1951*
was published in English in 1974.

ACHIEVEMENTS

George Seferis initiated a new spirit in Greek poetry
with the publication, in 1931, of his first book, *Turning
Point*. Influenced by the styles of French and English
poets, Seferis freed his verse from the excessive orna-
mentation that then encumbered Greek poetry, creating
a simple, direct style in the modern idiom and bringing
Greek poetry into a closer relationship with the modernism of Western Europe. Insisting that poetry should
be written in the language of everyday speech, he exploited the forms, themes, and diction of folk verse.
Very much aware of his heritage, he integrated the mythology and history of Greece with the situation of his
country and of humanity in general in the twentieth
century. Like Eliot, Seferis weaves a complex tapestry
of allusion in deceptively simple language; like Eliot,
he universalizes his profound sense of alienation, so
that his poetry, though distinctively Greek, speaks to
readers of all nationalities. The Greek sense of tragedy
that informs Seferis's work is not out of place in the
twentieth century.

BIOGRAPHY

George Seferis was born Giorgos Stylianou Seferiades
in Smyrna (now İzmir), Turkey. The city was largely
populated by Greeks then, and Seferis's memories of it
served as an inspiration to him for the rest of his life. It
was in Smyrna that he wrote his first poetry, at the age
of fourteen. Shortly thereafter World War I began, and
the Seferiades family left for Athens. There, Seferis
continued his secondary schooling at the First Classical
Gymnasium and graduated in 1917. His father, who
also wrote a few poems and made a few translations,
was an expert on international law and became a professor at the University of Athens in 1919. Seferis set
out to follow in his father's footsteps, studying law at

George Seferis (©The Nobel Foundation)

the Sorbonne in Paris from 1918 to 1924. During this period, he became familiar with French poetry, especially the works of Paul Valéry, Jules Laforgue, and other Symbolists, while continuing to write a few poems of his own.

After obtaining his degree at the Sorbonne, Seferis spent a year in London; anticipating a career in the Greek foreign service, he hoped to perfect his English. Thus, seven crucial years in Seferis's young manhood were spent away from Greece. In 1922, while Seferis was abroad, the city of Smyrna was burned and the Greek population there displaced. The "home" to which he had clung in his memories had ceased to exist, and he began to see himself in an Odyssean light, as a wanderer in search of home. After his return to Athens, he began a long career as a diplomat, working in the Ministry of Foreign Affairs. While serving as vice-consul in London in 1931, he first became acquainted with the works of Eliot and Ezra Pound, which would play an

important role in the development of his art. In the same year, he also published his first book of poetry, *Turning Point*, a volume that heralded the beginning of a new generation of poetry in Greece. His second volume, *The Cistern*, appeared in 1932; then, between 1934 and 1936, while Seferis was living in Athens, two more volumes of his poetry were published, *Mythistorema* and *Gymnopaidia*.

From 1936 to 1938, Seferis served as consul in Koritsa, Albania, and then became a press attaché to the Ministry of Foreign Affairs. He married Maria Zannou in 1941. As the Nazis rolled over Greece, Seferis joined the government in exile, spending the war in Cairo, Johannesburg, Pretoria, and Italy. After Greece was liberated, he returned to Athens, receiving the Palamas Prize for Poetry in 1946. He worked there until 1948, when he became consul attached to the Greek embassy in Ankara. In 1951, he was appointed to the same position in London, where he became a personal friend of Eliot. In 1953, he was promoted to ambassador to Lebanon, Syria, Jordan, and Iraq, and took up residence in Beirut. During his three years as ambassador, he visited Cyprus on several occasions, visits that would prove important not only in inspiring his later poetry but also in his diplomatic role as a member of the Greek delegation to the United Nations during the 1957 discussion concerning Cyprus.

Seferis was rewarded for his efforts with the ambassadorship to Great Britain. During his tenure there, he was awarded an honorary doctorate from Cambridge University, and in 1963, a year after he retired, he became the first Greek to receive the Nobel Prize in Literature. Many other awards soon followed, including honorary doctorates from Oxford, Thessaloníki, and Princeton. He was made an honorary foreign member of the American Academy of Arts and Letters and an honorary fellow of the Modern Language Association in 1966. Living in Athens at the end of his life, Seferis published very little, except for his *Three Secret Poems*. In March, 1969, he courageously attacked the Greek military dictatorship in a public statement; in the same year, he published one of his last poems, "The Cats of St. Nicholas," in an anthology of antigovernment poetry and prose, *Eighteen Texts*. He died in the fall of 1971 of complications following an operation for a duodenal ulcer. His funeral provoked a large public demonstration against the ruling junta, with thousands of people shouting "Immortal!" "Freedom!" and "Elections!"

ANALYSIS

George Seferis revitalized Greek poetry and brought it into the mainstream of twentieth century Western poetry. In his work, the long tradition of Greek poetry is wedded to the European avant-garde, producing (in the words of the Nobel Prize committee) a "unique thought and style." As an "orphan" of Smyrna, Seferis experienced at first hand the sense of alienation that characterizes much of the poetry of the twentieth century. The Smyrna he had known was destroyed, and there was no "home" to which he could return; the world was therefore strange and unfamiliar to him, distorted in some fundamental way. Seferis's life as a diplomat perhaps intensified his sense of alienation; at the same time, his wide experience allowed him to transcend individual sorrow to speak to the larger problems of the human condition.

Seferis was keenly interested in the stylistic and tonal experiments of the French Symbolists, especially Valéry and his "pure" poetry. In London, Seferis became acquainted with the poetry of Pound and Eliot, recognizing in their works the next step in the stylistic evolution that he had already begun. He abandoned strict meter and rhyme and avoided any sort of embellishment, keeping his imagery sparse.

Fundamentally, however, Seferis was Greek. His poetry springs from the traditions and heritage of his people, and though he altered substantially the shape of Greek poetry, he always worked from the raw materials provided by Greek folk songs, poetic forms, and mythology. In this approach, one immediately recognizes Seferis's kinship with Pound and Eliot, who also layered their texts with allusions, quotations, and mythological and historical parallels, though Seferis is more scrupulous in his treatment of his sources. He attempted to use the traditional decapentasyllable (a line of fifteen syllables with a caesura after the eighth and main accents on the sixth or eighth and on the fourteenth) in the expression of a contemporary sensibility, though it is the principal meter of folk poetry, dating back to

the Byzantine period. In addition, he was influenced heavily by Cretan literature of the sixteenth and seventeenth centuries, especially the seventeenth century epic romance *Erotokritos*, by Vitzentzos Kornaros. In this work, Seferis saw the possibilities of demotic Greek as a language for poetry. In addition to writing a brilliant commentary on *Erotokritos*, he incorporated phrases from it in his poem "Erotikos Logos," establishing links between the language of modern Greece and the Greek past, much as Eliot incorporates in his verse phrases from Geoffrey Chaucer, William Shakespeare, and numerous other major English authors.

As Lawrence Durrell has written, "When Eliot speaks of 'getting every ounce of tradition behind each word,' one thinks of Seferis, so deeply steeped in the ancient Greek tragedies, and yet so modern in his approach." Fragments of the past litter the landscape, and in attempting to find what they mean, Seferis, like Eliot, finds himself face-to-face with the vacuum at the core of modern existence.

Seferis published little in the last fifteen years of his life. His credo as a poet, at once consciously Greek and consciously international, is concisely stated in *A Poet's Journal*: "The free man, the just man, the man who is the 'measure' of life; if there is one basic idea in Hellenism, it is this one." Seferis's vision is dark, full of suffering and haunted by a sense of estrangement, but it is redeemed by his humanistic faith that man is the "measure" of life.

TURNING POINT AND THE CISTERN

Turning Point and *The Cistern*, Seferis's first two collections, marked a dramatic departure from the Decadent-derived poetry of the 1920's. Readers recognized in Seferis a different voice with something new to say. The poetry was stark, "Doric," but filled with original and surprising imagery. Seferis later commented that when he published *Turning Point*, he was aware of two things: He knew that he wanted to write simple poetry, and he knew that people would not like it. Seferis had not yet discovered the creative possibilities of free verse, and despite the demotic, conversational quality of the two collections, they show a careful attention to rhyme and meter. The characteristic starkness and sharpness of Seferis's work is already apparent in the first stanza of "Turning Point": "Moment, sent by a hand/ I had loved so much,/ you reached me just at sunset/ like a black pigeon." Consisting of only seventeen words (in the original Greek), the stanza is strongly evocative, emotionally powerful, yet finally enigmatic. As Peter Levi has observed, "There is a level at which the language of Seferis is simple, but with the apparent simplicity of ballads and chronicles, which is not simple at all."

This deceptive simplicity is further illustrated by the long poem "Erotikos logos," which is included in *Turning Point*. Composed of decapentasyllables in stanzas of four lines, the poem ends with the words, "The world is simple." Like Seferis's verse, which strives to appear simple yet is not, the world itself is simple yet opaque. In one sense, each line of the poem is clear, but if one tries to pin down the meaning of a given line or phrase, one finds oneself in a labyrinth of inferences, connotations, and allusions whose relationships to one another are as complex as the relationships among things in the world. Life is ultimately a mystery, out of human control, and pretensions to understand it (its "simplicity") finally only confirm humanity's terminal alienation. The imagery of "The Cistern" expresses this modern sensibility: "We are dying! Our gods are dying!/ The marble statues know it, looking down/ like white dawn upon the victim/ alien, full of eyelids, fragments,/ as the crowds of death pass by."

MYTHISTOREMA

Seferis's third collection, *Mythistorema*, was the first work of his maturity. In this volume, he abandoned strict meter and rhyme to work in his idiosyncratic free verse. Aware of the building political tensions and the rise of totalitarianism in Europe, Seferis conflated Greek myth and history in twenty-four concise poems with disturbingly violent imagery and an extraordinary number of allusions to classical myth and ancient literature. In Seferis's vision, the present is a desolate landscape of fragments. A coherent understanding of it is impossible, and one is left with the mere reverberations of voices from the past, echoes without meaning.

"THE KING OF ASINE"

One of the finest examples of Seferis's mature poetry is "The King of Asine," which ends *Logbook I*. The speaker of the poem relates that he has spent two years seeking the King of Asine, a Mycenaean ruler men-

tioned only once in Homer's *Iliad* (c. 750 B.C.E.; English translation, 1611; book 2, line 560), during the famous catalog of ships. The speaker has found a citadel covered with vines and a long beach, but even the wild doves have gone. He and his party have also found a gold burial mask that, when touched, makes an empty sound: "Hollow in the light/ like a dry jar in dug earth/ the same sound that our oars make in the sea." The King of Asine is a "void under the mask." His children are statues, his desires "the fluttering of birds." Though the mask replicates his face, a dark spot lies behind it—a dark spot symbolic of loss and the "void everywhere with us." Nothing is left but "nostalgia for the weight of a living existence/ there where we now remain unsubstantial. . . ." The poet, too, is a void. Nothing exists behind the words, just as the King of Asine exists only because of two words in Homer. Language itself thus becomes reality; behind it, there is nothing.

BOOK OF EXERCISES AND LOGBOOK II

Before fleeing the German invasion, Seferis published *Book of Exercises*, a collection of poems written between 1928 and 1937 that had not been included in his previous collections. A number of these poems involve a fictional character, Stratis Thalassinos (Stratis the Mariner), a persona used much as Eliot's J. Alfred Prufrock and Pound's Hugh Selwyn Mauberly are used. The collection also includes sixteen haiku, which, although not notably successful, are distinctively Seferis's work. In particular, number 4 expresses his vision of the mystical relationship between past and present: "Is it the voice/ of our dead friends or/ the gramophone?"

Logbook II was written in the various places of Seferis's exile with the Greek government; here, one finds the poet chronicling his wanderings, giving impressions of the many locales, some very exotic, to which his odyssey took him. Stratis Thalassinos appears again; in "Stratis Thalassinos on the Dead Sea," Seferis creates an image of Jerusalem during the war as a city of refugees with a Babel-like confusion of languages. People are shown as having little or no understanding of the city and its past and are led about like tourists with the refrain, "THIS IS THE PLACE GENTLEMEN!" One is reminded of T. S. Eliot's repetition of "HURRY UP PLEASE ITS TIME" in *The Waste Land* and the imagery of "Unreal City," which Eliot derived from Charles Baudelaire.

"LAST STOP"

"Last Stop," written at the last place where Seferis waited before returning to Greece at the war's end, has been called the most significant poem in the collection. His memories are painful, and it is not at all clear to him that the suffering of the war has been justified by the result. Nations lie in ruins, as they have in the past, some of them to be forgotten. Despite this, the poem's closing lines recall a hero who left the hospital with his wounds still open; Seferis quotes this hero's emblematic words: "'We advance in the dark/ we move forward in the dark. . . .'"

OTHER MAJOR WORKS

NONFICTION: *Dokimes*, 1947; *Treis meres sta monasteria tes Kappadokias*, 1953; *Delphi*, 1962 (English translation, 1963); *Discours de Stockholm*, 1964; *'E glossa stèn poiésé mas*, 1965; *On the Greek Style: Selected Essays in Poetry and Hellenism*, 1966; *A Poet's Journal: Days of 1945-1951*, 1974; *A Levant Journal*, 2007.

TRANSLATIONS: *Phoniko stèn ekklesia*, pb. 1935 (of T. S. Eliot's *Murder in the Cathedral*); *T. S. Eliot*, 1936; *Asma asmaton*, 1966 (of *The Song of Songs*); *E Apokalypse tou Ioanne*, 1966 (of *The Apocalypse of St. John*).

BIBLIOGRAPHY

Beaton, Roderick. *George Seferis*. 1991. Reprint. New Haven, Conn.: Yale University Press, 2003. A critical study of selected works by Seferis. Includes bibliographic references.

Hadas, Rachel. *Form, Cycle, Infinity: Landscape Imagery in the Poetry of Robert Frost and George Seferis*. Lewisburg, Pa.: Bucknell University Press, 1985. Compares the literary style and similarities of Robert Frost and Seferis. Includes a bibliography and an index.

Kapre-Karka, K. *Love and the Symbolic Journey in the Poetry of Cavafy, Eliot, and Seferis: An Interpretation with Detailed Poem-by-Poem Analysis*. New York: Pella, 1982. A critical study of selected works by three poets. Includes an index and bibliography.

_____. *War in the Poetry of George Seferis: A Poem-by-Poem Analysis*. New York: Pella, 1985. A critical study of selected works by Seferis. Includes an index and bibliography.

Madias, Markos. *George Seferis: The Strong Wind from the East*. River Vale, N.J.: Cosmos, 1997. A biography, translated from the Greek, of Seferis that looks at the effect of Asia on the writer.

Thaniel, George. *Seferis and Friends*. Toronto, Ont.: Mercury Press, 1994. Entertaining and informative correspondence from Seferis's wide circle of friends and acquaintances, including Henry Miller, T. S. Eliot, and Lawrence Durrell.

Tsatsou, Ioanna, and Jean Demos, trans. *My Brother George Seferis*. St. Paul, Minn.: North Central, 1982. An in-depth biography. Includes index.

J. Madison Davis

JAROSLAV SEIFERT

Born: Prague, Bohemia, Austro-Hungarian Empire (now Czech Republic); September 23, 1901
Died: Prague, Czechoslovakia (now in Czech Republic); January 10, 1986

PRINCIPAL POETRY

Město v slzách, 1921 (*City of Tears*, 1998)
Samá láska, 1923 (*Only Love*, 1990; revised as *Svatební cesta*, 1938; translated as *Honeymoon Ride*, 1990)
Na vlnách TSF, 1925 (*Over the Waves of TSF*, 1990)
Slavík zpívá špatně, 1926 (*The Nightingale Sings Out of Tune*, 1990; also known as *The Nightingale Sings Badly*, 1998)
Poštovní holub, 1929 (*Carrier Pigeon*, 1998)
Jablko z klína, 1933 (*An Apple from Your Lap*, 1998)
Ruce Venušiny, 1936 (*The Hands of Venus*, 1998)
Zpíváno do rotačky, 1936 (*Songs for the Rotary*, 1998)
Jaro, sbohem, 1937, 1942 (*Good-bye, Spring*, 1998)
Osm dní, 1937

Zhasněte světla, 1938

Vějíř Božený Němcové, 1939 (*Božena Němcová's Fan*, 1990)

Světlem oděná, 1940 (*Robed in Light*, 1998)

Kamenný most, 1944

Přilba hlíny, 1945 (*A Helmetful of Earth*, 1998)

Prsten Třeboóské Madoně, 1946, 1966

Ruka a plamen, 1948

Píseó o Viktorce, 1950 (*Song About Viktorka*, 1990)

Koncert na ostrově, 1965 (*Concert on the Island*, 1998)

Halleyova kometta, 1967 (*Halley's Comet*, 1987)

Odlévání zvonů, 1967 (*The Casting of the Bells*, 1983)

Nejkrásnější býacute;vá šílená, 1968

Morový sloup, 1977 (*The Plague Column*, 1979; also known as *The Plague Monument*, 1980)

Deštník z Piccadilly, 1979 (*An Umbrella from Piccadilly*, 1983)

Býti Básníkem, 1983 (*To Be a Poet*, 1990)

The Selected Poetry of Jaroslav Seifert, 1986

Dressed in Light, 1990

The Early Poetry of Jaroslav Seifert, 1997

A Sbohem, 1999

The Poetry of Jaroslav Seifert, 1998

Treba vám nesu ruze, 1999

The Vrtba Garden, 2006 (photographs by Lada Panchartkova)

OTHER LITERARY FORMS

For much of his life, Jaroslav Seifert (ZI-furt) worked as a journalist, and he wrote countless newspaper articles. During the decade after World War II, Seifert was under attack, vilified by the adherents of Socialist Realism, and withdrew from public life. His publications were limited to editing the works of various Czech authors, to translating—his translation of the biblical Song of Songs is outstanding—and to writing poetry for children.

Seifert's memoirs, *Všecky krásy světa* (1981; *Autobiography*, 1985), were first published in Czech in Toronto; a parallel edition under the same title, with minor deletions and alterations, was published shortly afterward in Prague. Seifert also produced children's literature in *Maminka: Yybor básni* (1954; *Maminka*, 1991).

ACHIEVEMENTS

The critic René Wellek once observed, "Lyrical poetry was always the center of Czech literature." One reason for this is that poets have probably expressed the concerns and aspirations of the Czech people better than writers in other genres. Jaroslav Seifert was the author of nearly thirty volumes of poetry, and he won the Nobel Prize in Literature for 1984. He was a member of one of the most remarkable groups of poets in the history of Czech literature, along with Vítězslav Nezval, Konstantin Biebl, František Halas, and Vladimír Holan. They were all born around the turn of the century, began to write when Czechoslovakia gained its independence after World War I, and took part in the numerous literary movements that flourished during the next two decades. They also lived through World War II, which their work records in depth, as well as the imposition of communism on Czechoslovakia. Seifert survived the period of Stalinism, participating in the Prague Spring of 1968. He was honored by the government in 1966 and was named a National Artist; he served as acting chairman of the Union of Czechoslovak writers in 1968; and he was its chairman in 1969-1970. In addition, he received state prizes for his verse in 1936, 1955, and 1968. Holan, Halas, Biebl, and Nezval all died before Seifert; he was the last surviving member of this extremely talented group of poets, dying at the age of eighty-four.

Seifert was remarkably popular in Czechoslovakia, both as a poet and as a symbol of freedom of expression for writers under an oppressive regime. In 1968, he condemned the Soviet invasion of his country and was one of the original signers of the Charter 77 Civil Rights movement.

BIOGRAPHY

Jaroslav Seifert was born in 1901 in Prague, in a working-class neighborhood called Žižkov. Throughout his life, Seifert liked to recall his childhood in this part of Prague with its strong proletarian flavor, many tenements, railroad tracks, taverns, and its own dialect. Seifert's mother was Catholic, his father an atheist and socialist. Although his parents were poor, Seifert was able to attend a *gymnasium* (academic secondary school), from which, however, he was not graduated;

he left the *gymnasium* early and started working as a journalist.

Seifert wrote his first poems during World War I, when the future Czechoslovakia was still a province of the Austro-Hungarian Empire. Czechoslovakia became independent in October, 1918; Seifert was associated with the left wing of the Social Democratic Party and became one of the first members of the Communist Party when it was organized in 1921. Although "workers' poetry" was fashionable at the time, Seifert was one of the few practitioners who actually came from a working-class background.

The evolution of Seifert's poetry in the 1920's and 1930's is almost identical to the general evolution of Czech poetry during the period, proceeding from one major movement to the next. Seifert's friends, especially Karel Teige and Stanislav Neumann, weaned him from his earlier "proletarian poetry" and brought him closer to avant-garde artistic circles. Seifert joined them in founding a group called Devětsil; the name comes from a medicinal herb and flower that means, literally, "nine strengths." The group was inspired both by the Russian Revolution and by the heady atmosphere of freedom and national independence at the end of World War I. Its aim was nothing short of the rebuilding of the world.

Seifert also took part in the important Poetism movement that left its imprint on almost all the arts in Czechoslovakia after 1924. Poetism was influenced both by Franco-Swiss Dadaism and by Surrealism. It was an avant-garde movement oriented toward the future, considering all aspects of life as art forms—in the future, art would become life, and life would become art. For the Poetists, poetry became an imaginative game of chance associations of ideas, images, and words, often illogical and paradoxical. Sound effects were strongly emphasized in poetry, as well as fresh, startling rhymes; logical connections were loosened. The subject matter of poetry was broadened to include areas previously considered to be nonpoetic, such as science, technology, and exotic information. The poets drew on all the arts for their inspiration: film, music, the ballet, pantomime, the circus, and the music hall. The movement represented a sharp break with proletarian poetry. In morality, the poets tended to be skeptical;

they were indulgent in sensual aspects of life and art, and often generalized their enthusiasms. They are sometimes accused of artistic insincerity, but they performed the great service of expanding the frontiers and technical devices of poetry.

In the early 1920's, Seifert wrote for a variety of newspapers and reviews. He was a reporter for a Communist newspaper in Prague, then in Brno, the Moravian capital; later, he worked for a Communist bookstore and publishing house in Prague and edited a Communist illustrated magazine. During this time, Seifert also traveled; he went to northern Italy and France. He also went to the Soviet Union in 1925 and 1928.

By 1929, Seifert believed that the closely knit circle of Devětsil had outlived its purpose, and he became disenchanted with the new leadership of the Communist Party. With eight other Czech Communist writers, he

Jaroslav Seifert (©The Nobel Foundation)

signed a letter protesting the new party line and cultural program. He was expelled from Devětsil and the Communist Party, which he never rejoined.

The 1930's saw a great shift of taste in Czech literature. The previous decade had sought liberation from tradition in theme, form, and style. The pendulum began to swing back, and there was a decline in free verse and a return to punctuation in poetry. Formerly avant-garde writers began to use classical forms such as the sonnet and rondel. Seifert, too, used regular, compact, stanzaic verse forms during the 1930's, with ingenious rhymes and frequent refrains. He showed an unsuspected gift for pure lyrical poetry, especially the poetry of love, with a new sense of spiritual or moral values. It was during this beleaguered decade that Seifert found and developed the two major themes that were to mark his poetic output and were to become the basis of his reputation: the theme of love for women and his stance as a national poet. He wrote his cycle of elegies on T. G. Masaryk, *Osm dní* (eight days), in 1937. Masaryk, the president-liberator, symbolized the independence of Czechoslovakia, and his somber funeral was an occasion for both nationalistic pomp and an outburst of lyric verse. Seifert's volume was reprinted six times before it satisfied popular demand. Seifert's next collections turned to children's poetry and the writer Božena Němcová; during World War II, Seifert published three collections, and most of the poems were about Prague, which comes to symbolize the continuity of Czech history. *Přilba hlíny* (helmut of clay) celebrates the May, 1945, uprising in Prague and the subsequent liberation of the city.

After the liberation, Seifert again became active in journalism, but he was attacked by the new Communist regime; in an article titled "Not Our Voice," one minor critic accused him of being alien, bourgeois, and even anti-Communist. Seifert was forced to withdraw from public life. It was only after 1954, following the death of Joseph Stalin, that he was able to publish selections from his past works and some new poetry. In 1956, he spoke from the platform at the Second Congress of the Union of Czechoslovak writers, advocating that writers express ethical conscience, civic consciousness, and public commitment—in his words, "May we be truly the conscience of our people."

After a decade of serious illness, Seifert emerged with a surprising new poetic manner. In *Koncert na ostrově* (concert on the island), he gave up much of his songlike intonation, rhyme, and metaphor for the sake of simpler, declarative free verse. It was during the Prague Spring, the time of maximum liberalization, when Alexander Dubček became leader of the Czech Communist Party, that Seifert was named a National Artist of Czechoslovakia. In August, 1968, after the invasion of the country by the Soviet Union, Seifert rose from his sickbed, called a taxi, and went to the building of the Union of Writers. Those present elected him acting chairman of the independent Union of Writers. A year later, the union was dissolved. Isolated and sick, Seifert continued to write; his poems were typed and distributed in copies by individual readers. He lived in a suburb of Prague, Břevnov, helping anyone who called on him and writing reminiscences of his long life as a poet. Between 1968 and 1975, only sections from his old works were published in Czechoslovakia, but some new poems were published in Czech in periodicals abroad. He became an original signer of Charter 77. Illness required him to be frequently hospitalized; in 1984, he received the Nobel Prize in his hospital bed, where television crews and reporters descended on him, asking for interviews. His son-in-law and secretary, Daribor Plichta, was to go to Stockholm to receive the Nobel Prize on behalf of the ailing Seifert, but the Czechoslovak government refused to give Plichta an exit permit. In 1985, Seifert was well enough to leave the hospital and return home, where he continued to write poetry. He died a year later.

ANALYSIS

Jaroslav Seifert's life and poetry are closely interwoven, and it is a mistake to separate them. He took part in all the major poetic movements of his long life. During some of these phases, it is possible to say that he was surpassed by a friend and colleague. Perhaps Neumann wrote superior poems of political commitment during the 1920's, and in the 1930's perhaps Josef Hora expressed the sense of attachment to the native land better than anyone else in his monumental poem "Zpěv rodné zemi" ("Song of the Native Land"). Indignation at the violent excesses of Communism was the most powerfully rendered in Halas's superb "Potopa" ("The Deluge"). Holan's output of meditative lyrics, published during the decade after World War II, was especially impressive. However, it is futile to contrast Seifert to these poets as if they were competitors: They were often remarkably close and engaged in similar endeavors, and Seifert wrote poems addressed to most of these poets. Seifert's own poems are consistently interesting, of remarkably high quality, and unique.

Seifert's main themes were the love of woman and the celebration of what is most positive in life. His finest collections were probably written after World War II, when these themes were increasingly associated with his defense of the individual conscience. Before the war, in the words of Arne Novák, Seifert was "a poet readily inspired by contemporary events and an unusually fluent improviser; he was a master of intimate, emotional, and highly musical verse." It should be added that he was able to express the feelings and aspirations of a remarkably broad audience. After the war, unable to publish regularly, he was to increase the depth and resonance of his poems until the end of his life.

LOVE AS PROTEST

In Western European countries and the United States, there has been some confusion about Seifert's emphasis on women, on the sensual love for them and their beauty, which he consistently expressed in his poems from 1930 onward. Sensuality, sexuality, love: These are often thought to be asocial, purely private concerns. In Eastern Europe, however, they assume a much greater importance. They are central to that domain where the individual man or woman still has freedom, where the state is unable to intrude, and where a human being is able to wrest a small, habitable space from a hostile environment. There a person is able to express love, intimacy, and his or her most positive values. Love becomes a form of protest and of personal commitment, even of heroism. Seifert was able to express this theme in language that is not abstract but very concrete and specific, not moralistic or sanctimonious but frequently erotic. This is the unique synthesis of Seifert: The poems appear to be about specific experiences, but at the same time they are always more than

this. He could define heaven and hell in these concrete terms, from "Jen jednou" ("Once Only"):

> Hell we all know, it's everywhere
> and walks upon two legs.
>   But paradise?
> It may be that paradise is only
> a smile
>   we have long waited for,
> and lips
>   whispering our name.
> And then that brief vertiginous moment
> when we're allowed to forget
> that hell exists.

Although many of Seifert's poems about women may appear at first glance to be simply erotic, about his desire for an individual woman, he almost always manages to raise that desire to a higher degree of generality, simultaneously maintaining the utmost concreteness and specificity. He writes in his poem, titled "Vlastní životopis" ("Autobiography"), "But when I first saw/ the picture of a nude woman/ I began to believe in miracles." This notion of a "miracle" stayed with him as a measure of what was most positive, of the highest value. Toward the close of his life, in "Merry-Go-Round with White Swan," he wrote:

> Goodbye. In all my life I never committed
> any betrayal.
> That I am aware of,
> and you may believe me.
>
> But the most beautiful of all gods
> is love.

The notion of a principle, and fidelity to it, might be easily missed. The strength of Seifert's notion of love is that it is both a positive moral concept and concretely erotic (entirely un-Calvinistic) at the same time.

A skeptical reader might ask, Is this love singular or plural? Does Seifert write of one woman, or several, or many? Or all women? Seifert moves from the singular to the plural with great ease, and the answer is that love is both singular and plural, one woman and many, concrete and universal. In addition, the concept is expanded in Seifert's many poems about Prague, which becomes "her," a distinctly feminine presence.

LOVE DEFINED BY ITS OPPOSITE

The notion of love is often defined in terms of its opposite:

> Those who have left
> and hastily scattered to distant lands
> must realize it by now:
> The world is horrible!
>
> They don't love anyone and no one loves them.
> We at least love.
>
> So let her knees crush my head!

A passage such as this one might be misread by a Western reader, who lives in a democracy and assumes a sharp dividing line between private life and society; this dichotomy is upheld by democratic laws, rights, and institutions. In a totalitarian society, however, the division is abolished. The individual must create his freedom and positive values by his own efforts on a daily basis.

In another passage, love is again defined in terms of its opposite. Here it is opposed to war, presumably World War II; once again the love is not escapist, but raised to a higher level of generalization and affirmation:

> The many rondels and the songs I wrote!
> There was a war all over the world,
> and all over the world
> was grief.
> And yet I whispered into bejewelled ears
> verses of love.
> It makes me feel ashamed.
> But no, not really.

Although such a passage might seem, on a superficial level, to mock feats of armed resistance, it should be read carefully. The love here is raised to a principle, it is almost a weapon used against war. Seifert is modest and shies away from large claims or abstract words; usually he seems whimsical, his agile verse leaps from image to image, but the reader should not be fooled by the self-demeaning manner. The jeweled earrings do belong not only to a soft, attractive body (here unseen, carefully removed from the picture) but also to an object of intense devotion, menaced by the war but momentarily beyond its reach.

THE CASTING OF THE BELLS

Love is also defined and contrasted to another opposite—death. Especially in *The Casting of the Bells*, Seifert looks forward to his own death, which serves as a foil for his theme of love. In "Dvořákovo requiem" ("A Requiem for Dvořák"), he describes a place on the Vltava River where two lovers killed themselves by drowning. Most of the poem describes the efforts to drag for the couple with hooked poles and the reactions of the men as they finally see the naked body of the girl. In the hands of another poet, this might easily degenerate into an exercise in necrophilia or voyeurism. However, Seifert maintains—surely, deliberately—the contrast between death and the beauty of life throughout:

> The men in the boat called to the shore:
> "Drag it out, boys!"
> Well, you know, there were many of them.
> As if stuck to the ground in iced terror,
> not one of them moved.

The ending of the poem occurs not with the conclusion of this scene but the next day, "a peaceful, normal day" when "The grass-pillows smelled hot/ and invited lovers again/ to the old game." The entire volume of *The Casting of the Bells* is a sustained meditation on imminent death and on life. The notion of the "casting" of a bell is a metaphor for the body, which is "cast" or formed by sexual desire. Paradoxically, some poems in the volume are among Seifert's most positive.

"THE BLOW"

Seifert creates a similar structure of contrasts in his cycle of poems on the bombing of the town of Kralupy during World War II. He was forced to take cover in a cemetery, behind a low grave in "Uder" ("The Blow"). When the dead girl buried there "gave me her hand," Seifert "held" it and was able to resist the explosions coming from the town nearby. The gesture became an affirmation of life, and of Seifert's strong ties to what is most positive in life: Even the dead, through the feeling of love they once felt—human, sexual, and erotic—are able to participate in these ties.

THE PLAGUE COLUMN

Seifert most explicitly contrasts love to totalitarian politics in *The Plague Column*. As in Albert Camus's novel *La Peste* (1947; *The Plague*, 1948), Seifert's concept of a plague is allegorical and refers to contemporary history. The plague goes on and on:

> Don't let them dupe you
> that the plague has come to an end:
> I've seen too many coffins hauled past.

> The plague still rages and it seems the doctors
> are giving different names to the disease
> to avoid panic.

The "plague" is the communism of the 1970's; it is also a grisly time of burning corpses and "cynical drinking songs." Like the young Seifert, the older poet again has an oppositional politics "in the name of love," though his politics is now anticommunist rather than procommunist. Love is given its maximal meaning not only as a foil to death, and to war, but also to the rampant "plague" of political terror.

LATE POEMS

This theme of love also has its special style. It closely resembles the alert and highly agile style that Seifert developed in his last three volumes. It is flexible and allusive, moves in unexpected directions, and is always surprising. Seifert is an extremely subtle poet. The translations of his work vary widely in quality; different translations of the same passage in Czech can give rise to totally different interpretations—what might seem whimsy to one reader may appear to be sharp irony to another, and the American or English reader relying on translations of Seifert should beware. The unique style of Seifert's last volumes is characterized above all by intimacy, also by freedom and sensuality. He harks back to his style during the period of Poetism, with its Surrealist and Dadaist overtones, but it has more depth and follows the contours of thought, the rhythms of intimate impulse and feeling, with far greater closeness and fidelity. As Seifert told a French interviewer near the end of his life:

As one grows older, one discovers different values and different worlds. For me, this meant that I discovered sensuality.... All language can be thought of as an effort to achieve freedom, to feel the joy and the sensuality of freedom. What we seek in language is the freedom to be able to express one's most intimate thoughts. This is the basis of all freedom.

Style, too, can be a function of a principle of love, of those most positive values that Seifert opposes to political repression. Professor Eduard Goldstücker, chairman of the Czech Writers Union in 1968 and subsequently exiled, emphasized Seifert's consistent role as a poet of resistance when he wrote in 1985: "Seifert's poems were always in the front line of resistance. In those dark years [of occupation by the Germans] he became the poet of his people, and he has remained so until this day."

OTHER MAJOR WORKS

NONFICTION: *Hvězdy nad rajskou zahradou*, 1929; *Všecky krásy světa*, 1981 (*Autobiography*, 1985).

CHILDREN'S LITERATURE: *Maminka: Ybor básni*, 1954 (*Maminka*, 1991).

MISCELLANEOUS: *Dílo*, 1953-1970 (collected works).

BIBLIOGRAPHY

French, Alfred. *The Poets of Prague: Czech Poetry Between the Wars*. New York: Oxford University Press, 1969. Provides the larger context for Seifert's work in its formative phase, including poems by all the major poets of his generation in translation and the original Czech for comparison.

Gibian, George. Introduction to *The Poetry of Jaroslav Seifert*. North Haven, Conn.: Catbird Press, 1998. A brief biography that focuses primarily on Seifert's literary activities and explores his literary ancestry and evolution as a poet. In a country in which poetry is highly regarded, Seifert achieved the status of a national poet who was widely respected and loved.

_____. "The Lyrical Voice of Czechoslovakia." In *The Selected Poetry of Jaroslav Seifert*. New York: Macmillan, 1986. Concise, insightful essay on Seifert's life and work by the dedicated editor who created one of the best anthologies of Seifert in English. Includes vivid description of Gibian's face-to-face meetings with Seifert in Prague. Seifert's poetry translated by Ewald Osers, prose by Gibian.

Iggers, Wilma A. "The World of Jaroslav Seifert." *World Literature Today* 60 (Spring, 1985): 8-12. Scholarly interpretation of Seifert's career, filling in some of Seifert's lesser-known literary associations.

Loewy, Dana. Introduction to *The Early Poetry of Jaroslav Seifert*. Translated by Dana Loewy. 1997. Reprint. Evanston, Ill.: Northwestern University Press, 1999. In his introduction, Loewy disavows claims by Seifert critics that his early work is untranslatable. Although some aspects of his poetry will be lost, his "musicality, playfulness, and lyricism can be imitated in English with the help of internal rhymes, half-rhymes, and assonance."

Parrott, Sir Cecil. Introduction to *The Plague Column*, by Jaroslav Seifert. Translated by Ewald Osers. London: Terra Nova Editions, 1979. Appreciative essay on Seifert's career, by a journalist who was an eyewitness to much of it, with particular awareness of the political subtleties.

Sternstein, Malynne M. *The Will to Chance: Necessity and Arbitrariness in the Czech Avant-garde from Poetism to Surrealism*. Bloomington, Ind.: Slavica, 2007. Provides the context in which Seifert's poetry developed as well as his place in it.

John Carpenter

ANTONI SŁONIMSKI

Born: Warsaw, Poland; November 15, 1895
Died: Warsaw, Poland; July 4, 1976

PRINCIPAL POETRY
Sonety, 1918
Czarna wiosna, 1919
Harmonia, 1919
Prada, 1920
Godzina poezji, 1923
Droga na Wschód, 1924
Z dalekiej podrózy, 1926
Oko w oko, 1928
Wiersze zebrane, 1929
Okno bez krat, 1935
Alarm, 1940
Popiól i wiatr, 1942
Wybór poezji, 1944
Wiek klęski, 1945

Poezje, 1951
Liryki, 1958
Nowe wiersze, 1959
Rozmowa z gwiazda, 1961
Wiersze, 1958-1963, 1963
Poezje zebrane, 1964
Mlodość górna: Wiek klęski, Wiek meski, 1965
138 wierszy, 1973
Wiersze, 1974

OTHER LITERARY FORMS

The poetic output of Antoni Słonimski (slawn-YIHM-skee) forms a relatively small part of his voluminous work. He was especially prolific as an author of nonfiction. During the 1930's, and again during the 1960's and 1970's, Słonimski's name was associated with the feuilleton even more than with poetry. He undoubtedly was one of the most accomplished masters of the *felieton*, a specifically Polish hybrid consisting of elements of literary essay, political column, and satirical lampoon. Before World War II, his popularity was also the result of his vitriolic criticism (particularly theatrical reviews), comedies in the manner of George Bernard Shaw, and science-fiction novels with some of the flavor of H. G. Wells. In 1966, he published *Jawa i mrzonka*, two short stories consisting of first-person monologues. Toward the close of his life, he published his memoirs, *Alfabet wspomnień* (1975).

ACHIEVEMENTS

Throughout the sixty years of his literary career, Antoni Słonimski successfully reached a large readership and exerted a powerful moral influence on opinions and attitudes in Polish society. His political position was that of an independent intellectual with pronounced liberal and democratic views. Especially in the 1930's, as both right-wing and left-wing groups in Poland grew dangerously radical, Słonimski stood out as the most prominent defender of common sense, human rights, and civil liberties, always the first to ridicule totalitarian or chauvinist follies in his immensely popular feuilletons. He maintained the same position during the war, which he spent in exile; in postwar Poland, his intransigent stance exposed him more than once to the ill will of the communist regime. In the last decades of his life, Słonimski, while he was still actively participating in Poland's literary life, was generally considered to be a living symbol of the best traditions of the Polish liberal intelligentsia. His funeral in Laski, near Warsaw, underlined his influence as it became a silent demonstration by independent-minded intellectuals.

Unlike Słonimski's unquestionable moral authority, his reputation as a poet has been subject to many critical reevaluations. He entered the literary scene in approximately 1918, as cofounder of an iconoclastic poetic group, Skamander, whose innovation consisted primarily of denying the validity of the post-Romantic tradition under the new circumstances of regained national independence. Very soon, however, the young rebels from Skamander, acclaimed as the Polish Pléiade, achieved prominent positions in the literary establishment while becoming artistically more and more conservative, especially in comparison to various avant-garde movements of that time. Słonimski, in particular, can be viewed as the most rationalistic, traditional, direct, and "public" among the Skamander poets.

By no means an artistic innovator, he was still highly esteemed for his integrity and immediacy of appeal; his *Alarm*, for example, written in 1939 in Paris and repeatedly broadcast to Poland, has certainly become the most remembered Polish poem of the entire war period. In the postwar years, Słonimski's willful defense of traditional artistic devices did not obstruct his own interesting development as a poet, and his final rapprochement with the Christian philosophical tradition (although he remained an agnostic) enriched his late poetry with a new, metaphysical dimension. Against the background of twentieth century Polish poetry, his poetry appears, even in the eyes of his opponents, as an unmatched example of clarity, precision, and moral sensitivity, happily married to a sense of humor.

BIOGRAPHY

The son of a Warsaw physician, Antoni Słonimski was born and reared in a family proud of its Jewish ancestors, including an eighteenth century inventor and mathematician. The poet's father was a member of the Polish Socialist Party and professed the progressivist and rationalistic ideology of Polish positivism. Initially, Słonimski chose the career of an artist rather than that of a writer. He studied painting in Warsaw and Munich, and although his first poem was published as early as 1913, he was not yet giving his writing any serious thought. Instead, he was making his living by drawing cartoons for satirical weeklies. Only in 1918 did he publish his first sonnets, which he later considered his actual debut.

In the last years of World War I, Słonimski entered into friendly relations with several other young poets, especially Julian Tuwim and Jan Lechoń. Together they created in 1918 a poetic cabaret, Picador, which two years later evolved into a poetic group called Skamander (which also included Jarosław Iwaszkiewicz and Kazimierz Wierzyński). In a few years, the five Skamander poets gained an astonishingly large following; for the next two decades, if not more, the mainstream of Polish literary life was dominated by them and their informal school. Their influence found a particularly efficient outlet in *Wiadomości Literackie*, a literary weekly of liberal orientation, to which Słonimski was perhaps the most prolific contributor. This weekly published most of his poems and articles, as well as his caustic theatrical reviews and, above all, his "Kroniki tygodniowe," the enormously popular weekly "chronicles," or feuilletons. The success of these chronicles reduced for a while Słonimski's lyrical productivity. Although between 1918 and 1928 he had published many books of poems, during the next decade only one new collection appeared. Instead of poetry, in the 1930's he wrote mostly nonfiction of various sorts, ranging from purely nonsensical parodies to serious publications, including a report on his trip to the Soviet Union, *Moja podróż do Rosji* (1932), interesting as a document of his fascination with "progress" and, at the same time, his unequivocal repugnance for the horrors of totalitarianism. At that time, his uncompromising liberal stance earned for him many violent attacks from both the Left and the Right.

As a Jew and an outspoken liberal, Słonimski had every reason to fear both Nazis and communists; Słonimski left Warsaw in September, 1939, and found his way to Paris via Romania and Italy. After the fall of France, he escaped to London. He stayed there with his wife until 1946, editing the émigré monthly *Nowa Polska*; his wartime poetry collection, *Alarm*, was re-edited several times during the early 1940's. While in London, he also began to work for UNESCO (United Nations Educational, Scientific, and Cultural Organization). Even though he was officially repatriated in 1946, he soon returned to the West, to serve, until 1951, first as chairman of the literary section of UNESCO, then as director of the Polish Cultural Institute in London.

In 1951, Słonimski again returned to Poland with his wife, this time for good. Initially a cautious supporter of the new political order, he soon began to find himself more and more at odds with the Communist regime. His spectacular comeback to public life occurred in 1956, when, in the celebrated "thaw," he was elected president of the Polish Writers' Union, a position he held until 1959. In the 1960's he returned to his favorite genre, writing a new series of feuilletons for a satirical weekly, *Szpilki*.

The year 1968 brought about the culmination of Słonimski's fame as the grand old man of Poland's intellectual opposition. After having courageously contributed to the protest of Polish writers against the regime's anti-Semitic and anti-intellectual campaign, the poet became a target for personal attacks from the Communist Party leader, Władysław Gomułka. Słonimski was all but blacklisted, at least until the early 1970's, when he found a shelter in a Catholic weekly, *Tygodnik Powszechny*. There, in 1972, he began publishing his last series of feuilletons, later collected in *Obecność* (1973) and *Ciekawość* (1981). The publication of *138 wierszy* in 1973 initiated the public reappearance of his poetry as well. His continuing participation in the protests of intellectuals, however, made him a target of state censorship until the end of his life. He died as a result of injuries suffered in a car accident.

ANALYSIS

Antoni Słonimski occupies a unique place in twentieth century Polish poetry as a result of a fundamental paradox in his work: his self-contradictory attitude toward tradition. As a man of ideas, he had always been in favor of progress, common sense, and tolerance; he unflaggingly fought all forms of obscurantism. The course of contemporary history, however, turned such efforts into their opposite: What initially was a progressive and modern stance soon began to appear as a defense of traditional, old-fashioned, outdated values. Słonimski's poetry seems therefore to be a peculiar combination of modern problematics and conservative artistic means; the poet himself appears as a champion of the public weal who is paradoxically aware of his quixotic loneliness.

THE SKAMANDER POETS

This apparent rift can be traced back to the very beginnings of Słonimski's literary career. As a member of a group of young poets, later called Skamander, he provided the chief battle cry in a couplet from one of his early poems: "My country is free, is free. . . . So I can throw Konrad's cloak off my shoulders." Konrad, the name of poet Adam Mickiewicz's Romantic hero, symbolizes here the whole tradition of national martyrdom as embodied in messianic poetry of the great Polish Romantics. Under the circumstances of Poland's newly regained independence, such a tradition seemed nothing but a needless burden, and Słonimski, like the other Skamandrites, at first rejected the Romantic heritage ostentatiously and totally.

PARNASSIANISM

Słonimski's individual way of doing this, however, was rather atypical. Apart from a long poem, *Czarna wiosna* (confiscated by government censors in 1919), in which, by way of an exception, he gave vent to anarchic slogans in an expressionistic style, he appeared in his early poems (most of them sonnets) as an utterly classical and harmonious Parnassian, very much in the spirit of José-Maria de Heredia. The only difference from the original Parnassianism was that Słonimski was using the classical forms not for art's sake, but rather to pose questions of an overtly ethical nature and to propound an active attitude toward contemporary reality. This peculiar manner, in which classical devices are used for anticlassical purposes and moral earnestness is disguised as aestheticism, remained a trademark of his poetry in later years.

This does not mean, however, that Słonimski's later work did not evolve. In fact, in his poems written in the mid-1920's, there is no trace of his youthful rejection of the Polish Romantic tradition. On the contrary, collections such as *Godzina poezji, Droga na Wschód*, and *Z dalekiej podrózy* enter into an explicit dialogue with the shadows of the greatest poets of the Polish nineteenth century, even going so far as to imitate Romantic verse forms. What attracted Słonimski to Romanticism, however, was not its messianic obsession. Rather, his rationalistic and liberal mind discovered in the native Romantic tradition a powerful current of humanism and universalism, according to which the brotherhood of humankind should always weigh more than nationalistic prejudices. This is explicit in one of Słonimski's most overt lyrical manifestos, "He Is My Brother."

PESSIMISM OF THE 1930'S

In the 1920's, Słonimski could have been accused, not without justification, of being a naïve optimist who professed Wellesian confidence in progress and the ultimate triumph of reason. His beliefs, however, underwent an important modification in the course of the next decade. The ominous course adopted by the European powers in the 1930's forced the poet to give up, at least partly, his outdated positivist illusions. It was becoming more and more apparent that the development of science and technological progress did not necessarily go hand in hand with the ethical improvement of humankind. Therefore, the rapid growth of pessimistic and even catastrophic tendencies that marked Polish literature in the 1930's found its reflection also in Słonimski's work.

Nevertheless, his volume *Okno bez krat* is pessimistic only as far as its picture of the contemporary world is concerned; evil is still seen as humankind's irrational and passing folly, capable of being overcome. Accordingly, Słonimski's poetry in this period became even more "public" and utilitarian; in *Okno bez krat*, he does not hesitate to resort to what could be termed poetic publicism, characterized by a didactic or satirical tone; an increased use of rhetorical devices; regular verse; and simple, transparent, sometimes quite prosaic language.

If such stylistic features seem to prove that, in the 1930's, Słonimski still believed in the didactic effectiveness of poetry, one must be aware that, on the other hand, some growing doubts were also often expressed in his poems of that period. His personal experiences (he constantly was being vilified, especially by the nationalistic Right, for his pacifism and supposed lack of

patriotic feelings) certainly had much to do with his perplexity. At any rate, the theme of the poet's loneliness among a hostile crowd recurs in his poems written at that time. Since they alluded clearly to the archetypal image of the ostracized prophet, Słonimski's poems of the 1930's would have taken on a thoroughly Romantic aspect were it not for his infallible rationalism and ironic sense of humor.

POPIÓL I WIATR

If Słonimski ever relinquished his self-irony and detachment, it was perhaps in his wartime poetry, in which the fate of the exiled poet quite naturally found its precedents in the biographies of Polish Romantics. Especially in the long poem *Popiól i wiatr*, Słonimski attempted to revive the century-old genre initiated by Mickiewicz's *Pan Tadeusz: Czyli, Ostatni Zajazd na litwie historia Szlachecka zr. 1811 i 1812 we dwunastu ksiegach wierszem*, 1834 (*Pan Tadeusz: Or, The Last Foray in Lithuania, a Tale of Gentlefolk in 1811 and 1812, in Twelve Books in Verse*, 1917). Like the latter, it is a nostalgic tale in which the exiled poet recalls the images of places and years that now seem to be irretrievably lost. What is striking is that Słonimski's rationalistic humanism remains intact, even in those poems in which he speaks with pain and indignation about the horrors of the war. Even at this darkest moment, he hopes against hope that, once the war is over, humankind will recover from its moral degradation and reconstruct the system of its fundamental ethical values.

THE 1960'S AND 1970'S

This belief seemed to be corroborated by the quite literal reconstruction of Poland in the immediate postwar years, which Słonimski greeted with enthusiasm and renewed hope. Very soon, however, his liberal principles—consisting, above all, in caring about the fate of the individual rather than some mythical "historical necessities"—prompted him to an ever-growing skepticism about the possibilities of the new political system and the truth of its slogans. It is worth noting that this time, his adoption of an independent stance as a defender of traditional values had something more to it than superficial common sense. In the 1960's and 1970's, Słonimski's poetry acquired a wider philosophical perspective. While remaining classical and rationalistic in its style and rhetoric, it became essentially tragic in its vision of existence. The symbolic figures of Hamlet and especially Don Quixote organize key images in these later poems, serving as metaphors for the unresolvable contradictions of human fate. Słonimski realized painfully that the human being is reduced to nothingness if placed against an indifferent universe and hostile history; he nevertheless refused to accept this situation, remaining, as he himself put it, "unreconciled with the absurdity of existence." The human spirit, doomed to fail in most cases, nevertheless must cope with adversity, not because there is any guarantee of victory, but because "only the human thought, free and fearless, can justify the subsistence of that feeding ground called 'the world.'" Within this existential context, the role of the poet is compared, with a certain amount of self-disparaging irony, to that of Don Quixote: His defense of illusory values may seem objectively useless and ridiculous, but it is precisely this hopeless struggle that makes him worth remembering.

In the last years of Słonimski's life, the supposedly outmoded poet was rapidly gaining in topicality and importance. His individual development coincided with society's tendency to seek genuine spiritual values in a world degraded by fear and deceit. Słonimski, old enough to ignore the postwar avant-garde yet young enough to grasp the spirit of the modern age, was able to contribute significantly to that spiritual revival.

OTHER MAJOR WORKS

LONG FICTION: *Teatr w więzienia*, 1922; *Torpeda czasu*, 1924; *Dwa końce świata*, 1937.

SHORT FICTION: *Jawa i mrzonka*, 1966.

PLAYS: *Wieża Babel*, pb. 1927; *Murzyn warszawski*, pr. 1928; *Lekarz bezdomny*, pb. 1930; *Rodzina*, pb. 1933.

NONFICTION: *O dzieciach, wariatach i grafomanach*, 1927; *Mętne łby*, 1928; *Moja podróż do Rosji*, 1932; *Moje walki nad Bzdurą*, 1932; *Heretyk na ambonie*, 1934; *W beczce przez Niagare*, 1936; *Kroniki tygodniowe, 1927-1939*, 1956; *Wspomnienia warszawskie*, 1957; *W oparach absurdu*, 1958, 1975 (with Julian Tuwim); *Artykuły pierwszej potrzeby*, 1959; *Gwalt na Melpomenie*, 1959; *Załatwione odmownie*, 1962, 1964; *Jedna strona medalu*, 1971; *Obecność*, 1973; *Alfabet wspomnień*, 1975; *Ciekawość*, 1981.

BIBLIOGRAPHY

Gillon, Adam, and Ludwik Krzyzanowski, eds. *Introduction to Modern Polish Literature*. Rev. ed. New York: Hippocrene Books, 1982. Provides translations of selected works and a brief biographical background of Słonimski.

Keane, Barry. *Skamander: The Poets and Their Poetry, 1918-1929*. Warsaw: Agade, 2004. Discusses the formation of Skamander and the poets' beliefs. Centers on Słonimski and provides a critical analysis of his work.

Miłosz, Czesław. *The History of Polish Literature*. 2d ed. Berkeley: University of California Press, 1983. Offers a historical background for the works of Słonimski. Includes bibliographic references and an index.

Polonsky, Antony, and Monika Adamczyk-Garbowska, eds. *Contemporary Jewish Writing in Poland: An Anthology*. Lincoln: University of Nebraska Press, 2001. Contains a short biography of Słonimski as well as translations of prose and poetry. Describes his poetry as characterized by a struggle between emotional content and classical form.

Stanisław Barańczak

JULIUSZ SŁOWACKI

Born: Krzemieniec, Poland; September 4, 1809
Died: Paris, France; April 3, 1849

PRINCIPAL POETRY

Poezye, 1832 (2 volumes), 1833 (3 volumes; includes *Żmija*, *Arab*, *Lambro, powstańca grecki*, and *Godzinna myśli*)

Anhelli, 1838 (English translation, 1930)

Poema Piasta Dantyszka o piekle, 1839

Trzy poemata, 1839 (includes *Wacław*, *W Szwajcarii* [*In Switzerland*, 1953], and *Ojciec zadż umionych* [*The Father of the Plague-Stricken*, 1915])

Grób Agamemnona, 1840 (*Agamemnon's Grave*, 1944)

Beniowski, 1841
Genezis z ducha, 1844
Król-Duch, 1847

OTHER LITERARY FORMS

The dramatic works of Juliusz Słowacki (slawv-AHT-skee) are among the most highly esteemed offerings in the repertory of the modern Polish theater. Despite his early death, Słowacki managed to complete close to twenty full-length plays of great variety. Six of these works are especially popular with Polish audiences: *Maria Stuart* (pr. 1832; *Mary Stuart*, 1937), *Kordian* (pb. 1834), *Balladyna* (pb. 1839; English translation, 1960), *Lilla Weneda* (pb. 1840), *Mazepa* (pb. 1840; *Mazeppa*, 1930), and *Fantazy* (pb. 1866; English translation, 1977). The subject matter of these plays stemmed more from his literary and historical studies than from his personal experiences. Among the literary influences that shaped these works, those of Greek drama, William Shakespeare, and the French Romantic theater are especially prominent. Elements derived from Polish balladry and Slavic folklore also contribute to the stylistic diversity manifested in these plays.

Later in life, Słowacki came increasingly under the influence of the seventeenth century Spanish playwright Pedro Calderón de la Barca, an influence evident in works such as *Ksiądz Marek* (pb. 1843; Father Mark) and *Sen srebrny Salomei* (pb. 1844; the silver dream of Salomea). Although both of these works are set in the Polish Ukraine, they combine elements of Spanish mysticism and Christian self-sacrifice in a manner that is reminiscent of Calderón's sacramental dramas. Also noteworthy is Słowacki's free-verse adaptation of Calderón's *El príncipe constante* (pr. 1629; *The Constant Prince*, 1853), which has become one of the featured plays in the repertory of the Laboratory Theater in Wrocław in the production directed by its founder, Jerzy Grotowski.

None of these dramatic works was ever performed onstage during Słowacki's lifetime; his writings were prohibited from being published in his homeland as a result of his political activities as an émigré. One of the positive literary by-products of this political exile can be found in the letters that Słowacki wrote to his mother during a period of nearly two decades. Now regarded as masterworks of Polish Romantic prose, they also contain instructive comments pertaining to the poet's works in progress.

ACHIEVEMENTS

Juliusz Słowacki, like Adam Mickiewicz, is honored in his homeland not only for his literary genius but also for his lifelong dedication to the cause of freedom. In 1927, the newly independent Polish state arranged for his remains to be transported from a cemetery in Paris back to Poland for interment in the royal crypt of the Wawel Castle in Kraków, amid the tombs of Poland's kings and national heroes. Słowacki's sarcophagus is to be found alongside that of Mickiewicz, the man whom he had always regarded as his archrival for the title of national *wieszcz* (bard). Although Mickiewicz is universally regarded as Poland's greatest poet, Słowacki, especially in his later works, transcended the limits of Romanticism and developed poetic techniques that anticipated those used by the French Symbolists and the English Pre-Raphaelites. Because he was a herald of future artistic trends, Słowacki became the guiding star for those Polish poets who were adherents of a neo-Romantic literary movement known as Młoda Polska (Young Poland), a group of writers who came of age around 1890. For them, his work was a source of inspiration for both theme and technique.

Oddly enough, very few of Słowacki's lyric poems were published in his lifetime. It was only from 1866 onward, when Antoni Malecki began to bring out an edition of the poet's collected works that incorporated many unpublished manuscripts, that the reading public in Poland became aware of Słowacki's lyric as well as epic and dramatic genius. By virtue of his accomplishments in all three genres, he is now ranked second only to Mickiewicz in the pantheon of Polish poets. If Mickiewicz may be said to be the Lord Byron of Polish literature, then Słowacki must surely be its Percy Bysshe Shelley.

BIOGRAPHY

Juliusz Słowacki left his homeland in 1831 when he was only twenty-two years old and was destined to spend the rest of his life in exile. Up to that year, he had lived in three Polish cities. He was born in the town of Krzemieniec on September 4, 1809 (August 23, Old Style). Located in the province of Volhynia, Krzemieniec was an important cultural center in eastern Poland at the time of Słowacki's birth because, in 1805, a prestigious lyceum had been established there. The poet's father, Euzebiusz Słowacki, taught literature and rhetoric at the lyceum, and his mother, Salomea né Januszewska, was a highly cultivated woman of sentimental temperament. Both parents were passionately devoted to their only child. When Słowacki was a few years old, the family moved to the city of Wilno so that his father could assume a professorship at the university there. The elder Słowacki died suddenly in 1814, and three years later, the boy's mother married August Bécu, a medical professor at the University of Wilno, who was himself a widower and the father of two young daughters. Słowacki, somewhat frail in health and the only male child in the new household, led a

pampered life and was strongly encouraged to pursue his musical and literary interests. In 1824, however, this sheltered life came to an abrupt end when Bécu was struck by lightning and killed. Słowacki's mother decided to return to Krzemieniec, leaving her son in Wilno, where he could train for a career in law at the university. Słowacki completed the prescribed course of studies in three short years and, at the young age of nineteen, became an employee of the ministry of finance in Warsaw, capital of the Russian-dominated kingdom of Poland.

Słowacki frequently attended the theater in Warsaw and soon completed two plays that he planned to publish in an edition of his works to date. Before arrangements for the printing of this two-volume set could be completed, an armed insurrection against the country's Russian overlords broke out in November, 1830. Although Słowacki had been largely apolitical up to that time, he immediately embraced the insurrection's cause as his own and composed an ode to freedom in its honor. Because of his delicate physical constitution, he was unfit for military service; he did, however, place himself at the disposal of the Polish revolutionary government and was eventually sent on a diplomatic mission to London during the summer of 1831. While in London, he mixed business with pleasure and managed to see Edmund Kean in a performance of Shakespeare's *Richard III*. After several weeks in London, Słowacki moved to Paris. By this time, it was clear that the November Insurrection was doomed to defeat, and he made no attempt to return to Warsaw. After the Poles capitulated to the Russians in September, 1831, Słowacki decided to settle in Paris, where he was soon joined by many of his compatriots. In a move that has come to be called the Great Migration, some ten thousand Poles left their homeland for sanctuary in the West and gathered in cities such as Paris, London, Geneva, and Rome. Unlike most of the other émigrés who left Poland to escape Russian retribution, Słowacki always had sufficient funds to meet his living expenses, for his father had established an annuity for him. Moreover, he invested these modest sums wisely

Juliusz Słowacki (©CORBIS)

in stocks, and thus he acquired the wherewithal to pursue his literary ambitions free from any financial restrictions.

Słowacki made his belated literary début in Paris by publishing at his own expense the two-volume set of his works to date which he had planned to publish in Warsaw before the insurrection. He then anxiously awaited his compatriots' reaction. One of the few people interested enough to read his works was Mickiewicz, slightly more than ten years Słowacki's senior and already regarded as the foremost Polish poet of his generation. Since Słowacki's verse was at this time almost wholly devoid of any political or religious ideology, Mickiewicz dismissed these volumes as being "a church without a God inside." In view of the indifference shown toward his work, Słowacki decided to leave for Switzerland toward the end of 1832 and spent the next three years there writing zealously. During the winter of 1836, Słowacki left Switzerland to join relatives from Poland on a grand tour of Italy. While in Rome, he met a Polish poet a few years his junior, Zygmunt Krasiński; it was Krasiński who first recognized Słowacki's literary genius. Much encouraged, Słowacki then decided to accompany two compatriots on a trip to Greece and the Near East. After his return to Europe ten months later, he remained in Florence for a year and a half before rejoining the émigré community in Paris in December, 1838.

Once back in Paris, Słowacki gradually gained recognition for his literary endeavors and also became a key figure in the political debates concerning the future of Poland. In 1846, amid all this activity, Słowacki discovered that he had contracted tuberculosis. Despite this affliction, he rushed off to the aid of his countrymen when an insurrection broke out in Prussian Poland in 1848. This revolt proved to be short-lived, but he did manage to arrange a meeting with his mother in the Silesian city of Breslau. The encounter was a sad one, for both realized that his days were numbered. Returning to Paris, he worked feverishly in an unsuccessful attempt to complete the epic poem *Król-Duch* (king-spirit). Death overtook him on April 3, 1849. Oddly enough, his compatriot Frédéric Chopin was to die in Paris a few months later from the identical malady and at exactly the same age.

ANALYSIS

Juliusz Słowacki's life was destined to unfold amid the political turmoil that arose as a result of the partitioning of Poland by Russia, Prussia, and Austria during the closing decades of the eighteenth century. The annexation of Polish territory by its more powerful neighbors occurred in three stages. The first partition took place in 1772; the second, in 1793; and the third, in 1795. Each of the three cities in which Słowacki spent his youth—Krzemieniec, Wilno, and Warsaw—came under Russian occupation in 1795. Thus, the restoration of Poland's independence was the central concern of Słowacki's life and work. His fellow poets Mickiewicz and Krasiński were similarly preoccupied with their country's fate, but Słowacki differed from them on a great many social and political issues. One crucial difference pertains to the status of the Polish nobility (*szlachta*) and its role in Poland's future national life. Up to the time of the partitions of Poland in the eighteenth century, all political power was vested in the nobility, and the masses were completely disenfranchised. The Polish nobility, otherwise known as the gentry, was a relatively large class constituting approximately 10 percent of the population. They regarded themselves as the "nation" (*naród*) and felt that they had a moral right to exploit the "people" (*lud*). Although Słowacki himself was technically a member of the gentry, he held a highly critical attitude toward this social class. While both Mickiewicz and Krasiński wanted the gentry to dominate the political and cultural life of a reconstituted Polish state, Słowacki advocated a social revolution that would give the people a greater stake in the cause of national liberation. It was thus in the people that he soght to find Poland's "angelic soul."

Słowacki's distrust of the political ambitions of the gentry, moreover, led him to take an extremely pessimistic view of the prospects for restoring Poland's independence in the immediate future. Mickiewicz believed that the task would be accomplished by his generation of Polish émigrés. Indeed, in Mickiewicz's messianic vision, the émigrés were depicted as destined to be the saviors not only of Poland itself but also of the entire world. In response to such notions, Słowacki composed *Anhelli*, an epic that deals with a group of Polish exiles who are annihilated in the frozen wastelands of Siberia. It is clear that Słowacki, at least on a symbolic level, meant to equate the fate of these exiles with that of their counterparts in Western Europe. Since Poland did not regain its nationhood until after World War I, Słowacki's position has been vindicated by the judgment of history.

By the fall of 1831, following the failure of the November Insurrection of 1830, Słowacki had already settled down in Paris with numerous other Polish refugees, including Mickiewicz and Chopin. In 1832, at his own cost, Słowacki published a two-volume set of his works to date, issued under the title *Poezye* (poems), the second volume of which consisted of the two plays that he had written in Warsaw, *Mindowe Król Litewski* (pb. 1829) and *Mary Stuart*. Among the narrative poems in the first volume were several juvenile verse tales of an exotic character enveloped in an atmosphere of Romantic pessimism reminiscent of Lord Byron. These works also reveal the strong influence of Mickiewicz's *Ballady i romanse* (1822; ballads and romances), the publication of which assured the triumph of the Romantic movement in Poland.

ŻMIJA

Among these verse tales in which Słowacki's pessimistic frame of mind manifested itself are *Żmija* (the viper) and *Arab*. The plot of *Żmija* combines Turkish and Cossack milieus. The protagonist is a young Turk who is the son of a powerful pasha. The pasha is overthrown and imprisoned by an ambitious rival, and at the same time, the son's bride is abducted and placed in the culprit's own harem. The young Turk, obsessed by a desire for revenge, runs off and seeks refuge with the Cossacks. He adopts the name Żmija and eventually becomes a hetman. Returning to his homeland at the head of a Cossack army, he succeeds in subduing the opposing forces but dies during individual combat with his archenemy. The work is meant to dramatize the plight of an individual who is compelled by cruel circumstance to abandon his whole way of life, to fight unequal battles with utmost courage, and still to lose in the end despite all his great sacrifices.

ARAB

Similarly bleak in outlook is *Arab*, a tale with an Islamic setting in which the central character is unable to tolerate the existence of human happiness. He therefore feels obliged to inflict injury on happy people whenever he encounters such individuals. On one occasion, for example, the Arab meets a man who is the only survivor of a caravan that was attacked by a band of robbers. Among the victims of the attack were the sons of the survivor, and he is so filled with remorse over his loss that he wishes to join his offspring in death. The Arab, true to his nature, prevents the bereaved father from embracing death and thereby forces him to continue living a life of unremitting sorrow. Słowacki never truly clarifies the motivation of this self-appointed tormentor, but the poem may be a reflection of the author's conviction that the reasons for humanity's terrestrial misfortunes are fundamentally inexplicable.

LAMBRO, POWSTAŃCA GRECKI

Before leaving Paris for Switzerland at the end of 1832, Słowacki made arrangements for the printing of another volume of poetry; this third volume duly appeared in the following year, when Słowacki was residing in the outskirts of Geneva. One of the two major poems included in this volume, *Lambro, powstańca grecki* (Lambro, Greek insurgent), is a verse tale that describes a Greek hero's fight against the Turks for the sake of his homeland's independence. Lambro, after leading his countrymen in many a valiant battle, becomes disillusioned with the shortcomings of his Greek contemporaries and decides to retreat to the mountains to purge himself from petty thoughts through contact with the grandeur of nature. Instead of experiencing spiritual rejuvenation, however, Lambro finds that life in isolation merely increases his own moral vulnerability, and he soon dies under the euphoric effects of hashish. Thus, in the end, both the leader and the rank and file are found to be wanting in moral strength. It is quite apparent that Słowacki was criticizing his fellow Poles, rather than the Greeks. Here, the diffuse psychological pessimism of his earlier works acquired a concrete political focus: a somber assessment of the prospects for achieving the restoration of Polish liberty in the near future.

GODZINNA MYŚLI

Godzinna myśli (hour of thought), the other major poem in Słowacki's third volume, may be characterized as an elegiac autobiographical sketch in verse form. Set in Wilno and its environs, the poem depicts the trials and tribulations of an adolescent poet who is coming of age. The poem's sketchy plot reflects Słowacki's relationship with two people: Ludwik Szpicnagel, his first close friend, and Ludwika Śniadecka, his first (unrequited) love. Both were a few years his senior and had fathers who were professors at the university. Szpicnagel, despite the promise of a brilliant academic future, committed suicide for unknown reasons, while Śniadecka, already in love with a Russian officer, proved unresponsive to Słowacki's courtship. The poet's despair and melancholy are, for the most part, poured into a classical mold, but from time to time, Słowacki's style reverts to the sensuous diction characteristic of the Baroque era. With this work, Słowacki may be said to have hit his stride as a poet of genius.

IN SWITZERLAND

Słowacki lived in Switzerland for three years—at first in a suburb of Geneva, later near Lausanne. During this period, he wrote five full-length dramas, including the masterworks *Kordian* and *Balladyna*. He did, however, interrupt his literary activity occasionally to visit the salon of Mrs. Wodzińska in Geneva to pay court to the Polish aristocrat's eldest daughter. This enchantress, named Maria, enjoyed a degree of celebrity herself, since it was common knowledge that Chopin was madly in love with her. On one occasion, Słowacki went on a long excursion into the Alps with Maria and other members of her family, and this experience inspired him to write the love idyll titled *In Switzerland*, a work begun during his Swiss sojourn and later completed in Italy.

Set amid the scenic splendor of the Alpine countryside, the idyll consists of a number of episodes in the life of a pair of lovers. The reader is told of their meeting, their marriage, the premature death of the bride, and the young man's subsequent departure from Switzerland. Except for a hermit who marries them, there are no other characters in the poem but the young lovers themselves, and even they are never identified by name. The young woman is generally said to be modeled after Maria Wodzińska, but it is difficult to regard the lovers as full-blooded people, for neither their speech nor their movements are precisely defined. The same lack of definition pertains to the Alpine countryside itself,

which appears as though recollected in a dream. In short, the idyll is a poem of great delicacy in which shifting moods are mirrored in a landscape of the mind. Słowacki's *In Switzerland* has often been likened to Shelley's *Epipsychidion* (1821) in terms of musical texture, and it is difficult to imagine how either work could be successfully translated into another tongue.

WACŁAW AND THE FATHER OF THE PLAGUE-STRICKEN

The publication of *In Switzerland* was deferred until 1839, at which time it appeared in the volume titled *Trzy poemata* (three poems) along with the narrative verse tales *Wacław* and *The Father of the Plague-Stricken*. Conceived as a sequel to Antoni Malczewski's highly acclaimed epic poem *Maria* (1825), *Wacław* is set in the Ukraine and delineates the treasonous activities and dreadful death of a powerful landowning magnate. It is generally considered to be the weakest of Słowacki's mature works. *The Father of the Plague-Stricken*, on the other hand, is one of his most popular narrative poems. During his visit to Egypt, Słowacki was quarantined for two weeks in a desert oasis, where a doctor told him a story about an Arab who, while in quarantine for a three-month period, lost his wife and all seven of their children. In his poem, Słowacki casts the father in the role of narrator and has him relate the circumstances accompanying each individual death. After his release from quarantine, the emotionally devastated father can find no further joy in life and simply wanders aimlessly. As time passes, however, the father gradually becomes reconciled to his fate, and he tells his tale with a certain degree of philosophical detachment. Many critics see the influence of Dante at work in this poem, directing attention to the parallels between Słowacki's theme and the situation described in the thirty-third canto of Date's *Inferno* (from *La divina commedia*, c. 1320; *The Divine Comedy*, 1802), in which Count Ugolino relates how he was compelled to watch his four sons die slowly from starvation. *Poema Piasta Dantyszka herbu Leliwa o piekle* (Piast Dantyszek's poem on Hell), Słowacki's subsequent attempt to imitate Dante more overtly, is far less successful, little more than a coarse political satire directed at contemporary Russian and Polish political figures, including Czar Nicholas himself.

PODRÓŻ NA WSCHÓD AND ANHELLI

The pair of works titled *Podróż na wschód* (1836; journey to the East) and *Anhelli* were the chief literary by-products of Słowacki's ten-month trip to Greece and the Near East during the years 1836 and 1837. Composed in sestinas, *Podróż na wschód* is a loosely structured travel diary that records Słowacki's voyage from Naples to Greece as well as his subsequent wanderings in that country. The narrative is, however, interrupted frequently by digressions in which the poet expatiates on various topics of personal concern. Some of *Podróż na wschód* was written while traveling, and other parts were composed later, in Italy and France. Published posthumously, it is an unfinished work. In 1840, however, Słowacki published the eighth canto independently, under the title *Agamemnon's Grave*. Here the poet meditates at a grotto that was then believed to be the burial chamber of Agamemnon. Słowacki recalls the legendary heroism of the ancient Greeks and bemoans the defects in both his own character and that of his countrymen. With a fury reminiscent of the invective that Dante directs at Florence in his *Inferno*, Słowacki angrily denounces the Polish gentry and attributes Poland's extinction as a nation to its self-indulgent behavior. He then predicts that Poland will not be restored to independence until there is a transformation in the national psyche, and he appeals for the liberation of its angelic soul, still imprisoned within a hardened skull.

Departing from Greece, Słowacki continued to Egypt and then to Palestine. While in Jerusalem, he prayed all night in the church containing Christ's tomb and ordered a Mass to be said for Poland. Słowacki next visited Lebanon, where he decided to spend a few weeks in contemplation at a local monastery to work on the first draft of *Anhelli*. Written in poetic prose with biblical affinities, it describes the plight of Polish deportees in the frozen wastelands of Siberia during the years following the failure of the November Insurrection. Like the Polish émigrés who settled in Western Europe, the exiles depicted in *Anhelli* begin to quarrel among themselves and soon divide into three main political factions—those of the gentry, the democrats, and the religionists. On one occasion, to determine which of these parties has the blessing of God, the exiles decide to crucify a representative from each of the three competing ideologies in the belief that the individual who survives the longest will thereby demonstrate the rightness of the cause that he champions. This trial-by-ordeal miscarries, however, and the bickering continues. The one pure soul among the exiles is a youth known as Anhelli (a name which, incidentally, sounds very much like the Polish word for angel). This angelic soul is singled out by a Siberian shaman who initiates him into the mysteries of the occult. Late in the story, Anhelli is visited by two angels, who inform him that all his fellow exiles have perished and that the darkness of winter is about to descend on his homeland for eternity. He immediately offers his own life as a sacrifice, in the hope that Poland will be resurrected at some future date. The Lord deigns to accept his sacrifice but makes no commitment concerning Poland's final fate. Before Anhelli's corpse is cold, however, a mysterious knight on a fiery steed appears and sounds a call to arms. Thus, the reader concludes that Anhelli's sacrifice of the heart has not been in vain, and that the resurrection of Poland will someday come to pass.

BENIOWSKI

Up to the time of the publication of the first five cantos of *Beniowski*, a mock-heroic epic composed in ottava rima, the Polish émigré community paid scant attention to any of Słowacki's writings. With the appearance of *Beniowski* in 1841, however, Słowacki achieved not only personal fame but also a degree of notoriety. Popular response to *Beniowski* centered on the satirical attacks against well-known persons, periodicals, and political factions that were made within its pages. To create a vehicle that would accommodate such freewheeling criticism of his countrymen and their follies, Słowacki decided to pattern his poem after Lord Byron's *Don Juan* (1819-1824, 1826). Thus, he was able to insert materials unrelated to the formal narrative. Because of the frequently scandalous character of these digressions, the reader soon becomes more interested in Słowacki's personal views on sundry topics than in the actual adventures of the epic's eponymous hero. At the conclusion of the fifth canto, for example, Słowacki stages an inspired "gigantomachy" in which Mickiewicz is cast as Hector, a symbol of Poland's past, and he himself is depicted as Achilles, a herald

of his country's future. Even though he defeats Mickiewicz in this poetic duel, he is magnanimous in victory, according his beaten rival an honored place on the
heavenly scroll where the names of great poets are inscribed.

The main character in this epic is a historical per-
sonage, Maurycy Beniowski, a man of mixed Polish
and Hungarian ancestry and a former officer in the
Austrian army. In the 1760's, Beniowski decided to go
to the Polish Ukraine to join members of the gentry
class in an armed insurrection against the Russian-
dominated Polish government. The Russians intervened, and Beniowski was arrested and exiled to the island of Kamchatka. He escaped to Japan and, after a
brief stay in France, went to Madagascar, declaring
himself to be the island's king. He died while leading
the natives in a revolt against the French. Słowacki,
however, departs from the historical facts and transforms Beniowski into a young Polish nobleman who,
after losing his estate, joins the anti-Russian conspiracy. He is then sent to the Crimean peninsula on a diplomatic mission for the conspirators. Despite many perilous adventures, Beniowski manages to return to Poland
at the head of a regiment of Tartar cavalry. A romantic
interlude in which Beniowski falls in love with the
daughter of a comrade-in-arms completes the plot of
Słowacki's epic. Słowacki probably intended to add
further cantos, but he apparently lost interest in continuing the epic once he had been converted to Andrzej
Towiański's mystical theological doctrines.

GENEZIS Z DUCHA

On July 12, 1842, Towiański, a religious mystic
from Wilno, had a long talk with Słowacki and succeeded in converting him to his doctrine. Towiański
had been in Paris since September, 1841, and had already converted Mickiewicz to his inner circle. His
teachings emphasized the central importance of the Hebrew, French, and Polish peoples in God's scheme for
establishing the kingdom of heaven on Earth as well as
the crucial role to be played by great individuals in fur-
thering the historical manifestation of the Divine Will.
Even though Słowacki broke with his spiritual mentor
over a political question in November, 1843, he never
abandoned the basic tenets of Towiański's religious
credo. Using these precepts as a point of departure,

Słowacki went on to develop a highly original philosophy of his own, set forth in *Genezis z ducha* (genesis
from the spirit) and *Król-Duch*. Both of these works are
based on Słowacki's belief in the supremacy of spirit
over matter.

In the prose poem *Genezis z ducha* Słowacki presents his readers with a vision of cosmic evolution that
has strong affinities with the theories propounded in the
twentieth century by the French Jesuit Pierre Teilhard
de Chardin. Written at Pornic on the Atlantic coast, it
opens with a meditation on the ocean, the cradle of
life. Inspired by its protean form and erratic sound, the
poet proceeds to explore the mysteries of evolution
from inorganic matter to humanity itself. All existing
forms, he argues, are progressive manifestations of
spiritual forces that pervade the universe. This evolutionary process, moreover, will not be complete until
humankind assimilates the spiritual force of Christ's
nature. To reach this goal, people need leaders, for
whom Słowacki invents the term "king-spirits." At
times, whole nations may perform the function that he
attributes to the "king-spirits," and Słowacki asserts
that Poland, purified by its sufferings, has assumed this
role.

KRÓL-DUCH

The manifestation of the spirit on the historical level
is examined in *Król-Duch*, an epic poem written in
ottava rima and divided into segments called "rhapsodies." Here, Słowacki employs the concept of metem-
psychosis that is derived from the tenth book of Plato's
Politeia (fourth century B.C.E.; *Republic*, 1701), in
which the Orphic doctrine of reincarnation is propounded in the section titled "The Myth of Er." In
Słowacki's vision, a Greek warrior named Er embraces
the idea of Poland while awaiting his next reincarnation, and upon rebirth he assumes the identity of Popiel,
the legendary Polish king of prehistory. This semi-
mythical figure is reputed to have been a cruel tyrant,
but Słowacki assigns him the task of hardening the
minds and bodies of his placid Slavic subjects in order
to prepare them to do battle with the German maraud-
ers, who threaten the Polish nation with extinction. The
series of reincarnations continues, the king-spirit passing on from Popiel to Mieszko, the king who brought
Poland into the comity of Christian nations in 966.

Other reincarnations follow, carrying on the historical mission of Poland. The figures that Słowacki selects to embody the king-spirit were well known to Polish readers, and this work may be read as a historical romance if one chooses to do so—just as one may appreciate Dante's *The Divine Comedy* without subscribing to his theological presuppositions. *Król-Duch* is, in fact, the closest counterpart to *The Divine Comedy* in Polish literature, and many regard it as Słowacki's finest work, despite the fact that he was only able to give final form to the first of the five rhapsodies that constitute its text.

LYRIC POEMS

Słowacki's lyric poetry makes up a relatively small part of his total work. He wrote approximately 130 lyric poems, of which only thirteen appeared in print during his lifetime. A large number of the unpublished poems remain unfinished, but some are highly polished, and it is difficult to understand why he made no attempt to publish them. Słowacki's language is highly creative, owing its unconventional character to his preference for unusual words, neologisms, uncommon rhymes, and metrical virtuosity. His work in this genre, moreover, covers a wide range of themes, Perhaps the weakest are those that treat love, for it is always thwarted love, not its triumph, that interests the poet. More varied are those poems dealing with friendship, such as the ones written for Szpicnagel and Krasiński, as well as those pertaining to historical figures and contemporaries in the émigré community. There are, strangely enough, two poems addressed to Słowacki's mother. Patriotic revolutionary themes first make their appearance in connection with the November Insurrection and become an inexhaustible source of poetic inspiration from then on. After the summer of 1842, when Słowacki became a convert to Towiański's messianic doctrines, his lyric poems undergo a marked change in tone. The pessimism recedes and is replaced by a mood of mystical exaltation. With a newly found faith in his mission and in himself, Słowacki enters into a close communion with God—viewing God as his ally in the cause of Poland and expressing gratitude for his own transformation into "a vessel of grace."

There are, it is interesting to note, four poems in which Słowacki expresses resentment toward the papacy for its failure to support Poland's struggle for freedom. In an untitled poem on this theme composed in 1848, Słowacki actually makes a prophecy to the effect that a Slavic pope will someday occupy the chair of Saint Peter.

> In the midst of dissension the Lord God suddenly
>   rings an enormous bell.
> Behold! He throws open his earthly throne to a pope
>   from Slavic realms.
> . . . .
> We need strength so as to rejuvenate this lordly world
>   of ours:
> A Slavic pope, a brother to humankind, comes to aid
>   us in this task.
> Look and see how he anoints our bodies with the
>   balms of the world,
> While a celestial choir of angels bedecks his throne
>   with resplendent flowers.

This poem is among the last that Słowacki wrote, and nowhere does he demonstrate the vatic powers of a national bard more fully. When the announcement "Habemus Papam!" was made on October 16, 1978, the world learned to its astonishment that the papal designate was a cardinal from Kraków named Karol Wojtyła.

A fruitful insight into the nature of Słowacki's approach to poetry is contained in an article titled "A Few Words About Juliusz Słowacki," written by his friend Krasiński. Here, Krasiński compares Słowacki with Mickiewiez and contends that the former's poetic style is "centrifugal" while the latter's is "centripetal." In place of the concreteness and tangibility that characterizes Mickiewicz's work, Słowacki's poetry manifests a dispersing tendency that is cosmic in its range. In Mickiewicz, moreover, one senses a poet who is exercising strict control over his language, while Słowacki appears at times to be engaged in a form of automatic writing. His imagery, as a consequence, is frequently diffuse and indistinct in a way that is reminiscent of the aesthetic qualities embodied in the paintings of the nineteenth century English artist J. M. W. Turner. Like Turner, Słowacki has a profound interest in color, and his poetry therefore shares many of the coloristic attributes of that written in Poland during the Baroque period. Musicality is, by the same token, another feature of Słowacki's verse that sets it apart from the more natural speech intonations to be found in that of Mickiewicz. Because of such significant stylistic differences, the poetical works of Słowacki and Mickiewicz are best viewed as complementary. It is, therefore, highly appropriate that the mortal remains of Słowacki and Mickiewicz now rest side by side in the royal crypt of the Wawel Castle in Kraków. They are, it should be noted, the only poets who have been accorded the signal honor of interment at the site of this Polish equivalent to Westminster Abbey.

OTHER MAJOR WORKS

PLAYS: *Maria Stuart*, pb. 1832 (*Mary Stuart*, 1937); *Mindowe Król Litewski*, pb. 1832 (wr. 1829); *Kordian*, pb. 1834; *Balladyna*, pb. 1839 (wr. 1834; English translation, 1960); *Lilla Weneda*, pb. 1840; *Mazepa*, pb. 1840 (*Mazeppa*, 1930); *Ksiądz Marek*, pb. 1843, *Agezylausz*, pb. 1844; *Książę niezłomny*, pb. 1844; *Sen srebrny Salomei*, pb. 1844; *Beatrix Cenci*, pb. 1866 (wr. 1839); *Fantazy*, pb. 1866 (wr. 1841; English translation, 1977); *Horsztyński*, pb. 1866 (wr. 1835); *Złota czaszka*, pb. 1866 (wr. 1842); *Zawisza Czarny*, pb. 1889 (wr. 1844); *Samuel Zborowski*, pr. 1911 (wr. 1845).

NONFICTION: *Podróż na wschód*, 1836.

MISCELLANEOUS: *Dzieła wszystkie*, 1952-1960 (complete works, including *Podróż na Wschód*, wr. 1836; Juliusz Kleiner, editor); *Poland's Angry Romantic: Two Poems and a Play*, 2009 (includes *Balladina*, *Agamemnon's Tomb*, and *Beniowski*).

BIBLIOGRAPHY

Cochran, Peter. Introduction to *Poland's Angry Romantic: Two Poems and a Play*, by Juliusz Słowacki. Edited and translated by Peter Cochran et al. Newcastle, England: Cambridge Scholars, 2009. An informative introduction that provides biographical background and critical analysis.

Dernałowicz, Maria. *Juliusz Słowacki*. Warsaw: Interpress, 1987. A short biographical study of the poet's life and work. Includes an index.

González, Fernando Presa. "Polish Literature in the Great Emigration of 1830: Adam Mickiewicz, Juliusz Słowacki, and Zygmunt Krasiński." In *Literature in Exile of East and Central Europe*, edited by Agnieszka Gutthy. New York: Peter Lang, 2009.

Takes up the topic of the Great Emigration and Słowacki, focusing on his writings.

Kridl, Manfred. *The Lyric Poems of Julius Słowacki*. The Hague, the Netherlands: Mouton, 1958. A critical assessment of the poetic works of Słowacki. Includes bibliographic references.

Krzyżanowski, Julian. *A History of Polish Literature*. Warsaw: PWN-Polish Scientific, 1978. A study of Polish literature that includes coverage of Słowacki. Bibliography and index.

Miłosz, Czesław. *The History of Polish Literature*. 2d ed. Berkeley: University of California Press, 1983. A scholarly study of Polish literature that includes a discussion of the role of Słowacki. Bibliography and index.

Treugutt, Stefan. *Juliusz Słowacki: Romantic Poet*. Warsaw: Polonia, 1959. A critical analysis of Słowacki's poetic works.

Victor Anthony Rudowski

EDITH SÖDERGRAN

Born: St. Petersburg, Russia; April 4, 1892
Died: Raivola, Finland; June 24, 1923

PRINCIPAL POETRY

Dikter, 1916 (*Poems*, 1980)
Septemberlyran, 1918 (*The September Lyre*, 1980)
Brokiga iakttagelser, 1919 (*Motley Observations*, 1980)
Rosenalteret, 1919 (*The Rose Altar*, 1980)
Framtidens skugga, 1920 (*The Shadow of the Future*, 1980)
Landet som icke är, 1925
Min lyra, 1929
Edith Södergrans dikter, 1940 (*The Collected Poems of Edith Södergran*, 1980)
We Women: Selected Poems of Edith Södergran, 1977
Love and Solitude: Selected Poems, 1916-1923, 1980, 1985
Poems, 1983
Complete Poems, 1984

Other literary forms

Edith Södergran (SUH-dur-grahn) died of tuberculosis at the age of thirty-one, and many of her works were published posthumously. She left behind a remarkable collection of letters to Hagar Olsson, a critic and novelist whose favorable review of Södergran's *The September Lyre* led to a close friendship between the two young women. Södergran's correspondence with Olsson was published under the title *Ediths brev: Brev från Edith Södergran till Hagar Olsson* (Edith's letters: letters from Edith Södergran to Hagar Olsson) in 1955. The letters appeared in translation in *The Poet Who Created Herself: The Complete Letters of Edith Södergran to Hagar Olsson with Hagar Olsson's Commentary and the Complete Letters of Edith Södergran to Elmer Diktonius* (2001).

Achievements

Edith Södergran's poetry met with a baffled and even hostile reception in her own day, with a few notable exceptions, and even caused a journalistic debate as to her sanity. Writing in a period when Nordic verse still supported traditional values of regular meter and rhyme, Södergran espoused free verse and arrived—apparently on her own initiative—at something like the "doctrine of the image" laid out by Ezra Pound in 1912, derived by him in part from his study of the first poems of H. D. Therefore, shortly before her death, Södergran was hailed in the Finno-Swedish journal *Ultra* as the pioneer of Finnish modernism.

By the 1930's, Södergran's home in Raivola (later Rodzino) had become an unofficial shrine for younger poets, and Södergran's work was revered by a number of successors, among these Gunnar Ekelöf, the Swedish poet, and Uuno Kailas, the Finnish writer. Her courageous rejection of verse conventions inspired later poets to do the same. Her canon makes clear the expressionistic elements in the modernist temper, and in granting pride of place to irrational forces, Södergran (wittingly or not) aligned herself with such contemporaries as D. H. Lawrence, James Joyce, and André Breton. In the words of George Schoolfield, "Her simple directness, enlivened by her genius for the unexpected in language, is seen to best advantage when [she] is overwhelmed by forces outside herself." This primordial and homespun receptivity has proved to be a highly prospective stance, and accounts for Södergran's continuing popularity, enhanced by the feminist movement's reexamination of women's writing, spreading far beyond the boundaries of Norden, and gaining momentum more than sixty years after her death.

Biography

Edith Södergran was born on April 4, 1892, in the cosmopolitan city of St. Petersburg (called Leningrad during the years of the Soviet Union), the principal Baltic seaport and then capital of Russia. Her father, Mattias Södergran, came from a family of farmers who, while they lived in northwestern Finland, were of Swedish stock. Her mother, Helena Holmroos, Mattias's second wife, was the daughter of a prosperous industrialist, also of Finno-Swedish descent. When she was three months old, Södergran's family moved to Raivola, a village in the Finnish province of Karelia, close to the Russian border. Thenceforth, the family divided their time between St. Petersburg, where they wintered, and Raivola. Södergran received a sound education at a German church school, studying the literature of France, Russia, and Germany. Her apprentice verse was written in German, which she learned not only in school but also at the sanatorium in Davos, Switzerland; she was a patient there from 1912 to 1913 and again from 1913 to 1914. Heinrich Heine provided the model for much of Södergran's early writing.

Södergran's father died of tuberculosis in 1907, after which his family ceased to reside in St. Petersburg. In 1908, Södergran was discovered to be tubercular, and between 1909 and 1911, she was on several occasions confined to a sanatorium at Nummela, in Finland. Nummela was the only place she lived where Swedish was the primary language; otherwise, Södergran spoke Swedish mainly with her mother.

It is believed that the philologist Hugo Bergroth was instrumental in persuading Södergran to write in Swedish. Nevertheless, she had very little knowledge of the literature of that language, beyond the work of two nineteenth century authors, C. J. L. Almqvist, whose novel *Drottningens juvelsmycke* (1834; *The Queen's*

Diadem, 1992) she found fascinating, and Johan Ludvig Runeberg, with his aphoristic lyrical poems. Her interest, rather, lay elsewhere—in such German expressionists as Else Lasker-Schüler and Alfred Mombert, in Victor Hugo (whose *Les Misérables*, 1862; English translation, 1862; captured her attention), in Rudyard Kipling (particularly his *The Jungle Book*, 1894), in Maurice Maeterlinck, in Walt Whitman, and in the Russians Konstantin Dmitrievich Balmont and Igor Severyanin.

A turning point in Södergran's life was her love affair, during her early twenties, with a married man, an affair of the kind customarily known as unhappy. Presumably it was not consistently so. For a poet so able to live with paradox, the relationship may have been, after all, deeply inspirational. Certainly, the affair virtually coincided with an intense period of production, during which she wrote the first of her mature works. Södergran's sense of her own poetic powers had been waxing throughout these two years, 1915 and 1916, and had given her the impetus to visit Helsinki to show her manuscripts to Arvid Mörne, the poet, and Gunnar Castrén, the critic. The literary world of Helsinki was unreceptive to her work; her first book, *Poems*, prompted one reviewer to wonder whether her publisher had wanted to give Swedish Finland a good laugh, and in general, reactions ranged from amused bewilderment to open ridicule. Södergran appears to have been taken completely aback by such uncomprehending hostility; her naïveté, one of the strengths of her poetry, was in this respect a major weakness of her person, and it caused her many painful passages.

However, resilience was hers in equal measure, and before long, Södergran regained equilibrium, coming to think of herself (indeed, quite properly) as a literary pioneer. Her sense of mission grew with her reading of Friedrich Nietzsche, whose influence may be traced throughout her subsequent work. Will in the sense of libido becomes a fundamental drive that her poetry not only acknowledges but also would advance. In "Mitt liv, min död och mitt öde" ("My Life, My Death, My Fate," composed in 1919, published in *Landet som icke är*), Södergran writes:

> I am nothing but a boundless will,
> a boundless will, but for what, for what?
> Everything is darkness around me.
> I cannot lift a straw.
> My will wants but one thing, but this thing I don't know.
> When my will breaks from me, then shall I die:
> All hail my life, my death and my fate!

She praises the moment when these three abstract, powerful forces unite into the one action, the moment of discovery, when the alienation of categories is banished by the wholeness, the good health, of choice, when the will to choose and the will to be chosen fuse, banishing both subjective and objective, to disclose the truth: that life, death, and one's fate are all of a piece, compose one single motion. The "I" one was until that moment "dies" and is replaced by the "I" who has chosen, having discovered that "thing" which until then one had not known.

Resilient though she was, however, Södergran was increasingly ill. More than her personal world was in turmoil. World War I, in which Russia was then engaged, led to the Russian Revolution of 1917. Raivola, astride a trunk line of the railroad from St. Petersburg, witnessed both troop transports and refugee trains passing through, and with the revolution, Södergran and her mother found themselves destitute, for St. Petersburg had been their source of funds. In this same year, 1917, Finland declared its independence from Russia, and the ensuing civil war resulted in near starvation for the poet and her family. At the same time, however, to behold so many other substantially afflicted persons helped Södergran place her own hardships in perspective. She learned quickly from her experiences. Huge, irrational forces had been unleashed, yet Södergran had the grace to recognize her world. In her introduction to *The September Lyre*, she observes:

> My poems are to be taken as careless sketches. As to the contents, I let my instincts build while my intellect watches. My self-confidence comes from the fact that I have discovered my dimensions. It does not behoove me to make myself smaller than I am.

To some extent, this was surely a whistling in the dark. Two further books of poetry were met with tremendous hostility. There was one favorable review, however, by Olsson, and to this Södergran responded with incredulous joy. The two became fast friends, albeit mainly through correspondence. (Invited to visit Olsson in Helsinki, Södergran declined: "Insomnia, tuberculosis, no money. We live by selling our furniture.") They met only a few times, but their correspondence flourished.

Södergran became a convert to anthroposophy, the belief of Rudolf Steiner, and thence to a primitive Christianity, which replaced for her the writing of poetry. She returned to poetry, however, shortly before her death, on June 24, 1923, at Raivola. The posthumous publication of her previously uncollected poems from 1915, under the title *Landet som icke är* (the land which is not), established her as a major poet. Subsequent collections and volumes of selected poems continue to appear, enhancing Södergran's reputation and securing for her an ever-widening audience.

ANALYSIS

The power of Edith Södergran's poetry stems from the complex mixture of its elements. She gives the impression of being very straight-spoken, yet for all that, most of her poems are deeply enigmatic. Her choice of subjects is usually appropriate to this technique. One is reminded of a child at that stage where puberty startles it out of one kind of consciousness into another. This is the age when the "big" questions come up: What is outside the universe? What was before time began? What is death? What shall be my destiny? And love—what is love?

Somehow, Södergran survived the subsequent stages of her life to produce virtually intact poems of a childlike naïveté wedded to a maturity that feels precocious—the precocious intelligence of the thirteen-year-old who has recently realized that she is more far-seeing than her elders and that she sees more clearly into the heart of adult life because she is so new to it. This image, subliminal in so many of her poems, of a gravely joyous child gazing directly into adulthood and finding it at once wanting and yet (wisely) sufficient, wreathes her poetry in an aura of heartbreak. All the mysterious grand abstractions—death, life, love, pain, happiness, grief, instinct, hell—framed by the pubescent as essential questions to be answered are answered

in Södergran's poetry, as in life, with an image that may at first appear as basically haphazard but which one then comes to apprehend as intuitively adequate. Life proves to be not the wondrous thing one had at thirteen thought it to be; it turns out, however, in its difference from the ideal, to be something (a state of affairs that is recognized, by a sudden twist of maturity, to be in itself wondrous).

Södergran does not incorporate undigested personal experience into her work. Her experience is nearly always universalized, through either a symbol or (more interestingly) some less predicated distancing technique—or a combination of both, as at the end of part 2 of "Dagen svalnar . . ." ("The Day Cools . . . ," from *Poems*, 1980):

> You cast your love's red rose
> into my white womb—
> I hold it tight in my hot hands,
> your love's red rose that will shortly wilt . . .
> O thou master, with the icy eyes,
> I accept the crown you give me,
> that bends my head towards my heart.

This passage demonstrates Södergran's ability to qualify the symbol with realism and realism with its own stylization: "head" being a symbol for thought, rationality, as distinct from feeling, impulse, symbolized by heart, yet at the same time as she is using this symbolic language to imply that, in love, the head is brought nearer to the heart, she is also stating the fact that, in the act of love, the neck can bend the head forward, bringing it literally closer to the heart, but perhaps only literally. The physical undoes the symbolic, even as the latter transcends the physical. The same double movement is present throughout this poem: The presence of the physical both renders the symbolism ironic ("red rose" is so obviously a penis) and accounts for it, explains away its symbolism, even while the symbolic is raising the sad physical facts to a transcendent plane, as though from lust to love.

"DISCOVERY"

In this technique, the essential ambiguity of such a situation is preserved intact, preserved from the poet's intentions and from the reader's everlasting demand for assurance. Is the "master" subject only to "higher" motives? That one may doubt this is suggested in "Upp-täckt" ("Discovery," from *The September Lyre*):

> Your love darkens my star—
> the moon rises in my life.
> My hand is not at home in yours.
> Your hand is lust—
> my hand is longing.

Here, Södergran lays out neatly the two halves of the picture, the "fifty-fifty" of the heterosexual fix. His love, although desired (in fact, "longed for"), threatens to overwhelm the woman, who senses that her own "star" (her own sense of self and particular destiny) is being obscured by the male presence, no doubt filled with assumptions and demands, obscured in the way that the light of a star is blocked when the full moon rises. Panicked, she retreats: "My hand is not at home in yours." Presumably she had felt otherwise about this man. Thus she leads herself to her "discovery": He lusts, while she longs. He also longs, as no doubt she also lusts; it is a question of which emotion is primary. Enlightened, however sadly, the poet, through observing this dynamic, gives herself back to herself and finds her star. Able to describe the process, she finds a power within herself to withstand it. It is noteworthy that Södergran is not deterred from her use of natural imagery by preexisting symbolic meaning: that the moon, for example, is customarily a symbol of the female.

"FOREST LAKE"

Such nature imagery permeates Södergran's work from start to finish. Whole poems are built from observations of the landscape and weather of Raivola. "Skogssjön" ("Forest Lake," from *Poems*, 1980) is a striking example of this:

> I was alone on the sunny strand
> by the forest's pale blue lake,
> in the heavens floated a single cloud
> and on the water a single isle.
> The ripening summer's sweetness dripped
> in beads from every tree
> and into my opened heart ran
> down one little drop.

Nature burgeons on all sides in supernumerous abundance, while in the felt middle of it all, the human singularity (which remarks not only the various signs of its own condition—cloud, island, lake, each one a singular—but also, the signs of its opposite state—the "beads" that drip from "every tree") inevitably, inescapably one feels, selects for itself that which most speaks to it of itself from out of the swarming possibilities. One senses at once the rightness of this as well as the sadness. In the phrase "one little drop," a pathos inheres: Why so little, when one is offered so much? However, the poem offers also a sense of this as sufficient; it is characteristic of Södergran's poetry to play between senses of pathetic inadequacy and grateful, if humble, plenitude.

"THE DAY COOLS . . ."

Sometimes the speaker senses herself as the source of the inadequacy, as in part 4 of "The Day Cools . . .":

> You sought a flower
> and found a fruit.
> You sought a well
> and found a sea.
> You sought a woman
> and found a soul—
> you are disappointed.

The irony of the situation, which she sees and names so clearly, does not completely expunge the guilt of the speaker. Somehow, one feels, she holds herself to blame for being so much more than the seeker expected to find. She is caught in the patriarchal trap, even as she would, with her vision and fluency, transcend it. Indeed, for her to testify otherwise would be an impossible distortion of reality, one that would demean her import and that of her fellow sufferers.

The simple symmetry of this poem reminds one of Södergran's courage in discarding so many of the conventional signs of verse. Perhaps it was as much a blind plunge forward as a reasoned decision; no matter, the result is the same. Whether the reader indeed interprets her poems, as she advised, as "careless sketches," or, disregarding that phrase as one born of a strictly temporary bravado, one views them as finished pieces is irrelevant. Certainly, she did not abjure regular meter and rhyme out of inability; while still a schoolgirl, she composed hundreds of verses in the manner typical of Heine.

While at Davos, Södergran learned something of

the current furor and ferment at work in European art and letters, and possibly of free verse. Above all, however, her writing is instinct with craft; Södergran has no need to make a display of her talent in more conventional terms because so many of her poems bear this out at the microscopic level.

"NOTHING"

If there are infelicities in Södergran's poetry, they are those inherent in writing poetry whose rhythms are at times those of prose. One notes the occasional deafness to the echoes of what is being said. In "Farliga drömma" ("Dangerous Dreams," from *Landet som icke är*), she inquires, "Have you looked your dreams in the eye?" her own eye on the object of her poem, distracting her from the faintly ridiculous literal picture presented. Because both "dreams" and "look in the eye" are clichés, it is not easy to remember that they allude to specifics. Her practice of personifying abstractions gets her into trouble sometimes, "My soul can only cry and laugh and wring its hands," as in "Min själ" ("My Soul," from *Poems*, 1980), or "Will fate throw snowballs at me?" as in "Hyacinten" ("The Hyacinth," from *The Shadow of the Future*). However, there is a charm of sorts in these minor ineptitudes, some echo of the child just learning to put words together; surely this is one with her ingenuousness and directness. The person who senses her soul as real, as real as her body, is blind to the unintended image offered of a pair of bodiless hands "wringing" each other; this is the same person who can write of the abstraction nothing, in "Ingenting" ("Nothing," from *Landet som icke är*):

> We should love life's long hours of illness
> and narrow years of longing
> as we do the brief instants when the desert flowers.

In this poem, Södergran is reminiscent of John Keats in "To Autumn"—the spiritual definition of "iron" circumstance which allows one room to live. It is a wonderful benignity, won at what cost from malign condition, and not at all ironic. There are certainly poems of less mitigated bitterness, but even with these, one feels that in the act of naming the enemy, Södergran has won the only release truly possible from the shadow of death and death-in-life. Through the storms within her own

organism, as through the storms without (war, revolution, poverty, and hunger) she looked steadily into the heart of things. In a very late and striking poem, "Lander som icke är" ("The Land That Is Not," from *Landet som icke är*), she wrote

> I long for the land that is not,
> because everything that is, I'm too weary to want.
> The moon tells me in silvery runes
> of the land that is not.
> The land where all our wishes shall be wondrously
>   fulfilled,
> the land where our shackles drop off,
> the land where we cool our bleeding forehead
> in moon-dew.
> My life was a feverish illusion.
> But one thing I have found and one I have really won—
> the way to the land that is not.

The poem has a further stanza but should have ended here. Södergran's gift for discerning the positive in the negative has seldom been more strongly realized. Through her genius, the reader comes to understand how the negative is so qualified, somewhat as "faery lands forlorn" in Keats's "Ode to a Nightingale," and that a simple act of the imagination may transform nothingness into a vision more sustaining than anything that blank materialism affords.

OTHER MAJOR WORKS

NONFICTION: *Ediths brev: Brev från Edith Södergran till Hagar Olsson*, 1955; *The Poet Who Created Herself: The Complete Letters of Edith Södergran to Hagar Olsson with Hagar Olsson's Commentary and the Complete Letters of Edith Södergran to Elmer Diktonius*, 2001 (translated and edited by Silvester Mazzarella).

BIBLIOGRAPHY

Jones, W. Glyn, and M. A. Branch, eds. *Edith Södergran*. London: University of London Press, 1992. A collection of nine biographical essays dealing with Södergran's life and works. Includes bibliographical references and indexes.

Katchadourian, Stina. Introduction to *Love and Solitude: Selected Poems, 1916-1923*, by Edith Södergran. 3d ed. Seattle, Wash.: Fjord Press, 1992. Katchadourian's introduction to this translation of a selection of Södergran's poetry offers some biographical and historical background for her life and works.

Lindqvist, Ursula. "The Paradoxical Poetics of Edith Södergran." *Modernism/Modernity* 13, no. 1 (2006): 813-818. Examines the paradoxical nature of Södergran's poetry, which contains a complex mix of themes.

Schoolfield, George C. *Edith Södergran: Modernist Poet in Finland.* Westport, Conn.: Greenwood Press, 1984. A biography of Södergran detailing the historical background of her life and works. Includes bibliographic references and an index.

Södergran, Edith, and Hagar Olsson. *The Poet Who Created Herself: The Complete Letters of Edith Södergran to Hagar Olsson with Hagar Olsson's Commentary and the Complete Letters of Edith Södergran to Elmer Diktonius.* Translated and edited by Silvester Mazzarella. Chester Springs, Pa.: Dufour Editions, 2001. These letters to Södergran's critic and friend Olsson and to the poet and composer Diktonius reveal a great deal about the poet's thoughts. Olsson's commentary provides additional background.

Valtiala, Nalle. "Edith Södergran: When Karelia Was the Centre." In *Centring on the Peripheries: Studies in Scandinavian, Scottish, Gaelic, and Greenlandic Literature,* edited by Bjarne Thorup Thomsen. Norwich, England: Norvik Press, 2007. This essay looks at the innovations of Södergran and her influence on subsequent Scandinavian literature.

Witt-Brattstrom, Ebba. "Towards a Feminist Genealogy of Modernism: The Narcissistic Turn in Lou Andreas-Salomé and Edith Södergran." In *Gender, Power, Text: Nordic Culture in the Twentieth Century,* edited by Helena Forsås-Scott. Norwich, England: Norvik Press, 2004. Examines Södergran and the mistress of Rainer Maria Rilke, looking at the development of modernism from a feminist perspective.

David Bromige

DIONYSIOS SOLOMOS

Born: Zakynthos, Greece; April 8, 1798
Died: Corfu, Greece; November 21, 1857

PRINCIPAL POETRY

Rime improvisate, 1822
Imnos is tin eleftheria, 1823 (*The Hymn to Liberty,* 1825)
Is ton thanato tou Lord Byron, 1824
Lambros, 1834 (partial), 1859
Ta euriskomena, 1859 (collection of works including the foregoing as well as *Eleftheroi poliorkimenoi, To Kritikos,* and *Porphyras*)
Hapanta, 1880, 1948-1960 (collected works)
Faith and Motherland: Collected Poems, 1998
The Free Besieged, and Other Poems, 2000

OTHER LITERARY FORMS

Although verse was the major form of expression of Dionysios Solomos (saw-law-MAWS), he published two works of prose. *Dialogos* (1824) is Solomos's defense of the demotic language of Greece, a kind of rebuttal to Adamantios Koras and other proponents of the *katharevousa,* the purist tongue. Solomos asserted that the language of the people belongs only to them, and no external forces can change it. It was also part of his credo that the poet, as a custodian of the language, must enrich and ennoble it from within. The twenty-five or thirty pages of *Dialogos* (one part of the work has been lost), written in the form of a conversation between a poet, a friend, and a philosopher, have served as the prototype of modern Greek prose. Solomos's other prose work is *I yineka tis Zakynthos* (1927, 1944; *The Woman of Zakynthos,* 1982), an enigmatic, fragmentary work set at the time of the fall of Missolonghi.

ACHIEVEMENTS

Dionysios Solomos is the national poet of modern Greece. The first four stanzas of his *The Hymn to Liberty* were proclaimed by King Otto in 1865 as the Greek national anthem, and Greek schoolchildren have been learning and memorizing Solomos's verses for more than 150 years. His use of demotic Greek—the spoken language of everyday life—prepared the way for the extraordinary flowering of Greek poetry in the twentieth century.

Solomos has been the subject of studies in Italian, Dutch, French, German, Romanian, and Turkish, as well as English. The critic M. Byron Raizis has estimated that scholarly works on Solomos "approach the one-thousand mark." Because Solomos wrote in Italian in the early years of his apprenticeship, he has been especially interesting to Italian poets and critics.

Solomos's contemporaries acknowledged him as the founder of modern Greek poetry: He took it upon himself to become a Greek Dante, a poet who would use the vernacular, the language of the people, to praise his countrymen's struggle for liberation and to sing of the pains, the values, and the joys of the land of his birth. What Alexander Pushkin, who was born a year later, came to mean to the Russians, Solomos came to mean to the Greeks. Like Pushkin's lyrics, Solomos's Romantic verse lauded freedom and castigated tyranny. Solomos is regarded as the quintessence of the national genius; it is no wonder that after his death, the Greek poet was given a state funeral, which was followed by public mourning throughout Greece.

It is not only for his poetry, then, that Solomos is important. He was the bard of the Greek War of Independence; he introduced Romanticism to Greece; and perhaps most important, he gave dignity to demotic Greek, the language of the people, at a time when pretentious literati in Greece were working hard to impose the purist tongue on the recently freed, tormented country.

In contemporary Greece, Solomos's appeal transcends ideological boundaries: He is loved by conservatives, for he represents that old spirit of the disciplined artist, the pioneer of Hellenic values. The leftists honor him for praising the virtues of struggle and for dramatizing the plight of the oppressed. The Greek Orthodox Church has embraced him for praising the religious values of his land and for his acceptance of the Church's role in the war of liberation from the Turks. He is admired by Greek youth, who respond to the youthful energy and simplicity of his patriotic and romantic verse. Solomos's achievement as a Greek poet is unquestioned and unshakable.

BIOGRAPHY

After the fall of Constantinople in May, 1453, Greece, under oppressive Ottoman rule, remained a cultural wasteland for nearly four hundred years. When Crete fell to the Turks in 1669, the Solomos family migrated to the Heptanesian island of Zakynthos, having first been honored by the Venetian administrators in Crete with titles of nobility. After one generation, Count Nicholas Solomos, the poet's father (acknowledged as count by the Venetian authorities of Zakynthos), succeeded in acquiring the tobacco monopoly of the island, and in a few years, the shrewd businessman had amassed a large fortune. Dionysios Solomos was born to Count Nicholas in 1798; at his birth, his father was sixty-one and his mother, the count's maid, only seventeen years old. When Solomos was seven years old, he came under the tutelage of an Italian priest, Santo Rossi, then living in exile on Zakynthos because of his liberal views. Father Rossi taught the precocious boy not only the language of Italy but also its culture and literature.

After the death of his father, Solomos (accompanied by Rossi) was sent to Italy for a more sophisticated, more systematic education. In 1807 and 1808, in Venice and Cremona, the youth studied Latin and Italian philology. He was introduced to liberal ideas, to Romantic aestheticism, and to the works of Vergil, Dante, and Petrarch, who were to influence his poetry. From 1812 to 1814, he wrote his first Italian verse. The fall of 1815 found the seventeen-year-old Solomos studying law at the University of Pavia. Although he received his first certificate of law, literature was his consuming interest. In Milan in 1817, Solomos met the famous poet and translator of Homer, Vincenzo Monti. Legend has it that the young Greek got into an argument with Monti over a certain passage in Dante's *Inferno* (in *La divina commedia*, c. 1320; *The Divine Comedy*, 1802). "Nobody should rationalize so much," Monti chastised the youth. "One should feel, feel." Solomos's reply has been repeated with pride by his biographers: "First the mind must understand vigorously, and then the heart must feel warmly what the mind has comprehended."

Solomos's return to Zakynthos in August, 1818, presented him with a challenge: How could he thrive intellectually in a place that did not have the cultural fervor of the Italy of his adolescence? There were some intellectuals on the island, but not of the caliber of Ignazio Baretta, Mateo Butturini, or Monti. Nevertheless, Zakynthos was not intellectually barren: Andreas Kalvos, a contemporary of Solomos and a great poet himself, was born in Zakynthos, though there is no indication that he ever met Solomos. The island, too, was the birthplace of Ugo Foscolo (a half-Greek poet who wrote in Italian, a giant of the Romantic movement), whom Solomos did befriend, as in due course he befriended several other Zakynthos intellectuals.

Italian gave way to the Greek language in Solomos's verse soon after his return to Zakynthos. His sonnets and religious poetry still manifested his Romantic tendencies, along with the techniques of prosody that he had learned in Cremona and Venice. He had not yet achieved the mastery of the demotic that would distinguish his later verse.

Solomos's serious Greek verse began, in fact, when Spyridon Trikoupis visited Zakynthos. Trikoupis was a politician and the foremost historian of the Greek War of Independence. A relative of the Greek leader Alexandros Mavrokordatos, Trikoupis had come to Zakynthos to meet Lord Byron. When Trikoupis met Solomos at the end of 1822, the latter read him his Italian "Ode per prima messa." Trikoupis fell silent for a moment and then told Solomos that what their country needed was a Greek poet. "Greece is waiting for her Dante," exclaimed Trikoupis. Solomos must have been both flattered and challenged. He had not actively joined the fight against the Turks, partly because of his reclusive personality and partly because the Greek revolutionaries, though heroic, were cantankerous and uneducated villagers. There is no indication, in fact, that the poet ever visited the Greek mainland. The meeting with Trikoupis, however, sparked in the young poet a patriotic sense of literary duty. Though he never forsook his Italianate learning, he turned to Greek themes and the Greek language.

Some six months after meeting Trikoupis, Solomos completed the 158 quatrains that constitute *The Hymn to Liberty*. The long poem (whose first stanzas became the Greek national anthem) reenacts scenes from the Greek War of Independence and exalts the glory of Greece and of Greek freedom. Solomos's diligent ef-

fort to improve his Greek and to become the Greek poet par excellence must have also been inspired by the publication of Claude Fauriel's *Chansons populaires de Grece* (1824), in which the Frenchman praised the Greek language as "the most beautiful of the European languages and the one . . . suited to perfection." Fauriel further prophesied that "modern Greek will soon be a language which, without resembling ancient Greek more than it now resembles it, will have no reason to envy it." Years later, Solomos would collaborate with Fauriel.

In 1928, when most of Greece had been liberated, Solomos moved from Zakynthos to the island of Kerkyra (Corfu). By then, Solomos had become famous throughout Greece, and on Corfu, he found the solitude that he sought. There, he pursued more vigorously his studies in the German Romantic movement, in particular the works of Friedrich Schiller. Though a more prolific decade was behind him, the decade that followed was to be more impressive in terms of the quality of his work. On Corfu, Solomos honed and refined his poetry, working on his fragmentary *The Woman of Zakynthos*, on *Eleftheroi poliorkimenoi* (the free besieged), and on *To Kritikos*, revising his *Lambros*, and writing his serene "Funeral Ode" and "To an English Lady."

Temperamental, especially during his years on Corfu, Solomos manifested a disquieting propensity to leave his works incomplete. An extreme perfectionist, he destroyed almost as many manuscripts as he was able to complete. Kostis Palamas, Solomos's successor as the poet of the Greek people, discerned a duality in Solomos's nature: the dedicated, patient, profound creator opposed to the impetuous, bored, immature man who could not complete his work when he felt disheartened and unsatisfied. Other critics, in examining his character, have pointed to the distractions of a prolonged legal battle: John Leontarakis, Solomos's half brother, sued to prove, both for inheritance purposes and out of vindictiveness, that he, John, was the only legitimate son of Count Nicholas. The trial that ensued lasted from 1833 to 1838 and embittered Solomos greatly, since he had helped his half brother both socially and financially. This humiliating episode, and the poet's own restless nature, explain—as well as anything can explain—his inability to finish many of his poems.

The litigation with his half brother—finally won by Solomos—caused the poet to retreat even more into his solitude. "There is no doubt," he wrote to his friend George Markoras, "that one can live well only alone." It was probably at this time that Solomos began drinking, which may well have affected both the quality as well as the quantity of his subsequent work. Solomos's struggle for perfection, however, overcame all the crises that held him back. Indeed, he wrote his best poetry during the last twenty years of his life: *To Kritikos*, *Eleftheroi poliorkimenoi*, and *Porphyras* were written during this period. The obstacles in his life were counterbalanced by the recognition he received not only in Greece but also throughout Western Europe. In 1849, King Otto of Greece bestowed on Solomos the Golden Cross of the Royal Order of the Savior. By then, Solomos was respected even among the envious mainland writers.

Despite his preference for solitude, Solomos had a select group of friends while living on Corfu. James Polylas, who selflessly collected and edited Solomos's works posthumously (in *Ta euriskomena*), was one of the most loyal; Nicholas Mantzaros, the composer who set the lyrics of *The Hymn to Liberty* to music, was another. Solomos never married, and no evidence of a love affair exists.

From 1847 to 1851, Solomos returned to writing verse in Italian, which some critics see as evidence of his disappointment with his output in Greek. However, even when he wrote in Italian, most of his themes remained Greek ("To Orpheus," "The Greek Mother," "The Greek Vessel"). It was also during this period, between 1847 and 1849, that he wrote one of his greatest works in Greek, *Porphyras*.

During the last decade of his life, Solomos's health deteriorated. He suffered a cerebral stroke in 1851, and his niece's suicide caused him further depression that year; fits of melancholy continued until his death. On November 21, 1857, he died of a stroke. It is alleged that on his deathbed, the poet remembered the beloved mentor of his youth, Rossi, and that in gratitude to him, he recited stanza 95 of *The Hymn to Liberty*, where Liberty is seen allegorically in imagery of light:

> Fiery gleams of flashing cluster
> Hang from lip, eye, forehead bright,
> Hand and foot are clothed in luster,
> And around you all is light.

ANALYSIS

It is unfortunate that Dionysios Solomos's poetry is almost totally resistant to translation. Just as Robert Burns's musical lines suffer greatly in translation into other languages, and just as Pushkin's lyric Russian is frustrating to translators, so Solomos and his lyric rhyming lines lose a great deal in translation. It is difficult to convey the exquisite music of his stanzas, his struggle to achieve perfection with each poem, his admirable development in diction and form. A good translation will communicate only in part the energy of his language, but even in translation, one can still appreciate Solomos's love of freedom and his loathing of oppression, his compassion for the humble and his bewilderment with the injustices of destiny.

Solomos started to write seriously upon his return from Italy in 1818. His early poems, written in Italian, are more mature and precise than the naïve and imperfect poems that he wrote when he first experimented with the Greek language. His earliest poems were written in short, flexible trochaic and iambic lines; when he attempted decapentasyllabic couplets, in imitation of the Greek folk song, the prosody appeared contrived and superficial.

Among these early poems, there are many that are pastoral in nature, such as "The Death of the Shepherd," "Eurykome," and "The Death of the Orphan Girl." Most typical of Solomos's work at this stage is "The Mad Mother," a moving poem about the tragic death of a child; the Romantic elements are obvious. Here, Solomos employs a favorite theme: the suffering of a gentle woman at the hands of fate. "The Unknown Woman" and "Xanthoula" are two more sophisticated poems with this theme. In the best of these early poems, Solomos avoids emotional description, though emotional connotations are cleverly insinuated.

THE HYMN TO LIBERTY

Solomos was profoundly inspired by the revolution of 1821. In his *Dialogos*, he exclaimed: "Have I anything else in my mind but liberty and the language?" In

1823, he completed *The Hymn to Liberty*, a vigorous paean to Greek freedom that bought instant fame to the twenty-five-year-old poet. Here, the poet, surveying the ordeals and ideals of the enslaved Greeks, intertwines the essence of freedom with the whole destiny of the Greek nation, as he recounts, one by one, both the sacrifices and the achievements of the Greek fighters.

The Hymn to Liberty begins as the poet, addressing Liberty, visualizes her rising from the bones of slain Greek heroes. He recognizes her from her gaze and from the sharpness of her sword; as she paces across the blood-soaked hills and valleys, he greets her with joy and pride: "Hail, oh Hail, Liberty!" The poem goes on to relate the Greeks' struggles for freedom, and the blood shed on Liberty's behalf—the Battle of Tripolis, the destruction of Corinth, the naval victories. The tempo is rapid, robust, and rolling; the trochaic stanzas move from image to image without sacrificing smooth transitions or unity. For 140 or so of the poem's 158 stanzas, Liberty is both the inspiration and the unifying force.

In the last section, however, the poem loses direction as Solomos summons the great powers of Europe to help "the defenders of the Cross." The references to Liberty, her actions, words, and inspiring presence are abandoned as the poet chastises the larger powers of Europe for having turned their backs on Greece for centuries.

IS TON THANATO TOU LORD BYRON AND "KATASTROPHI TON PSARON"

Solomos's next patriotic work, *Is ton thanato tou Lord Byron* (on the death of Lord Byron), is inferior to *The Hymn to Liberty*, which it resembles in both meter and subject matter. Though artistically a failure, this long poem served its purpose in expressing the gratitude of the Greek nation to the famous philhellene. That Solomos's craft was not deteriorating at this stage of his career is manifested by the short poems written during this period, from 1824 to 1827. "Katastrophi ton Psaron" (the destruction of Psara) is a short lyric that all Greek children learn by heart (the town of Psara had just been burned to the ground by the Turks when the poem was written):

On Psara's dark and desolate stone
Glory softly walks all alone
Musing over her son's noble deeds
As her hair is adorned by a wreath
Made of some yet unrazed weeds
That remained on the wasted heath.

LAMBROS

Lambros is a melodramatic tale about a young man (Lambros) who fathers three sons and a daughter out of wedlock with a teenage beauty named Maria. Lambros, while fighting the Turks, meets a young man who turns out to be a girl in disguise. He falls in love with her and seduces her, only to discover that she is the daughter he had long ago left behind. The daughter drowns herself in a lake, and Lambros returns to tell Maria what has happened. Grief is followed by their agreement to marry each other. As their three sons accompany them to the church, however, Lambros, overwhelmed by pain and shame, drowns himself, and Maria, after going insane, also drowns herself in the same lake. Though *Lambros* is maudlin by modern standards and though it lacks unity, there is robust emotion in it and much pathos. The Byronic influence is evident in the fifteen-syllable lines of its octaves.

TO KRITIKOS

Like *Lambros*, *To Kritikos* (the Cretan) is a tragic narrative of romantic love. Its prosody and its theme were inspired by the Cretan epic *Erotokritos* (seventeenth century), and its musicality, simplicity, and skillful syntax have been highly praised by critics. An incomplete work, *To Kritikos* is oneiric in content and decapentasyllabic in meter. The passionate, musical, and well-controlled work is about a Cretan youth found at sea at night, trying to rescue his beloved. The girl is his only contact with life. Everyone in his family has been disgraced and destroyed by the Turks. His struggle with the irrational, unpredictable sea is juxtaposed to his struggle against the Turks in Crete.

Early in the poem, there appears to the youth a "moonlight-dressed" maid. When she stares at the stars, they stop twinkling, and she makes the light seem brighter. The youth feels that he has seen her before; indeed, the girl is a "Platonic memory." The Hungarian critic Andrei Horvat has said that she is an angel of beauty and goodness descended from the Platonic heaven. The young Cretan's epiphany is accompanied by a heavenly sound, as if to complete the harmony of the senses. In keeping with classical Greek notions of form and concept, Solomos here weds the ideal and the real—an endeavor that would be successful in many of his poems. What Solomos intended to symbolize with the moonlight-dressed girl may be suggested by his later poem, *Eleftheroi poliorkimenoi*, in which a "light-vested" maid symbolizes life and nature, which, along with freedom, are most dear and most inspiring to the Cretan lad.

After four thunderbolts strike the sea, a calmness reigns everywhere, and in his beloved's embrace, the youth breathes a fragrance that he compares to a flower garden amid the silence. From that moment, the narrator-youth says, his hand can no longer grasp the knife: The warrior has turned poet and lover. In marvelous synesthesia, the youth hears his beloved's eyes within him and is touched by her smile. Both tears and smile are inspirational, and the Cretan becomes more eloquent, so that the lines that follow are among Solomos's most beautiful. Although the youth turns to his beloved only to find her dead, Solomos suggests that the Cretan has triumphed: He has experienced true wonder and beauty; he has become a poet. In both *To Kritikos* and *Lambros*, Solomos tried to prove that demotic Greek was capable of expressing the loftiest emotions and not merely mundane realities.

ELEFTHEROI POLIORKIMENOI

Eleftheroi poliorkimenoi is a long poem that many regard as Solomos's finest work. Solomos's intent was to show how moral strength triumphs over physical violence. The heroes of the poem are the masses, the people; the poet dramatizes the plight of the besieged at Missolonghi, who, for more than a year and against unbelievable odds, withstood the Turkish attacks. The lyricism of this work reaches heights unequaled in all Greek poetry. Though incomplete, *Eleftheroi poliorkimenoi* has the peculiar fascination of the fragmentary, a quality it shares with the Hermes of Praxiteles and the Venus de Milo. Solomos began the poem in 1826—the year when Missolonghi, after its inhabitants' heroic stand, fell to the Turks—and worked on it until his death.

The poem changes metric form as it moves along, and parts of it, in fact, are in prose. Spring in all its glory and the beauty of nature ("April of the golden hair is dancing with Eros") aim to weaken the resolve of the Missolonghians to die fighting for their freedom ("on such a day dying is death a thousand times"). It is a time of the year when human beings would love to live forever. The besieged are confronted with the temptation to embrace the loveliness and pleasure surrounding them. The patriotic sense of duty that sustains them in the face of such temptation is best exemplified in the scene with a young orphan girl. An angel descends and offers the doomed girl, whose lover has already been killed in battle, a pair of wings with which to escape. She proposes to accept the wings, not to fly away, but to wrap them round her and wait for death in solidarity with the other heroic women.

It was with such a sense of duty in mind that Solomos originally named his incomplete masterpiece "The Obligation." The defenders of Missolonghi, like their ancestors in ancient tragedy, place glory above hope and duty above expedience. The overriding moral imperative is to live free or die. The poem's theme is the struggle between ethical duty and merciless necessity. That the Greeks of Missolonghi will be defeated is not the issue; rather, the question is their actions in the face of defeat.

PORPHYRAS

During the last decade of his life, Solomos composed *Porphyras*, which some critics regard as his masterpiece. Though the poem is incomplete, its greatness is evident: Its rhythms, diction, humane theme, and poetic treatment of ideas are superb. The poem was inspired by the news that an English soldier had been devoured by a shark (called *porphyras* by the islanders of Corfu) in the port of Corfu. Solomos makes the soldier, as he struggles between sea and sky, a symbol of spiritual strength fighting against the aggressiveness and obstinacy of matter—purity against barbarity. When the young Englishman is confronted with "reasonless and monstrous strength," he finds in a moment of self-awareness the strength to resist and to acknowledge his being: "Before the noble breath was spent, his soul was filled with joy./ Suddenly in a lightning flash the young man knew himself."

Solomos must be seen not only as a poet but also as a patriot and a humanist, a man who preached a higher sense of morality. He must also be recognized as one of the major pioneers of modern Greek poetry.

OTHER MAJOR WORKS

NONFICTION: *Dialogos*, 1824; *I yineka tis Zakynthos*, 1927, 1944 (*The Woman of Zakynthos*, 1982).

BIBLIOGRAPHY

Coutelle, Louis, Theofanis G. Stavrou, and David R. Weinberg. *A Greek Diptych: Dionysios Solomos and Alexandros Papadiamantis*. Minneapolis, Minn.: Nostos Books, 1986. A historical and biographical study of two nineteenth century Greek authors. Includes bibliographical references.

Dimoula, Vassiliki. "The Nation Between Utopia and Art: Canonizing Dionysios Solomos as the 'National Poet' of Greece." In *The Making of Modern Greece: Nationalism, Romanticism, and the Uses of the Past (1797-1896)*, edited by Roderick Beaton and David Ricks. Burlington, Vt.: Ashgate, 2009. Describes Solomos as moving from the documentary to the utopian in his writings. Discusses the nature of nationalism in Solomos's work and how he has been misinterpreted and misrepresented for political purposes. Especially informative as it brings in the viewpoints of many Greek critics.

Mackridge, Peter. *Dionysios Solomos*. New Rochelle, N.Y.: Aristide, 1989. A biography and critical analysis of Solomos's works. Includes bibliographical references.

Raizis, M. Byron. *Dionysios Solomos*. New York: Twayne, 1972. An introductory biography and critical study of selected works by Solomos. Includes bibliographic references.

Tsianikas, Michalēs, and Vrasidas Karalēs, eds. *Pages of Dionoysios Solomos*. Blackheath, N.S.W.: Brandl and Schlesinger/Modern Greek Studies Association of Australia and New Zealand, 2002. Contains analysis of the life and poetry of Solomos in English and in Greek.

Minas Savvas

GASPARA STAMPA

Born: Padua(?) (now in Italy); c. 1523
Died: Venice (now in Italy); April 23, 1554

PRINCIPAL POETRY

Rime, 1554
Selected Poems, 1994

OTHER LITERARY FORMS

Gaspara Stampa (STAHM-pah) is remembered only for her poetry.

ACHIEVEMENTS

Gaspara Stampa produced only one lyric collection during her short life: the *Rime*. Modeled after Petrarch's prototypical *canzoniere*, Stampa's work offers modern readers exceptional insight into the artistic aspirations and literary ideals of the Italian Renaissance, a period that cherished creative imitation. Like many of her contemporaries, Stampa emulated the language, form, and thought of the traditional master. In a period that did not favor radical innovation, the *Rime* kept to the forms favored by Petrarch—the sonnet, madrigal, and sestina—as well as to his basic motifs, rhetorical devices, and conventional images.

In addition, Stampa employed the standardized lyric vocabulary formulated by Petrarch and adopted by his followers. Stampa's borrowings from Petrarch are numerous and acknowledged. The very structure of her opus follows an established format for collections of love poetry in the sixteenth century. Like Petrarch, she presents a love story as it unfolds in a series of inner conflicts in an atmosphere of painful self-awareness; like him, she orders the loose threads of her plot line in a chronological fashion. Nevertheless, both master and disciple transcend the barriers of biographical or realistic experience and enter the realm of universality. Nor was Stampa a mere copier. Her reworking of the Petrarchan model enriches her verse by constantly functioning as a sounding board against which her own words echo forcefully. Like the most successful *Petrarchisti*, she manipulates her borrowings so that the atmosphere of the original is transferred to the new composition. This "translation" is all the more significant because Stampa was forced to operate within the masculine lexicon of the dominant Petrarchan/Neoplatonic code. One of the privileged women who received a solid education in the sixteenth century, she was one of the first poets to express the woman's view of the love experience.

Stampa's feminine sensibility is clearly expressed in her poetry. Even within the confines of her creative imitation, the writer possesses a singular lyric personality, easily recognizable for its sincerity of expression, lack of rhetorical affectation, and emotive power, in contrast to the repetitive monotony of numerous other Petrarchan adherents. These very qualities, justly appreciated by modern readers, were the probable cause for her lack of popularity in her own day. Insufficiently erudite and controlled, Stampa's compositions lacked the formal dress and decorum so admired during the late Renaissance. A minor player on the stage of Venetian culture, Stampa had little influence and no resonance. After centuries of critical neglect, however, she has come to be recognized as one of the great love poets of her tradition. The rich psychological nuances of her sonnets and the extraordinary musicality of her madrigals, joined with the spontaneity of her discourse, separate her from the scores of Petrarchan imitators and make her one of Italy's foremost women writers and one of the best lyric poets of the Renaissance.

BIOGRAPHY

Very little is actually known about the historical Gaspara Stampa. Documentation of her life is scarce, and most data are limited to contemporary letters and occasional poems dedicated to her. Even the exact year and location of her birth are uncertain, as is the social status of her family, although some evidence suggests that her father had been a successful Paduan jeweler whose trade permitted a comfortable bourgeois existence. Some information can be drawn from the *Rime*, although it is not always wise to use the poetry as a biographical source. It appears that sometime after 1530, the three Stampa children were taken to Venice by their widowed mother and were given a good Humanistic education. The daughters, Gaspara and Cassandra, demonstrated exceptional musical aptitude

and soon achieved excellent reputations as musicians, while their brother, Baldassare, was becoming greatly admired as a promising young poet before his untimely death in 1544. The siblings, particularly Baldassare, participated actively in the social world of the Venetian *ridotti*, or salons, meeting some of the most prominent artists, musicians, patrons, and intellectuals of the time. It was a sophisticated environment where the nobility freely mingled with dandies, foreigners, students, and courtesans. It was an ambiance generally inaccessible to the maidens and matrons of the city, who lived a sheltered existence. Gaspara and Cassandra had a *ridotto* of their own, where they entertained guests with song and poetry.

Sometime in 1548, at such a gathering, Stampa met Count Collatino di Collato, a feudal gentleman-warrior known for his patronage of artists and musicians. The romantic involvement of Stampa and the count became literary history. For the first time, the young woman seriously devoted herself to poetry, producing hundreds of compositions dedicated to the man and the love that would dominate her life for three years. Collatino was an indifferent lover, however, and after a series of separations and conflicts, the two ended their affair.

Stampa found consolation in her art and in another man, the patrician Bartolomeo Zen, who appears in a limited number of sonnets in the *Rime*. Stampa died in 1554, barely thirty, having published only three of her numerous sonnets in an anthology. Her complete opus was edited posthumously by Cassandra and appeared a few months after the poet's death. Then, for two hundred years, the writer and her work were forgotten.

The fictional Gaspara Stampa first appeared in 1738, in a biographical sketch accompanying the second edition of the *Rime*. A direct descendent of Collatino, Count Antonio Rambaldo, wrote this short profile of Stampa, and thus began the first of her legends. Describing Stampa as a sweet young noblewoman of great talent, the count accused his ancestor of cruelty and betrayal leading to the unnatural and untimely death (by poison?) of the distraught lady. This version of Stampa's life appealed to the Romantic soul, and a number of fictional renderings followed, including one novel and two plays. Stampa had become a female Werther, an unwary virgin doomed to unhappiness and death.

This mythical Stampa was ravished in 1913 when a literary scholar, Abdelkader Salza, concluded that the poet had not been a young innocent but a high-class prostitute, a courtesan. Given the independence of Stampa's life, her known participation in the Venetian demimonde, and her sexual liberty, such a conclusion remains plausible but unproved; Gaspara may also have been a *virtuosa*, or professional musician, for example. The critical debate concerning the poet's social and moral standing raged for decades, involving some of Italy's major literati. As a result, another legend was born: The eternal *appassionata* emerged to replace the virginal victim. In such a biographical furor, Stampa's *Rime* was interpreted variously as a document, a diary, even an epistolary novel in verse. The historical figure and the fictional protagonist merged, and, in the process, the poet was ignored. It is only during the past fifty years that some literary critics have begun to evaluate the artist and separate her from the woman, discovering that Stampa was a serious writer, cognizant of the difficulties of her craft and of the need to develop a personal style that would adequately express what she wished to convey.

ANALYSIS

Most modern editions of the *Rime* are based on the one prepared in 1913 by Salza, who divided Gaspara Stampa's poetry into two major groupings: the "Rime d'amore" (love poems) and the "Rime varie" (miscellaneous poems). The former includes more than two hundred compositions, preponderantly sonnets, which chronicle the poet's love for Collatino and, later, Zen. The latter contains Stampa's occasional poetry, addressed to friends, acquaintances, and celebrities. Salza's edition concludes with eight religious sonnets, extracted from their original positioning among the love poems, so that the text ends on a morally contrite and uplifting note probably not intended by the author.

The miscellaneous poems are Stampa's most conventional works, often mere exercises in the art of writing. Adhering to shared literary expectations and the collective Petrarchan taste, they are expressions of social courtesy, gallantry, polite exchange, and encomium. Their function was public, in a century that utilized poetry as a tool of communication and flattery.

Nevertheless, the "Rima varie" offer clear indications of Stampa's personal attitudes toward poetry, poetics, and her own accomplishments. Most of her addressees were avowed, if occasionally innovative, members of Venice's Petrarchan literary elite. Their relationship to Stampa was primarily artistic, poetry functioning as the common social denominator. In her laudatory verse, Stampa is often concerned with the intellectual and stylistic attainments of those to whom her poems were addressed. By praising them, she is making an express value judgment on conventional Petrarchianism, accepting it as the ideal poetic model and stating that fame can be obtained through successful emulation.

From reading the "Rima varie," it appears that the poet had a well-formulated critical criterion, by which she judged her own work and that of others—a criterion based on the theory of creative imitation. Whereas she praises her fellow poets, Stampa projects an air of artistic insecurity in regard to her own abilities, declaring time and again that her "style" is inadequate, that she lacks sufficient eloquence, that her technique is crude. Often the poet suggests that her artistic failure is a result of her gender. The frailty of women is presented as implying intellectual inferiority as well, in a series of negative qualifiers Stampa uses to describe herself, ranging from "vile" to "humble." Within her cultural environment, these disclaimers and confessions of inadequacy were Stampa's way of defining herself as an unsatisfactory *Petrarchista*, a writer who aspires to great art but fails.

PETRARCHANISM

The Petrarchan origin of Stampa's poetry is undeniable and indeed is clearly acknowledged by the poet herself in the *Rime*'s opening sonnet, which both paraphrases and pays homage to Petrarch's prefatory poem to *Rerum vulgarium fragmenta* (1470, also known as *Canzoniere*; *Rhymes*, 1976). Similar paraphrases open many Renaissance collections of love poetry, immediately acknowledging their artistic origins in the medieval master. In Stampa's case, this declared derivation serves two purposes. On one hand, the poet directly associates her compositions with those of their literary source; on the other, she also contrasts the two works by altering the premises of the sonnets. Thus, Stampa's prefatory sonnet informs the reader that she is about to construct an exemplary love story in the pattern established for *canzonieri*, but it also declares that Petrarch's moral environment is not operative in this Renaissance work. Petrarch had from the outset of his collection emphasized the victory of the soul over earthly *vanitas*; Stampa, the disciple, retains none of her master's religious conflicts.

The first sonnet of Petrarch's *Rhymes* had emphasized spiritual repentance; the first sonnet of the *Rime* proposes the unending exaltation of human love, not its moral rejection. From the beginning, Stampa distinguishes her poetic universe from Petrarch's and initiates her subversive interpretation of the model. Here, and throughout her collection, Stampa divests her borrowings of their original moral and religious implications. She uses Petrarchan themes, images, metaphors, poetic devices, forms, vocabulary, and even whole lines but rejects the Christian consciousness that shapes the psychological ambiance of the medieval source. One example is the poem "La vita fugge," which replicates the first line of a famous Petrarchan sonnet. Both poems are concerned with the passage of time and the ensuing emotions of loss and dread, but Stampa purposely distorts the original's premises. Whereas Petrarch had been preoccupied with time wasted in transient pleasures, Stampa regrets the loss of pleasure in the transience of time. What had been a poem of spiritual suffering is transformed into a complaint against the fleeting nature of earthly love. In similar fashion, Stampa's anniversary poems—also derived from Petrarch's *Rhymes*—engage in an argument with their model. In contrast to Petrarch's Good Friday, a feast of death, Stampa proposes Christmas, a celebration of birth, as the anniversary of her love.

Stampa's rejection of Petrarch's spiritual battles places her directly in the more naturalistic world of the Renaissance but does not negate her greatest contact with his poetic universe. It is in the act of loving and in psychological self-awareness that Stampa comes closest to her literary mentor. Both are exceptional landscapers of their interior worlds, delving into the deepest recesses of emotion and thought. For both, the principal issue is love. More intense than Petrarch's collection, Stampa's "Rime d'amore" is compactly powerful in its analysis of the states and stages of loving. Nothing

deflects the poet from her theme. Love is omnipresent in the *Rime*, an overwhelming force that controls the poetic persona, ranging from feelings of extreme joy to painful masochism.

Equally present is the beloved, principally Collatino, who is never named directly but who is consistently idealized. The beloved is the poet's *signore*, or lord, concurrently feudal master, gentleman, superior, and god. To create such an exceptional figure, Stampa borrowed from both Petrarchianism and Platonism, easily associating him with abstractions such as the true, the beautiful, and the good as well as linking him poetically to the representation of Christ in the anniversary poems. Like an idol, the beloved receives amorous tributes but does not reciprocate, being enamored of his own beautiful self. Stampa deifies her man, rendering him as a Platonic emanation, a translucent reflection, or an immaterial beauty. She compares him to the planets, the elements, and the seasons, attributing mystical qualities to him. He is a celestial Mars, an Apollo, and an Adonis—a figure of myth, not a mere man. In keeping with Stampa's Petrarchan inspiration, however, this idol is also a cruel beloved, a pagan icon who demands immolation as a sacrifice for love. Even the Platonic desire to acquire beauty through union with the loved one becomes a means of torment, for union—understood physically as well as spiritually—is denied through separation, abandonment, and rejection. The glorification of the beloved in Stampa is concurrent with the self-denigration of the lover. The Stampean persona loses self to love, as exemplified by the figure of Echo, the nymph who had wasted away for love of Narcissus (the Count?), retaining only her voice (poetry?). Gaspara also associates love with death, in Platonic terms, for the lover is lost to the beloved. To these standard themes, the poet adds the novel one of jealousy, whose pain survives even as the persona's identity withers.

LANGUAGE

It is Stampa's language that most clearly separates her from the other imitators of Petrarch and lyric poets of the sixteenth century. Common, everyday speech often intrudes into the courtly diction of emulation. The poet tends toward spoken language, creating an atmosphere of directness and sincerity often lacking in the work of her more polished contemporaries. To achieve such spontaneity, Stampa employs direct and indirect discourse, dialogue, apostrophe, invocation, and direct address. Her verse is also unique for its musicality. Given her instrumental and vocal training, it is not surprising that her poems are often melodious, rhythmic, and aurally suggestive, linking her to the later contributions of the Arcadian school and the melodrama of Pietro Metastasio. Stampa's lyric idiom has a distinct identity, a private language that unites conventional style, colloquialisms, musical cadence, and directness.

SENSUALITY

Also unique to Stampa is her sensual honesty. Her poetry is not explicitly erotic, but it is sensuous, its sexuality being contained by the generalities of Petrarchan diction. The carpe diem theme, the call to the beloved to enjoy pleasure and beauty before they disappear in time, links some of her poetry to that of Christopher Marlowe, Robert Herrick, and Andrew Marvell. The pain and negativity of love found in Stampa is also given rhetorical dress in her unusual use of the hyperbole. Just as the Petrarchan antithesis had served Stampa well in describing the dichotomy of loving, so the conceit serves to express love's pain and imperiousness, as well as the beloved's cruelty. Contradictory feelings, the tensions and extremes of emotion, frustration, passion, anger, and hopelessness are dramatized through language. It is this emotive tension that separates Stampa from other lyric poets in her century, justifying her famous line: "Love has made me such that I live in fire."

BIBLIOGRAPHY

Bassanese, Fiora A. *Gaspara Stampa*. Boston: Twayne, 1982. Comprehensive and authoritative, this rare full-length critical study of Stampa in English synthesizes the full range of continental scholarship, with sound original conclusions. Annotated bibliography of Italian sources is also useful.

Benfell, V. Stanley. "Translating Petrarchan Desire in Vittoria Colonna and Gaspara Stampa." In *Translating Desire in Medieval and Early Modern Literature*, edited by Craig Barry and Heather Hayton. Tempe: Arizona Center for Medieval and Renais-

sance Studies, 2005. Traces the Petrarchian influence in the poetry of Stampa and the poet Vittoria Colonna, particularly in the area of desire.

De Rycke, Dawn. "On Hearing the Courtesan in a Gift of Song: The Venetian Case of Gaspara Stampa." In *The Courtesan's Arts: Cross-Cultural Perspectives*, edited by Martha Feldman and Bonnie Gordon. New York: Oxford University Press, 2006. This essay concentrates on the madrigals and works that Stampa set to music. An accomplished lute player and singer, she performed her works in public. Another chapter in this work, "The Courtesan's Voice: Petrarchan Lovers, Pop Philosophy, and Oral Traditions," by Feldman also discusses Stampa and places her in context, briefly touching on the debate over whether she was a courtesan.

Moore, Mary B. *Desiring Voices: Women Sonneteers and Petrarchism*. Carbondale: Southern Illinois University Press, 2000. Places Stampa within a larger European poetic community, providing feminist insights. Devotes a chapter to Stampa, with new translation of several poems.

Philippy, Patricia Berrahou. *Love's Remedies: Recantation and Renaissance Lyric Poetry*. Lewisburg, Pa.: Bucknell University Press, 1995. A chapter on Stampa elucidates her position in Italian literature and her deviation from the established male Petrarchan conventions.

Stampa, Gaspara. *Gaspara Stampa: Selected Poems*. Edited by Laura Anna Stortoni and Mary Prentic Lillie. New York: Italica Press, 1994. A bilingual edition, with new translations and notes. The introduction is particularly helpful with its insights into Stampa's life and times. The translations are both lyrical and faithful. A chronology of Stampa's life prefaces the text.

Warnke, Frank J. *Three Women Poets: Renaissance and Baroque*. Lewisburg, Pa.: Bucknell University Press, 1987. Presents a convincing argument that Stampa is the prime female poet of Italy. Ranks her in skill with Louise Labé and Sor Juana Inés de la Cruz. Good translations of the poetry of each poet are provided, and the comparisons of the three are particularly enlightening.

Fiora A. Bassanese

STATIUS

Born: Neapolis, Campania (now Naples, Italy);
between 40-45 C.E.
Died: Neapolis, Campania (now Naples, Italy);
c. 96 C.E.

PRINCIPAL POETRY
Thebais, c. 90 (*Thebaid*, 1767)
Silvae, c. 91-95 (English translation, 1908)
Achilleid, c. 95-96 (English translation, 1660)

OTHER LITERARY FORMS

The reputation of Statius (STAY-shuhs), for good or ill, rests on his poetry, although he did write in other forms. A lost work, "Agave," is mentioned by the satirist Juvenal, who says that Statius wrote it for the mime Paris. More important are the prose prefaces that Statius wrote to begin each of the books of the *Silvae*, which some critics argue are a new type of introduction in prose to a collection of poetry. Statius used the preface to describe the contents of the book and the circumstances under which some of the poems were composed as well as addressing apologies and flattering remarks to the audience.

ACHIEVEMENTS

Statius set himself an ambitious goal when he chose to write epics. He lived to see the completed *Thebaid* published about 90 C.E. (a privilege granted neither Vergil nor Lucan); the poem ends with a burst of pride, expectation, and just a little humility:

Wilt thou endure in the time to come, O my *Thebais*, for twelve years the object of my wakeful toil, wilt thou survive thy master and be read? Of a truth already present Fame hath paved thee a friendly road, and begun to hold thee up, young as thou art, to future ages. Already great-hearted Caesar deigns to know thee, and the youth of Italy eagerly learns and recounts thy verse. O live, I pray! nor rival the divine *Aeneid*, but follow afar and ever venerate its footsteps. Soon, if any envy as yet o'ercloads thee, it shall pass away, and, after I am gone, thy well-won honours shall be duly paid.

Statius's wish for lasting fame was granted—at least until recent years. Neither Gaius Valerius Flaccus's *Argonautica* (first century C.E.; English translation, 1863) nor Silius Italicus's *Punica* (first century C.E.; English translation, 1933), the only other Flavian epics, enjoyed the prominence of Statius through the medieval and Renaissance periods of European literature. In the late fourth century, Claudian used the *Silvae* as models for his own occasional poems, and a little later Sidonius Apollinaris copied more from Statius than from Vergil. In the fifth century, Lactantius Placidus wrote an allegorizing commentary on the *Thebaid*; in the sixth century, Fulgentius saw a Christian psychomachy in both Statius and Vergil. Later, both Petrarch and Desiderius Erasmus listed Statius among their favorite classical poets. Giovanni Boccaccio, too, was indebted to Statius. Because of possible Christian interpretations and because of the romantic, adventuresome nature of his stories, Statius was very popular throughout the medieval period and into the Renaissance, but nowhere is his influence more apparent than in the works of Dante and Geoffrey Chaucer.

In *La divina commedia* (c. 1320; *The Divine Comedy*, 1802), Dante and his guide, Vergil, meet Statius in Purgatory. Statius, who reveals that he had in life been a secret Christian, has just finished his penance for the sins of sloth and prodigality and becomes Dante's model for the released soul, passing from Purgatory into Heaven. As such, Statius travels with Vergil and Dante, the pilgrim from canto 21, to canto 30, when Vergil disappears and Statius continues with Dante until they cross into Paradise in canto 33. Dante calls the two "the good escorts" and "my poets." C. S. Lewis, noting that every one of Statius's major characters can be found somewhere in *The Divine Comedy*, argues persuasively that as much as Dante loved Vergil, as a medieval Christian, he was more comfortable with the worldview implicit in the *Thebaid*. Lewis concludes, "It was not perverse of Dante to save Statius and damn Vergil."

Chaucer, too, found Statius to be a valuable source, although he probably was more familiar with Ovid and Boethius. A number of works of Chaucer show evidence of direct borrowings from the *Thebaid*, and there are additional borrowings through Boccaccio.

"The Knight's Tale," for example, comes to Chaucer through Boccaccio's *Teseida delle nozze d'Emilia* (1339-1341; *The Book of Theseus*, 1974), and is itself the source for John Fletcher and William Shakespeare's *The Two Noble Kinsmen* (pr. c. 1612-1613) and John Dryden's "Palamon and Arcite." Chaucer mentions Statius by name in *House of Fame* (1372-1380), where his statue is on an iron pillar, coated with tiger's blood, upholding the fame of Thebes and Achilles. Chaucer mentions Statius by name again in the envoi to *Troilus and Criseyde* (1382), the work influenced more than any other by Statius: "Go, litel bok . . . And kis the steppes, where as thow seest pace/ Virgile, Ovide, Omer, Lucan, and Stace."

Statius has been admired and imitated to a lesser extent by other famous writers (Edmund Spenser, John Milton), and some not so famous (John of Salisbury, Joseph of Exeter, John Gower, John Lydgate). The eighteenth century, however, was the last period in English literature when Statius was uncritically admired. Alexander Pope and Thomas Gray each translated parts of the *Thebaid*, but when J. H. Mozley prepared the Loeb translations of Statius in 1928, he recorded no modern edition of either the *Thebaid* or *Achilleid*. Modern readers have criticized Statius for being artificial, florid, sentimental, bombastic, episodic, trivial, pedantic, heavily mythological, digressive, obscure, and baroque in the worst sense. Even friendly critics have been circumspect, choosing to praise only parts of the work. Among later scholars, some have seen structure and purpose and others have found none. In choosing the elements of his story, in expressing them in poetic language, in arranging the parts, in developing the themes, Statius reshapes the style of his great predecessors Vergil, Ovid, and Lucan, within the context of the polished and autocratic age of Domitian. Statius tries to make a virtue of excess, a choice that reflects the time in which he lived and the cultured circle for which he wrote. Statius's style is not Vergil's, but what Statius does, he does better than anyone else.

BIOGRAPHY

Most of what is known about Publius Papinius Statius comes from what he himself chose to tell in the *Silvae*. Statius was born between 40 and 45 C.E. in Neapolis, into a family of modest circumstances and a cultural blend of the Roman and the Hellenic. His father was a schoolmaster who had won poetry contests in both Italy and Greece and had translated Homer into prose. Statius senior had written a poem on the ambitious topic of the civil wars of 69 C.E., and at the time of his death, he was contemplating another on the eruption of Vesuvius. Statius gives his father credit for his education and even for guidance in the composition of the *Thebaid*. His father, then, and Vergil, whose tomb he visited, and Lucan, whose birthday he commemorates, were his great mentors.

Statius moved from Neapolis to Rome and earned a living with his writing. Juvenal, the only contemporary to mention him, says that Statius gave recitations of the *Thebaid* to enthusiastic audiences but would have starved had he not sold material to a famous mime named Paris. Nowhere, however, does Statius himself complain about finances. He addresses each of the first four books of the *Silvae* to a different wealthy and influential friend and seems to have enjoyed the patronage of Domitian. Statius and Martial knew many of the same important people, but neither poet mentions the other.

In Rome, Statius married a widow named Claudia. She and Statius were childless, although the poet speaks with affection about Claudia's daughter from a previous marriage and with real grief about his adopted son, a freed slave who died as a child. Statius and Claudia lived together, apparently happily, for many years. It is in the poem addressed to her that Statius says he won Domitian's poetry competition at Alba, but later lost in the Capitoline contest of 94 C.E. In the *Silvae*, he entreats Claudia, who knows, he says, how sick he has recently been and how hard he labored over the *Thebaid*, to return with him to Neapolis. This she apparently did, and the poet is presumed to have died there about 96 C.E. Statius himself saw the *Thebaid* published about 90 C.E. and the first four books of the *Silvae* between 91 and 95 C.E.; book 5 of the *Silvae* and the fragment *Achilleid* were published by an anonymous editor after Statius's death.

ANALYSIS

Statius wrote in the middle of what has been called the Silver Age of Latin literature. A contemporary of

Gaius Valerius Flaccus, Quintilian, and Martial, Statius was heavily influenced by his Neronian predecessors Seneca and Lucan. Statius's poetry was written during the reign of Domitian, a patron who must have been difficult to please, fancying himself (as he did) both a poet and a god. Statius's poetry exemplifies much of what is typical of Silver Age poetry. He was a skilled writer of Vergilian hexameters, heavily influenced by various schools of rhetoric, and fond of mythology, intellectual display, epigram, and description. On these matters, there is consensus. About the other characteristics of Statius's work, there is not. Critics have disagreed over whether psychological power was a strength of Statius, whether Stoicism is present in his works, and whether *Thebaid* has a morally redemptive message. In general, however, modern critics have come to look more favorably on his works than earlier scholars did.

SILVAE

Statius believed the *Thebaid* to be the work through which he would achieve immortality, but a good deal of attention has been paid to the *Silvae*, occasional poems he himself describes as "produced in the heat of the moment and by a kind of joyful glow of improvisation." The *Silvae* comprise thirty-two poems in five books. The first four books were arranged by Statius from a presumably much larger number of light poems and published between 91 and 95 C.E.; book 5 lacks the same kind of prose preface that begins books 1 through 4 and probably was published posthumously. The *Silvae* were known and admired until the Carolingian Age, after which they were lost. They were rediscovered by the scholar Poggio in 1417.

The poems of the *Silvae* were like earlier lyric and elegiac poems in subject, but they differed from the earlier poems in their meter, their length, and their concern for rhetorical form. The same can be said for a comparison between Statius and his contemporary, Martial. Martial wrote epigrams on the same topics as seven of Statius's poems (for example, the marriage of Stella and Violentilla, the death of Claudius Etruscus's father, and a statue of Hercules), but the forms of their works are very different. The poems of the *Silvae* are predominantly written in dactylic hexameter, but four are hendecasyllabic, and there is one each in Sapphics and Alcaics. The length of the poems varies from 19 to 293

lines, with the average a little more than 100 lines. Many of the poems can be identified with a particular rhetorical type. There are multiple examples of the *epicedion* (consolation) and *ekphrasis* (description), and less numerous examples of the *epithalamium* (marriage song), *proempticon* (farewell), *genethliacon* (birthday poem), and others.

This range of rhetorical types alone might make the reader raise an eyebrow at Statius's repeated protests that the *Silvae* are but "trifling pieces." Indeed, later scholarship has found remarkable patterns within and among these "trifling" poems. Critics have found a recessed-panel organization, in which poems are balanced around a central point. The pattern may be determined by the rhetorical type, the meter, the theme, or the length of individual poems. The predominant theme is of nature, worked and reworked along with other themes, such as art, death, travel, and family ties. In the *Silvae*, nature is for the most part ordered by the hand of humanity or God. This is interesting in the context of the word *silva*, the basic meaning of which is "forest" and, by extension, "material." Patterns are established only to be broken or left incomplete.

The poems of the *Silvae* are diverse, and opinion about them varies. Hardest for the modern reader to appreciate are the long and seemingly digressive poems and the poems to or about Domitian. H. E. Butler's comments in *Post-Augustan Poetry from Seneca to Juvenal* (1909) are notorious: Butler says he cannot quote *Silvae* poem 4, book 3, calling it "one of the most disgusting productions in the whole range of literature." Of Domitian, Butler says: "The emperor who can accept flattery of such a kind has certainly qualified for assassination." It is true that Statius wrote flattery, but in the years before Domitian's death by assassination in 96 C.E., those who did not, did not write. It is strange that Martial, who flattered the tyrant just as much but lived to retract his words, does not suffer, as Statius does, from the charge of sycophancy.

Several of Statius's occasional poems, particularly those in *Silvae*, do have the ability to charm even the modern reader. Poem 3, book 2, a birthday gift to Atedius Melior, tells a myth explaining why a plane tree on Melior's land grows bent over a lake. In comic hendecasyllables, poem 9, book 4, teases Plotius Grypus for returning a worthless book in exchange for a valuable one. Also in hendecasyllables (Statius says that he will not be so bold as to write in Lucan's own meter) is poem 7, book 2, a birthday poem praising Lucan, the author of the *Bellum civile* (60-65 C.E.; *Pharsalia*, 1614). This birthday poem is atypical because Lucan was already deceased, and so his *genethliacon* has some of the characteristics of an *epicedion*. Other *epicedia* that show real emotion are Statius's laments on the deaths of his father and his adopted son. In a lighter vein is the mock *epicedion* on the death of Melior's parrot. Perhaps the most famous and most admired of all of Statius's poems is poem 4, book 5, the gentle, nineteen-line poem "To Sleep."

The poems of *Silvae* are also read for extraliterary reasons. In this work, Statius presents a vivid picture of life in the Flavian Age: Places, people, and events are drawn in bold strokes. The reader becomes acquainted with the men to whom Statius dedicates the first four books of the *Silvae*: L. Arruntius Stella, a patrician poet whose marriage Statius celebrates; Melior, another of his rich patrons; Pollius Felix, a wealthy Epicurean; and Vitorius Marcellus, an accomplished man of equestrian family who eventually became a praetor. There are also historians, art collectors, imperial secretaries, politicians, orators, the son of a freedman, and a eunuch. Statius describes sumptuous villas, marble baths, a temple of Hercules, and a statue of the same god. He also shows people enduring a death or celebrating a birth, setting out on a journey, beginning or enjoying a happy marriage. He shows both how people—and poets—survive under despotism and, in a more light-hearted vein, what goes on at a Saturnalia celebration. The *Silvae* are as polished and full of artifice as the age they so succinctly describe.

THEBAID

Thebaid is no less polished and full of artifice. Statius says that he worked on the epic for twelve years, and on it, he believed, rested his claim to enduring fame. Still, he claims not to rival the "divine *Aeneid*" (c. 29-19 B.C.E.; English translation, 1553) but only to follow in its footsteps. Statius's debt to Vergil is real, but no less real than his debt to later authors, particularly Lucan. Statius treads a middle ground. He takes from Vergil without seeking to duplicate his classi-

cism; he also takes from Lucan without trying to emulate his new type of epic. Consider the opening lines of *Thebaid*:

> Fraternal rage, the guilty Thebes alarms,
>
> The alternate reign destroyed by impious arms,
>
> Demand our song. . . .

This does not have the classical directness of Vergil's "Arma virumque cano" ("I sing of arms and the man"), but Statius tells the reader, as does Vergil, exactly what the topic will be. Echoing Lucan's "cognatasque acies," Statius will write of "Fraternas acies," the action around which all other action revolves. He begins with a profession of ignorance as to where he should begin the Theban story and with flattery of Domitian, both of which are to be expected. The first because such a catalog displays Statius's range of learning, and the second because it was a prudent necessity. The forty-six lines of the proem are carefully arranged. The opening lines tell the reader that this will be a story, not of a single hero, but of "strife of brethren" and "impious hatred" and "the guilty tale of Thebes." After the catalog of associated stories he chooses to eschew, Statius returns to his topic:

> And fix, O Muse! the barrier of thy song,
>
> At Oedipus—from his disasters trace
>
> The long confusion of his guilty race.

Then, after the obligatory obeisance to Domitian, Statius ends the proem with another reiteration of his topic, mentioning again the Theban wars fatal to the two brothers and to many other heroes. The four heroes Statius names are not random choices: Each is an ally of Polynices, killed in a different one of the four books directly preceding the fatal duel between Polynices and Eteocles in book 11.

Just as Achilles' wrath and his great oath in book 1 of Homer's *Iliad* (c. 750 B.C.E.; English translation, 1611) control the subsequent action of that epic, so do Oedipus's hate and his great curse control the action of *Thebaid*. A paradoxical situation is presented in which the blind Oedipus hides in physical darkness but is haunted by "the fierce daylight of the mind." He invokes the gods of Tartarus, Styx, and Tisiphone to advance an "unnatural wish." Oedipus, however, builds his case and the suspense for twenty more lines before he explicitly identifies his unnatural wish: namely, to have his two sons destroy each other. Oedipus pronounces this curse even though he realizes that it is evil. Like Achilles, Oedipus lives to regret his oath, which is completed only in book 11 when Polynices and Eteocles kill each other in a duel. Only then, too late, does Oedipus grieve and regret. As he does, he admits that mercy has entered his heart and declares that Nature has conquered him. The mention of mercy is a foreshadowing of the remarkable scene in book 12 of the Altar of Mercy at Athens, to which the Argive women go as suppliants. The scene of the Altar of Mercy has been called the most famous and the most influential passage in Statius. Oedipus's address to Nature is also remarkable. This is the same *Natura* to whom the Argive women and Theseus appeal in book 12. C. S. Lewis, in *The Allegory of Love* (1936), traces in Statius a tendency to make the old Olympians mere figures of a specific trait (for example, Mars represents war) and to make abstractions, such as *Clementia*, *Pietas*, or *Virtus*, almost gods. The idea of *Natura*, for example, is both very Stoic and very medieval. It is a short step from here to allegory.

Another example of this tendency occurs directly as a result of Oedipus's curse in book 1. The Fury Tisiphone, who rises to fulfill the curse, while related to Vergil's and Seneca's Furies, is more allegory than snaky goddess. A figure of violence and madness, she embodies Oedipus's spiritual state. It was for such purposes that Statius reinstated the divine machinery which Lucan had banished from his epic. Tisiphone swoops down upon Thebes and stirs up discord, and the two sons of Oedipus are infected. Neither of the brothers is without guilt, as the short but skillful speech by an anonymous Theban makes clear, but Eteocles has more opportunity to do wrong and so appears more tyrannical.

In contrast to the violence, disorder, and darkness on Earth shines Jupiter's realm in Heaven. Jupiter, the supreme but not capricious ruler, states his conviction that not only Thebes but also Argos must be destroyed because of the misdeeds of their inhabitants. Juno objects, pleading for Argos in a polished rhetorical set piece. However, the crimes of humankind demand retribution. Juno bows to Jupiter's dictates, as she does in *Iliad*; thus, chaos on Earth is contrasted to the harmony and compliance in Heaven.

In book 1 of *Iliad*, Homer shows men in council and gods in council; Statius gives an internalized or indirect picture of his two human protagonists, shows the gods in council, and continues the first book of his epic. Thus, the pattern of a debate in the Greek camp contrasted to a debate in Heaven is expanded and complicated. Book 1 of *Thebaid* has a tripartite construction: Thebes, Heaven, Argos. After Jupiter's reinforcement of Oedipus's curse, the action turns to Polynices and his journey to Argos. This disenfranchised son is really no better than his brother Eteocles. He wishes not so much to excel in his own right as to humiliate his brother. He journeys to Argos through a storm that mirrors his internal state. Statius probably had in his mind two famous storms (*Aeneid*, book 1; *Pharsalia*, book 5); in turn, his storm probably inspired an episode in Spenser's *The Faerie Queene* (1590, 1596): Britomart's fight to gain entrance to a pigsty during a terrible storm resembles Polynices' fight with Tydeus when both arrive at Argos simultaneously.

Polynices and Tydeus fight before they speak. They are, as King Adrastus of Argos says, full of furor. They are in direct contrast to Adrastus, who stops their fight, predicting that a friendship may come from it. His prediction proves true: Polynices gives to Tydeus the affection more naturally owed to his brother. The two intruders, however, will change Adrastus more than he changes them. When they appear, Polynices is wearing a lion's skin, Tydeus a boar's. They are the boar and the lion who Apollo prophesied would wed Adrastus's daughters, and they bring Adrastus from his soft peace to the hardship and loss of war.

Much of the celebration with which book 1 ends is occupied with the praise of Apollo and Adrastus's telling of the myth of Coroebus, who appeases a god's anger by his *pietas* (dutifulness). Some critics have viewed this myth as a digression, but others see it as related to the work's main themes. The king and his daughter, her disastrous union with a stranger, the Fury-like monster, the abandoned babe, Coroebus and his companion who set out to save their city—all these characters from the myth are types that appear elsewhere in the epic. Coroebus tells Apollo that he killed the god's monster because of his *pietas* and his "consciousness of right." Indeed, Coroebus is a symbol of *pietas*, governed by it as was pious Aeneas in Vergil's epic. Oedipus and his sons are impelled by the opposite emotion. The first word after the proem is *impia*; madness and hate replace *pietas* in Oedipus, Polynices, and Eteocles, and the results are violence and death for all surrounding them. It is a measure of Adrastus's failure that he dismisses the importance of Polynices' parentage. After telling the myth, he says to Polynices, "Cease to lament, or to recount the woes of thy fathers: in our house also hath there been many a fall from duty (*pietas*), but past error (*culpa*) binds not posterity." Here from Adrastus's own lips comes confirmation that Jupiter's damnation of Argos is just; the reader also sees how mistaken Adrastus is about the nature of error.

Book 1 of *Thebaid* is a masterful beginning of an ambitious work. It sets in motion Oedipus's curse and Jupiter's decree, both of which are finally fulfilled with the deaths of Eteocles and Polynices in book 11. In book 1, the madness of impoverished Thebes is contrasted to the peace of luxurious Argos; later, the failings of both cities are apparent in comparison to Athens, just as the failings of Eteocles and Adrastus are more apparent in comparison to Athens's king, Theseus. Journeys, tyrants, city types, *pietas* or its lack—all these motifs establish parallels and contrasts between the first book of the *Thebaid* and the last, helping to unify the epic. Book 1 establishes the guilt and horror that will be expiated only in book 12. It contains a lengthy mythological digression which, like the later Hypsipyle episode, reinforces important themes. Book 1 also provides contrasting models of behavior, ruled respectively by *pietas* and by *furor*, demonstrating the strength of the one and the destructiveness of the other. With its rhetorical display, skillful descriptive passages, romance, and violence, the first book is representative of the craftsmanship of the whole *Thebaid*.

The most memorable passages of the *Thebaid* are unusual for their variety. Many of the finest passages are dramatic: the storm in book 1 that culminates in the fight between Polynices and Tydeus; the descent of Amphiareus alive into the underworld and his speech to the deities there; the deeds of Argia and Antigone in book 12, culminating in the cremation of Polynices with Eteocles, when even in death a double flame signals their continued hatred. There are critics who believe that some of Statius's dramatic passages are too extreme, going beyond good taste in their attempt to thrill the audience, such as Tydeus in book 8 gnawing on the head of his dead foe as he himself dies (an episode imitated by Dante in the *Inferno*). Other passages have been criticized for carrying realism to the point of absurdity, such as when Tiresias is so horrified by the visions he calls from the underworld that his hair stands on end, carrying his chaplet with it. More often, however, Statius is remembered for his fine descriptions of characters such as Tisiphone in book 1 and of places such as the abode of Mars in book 3. In contrast to the violence and horror of most of the *Thebaid*, two of Statius's most famous descriptions are of the Abode of Sleep in book 10 and the Altar of Mercy in book 12.

As a writer, Statius reflected his age. He borrowed extensively from his predecessors, Homer, Vergil, Ovid, and Lucan. Statius was imbued with the rhetorical style and the Stoicism of the time. His *Thebaid* is cruel and violent but ends with *pietas* triumphing over wickedness. His *Silvae* provide a mirror of the people and places of the Flavian era. Statius excels at description, using any number of rhetorical or metrical tricks to achieve his end—often a scene of horror or pathos. Both his style and his stories are extreme, but he was admired from his own time through the medieval period and the Renaissance into the eighteenth century. A poet so admired by Chaucer and Dante well deserves any reconsideration he receives.

BIBLIOGRAPHY

Dominik, William J. *The Mythic Voice of Statius: Power and Politics in the "Thebaid."* New York: E. J. Brill, 1994. Examines in detail the thematic design of the *Thebaid* and explores the poem's political undercurrents.

_____. *Speech and Rhetoric in Statius's "Thebaid."* New York: Olms-Weidmann, 1994. Presents a critical analysis of the stylistic, narrative, and thematic functions of the characters' speeches in the *Thebaid*.

Ganiban, Randall Toth. *Statius and Virgil: The "Thebaid" and the Reinterpretation of the "Aeneid."* New York: Cambridge University Press, 2007. Compares the two epics and argues that Statius reinterprets the "politics and moral virtues of kingship" in the *Aeneid*.

Lovatt, Helen. *Statius and Epic Games: Sport, Politics, and Poetics in the "Thebaid."* New York: Cambridge University Press, 2004. Rereads the *Thebaid* through the games in book 6 and how they relate to the rest of the book.

McNelis, Charles. *Statius' "Thebaid" and the Poetics of Civil War.* New York: Cambridge University Press, 2007. Examines how the *Thebaid* reflects the theme of internal discord through its narrative strategies. Argues that it employs a new mode of epic closure involving individual means of resolution.

Newlands, Carole. *Statius' "Silvae" and the Poetics of Empire.* New York: Cambridge University Press, 2002. Sees *Silvae*, written late in the reign of Domitian, as expressing the tension of that time and praising imperial majesty and private wealth.

Smolenaars, Johannes Jacobus Louis, Harm-Jan van Dam, and Ruurd R. Nauta, eds. *The Poetry of Statius.* Boston: Brill, 2008. Essays discuss elements within *Silvae* and *Thebaid*, place them in context, and compare them to other works.

Vessey, David. Introduction to *Statius: "Thebaid."* Translated by A. D. Melville. Oxford, England: Clarendon Press, 1992. Provides a general introduction to the *Thebaid* as well as a summary of the poem and a list of principal characters.

Zeiner, Noelle K. *Nothing Ordinary Here: Statius as Creator of Distinction in the "Silvae."* New York: Routledge, 2005. Uses philology, archaeology, and social theory to provide a reinterpretation of *Silvae*. Examines the material and nonmaterial forms of wealth in the work and how they influenced personal distinction.

Elizabeth A. Holtze

ANNA SWIR

Born: Warsaw, Poland; February 7, 1909
Died: Kraków, Poland; September 30, 1984
Also known as: Anna Świr

PRINCIPAL POETRY

Wiersze i proza, 1936
Liryki zebrane, 1958
Cudowna broda szacha, 1959
Z dawnej Polski, 1963
Czarne słowa, 1967
Wiatr, 1970
Jestem baba, 1972 (*I'm the Old Woman*, 1985)
Poezje wybrane, 1973
Budowałam barykadę, 1974 (*Building the Barricade*, 1979)
Szczę liwa jak psi ogon, 1978
Wybór wierszy, 1980
Śląski opowieści, 1982
Happy as a Dog's Tail, 1985
Radość i cierpienie: Utwory wybrane, 1985
Fat Like the Sun, 1986
Talking to My Body, 1996
Poezja, 1997
Mówię do swego ciała, 2002 (*Talking to My Body*, 1996)

OTHER LITERARY FORMS

Though Anna Swir (sfihr) began writing and publishing poetry in the 1930's, she was known principally as the author of children's stories and plays until later in her career. Not until decades after World War II was Swir able to develop the spare, economical style that characterizes her mature work and has drawn so many admirers. Although Swir did not write literary criticism, her translator and fellow poet Czesław Miłosz, in the introduction to *Talking to My Body*, quotes several of Swir's memorable aphorisms about writing, including "the poet should be as sensitive as an aching tooth."

ACHIEVEMENTS

The bilingual edition of Anna Swir's *Building the Barricade*, with translations by Magnus Jan Kryński and Robert A. Maguire, won the Polish Authors' Association's ZAiKS Prize in 1979. Though Swir's work was not always well received in her native Poland because of her feminism and her uneasy relationship with Catholicism, her reputation has improved greatly, partially because of the support of Miłosz, who wrote an appreciative monograph on her work in 1996. In the West, she has achieved a rare degree of recognition and popularity. Her poems have been received with high enthusiasm since English translations of her books began appearing in the late 1970's and 1980's and after Miłosz chose twelve of her poems for inclusion in *A Book of Luminous Things: An International Anthology of Poetry* (1996).

BIOGRAPHY

Anna Swir was born Anna Świrszczyńska in Warsaw, Poland, on February 7, 1909. The daughter of an impoverished painter and a local beauty, Anna grew up in her father's studio and struggled to help support her family by looking for jobs while she was still young. While working her way through college, she studied medieval Polish literature. She drew from this tradition and her interest in visual art as she wrote her first poems, which were published in the 1930's. Miłosz describes these impersonal verses as "sophisticated miniatures" and writes that "the form of the miniature was to return later, while the reticence about her personal life was to disappear."

Swir became a member of the Resistance after the Nazi invasion of Poland in 1939, working as a waitress under the occupation while writing for underground journals and participating in clandestine poetry readings. In August and September of 1944, during the Warsaw Uprising, she served as a military nurse, treating soldiers at a provisional military hospital. At one point, she expected to be executed for her Resistance activities, as she recounts in "Waiting to Be Shot" (from *Building the Barricade*).

In 1970, with the publication of *Wiatr* (wind), Swir reached her mature style. Having reached her sixties, she was able to write the direct, unadorned poetry of physical experience that characterizes her best work. *I'm the Old Woman* continued her development as a feminist poet through sharply recollected vignettes of women's experiences. The publication of *Building the Barricade* in 1974, thirty years after the events of the uprising, suggests how much internal deliberation was required to create the deceptively simple and straightforward narratives dramatizing the tragedy of the destruction of her city.

In 1984, Miłosz, who was in the process of translating a book-length selection of Swir's poems, wrote to the poet to inform her of the project. Though she told him that she was pleased that he was translating her poetry, she did not disclose that she was in the final throes of the cancer from which she would die in a matter of weeks. Over the following years, her reputation as a poet would grow with the posthumous publication of *Radość i cierpienie* (suffering and joy), a loving tribute to her relationship with her parents, and an expanding series of translations and criticism.

ANALYSIS

In the introduction to one of Anna Swir's poems in *A Book of Luminous Things*, Miłosz notes that her work can be seen as an extension of a classic trope in poetry, the conversation between the body and the soul. This motif, seen in such poems as Andrew Marvell's "A Dialogue Between the Soul and the Body," is recast for a world that has seen such calamities as the emptying of the Warsaw ghetto and the annihilation of the city. Swir's presentation of the motif is not a dialogue between equals that attempts to arrive at a satisfying metaphysical conclusion. Rather, her world is one in which nothing beyond the physical can be imagined, in which bodies are prey to malice or injury, sickness, and age. The remarkable aspect of the poems is that while they are almost entirely body-driven, they are not simply written from the perspective of the body, but from a separate vantage that can see, critique, and lament the shortcomings of a physical existence and celebrate the pure joys of bodily delight and ecstasy. It is this consciousness that comments on the life of the body, while realizing that nothing can be experienced or accomplished beyond it. In the introduction to *Talking to My Body*, Miłosz posits that "her poetry is about not being identical with one's body, about sharing its joys and pains and still rebelling against its laws."

It is perhaps fitting that a poetry that centers on

the body should be written in such an unadorned, naked style. All artifice, including figurative and self-consciously poetic language, has seemingly been stripped from the finished poems, which appear to be transparent accounts of mundane yet universal moments in human lives. The artistry of the poems lies in the immediacy of the accounts, as the reader responds to the perfectly chosen, evocative scenes produced with conversational language. The repetition of phrases and events through both poem and collection allows for a subtle building of emphasis and intensity, which is all the more remarkable when the reader considers how artless it appears.

BUILDING THE BARRICADE

Building the Barricade, a narrative of the Warsaw Uprising, gains its intensity from the directness of its presentation. The poems, which describe the futile effort of the city's inhabitants to fight off the overwhelming manpower and firepower of the Nazi army, are presented from the perspective of the resistance, "the tavern-keeper, the jeweler's mistress, the barber,/ all of us cowards" ("Building the Barricade"). While the poems are divided between those with a first-person speaker and those written from a more reportorial stance, all share the same immediacy, as those in the city are moved by the immense stress of the conflict to seek basic human consolations together. In certain of the poems, the speaker is a nurse in a military hospital, attempting to comfort dying soldiers. In "When a Soldier Is Dying," the nurse repeats to a wounded youth the calming words, "you will live, my beautiful,/ my brave boy." The poem ends as the soldier smiles and begins to close his eyes, not knowing ". . . that such words/ are said to a soldier/ only when he is dying."

HAPPY AS A DOG'S TAIL

Happy as a Dog's Tail consists primarily of love poems; this is most clearly the work that Miłosz defined as somatic poetry, though it differs from most poetry of the sort in that it is not confessional in its representation of physical moments. "A Woman Talks to Her Thigh" consists of a dialogue between the body and the self. The poem begins, "It is only thanks to your good looks/ I can take part/ in the rites of love" and ends with praise for the thigh and its ". . . clear, smooth charm/ of an amoral little animal." The separation between the consciousness of the speaker and her body, however, can become isolating; when the needs of the body are satisfied, the self's sensations of alienation can be heightened. In "What Is a Pineal Gland," a woman looks at her sleeping lover with the familiar query, "Do you belong to me?" Her immediate answer, however, is atypical and extreme: "I myself do not belong to you." Dividing herself from her body, the speaker first moves internally, examining the lungs and viscera, and contemplating the work about which "I know so little." The self, realizing its essential division from the solid and stable body, then rises above the scene: "It's cold here./ Homeless, I tremble looking/ at our two bodies/ warm and quiet."

TALKING TO MY BODY

Talking to My Body is largely a reissue of the work Miłosz and Leonard Nathan produced for *Happy as a Dog's Tail* and was released in a Polish edition in 2002. It begins with a new suite of translations from Swir's posthumous collection, *Radość i cierpienie*. These tender poems speak lovingly and directly of Swir's relationship with her parents, the painter father whose works are largely unknown to the art world, but who retains his artistic integrity, and her mother, who continually makes sacrifices in her attempt to create domestic stability. Although Swir repeatedly refers to her father as a "madman" and her parents' marriage as a curse, the collection is a celebration of her childhood and their mutual emotional reliance. Despite their poverty, it is clear that the family feels that their artistic commitment confers a degree of social status; in "Soup for the Poor," in which Swir describes her mother standing in a soup kitchen line, she writes that "Mother was afraid/ that the janitor's wife would see her./ Mother after all was/ the wife of an artist." While autobiographical, the selections build into something of a *Künstlerroman*, the story of a young artist's coming of age, as Swir dramatizes the preserving power of art, as well as its liabilities and shortcomings. This aspect of the collection is perhaps best articulated in the masterpiece in miniature, "I Wash the Shirt." The poem narrates the moment after her father's death when Swir washes his shirt for the final time, eliminating the sweat that was uniquely his: "From among all the bodies in the world,/ animal, human,/ only one exuded that sweat." As she destroys the bodily connection with her father, she notes, "Now/ only paintings survive him/ which smell of oils." The great pathos of that final sentiment is the same contradiction that runs through her poetry and lends it so much of its human power: Although it is the potential permanence of art that transmits Swir's voice to readers, her poems continue to assert that artistry fails in significance when compared with the body, even with all its inadequacies and complications.

OTHER MAJOR WORK

PLAY: *Teatr poetycki*, pb. 1984.

BIBLIOGRAPHY

Carpenter, John R. "Three Polish Poets, Two Nobel Prizes." *Kenyon Review* 20, no. 1 (1998): 148-156. Compares *Talking to My Body* with translations of the verses of two other Polish poets, *Facing the River: New Poems* (1995), by Czesław Miłosz, and *Sounds, Feelings, Thoughts: Seventy Poems by Wisława Szymborska* (1981).

Hacht, Anne-Marie, ed. *Poetry for Students*. Vol. 21. Detroit: Thomson/Gale, 2005. Contains an analysis of Swir's "Maternity," as well as context and criticism.

Jason, Philip K., ed. *Masterplots II: Poetry Series*. Rev. ed. Pasadena, Calif.: Salem Press, 2002. Contains an in-depth analysis of the poem "I Wash the Shirt."

Levine, Madeline. Review of *Happy as a Dog's Tail*, by Anna Swir. *Partisan Review* 57, no. 1 (1990): 145-150. Places Swir in context by discussing other contemporary Polish poets, including Miłosz and Adam Zagajewski, while commenting on questions of feminism and the mediation of the body in her work.

Miłosz, Czesław. "A Body of Work." *Threepenny Review* 6 (1985): 4-5. This short biography touches on some thematic considerations of Swir's work and discloses Miłosz's rationale in deciding to translate Swir's poetry. An adapted version of this essay was reprinted as the introduction to *Happy as a Dog's Tail*, and was rewritten and used as the introduction of *Talking to My Body*.

Miłosz, Czesław, and Leonard Nathan. "A Dialogue on

the Poetry of Anna Swir." *Trafika* 2 (1994): 193-200. Two of Swir's translators discuss the poems, including issues regarding the poet's conception of the body, her dissimilarity to other international poets, and her reception in the United States. An expanded version of this conversation was included as the afterword to *Happy as a Dog's Tail* and a slightly edited version as the afterword to *Talking to My Body*.

Todd Samuelson

WISŁAWA SZYMBORSKA

Born: Bnin (now part of Kórnick), Poland; July 2, 1923

PRINCIPAL POETRY

Dlatego żyjemy, 1952
Pytania zadawane sobie, 1954
Wołanie do Yeti, 1957
Sól, 1962
Sto pociech, 1967
Poezje, 1970
Wszelki wypadek, 1972
Wielka liczba, 1976
Sounds, Feelings, Thoughts: Seventy Poems by Wisława Szymborska, 1981
Ludzie na moście, 1986 (*People on a Bridge*, 1990)
Poems, 1989
Koniec i początek, 1993
View with a Grain of Sand: Selected Poems, 1995
Widok z ziarnkiem piasku, 1996
Nic dwa razy: Wybór wierszy = Nothing Twice: Selected Poems, 1997
Poems: New and Collected, 1957-1997, 2000
Miracle Fair: Selected Poems of Wisława Szymborska, 2001
Monolog psa zaplątanego w dzieje, 2002 (*Monologue of a Dog: New Poems*, 2006)
Wiersze, 1946-1996, 2006
Zmysł udziału: Wybór wierszy, 2006
Here: New Poems, 2010

OTHER LITERARY FORMS

Wisława Szymborska (shihm-BAWR-skuh) is primarily a poet, but she also published several collections of short articles written during her career as a columnist at the weekly *Życie Literackie* from 1968 to 1981. *Lektury nadobowiązkowe* (1973; nonrequired reading) is a collection of witty, short essays inspired by a vast and eclectic selection of books ranging from the classics of literature to cooking and gardening manuals. Szymborska began publishing *Lektury nadobowiązkowe* in the daily *Gazeta Wyborcza* in the mid-1990's.

In *Życie Literackie*, Szymborska also hosted (anonymously) a column for aspiring writers. Her witty responses to hopeful writers have been collected in the volume *Poczta literacka* (literary mail, 2000).

ACHIEVEMENTS

Wisława Szymborska is known as the first lady of Polish poetry. Her poetry is elegant, witty, and delightfully intelligent. Szymborska is that rare phenomenon:

Wisława Szymborska (AP/Wide World Photos)

a poet of universal appeal. Her poems—beloved by both demanding intellectuals and high school students—introduced humor, irony, and wit into the dreary reality of Communist Poland. Her work, however, is by no means of merely local consequence. Szymborska's poetry has been translated into nearly all European languages, as well as into Hebrew, Chinese, Japanese, and Hindu.

Szymborska received numerous literary awards, including the City of Kraków Award, the Polish Pen Club Award, the Solidarność Award, the Jurzykowski Foundation Award, the Kallenbach Foundation Award, the Goethe and Herder Prizes, and the Nobel Prize in Literature for 1996. Szymborska is also known for her superb translations of French poetry, especially of the sixteenth and seventeenth centuries.

BIOGRAPHY

Wisława Szymborska was born in Bnin (now Kórnick), a small town situated near Poznań in the western part of Poland. When she was eight years old, her family moved to Kraków, the city that the poet made her home for life. There, Szymborska went to a prestigious school for girls, run by nuns of the Saint Ursula order. Her education was interrupted by the outbreak of World War II; she had to continue her schooling at clandestine classes, whereby she received her high school diploma. After the war, Szymborska studied sociology and Polish philology at the Jagiellonian University, but neither of those fields held enough interest for the young poet. She left the university in 1948 and embarked on a number of proofreading and editorial jobs.

In 1953-1981, Szymborska worked for the weekly *Życie Literackie*, where she was responsible for two extremely popular columns: *Poczta literacka*, featuring responses to aspiring writers and *Lektury nadobowiązkowe*, a series of playful commentaries on all sorts of reading matter.

In the early 1950's, Szymborska became a member of Polska Zjednoczona Partia Robotnicza (PZPR), the official party of the Communist regime. She gave up her membership in 1966, disillusioned by the party's policies—a decision requiring considerable courage in the political climate of the time. Szymborska became part of the Kraków underground literary movement and cooperated with the monthly *Pismo*. She was one of the founding members of Stowarzyszenie Pisarzy Polskich (Polish Writers' Association), created in 1988 and legalized the following year.

After she left *Życie Literackie*, Szymborska refused to form permanent professional ties with any institution. The poet became known for her reclusive ways; she shunned publicity, rarely appeared in the media, and would speak about herself only with the greatest reluctance. She very seldom left Kraków. When she received the Nobel Prize in Literature, she reacted with joy but also apprehension; she knew that this international honor would interfere with her fundamentally private lifestyle.

Szymborska has been known to write about four or five poems intended for publication per year—a slow pace fully rewarded by the quality of her poetry. The author of limericks, she has also created collages, which she produced out of newspaper scraps and mailed to her friends in the form of postcards. These pieces, reminiscent of Surrealist and Dada games, combine elements of the quotidian to give them unexpected (and often ironic) meanings—a method characteristic also of Szymborska's poetic technique.

ANALYSIS

The two key qualities of Wisława Szymborska's poetry are curiosity and a sense of wonder. She has the ability to look at things as if seeing them for the first time. In her curious eyes, nothing is ordinary; everything is part of the ongoing "miracle fair." Her poetry forces the reader to abandon schematic thinking and to distrust received wisdom. On the level of language, this distrust is expressed through a constant play with fixed phrases and clichés. Both language and thought are turned upside down, revealing new and surprising meanings. Such poetry is very humorous, but it also conveys a sense of profound philosophical discomfort, prompting the reader to probe deeper and to adapt new perspectives. Szymborska's poems skillfully combine seriousness and play, seemingly opposite categories that, in the eyes of the poet, are of equal value.

DLATEGO ŻYJEMY

The earliest poems of Szymborska, published in newspapers in the years following World War II, dealt with experiences common to the poet's generation: the trauma of the war, the dead child-soldiers of the Warsaw Uprising, and the hope for a new, peaceful future. These poems were not included in Szymborska's first two collections, *Dlatego żyjemy* (this is why we live) and *Pytania zadawane sobie* (the questions we ask ourselves). By the 1950's, the political climate in Poland had changed considerably; poetry was to become an extension of state propaganda and a reinforcement of the official ideology. For a time, Szymborska naïvely subscribed to this agenda. Her first two collections give testimony to her youthful political beliefs. Later, the poet would disown her early work; however, the brief period of idealism and the subsequent disillusionment taught her to distrust totalizing ideologies of any kind.

Although the primary theme of Szymborska's earliest collections was the building of the perfect socialist state, some poems dealt with nonpolitical subjects such as love, intimacy, and relationships between people. Stylistically, these early poems bettered typical products of socialist propaganda and contained a promise of Szymborska's later achievements. Nevertheless, most critics (as well as the poet herself) prefer to begin discussions of Szymborska's oeuvre with her third collection.

WOŁANIE DO YETI

Wołanie do Yeti (calling out to Yeti) marks a turning point in the work of Szymborska and is considered her true literary debut. The poet cuts away from the earlier political creed; her former assurance is replaced by a profound distrust. This change of heart is expressed in the poem "Rehabilitacja" ("Rehabilitation") in which the speaker refers to her deluded head as "Poor Yorick." By 1957, Szymborska had become a poet of doubtful inquiry and profound uncertainty.

Wołanie do Yeti introduces a number of themes and devices that would become permanent features of Szymborska's poetics. The poem "Dwie małpy Brueghla" ("Brueghel's Two Monkeys") exemplifies both the poet's characteristic use of the anecdote and her growing interest in looking at the human world from a nonhuman perspective. The speaker in the poem is taking a final exam in "the History of Mankind" while the two monkeys look on:

One monkey stares and listens with mocking disdain,
The other seems to be dreaming away—
But when it's clear I don't know what to say
He prompts me with a gentle
Clinking of his chain.

Similarly, the poem "Z nieodbytej wyprawy w Himalaje" ("Notes from a Nonexistent Himalayan Expedition") portrays the achievements of humankind, as presented to a nonhuman listener. Characteristically, Szymborska creates a hypothetical, alternative world, thus making possible her imaginative investigations.

These poems mark the beginning of Szymborska's poetic anthropology: her study of the condition of human beings in the world, as observed and analyzed from various unexpected perspectives. *Wołanie do Yeti* reveals another seminal feature of Szymborska's poetics: her skillful use of irony as a cognitive and poetic category.

SÓL

The publication of *Sól* (salt) in 1962 was pronounced a major literary event. This collection gives a taste of Szymborska's mature style, with its brilliant paradoxes, its skillful intertextuality and allusions, and its mastery of puns, antitheses, and metonymy. The poet also develops her characteristic art of phraseological collage, playing with readers' linguistic expectations, as in the lines: "Oh, not to be a boxer but a poet,/ one sentenced to hard shelleying for life," or "written on waters of Babel."

Sól contains a number of very private, intimate poems, which is quite unusual in Szymborska's work. An important theme is communication between two people, or, rather, the impossibility or breakdown of communication, as in the poem "Wieża Babel" ("The Tower of Babel"). While this poem explores the failure of a dialogue between a man and a woman, the poem "Rozmowa z kamieniem" ("Conversation with a Stone") reveals the futility of human attempts at communicating with nature. The speaker "knocks at the stone's front door," but the stone remains inscrutable:

. . . You may get to know me, but you'll never know
    me through.
My whole surface is turned toward you,
all my insides turned away. . . .

Another important theme developed in *Sól* is the dichotomy of nature and culture, biology and art. This problem appears in poems such as "Woda" ("Water"), "Muzeum" ("Museum"), and "Kobiety Rubensa" ("Rubens Women"), a playful poetic parody of the Baroque style:

Daughters of the Baroque. Dough
thickens in troughs, baths steam, wines blush

. . . .

O pumpkin plump!

The Baroque giantesses' "skinny sisters woke up earlier,/ before dawn broke" and "went single file/ along the canvas's unpainted side." This image reveals other key features of Szymborska's poetic imagination: her incessant search for the other side of the picture, her defense of those excluded and pushed to the margins, and her love of exceptions.

STO POCIECH

In "Mozaika bizantyjska" ("A Byzantine Mosaic"), from the next collection, *Sto pociech* (no end of fun), the Baroque situation is reversed—here slenderness is the norm, and everyone is offended by the sight of a fat baby. *Sto pociech* explores a number of other cultural myths, ancient and modern. This collection also shows Szymborska's fascination with discourses of biological sciences in general and the theory of evolution in particular. This fascination is linked to the poet's desire to extend the language of poetry to include discursive modes commonly labeled as nonpoetic.

Another major theme in *Sto pociech* is time, and art's ability to suspend it. While "Pejzaż" ("Landscape") deals with the art of painting, "Radość pisania" ("The Joy of Writing") is a hymn to "The joy of writing./ The power of preserving./ Revenge of a mortal hand."

WSZELKI WYPADEK

Szymborska's sixth collection, *Wszelki wypadek* (could have), confirms her reputation as a philosophical poet. Critics point out her affinities with existentialism, Positivism, and, most important, the French Enlightenment. Moreover, Szymborska's poetry has strong links with the rhetorical tradition. Many of her poems are structured around questions, dialogues, or theses with supporting examples. Moreover, in a typical rhetorical approach, the poet strives to make even the most difficult problems appear accessible: "Don't bear me ill will, speech, that I borrow weighty words,/ then labor heavily so that they may seem light."

The title poem of the 1972 collection, "Wszelki wypadek," ("Could Have"), introduces the weighty theme of necessity and coincidence: "It could have happened./ It had to happen." Similarly, "Pod jedną gwiazdką" ("Under One Small Star") begins: "My apologies to chance for calling it necessity./ My apologies to necessity if I'm mistaken, after all."

Wszelki wypadek confirms Szymborska's distrust of fundamentalism. The poet presents the world as relative. She speaks to the reader from shifting and surprising perspectives. "Wrażenia z teatru" ("Theater Impressions") describes her favorite act of a tragedy—the sixth, after the curtain has fallen. In "Prospect" ("Advertisement"), the speaker is a tranquilizer:

> Sell me your soul.
> There's no other buyer likely to turn up.
>
> There's no other devil left.

WIELKA LICZBA

Szymborska's next collection, *Wielka liczba*, which opens with the title poem, "Wielka liczba" ("A Large Number"), and closes with "Liczba pi" ("Pi"), juxtaposes the amazing vastness and multiplicity of the world against the limitations of human perception and cognition. The world evokes a childish delight but also despair: There are "four billion people on this earth" but the poet's imagination is still "bad with large numbers/ . . . still taken by particularity." Faced with excess, the poet defends the particular. Confronted with the cosmos, she rehabilitates the quotidian: for example, the soup "without ulterior motives" described in the warmly ironic portrait of her sister, or the "silver bowl" that might have caused the biblical Lot's wife to look back, against the angel's orders. As always, Szymborska is fascinated with particularities and complexities, with human imperfections.

PEOPLE ON A BRIDGE

In *People on a Bridge*, Szymborska addresses political questions for the first time since *Wołanie do Yeti*. The problems of human history and civilization appear next to the themes of chance, necessity, abstraction, and particularity continued from the preceding collections. "Our twentieth century was going to improve on the others" begins "Schyłek wieku" ("The Century's Decline"), while "Dzieci epoki" ("Children of Our Age") warns: "We are children of our age,/ it's a political age." Here, Szymborska's irony is at its most poignant and subtle. This collection also marks the beginning of the poet's effort to deal with death: "There's no life/ that couldn't be immortal/ if only for a moment."

KONIEC I POCZĄTEK

Koniec i początek (the end and the beginning) contains a number of very private poems, many elegiac in tone, dealing with memory and loss. In "Kot w pustym mieszkaniu" ("Cat in an Empty Apartment"), the death of a human being is shown from the perspective of a cat. "Nic darowane" ("Nothing's a Gift") reminds the reader that: "Nothing's a gift, it's all on loan" and "I'll have to pay for myself/ with my self." In "Może być bez tytułu" ("No Title Required"), the poet poses the metaphysical questions: what is important and what is not? How can we be certain? In comparison with Szymborska's earlier work, the poems in this collection are more direct, less dependent on masks and role-playing. However, the poet retains her propensity for unusual perspectives. In "Wielkie to szczęście" ("We're Extremely Fortunate"), she claims: "We're extremely fortunate/ not to know precisely/ the kind of world we live in." Such knowledge would require adopting a cosmic point of view, from which "the counting of weekdays" would seem "a senseless activity," and "the sign 'No Walking On The Grass'/ a symptom of lunacy." There is irony here, but also a great tenderness toward the counting of days and the grass—a human quotidian.

POEMS: NEW AND COLLECTED, 1957-1997

Poems: New and Collected, 1957-1997 contains nearly all of Szymborska's poems that had appeared in book form, from *Wołanie do Yeti* to *Koniec i początek*, with a suite of new poems. The masterful translations were executed by Stanisław Barańczak, a Polish poet of the younger Generation of '68 who is considered one of the most linguistically gifted poets and one of the most fluent and prolific translators of his time, and by Clare Cavanagh, an exceptional critic and Barańczak's longtime collaborator. Their work is confident and colloquial, but attuned to the source's playful elaborations, containing the ". . . ill-timed tails, horns sprouted out of spite,/ illegitimate beaks, this morphogenetic potpourri, those/ finned or furry frills and furbelows . . ." of the poems' menagerie.

The poems, when viewed as a body, show Szymborska to be a champion of individuality and imagination. The impersonal provinces of science and art are transformed into conjectural scenarios that feel lived and human. For example, the simple observation of the lifelike qualities of a classical painting becomes the monologue "Landscape," which begins, "In the old master's landscape,/ the trees have roots beneath the oil paint." Szymborska is not merely content to use poetry's transformative power to create reality out of artifice, but also drawn to the life intimated in the painting; the speaker of the poem is a woman portrayed as a small part of the landscape. The historical limitations of her experience lend the poem its authenticity: "I know the world six miles around./ I know the herbs and spells for every pain.// I've never seen my children's father naked." The poem ends by drifting toward the "unpainted" life that continues beyond the limits of the artistry: "The cat hops on a bench,/ the sun gleams on a pewter jug."

The premise of "Discovery" is, once again, presented in its first lines: "I believe in the great discovery./ I believe in the man who will make the discovery./ I believe in the fear of the man who will make the discovery." The anaphora opening the poem, with the phrase "I believe" beginning its first three lines, suggests that the poem may be a credo or article of faith. The structure of the lines, however, with each successive line building on the previous, seems more characteristic of a nursery rhyme. This undercutting of supposed belief initiates the irony of the poem. The poem itemizes the manner in which the discovery goes unreported, its notes and instruments destroyed. However, even though the poet continues to underscore her assurance that the decision to turn away from the never-explained breakthrough could be made for the betterment of humanity, even at personal sacrifice—"I believe in the refusal to take part./ I believe in the ruined career."—the poem ends with the deflating line, "My faith is strong, blind, and without foundation."

MIRACLE FAIR

Miracle Fair is a selection of Szymborska's work translated by Joanna Trzeciak, a Ph.D. student at the University of Chicago who has had great success in placing her translations in many of the highest-profile literary magazines in the United States. Perhaps out of a desire to avoid competition with Barańczak and Cavanagh's monumental project, Trzeciak has not arranged Szymborska's poems chronologically by book, but rather has divided them into six general themes, which she has titled with quotations from the poems, such as ". . . the unthinkable is thinkable . . ." or ". . . of human kind for now. . . ." This collection covers the full range of Szymborska's poetry, presenting poems that had never before been published in English, including a sampling of the poet's early work, as well as occasional poems and pieces. Each theme is introduced with one of Szymborska's collages, providing a spark of visual wit that acts as an analogue to the verbal tonalities of the poems.

Though critics have commented on Szymborska's consistency of quality and method throughout her volumes, one effect of Trzeciak's thematic organization is to emphasize the ways in which certain themes have played through her work, providing a larger web of meaning. For example, the poems in the section ". . . too much has happened that was not supposed to happen . . ." all concern the problems of politics and the brutality of war, with poems such as "Torture" and "Starvation Camp at Jasło." Unsurprisingly, these poems tend to begin with a compellingly presented supposition, which is then complicated over the course of the poem's meditations; frequently, they show the poet expressing one of her supreme values, human empathy.

"The End and the Beginning," the title poem from the 1993 collection *Koniec i początek*, begins with the provocative assertion, "After every war/ someone has to clean up./ Things won't/ straighten themselves up, after all." Initially, the tone seems to minimize the human cost of war, and the reader may object to the matter-of-fact manner that suggests that the aftermath of a battle is no different from the domestic labors of a weekend cleaning: "Someone has to get mired/ in scum and ashes,/ sofa springs,/ splintered glass,/ and bloody rags." However, among the laborers, while there are many who recall the circumstances of the destruction ("Someone, broom in hand,/ still recalls the way it was"), others are losing interest. Finally, "In the grass that has overgrown/ causes and effects,/ someone must be stretched out/ blade of grass in his mouth/ gazing at the clouds." The triumph of ordinary life, with the escape offered by the natural world and the imaginative suggestion of the clouds, continues despite the privations of history. Nevertheless, one teasing conundrum that remains suggested by the poem's title, in the temporal reversal of beginning and end, is whether the end of the war is leading to the beginning of peace and life, or to the beginning of forgetfulness that will lead, inexorably, to another war.

OTHER MAJOR WORKS

NONFICTION: *Lektury nadobowiązkowe*, 1973, *Nonrequired Reading: Prose Pieces*, 2002.

TRANSLATIONS: *Poezje wybrane*, 1964 (of Charles Baudelaire); *Poezje*, 1977 (of Alfred de Musset).

MISCELLANEOUS: *Poczta literacka*, 2000.

BIBLIOGRAPHY

Aaron, Jonathan. "In the Absence of Witnesses: The Poetry of Wisława Szymborska." *Parnassus: Poetry in Review* 11, no. 2 (1981/1982): 254-264. An insightful overview of the major themes in Szymborska's poetry based on the 1981 English-language collections of her poems.

Anders, Jaroslaw. *Between Fire and Sleep: Essays on Modern Polish Poetry and Prose*. New Haven, Conn.: Yale University Press, 2009. Contains an essay in which Anders examines the poetry of Szymborska.

Cavanagh, Clare. "Poetry and Ideology: The Example of Wisława Szymborska." *Literary Imagination* 2, no. 1 (1999): 174-190. An analysis of Szymborska's poetry written by its American translator. Cavanagh emphasizes the dialogical character of Szymborska's work, as well as its affinities with poststructuralist thought.

Constantakis, Sara, ed. *Poetry for Students*. Vol. 31. Detroit: Thomson/Gale Group, 2010. Contains an analysis of Szymborska's "Some People like Poetry."

Czerniawski, Adam, ed. *The Mature Laurel: Essays on Modern Polish Poetry*. Chester Springs, Pa.: Dufour, 1991. A collection of essays dealing with twentieth century Polish poets. Two important articles on Szymborska appear in the collection: Adam Czerniawski, "Poets and Painters," and Edward Rogerson, "Anti-Romanticism: Distance."

Krynski, Magnus J., and Robert A. Maguire. Introduction to *Sounds, Feelings, Thoughts: Seventy Poems by Wisława Szymborska*. Princeton, N.J.: Princeton University Press, 1981. This good English-language collection of Szymborska's poetry contains an excellent introduction discussing the poet and her work.

Legezynska, Anna. *Wisława Szymborska*. Poznań, Poland: Rebis, 1996. This extremely helpful work contains Szymborska's biography and a careful analysis of each poetry collection. In Polish.

Miłosz, Czesław. Introduction to *Miracle Fair*. New York: Norton, 2001. A compelling introduction by Szymborska's fellow poet and Nobel Prize winner. This appreciation of Szymborska's work emphasizes the poet's probing of consciousness, but also her ability to bring joy to the reader, despite the grimness of her poetry.

Milne, Ira Mark, ed. *Poetry for Students*. Vol. 27. Detroit: Thomson/Gale Group, 2008. Contains an analysis of Szymborska's "Conversation with a Stone."

Serafin, Steven, ed. *Twentieth-Century Eastern European Writers: Third Series*. Vol. 232 in *Dictionary of Literary Biography*. Detroit: Gale Group, 2001. Contains a brief essay on Szymborska examining her life and works.

Magdalena Mączyńska
Updated by Todd Samuelson

T

TORQUATO TASSO

Born: Sorrento, Kingdom of Naples (now in Italy);
March 11, 1544
Died: Rome, Papal States (now in Italy); April 25,
1595

PRINCIPAL POETRY

Rinaldo, 1562 (English translation, 1792)
Gerusalemme liberata, 1581 (*Jerusalem Delivered*,
1600)
Rime, 1581, 1591, 1593 (*From the Italian of
Tasso's Sonnets*, 1867)
Gerusalemme conquistata, 1593 (*Jerusalem
Conquered*, 1907)
Le sette giornate del mondo creato, 1607

OTHER LITERARY FORMS

The literary work of Torquato Tasso (TAS-oh) begins and ends with his discussions of poetic theory. As early as 1561 but certainly before 1570, he had composed *Discorsi dell'arte poetica* (1587; discourses on the poetic art), and he published a much revised and expanded version of the same work, *Discorsi del poema eroico* (1594; *Discourses on the Heroic Poem*, 1973) the year before his death. The latter is both a defense of Tasso's own epics and an influential statement of Renaissance critical theory. Tasso's *Dialoghi* (1581) embraces a variety of subjects and often includes Tasso himself as one of the speakers; these dialogues are modeled after those of Plato. Tasso's *Lettere* (1587, 1588, 1616-1617), numbering as many as seventeen hundred, constitute a rich source of information about his life in elegantly crafted prose. Tasso's pastoral drama *Aminta* (pr. 1573; English translation, 1591), celebrates love and has been far more influential than his tragedy of mistaken identities and incest, *Il re Torrismondo* (pb. 1587; the King Torrismondo).

ACHIEVEMENTS

Torquato Tasso's importance in the history of letters is twofold: His own prodigious work has great merit, and he exerted enormous influence on artists who followed him. Tasso, the representative genius of the late Italian Renaissance, was the creator of Christian epic. In him, the erudition of classical literature and Aristotelian poetic theory combined with the force of the Counter-Reformation and court life to produce *Jerusalem Delivered*. His reputation as a writer rests on this epic, his superb pastoral drama *Aminta*, some of his lyric poetry, and his synthesis of epic poetic theory.

Tasso enjoyed almost immediate renown both in and out of Italy. The romance *Rinaldo* showed promise, but *Aminta*, on the theme of innocent and natural love triumphing over various adversities of law and circumstance, established his reputation as a poet. *Jerusalem Delivered*, completed three years later, touched off a spirited controversy over poetic theory, with comparisons to Homer, Vergil, and Ludovico Ariosto that always recognized Tasso's stature, whether the commentary was hostile or admiring. Tasso's epic also excited interest in England. As early as 1584, a Latin translation of *Jerusalem Delivered* by Scipio Gentili was published in London. Edmund Spenser in his 1587 "Letter to Raleigh" mentioned Tasso as one of his models for *The Faerie Queene* (1590, 1596). In 1594, the second part of the British play *Godfrey of Bulloigne* was performed by the Admiral's Men. Also in 1594, Richard Carew published the Italian text and English translation of the first five cantos of *Jerusalem Delivered*. In the early seventeenth century, Tasso influenced Samuel Daniel, Michael Drayton, Abraham Cowley, and John Milton. Later Tasso's reputation suffered an eclipse, although John Hoole's 1763 translation of *Jerusalem Delivered* into heroic couplets was very popular. The nineteenth century saw as many as eight new translations of the epic, the most influential being Jeremiah Holmes Wiffen's 1824 version in Spenserian stanzas. Whether Tasso's epic was read for its own sake or used as a source, it was admired for its love stories. Leigh Hunt, for example, chose the romantic trials of Olindo and Sofronia, Tancred and Clorinda, and Rinaldo and Armida for his *Stories from the Italian Poets* (1846).

Early in the twentieth century, however, many critics evinced little sympathy for Tasso's works or his reputation.

That reputation, the picture of a man driven to or feigning madness because of persecutions endured for love, was fostered by the biography *Vita di Torquato Tasso* (1621), published by the poet's friend G. B. Manso. As early as 1594, a now lost play, *Tasso's Melancholy*, was performed in London. The Romantic age saw in Tasso's writings his supposed love for Leonora d'Este and made Tasso a symbol of the suffering artist. The legend that grew up around his life inspired the drama *Torquato Tasso* (pb. 1790; English translation, 1827) by Johann Wolfgang von Goethe and the monologue *The Lament of Tasso* (1817) by Lord Byron, in addition to numerous musical and pictorial works. Psychological interest in Tasso has not completely disappeared, but interest in his legend no longer overshadows the worth of his writing.

BIOGRAPHY

Torquato Tasso was born on March 11, 1544, in Sorrento, the son of the poet and courtier Bernardo Tasso and Porzia de' Rossi. He began his education in Naples with Jesuit teachers. His family life was disrupted first when young Tasso followed his father, exiled from the Kingdom of Naples, to Rome in 1554, and again in 1556 when his mother died unexpectedly. Perhaps influenced in choice of genre by his father's recently completed epic *Amadigi* (1560) and in choice of a subject by his sister's escape from an Ottoman attack on Sorrento, Tasso wrote 116 stanzas of what was to become later his epic *Jerusalem Delivered* but laid aside the story of Godfrey and the First Crusade when his father sent him to Padua to study law in 1560. In Padua, law was far less interesting than Sperone Speroni and the discussion of philosophy, rhetoric, and poetic theory. Tasso wrote and published the chivalric romance *Rinaldo* and began writing Petrarchan love lyrics. After a period of study interspersed with escapades at the University of Bologna, he returned to Padua, probably where he wrote *Discorsi dell'arte poetica*. In 1565, Tasso left school (without a degree) for Ferrara and the service of Cardinal Luigi d'Este.

In Ferrara, Tasso resumed work on his epic on the liberation of Jerusalem. He also wrote lyrics for the two sisters of Duke Alfonso II, Lucrezia and Leonora d'Este. Tasso suffered the death of his father in 1569; in 1570, he traveled to Paris, his only trip outside Italy.

Entering the service of Duke Alfonso in January, 1572, Tasso began a very productive period of his life. His pastoral masterpiece *Aminta* was performed in 1573; he began a tragedy based on classical models in 1574; and he completed *Jerusalem Delivered* in 1575 at the age of thirty-one. Although he was eager to publish his epic, Tasso submitted it to the criticism of Scipione Gonzaga and others. Tasso wished nothing in his work to offend either poetic theory or Roman Catholic Church doctrine, but he could not bear the criticism that resulted. He left Ferrara only to return; he felt spied on and attacked a servant with a knife; he was placed under guard, but escaped to stay with his sister in Sorrento. Tasso returned to Ferrara, then soon left to wander through Mantua, Padua, Venice, Urbino, Pesaro, and Turin before returning again to Ferrara in 1579. This time, his accusations and irrational behavior led

Torquato Tasso (Library of Congress)

Duke Alfonso to imprison him in Sant'Anna, where Tasso remained for seven years.

Biographers have variously attributed Alfonso's imprisonment of Tasso to the duke's anger at Tasso's love for Alfonso's sister, pique at the suggestions that his poet wished to find a new patron, fear over what Tasso might reveal to the Inquisition, or the sincere concern of an exasperated ruler to save all concerned, including Tasso himself, from the effects of real madness. Regardless of the causes of Tasso's madness or melancholy, the conditions of his long imprisonment did not prevent him from writing, although it did prevent him from having any control over the many unauthorized editions of his works published in those years. During the years of his imprisonment, Tasso composed more than four hundred letters, many of his dialogues, considerable occasional poetry, and an *Apologia* (1586) for *Jerusalem Delivered*.

Released from prison in 1586, Tasso first went to Mantua, where he completed his tragedy, renaming it *Il re Torrismondo*. He traveled restlessly and published his earlier epic, *Jerusalem Conquered*. He also composed a number of religious poems, one of which was the religious epic *Le sette giornate del mondo creato* (the seven days of the creation of the world). The last of Tasso's many journeys was to Rome, where he was to be crowned poet laureate by the pope. Tasso became ill, however, and died at the monastery of Sant'Onofrio on April 25, 1595.

ANALYSIS

It is apparent that, from the first, Torquato Tasso set out to reconcile a number of seeming opposites in his work: lyric and heroic, myth and history, fantasy and religion, romance and epic, popular variety and Aristotelian principle. The tension of this attempt at synthesis caused Tasso to abandon his early draft of an epic poem for a series of less ambitious compositions. Many critics believe that the tension remains unresolved.

Tasso's lyric voice is amply represented in the almost two thousand short poems produced throughout his life. Many of them are imitative of Petrarch. In 1589, Tasso planned to publish his poems in separate volumes according to subject—amorous, encomiastic, and sacred. The love poems are among the earliest lyrics, sometimes linked to historical women such as Lucrezia Bendidio or Laura Peperara, but often general and diffuse in praise of beauty, love, and emotion. Rich in poetic devices, the lyrics luxuriate in the suffering of the poet.

If the middle style characterizes Tasso's amorous verse, the grand style characterizes his encomiastic verse. Many of these poems in praise of influential men risk being sterile or self-serving, but they can also be poignant. Many of the lyrics written in Sant'Anna are pleas for help or pardon, addressed to Duke Alfonzo, the Ferrara princesses, or the duke of Urbino. The Sant'Anna lyrics exhibit a remarkable variety in tone and mood and include a famous and atypical sonnet addressed to the cats of the prison.

RELIGIOUS LYRICS

Tasso's religious lyrics reflect both personal experience and the general tenor of the Counter-Reformation. There are sonnets, canzones, madrigals, and ballads. They are concerned with both his personal fears and common religious themes such as "Le lagrime di Gesu Cristo" ("The Tears of Jesus Christ"), "Le lagrime di Maria Vergine" ("The Tears of the Virgin Mary"), and "Monte Oliveto" ("Mount Olivet"), a poem on the founding of the religious order that sheltered Tasso in Naples in 1588. The poems reflect the restlessness, melancholy, and personal suffering that are also present in so many of Tasso's other works. Just as Erminia in *Jerusalem Delivered* finds a temporary respite from her troubles in a pastoral sanctuary, so various people in the sonnets retire from the world to an idealized, cloistered life that Tasso envies but cannot join. Tasso's sacred verse is similar in language, style, and tone to his secular verse.

LE SETTE GIORNATE DEL MONDO CREATO

Le sette giornate del mondo creato illustrates some of Tasso's characteristic strengths and weaknesses. Tasso wrote the poem about the Creation between 1592 and 1594 after he had finished *Jerusalem Conquered*, a version of his great epic that he felt to be immune from any possible religious or stylistic criticism, and this new theme would allow him to expand his unimpeachable views. *Le sette giornate del mondo creato* is eight thousand lines of blank verse. It is derivative of pagan authors, the Bible, the Church fathers, and Renaissance writers including Guillaume du Bartas. It is neither original nor coherent, although it does attempt to reconcile Aristotle and the Neoplatonists. It is digressive; it succumbs to superfluous praise of noble contemporaries, such as the pope; it subordinates art to moral lesson. For all this, the poem also sees in nature a reflection of the poet's own circumstance. Even at the end of his life, Tasso reflects his person in his art: doubt, suffering, a love of the marvelous, and the lyric mood in epic expression.

RINALDO

Tasso seems always to have aspired to the writing of epic and, like Vergil, trained for his magnum opus by writing less noble works. *Rinaldo* is just such an exercise. It is a romance in the tradition of Ariosto's *Orlando Furioso* (1516, 1521, 1532; English translation, 1591) or Bernardo Tasso's *Amadigi*. *Rinaldo* is composed of twelve cantos of ottava rima, preceded by an address, "A i lettori" ("To the Readers") which discusses his artistic choices. Tasso was influenced by the study of Aristotle, which blossomed following new translations of and commentaries on Aristotle's *De poetica* (c. 334-323 B.C.E.; *Poetics*, 1705). Tasso claims to follow Aristotelian precedent and to improve on Ariosto by limiting the action to the unity of a single hero and eliminating personalized prologues to each canto. Tasso, however, places the enjoyment of his readers above even Aristotle, and so the unity of action in Tasso's plays will admit considerable variety, along with love interest and marvels.

Both Tasso's method and his material are derivative. Commentators have found in *Rinaldo* echoes of Bernardo Tasso, Petrarch, Matteo Maria Boiardo, and Ariosto, as well as Homer, Theocritus, Vergil, Ovid, and others. The story tells of the trials endured by the protagonist in his search for glory and love. Rinaldo, Orlando's cousin, falls in love with Clorice, the sister of the king of Gascony, but must undergo many adventures on land and sea before at last rescuing Clorice from the infidels and marrying her. There are battles, magic, the glitter of the court, and the suffering of love. Just as Rinaldo in *Jerusalem Delivered* is seduced by Armida but ultimately renounces passion in favor of duty, so is this Rinaldo temporarily wooed away from his true love by the alluring Floriana. When Rinaldo ul-timately rejects Floriana, she, like Armida, attempts suicide but is saved. In another incident, Clizia is accidentally shot by her husband just as Clorinda is slain by the unsuspecting Tancred in *Jerusalem Delivered*. *Rinaldo* is the story of the education of a young knight who must prove himself both moral and brave in order to win his love. In theme, incident, style, and tone, this early romance prepares for the epic that follows. *Rinaldo* was written in ten months and published in 1562 when Tasso was only eighteen years old. It was immediately popular, going through six editions during Tasso's lifetime.

JERUSALEM DELIVERED

Tasso then returned to the 116 stanzas of the *Jerusalem Delivered*, which he had begun in 1559. Manuscripts of that text, an intermediate version of about 1570, and the final version of 1575 all survive, and comparisons of the three show some of the poem's development. The original *Jerusalem Delivered* was militaristic and moralistic. It described the arrival of the Christian army, an unsuccessful negotiation, and the anticipation of strife. Almost half of these stanzas survive in the final version of *Jerusalem Delivered*, but there are no love adventures and no supernatural marvels. Tasso expanded his epic to six cantos by 1566, and by 1570, the whole poem had been written. In the 1570 version, Armida and the accompanying love interest were present, but the poem's protagonist was still Ubaldo, a forebear of the duke of Urbino. Significant changes and deletions occurred before the poem, first called *Il Goffredo*, was completed in 1575.

The twenty cantos of ottava rima, which now followed the exploits of an imaginary Rinaldo d'Este rather than Ubaldo, were submitted by Tasso to his friend Gonzaga and others for suggestions for further revision. The period of revision lasted for two years. Tasso did alter some things, but the most sweeping criticisms were followed only when Tasso rewrote the epic as *Jerusalem Conquered* in 1593. Tasso was imprisoned in Sant'Anna when the first unauthorized and incomplete version of his epic was published in 1580 under the title *Godfrey*. This was followed in 1581 by a complete but still unauthorized edition printed by Angelo Ingegneri, who was responsible for naming the epic *Jerusalem Delivered*. Tasso himself apparently collaborated with Febo Bonnà in preparing two corrected editions that followed in the same year.

Jerusalem Delivered is a conscious effort to exceed the accomplishments of Homer, Vergil, and Ariosto. Tasso wished to surpass his predecessors by reconciling the antithetical genres represented by those authors—classical epic and chivalric romance—all within the context of Christian history. He refused to admit that romance is a genre distinct from epic. Judith Kates, in her 1974 essay "Revaluation of the Classical Heroic in Tasso and Milton" persuasively argues that Tasso is the creator of Christian epic.

Jerusalem Delivered is the story of the First Crusade, in which Godfrey of Boulogne recaptures the Holy City from the Turks. As a subject, it is neither too ancient nor too modern. In canto 1, the Archangel Gabriel tells Godfrey, who is discovered praying, that he has been elected commander of the army about to set out for Jerusalem. Pagan defenders reinforce the city and the fortunes of war sway back and forth, with each side aided by supernatural agents of good or evil. After a last terrible battle, the victorious and bloodstained Godfrey leads his men in prayer at the Sepulcher of Christ. C. M. Bowra, in *From Vergil to Milton* (1963), sees the three main heroes as representative of three different ideal virtues. The historical Godfrey is here the consummate Christian leader, renowned for wisdom and piety. He is a Christian Aeneas, subordinating even personal glory to divine plan. The nonhistorical Rinaldo, in comparison, comes close to exemplifying a Homeric ideal. He is an Achilles, with "a brave heart impatient of repose" and "a burning boundless thirst for fame." Tancred exemplifies the courtly virtues and suffers from the courtly malady, laid low by a doomed love "which feeds on grief and grows forevermore."

These Christian warriors are opposed by an array of pagan heroes, the mightiest of whom are Argante and Solyman, differentiated and noble as much as any mortal outside a state of grace can be. The most memorable pagans, however, are women, exhibiting and eliciting very different types of love. The three women, Clorinda, Erminia, and Armida, are very different manifestations of an ideal of feminine beauty and love. Clorinda is an Amazon, like Vergil's Camilla, but also capable of tears, when she is moved by the plight of the lovers Olindo and Sophronia (canto 2), and of forgiveness, when she experiences God's grace through baptism at the moment of her death (canto 12). She is loved by Tancred, who unwittingly kills her, as Achilles did Penthesilea. Erminia, in contrast, epitomizes shy and delicate tenderness. Her love for Tancred is revealed only at the end of the epic, but Tasso leaves its resolution ambiguous. Nevertheless, it allows the poet to include two famous episodes: Erminia's venture, dressed in Clorinda's armor, to look for Tancred (canto 6), and her sojourn among shepherds (canto 7), a pastoral idyll in which the evil life of a court suffers by comparison with the humble, tranquil life of shepherds. Armida, the third pagan woman, is a temptress who, like Circe, changes men into nonhuman forms and, like Dido, seduces heroes from their heaven-appointed duty. Armida's garden (canto 16) is the pattern for Spenser's Bower of Bliss (*The Faerie Queene*, book 2, canto 12). Her enchantments based on sensual beauty are effective against all but direct heavenly intervention. Even when Tasso ends a love story happily, as here when Armida submits to Rinaldo and to Christianity with the words of the Virgin at the Annunciation, the lasting impression is one of tears and suffering.

The whole problem of justifying the love interests in the epic concerned Tasso very much. He set out to surpass Ariosto, and considered *Jerusalem Delivered* to be superior to Ariosto's *Orlando Furioso* in many respects. Tasso's epic conforms to ancient poetic theory, as he proves in his *Discorsi dell'arte poetica*, and expands upon in *Discourses on the Heroic Poem*. It also expresses the true piety of a man of the Counter-Reformation. The classical and religious elements are as much a part of the epic as are the love episodes, although the latter are what readers of all ages have tended to remember.

Tasso writes in an elevated style, decorous and humorless, describing a single action and beginning in medias res. The scope of the action encompasses Heaven, Earth, and Hell. He uses supernatural elements, Homeric similes, and a Latinate vocabulary. In addition to the correspondences between Tasso's characters and characters from previous epics (such as Godfrey/Aeneas or Rinaldo/Achilles), specific actions are reminiscent of earlier epic scenes: God the Father ratifies his decrees with a nod similar to that of Homer's Zeus; a statue of the Virgin, rather than the Palladium of Troy, is stolen; there are night sorties, single combats, troop reviews, espionage missions, the burning of enemy strongholds, and a beautiful woman who stands on the battlements and names the enemy combatants on the field below.

Tasso never forgets, however, that he is writing a Christian epic. As much as he admires the classical tradition, he sees it as deficient in several respects. Tasso speaks of his epic as an allegory in a letter in which he calls Godfrey "the head" and Rinaldo "the right hand." Later, the Bonnà editions of *Jerusalem Delivered* include Tasso's *Allegoria del poema* (1581), in which Tasso claims that the entire plot of his epic ought to be read as a continuous allegory. Spenser seems to have believed this, but some modern critics dismiss the *Allegoria del poema* as an afterthought, a ruse to placate the Inquisition and excuse the marvels and love interest.

Despite their classical and romantic antecedents, Tasso's characters are always judged from a Christian perspective. Admitting the nobility of an Argante or the seductive power of an Armida does not alter this fact. Some critics see the shape of Tasso's epic as reflecting the workings of Providence through history. All the diverse episodes are subordinated to this perspective and ranked by it. *Jerusalem Delivered* is divided into twenty cantos, not the usual twelve or twenty-four. The action divides these cantos in half, with the pagans in ascendance throughout the first half, the Christians throughout the second. The first half begins with the action of God, the second with that of Godfrey. The poem also divides into quarters, with Rinaldo present and active in the first and last sections, absent and enchanted in the middle two. Lastly, the poem exhibits mirror-symmetry, in which each pair of cantos, starting with the first and last, deals with parallel or opposite material. For example, Argante enters the action in canto 3 and is killed in canto 19; the Crusaders first see Jerusalem in canto 3 and first breach its walls in canto 18.

JERUSALEM CONQUERED

Near the end of his life, Tasso himself completed a version of his epic so substantially revised that it de-

served and was given a new name, *Jerusalem Conquered*. The new poem, in twenty-four books instead of twenty cantos, is increasingly allegorical and doctrinaire. It purges many of the most fondly remembered episodes (Sophronia and Olindo, Erminia among the shepherds, the trip to the Fortunate Islands) and the most magical or sentimental ones (Armida transforming the knights into fish, the reconciliation of Rinaldo and Armida). Diction is smoothed; Homeric elements are increased; and many characters are renamed (Rinaldo becomes Riccardo, for example). Tasso considered *Jerusalem Conquered* to be far superior to his earlier epic; critics have not agreed with him, however, and have either dismissed the poem or vilified it.

This, however, does not negate Tasso's achievements. He is a consummate storyteller. He epitomizes the Renaissance in his veneration of classical learning and human worth. He redefines the meaning of "heroic" by transforming both the epic poem and its heroes to conform to religious ideals and his own emotional sensibility. No poet more effectively reflects the Renaissance spirit while anticipating the Romantic.

OTHER MAJOR WORKS

PLAYS: *Aminta*, pr. 1573 (verse play; English translation, 1591); *Il re Torrismondo*, pb. 1587 (verse play).

NONFICTION: *Allegoria del poema*, 1581; *Dialoghi*, 1581; *Apologia*, 1586; *Discorsi dell'arte poetica*, 1587; *Lettere*, 1587, 1588, 1616-1617; *Discorsi del poema eroico*, 1594 (*Discourses on the Heroic Poem*, 1973).

BIBLIOGRAPHY

Brand, C. P. *Torquato Tasso*. New York: Cambridge University Press, 1965. A classic biography and critical work on Tasso. Discusses the author's use of historical sources, gives a detailed account of his life, and analyzes his major works. Includes an interesting essay on the legend of Tasso's life and presumed madness, and ends with a lengthy chapter on the poet's contribution to English literature. Bibliographic references are included in the notes.

Cavallo, Jo Ann. *The Romance Epics of Boiardo, Ariosto, and Tasso: From Public Duty to Private Pleasure*. Buffalo, N.Y.: University of Toronto Press, 2004. Examines the epics of Tasso, Matteo

Maria Boiardo, and Ludovico Ariosto within their literary contexts. Cavallo places emphasis on genre, ideology, and politics, and how these writers influenced one another.

Finucci, Valeria, ed. *Renaissance Transactions: Ariosto and Tasso*. Durham, N.C.: Duke University Press, 1999. This collection of essays represents a cross-section of critical approaches to "foster a dialogue" among schools of thought on *Jerusalem Conquered* and its relationship with Ariosto's work.

Gariolo, Joseph. *Lope de Vega's "Jerusalén conquistada" and Torquato Tasso's "Gerusalemme liberata" Face to Face*. Kassel, Germany: Edition Richenberger, 2005. Compares Lope de Vega Carpio's *Jerusalén conquistada* (1609) and Tasso's *Jerusalem Conquered*. Looks at the influence of Tasso's work on that of Lope de Vega and provides considerable analysis of both works.

Günsberg, Maggie. *Epic Rhetoric of Tasso: Theory and Practice*. Oxford, England: Legenda, 1998. An in-depth study of *Jerusalem Delivered*.

Sherberg, Michael. *Rinaldo: Character and Intertext in Ariosto and Tasso*. Saratoga, Calif.: ANMA Libri, 1993. Part 2 examines Tasso's treatment of the Carolingian "knight," which downplays Rinaldo's rebellious nature and actions while expanding his character, especially through psychological depth.

Zatti, Sergio. *The Quest for Epic: From Ariosto to Tasso*. Buffalo, N.Y.: University of Toronto Press, 2006. Examines Tasso's *Jerusalem Conquered* and Ludovico Ariosto's *Orlando Furioso*. Zatti has written books examining both authors' works as well as works explaining the development of the epic.

Elizabeth A. Holtze

ESAIAS TEGNÉR

Born: Kyrkerud, Sweden; November 13, 1782
Died: Östrabo, Sweden; November 2, 1846
Also known as: Esaias Tegnerus

PRINCIPAL POETRY

Svea, 1811 (English translation, 1840)
Epilog vid magister-promotionen i Lund: Den 22 Juni, 1820, 1820 (*Epilogue at the Master's Presentation*, 1829)
Nattvardsbarnen, 1820 (*The Children of the Lord's Supper*, 1841)
Axel, 1822 (English translation, 1838)
Frithiofs saga, 1825 (*Frithiof's Saga*, 1833)

OTHER LITERARY FORMS

Esaias Tegnér (tehng-NAYR) wrote the vast majority of his literary output in poetic forms; however, he did write sermons (*kyrklinga tal*) and other ecclesiastical works in his role as bishop of Växjö, and gave orations on other writings as a member of the Swedish Academy. Perhaps the most notable of the orations was his academic address on Johan Gabriel Oxenstierna, his predecessor in the academy, in which he influentially stated that language, as such, had fallen from the pure imagistic state for which it could only be a metaphor. Both his church and secular writings show Tegnér's considerable learning in Greek; in his lifetime, he was not only Sweden's foremost poet but its foremost academic philologist.

ACHIEVEMENTS

Esaias Tegnér was the first Swedish writer to make a serious impact on world literature. Although Romanticism and its concomitant interest in folklore and legend played a part in this achievement, Tegnér's influence can be attributed mainly to his aesthetic sensitivity, his distinct and independent character, and the way his verse often espoused attitudes in direct contrast to those that might have been expected of it. Tegnér also demonstrated that a poet of feeling and authenticity could also be a figure of great learning and retain a deep respect for the past.

BIOGRAPHY

Esaias Tegnér was born into a family that had begun as peasants and over several generations had become educated and aspired to middle-class status; his surname, "Tegnér," was an abbreviation of "Tegnérus," a Latin name adapted from the family's earlier residence in the village of Tegneby in the province of Småland. Tegnér's parents urged him to seek as much education as possible, and when Esaias had exhausted the resources of the local tutor, his elder brother, Lans Gustaf, took him to the Myhrman family household, whose children he was tutoring. Esaias fell in love with one of the Myhrman daughters, Anna, whom he married in 1806. By then, Esaias Tegnér had matriculated at the University of Lund, the leading academic institution in southern Sweden, where he became a professor upon graduation.

In 1808, Tegnér composed his first major poem, "Battle Song for the Swedish Militia," followed by the 1811 "Svea," which won the Swedish Academy prize. Both poems were patriotic manifestos urging Sweden to join the revolutionary Napoleonic cause and declare war on Russia; in the end, Sweden switched sides, came out against Napoleon Bonaparte, and became one of the victors in the Napoleonic Wars. Even as he wrote his best lyric poems, Tegnér was disappointed by this turn of events.

In 1822, he faced a crossroads in his life when he was offered the bishopric of the city of Växjö. Although Tegnér was not a conspicuous adherent of the Lutheran Church, in Sweden, any man of letters automatically took holy orders, and the offer of the position of bishop was not unlike the offer of a full professorship in the modern academic world. Tegnér felt conflicted not because of religious reasons but rather because leaving Lund for Växjö would have meant abandoning the young women with whom he had recently become infatuated, Euphrosyne Palm and Baroness Martina von Schwerin. These intellectual friendships laced with romance took on added importance for Tegnér as a contrast to the official responsibilities of his new Episcopal role, and his bitterness over having to abandon them led to melancholy fits in the 1820's, even as his most acclaimed work, *Frithiof's Saga*, was published in 1825. Tegnér was ill or distracted during much of his time as bishop, eventually going to the German principality of Schleswig for convalescence. He still maintained his literary productivity and had contacts with writers in many countries, including the United States. He returned to Växjö in the early 1840's and died in 1846.

ANALYSIS

Esaias Tegnér's early years as an academic in Lund are captured in "Kannick" (the church house). In the poem, he contrasts the active lives of Lutheran pastors who can marry with the ascetic lives of medieval Catholic monks who could not, as innocent outdoor frolics with young girls turn into loving marriages; the possibility of a good clergyman being able to fall in love was a keynote of Tegnér's biography. "Flyttfåglarna" (birds of passage) is a mock-celebration of poets who yearn for the sun and migrate to the south during the winter, but then wish to return to the bracing climes of their northern origin. The poem also carries a secondary scene of Sweden's own marginality with respect to the rest of Europe, canvassing both the benefits and liabilities of that position. "Sången" (song) is Tegnér's most adamant rejection of Romantic melancholy; he embraces sound, strenuous moral optimism, a position all the more poignant because of the unhappiness of Tegnér's later life. Even "Mjeltsjukan" (melancholy), written in the late 1820's during a period of emotional turmoil, shows the speaker, far from exulting in self-pity, wishing he could recover his self-assurance and sanity.

Epilogue at the Master's Presentation was written for the conferral of degrees on the graduating students at Lund. Using the metaphor of laurel and its fanciful origins in Apollo's pursuit of Daphne, who is turned into the plant, Tegnér sees this myth as an image of a larger ideal, but also shows how any linguistic sign is only a partial manifestation of the implied reality behind it. Tegnér's emphasis, though, is not skeptical, but oratory, as he urges the young graduates not just to live a life of joy and learning but also to engage in a fiery, concerted struggle against ignorance and illiberalism, in favor of truth and enlightenment. That the travails of his later life and his ambivalence about becoming a bishop soon made him unable to fully espouse these ideals himself is a further irony.

Tegnér's becoming a bishop highlights two aspects

of Romanticism: the writers' tendency to become more conservative as they grew older and their distaste for the aftermath of the French Revolution and its unshackling of religious belief from incipient Enlightenment secularism. Both tendencies, though, are somewhat eccentric. In Tegnér's case, his belief in Christianity was not that fervent; his assumption of a pastoral and then episcopal vocation was more a solution to the question of what to do with his life than an urgent calling, and his performance in the ministry, though both competent and compassionate, was marked by neither theological revelation nor dogmatic ardor. This was noted by the later poet Gustaf Fröding in his "Hans högvördighet biskopen i Växiö" (the Right Reverend the Lord Bishop of Växjö), in which he portrays Tegnér as scandalizing onlookers with his recitation of pagan-sounding poet credos; however, according to Tegnér translator Judith Moffett, Tegnér had lost much of his animating poetic force and was more scatter-brained than Dionysian as a bishop. Tegnér, though as disappointed in the outcome of the French Revolution as his contemporaries, did not retreat into a chastened conservatism, but rather espoused the ideals of liberty and democracy, even though these were not fully achieved in the Europe of his time. Tegnér, however, never saw himself as a Romantic; his aesthetics probably are closer to the Weimar classicism represented by Johan Wolfgang von Goethe and Friedrich Schiller than later Romantics such as Finnish writer Johan Ludvig Runeberg.

FRITHIOF'S SAGA

Frithiof's Saga chronicles the conflict between family identity and romantic love; Frithiof, a hero who nobly serves the family of the king, is finally destroyed not so much by any antagonist on the battlefield but by the jealousy and prejudice of the brothers, Helgi and Hafldan, of his beloved, Ingeborg. Written in rhyming couplets with lines of fourteen beats, the poem mimics epic rhythms yet is a psychological drama as much as it is a sanguinary struggle. It is characterized by subtle, melancholy emotion that adds both a psychological dimension and a nuance of reserve to the original saga.

Frithiof's Saga was part of the movement—occasioned by James Macpherson's Ossian forgeries (which Tegnér read to learn English), Bishop Thomas Percy's

Reliques of Ancient Poetry (1765), and the crafted ballads of Sir Walter Scott—toward infusing the polished veneer of a European poetry long influenced by neo-classical models with the vigor and force of folk poetry that had survived through oral tradition. The confidence and reach of Tegnér's verse, for example, far exceeded that of his Swedish predecessor Carl Michael Bellman, whose lyric energy had been stifled by the conventionality of the forms in which it was encased.

Tegnér's popularity in Europe was, in turn, partially due to Romantic nationalism and to Dutch and German scholars feeling an ethnic kinship with Scandinavians, particularly since Scandinavia was then regarded, because of a misreading of Jordanes's *Getica* (c. 551; *The Origin and Deeds of the Goths*, 1908), as the fount of Gothic and therefore Germanic identity. Thus there was a racial component to his vogue. On the other hand, Tegnér's reception, especially in Germany, was tinged with the cosmopolitan ideal of *Weltliteratur* or "world literature," advocated by Goethe. In this light, material such as *Frithiof's Saga* was welcome not out of atavistic primitivism but out of a sense of cultural variety and the need for there to be different kinds of literature, not necessarily the most polished, urbane, and conventional.

This aspect of Tegnér's work was seized on by American poet Henry Wadsworth Longfellow, whose *The Song of Hiawatha* (1855) was influenced by *Frithiof's Saga*. Some critics view the influence of *Frithiof's Saga* to be less than that of Elias Lönnrot's *Kalevala* (1835, enlarged 1849 as *Uusi Kalevala*; English translation, 1888), but Longfellow's technique was informed not only by Lönnrot's air of oral, collective anonymity but also by Tegnér's ability to consciously refashion archaic material in a way that exhibited the conscious, refined touch of the poet. In his tribute poem to Tegnér, "Tegnér's Drapa," Longfellow overtly states that he wants the life and breadth of Scandinavian poetry without the violence, killing, and, it is implied, the monocultural ethnic identity. Far more a cosmopolitan than a source-hunter, Longfellow appreciated the universality and idealism of Tegnér's work in a way that the poet might well have appreciated it.

For whatever reason, Tegnér's name did not remain a permanent part of world literature; he dropped from consideration outside Sweden. However, he has remained a touchstone for all Swedish poetry, and his oeuvre awaits the discovery of comparative Romantic-period scholars, who would find in him a figure that would bear fruitful comparison to more frequently studied writers in German and English.

OTHER MAJOR WORK

NONFICTION: *Esaias Tegnérs brev*, 1953-1976 (11 volumes, Nils Palmborg, editor).

BIBLIOGRAPHY

Beijborn, Ulf. "Tegnér and America." In *Scandinavians in Old and New Lands*, edited by Philip K. Anderson. Chicago: Swedish-American Historical Society, 2004. Focuses on the Longfellow-Tegnér encounter as well as Tegnér's views of America; could be more aesthetically minded but still provides valuable information.

DuBois, Thomas A. "Frithiof's Motley Cousins: On the Perils of Using Folklore to Create a National Epic." In *The Nordic Storyteller: Essays in Honor of Niels Ingwersen*, edited by Susan Brantly and Thomas A. DuBois. Newcastle, England: Cambridge Scholars, 2009. Remarks on the contradictions between the epic, lyric, and folkloric strains in Tegnér's verse.

Gustafson, Lars. *Forays into Swedish Poetry*. Austin: University of Texas, 1978. One of the leading twentieth century Swedish men of letters places Tegnér in the context of his country's literary tradition; the most accessible introduction for the beginning student.

Hilen, Andrew. *Longfellow and Scandinavia*. New Haven, Conn.: Yale University Press, 1947. Still the best source for Longfellow's borrowings from Tegnér, which provided the Swedish poet with his widest visibility in the English-speaking world.

Moffett, Judith. *The North! To the North!: Five Swedish Poets of the Nineteenth Century*. Carbondale: Southern Illinois University Press, 2001. Moffett's translation of Tegnér's lyrics is accompanied by a thorough introduction about his career and place in Swedish poetry; she also provides a partial translation of *Frithiof's Saga*.

Nicholas Birns

THEOCRITUS

Born: Syracuse, Sicily (now in Italy); c. 308 B.C.E.
Died: Syracuse, Sicily (now in Italy); c. 260 B.C.E.
Also known as: Theocritus of Syracuse

PRINCIPAL POETRY

Idylls, c. 270 B.C.E. (first pb. 1566; English translation, 1684)

OTHER LITERARY FORMS

As an adherent to the Callimachean belief in short, polished poetic forms, Theocritus (thee-OK-ruht-uhs) probably did not attempt epic, dramatic, or didactic poetry—though a late reference work, the *Suda* (tenth century), does mention two supposedly large works or collections, *The Heroines* and *The Daughters of Proetus*, known only by their titles.

ACHIEVEMENTS

Although Theocritus wrote in a variety of forms—pastorals, erotic lyrics, mimes, hymns, encomia, miniature epics, and epigrams—he is best known in the history of literature as the creator of pastoral poetry, which was to become a very sophisticated literary tradition in Western Europe. It has been argued that Theocritus himself produced and published a collection of his rustic poems, which established his identity and reputation as a pastoral poet, but there is no external evidence for such a collection. Rather than a fixed formula, the pastoral idyll was for Theocritus a loosely defined species of sketch set in the central or eastern Mediterranean countryside and peopled by herdsmen with a fondness for poetry and music. Love motifs are common in these rustic landscapes, as are recitations of poetry made up by herdsmen for some small occasion such as a casual singing match. It was for Vergil, writing nearly 250 years later, to add layers of sentiment and allegory to Theocritus's semirealistic and self-contained country scenes, and it was largely through Vergil that Theocritus made his mark on European letters. Elements of the pastoral appeared here and there in earlier Greek literature: musical or poetic herdsmen in Homer and Hesiod, a lament for Daphnis in Stesichorus, rustic settings in Euripides and even in Plato's *Phaedros* (fourth century B.C.E.; *Phaedrus*, 1792), mime in the works of Sophron and Epicharmus in the fifth century B.C.E., and the prominence of erotic motifs in much late classical poetry, drama, and fiction. It is hard, in fact, to assess the originality of Theocritean pastoral because so much of what was written in the fourth century B.C.E. has been lost, but it was early claimed and has never been disproved that Theocritus was the one who brought the elements of the pastoral or bucolic idyll together in a definitive way.

Theocritus's pastoral poems share with the other idylls a distinctive, pungent realism that gives his vignettes a flavor of authenticity, as if the reader were witnessing actual scenes of Hellenistic country and city life. The effect is achieved in part by Theocritus's use of a Doric dialect like that of his native Sicily, chosen partly for its phonetic qualities, but also, no doubt, because it bypassed the literary Attic, Ionic, and Aeolian usages, which were associated in his readers' minds with earlier Greek poetry. The realistic effect is also the result of his preference for everyday characters belonging to the lower social and economic ranks. A mythical King Oedipus or Medea could be representative of the human condition to a classical (or neoclassical) theater audience, but neither could be as typical as the Alexandrian housewives in idyll 15 or as real as the Coan peasant-poets in idyll 7. Theocritus's achievement is therefore not confined to the creation of pastoral poetry. Of the twenty-two idylls attributable to him, only eight are pastoral, and no more than a half dozen of his twenty-six epigrams are rustic.

The balance of his poems survived, one must suppose, because they are vivid and credible epiphanies of the Hellenistic world that Theocritus inhabited. Granted, Theocritus's realism is not as literal as it is made to seem: His Doric Greek is an artificial patois drawn from a variety of dialects within the Dorian family, and his fictions are too artfully concocted to be real slices of rustic or urban life—this is the paradox of all literary realism. It is a more striking paradox that the creator of the genre that was to become the most artificial in European belles lettres should also have been one of the first great masters of literary realism.

Biography

Little is known with certainty about the life of Theocritus. Born in or near Syracuse around 308 B.C.E., he traveled as a young man to the Aegean island of Cos. The reasons for this sojourn are unknown. Family connections may have provided an initial foothold there, but the existence of a kind of medical center and school outside the city of Cos, the Asclepieion, where his friend Nicias was a student, could have been the main attraction for him. A detailed knowledge of eastern Mediterranean plant life in the *Idylls* suggests that Theocritus made a special study of botany in that age when plants were the chief source of medication. Another possible motive was the community of poets around Philetas, a distinguished scholar and poet who had been the tutor of the Egyptian monarch Ptolemy Philadelphus. Idyll 7, "The Harvest Festival," is a lightly disguised tribute to this group, of which Theocritus counts himself a member under the alias Simichidas. The idea of a herdsman-poet may have evolved from a self-sufficient commune headed by Philetas, dedicated to the pursuit of writing in a setting that (like Epicurus's famous garden in Athens) insulated its members from the distractions of city life. From this perspective, the combination of goatherding and poetry would have been a sensible expedient rather than the affectation it became in later ages.

It was probably on Cos that Theocritus had his first success as the creator of a new style of poetry, the pastoral. He was noticed in Alexandria, and at some point, no doubt with the encouragement of his mentor Philetas, Theocritus sought the patronage of the royal court. Idyll 16 is evidence of an earlier unsuccessful bid for the patronage of Hiero II of Syracuse. With Ptolemy, Theocritus was apparently more successful, as his praises of the Egyptian monarch in idylls 14 and 17 suggest. It was during the reign of Ptolemy II Philadelphus (285-246 B.C.E.) that Theocritus lived in Alexandria, some time between 278 B.C.E. and the summer of 270 B.C.E. The nature and extent of his contact with Callimachus and Apollonius Rhodius is uncertain, but it was fruitful, and together the three became the leading poets of the Hellenistic Age, placing an "Alexandrian" stamp on literary tastes for the two and a half centuries culminating with Vergil, Horace, and Ovid.

Ptolemy himself promoted science and scholarship in Alexandria by establishing the museum and library in the royal quarter and gathering under his patronage one of the most remarkable assemblages of talent in history. In this most cosmopolitan of all settings, far from the fields of Cos, Theocritus was in the company not only of gifted literary contemporaries, but of Archimedes (a fellow Syracusan) and the geometer Euclid as well—and also enjoyed access to the largest library ever assembled to that date. Already famous for his pastoral poetry, Theocritus turned here to court poetry, *epyllia* (miniature epics), and mimes that dramatized the lives of ordinary city people. Nothing is known about the circumstances of Theocritus's death, but most authorities believe he died around 260 B.C.E.

ANALYSIS

Theocritus wrote in a number of poetic types, but the three most typical are the pastoral idylls (numbers 1, 3, 4, 5, 6, 7, 11), the mimes (numbers 2, 10, 14, 15), and the *epyllia* (numbers 13, 22, 24). Except for the epigrams, which are mostly in the elegiac couplets customary for fictive inscriptions in the Hellenistic Age, Theocritus's poems are set in the same dactylic hexameter that Homer used. In English, they are called "idylls," a somewhat misleading generic term suggesting peace, tranquillity, and an Arcadian pleasantness—associations relevant only to the pastoral idylls. Even the Greek *eidullion* was not Theocritus's word; a diminutive of *eidos* (form), it means something like "little form," or "short separate poem." It is sometimes explained as meaning "little picture"; although Theocritean poetry is not especially pictorial, the poet did excel in drawing vignettes, and vivid presentation is a special Theocritean talent.

The pastoral, or bucolic (from *boukolos*, "cowherder"), idylls are not written in accordance with strict rules; consequently, idylls 4 and 10 may or may not be considered strictly pastoral, the former because it has no song recited within it, the latter because the singers are agricultural workers, not herdsmen. In any case, the herdsman-poet is the hallmark of the genre, and some kind of poetic recitation usually occurs in the course of the poem. Exceptions are sometimes called rustic mimes, in accordance with the convention that poetry

Theocritus (Hulton Archive/Getty Images)

set in the country is not pastoral without the herdsman-poet and the song within the song. An early ancestor of pastoral song may be the Linos song performed in the vineyard on the shield of Achilles in book 18 of Homer's *Iliad* (c. 750 B.C.E.; English translation, 1611). Closer to the literary beginnings of pastoral is the legendary Sicilian cowherd-poet Daphnis, whose death on the slopes of Mount Etna is the subject of Thyrsis's song in idyll 1. Another source of pastoral is the singing matches observed in ancient and modern times in Sicily, southern Italy, and Greece. It is still sometimes said, on the weakest of evidence, that pastoral has ritual origins connected with a Sicilian cult of Daphnis, but such speculations have little to do with what Theocritus wrote.

The rustic setting on which pastoral depends has moral overtones even in Theocritus, although they were given more explicit emphasis by Vergil and his successors. Theocritean shepherds do not moralize on the superiority of country to city life, but they are creatures of instinct whose fluency in describing their restful surroundings gave rise to a literary topos: the *locus amoenus*, or pleasant spot, where a spreading tree provides shelter from the noonday sun, cicadas chirp in the background, cool waters babble nearby, and grasses offer a natural couch in the shade. The locale is otherwise left to the reader's imagination; Vergil placed his shepherds in Arcadia for its remoteness from Italy, but in Theocritus the *locus amoenus* could be anywhere in the eastern Mediterranean. Idylls 4 and 5 are in southern Italy, idyll 7 on Cos, the rest unspecified. Unlike earlier Greek poetry, which was addressed to a particular *polis* and therefore specific as to location, Theocritean pastoral is addressed to the *oikoumenē*, or civilized world in general, and downplays the specifics of place. Pastoral is an escape to any rustic spot where the sun shines, trees make shade, and shepherds sing. The timelessness of Theocritus's themes and situations also contributes to pastoral's escapism. Like the pleasant spots where they loaf, his shepherds belong to any generation or century; unlike their urban counterparts, they are in no hurry, having nowhere to go and nothing to do but watch their herds and sing about love.

Eros was a favorite Hellenistic topic, being both timeless and apolitical, and in Theocritus, it is the chief disturber of the midsummer calm. Even love is toned down, however, to reduce its potential for tragedy or pathos. Daphnis dies because of love in idyll 1, but the reader is never told exactly how or why, and the whole business is only a shepherd's prize poem, not a firsthand narrative. The goatherd's serenade to Amaryllis in idyll 3 paints the lover's country pathos in quaint rather than tragic colors, so that his threats of suicide are no more believable than his warning that the wolves will eat him. The one-eyed Polyphemus's love for the sea nymph Galatea in idylls 6 and 11 is comic for the same reasons. The carnality in idylls 4 and 5 is no more than a whiff of goatishness to liven up a scene. The love stories in idyll 7 come naturally to the singers, who seem not at all involved in the tales they tell of unrequited love (pastoral love is always unrequited); it is only a song. Love ripples the serenity of pastoral life from time to time, but it never makes waves.

In Theocritean pastoral, therefore, very little happens and nothing of much consequence is discussed. Its characters are unreflective, its actions involve no crisis and little tension, nor does the larger world of change, cities, wars, or politics intrude. In fact, most of the concerns that may be said to lie at the core of literature seem to be excluded from the Theocritean version of pastoral. Its underlying mythos, as Charles Segal has noted, is "a return to origins, to childhood, to simplicity, and to clarity of feeling." Unlike (for example) much prose fiction of the American South in which a similar return is suggested, the Theocritean return contains few deep reverberations. Theocritus turns his back on the goings-on and the interests of his time: the passion for learning shared by his contemporaries Callimachus, Apollonius Rhodius, Herondas, and others; the life of the great Hellenistic courts and the intrigues of their kings; the emotionalism of much Hellenistic poetry and art, the cosmopolitanism of the Hellenistic cities, and the expanding ethical horizons of the age in which he lived—all are forgotten in the quiet simplicity of the pastoral idylls. Recent scholarship has shown it to be a poetry of subtlety and some complexity, but it is a poetry that avoids depth of meaning. In one respect alone, it can be said that Theocritus brought his readers into contact with the serious thinking of his time. Both Stoic and Epicurean philosophies held that the highest truths lie in the rhythms of nature and the basic instincts common to humans and animals. By leading the way to a pastoral life of nature and instincts, Theocritus dramatized a simpler and perhaps better world for his citified readers. Pastoral is therefore essentially an urban form, and Theocritus's initial success as a poet probably came from an urban audience's vicarious participation in that simpler world.

The line between pastoral and mime is not easy to draw, because all pastoral is also mime—that is, a dramatized scene with one or more characters, emphasizing character in a single situation rather than action in a plot. Pastoral mime typically brings two herdsmen together in a situation which elicits song. Sometimes—in the beginning of idyll 1 and throughout idyll 5—the speech is amoebean, with the second speaker trying to cap the verses of his rival. In idylls 6, 7, and 10, the singing contest takes the form of one song from each of two performers, a modification of the folk contests which must have influenced Theocritus in his creation of pastoral. In this perspective, both pastoral and mime are sketches from life, imaginary conversations done into verse and a made-up Doric dialect.

IDYLL 2

Idyll 2 is a dramatic monologue, but there is nothing pastoral about it, nothing of the male bucolic world in which women are mentioned only as objects of love's unhappy passion. Here, for the first and only time in Theocritus, a single woman is the speaker, and the reader sees through her eyes Theocritus's favorite theme: love's unhappiness. The comic stage had begun in the previous generation to present love stories with happy endings, but romantic love was not yet a cultural attitude, and when Hellenistic poets wrote of love, it was more often than not in the tradition of destructive passion. It was the same tradition that produced the tragedy of Dido in the *Aeneid* (c. 29-19 B.C.E.; English translation, 1553) In idyll 2, the woman in love is Simaetha, recently struck with a sudden passion for Delphis, a young playboy, as he was walking back from the gymnasium. In his careless way, he has made love to her and gone on to other conquests, leaving her the victim of an aroused passion. However, Simaetha is not the victim of a male seducer. As her own account of the encounter with Delphis reveals, she is the one who suffered love at first sight and took all the initiative, to the point of pushing him down on her bed. Now she is given another traditionally male role to play—that of the forlorn lover—as she calls upon the feminine powers of darkness, Selene, Hecate, Aphrodite, and Artemis, to make her lover return or to hurt him if he refuses. For all this, she is a figure of pity; her nighttime monologue, punctuated by the refrains of her spells to bind a lost lover, could well be Theocritus's masterpiece. It is an evocative and realistic portrayal of a woman in a state of passionate obsession, representative of the interest which Hellenistic poets shared in this subject.

IDYLL 15

Another Theocritean masterpiece, idyll 15, also looks to the life of women, but in a lighter vein. Gorgo and Praxinoa are two young matrons from Syracuse who are living in Alexandria. Here, Theocritus's interest is not in a woman's crisis, but in the ordinary life of lively but unsophisticated women. The occasion is the autumn festival of Adonis, the lover of Aphrodite whose death symbolized the annual withering of vegetation. Queen Arsinoe has opened the Ptolemaic palace for a public viewing of the artworks created for the occasion: the dead or dying Adonis represented in a tapestry, a couch with figures of Adonis and Aphrodite embracing, and an impressive array of surrounding adornments. The two ladies take this opportunity for time out from their domestic routine, and the reader overhears their conversation as they meet at Praxinoa's house, walk through the streets of Alexandria, and marvel at the display before them in the palace. The scenes of everyday life include a singer performing an "Adonis" song, which Walker calls "a deliberately parodistic example of Alexandrian kitsch." The whole is a tour de force of representation. The matrons are contemptuous of their husbands and sharp-tongued when jostled in the crowd, but Theocritus's intent is not entirely malicious, and the reader gets a persuasive view of a subject that other Greek poets chose to ignore: "a page torn fresh out of the book of human life," as Matthew Arnold called it.

IDYLLS 10 AND 14

Idylls 10 and 14 are skits of the male world, the first representing two hardworking reapers (not the idle herdsmen of the pastoral idylls) who exchange songs. The lovesick Bucaeus sings a clumsy ode to a skinny, sun-blackened girl named Bombyca (after the pipes she plays for the field hands), and the pragmatic Milon answers with a brace of Hesiodic couplets of advice to the farmer that sound as if they came from some ancient farmer's almanac. The characters who converse in idyll 14 are also men, but through their conversation, the reader gets a glimpse of a woman, Cynisca, who has left the lovesick Aeschinas for a gentler boyfriend after he has beaten her up in a jealous rage. Thyonichus advises his friend to enter the service of Ptolemy as a mercenary to forget his troubles. Both mimes are humorous commentaries, the one on a lover's blindness to his girl's plainness, the other on a quick-tempered lover's inability to treat decently a mistress he finds it so hard to do without.

IDYLLS 13, 22, AND 24

One important difference between Theocritus's pastoral and his mimes is that the latter present their subjects in low mimetic style, with a characteristic capacity for irony, humor, and parody, while the pastorals temper those features with a lyricism in the presentation of pastoral life. The *epyllion*, or "little epic," was a Hellenistic attempt to revive characters and stories of a high mimetic form in an age when the epic was becoming obsolete. Callimachus wrote a homey interlude in the exploits of Theseus in the *Ekalē* (n.d.; *Hecale*, 1958), of which some fragments still survive. Theocritus's "Hylas" (idyll 13) shows Heracles distraught over the loss of his young companion, taken by the nymphs of a pool where he had come for water during the expedition of the Argonauts. The point of this short narrative, addressed to the poet's friend Nicias, is that although love can upset the stoutest heart, man—like Heracles in this story—must eventually return to his tasks. The episode also appears in the *Argonautica* (third century B.C.E.; English translation, 1780) of Theocritus's contemporary Apollonius Rhodius, perhaps written before this version. Theocritus's poem has been much admired. It is the subject of a well-known Victorian painting by J. W. Waterhouse, *Hylas and the Nymphs*, and Alfred, Lord Tennyson, was so moved by Theocritus's poem that he is said to have exclaimed, "I should be content to die if I had written anything equal to this!"

Idyll 22, "The Dioscuri," describes in its first part an episode in the *Argonautica* involving a boxing match between Polydeuces and Amycus; the second part, describing a duel between Castor and Lynceus, is a pastiche of Homeric formulae from the *Iliad* and does its author little credit.

"Little Heracles" is the title of idyll 24, apparently composed for a contest. It is a reworking of Pindar's first Nemean ode (fourth century B.C.E.), in which the story is told of how the infant Heracles killed the snakes sent by Hera to devour him. The poem's movement from the heroic to the domestic follows a Hellenistic tendency to domesticate epic themes, and Heracles' emergence as what anthologizer Anna Rist calls "a Hellenistic gentleman, complete with all proper accomplishments" is a reminder that the royal house of Ptolemy, Theocritus's patron, claimed descent from Heracles.

Theocritus was a major writer in a period that produced no great literature. It is of little use to disparage his work as lacking in profundity, because it was subtlety and polish rather than scope and depth that the poets of the age prized. He was Hellenism's keenest observer of men and women; he expanded the vision of the age with his choice of subjects, his lyric powers, and his detailed representations. Finally, his pastoral myth has provoked the imaginations of great poets for more than two millennia.

BIBLIOGRAPHY

Burton, Joan B. *Theocritus's Urban Mimes: Mobility, Gender, and Patronage*. Berkeley: University of California Press, 1995. Burton presents sophisticated readings of Theocritus's urban mimes. Unlike Theocritus's bucolic poems, which focus on the male experience, all his urban mimes represent women in more central and powerful roles, reflecting the growing visibility of Greek women at the time.

Gutzwiller, Kathryn J. *Theocritus's Pastoral Analogies: The Formation of a Genre*. Madison: University of Wisconsin Press, 1991. Examines Theocritus as the originator of the pastoral.

Haber, Judith. *Pastoral and the Poetics of Self-Contradiction*. New York: Cambridge University Press, 1994. A review of the origins and development of the pastoral tradition, with an especially acute focus on the criticism and interpretations of Theocritus over the centuries.

Halperin, David. *Before Pastoral: Theocritus and Ancient Tradition of Bucolic Poetry*. New Haven, Conn.: Yale University Press, 1983. A reexamination of Theocritus's place as the originator of the pastoral poetry. Halperin credits him with more originality and greater influence than do previous critics.

Hubbard, Thomas. *Pipes of Pan*. Ann Arbor: University of Michigan Press, 1998. A review of the pastoral tradition from ancient Greece to the European Renaissance, with special attention paid to Theocritus as originator and prime exponent.

Hunter, Richard. *Theocritus and the Archaeology of Greek Poetry*. 1996. Reprint. New York: Cambridge University Press, 2006. An interesting study of the historical and literary context of the Greek

Archaic Age from which Theocritus's poems emerged. Focuses more on the hymns, mimes, and erotic poems of Theocritus than on his pastorals.

Payne, Mark. *Theocritus and the Invention of Fiction.* New York: Cambridge University Press, 2009. Provides extensive analysis of Theocritus's poetry and its legacy.

Rosenmeyer, Charles. *The Green Cabinet: Theocritus and European Pastoral Lyric.* Bristol, England: Bristol Classical, 2004. Examines the pastoral poems of Theocritus and his influence on later pastoral poets.

Walker, Steven F. *Theocritus.* Boston: Twayne, 1980. A study providing a solid introduction and background to the author, his world, and his works.

Zimmerman, Clayton. *The Pastoral Narcissus: A Study of the First Idyll of Theocritus.* Lanham, Md.: Rowman and Littlefield, 1994. Links Theocritus's poem on Narcissus to the visual arts in the Hellenistic period.

Daniel H. Garrison

THEOGNIS

Born: Megara(?), Greece; c. seventh century B.C.E.
Died: Megara(?), Greece; c. sixth century B.C.E.
Also known as: Theognis of Megara

PRINCIPAL POETRY

Theognidea, seventh or sixth century B.C.E.
The Elegies of Theognis, and Other Elegies
    Included in the Theognidean Sylloge, 1910

OTHER LITERARY FORMS

Theognis (thee-OG-nuhs) is remembered only for his poetry.

ACHIEVEMENTS

The words of Theognis transcend their age, occasion, and audience. Although his images, assumptions, and advice were based on an archaic value system, much of what he wrote still has currency in the twenty-

first century. Theognis predicted the universal acceptance and immortality of his poetry. Time has proved him an accurate seer. After all, poverty is still painful; youth is still fleeting; ships of state are still capsized; true friends are few.

BIOGRAPHY

Verses 22 and 23 of the *Theognidea* assert that they are "the words of Theognis the Megarian, known by name among all men." This assertion provides most of the available information about him. No ancient biography survives, and perhaps none ever existed. The dates and even the place of his origin are disputed. Because Plato makes him a citizen of the Megara in Sicily, this view has had its adherents; most often, however, he is associated with Megara on the Isthmus of Corinth, near Athens.

The few historical allusions in the *Theognidea* span a period from the seventh to the fifth century B.C.E. Passages that seem to anticipate a tyranny at Megara were presumably composed before the actual tyranny of Theagenes, which perhaps began about 630; the threat from the Medes in verses 764 and 775 should be the invasion of Xerxes in 480. Some medieval sources place the floruit of Theognis between 552 and 541 B.C.E. The tenth century lexicon, the *Suda*, gives the fifty-ninth Olympiad, 544 to 541, as his floruit. The dates of the 630's and 544 to 541 have gained the most favor. Passages that seem earlier and later than the chosen floruit are explained as anonymous compositions included before about 300 B.C.E. among the genuine poems of Theognis.

In verses 19 to 23 of the *Theognidea*, Theognis claims to put a *sphregis*, or seal, on his words so that it would be obvious if they were stolen. This *sphregis* is commonly assumed to be the name of Kyrnos, a youth to whom these verses are addressed. Accordingly, the name Kyrnos or his patronymic, Polupaides, in a poem identifies it as genuinely by Theognis. Thus, of almost fourteen hundred verses attributed to Theognis, about one-fourth are usually considered genuine, with Theognis's name attached to the whole because of the predominance and prominence of the Kyrnos poems.

A radically different view sees the name of Theognis as generic, traditionally associated with Megarian gnomological elegiac poetry. From this perspective, the chronological range of the poetry has no significance; the poetry was composed over time. The *sphregis* becomes the message of the poetry, the traditional code of behavior for the aristocracy.

ANALYSIS

Named after Theognis, the *Theognidea* is a collection of elegiac poetry addressed to aristocratic audiences of Archaic Greece. The poems are paraenetic and didactic; that is, they seek to give counsel and to teach. One ancient name for the collection is *Gnomology*, a compilation of gnomic statements or maxims. Theognis's favorite terms, "the good" and "the bad," originally had connotations relating to birth, status, and politics; nevertheless, they are not tied down by names, events, or places. Because his advice was adaptable to time and circumstances, he spoke to "the good" everywhere.

Many of Theognis's observations are now so familiar as to seem clichés. Most were traditional wisdom even for the poet: There is no place like home; youth is fleeting; poverty is painful. On the other hand, some seem fresh. For example, the increasingly widespread phenomenon of coined money made an impact on Theognis's poetry. Not found in Homer and Hesiod are such derivative images as Theognis's counterfeit friend and need for a touchstone to test purity of character, images that were developed by Plato and others.

Theognis is often cited for confirmation or quibbling in the works of ancient and medieval authors. The poems of the *Theognidea*, however, were transmitted through medieval manuscripts rather than from scattered citations, as was the case with most Archaic elegiac, iambic, and melic poetry. The perceived usefulness of the counsel undoubtedly contributed to its survival.

THEOGNIDEA

The *Theognidea* is divided into two books of unequal length. Scholar Martin L. West concludes that the division was made about 900 C.E. The second book contains fewer than two hundred verses, concerned with various aspects of pederasty. These verses had originally been scattered throughout the collection. The theme of pederasty is consonant with other preoc-

cupations of the *Theognidea*: status and wealth, the faithfulness of friends, moderation and excess. The author of the elegies upholds the mores and privileges of the aristocracy against encroachment by an increasingly aggressive "middle class."

Most of the poems consist of one or two couplets. Two of the longer passages, 19 to 38 and 237 to 254, bound a core thought by all scholars to be genuine. The first of the longer passages begins with Kyrnos's name, identifies Theognis as author, and introduces the problem of the seal. Within the core passage, the poet declares his intentions:

> Being well-disposed to you, I shall advise you,
>   Kurnos, on such things as I myself learned from the
>   good when I was a youth.
> Be wise; amass neither honors nor glories nor wealth
>   at a price of either shameful or unjust deeds.
> Just know these things: do not associate with bad
>   men, but keep yourself always with the good.
> Drink and eat beside them; sit with them and please
>   them; their power is great.
> For from the noble you will learn noble things, but if
>   you mix with the bad, you will lose
>   even the sense you now have.
> Learn these things and associate with the good; at
>   some time you will say that I give good counsel to
>   my friends.

In verses 237 to 254, the poet claims to have given Kyrnos immortality. Kyrnos will be present at every banquet and feast, in poems sung to the accompaniment of an oboe. The immortality of Kyrnos assumes the immortality of Theognis's poetry through its being sung at banquets and feasts—that is, at symposia. As the symposium was an institution of the leisure class, so the poetry passes on the values of this class. The good and noble are the aristocrats; the bad are those with unimpressive pedigrees, whose wealth requires that they be noticed. The poet cannot deny this notice, but it is hostile and scornful.

THE SKOLIA

As Plato's *Symposion* (fourth century B.C.E.; *Symposium*, 1701) suggests, after the consumption of food and along with the consumption of wine, demonstrations of cleverness contributed to the entertainment on such occasions. The poems of the *Theognidea* agree in tone and content with the drinking songs, or *skolia*, collected in the *Deipnosophists* (second century C.E.; learned men at dinner) of Athenaeus. Some are riddles; some make observations on the symposium itself: A man who chatters all the time is a nuisance and is invited only by necessity. A guest should not be forced to go home or forced to stay. One who drinks too much also talks too much and makes a fool of himself. He who has drunk very much but is still sensible is unsurpassed. A symposium is pleasant when everything is said in the open and there are no quarrels. When drunk, the wise and foolish are indistinguishable. Wine shows the mind of a man. At a banquet, it is good for one to sit beside a wise man and to go home having learned something. Drink when people drink; when sad, drink so no one will know. Many are friends over food and drink, but few can be relied on in a serious matter.

FRIENDSHIP

The task of distinguishing true friends from false requires the versatility of Odysseus. The poet adjures his heart to cultivate a changeful character, to be like his companion, to have the temperament of the octopus, which looks like the rock to which it clings. The poet frequently advises testing a friend before trusting him in a serious matter. The antitheses of tongue and deed and tongue and thought are marked; men love deceit. Kyrnos should, therefore, speak as if he were a friend to all but become involved with no one in anything serious. A man who says one thing and thinks another cannot be a good friend. Some friends are counterfeit; the poet longs for a touchstone. Blessed is he who dies before having to test his friends.

Theognis's apparent pessimism concerning friendship is part of a more general pessimism typical of Archaic poetry. In Homer's *Iliad* (c. 750 B.C.E.; English translation, 1611), a generation of people is like a generation of leaves. The best possibility for humans is a mixture of good and evil. Theognis says that the best thing for those on Earth is not to be born; for one born, it is best to die as quickly as possible. Death is preferable to oppressive poverty, and poverty forces people into wickedness. Wealth confers honor; wealth and poverty should be distributed according to personal worth, but they are not. Divine favor gives money even to one completely worthless; few have virtue.

MODERATION

Since wealth does not belong only to the good, it cannot carry a completely positive valence. The wealth of wicked men who lack sound judgment and are unjust leads to excess, to hubris. Examination of the passages in which hubris appears reveals that in the diction of the *Theognidea*, the context of hubris is always, although not always overtly, political. The greatest danger of hubris is that it causes the destruction of cities. For private gain, the bad give unjust judgments and injure the people; from hubris comes factionalism, internecine killings, and tyrants. On the other hand, the gods give political moderation, *gnome*, as the best thing for mortals; all things are accomplished through moderation.

Theognis uses many other terms for political moderation. The most familiar, *sophrosune*, is explicitly opposed to hubris, but Theognis's most striking call to political moderation begins with the phrase *meden agan*. The phrase *meden agan* (nothing in excess) was carved on the entrance to the temple of Apollo at Delphi and was associated with the wisdom of the Seven Sages. *Gnothi sauton* (know yourself) was inscribed with *meden agan*; the two warnings against hubris are important for interpreting much of classical Greek literature, especially tragedy and the *Historiai Herodotou* (c. 424 B.C.E.; *The History*, 1709) of Herodotus.

The middle way is urged in several poems beginning with *meden agan*: Do not in any way strive too eagerly; the middles of all things are best. The opportune moment is best for all the deeds of humans. Do not in any way too much glut your heart with difficulties or rejoice too much in good things, because it is the mark of a good person to bear everything. Comparison with other injunctions shows the pattern of the negative command followed by a reinforcing positive statement. These reinforcing statements are separable from the particular commands, and both are reusable. Since the diction of Solon, Hesiod, Homer, and others shows the same pattern, similarities of Theognis to other poetry can be attributed to the traditional nature of the language and the general importance of moderation in the Archaic value system.

SEA AND SAILING IMAGERY

That the dominant metaphors in the *Theognidea* concern the sea and sailing is perhaps natural, because

Greece is surrounded by water, and the major Archaic city-states all founded colonies overseas. Not only was sailing vital to Greek economic life, but also, as the *Odyssey* (c. 725 B.C.E.; English translation, 1614) suggests, it was vital to the Greek psyche. On the wings of Theognis's poetry, Kyrnos will be universally known, borne easily over the boundless sea. The poet advises that doing a favor for a bad man is like sowing the sea. A bad man should be avoided like a bad harbor. Like a ship, the poet keeps his distance from one whom time has exposed as a counterfeit friend. A boy was rough but relented; after the storm, the poet rests at anchor with night coming.

The ship can also be the ship of state. The first extant examples of this image are found in two fragments of the Greek poet Alcaeus; the best known is in the Augustan poet Horace. Theognis is an important link in the transmission of the metaphor. It appears in verses 575 to 576 and verses 855 to 856, but it receives extended treatment in verses 667 to 682. The wealth of the poet is not equal to his character. The state is beset by difficulties that could have been foreseen but were not. The skilled helmsman has been displaced. There is no order, no concern for the common good. The bad rule over the good. The ship is in danger of being swallowed by the waves. The poet calls his extended metaphor a code to the good, but one comprehensible even to a bad man if he is wise.

PEDERASTIC POEMS

Pausanias's encomium of Eros in the *Symposion* (fourth century B.C.E.; *Symposium*, 1701) of Plato sheds much light on the pederastic poems of the second book of the *Theognidea*. According to Pausanias, pederasty is acceptable in a context of moral improvement. The lover aims to make the young man better; the beloved gratifies his lover in the hope of becoming better. In Theognis, the situation is much the same. Through his association with the poet, the young Kurnos learns how to conduct himself, how to interact with his own kind, and what attitudes to adopt toward social inferiors. Because the role of beloved can be played for only a short time, he learns the part of the lover also, able to take his turn. As an institution, pederasty tightened the bonds of aristocratic solidarity.

Many of the pederastic poems are facetious, befit-

ting their sympotic setting. A boy is advised to quit running away, since he will not be of an age for long. As long as the boy's cheek is smooth, the poet will fawn on him, even if the price is death. Love is bitter and sweet, hard and soft. The poet laments the public exposure of his love for a boy, but he will endure the attacks; the boy is not unseemly. Finally, in verses 1345 to 1350, the poet adduces a mythic exemplum:

> Loving a boy has been something pleasant since the
>   son of Kronos, the king of the
> immortals, was in love with Ganymede.
> He snatched him up and carried him off to Olympus
>   and made him a divinity while he
> had the lovely flower of his boyhood.
> So do not marvel, Simonides, that I too was shown
>   conquered by love of a pretty boy.

BIBLIOGRAPHY

Compton, Todd. "Theognis: Faceless Exile." In *Victim of the Muses: Poet as Scapegoat, Warrior, and Hero in Greco-Roman and Indo-European Myth and History*. Washington, D.C.: Center for Hellenic Studies, 2006. A biography of Theognis that considers the poet a faceless exile.

Edmunds, Lowell. "The Seal of Theognis." In *Poet, Public, and Performance in Ancient Greece*, edited by Lowell Edmunds and Robert Wallace. Baltimore: The Johns Hopkins University Press, 1997. Traces the relationship of the poet and his work to his audience, who are seen as less readers and literary enthusiasts than fellow citizens in the polis and friends of the poet's tribal group. The fundamental effect sought in Theognis's work is therefore not aesthetic but political.

Figueire, Thomas, and Gregory Nagy, eds. *Theognis of Megara: Poetry and the Polis*. Baltimore: The Johns Hopkins University Press, 1985. This collection of essays examine a number of topics but focuses especially on the relationship between Theognis's work and his native city of Megara. The result is a combination of poetic, literary, social, and historical insights.

Hubbard, Thomas. "Theognis' *Sphregis*: Aristocratic Speech and the Paradoxes of Writing." In *Politics of Orality*, edited by Craig R. Cooper. Boston: Brill,

2007. Hubbard notes that although many modern scholars have come to view the works collected under the name of Theognis as a local tradition of aristocratic poetry, the *sphregis*, or seal, refers to an individual and casts doubt on this theory. He discusses the passage in detail.

Schmidt, Michael. *The First Poets: Lives of the Ancient Greek Poets*. New York: Knopf, 2006. Contains a biography of Theognis that analyzes his work.

Walker, Jeffrey. "Theognis' Octopus: On Poetry as Rhetorical Transaction." *Rhetoric and Poetry in Antiquity*. New York: Oxford University Press, 2000. Study examines the poetry of Theognis, using his statement that he should be like the octopus, which adapts to its situation.

Carrie Cowherd

GEORG TRAKL

Born: Salzburg, Austro-Hungarian Empire (now in Austria); February 3, 1887
Died: Kraków, Galicia, Austro-Hungarian Empire (now in Poland); November 3, 1914

PRINCIPAL POETRY

Gedichte, 1913
Sebastian im Traum, 1914
Die Dichtungen, 1918
Aus goldenem Kelch, 1939
Decline: Twelve Poems, 1952
Twenty Poems of Georg Trakl, 1961
Selected Poems, 1968
Poems, 1973
Georg Trakl: A Profile, 1983

OTHER LITERARY FORMS

Although Georg Trakl (TROK-uhl) is remembered primarily for his poetry, he did compose two one-act plays (*Totentag*, pr. 1906, and *Fata Morgana*, pr. 1906), but he later destroyed the manuscripts. His letters can be found in his collected works.

ACHIEVEMENTS

Georg Trakl was one of the major poets of German literary expressionism (with Georg Heym and Gottfried Benn). Today, he is ranked by many critics and readers as one of the outstanding poets of the early twentieth century. Like Rainer Maria Rilke, Stefan George, and Hugo von Hofmannsthal, who were his contemporaries, Trakl developed the heritage of Romanticism and French Symbolism into a very personal poetic diction, which, in spite of its individual and original tone, shares some significant stylistic and philosophical features with the work of Trakl's fellow expressionist writers and artists. Trakl's rank as a poet was recognized during his lifetime only by a few (among whom was Rilke). Because the National Socialist regime in Germany and Austria rejected expressionism, claiming it to be a form of degenerate art, Trakl's achievement was fully recognized only after the end of World War II. His work has been particularly influential in Germany, France, and the United States.

BIOGRAPHY

Georg Trakl was born in Salzburg, on February 3, 1887. During high school, he decided to become a pharmacist. After serving his pharmaceutical apprenticeship, he studied pharmacy for four semesters in Vienna and earned his degree in 1910. Trakl wrote two one-act plays (*Totentag* and *Fata Morgana*), both of which were performed in Salzburg. The failure of the latter prompted him to destroy the manuscripts of both plays.

Trakl's earliest poems were written during the last years of the first decade of the twentieth century. In 1910 and 1911, Trakl served in the military as a dispensing pharmacist. After several unsuccessful attempts at a career as a pharmacist, he fell into severe depression and sought refuge from a hostile reality in drugs, to which he had easy access. He would have been unable to cope had it not been for the friendship and patronage of Ludwig von Ficker, publisher of the Austrian journal *Der Brenner*. Ficker published in his journal almost all of Trakl's poetry written between 1912 and 1914. He was one of the few who recognized Trakl's poetic genius during the poet's lifetime. Be-

Georg Trakl (Getty Images)

sides his friendship, Ficker offered Trakl shelter and financial help.

In late August of 1914, with the outbreak of World War I, Trakl, who was serving as a lieutenant in the medical corps, was sent into combat. After the Battle of Grodek in Galicia, he was ordered to care for ninety seriously wounded fellow soldiers who were housed in a barn. Not having the medical training and expertise necessary to help the wounded, Trakl was overwhelmed by the gruesome experience and suffered a nervous breakdown. Comrades prevented him from shooting himself. A few weeks later, he was sent to the garrison hospital at Kraków for observation and psychiatric care. There, he was confined to a cell with another officer who was suffering from delirium tremens. On the night of November 3, 1914, Trakl died from an overdose of cocaine. The question of whether his death was accidental has remained unanswered.

ANALYSIS

Georg Trakl's poetry can be divided into three phases that followed one another within the brief period of approximately eight years. During these years, Trakl's poetic diction underwent profound changes. His early poetry (that written prior to 1909) reflects his groping attempts to find his own "voice." In the early poems, Trakl is unable to free himself fully from the Romantic and neo-Romantic stereotypes of German poetry. His major themes are sorrow, loneliness, the past, and biblical and erotic scenes. His extensive use of the refrain and of four trochee sequences also betrays the influence of Romantic writers, particularly Friedrich Hölderlin and Novalis. Trakl admired the nineteenth century French poet Charles Baudelaire as well as Johann Wolfgang von Goethe, Friedrich Nietzsche, and Fyodor Dostoevski, all of whom left their mark on his writings. A noteworthy feature of Trakl's early poems is the presence of the first-person singular, which in his later poems dissolves to a point beyond recognition. This "I" and its inner world of feelings is distinguishable from externally perceived reality, even though, as in Romantic poetry, the boundary between a mimetic presentation of objects discernible to the senses and a configuration of images expressing the vision of the poet's "inner eye" is often impossible to delineate.

Between 1909 and 1912, Trakl's style changed noticeably. Whereas the early poems frequently show hypotaxis, the poems of this middle phase are predominantly paratactical. The reflective element that is still present in Trakl's earlier poems disappears and gives way to a more "lyrical" or musical principle, and semantic and syntactical patterns are selected according to the interplay of emotional impulse and sound patterns. The emotional impulse translates itself into language in the form of many emotionally charged verbs, such as "threaten," "shiver," "tremble," "be silent," and "hark." The same anthropomorphic tendency that informs Trakl's use of verbs can be observed in his adjectives, most of which do not increase the visibility of his images but convey a vague yet suggestive emotional aura: for example, "lonely," "quiet," "horrible," "sweet," and "wonderful." Regarding sound composition, Trakl's drafts show clearly that he often changed words and made other revisions for purely "musical" reasons. As mentioned earlier, the first person dissolves into a number of objectified protagonists. Whereas Trakl's early poems still reflect an unshaken belief in a divine order of the universe represented by the symbols of the Christian Church, this belief appears to be shattered in the second phase.

Another, more significant change, however, allows one to distinguish between Trakl's poetry of the early phase and that of the second phase. The mimetic relation of poetic expression and the real world as experienced through sensory perception gives way to a new "visionary" approach, an "inner landscape" that defies the laws of realistic and logical presentation and thus poses many hermeneutical problems.

The third and last phase of Trakl's poetry developed in late 1912. The most noticeable changes are evident in a free rhythmical structure (without rhyme) and in a return to hypotaxis. Even though this means a loss in the musical quality of Trakl's late poems, his new free verse makes assonance and alliteration more obvious. It also allows Trakl's images greater visibility, for they are no longer veiled by rhyme and by a regular metrical pattern. The contrasting themes of sinfulness and purity that permeate the poems of the second phase culminate in the third phase in the creation of the mythical figure of a surrogate god, Elis, who represents the ideal of ethical purity.

In spite of its visionary quality, Trakl's poetic "world" never completely emancipates itself from the "real" world. Rather, the reader observes a gradual dissociation from a realistic representation, a shift toward the imaginary. This is why Trakl can indeed be called an expressionist, since the expressionist artist does exactly what Trakl attempts in his poems: He turns away from a realistic or naturalistic approach to the representation of reality. He no longer copies, imitates, reproduces. He follows the emotional impulse of his inner vision and expresses it, whether this means deforming or distorting reality as it is known, changing its perceptual and logical structure at will, or shifting from a representational to an abstract creative mode.

"IN WINTER" AND "THE OCCIDENT"

Compare the first stanza of "Im Winter" ("In Winter") from *Gedichte* (poems):

> The field shimmers white and cold.
> The sky is lonely and vast.
> Jackdaws circle over the pond
> And hunters descend from the forest.

with the first stanza of "Abendland" ("The Occident," fourth version) from *Sebastian im Traum* (Sebastian in dreams):

> Moon, as if something dead emerged
> From a blue cave,
> And many blossoms fall
> Across the rocky path.
> Someone sick weeps silver tears
> Near the evening pond;
> In a black boat
> Lovers drifted beyond toward death.

The text of "In Winter" is clearly mimetic. It can at least be taken as the realistic description of a winter landscape, even though the scene depicted might be an imaginary one. The second example, however, no longer presents a view of reality as it is traditionally and normally perceived. The images joined together in the stanza from "The Occident" can still be construed, with some effort on the part of the reader, as the evocation of a moonlit night in spring. However, who is "someone sick," and why are the lovers in their black boat moving toward death? This stanza seems to have originated in a dream.

ABSTRACT AND ABSOLUTE TECHNIQUES

Because the poetic images unfold an inner landscape, the reader can no longer be sure whether he is to take them at their face value. Trakl scholars have long claimed that many images in Trakl's mature poetry are "ciphers"—that they point to a meaning other than their own. As part of a code, they have to be "deciphered," since they are poetic signs that stand for a signified meaning. Trakl's poetry, however, defies reduction to a system of ciphers, the meanings of which can be revealed by comparing all the contexts of a given cipher in the poet's work. Often such a contextual comparison yields a variety of different meanings, some of which are contradictory. This is true particularly in the case of Trakl's use of colors. Almost none of his color adjectives or nouns can be given a fixed meaning. An exception is the color "blue." It frequently appears in the context of images referring to God, to biblical scenes, to childhood, or to animal life. The common semantic ingredient in all these images is the concept of innocence. The words "blue" and "blueness" also sometimes convey the idea of salvation. The cipher "blue" thus stands for a positive semantic content, one that is opposed to the notions of darkness, death, decay, or decline, which are prevalent in Trakl's poetry.

Some scholars have maintained that in those cases in which a cipher cannot be assigned a constant meaning abstracted from contextual comparison, Trakl uses "absolute ciphers"—that is, ciphers that are part of a code that is beyond decoding, because its "connection" with any signified meaning has been disjoined. Because of this disjunction of word and denoted content, the poet's language withdraws to a certain degree from reality, forming its own Hermetic network of ciphers with multiple semantic content. If no common-meaning denominator can be abstracted from a given number of contexts, the image has to be interpreted within the context of the individual poem.

With caution, one can compare Trakl's poetic strategies to certain similar techniques in the paintings and sculptures of the artists of German expressionism. The latter no longer use colors in a realistic fashion (Franz Marc, for example, paints blue horses). Color in expressionist paintings takes on a symbolic emotional quality that originates in the artist's creative intuition. It is the artist's inner creative "vision" that seeks out its equivalents from the realm of real things for the purpose of artistic expression (regardless of any "realistic" modes of representation). Therefore, it is not a given outer reality that calls for mimetic reproduction in the work of art. Just as Trakl's poetic images lose their realistic and mimetic content and become imbued with an elusive and highly subjective emotional content, expressionist paintings exhibit a tendency toward loss of detail and toward elementary, "essential" forms, a tendency that ultimately leads to nonrepresentational art. This loss of the mimetic mode can be compared to the configurations of images in Trakl's mature and late poetry, which are no longer transparent with a rationally definable meaning "behind" the poetic ciphers. The ensuing darkness and elusiveness of Trakl's poetry (in conjunction with its musical quality) accounts for the often-noted enchanting and captivating effect of his verse.

PHILOSOPHICAL PERSPECTIVE

In spite of all the melodic obscurities in Trakl's poems, it is possible to abstract from his texts a relatively comprehensive view of life. Although Trakl does not offer a full-fledged and systematic "philosophy," his poems are informed by a rather consistent and, at the same time, diversified philosophical perspective that is based on his rejection of many aspects of modern reality. Like most of the expressionists of his generation, Trakl experienced modern industrialized society with its metropolitan cities as a pain-inflicting alien world of which he wanted no part. In Trakl's case, this phobia concerning modern reality was almost paranoiac. The poet's patron, Ficker, reported that he once took Trakl to a large bank in order to deposit a certain sum in Trakl's name. The sight of this institution made Trakl physically ill, and he left the building trembling and perspiring heavily.

If there is an underlying guiding principle in Trakl's thought and poetic style, it is his dread of life in a totally administered, technologically manipulated, and utterly commercialized world. His poetry becomes the expression of his unwillingness to cope with such a life. This is why poetry is the theater of his inner visionary world, which ignores the accepted rules and laws of normal reality. Literature functions as a sanctuary that, while it still reflects some of the evil of life, contains the features of a better antiworld. Trakl's poetic world is shaped not only by a modern version of Romantic escapism, with all its magical and morbid charm, but also by the harshness of industrial society.

For Trakl, the effects of such a society are manifold. Humans feel forlorn, like strangers in this world. They wander through life without goals. The big cities epitomize the plight of modern humans, who turn into anonymous beings in a mass society. In an astonishingly prophetic vision, Trakl sees Europe's metropolitan cities destroyed by fire. The poet does not deplore his somber foreboding, since, in his view, humanity's quest for ethical purity and spiritual nobility is being severely undermined by the brutal, materialistic impact of modern city life.

Trakl seems unable to find any solace in Christianity. Nevertheless, his poems contain numerous biblical references, many of which are an integral part of descriptions of landscapes. It must remain an open question whether Trakl secularizes the religious content of certain biblical words and phrases or whether he imbues nature with a new religious quality. He frequently claims in his poetry that religion is no longer alive. Having degenerated into a lifeless ritual, it has ceased to be a guiding and sustaining power in the life of modern humanity. Where religion fails, the door to the realm of God can be reopened only through the use of drugs, as expressed in Trakl's poem "Traumerei am Abend" ("Daydreaming in the Evening"), from *Gedichte*.

Among the abstract concepts (which are not images and thus not ciphers) that recur in Trakl's poetry are decay, disintegration, disease, and, ultimately, death. These concepts all point to a facet of reality that elicits the poet's lament even though it cannot be regarded as the fruit of modernity. Trakl often links decay and disintegration with humanity's sinfulness and with an undefined sense of guilt from which humanity cannot be freed.

MELANCHOLY

The mood in many of Trakl's poems is one of melancholy, anxiety, and desperation. Subdued emotions such as melancholy, however, prevail over the harsher expressions of negative emotions. The poet frequently establishes a connection between expressions of negative emotions and the themes of decay and sinfulness, which are in turn interrelated.

Trakl's view of life and human destiny is a somber and often gloomy one. Having become alienated from his world, especially from the world of the big city, humans find no comfort in religion and thus blindly pursue a meaningless life, drifting in the stream of time. Because everything ends in decay or death, time can be equated with suffering. In such a view, reality is difficult to love or even to accept. Nevertheless, life offers beauty and peace to those who know how to look for them in a hostile world. In Trakl's poems, one indeed finds a peculiar fusion of threatening and attractive features. It is hard to decide whether the positive ingredients belong to the descriptive-mimetic dimension in Trakl's work—which is, after all, still present to some

degree—or whether they are the product of his inner poetic intuition. Nonmimetic expression and mimetic rendering of perceived impressions are often hardly distinguishable in Trakl's texts.

STYLISTIC DEVICES

A closer look at Trakl's principles of poetic composition reveals that the expressionist style breaks down in many different ways the established, "normal" modes of perception and logical thinking. The new expressionist "perspective" that emerges in Trakl's mature poetry disengages one from the customary and conventional manner in which one grasps phenomenal reality as it appears to one—to one's senses and one's mind.

Trakl's "arsenal" of images, protagonists (the sister, the boy, the dreamer, the lovers, the child, the hunters, the shepherd, the farmer, the monk, the lepers), and abstract concepts is surprisingly small. The immense variety of the real world has been drastically reduced to a small number of images and concepts that are presented in various guises and which appear in ever-new configurations. This reduction represents a subtle first step toward the expressionist, nonmimetic mode of poetic composition.

Another stylistic device derived from the same basic artistic premises might be called "defocusing." Trakl likes to use nouns derived from past participles or adjectives. In the first stanza of "The Occident" (fourth version), one finds expressions such as *ein Totes* ("something dead") or *ein Krankes* ("something sick"). The image has been reduced to its essential core (being dead, sick, and so forth), but no further individualizing details are given. It is almost impossible for the reader to "picture" anything concrete when such blurred images are evoked.

A very effective as well as expressive technique, the nonmimetic thrust of which goes far beyond mere defocusing, is the tendency to present images that denote destruction, dismemberment, and dissolution. This is a stylistic device used by many expressionist writers and artists. Here is an example taken from one of Trakl's late poems: ". . . the black face,/ That breaks into heavy pieces/ Of dead and strange planets." This "destructionism" can be interpreted either as a symptom of the broken and fragmented quality of reality itself (Trakl wrote to his friend Ficker in November, 1913: "It is such a terrible thing when one's world breaks apart") or as the poet's attempt to destroy symbolically a world with which he can no longer identify.

Synesthesia and stylistic devices that run counter to the customary ways of perception constitute yet another (though certainly not new) technique that allows the creative intuition of the expressionist to deform the established structure of reality. Trakl likes to blend heterogeneous qualities and processes that defy the norms and the logic of the real world: Walls are "full of leprosy," and the laughter of a human being "sinks into the old well." Inanimate objects take on human qualities, and vice versa.

The poetic inversion of customary modes of perception extends also to the presentation of time in Trakl's poetry. There are passages of lyrical prose in which the present tense alternates in a completely unrealistic way with the past tense. Furthermore, the "unborn" as well as the "dead" appear and speak in Trakl's poems, and time is sometimes experienced as "standing still," its flow abruptly changed to a state of dreamlike timelessness.

Trakl's lyrical transmutation of reality also leads to the dissolution of the conventional structure of space. The notions of "above" and "below" or "near" and "far" lose their accepted meaning when the poet writes such lines as "A white shirt of stars burns the shoulders which wear it" or "The autumn moon dwells silently near your mouth."

As mentioned earlier, the first-person singular, so frequently found in Trakl's early poetry, disappears in the poems written after 1909. It undergoes various transformations that show a tendency toward objectivization. The "I" becomes part of (or fused with) the images of the poet's imaginary world. It can turn into a "you"; that is, the poet addresses himself in the second person. Parts of the human being who once referred to himself as "I" now represent the lost "whole": "a heart," "the soul," "the forehead," "a face," "a head." A further step toward this objectivist direction can be seen in Trakl's use of unindividuated, anonymous human protagonists (the "stranger," the "lonely one," the "beholder," the "wanderer"). Here it is no longer possible to verify with any degree of accuracy whether such

protagonists are indeed projections of the poet's self.

Since the expressionist world of Trakl's poems is a world that does not obey the laws of reality, it is small wonder that one finds it populated with mythical figures such as fauns, nymphs, Tritons, Satyrs, and dryads. The appearance of demons and ghosts occasionally contributes to the dreamlike atmosphere that is so characteristic of many of Trakl's texts.

Not only is the world described by Trakl an imaginary and in many ways an unreal one, but also the beholding subject, whether intended to be identical with the poet or not, appears in Trakl's poems as one who has lost the ability to experience reality in a normal, conscious, and sober way. The beholder either is a dreamer or is described as under the influence of alcohol or drugs (an obvious autobiographical reference). Dreaming and intoxication derange the mind in its attempt to order the stimuli received from reality.

In Trakl's poetry, the derangement of the world as conventionally perceived allows the construction of a new visionary world. This "inner landscape" becomes a haven for the poet, who finds himself unable to cope with the harsh realities of modern industrialized society. Deforming and transmuting reality, however, need not be interpreted only as an escapist gesture. It is equally significant as a gesture of protest (an elegiac rather than a strident one) against the threatening aspects of modernity.

OTHER MAJOR WORKS

PLAYS: *Fata Morgana*, pr. 1906 (lost); *Totentag*, pr. 1906 (lost).

MISCELLANEOUS: *Gesammelte Werke*, 1949-1951 (3 volumes); *Dichtungen und Briefe*, 1969 (poetry and letters); *Poems and Prose: A Bilingual Edition*, 2005.

BIBLIOGRAPHY

Graziano, Frank, ed. *Georg Trakl: A Profile*. Durango, Colo.: Logbridge-Rhodes, 1983. This biographical study of Trakl's work concentrates on the poet's family relations, drug addiction, poverty, and depression as well as the influence of World War I.

Jason, Philip K., ed. *Masterplots II: Poetry Series*. Rev. ed. Pasadena, Calif.: Salem Press, 2002. This set contains summaries and analyses of the poems

"Evening Song," "Grodek," "The Heart," "Helian," "The Occident," and "Psalm."

Lehbert, Margitt. Introduction to *The Poems of Georg Trakl.* Translated by Margitt Lehbert. London: Anvil Press Poetry, 2007. The translator's introduction to this poetry selection provides valuable information about his life and some literary criticism.

Rolleston, James. "Choric Consciousness in Expressionist Poetry: Ernst Stadler, Else Lasker-Schüler, Georg Heym, Georg Trakl, Gottfried Benn." In *A Companion to the Literature of German Expressionism*, edited by Neil Donahue. Rochester, N.Y.: Camden House, 2005. Discusses the expressionist poetry of Trakl and several other poets. Other essays in this work discuss German expressionism in general.

Sharp, Francis Michael. *The Poet's Madness: A Reading of Georg Trakl.* Ithaca, N.Y.: Cornell University Press, 1981. Critical interpretation of selected poems by Trakl. Includes the texts of poems in English and German.

Williams, Eric. *The Mirror and the Word: Modernism, Literary Theory, and Georg Trakl.* Lincoln: University of Nebraska Press, 1993. A critical study of Trakl's works that focuses on his contributions to modernism in Austria. Includes bibliographical references and index.

_____, ed. *The Dark Flutes of Fall: Critical Essays on Georg Trakl.* Columbia, S.C.: Camden House, 1991. A collection of essays on the works of Trakl. Includes bibliographical references and index.

Christoph Eykman

TOMAS TRANSTRÖMER

Born: Stockholm, Sweden; April 15, 1931

PRINCIPAL POETRY

17 Dikter, 1954
Hemligheter på vägen, 1958
Den halvfärdiga himlen, 1962
Klanger och spår, 1966
Kvartett, 1967
Mörkerseende, 1970 (*Night Vision*, 1971)
Twenty Poems of Tomas Tranströmer, 1970
Windows and Stones: Selected Poems, 1972 (translated by May Swenson)
Elegy: Some October Notes, 1973
Stigar, 1973 (original poems and translations of Robert Bly's and János Pilinszky's poetry)
Citoyens, 1974
Östersjöar, 1974 (*Baltics*, 1975)
Selected Poetry of Paavo Haavikko and Tomas Tranströmer, 1974
Friends You Drank Some Darkness: Three Swedish Poets, 1975 (with Harry Martinson and Gunnar Ekelöf)
Sanningsbarriären, 1978 (*Truth Barriers: Poems by Tomas Tranströmer*, 1980)
Dikter, 1954-1978, 1979
How the Late Autumn Night Novel Begins, 1980
Det vilda torget, 1983 (*The Wild Marketplace*, 1985)
Collected Poems, 1987 (translated by Robin Fulton)
The Blue House = Det blå huset, 1987
Tomas Tranströmer: Selected Poems, 1954-1986, 1987 (edited by Robert Hass)
Sorgegondolen, 1996 (*Sorrow Gondola*, 1997)
New Collected Poems, 1997 (translated by Fulton)
Samlade dikter, 1954-1996, 2001
The Half-Finished Heaven: The Best Poems of Tomas Tranströmer, 2001 (translated by Bly)
Den stora gåtan, 2004
The Deleted World, 2006 (translated by Robin Robertson)
The Great Enigma: New Collected Poems, 2006 (translated by Fulton)

OTHER LITERARY FORMS

The reputation of Tomas Tranströmer (tron-STRUHM-ur) rests primarily on his poetry. *Minnena, ser mig* (1993; *Memories Look at Me: A Memoir*, in *För levende och döda*, 1989; *For the Living and the Dead: New Poems and a Memoir*, 1995), offers the poet's own insights into his work. In 2001, a volume of correspondence between Tranströmer and Robert Bly was published as *Air Mail: Brev, 1964-1990*.

ACHIEVEMENTS

In part because Tomas Tranströmer is essentially a poet of images—an aspect of poetry that can be conveyed virtually without loss from one language to another—he is the most widely translated contemporary Scandinavian poet, and his work has been highly influential abroad as well as in his native Sweden. He has been honored with the Bellman Prize (1966), the International Poetry Forum's Swedish Award (1971), the Petrarch Prize (1981), and a lifetime subsidy from the Swedish government. In 1982, Tranströmer became a member of the Swedish Bible Commission to work on a translation of the Psalms. In 1983, he received the Bonnier Prize for Poetry; in 1988, the Pilot Prize; in 1990, the Nordic Council Prize as well as the prestigious Neustadt International Prize for Literature, often seen as a precursor to the Nobel Prize; in 1992, the Horst Bienek Prize; and in 1998, the Ján Smrek Prize. In 2007, he was presented with the Lifetime Recognition Award from the Griffin Trust for Excellence in Poetry.

Tomas Tranströmer (Swedish Information Service)

BIOGRAPHY

Tomas Gösta Transtömer was born on April 15, 1931, in Stockholm, Sweden. His grandfather and other, more distant ancestors were ship pilots, and his father was a journalist. When Transtömer was a child, his parents were divorced; from that time onward, he had a very close relationship with his mother, whose death, many years later, affected him greatly. From 1960 to 1965, he served as a psychologist at Roxtuna, a prison for juvenile offenders; in 1967, he moved to Västerås, where, until 1990, he worked with disabled persons. This position allowed him to devote more time to his wife and two daughters, to playing the piano, and especially to writing. In 1990, he suffered a stroke. Though he was silent for several years, he has continued to write and publish and to make occasional public appearances.

In his early sixties, Transtömer published memoirs of his early and adolescent years. In these, one learns of his formative and familial school experiences, his interests in entomology and natural history, the war, the extreme anxiety that pervaded his life for a brief period, and the influence that museums and libraries have exercised on him.

ANALYSIS

Tomas Transtömer's development as a poet has been marked by an extraordinary clarity of purpose. His first slim volume, *17 Dikter* (seventeen poems), acknowledged in Sweden as the debut of a major talent, set the pattern for his career. By publishing a collection comprising a mere seventeen poems, none of which is long, Transtömer made a contract with his readers, a contract that is still binding: He has continued to publish slim volumes in which each poem is invested with all the care and intensity he can bring to it. Few contemporary poets have demonstrated this unassuming but absolute confidence in themselves and in their medium. The sparsity of Transtömer's output might suggest that he is a hermetic poet, a creator of perfect verbal artifacts. Nothing could be further from the truth. For Transtömer, the poem is an instrument of vision and a means of communication:

My poems are meeting-places. Their intent is to make a sudden connection between aspects of reality that conventional languages and outlooks ordinarily keep apart. Large and small details of the landscape meet, divided cultures and people flow together in a work of art, Nature meets Industry etc. What looks at first like a confrontation turns out to be a connection.

Tranströmer's own definition of his aims cannot be bettered. His poems are indeed "meeting-places" for different levels of reality, brought together in the striking images that are the hallmark of his art.

A precise development can be traced through many of Tranströmer's books. His *17 Dikter* consists primarily of brief lyrical pieces that depict local natural manifestations. Multiple and complex images, metaphors, and similes provide a strong poetic center. In his second and third volumes, *Hemligheter på vägen* (secrets on the road) and *Den halvfärdiga himlen* (the half-finished heaven), Tranströmer continues his lyric homage to nature but expands to an international perspective; here, one finds some narrative verse as well as pieces on music, dreams, and other themes. Telegraphic and imagistic, these are simple poems with complex messages. It is in *Klanger och spår* (resonance and tracks) and *Night Vision* that Tranströmer makes such excellent use of his transitional method. These two volumes contain fewer nature poems and concentrate more on personal revelations that presumably function as actual catharses. *Stigar*, which along with his own poems includes Tranströmer's translations of Bly and the Hungarian poet János Pilinszky, is an extension of his earlier concerns, including nature, creativity, and even subtle political themes, while *Baltics*, with its long lines, prosaic quality, and motifs drawn from the poet's family history, is something entirely new. *Truth Barriers* assimilates the lyric, the prose poem, and many of the poet's thematic interests that have remained fairly constant for thirty years—particularly the mystical, quasi-religious respect for truth and the cosmos that has always informed Tranströmer's verse.

In Tranströmer's work, one finds a diversity of interests, forms, and methods. His poetry is often insightful, striking in its richness of image and metaphor, but it can also be plodding, prosaic, and uninteresting. In an age of excruciating prolixity, Tranströmer is distin-guished by the concision of his verse, reminiscent of Salvatore Quasimodo's late lyrics. Only infrequently does this succinct quality result in obscurity, for Tranströmer's verse, though at times oblique, is never deliberately arcane. One of the finest poets of his generation, Tranströmer has continued to grow, his later work confirming the earlier assessments. Bly observes that his "poetry of silence and depths" has influenced many American poets.

A typical poem by Tranströmer is short, lyric, telegraphic, strongly imagistic, and autobiographical; his recurring themes include philosophical problems, music, dreams, awakenings, obstacles, frontiers, and especially nature. However, if his is a poetry informed by nature—by black-backed gulls and ants, forests and mountains, water and storms—the poet transcends his natural imagery in a flight of continual self-discovery. This is where he differs so radically from many of his Scandinavian predecessors: Tranströmer's descriptive imagery is often merely the key through which the speaker achieves understanding of his specific situation. In "Agitated Meditation" (from *17 Dikter*), Tranströmer depicts a storm's effects and a "grey shark's belly," which logically leads to the ocean floor; this is followed by an algae-encrusted crutch, but the poem concludes with metaphysical precision: "He who/ wanders to the sea returns petrified."

"THE OPEN WINDOW"

Tranströmer frequently achieves such shifts in perspective by a method that might be termed "transitionalism." "Det öppna fönstret" ("The Open Window," from *Night Vision*) begins with a matter-of-fact, first-person narrative: "I shaved one morning standing/ by the open window/ on the second story." This mundane, prosaic tone is sustained for several lines; the crucial transition occurs when the narrator's electric razor, which has begun to hum with a "heavier and heavier whirr," suddenly becomes a helicopter on which the narrator is a passenger. "Keep your eyes open!" the pilot shouts to him; "You're seeing this for the last time!" The speaker looks down on the things of the Earth, houses and beetles and all, asking: "The small things I love, what do they amount to?" As he looks, he feels an increasing sense of urgency, and the poem concludes with the manifest need to see everything:

Fly low!
I didn't know which way
to turn my head—
my sight was divided
like a horse's.

"AN ARTIST IN THE NORTH"

This is Tranströmer's favored method: a description of a physical situation metamorphosed into aphoristic reflections on spiritual or psychological states—a method exemplified in one of his finest poems, "En konstnär i norr" ("An Artist in the North," from *Klanger och spår*, translated in *Windows and Stones*). The poem is a monologue spoken by the composer Edvard Grieg while on retreat in a small mountain hut. In the first three stanzas, Grieg recalls his past activities, including his triumphs as a conductor; now his only companions are a piano, the mountains, and a "peculiar light [that] leaks in directly from the trolls." In this setting, Grieg admonishes himself to

> Simplify!
> And hammer blows in the mountain came
> came
> came
> came one spring night into our room
> disguised as heartbeats.

This is Tranströmer at his apex, echoing Grieg's music and concluding enigmatically,

> Battlegrounds within us
> Where we Bones of the Dead
> fight to come alive.

Struggle, influences, the act of composing at the piano—all these are contained in this final onslaught. There can be little doubt that the need to simplify and the internal struggle are equally applicable to the creation of Tranströmer's poetry.

BALTICS

Baltics represents an extreme departure from Tranströmer's usual concise lyric pieces. A lengthy, often prosaic poem in six parts, it deals with the poet, his ancestors, and their Baltic environment. Because Tranströmer has come to value literal truth more than mere literary criteria, he emphasizes actual events, with the result that the poem often sounds like untransformed

historical narrative, complete with names, dates, and other facts. This content may alternate with various manifestations of nature, but regardless of content, *Baltics* is a sparse poem: Ships or wind, forest, and sea are all limned simply, and imagistic language is infrequent. In fact, although these pieces have unequal line lengths, they read, for all practical purposes, like prose poems, and at times they are as constricted as journal entries. What is important is not form, rhythm, or heightened language, but rather what the reader actually learns: Tranströmer's grandfather was a ship's pilot, he kept an almanac, and the ship's engine room had a pungent aroma; there is a font in a Gotland church on which the name of the twelfth century mason Hegwaldr is still inscribed.

When philosophical transitions do occur, as in the third part of *Baltics*, they are extremely esoteric, and it is difficult to connect the physical and the metaphysical realms. Occasionally, however, Tranströmer's true gift shines through, as when he draws a parallel between a jellyfish, which becomes formless when it is taken out of the water, and "an indescribable truth . . . lifted out of silence and formulated to an inert mass. . . ."

SORROW GONDOLA

Tranströmer's later poems are similar to their ancestors: short, sometimes succinct, explorations of an obvious manifestation that leads to an unusual or striking revelation. In *Sorrow Gondola*, "Midvinter" ("Midwinter") is an excellent example of how Tranströmer continues to transform the mundane into something entirely unexpected:

> A blue sheen
> radiates from my clothes.
> Midwinter.
> Jangling tambourines of ice.
> I close my eyes.
> There is a soundless world
> there is a crack
> where dead people
> are smuggled across the border.

This is ambiguously deceptive: The reader does not know if the dead are leaving, which is depressing and malign, or if they are returning (metaphorically, spiritually), which is uplifting and psychologically beneficial. Tranströmer, like Stéphane Mallarmé (as one critic observes), wants to mystify his readers with conundrums. Whereas Mallarmé often remains inexplicable and annoying, however, Tranströmer's ambiguity is, paradoxically, comprehensible and palliating.

In the same volume are a series of *haikudikter* (haiku) in four sections. Many poets have moved away from verbosity toward silence. Succinct, sparse, denuded poetic articulations reflect the minimalist aesthetic that view with the prolixity so typical of twentieth century fiction. Thus, Paul Celan, Robert Creeley, or Bob Arnold prefer to leave the interpretive work to the reader's imagination.

THE GREAT ENIGMA

The Great Enigma represents the first occasion that all of Tranströmer's poetry has been available in English translation. The collection is also the culmination of the labors of Robin Fulton, the Scottish poet who has made translating Tranströmer his work for three decades. To the poet's extensive audience who encounters his work exclusively in English, this edition adds to or replaces *The Half-Finished Heaven*, a generous range of poems from each of the author's collections, translated by his friend and fellow poet, Bly. It also completes another long-held standard, *Tomas Tranströmer: Selected Poems, 1954-1986*, edited by Robert Hass and drawn from the work of a wide number of translators (Bly, May Swenson, Samuel Charters, and Fulton among them).

Although Tranströmer has published slim volumes only periodically, and critics have noted that his production is of consistently high quality, a complete collection had not appeared before *The Great Enigma*. The opportunity to view the poems as a body is valuable, and reading the published work chronologically is an instructive way of charting some of the poet's recurring preoccupations, both thematic and formal, and the few movements away from his characteristic voice and style. One such variation is, perhaps, his growing preference for more compressed forms, which many critics have connected to his stroke in 1990 (though the movement toward the stark, aphoristic, and sometimes elliptical utterance had been building throughout the prior decade).

The new poems contained in *The Great Enigma* can be considered part of this movement. All are brief, and the majority of the selection is a series of haiku sequences; it is easy to view them as an offshoot of the poems written in the 1990's and published in *Sorrow Gondola*. (*Prison*, a collection of nine other haiku, written in 1959 and never before published, has also been included in the collection.) On the whole, the new poems lack the sense of open space and distance frequently seen in Tranströmer's work, both in the images of land and seascapes, and in the metaphysical introspection of the speaker, which so often finds itself at a moment in which the borders of the self are permeable and which may account for Tranströmer's many representations of dreaming, or the diffused sensation of the consciousness when beginning to wake. *The Great Enigma* haiku, however, are still concerned with the estrangement of the familiar, presented through Tranströmer's characteristically vivid images—"all over a whitewashed wall/ the flies crowd and crowd," or "a wind vast and slow/ from the ocean's library."

The final poem in the series, which provides the book with its title, encapsulates the poet's capacity for wonder in both the poem's transformations of perception, and the untouched beauty of the world:

> Birds in human shape.
> The apple trees in blossom.
> The great enigma.

If this poem presents the haiku at its most traditional, with the signifier of season tied to the common image of the blossoming tree, it is also fully characteristic of Tranströmer, as the images quietly depict the human in all its unfamiliar, evocative nature.

OTHER MAJOR WORKS

NONFICTION: *Air Mail: Brev, 1964-1990*, 2001 (with Robert Bly).

TRANSLATION: *Tolkningar*, 1999 (of many poets, including James Wright, Robert Bly, and Sandor Weores).

MISCELLANEOUS: *För levende och döda*, 1989 (*For the Living and the Dead: New Poems and a Memoir*, 1995).

BIBLIOGRAPHY

Adams, Ann-Charlotte Gavel, ed. *Twentieth-Century Swedish Writers After World War II*. Vol. 257 in *Dictionary of Literary Biography*. Detroit: Gale Group, 2002. Contains a brief biography of Tranströmer that also examines his works.

Bankier, Joanna. "Breaking the Spell: Subversion in the Poetry of Tomas Transtömer." *World Literature Today* 64, no. 4 (Autumn, 1990): 591. A discussion of several of Transtömer's poems that describe how socialization imposes a role and turns life into a set of ritualized performances that minimize stylized movement.

Bly, Robert. "Tomas Transtömer and 'The Memory.'" *World Literature Today* 64, no. 4 (Autumn, 1990): 570-573. A useful biocritical overview.

Fulton, Robin. Introduction to *New Collected Poems*, by Tomas Transtömer. Newcastle upon Tyne, England: Bloodaxe Books, 1997. An excellent brief biographical and analytical overview.

Ivask, Ivar. "The Universality of Openness: The Understated Example of Tomas Transtömer." *World Literature Today* 64, no. 4 (Autumn, 1990): 549. A profile of Transtömer and the international recognition he has found through his poetry.

Kaplinski, Jaan. "Presentation to the Jury." *World Literature Today* 64, no. 4 (Autumn, 1990): 552. Kaplinski describes Transtömer as one of the most outstanding poets of the present age and as a fitting recipient of the Neustadt International Prize for Literature. A listing of his works is offered.

Peterson, Katie. "Acts of Mind." Review of *The Great Enigma*. *Boston Review* 32, no. 3 (May/June, 2007): 45-46. A review of *The Great Enigma* that defines Transtömer's characteristic lyric poem as one in which nature provides the subject and the self becomes the object. The review also briefly compares the quality of the recent collections of English translations.

Rossel, Sven H. Review of *Tolkningar*. *World Literature Today* 74, no. 1 (Winter, 2000): 253. Rossel's review includes biographical information on Transtömer's career and work.

Sjoberg, Leif. "The Architecture of a Poetic Victory: Tomas Transtömer's Rise to International Preeminence." *Scandinavian Review* 78, no. 2 (Autumn, 1990): 87. Transtömer has enjoyed sensational publicity and critical acclaim. Reasons for this unusual success are outlined. Two of Transtömer's poems are included.

Soderberg, Lasse. "The Swedishness of Tomas Transtömer." *World Literature Today* 64, no. 4 (Autumn, 1990): 573. The poetry of Transtömer is examined, and ways in which his poetry can be described as being specifically Swedish are discussed.

Robert Hauptman
Updated by Todd Samuelson

TRISTAN TZARA
Sami Rosenstock

Born: Moineşti, Romania; April 4, 1896
Died: Paris, France; December 24, 1963

PRINCIPAL POETRY

La Première Aventure céleste de Monsieur Antipyrine, 1916
Vingt-cinq Poèmes, 1918
Cinéma calendrier du coeur abstrait, 1920
De nos oiseaux, 1923
Indicateur des chemins de coeur, 1928
L'Arbre des voyageurs, 1930
L'Homme approximatif, 1931 (*Approximate Man, and Other Writings*, 1973)
Où boivent les loups, 1932
L'Antitête, 1933
Primele Poème, 1934 (English translation, 1976)
Grains et issues, 1935
La Deuxième Aventure céleste de Monsieur Antipyrine, 1938 (wr. 1917)
Midis gagnés, 1939
Une Route seul soleil, 1944
Entre-temps, 1946
Le Signe de vie, 1946
Terre sur terre, 1946
Morceaux choisis, 1947
Phases, 1949

Sans coup férir, 1949

De mémoire d'homme, 1950

Parler seul, 1950

Le Poids du monde, 1951

La Première main, 1952

La Face intérieure, 1953

À haute flamme, 1955

La Bonne heure, 1955

Miennes, 1955

Le Temps naissant, 1955

Le Fruit permis, 1956 (wr. 1946)

Frère bois, 1957

La Rose et le chien, 1958

De la coupe aux lèvres, 1961

Juste présent, 1961

Selected Poems, 1975

OTHER LITERARY FORMS

Although the largest part of the work of Tristan Tzara (TSAH-rah) consists of a vast body of poetry—filling more than thirty volumes—he did experiment with drama, publishing three plays during his lifetime: *Le Coeur à gaz* (pb. 1946; *The Gas Heart*, 1964), *Mouchoir de nuages* (pb. 1924; *Handkerchief of Clouds*, 1972), and *La Fuite* (pb. 1947; the flight). His important polemical writings appeared in two collections: *Sept Manifestes Dada* (1924; *Seven Dada Manifestos*, 1977) and *Le Surréalisme et l'après-guerre* (1947; Surrealism and the postwar period). Much of Tzara's critical and occasional writing, which is substantial in volume, remains unpublished, including book-length works on François Rabelais and François Villon, while the published portion includes *Lampisteries* (1963; English translation, 1977), *Picasso et la poésie* (1953; Picasso and poetry), *L'Art Océanien* (1951; the art of Oceania), and *L'Égypte face à face* (1954).

ACHIEVEMENTS

Tristan Tzara's importance as a literary figure of international reputation rests primarily on his relationship to the Dada movement. Of all the avant-garde movements that challenged the traditional foundations of artistic value and judgment at the beginning of the present century, Dada was, by consensus, the most radical and disturbing. In retrospect, the Dada aesthetic, which was first formed and expressed in Zurich about 1916, seems to have been a fairly direct response to World War I; the Dadaists themselves suggest as much in many of their works during this period.

The harsh, confrontational nature of Dada is notorious, and Tzara was one of the most provocative of all the Dadaists. In his 1930 essay, "Memoirs of Dadaism," Tzara describes one of his own contributions to the first Dada soiree in Paris, on January 23, 1920, in which he read a newspaper while a bell rang. This attitude of deliberate confrontation with the conventional, rational expectations of the audience—to which the Dadaists juxtaposed their illogical, satirical productions—is defended by Tzara in his most famous polemical work, "Manifeste Dada 1918" ("Dada Manifesto 1918"), in which he asserts the meaninglessness of Dada and its refusal to offer a road to truth.

To escape the machinery of human rationality, the Dadaists substituted a faith in spontaneity, incorporating the incongruous and accidental into their works. Even the name by which the Dadaists called themselves was chosen rather arbitrarily. According to most accounts (although this report is subject to intense difference of opinion among Dadaists), it was Tzara himself who chose the word *dada*, in February of 1916, by opening a French dictionary to a randomly selected entry.

Tzara's achievements are not limited solely to his leadership in the Dada movement. Until recently, Tzara's later work—which is more optimistic in tone and more controlled in technique—has been overshadowed by his more violent and sensational work from the Dada period. It is now becoming apparent to many readers and critics that the Surrealist phase of Tzara's work, the little-known work of his post-Surrealist phase, and his early pre-Dada work in Romanian, are equally important in considering his contribution to modern literature. In the 1970's and 1980's, largely through the work of editors and translators such as Mary Ann Caws, Henrí Behar, and Sasa Panǎ, this work became more readily available.

BIOGRAPHY

Tristan Tzara, whose real name was Sami Rosenstock, was born on April 4, 1896, in Moineşti, a small town in the province of Băcău, in northeastern Romania. His parents were Jewish, his father a prosperous merchant. Tzara first attended school in Moineşti, where Romanian was spoken, but later, when he was sent to Bucharest for his secondary education, he attended schools where instruction was also given in French. In addition to languages, Tzara studied mathematics and music. Following his graduation in 1913, he attended the University of Bucharest for a year, taking courses in mathematics and philosophy.

It was during this adolescent period, between 1911 and 1915, that all Tzara's Romanian poems were written. His first published poems appeared in 1912 in *Simbolul*, a short-lived Symbolist review that he helped to edit. These first four poems were signed with the pseudonym S. Samyro. The subsequent poems in Romanian that Tzara published during this period were often signed simply "Tristan" or "Tzara," and it was not until near the end of this period, in 1915, that the first Romanian poem signed "Tristan Tzara" appeared.

In the fall of 1915, Tzara went to Zurich, in neutral Switzerland, where he became involved with a group of writers and artists—including Hugo Ball, Richard Huelsenbeck, Marcel Janco, and Hans Arp—who were in the process of forming an artistic movement soon to be called Dada. This period, between Tzara's arrival in Zurich in the fall of 1915 and February of 1916, was the germinating period of the Dada movement. The Dadaists' first public announcement of the birth of a new movement in the arts took place at the Cabaret Voltaire on the evening of February 5, 1916—the occasion of the first of many such Dada soirees. These entertainments included presentations such as "simultaneous poems," which confronted the audience with a chaotic barrage of words made incomprehensible by the din; recitations of "pure sound-poems," often made up of African-sounding nonsense syllables and recited by a chorus of masked dancers; satirical plays that accused and insulted the audience; and, always, the ceaseless manifestos promoting the Dada revolt against conformity. Tzara's work during this period was written almost entirely in French, and from this time on he used that language exclusively for his literary productions.

As the activities of the Zurich Dadaists gradually attracted notice in other countries, especially Germany and France, Tzara's own fame as an artist spread to an increasingly larger audience. The spread of Dada's fame from Zurich to other centers of avant-garde activity in Europe was aided by the journal *Dada*, edited by Tzara and featuring many of his most provocative works. Although this journal lasted only through five issues, it did draw the attention of Guillaume Apollinaire in Paris, and through him the devoted admiration of André Breton, who was later to be one of the leaders of the Surrealist movement. At Breton's urging, Tzara left Zurich shortly after the Armistice was declared, arriving in Paris in December of 1919.

For a short period between January of 1920, when the first public Dada performance in Paris was held, and May of 1921, when Breton broke his association with Tzara to assume the leadership of the developing Surrealist movement, Breton and Tzara organized an increasingly outrageous series of activities that frequently resulted in public spectacles. Fol-

Tristan Tzara (©Bettmann/CORBIS)

lowing Breton's break with the Dada group, Tzara continued to stage public performances in Paris for a time, collaborating with those who remained loyal to the Dada revolt. By July of 1923, however, when the performance of his play *The Gas Heart* was disrupted by a Surrealist counter demonstration, even Tzara regretfully admitted that Dada was effectively dead, a victim of its own destructive impulses. Tzara gave up the Dada ideal reluctantly and continued to oppose the Surrealists until 1929, when he joined the Paris Surrealist group, accepting Breton's leadership. Tzara's resumption of activities with Breton's group was also accompanied by an increasing move toward political engagement.

The same year that he joined the Surrealists, Tzara visited the Soviet Union, and the following year, in 1930, the Surrealists indicated their dedication to the Communist International by changing the name of their own journal, *La Révolution surréaliste*, to *Le Surréalisme au service de la révolution*. For Tzara, this political commitment seemed to be a natural outgrowth of his initial revolt, for, as he wrote later in *Le Surréalisme et l'après-guerre*: "Dada was born . . . from the deep feeling that man . . . must affirm his supremacy over notions emptied of all human substance, over dead objects and ill-gotten gains."

In 1935, Tzara broke with the Surrealists to devote himself entirely to the work of the Communist Party, which he officially joined at this time. From 1935 to 1937, he was involved in assisting the Republican forces in the Spanish Civil War, salvaging art treasures and serving on the Committee for the Defense of Culture. This political engagement continued during World War II, with Tzara serving in the French Resistance, all the time continuing to publish his work, despite widespread censorship, under the pseudonym T. Tristan. In 1946 and 1947, he delivered the lectures that make up *Le Surréalisme et l'après-guerre*, in which he made his controversial assessment of Surrealism's failure to influence Europe effectively between the wars. In 1955, Tzara published *À haute flamme* (at full flame), a long poetic reminiscence in which he reviewed the stages of his lifelong revolt and reaffirmed his revolutionary aesthetic. Tzara continued to affirm the authenticity of his position until his death in Paris at the age of sixty-seven, a victim of lung cancer.

ANALYSIS

Whatever else Tristan Tzara was—Dada instigator and polemicist, marginal Surrealist, Communist activist, or Romanian expatriate—his great skill as a poet is abundantly apparent. At his death, Tzara left behind a vast body of poems, extremely diverse in style, content, and tone. Important features of his work are his innovations in poetic technique and his development of a highly unified system of symbolic imagery. The first of these features includes the use of pure sound elements, descriptive ideophones, expressive typography, enjambment that creates complex syntactic ambiguities, and multiple viewpoints resulting in a confusing confluence of speaking voices. The second important feature includes such elements as Tzara's use of recurring verbal motifs and refrains, ironic juxtapositions, and recurring image clusters.

Tzara's earliest period extends from 1911 to 1915 and includes all the poetry he wrote in his native Romanian. Until recently, little attention has been given to Tzara's Romanian poetry. Several Romanian critics have noted the decisive but unacknowledged influence on Tzara of the Romanian poet Urmuz (1883-1923), virtually unknown in the West, who anticipated the strategies of Dada and Surrealism. Much of Tzara's early work, however, is relatively traditional in technique, although it must be remembered that this period represents his poetic apprenticeship and that the poems were written when he was between the ages of fifteen and nineteen. The poetry of this period often displays a curiously ambivalent tone, mixing a detached ironic perspective—which is sometimes gently sarcastic and at other times bitterly resentful—with an uncritically sentimental nostalgia for the past. In some of the poems, one of these two moods dominates, as in Tzara's bitterly ironic treatment of war's destructive effect on the innocence of youth in "The Storm and the Deserter's Song" and "Song of War," or the romantic lyricism of such highly sentimental idylls on nature as "Elegy for the Coming of Winter" and "Evening Comes."

PRIMELE POÈME

The most successful poems of this period—later collected as *Primele Poème*—are those which mix nostalgia with irony, encompassing both attitudes within a single poem. The best example of this type of poem is

"Sunday," whose conventional images of leisurely activities that occupy the inhabitants of a town on the Sabbath are contrasted with the bitter reflections of the alienated poet-speaker who observes the scene. The scene seems idyllic enough at first, presenting images of domestic tranquillity. Then the reflecting consciousness of the alienated speaker intrudes, introducing images that contrast darkly with and shatter the apparently false impression he himself has just created. Into the scene of comfortable regularity, three new and disturbing elements appear: the inescapable presence of death in wartime, the helplessness of parents to protect their children from danger, and the futility of art stagnated by Decadence.

VINGT-CINQ POÈMES

This successful mixture of sentimental lyricism with ironic detachment is developed to an even greater degree in Tzara's first collection of poems in French, *Vingt-cinq Poèmes* (twenty-five poems), a collection that, although published after he had already arrived in Zurich, still resembles in technique and content the early Romanian poems. In "Petite Ville en Sibérie" ("Little Town in Siberia"), there are a number of new elements, the most important of which are Tzara's use of typography for expressive purposes, the complex syntactic ambiguity created by enjambment, the rich confluence of narrative voices, and the appearance of images employing illogical juxtapositions of objects and qualities:

a blue light which flattens us together on the ceiling
it's as always comrade
like a label of infernal doors pasted on a medicine bottle
it's the calm house tremble my friend

This disorienting confluence of voices is deliberate, and it evokes in the reader a futile desire to resolve the collage (based on the random conjunction of several separate discourses) into a meaningful and purposeful poetic statement.

DE NOS OISEAUX

In Tzara's second period—extending from 1916 until 1924—he produced the Dadaist works which brought him international fame. To the collage technique developed in *Vingt-cinq Poèmes*, the poems that make up *De nos oiseaux* (of our birds)—the major

collection from this period—introduce several innovations, including pure sound elements such as African-sounding nonsense words, repeated phrases, descriptive ideophones, use of multiple typefaces, and catalogs of discrete, separable images piled one upon the other. Tzara's collage technique has become more radical in these poems, for instead of simply using the juxtaposition of speaking voices for creating ironic detachment, in the Dada poems the narrative itself breaks down entirely into a chaotic barrage of discontinuous fragments that often seem to lack any discursive sense. These features are readily apparent in "La Mort de Guillaume Apollinaire" ("The Death of Guillaume Apollinaire") and "Les Saltimbanques" ("The Circus Performers"), two of the best poems from *De nos oiseaux*.

"THE DEATH OF GUILLAUME APOLLINAIRE"

In his Dadaist elegy for Apollinaire, Tzara begins with a series of propositions that not only establish the resigned mood of the speaker but also express the feeling of disorder created in the reader by the poem itself. A simple admission of man's inability to comprehend his situation in the world is followed by a series of images that seem designed to convey the disparity the speaker senses between a world which is unresponsive to human needs (the unfortunate death of Apollinaire at such an early age is no doubt one aspect of this) and a world in which he could feel comfortable (and presumably learn to accept the death of his beloved friend):

if snow fell upward
if the sun rose in our houses in the middle of the night
just to keep us warm
and the trees hung upsidedown with their crowns . . .
if birds came down to us to find reflections of
    themselves
in those peaceful lakes lying just above our heads
THEN WE MIGHT UNDERSTAND
that death could be a beautiful long voyage
and a permanent vacation from flesh from structures
    systems and skeletons

The images of this poem constitute a particularly good illustration of Tzara's developing symbolic system. Although the images of snow falling upward, the sun rising at night, trees hanging upside down, and birds coming to earth at first appear unrelated to one another, they are actually related in two ways. First, Tzara is describing processes within the totality of nature which give evidence that "nature is organized in its totality." Humanity's sorrow over the inescapable cycles of life and death, of joy and suffering, is caused by a failure to understand that humans, too, are a part of this totality. Second, Tzara's images suggest that if one's perspective could only be reversed, one would see the reality of things properly. This method of presenting arguments in nondiscursive, imagistic terms was one of Tzara's primary poetic accomplishments, and the uses to which he put it in this elegy for Apollinaire were later expanded and developed in the epic scope of his masterpiece, *Approximate Man, and Other Writings*.

"THE CIRCUS PERFORMERS"

"The Circus Performers" illustrates Tzara's increasing use of pure sound elements in his work. The images of this poem attempt to capture the exciting rhythms of the circus performance that Tzara is describing. In the opening vignette of the poem, in what seems at first an illogical sequence of statements, Tzara merges the expanding and contracting rhythm of the verses with his characteristic use of imagery to convey thought in analogical, nondiscursive terms. Describing a ventriloquist's act, Tzara uses an image that links "brains," "balloons," and "words." In this image, "brains" seems to be a metonymic substitution for ideas or thoughts—that which is expressed by "words." Here the brains themselves are inflating and deflating, as are the balloons. What is the unstated analogical relation between the two? These words are treated like the words and thoughts of comic-strip characters—where words are enclosed in the "balloons" that represent mental space in newspaper cartoons. To help the reader more easily identify the analogy, Tzara has included an explanatory aside, enclosed in parentheses. A second example of Tzara's use of sound in this poem is the presence of "ideophones"—words that imitate the sounds of the actions they describe. Pure sound images devoid of abstract meaning are scattered throughout the poem.

APPROXIMATE MAN, AND OTHER WRITINGS

By all standards of judgment, *Approximate Man, and Other Writings*, a long epic in nineteen sections, is Tzara's greatest poem. It was Tzara's most sustained effort, its composition and extensive revisions occupying the poet between 1925 and 1931, the year that the final version appeared. Another important characteristic of the work is its epic scope, for *Approximate Man, and Other Writings* was Tzara's attempt to discover the causes of modern humanity's spiritual malaise, drawing on all the technical resources he had developed up to the time of its composition. The most important feature of the poem, however, is its systematic presentation of Tzara's revolutionary ideology, which had begun to reflect, in a guarded form, the utopian vision of Surrealism.

Approximate Man, and Other Writings is about the intrusion of disorder into modern life, and it focuses on the effects of this disorder on the individual. Throughout the poem, Tzara makes it clear that what he is describing is a general disorder or sickness, not a personal crisis. This is one of the key ideas that is constantly repeated in the form of a refrain: "approximate man like me like you reader and like the others/ heap of noisy flesh and echoes of conscience/ complete in the only element of choice your name." The most important aspect of the poem's theme is Tzara's diagnosis of the causes of this debilitating universal sickness, since this indicates in a striking way his newly found attitude of commitment.

The first cause of humanity's sickness is the very condition of being "approximate." Uncertain, changeable, or lacking commitment to any cause that might improve the world in which he lives, Approximate Man wanders aimlessly. For Tzara, the lost key for curing the sickness is commitment, as Tzara himself declared his commitment to the work of the Communist Party in 1935, shortly after the completion of this poem.

Humanity's sickness arises not only from inauthentic relationships with others but also from an exploitative attitude toward nature—an attitude encouraged by the development of modern technology. In Tzara's view, this modern belief in humanity's preeminent importance in the universe is a mistaken one, as is evident in "The Death of Guillaume Apollinaire," and such vanity contributes to the spiritual sickness of humankind.

Tzara finds a third cause of humanity's spiritual sickness in humans' increasing reliance on the products of their own alienated consciousness, especially reason and language. In *Approximate Man, and Other Writings*, Tzara's efforts to describe this solipsistic entrapment of humans by their own systems gives rise to many striking images, as in the following passages: "vapor on the cold glass you block your own image from your/ sight/ tall and insignificant among the glazed frost jewels/ of the landscape" and "I think of the warmth spun by the word/ around its center the dream called ourselves." These images argue that human reason is like a mirror in which the reflection is clouded by the observer's physical presence, and that human language is like a silken cocoon that insulates people from the external world of reality. Both reason and language, originally created to assist humans, have become debased, and to attain a more accurate picture of the world, humans must learn to rely on instinct and imagination. These three ideas, which find their fullest expression in *Approximate Man, and Other Writings*, form the basis of Tzara's mature poetic vision and constitute the most sustained expression of his critique of the modern sensibility.

Other major works

PLAYS: *Mouchoir de nuages*, pb. 1924 (*Handkerchief of Clouds*, 1972); *Le Coeur à gaz*, pb. 1946 (wr. 1921; *The Gas Heart*, 1964); *La Fuite*, pb. 1947.

NONFICTION: *Sept Manifestes Dada*, 1924 (wr. 1917-1918; *Seven Dada Manifestos*, 1977); *Le Surréalisme et l'après-guerre*, 1947; *L'Art Océanien*, 1951; *Picasso et la poésie*, 1953; *L'Égypte face à face*, 1954; *Lampisteries*, 1963 (English translation, 1977).

MISCELLANEOUS: *Œuvres complètes*, 1975-1991 (6 volumes).

Bibliography

Browning, Gordon Frederick. *Tristan Tzara: The Genesis of the Dada Poem: Or, From Dada to Aa*. Stuttgart, Germany: Akademischer Verlag Heinz, 1979. A critical study of Tzara's Dada poems. Includes bibliographical references.

Caws, Mary Ann. Introduction to *Approximate Man, and Other Writings*, by Tristan Tzara. Translated by Mary Ann Caws. Detroit: Wayne State University Press, 1973. This book is an excellent selection of English translations of Tzara's poetry, and the introduction provides a helpful guide to each phase of his work.

_____, ed. *Surrealist Painters and Poets: An Anthology*. Cambridge, Mass.: MIT Press, 2001. Contains translations of several prose pieces by Tzara as well as works by many of his contemporaries, providing an overview of the context in which he operated. Includes many illustrations.

Forcer, Stephen. *Modernist Song: The Poetry of Tristan Tzara*. Leeds, England: Legenda, 2006. Traces Tzara's development and changing poetry from his early works to publications in the 1950's.

Marcus, Greil. *Lipstick Traces: A Secret History of the Twentieth Century*. 1989. 20th anniversary ed. Cambridge, Mass.: Belknap Press, 2009. A highly original and accessible study of nihilistic movements in art, music, and literature, from Dada to punk rock. Tzara is only one of many figures discussed here, but this book deserves mention because of its broad historical scope and excellent analysis of the relationship between popular culture and the avant-garde.

Motherwell, Robert, and Jack D. Flam, eds. *The Dada Painters and Poets: An Anthology*. 2d ed. Cambridge, Mass.: Harvard University Press, 1989. A collection of Dada documents including journals, reviews, and manifestos that hold valuable biographical and historical details of the life and work of Tzara.

Peterson, Elmer. *Tristan Tzara: Dada and Surrational Theorist*. New Brunswick, N.J.: Rutgers University Press, 1971. A study of Tzara's aesthetics. Includes bibliographical references.

Richter, Hans. *Dada: Art and Anti-Art*. New York: Thames & Hudson, 1997. Through selections from key manifestos and other documents of the time, Richter records Dada's history, from its beginnings in wartime Zurich to its collapse in the Paris of the 1920's.

Sandqvist, Tom. *Dada East: The Romanians of Cabaret Voltaire*. Cambridge, Mass.: MIT Press, 2006. Looks at Dadaism in Romania, where Tzara was born.

Steven E. Colburn

U

MIGUEL DE UNAMUNO Y JUGO

Born: Bilbao, Spain; September 29, 1864
Died: Salamanca, Spain; December 31, 1936

PRINCIPAL POETRY

Poesías, 1907
Rosario de sonetos líricos, 1911
El Cristo de Velázquez, 1920 (*The Christ of Velázquez*, 1951)
Rimas de dentro, 1923
Teresa, 1924
Romancero del destierro, 1928
Poems, 1952
Cancionero: Diario poético, 1953 (partial translation as *The Last Poems of Miguel de Unamuno*, 1974)

OTHER LITERARY FORMS

Miguel de Unamuno y Jugo (ew-nah-MEW-noh ee HEW-goh) wrote prolifically throughout his life and produced numerous novels, short stories, dramas, and essays, as well as volumes of poetry. A mediocre dramatist who, under the influence of Henrik Ibsen, created talky stage works with uninspired characters, Unamuno achieved his greatest success with fiction, poetry, and the essay. His outstanding works of fiction include *Niebla* (1914; *Mist: A Tragicomic Novel*, 1928); *Abel Sánchez: Una historia de pasión* (1917; *Abel Sánchez*, 1947); and *San Manuel Bueno, mártir* (1931; *Saint Manuel Bueno, Martyr*, 1954). A philosophical author, Unamuno explored rich and complex ideas in all his works, regardless of genre. Particularly noteworthy are two long collections of essays, *Del sentimiento trágico de la vida en los hombres y en los pueblos* (1913; *The Tragic Sense of Life in Men and in Peoples*, 1921) and *La agonía del Cristianismo*, 1925 (in French as *L'Agonie du Christianisme*; in Spanish 1931; *The Agony of Christianity*, 1928, 1960), regarded by many critics as his central works.

ACHIEVEMENTS

Miguel de Unamuno y Jugo embodied the Spanish spirit and temperament in profound ways not seen in any Spanish writer since the Golden Age of Miguel de Cervantes, Lope de Vega Carpio, and Pedro Calderón de la Barca. In an oddly ironic twist, Unamuno began his career by attempting to "Europeanize" what he believed to be a backward Spain. Believing—as did many young Spanish artists—that Spain had lagged far behind the other European countries in its literature, art, music, and philosophy, Unamuno hoped to be able to take what was best in recent European advances and, by planting those seeds, allow new cultural life to grow in Spain. However, by the end of his prolific and distinguished career, Unamuno had not opened the windows of Spain so that new European light might shine on his land; instead, through his writing, he had given his country its own unique literary character. As artist and philosopher, Unamuno was a distinctly Spanish figure—a figure whose works the rest of Europe was forced to contemplate, explore, and assimilate. Throughout his career, Unamuno thrust Spain and the Spanish character at the rest of Europe, from his glorification of the Spanish landscape in such great poems as "Salamanca" and "On Gredos" to his assertion of the Spanish temper and the Spanish soul as it was mirrored in his own poetry and personality.

Unamuno was passionate in his convictions and claimed to understand philosophy only as poetry and poetry only as philosophy. In seeking to blur the distinction between poetry and philosophy, he was deliberately attempting to change the nature of poetry in his time. He had no interest in the elegance, decorum, and refinement of the poetry of his day. Poetry was held captive, in Unamuno's vision, by a precious "literatism," and he sought to free it from its literary bonds by proclaiming poetry the proper sphere of philosophy. Poetry could once again become a field of turbulent emotions and passionate thought if its smooth sheen of polished craft and beautiful art were fired by suffering, fear, doubt, and death. Even his seemingly most traditional poetic work, *Teresa*, a collection of love poems by a supposedly "unknown poet" to his beloved in the manner of Dante, Petrarch, or Torquato Tasso, is given a typical and characteristic twist by Unamuno. The po-

Miguel de Unamuno y Jugo (Library of Congress)

ems are written to the beloved after her death. The whole series is not an ordinary cycle of love poems, but rather a study of the "metaphysics of love" and the spiritual link between love and death.

Unamuno believed that the basis for all art must be religious, and he believed that much of the art of his time had become the mere eruption of petty egos. He had little regard for Charles Baudelaire, Paul Verlaine, or Stéphane Mallarmé, preferring the more ambitious, if less refined, work of Algernon Charles Swinburne, Robert Browning, and Walt Whitman. In creating poetry more concerned with substance than with form and in forcing large philosophical ideas back into the closed and refined poetry of his day, Unamuno not only made his poetry the living testament of a struggling soul, but also brought Spanish poetry into the forefront of the play of ideas in Europe.

BIOGRAPHY

Miguel de Unamuno y Jugo was born in Bilbao, Spain, an industrial center of the Basque province, on September 29, 1864. He remained in Bilbao until he

was sixteen and then attended the University of Madrid, where he received a doctorate in 1884. Returning then to the Basque region of northern Spain, he began to work as a tutor and to write articles for the local newspapers, all the while preparing himself for a teaching career. During this time, he also began work on his first novel, *Paz en la guerra* (1897; *Peace in War*, 1983) and devoted himself to the study of foreign languages. In 1891, he was appointed to the chair of Greek at the University of Salamanca. In that same year, he married Concepción Lizárraga (Concha), a woman who remained in the background when her husband became a public figure, but who gave him a refuge from the limelight, a happy home, and nine children. His devotion to her was absolute throughout his life.

In 1897, one of Unamuno's sons contracted meningitis, resulting in terminal hydrocephalus. As a result, Unamuno suffered a grave religious crisis and, after years of Roman Catholic upbringing and devoted observance of the faith, lost his trust in Catholicism. His spiritual struggle lasted for the rest of his life and came to be the major subject of many of his works—the torment of a soul that feels itself a Christian and yet is besieged by doubt.

Named rector of the University of Salamanca in 1900, Unamuno wrote extensively during the next fourteen years in many different forms—producing fiction, poetry, essays, and travel books—and completed his seminal philosophical work, *The Tragic Sense of Life in Men and in Peoples*. Dismissed from the rectorship in 1914, he continued to teach, to write prolifically, and to be an outspoken public figure. His forthright criticism of the dictatorship of Miguel Primo de Rivera resulted in the loss of his position at the university and his exile to Fuerteventura in the Canary Islands in 1924. Although he escaped to Paris, he was unhappy and longed to return to his native land. He moved to Hendaye, a border town that offered him a view of the Basque mountains and thus some contact with his land, his home, and his family.

Unamuno's exile came to an end in 1930 when Primo de Rivera was overthrown. Unamuno returned to Spain in triumph, and, after the establishment of the republic in 1931, the University of Salamanca reappointed him as rector; he was also elected deputy for the city of Salamanca to the Constituent Assembly. The same year his second great philosophical work, *The Agony of Christianity*, was published. Within two months in the spring and summer of 1934, Unamuno lost his wife and a daughter, Salomé, and that fall he retired as a professor and was named lifetime rector of the university. At the outbreak of the Civil War in July, 1936, Unamuno lent his support to General Francisco Franco but soon became disillusioned with the intolerance of the military leaders and openly denounced them in a speech delivered at the University of Salamanca on October 12, 1936. He was promptly dismissed from his post and was confined to his home, where he died of a heart attack on December 31, 1936.

ANALYSIS

In an essay titled "Mi religión" ("My Religion"), Miguel de Unamuno y Jugo states that he has expressed his religion in his "song," in the poetry to which he devoted so much of his literary career. His poems do not offer logical explanations or reasoned analyses of his faith; rather, they are the cries of his soul. Unamuno's poetry represents a great accomplishment in the field of religious verse, but perhaps more important, it records the spiritual journey of a tormented soul through all the avenues of hellish doubt and divine exultation, a brutally honest record of a human soul through all the vicissitudes of faith, doubt, love, despair, and hope. Only a handful of modern writers—among them August Strindberg, Fyodor Dostoevski, and John Berryman—have confronted religious questions and their effects on heart and mind with such honesty, energy, and passion.

Poetry became the natural place for Unamuno to set down his philosophical ideas. After his spiritual crisis of 1897, he broke with the faith of his childhood because he could no longer tolerate the certainties of a dogmatic faith, the notion that the existence of God and the principal mysteries of the Christian religion could be proven through human reason and then codified by a worldly institution. For Unamuno, doubt was the fuel of faith. He became the enemy of rational attempts to systematize religious faith and championed the antirational believer, one who strives toward knowledge and ultimately faith, but does so through the pain of doubt, suffering, and despair.

MEDIUM FOR PHILOSOPHY

In Unamuno's view, humans are defined by their yearning for immortality, but each person in his or her lifetime seeks that immortality and hence finds faith by a unique path. Poetry, Unamuno believed, could offer a place for the individual voice to express its unique pain, its unique insights. In poetry, the sacred flame that had been extinguished by dogma could be rekindled. That process could only begin, however, through suffering. In Unamuno's philosophical work, *The Agony of Christianity*, "agony" is used in the Greek sense of *agon* or struggle, not in the narrower modern sense of the product of pain. The struggle of each questioning soul is unique, and can only be expressed in a form such as poetry or fiction, which makes no pretensions to scientific objectivity.

As these emphases suggest, Unamuno was an important figure in the development of existentialism, standing between Søren Kierkegaard, a writer he admired deeply, and later thinkers such as Martin Heidegger, Jean-Paul Sartre, and Albert Camus. William Barrett observes that Unamuno's vision helped bring questions of life and death back into the philosophical arena and thus spurred the development of modern existential thought.

Indeed, poetry offered Unamuno an ideal medium for his philosophy. Fiction and drama required the transformation of his voice into other voices, the transformation of his life into other lives. In poetry, his voice could speak directly of its suffering, its pain, its ecstasy. Poetry opened itself to the display of pure emotion and could be a vehicle of antirationalism. In Unamuno's verse, structure and form are often deliberately subordinated to idea and content; the criticism—that his poetry lacked discipline—he wore as a badge of honor.

If he often neglected structure, however, Unamuno was obsessed with the precision and the perfection of the word. Poetry and the poet, in depending on the importance of the word, in caring for the precise truth of the word and in creating new life and new thoughts through the word, might reach toward the ultimate Word, the Word that was made flesh. Unamuno constantly asserts the parallel between the word in poetry and the Divine Word, even in his earliest poems, published in 1907. For example, in "¡Id con Dios!" ("Farewell, Go with God!"), he speaks directly to his own verse:

> Go with God, since with Him you came to take
> in me the form of words: like living flesh.

The role of the poet becomes the role of the priest, the function of art a sacred function, for in the creation of poetry the poet makes the Word flesh.

THE CHRIST OF VELÁZQUEZ

Unamuno's greatest poetic achievement, *The Christ of Velázquez*, is a long sequence of poems that meditate on Diego Velázquez's famous painting of the figure of Christ on the Cross. The poet never moves his eyes from the vision of the Savior; instead, he explores each element of the painting, each detail of the crucified body and each response of his own mind and heart. The canvas unveils to Unamuno the pain, the mystery, and the hope of all Christian thought, and he creates songs of complex beauty that explore his own love and fear, despair and hope. The titles of the individual poems in this "liturgical epic"—"Luna" ("Moon"), "Ecce Homo," "Dios-obscuridad" ("God-Darkness"), "Sangre" ("Blood"), "La vida es sueño" ("Life Is a Dream"), "Paz en la guerra" ("Peace in War"), "Alba" ("Dawn"), "Rosa" ("Rose"), and so on—offer hints as to the individual sparks of inspiration for each poem.

At first, all thought and the universe itself are embodied in the figure of the crucified man-God, as in the poem "Moon," where the whiteness of Christ's body against the enveloping darkness of the background offers the poet assurance of God's presence and light, just as the moon in the black night radiates the light of the invisible sun. As the poems proceed, however, Unamuno comes to focus solely on the body of Christ itself, examining each detail of his human form in poems titled, "Corona" ("Crown"), "Cabeza" ("Head"), "Pelo" ("Hair"), "Frente" ("Forehead"), "Ojos" ("Eyes"), "Orejas" ("Ears"), and so on. The body becomes the poems. Throughout all the poems, images hurtle wildly by, for the suffering figure contains the whole universe and becomes the link for wide-ranging thoughts.

Unamuno's ideas are presented antirationally and nonlogically, for thought resides in his response to Christ's Passion and all it suggests of life and death, humans and God, time and eternity, and not in reason

or analysis. The poems are sprinkled with references to and paraphrases from both Old and New Testaments, the sources of the quotations being duly noted in the margin. The sacred texts become natural elements of the individual poems as the poet deliberately blends his own voice with the Divine Word of the Almighty. Above all, Unamuno reproduces for the reader the promise of freedom from time and death that he feels as he views Velázquez's painting. The painter's art is re-created for the reader: Art becomes a source of hope.

CANCIONERO

Unamuno's last major work of verse, his *Cancionero* (book of songs), consists of more than fifteen hundred brief meditations and hymns. Published in 1953, many years after Unamuno's death, these compositions record the poet's thoughts from 1928 to 1936, constituting a kind of spiritual diary. Each of the poems was composed by Unamuno in the morning after he had read a chapter of the Bible. These meditations on biblical passages provided a measure of his spiritual state as he began to "resume . . . strife" for another day.

The poems of *Cancionero* reach the ideal form that Unamuno had long been seeking for his poetry; they do not pretend to be anything other than direct meditations and do not need any other subject than the Word of God and the mind and heart of the poet himself. They possess an intimacy and immediacy that go to the heart of Unamuno's philosophy. Moment by moment, the soul searches for the sacred, recording its quest with precision and reverence.

This immersion in and love for the details of life's reality follows from Unamuno's Christian beliefs. When God became man and descended to assume flesh, he invested earthly life with eternal importance. Thus, there is nothing odd in Unamuno's addressing poems to a dead dog, a wild reed, or the "Forefinger of the Right Hand" of the crucified Christ. All life, all matter provokes meditation. For Unamuno, poetry is meditation, a means to stretch the soul: "the deeper into yourself you go,/ the larger your boundaries, my soul."

LEGACY

Unamuno once wrote of Blaise Pascal that his *Pensées* (1670; *Monsieur Pascal's Thoughts, Meditations, and Prayers*, 1688; best known as *Pensées*) do not invite the reader to study a philosophy, but rather to become acquainted with a man, to penetrate the sanctuary of a soul bared to the quick. Unamuno's poetry makes the same invitation, for though it is philosophical poetry, the soul of the poet in all his complexity animates the poems. A poetry of philosophy, contemplation, meditation, religious hope, and the agony of doubt, Unamuno's verse is most memorable for the unique, unswervingly honest voice of the poet himself. Indeed, Unamuno's poetry is more dramatic than his dramas, for in his poetry, he brings his own character to startling life. Unamuno's intensity of personal vision combines with the ambition and universality of his themes and the precise energy of his language to create a poetry of richness, range, and lasting importance.

OTHER MAJOR WORKS

LONG FICTION: *Paz en la guerra*, 1897 (*Peace in War*, 1983); *Amor y pedagogía*, 1902; *Niebla*, 1914 (*Mist: A Tragicomic Novel*, 1928); *Abel Sánchez: Una historia de pasión*, 1917 (*Abel Sánchez*, 1947); *Tres novelas ejemplares y un prólogo*, 1920 (*Three Exemplary Novels and a Prologue*, 1930); *La tía Tula*, 1921 (*Tía Tula*, 1976); *San Manuel Bueno, mártir*, 1931 (*Saint Manuel Bueno, Martyr*, 1954); *Dos novelas cortas*, 1961 (James Russell Stamm and Herbert Eugene Isar, editors).

SHORT FICTION: *El espejo de la muerte*, 1913; *Soledad y otros cuentos*, 1937; *Abel Sánchez, and Other Stories*, 1956.

PLAYS: *La esfinge*, pr. 1909 (wr. 1898); *La difunta*, pr. 1910; *La princesa doña Lambra*, pb. 1913; *La venda*, pb. 1913 (wr. 1899); *Fedra*, pr. 1918 (wr. 1910; *Phaedra*, 1959); *El pasado que vuelve*, pr. 1923 (wr. 1910); *Raquel encadenada*, pr. 1926 (wr. 1921); *Sombras de sueño*, pr., pb. 1930; *El otro*, pr., pb. 1932 (wr. 1926; *The Other*, 1947); *El hermano Juan: O, El mundo es teatro*, pb. 1934 (wr. 1927); *Soledad*, pr. 1953 (wr. 1921); *Teatro completo*, 1959.

NONFICTION: *De la enseñanza superior en España*, 1899; *Nicodemo el fariseo*, 1899; *Tres ensayos*, 1900; *En torno al casticismo*, 1902; *De mi país*, 1903; *Vida de Don Quijote y Sancho según Miguel de Cervantes Saavedra, explicada y comentada por Miguel de Unamuno*, 1905 (*The Life of Don Quixote and Sancho*

According to Miguel de Cervantes Saavedra Expounded with Comment by Miguel de Unamuno, 1927); *Recuerdos de niñez y de mocedad*, 1908; *Mi religión, y otros ensayos breves*, 1910; *Soliloquios y conversaciones*, 1911 (*Essays and Soliloquies*, 1925); *Contra esto y aquello*, 1912; *Del sentimiento trágico de la vida en los hombres y en los pueblos*, 1913 (*The Tragic Sense of Life in Men and in Peoples*, 1921); *La agonía del Cristianismo*, 1925 (in French as *L'Agonie du Christianisme*; in Spanish 1931; *The Agony of Christianity*, 1928, 1960); *Cómo se hace una novela*, 1927 (*How to Make a Novel*, 1976); *La ciudad de Henoc*, 1941; *Cuenca ibérica*, 1943; *Paisajes del alma*, 1944; *La enormidad de España*, 1945; *Visiones y commentarios*, 1949; *Tratado del amor de Dios*, 2005 (wr. 1905-1908; *Treatise on Love of God*, 2007).

MISCELLANEOUS: *De Fuerteventura a París*, 1925; *Obras completas*, 1959-1964 (16 volumes).

BIBLIOGRAPHY

Ch'oe, Chae-Sok. *Greene and Unamuno: Two Pilgrims to La Mancha*. New York: Peter Lang, 1990. This comparison of the Christian fiction of Unamuno and Graham Greene sheds light on the religious themes employed by Unamuno in his dramatic works. Includes bibliography and index.

Ellis, Robert Richmond. *The Tragic Pursuit of Being: Unamuno and Sartre*. Tuscaloosa: University of Alabama Press, 1988. This work compares and contrasts the existentialism revealed in the works of Unamuno and Jean-Paul Sartre. Includes bibliography and index.

Gonzalez, Pedro Blas. *Unamuno: A Lyrical Essay*. Mountain View, Calif.: Floricanto Press, 2007. Provides literary criticism of his poetry as well as of two novels.

Hansen, Keith W. *Tragic Lucidity: Discourse of Recuperation in Unamuno and Camus*. New York: Peter Lang, 1993. A comparison of the political and social views of Unamuno and Albert Camus, as evidenced in their literary works. Includes bibliography.

Little, William Thomas. Introduction to *The Velázquez Christ*, by Miguel de Unamuno y Jugo. Translated by William Thomas Little. Lanham, Md.: University Press of America, 2002. Little provides a scholarly introduction and commentary on each of the poems in his translation of Unamuno's poem sequence.

Luby, Barry. *The Uncertainties in Twentieth- and Twenty-first Century Analytic Thought: Miguel de Unamuno the Precursor.* Newark, Del.: Juan de la Cuesta, 2008. Examines the philosophy of Unamuno as revealed in his writing, looking at truth, reality, religion, and language.

Nozick, Martin. *Miguel de Unamuno.* New York: Twayne, 1971. A basic biography of Unamuno that covers his life and works. Includes a bibliography.

Round, Nicholas G., ed. *Re-reading Unamuno.* Glasgow: Department of Hispanic Studies, University of Glasgow, 1989. This collection of papers from a conference on Unamuno provides literary criticism of his works. Includes bibliographies.

Sinclair, Alison. *Uncovering the Mind: Unamuno, the Unknown, and the Vicissitudes of Self.* New York: Manchester University Press, 2002. An examination of the fictional works of Unamuno in respect to his portrayal of the self. Includes bibliography and index.

David Allen White

GIUSEPPE UNGARETTI

Born: Alexandria, Egypt; February 8, 1888
Died: Milan, Italy; June 1, 1970

PRINCIPAL POETRY

Il porto sepolto, 1916
Allegria di naufragi, 1919
La Guerre, 1919
L'allegria, 1931, 1942 (includes revisions of *Il porto sepolto* and *Allegria di naufragi*)
Sentimento del tempo, 1933
Il dolore, 1947
La terra promessa, 1950
Gridasti, soffoco . . . , 1951
Un grido e paesaggi, 1952
Life of a Man, 1958
Il taccuino del vecchio, 1960
Morte delle stagioni, 1967
Dialogo, 1968
Giuseppe Ungaretti: Selected Poems, 1969
Vita d'un uomo: Tutte le poesie, 1969
Selected Poems of Giuseppe Ungaretti, 1975
The Buried Harbour: Selected Poems of Giuseppe Ungaretti, 1990 (Kevin Hart, translator and editor)
A Major Selection of the Poetry of Giuseppe Ungaretti, 1997

OTHER LITERARY FORMS

Giuseppe Ungaretti (ewng-gah-REHT-tee) published literary and critical essays as well as poetry. Perhaps as a consequence of the negative criticism his work drew at first, Ungaretti was concerned to show his connection with the greatest voices of the Italian literary tradition. In discussing the importance of Giacomo Leopardi, Petrarch, or the poets of the Baroque period, Ungaretti provided a framework that assists in the interpretation of his own work. These essays also contain autobiographical information and descriptions of travel and foreign places.

Ungaretti translated poetry by such diverse figures as William Shakespeare, William Blake, Luis de Góngora y Argote, Sergei Esenin, Jean Paulhan, Saint-John Perse, and Jean Racine. Notable for the English reader is Ungaretti's essay on Shakespeare's sonnets, "Significato dei sonetti di Shakespeare," in *Vita d'un uomo: Saggi e interventi* (1974; life of a man: essays and interventions), and an essay accompanying his translations of Blake.

ACHIEVEMENTS

With Eugenio Montale and Salvatore Quasimodo, Giuseppe Ungaretti stands as a leader of contemporary Italian poetry. His is the first modern poetic idiom in Italian. He renewed interest in, and criticism of, the tradition of Italian poetry and is considered the founder of the dominant school of poetry in Italy in the twentieth century, the Hermetic school. Though he never won the Nobel Prize in Literature, he had a significant international reputation and influence. He won the most prestigious prizes in Italy; the earliest was the Gonfaloniere

Prize in Venice in 1932, followed by the Premio Roma in 1949, the Premio Montefeltro from Urbino in 1960, and the Etna-Taormina International Poetry Prize in 1966. Outside Italy, his poetry was honored in 1956 when he shared the Knokke-le-Zoute Poetry Prize with Juan Ramón Jiménez and W. H. Auden; in 1970, he received the Books Abroad Award (now the Neustadt International Prize for Literature) at the University of Oklahoma.

Ungaretti was perhaps the major voice in establishing Leopardi as the most important traditional influence on Italian poetry of the first half of the twentieth century, for he found in Leopardi a bridge between his own poetics and the long Italian tradition that had begun with Petrarch. He also wrote significantly of Baroque poetry, of Shakespeare and Blake, and of several poets of the French tradition.

Difficult in its austere, understated beginnings, Ungaretti's poetry grew deeper and yet more complex as he became responsive to traditional metrics; indeed, he was often accused of purposeful obscurity. There was no doubt, however, that Ungaretti spoke to other poets, for when Francesco Flora called his poetry Hermetic because of its subjective content, involuted forms, and French Symbolist influences, he was unwittingly acknowledging Ungaretti's leading position in Italian poetry. Ungaretti himself, however, did not remain within what came to be called the Hermetic school. The Hermetics, it might be claimed, developed mannerisms and an abstruse poetic idiom. Ungaretti, with a possible exception here and there, though writing a difficult poetry, always used that difficulty to intensify communication, and not merely for its own sake.

BIOGRAPHY

Giuseppe Ungaretti was born on February 8, 1888, to Italian parents, Antonio Ungaretti and Maria Ungaretti, in Alexandria, Egypt. Ungaretti's parents had emigrated from an area near Lucca, Italy, to Egypt, where his father, who was employed for a short time at the Suez Canal site, contracted an illness that was to lead to his death in 1890. The Ungarettis had opened a bakery in the Arab quarter of the city, however, and Maria Ungaretti, after her husband's death, continued this business quite successfully.

Ungaretti's education was French, but he was familiar with the Italian intellectual scene in Alexandria. He knew the Italian writer Enrico Pea and frequented Pea's house, called the *baracca rossa*, a gathering place for anarchists. Between 1906 and 1912, Ungaretti's interests included politics, for he wrote and published some political essays. More important, however, Ungaretti came to know several writers both from Alexandria and abroad. He corresponded with Giuseppe Prezzolini, editor of the important literary magazine *La voce*. It was through Prezzolini, in part, that Ungaretti met many of the most notable writers and artists of his day when he finally left Alexandria in 1912, at the age of twenty-four, to travel to Italy and then to Paris.

Paris was the place of Ungaretti's first self-awakening. There, he met with men such as artists Pablo Picasso, Georges Braque, Fernand Leger, Giorgio Di Chirico; writer Max Jacob; sculptor Amedeo Modigliani; and the Italian Futurists. In 1913, Ungaretti followed Henri Bergson's courses at the Collège de France; in the same year, Mohammed Sheab, Ungaretti's friend since childhood, unable to adjust to European life,

Giuseppe Ungaretti (AP/Wide World Photos)

committed suicide. Ungaretti remembered him in the poem "In Memoria" ("In Memoriam"): "And only I perhaps/ still know/ he lived," he wrote, foreshadowing, his conviction that immortality is gained only in the memory of others.

By 1914, Ungaretti was in Italy, where he wrote the first poems later collected in *L'allegria* (the joy). In 1915, he was inducted into the Italian army and was sent to the Austro-Italian Front. The poems of *Il porto sepolto* (the buried port) were written while Ungaretti was on active duty; these poems also became a part of *L'allegria*. Ungaretti did not want to print the poems written at the front, because he felt that such an act would break the solidarity he had with his countrymen, but a friend of his, Ettore Serra, took them and insisted on publishing them in 1916. In 1918, Ungaretti was in Paris again. (Guillaume Apollinaire, a friend of Ungaretti, died soon after he arrived.) He stayed in Paris until 1921, supporting himself by working for an Italian newspaper. While there, he met and married Jeanne Duprix. During this time, Ungaretti's reputation was growing, and he began lecturing in France and Belgium.

In 1921, Ungaretti returned to Rome, where he was to live until 1936. Here the Baroque art of the city had a great impact on him, and eventually this influence led to the writing of *Sentimento del tempo* (the feeling of time). He continued his lecturing and worked in the press division of the Foreign Ministry. In 1925, a daughter, Anna Maria, was born, and in 1930 a son, Antonietto. In 1931, *L'allegria* was given its definitive title and published; this collection included the poems from 1914 to 1919. In 1932, Ungaretti received the Venice Premio Gondoliere, and in 1933, *Sentimento del tempo* was published.

In 1936, Ungaretti accepted a teaching position in Italian literature at the University of São Paulo, Brazil. His stay in Brazil was a dark time, for in 1937, his older brother, Constantino, died, and in 1939, his son, Antonietto, died after a mistreated attack of appendicitis. The trials Italy faced during World War II compounded Ungaretti's sense of loss, and his writing from this period represents a hiatus in the unfolding of his poetic vision. *Il dolore* (the grief), which emerged from this time, was published in 1947.

When Ungaretti returned to Italy in 1942, he accepted a position at the University of Rome. After the war, his right to retain his teaching post was disputed, for many criticized his apparent acceptance of fascism. In spite of this controversy, he retained his position and was very productive during the period following the war. Most of his translations were published during this time, as were several commemorative editions of his works. In his seventieth year, his wife, Jeanne, died.

During his last years, Ungaretti traveled around the world. In 1964, he gave a series of lectures at Columbia University in New York City. On a visit to São Paulo in 1966, Ungaretti met a young Brazilian poetess named Bruna Bianco, with whom he pursued a platonic love affair. *Dialogo* is a poetic dialogue between them. In 1967, *Morte delle stagioni* (death of the seasons), which collected the poems of Ungaretti's old age, was published. Ungaretti was to have one more passionate relationship, with a young Croatian girl, Djuna. In 1970, he traveled again to the United States to receive the Books Abroad Award at the University of Oklahoma. While on this trip, he developed bronchitis. He died in Milan on the night of June 1, 1970.

ANALYSIS

Giuseppe Ungaretti believed that great poets write "seemly biographies," for "poetry is the discovery of the human condition in its essence." Friendship, love, death, and the fate of humanity, the great lyric themes, are the subjects of Ungaretti's poetry. Though his poems show a contemporary concern for autobiographical material, they blend this material with the imagery of the poetic tradition. The form of this poetry is discontinuous, sensuous, and elusive. Metonymy, hyperbaton, ellipsis, surprising juxtapositions of images, and the cultivation of unusual language are all characteristic of Ungaretti's style.

As "seemly biography," Ungaretti's lifework developed with the movement of his experience. His first major collection, *L'allegria*, reflected his experience of World War I. *Sentimento del tempo*, written during his first extended stay in Rome, unfolded around a religious crisis. *Il dolore*, the book Ungaretti said he loved most, chronicled the poet's struggle to come to terms with the loss of his brother and son and the disaster Italy faced at the end of World War II. *La terra promessa* (the promised land) and the later works grew out of the realization that aging and its consequences, the fading of the senses and of feeling, offer a final challenge to the poet.

L'ALLEGRIA

Ungaretti's first major collection, *L'allegria*, includes revisions of two earlier collections, *Il porto sepolto* and *Allegria di naufragi*, which had been published separately, as well as a group of poems written in France just before World War I. *L'allegria* is a work of self-discovery. In his notes to *Il porto sepolto*, Ungaretti says that though his first awakenings came in Paris, it was not until the war that he fully came to know himself. The young Ungaretti was an atheist. There was for him no God, nor any Platonic ideals, somehow infiltrating time, to serve as a basis for life's meaning. The war and its desolate landscapes came to take on something of the significance of his youthful experience of the desert. The desert was a void—as such it represented the emptiness of blind existence—but the desert was also a space in which mirages could blossom. So, too, the war brought Ungaretti to the bones of existence, and there he discovered his courage. The self-discovery he spoke of was the courage to resist the sweep of objective, hence depersonalized, events that depress the human spirit and force it into a life of merely private pleasures and pains. Poetry was the courage to transform the worn images of everyday existence into the perfection of dreams, to find an eternal moment even in the face of desolation. Of all the poets of World War I, Ungaretti is arguably the most affirmative. He cries out in "Pellegrinaggio" ("The Pilgrimage"), "Ungaretti/ man of pain/ you need but an illusion/ to give you courage."

Also arising from Ungaretti's Alexandrian experience of the desert is his identification of himself as a Bedouin poet. This image emerges as central in *L'allegria* and recurs throughout his works in any number of transformations. Ungaretti implies in the use of this image that the poet cannot be submerged in the familiar. Movement and change nourish the quintessential condition of poetry, *disponibilità* ("availability to things"). The Bedouin nature of the poet is required by

the solitary reality that the emptiness of blind existence imposes on him. In "Agonia" ("Agony"), Ungaretti pulls these themes together:

> To die at the mirage
> like thirsty skylarks
> Or like the quail
> past the sea
> in the first thickets
> when it has lost
> the will to fly
> But not to live on lament
> like a blinded finch.

The migration of the Bedouin, like that of birds, is a kind of eternal return. Human individuals are not lost in time if they allow the mirage (beauty, or the flash of poetic insight) to beckon them to the depths of experience. The Bedouin poet's courage is his recognition that thirst and the loss of the will to fly are circumstances, as death is a circumstance. Though he knows that these will overtake him, they do not diminish his passion for flight and song. The poet is always moving back, but with openness; the truth he finds can be held in an image, briefly, but it can never become fixed or permanent. Ungaretti's spirit persists in its capacity to evoke the dream in the midst of the wasteland.

Ungaretti's poetic vision shares a great deal with that of the French Symbolists, for whom the world is a kind of nullity until it is transformed by human subjectivity—hence Charles Baudelaire's celebrated notion that humans know the world through "forests of symbols." In Ungaretti's "Eterno" ("Eternal"), there is a whole poetics in epigrammatic form: "Between one flower gathered and the other given/ the inexpressible null. . . ." If the gathering and giving of the flower stand for poetry, then every poem results from a struggle with the inexpressible, what Ungaretti calls the void, or blind existence. As in the Platonic idea of recollection, the soul perfects itself only through repeated struggles with forgetfulness until it gains real knowledge; so too, in Ungaretti, a movement through repeated loss and gain is implied. In his work, however, this movement is one of renewing, or re-creating, in such a way that the poet, thereby humankind, is brought in touch with his deepest nature.

In *L'allegria*, Ungaretti abandoned the rhetorical devices that had become rife in nineteenth century Italian poetry. He conceived the poet's task to be an "excavation of the word" to release its latent power and music. In "Commiato" ("Leavetaking"), Ungaretti addresses his friend Serra, saying, "poetry/ is the world humanity/ one's own life/ flowering from the word," and concluding, "When I find/ in this my silence/ a word/ it is dug into my life/ like an abyss." The abyss of which he speaks here is not the nullity between the gathered and the given word; it is, rather, the depth of memory that carries back beyond the individual into a mythic past. The abyss is present not in the expressive content of the words but in their power. "To find a *parola* ["word"]," Ungaretti declared in a note to the poems in *L'allegria*, "means to penetrate into the dark abyss of the self without disturbing it and without succeeding in learning its secret."

The culmination of this vision in *L'allegria* is found in "I fiumi" ("The Rivers"), which opens with a scene from the battlefront. It is evening, a world of moonlight; a crippled tree evokes the desolation of war. The poet recalls that in the morning, he had "stretched out/ in an urn of water/ and like a relic/ rested." This is a ritual act, a baptism, for the poem goes on to recount something of a rebirth. Each epoch of the poet's life is represented by a river—the Isonzo, the river of war; the Serchio, the river of his forefathers; the Nile, the river of his birth and unconsciousness; and the Seine, the river of awakening self-awareness: "These are the rivers/ counted in the Isonzo." In the ancient image of the river, Ungaretti captures the subjective moment in which all the branches of his existence blossom together. Such a moment is a consolation and a confirmation of a path but is at the same time evanescent. There is the tantalizing sense that while the outward rivers are in a moment of vision, harmonious with the flow of one's life, such moments do not last: "My torment/ is when/ I do not feel I am/ in harmony." Nevertheless, Ungaretti suggests that there is a power working through his experience that is not identifiable with himself: "hands/ that knead me/ give me/ rare/ felicity." One critic suggested that "hands" refers to the power of ancestors working through the poet and establishing a bond between him and his tradition. However one interprets this image, it is a statement of conviction that the poet has tapped the depths of his being. Unlike his friend Mohammed Sheab, who ". . . could not/ set free/ the song/ of his abandon," Ungaretti found his voice. The poem concludes: "Now my life seems to me/ a corolla/ of shadows."

SENTIMENTO DEL TEMPO

The poems of Ungaretti's second major collection, *Sentimento del tempo*, grew out of a confrontation with the spirit of Rome. Initially, Ungaretti was shocked by Baroque architecture, which seemed to lack unity. After that initial shock, he came to feel that in the Baroque style, things are "blown into the air," and the resultant fragmentation opens the way for a new ordering of things.

For Ungaretti, the Baroque bespeaks the absence of God. In Baroque art, the sense of absence is covered by an elaboration of sensuous detail and by the use of trompe l'oeil. Although Ungaretti saw in this expression of God's absence another manifestation of the emptiness of blind existence, the rhetorical responses of the Baroque did not appeal to him. Poetry was an exploration of the real; he would not abandon the concentrated forms of his first poems. Nevertheless, Baroque poetry gave him access to traditional meters and harmonies, and these he did employ. As he said in a note to *Sentimento del tempo*, he initially wanted to recover "the naturalness and depth and rhythm in the significance of each individual word," but his new project was "to find an accord between our traditional metrics and the expressive needs of today."

The traditional metrics of which he speaks were the hendecasyllable (as in Geoffrey Chaucer's "Whan that Aprill with his shoures soote/ The droghte of March hath perced to the roote") and the seven-syllable line, or *settinario*. These metrics are not simply imposed on his poetry. They are filtered through his intuition, syncopated, and brought together with a poetic style which remains staccato. Moments of passion are drawn out by the music of the line, which Ungaretti understood to be the actual rhythm of humanity's deepest self. The fragmented modern vision is sustained by underlying harmonies. A surface coherence of images achieved through rhetorical devices would be simply linear in its structure; musical harmonies in their polyvalence and rich suggestiveness make possible a multidimensional and deeper union of self and work.

Philosopher Bergson, with whom Ungaretti had studied in Paris, provided the poet with one of the central distinctions of his poetics. Bergson distinguished between two forms of memory: voluntary and involuntary. Voluntary memory is analogous to the sense of space that focuses on space as an aggregate of discrete parts. Life, however, is primarily temporal, not spatial, and this analogy between memory and space conveys the essentially superficial character of voluntary memory. In voluntary memory, a person stands in an extrinsic relationship to his or her past; forgetfulness is the essence of such a relationship. Ungaretti saw in this idea the psychological symbol for the void. What Bergson called involuntary memory, however, was as a unified flow. In involuntary memory, everything is retained. One gains access to involuntary memory through free action, action in which the past flows into and enriches the present. Ungaretti saw in involuntary memory the concept that would unify his poetics: Poetry was a mode of free action. Blending autobiographical elements with the appropriate imagery and language of the tradition, Ungaretti felt that he had returned to the living reality of poetry: a momentary making conscious of the collective unconscious.

Sentimento del tempo is written in several sections. "Fine di Crono" ("The End of Chronos") is both the title of a poem and the name of an important section of the work. Ungaretti presupposes a knowledge of the underlying myth: the murder of Chronos by his son, Zeus, who in his action revolted against the dark world of the Titans and successfully established the world of justice, the Olympian world. For Ungaretti, this revolution reflects the discovery of the deeper, liberating flow of memory beneath the fragmented memory of blind existence. Ungaretti, however, radically alters the traditional association of the Olympians with light. He associates the deeper sense of memory with the inner, subjective world of humans; hence, things must be drawn out of the daylight experience of life into the world of memory and imagination that he associates with night. In *Sentimento del tempo*, Ungaretti inverts the values of life and death. He carries this inversion as far as he can, making death the realm of perfection and day the realm of imperfection—imagery recalling Plato's dialogue *Phaedōn* (fourth century B.C.E.; *Phaedo*, 1675) in which Socrates argues that philosophy is a preparation for death. True life is the life of the spirit, and what most people take as life, the life of enjoyment, is death. Such a view expresses an ultimate human desire to give even death, that unknown standing wholly outside experience, a meaning.

The central collection of *Sentimento del tempo* is "Inni" ("Hymns"), whose subject is a religious crisis. Here Ungaretti introduces the idea of *pietà* (compassion, pity, or piety), which fuses the ancient notion of respect for ancestors with the Christian notion of love for all humankind. In these poems, Ungaretti's self-declared condition is that of alienation, and through *pietà*, he seeks a sense of solidarity with other people. This search adds a moral dimension to the ambitions of a poet whose earlier works might be taken as seeking purely aesthetic resolutions.

The poem in "Hymns" titled "La pietà" ("Pity") is the most important single poem in *Sentimento del tempo*. It opens with an echo of Ungaretti's earlier self-depiction as "a man of pain." "I am a wounded man," he declares dramatically, going on to describe himself as an exile. This sense of exile is the profoundest sense of being out of harmony with the depth of experience Ungaretti has yet expressed: "I have peopled the silence with names./ Have I torn heart and mind to shreds/ to fall into the slavery of words?/ I rule over phantoms." Ungaretti conjures up his previous work and throws its value into doubt. The absence of God confronts the poet with the possibility that he has built on sand. In this, he is like Michelangelo, whom he regarded as the greatest Baroque artist (and after a group of whose works this poem is titled).

The second section of "Pity" develops the inversion of death and life met within all sections of *Sentimento del tempo*. "They [the dead] are the seed that bursts within our dreams," he says. If there is a road open to God, it must be by way of memorial reawakening and restoration of the past. This is the very path that has led Ungaretti to the possibility of despair, but just as the desert had the double significance of the void and the mirage, so also might Ungaretti's religious despair be the other face of hope.

In "Pity," Ungaretti achieved something akin to prayer, but there was no discovery of a way back to a poetry of the divine. The poem's fourth section is, therefore, a portrayal of human life without God. "Man, monotonous universe," it begins. Every human action, considered by itself, is a frustration: "Nothing issues endlessly but limits." When man tries to turn toward God, "He has but blasphemies." This final line echoes the earlier ". . . do those who implore you/ Only know you by name?" "Pity" ends, then, without resolution. Ungaretti has moved away from the atheism of his early years—in fact, he embraced Roman Catholicism—but, in his poetry, the stance of this Bedouin poet is that of an agnostic who seeks to believe. There is no room for dogma here.

Scholar Glauco Cambon suggests that the metaphysical connection among memory, consciousness of the void, and "the dream of becoming" is paralleled in Ungaretti's later work by a moral connection among innocence, sin, and conscience. What had been, in the earlier work, the condition of humanity lost in blind existence deepens in the later work, taking on the significance of the Fall. Indeed, the next section of *Sentimento del tempo*, titled "La morte meditata" ("Death Meditated"), takes place in the Garden of Eden, and Eve is its central figure. Ungaretti gives a particularly modern shading to Eve by introducing an element of sensuality; he does this in order to include the sensuous, poetry's medium, in an image of restored innocence. As the symbol of restored innocence, Eve carries the double significance of death as a realm of perfection and as the realm of the terrible loss of innocence. If death is another face of blind existence, then Eve emerges against the void of death as the mirage emerges on the desert. Ungaretti's choice of a female symbol to express the restored innocence for which poetry strives is characteristically Italian, recalling Petrarch's Laura, Dante's Beatrice, and Leopardi's Silvia.

IL DOLORE

The poems of *Il dolore* grew out of Ungaretti's experience of profound loss. In a poem about his brother Constantino's death, he writes: "I have lost all of childhood—/ Never again can I/ Forget myself in a cry." This nihilistic chord underlies the "bitter accord" of the collection.

"Tu ti spezzisti" ("You Shattered") is the greatest poem of the collection. It opens with the alien Brazilian landscape—a landscape unnerving and threatening: "That swarm of scattered, huge, gray stones/ Still quivering in secret slings/ Of stifled flames of origin. . . ." The references to nonhuman creation call to mind the poetic task of inwardly re-creating the world, but this landscape is presented with a force and a strangeness that make such a task overwhelming, if not impossible. Against this landscape, Antonietto, Ungaretti's son who died, is likened to a small bird: on one hand, the recalcitrantly primitive and foreboding; on the other, the fragile but keenly alive. Disaster is inevitable. "How could you not have shattered/ In a blindness so inflexible/ You, simple breath and crystal." The oppressive powers that brought down this small life are focused by reference to the sun: "Too human dazzling for the ruthless,/ Savage, droning, tenacious/ Roar of naked sun."

The rest of *Il dolore* grows out of a preoccupation with the possible destruction of Italy. A notable aspect of these poems is the emergence of the figure of Christ. Like Michelangelo, who desired faith but from whom God hid himself, Ungaretti might be seen as an odd sort of agnostic. The Christ of Ungaretti's poems is modified by the poet's humanism.

LA TERRA PROMESSA

La terra promessa contains poems written in the early 1930's, although the volume was not published until 1950. If, as Ungaretti says, the dominant season of *Sentimento del tempo* is summer, then the dominant season of *La terra promessa* is autumn. In this season, as Jones comments, "detached as the aging mind becomes from the flesh, it begins to see the world as a sensational Pascalian abyss . . . , which neither the fancy nor the imagination can any longer bridge over." Pascal, however, took joy in the promised liberation from the senses, something that Ungaretti cannot do. There would be no way to the restoration of "innocence with memory" without the sensuous imagination. For Ungaretti, the separation of sense and mind—the dying of sense—which threatens to undermine the poet's immediate engagement with things can be overcome through memory. The poet returns to the memories of youth to restructure them out of the knowledge of a full life, breathing new life into them.

The "promised land" of which Ungaretti speaks is promised because it is the place of renewed innocence. This symbol repeats and transforms his attempt to resolve the problem which was central to his writing from the beginning: How, without absolutes, does one live a human life in time? The answer he gave should be seen against a guiding mythology. As he says in *Vita d'un uomo: Tutto le poesie*:

> Once upon a time there was a pure universe, humanly speaking . . . an absurdity: an immaterial materiality. This purity became a material materiality as a result of some offence perpetrated against the Creator by who knows what event. But anyway, through some extraordinary happening of a cosmic order, this material became corrupt—thereby time originated, and history originated. This is my manner of feeling things, it is not the truth, but it is a way of feeling: I feel things in this way.

This note to the poems of *La terra promessa* makes clear Ungaretti's mythological cast of mind. The Golden Age cannot be restored, but its power can be evoked by a process of memory akin to the ritual. Poems are such evocations, and in this collection, the rites of poetry are reconstitutions of memories through the informing insight of maturity. If old age is characterized by the decline, even death, of the senses, this does not imply that there is no bridge between the sensuous visions of youth and the understanding of old age. A purification of memory is possible, and such a purification leads back through the "tunnel of time" to innocence.

The key figure in this collection is Aeneas, though he never takes the stage, and the *Aeneid* (c. 29-19 B.C.E.; English translation, 1553) of Vergil is a source of much of its symbolic material. One of the most important poems of the collection is titled "Cori descrittivi di stati d'animo di Didone" ("Choruses Descriptive of Dido's States of Mind"). In this group of nineteen fragments, the passing of Dido's beauty is mourned. This image has obvious resonance with the image of Eve as a figure of lost innocence, but only to contrast Dido with Eve. Dido is ultimately lost. She is here, as she was for Vergil, the contrast to Aeneas's virtue. She has no inner spiritual world. If Dido negatively echoes Eve, Aeneas positively echoes the image of the Bedouin poet.

Ungaretti's lifework was to open a way to cultural origins by means of his adventure in language. For Ungaretti, whatever measure of salvation can be found is to be found only through history. Humans are alone, but through *pietà* they can move beyond their alienation toward solidarity with their fellows. The poet's access to the cultural flow of memory is gained through language. The language of poetry, Ungaretti said, is always in crisis, but this is a condition of its renewal. Through the purification of language, the poet hands on the tradition intact and creatively reworked. In doing so, he holds open the possibility of perpetual renewal.

OTHER MAJOR WORKS

NONFICTION: *Il povero nella citta*, 1949; *Il deserto e dopo*, 1961; *Innocence et memoire*, 1969; *Lettere a un fenomenologo*, 1972; *Vita d'un uomo: Saggi e interventi*, 1974.

TRANSLATIONS: *Traduzioni*, 1936 (various poems and authors); *Venti-due sonetti de Shakespeare: Scelti e tradotti da Giuseppe Ungaretti*, 1944; *Vita d'un uomo: Quaranta sonetti di Shakespeare tradotti*, 1946; *L'Après-midi et le monologue d'un faune di Mallarmé*, 1947; *Vita d'un uomo: Da Góngora e da Mallarmé*, 1948; *Vita d'un uomo: Fedra di Jean Racine*, 1950; *Finestra del caos*, 1961 (of Murilo Mendes); *Vita d'un uomo: Visioni di William Blake*, 1965.

BIBLIOGRAPHY

Godorecci, Maurizio. "The Poetics of the Word in Ungaretti." *Romance Languages Annual* 9 (1997): 197-201. A critical analysis of selected poems by Ungaretti.

Hacht, Anne Marie, and David Kelly, eds. *Poetry for Students*. Vol. 20. Detroit: Thomson/Gale, 2004. Analyzes Ungaretti's "Variations on Nothing." Contains the poem, a summary, themes, style, historical context, a critical overview, and criticism. Includes bibliography and index.

Jason, Philip K., ed. *Masterplots II: Poetry Series*. Rev. ed. Pasadena, Calif.: Salem Press, 2002. This set contains summaries and analyses of the poem "La pietà."

Jones, Frederic J. *Giuseppe Ungaretti: Poet and Critic*. Edinburgh: Edinburgh University Press, 1977. An assessment of Ungaretti's life and career. Includes bibliographic references.

Moevs, Christian. "Ungaretti: A Reading of 'Alla noia.'" *Forum Italicum* 25, no. 2 (Fall, 1991): 211-227. A critical study of one of Ungaretti's poems.

Re, Lucia. "Alexandria Revisited: Colonialism and the Egyptian Works of Enrico Pea and Giuseppe Ungaretti." In A *Place in the Sun: Africa in Italian Colonial Culture from Post-unification to the Present*, edited by Patrizia Palumbo. Berkeley: University of California Press, 2003. Examines the writings of Ungaretti and Pea, both of whom lived in Alexandria.

Suvini-Hand, Vivienne. *Mirage and Camouflage: Hiding Behind Hermeticism in Ungaretti's "L'allegria."* Market Harborough, Leicester, England: Troubador/Hull Italian Texts, 2000. Provides in-depth analysis of *L'allegria*, including the issue of hermeticism.

Robert Colucci

V

PAUL VALÉRY

Born: Sète, France; October 30, 1871
Died: Paris, France; July 20, 1945

PRINCIPAL POETRY

La Jeune Parque, 1917 (*The Youngest of the Fates*,
    1947; also known as *The Young Fate*)
Album de vers anciens, 1920 (*Album of Early
    Verse*, 1971)
Charmes: Ou, poèmes, 1922 (*Charms*, 1971)

OTHER LITERARY FORMS

The diverse and copious writings of Paul Valéry
(va-lay-REE) include plays, such as *Mon Faust* (pb.
1946; *My Faust*, 1960); musical drama such as *Amphion* (pr., pb. 1931; English translation, 1960), *Sémiramis* (pr., pb. 1934; English translation, 1960), and
Cantate du Narcisse (pr. 1939; *The Narcissus Cantata*,
1960); dialogues such as *Eupalinos: Ou, L'Architecte*
(1921; *Eupalinos: Or, The Architect*, 1932) and *L'Âme
et la danse* (1925; *Dance and the Soul*, 1951); the witty
Monsieur Teste series; essays on a wide range of subjects; translations (such as that of Vergil's *Eclogues*,
43-37 B.C.E.; English translation, 1575); numerous book
prefaces, speeches, and university lectures; and an extensive correspondence with many illustrious contemporaries, such as André Gide and Stéphane Mallarmé.
Dwarfing this work in terms of volume alone are the
nearly twenty-nine thousand pages of his notebooks,
which he kept from 1894 until his death in 1945. They
record his thoughts on such diverse subjects as psychology, mathematics, culture, and literary theory, and
are considered to contain some of the most beautiful prose ever written in the French language. Virtually the only literary form which Valéry did not attempt was the novel. He considered the genre, with
its contradictory demand to create a fictional reality, to be alien to his sensibilities, once remarking that
he was incapable of composing a work that began
with a line such as "The Marquise went out at five
o'clock."

ACHIEVEMENTS

The honors bestowed on Paul Valéry by the French
people attest the veneration in which he was held by his
fellow countrymen. His talents were also recognized
by many outside France. Not only was he instrumental
in acquainting the rest of the world with French culture, but also he enjoyed an international reputation as
a literary figure and as a keen analyst of politics and
culture. For a number of years, he served on the Committee on Intellectual Cooperation of the League of
Nations. In 1935, he became a member of the Academy
of Sciences of Lisbon. Highly respected by the British
and the Portuguese, he received honorary degrees from
the universities of Oxford (1931) and Coimbra (1937).
Valéry was the last member of a trio of poets with similar aesthetic ideals and compositional practices (the
other members were Charles Baudelaire and Mallarmé);
he was the last major French poet to use the strict rules
of French versification. The Surrealist poets, for example, although finding much to admire in his work,
preferred other methods of poetic composition, such as
automatic writing. Although Valéry left no literary disciples to practice his aesthetic ideals, his works and
literary philosophy interested and stimulated such diverse literary figures as T. S. Eliot, Rainer Maria Rilke,
Jorge Luis Borges, and Jean-Paul Sartre. Tzvetan
Todorov and other structuralists share with Valéry an
interest in the relationship between the component elements of a work, although Valéry focuses on the process of composition rather than on the analysis of the
resulting literary discourse. Todorov credits Valéry
with redefining the word "poetics" to emphasize literary language rather than rules of rhyme and versification. Others, such as New Novelist Jean Ricardou, find
Valéry's aesthetic in accord with their rejection of the
subjectivity, the false sense of "psychology," the insistence on verisimilitude, and the lack of compositional
rigor which they find characteristic of the traditional
novel. Thus, Valéry still speaks to a wide range of writers and readers, and the beauty of his poetry, the incisive observations and lucid prose of his notebooks, and

the continuing influence of his literary theories assure his continued importance in French literature.

BIOGRAPHY

Paul Valéry was born Ambroise-Paul-Toussaint-Jules Valéry on October 30, 1871, in the small French seaport of Sète. His childhood was bathed in the sunlight, blue sky and water, and salt air of this Mediterranean setting. The young Valéry disliked intensely the regimented nature of his schoolwork and spent much of his free time studying objects that greatly interested him: painting, architecture, and poetry, especially that of Baudelaire, Théophile Gautier, and Victor Hugo. Valéry's first poems were composed in 1884, at the age of thirteen.

In that same year, Valéry's family moved to Montpellier. The year 1887 was marked by his father's death; in 1888, he entered law school at the university in Montpellier. His first published poem, "Rêve," ap-

Paul Valéry (Roger Viollet/Getty Images)

peared in 1889 in a small literary review. During this period, Valéry spent many hours studying mathematics (an interest that he maintained all his life), physics, and music (he especially admired the music of Richard Wagner, which had a grandeur he judged both "visceral" and "structural").

In 1890, Valéry met Pierre Louÿs, a young Symbolist poet and editor. Louÿs was to have a great impact on Valéry's future; not only did he help to further Valéry's literary reputation, but also he introduced the young man to others who were to play significant roles in his life. An introduction to Louÿs's uncle, André Gide, sparked a lasting friendship and voluminous correspondence that was to span the next fifty years. Louÿs also introduced his friend to Mallarmé. For Valéry, Mallarmé's works exemplified such perfection of form and control of language that all other poetry seemed inferior by comparison. In their subsequent correspondence, Mallarmé praised the young poet's work, and, perhaps as a result of this encouragement, Valéry's literary output increased dramatically; several of his poems soon appeared in print in Louÿs's literary review, *La Conque*, and elsewhere.

Valéry's literary career had hardly begun, however, when he chose to turn away from poetry as his primary occupation in favor of a life of study and contemplation. His biographers have sought to explain this action by referring to a growing predilection for introspection among young French intellectuals, to their common dislike of the then-popular naturalistic novel and of objective and descriptive Parnassian poetry, to Valéry's feelings of inferiority in the face of the poetic perfection of his master, Mallarmé, and to Valéry's unrequited (and undeclared) love for a married woman, which left him frightened of his inability to control his strong feelings. No doubt these factors affected Valéry, but his decision in 1892 to devote his life to the cultivation of his intellect can just as easily be seen as a natural consequence of his introspective nature. His decision was greatly influenced by the intellectual and poetic theories of Edgar Allan Poe, which portrayed poetry as creating certain calculated effects. Valéry believed that the techniques required to produce these effects suppressed rather than expanded the intellect; thus, although he had already written several hundred poems, he concluded that the best path toward intellectual growth and wisdom was that of the thinker rather than the artist.

Thus began the period in Valéry's life somewhat erroneously termed the "Great Silence." For the next twenty years or so, he occasionally wrote and published, and he carried on an active social life, often frequenting Mallarmé's Tuesday evening salons and attending concerts and plays. In 1900, he married Jeannie Gobillard, niece of the Impressionist painter Berthe Morisot; the couple had three children. His main occupation during the years from 1892 to 1912, however, was the systematic and dispassionate study of the human mind. Charles Whiting indicates the great extent to which Valéry's method resembled that of René Descartes, in its insistence on intellectual independence, a rigorous method, the founding of all knowledge and certainty within the self, and the "ambition for reducing the process of the mind to measurable quantities." Perhaps in emulation of Leonardo da Vinci, Valéry began keeping a series of notebooks, in which he inscribed mathematical equations, aphorisms, ideas and their developments, bits of verse, and so on. By the time of his death, he had filled almost twenty-nine thousand pages.

During this period, the workings of international politics did not escape Valéry's attention. A prophetic essay on the threat posed by modern Germany, first published in England in 1897, was reprinted in France in 1915, and stirred the public's curiosity about Valéry. He published other works as well, including the essay "L'Introduction à la méthode de Léonard da Vinci" ("Introduction to the Method of Leonardo da Vinci") in 1895 and the philosophical tale "La Soirée avec Monsieur Teste" ("An Evening with Monsieur Teste") in 1896; the protagonist of the latter, Monsieur Teste, in many ways embodies Valéry's ideals of pure intellect and creative genius.

Although Valéry's family connections permitted him the leisure to pursue his interests, in 1897, he assumed a somewhat tedious clerkship with the War Ministry, and in 1900, he became private secretary to Edouard Lebey of the Havas Press Association. Valéry found the job with Lebey most stimulating, and it left him with ample free time for his own intellectual pursuits.

In 1912, Gide and the publisher Gaston Gallimard urged Valéry to prepare a collection of his poetry for publication. Reluctant at first, he finally began to edit and revise his early poems (eventually published in 1920 as the *Album of Early Verse*) and to compose a new poem, *The Young Fate*, which was published in 1917. The poem was astonishingly successful in spite of its extreme Hermeticism; it secured Valéry's reputation as a great poet, and it is still considered one of the finest French poems of the twentieth century.

His work on *The Young Fate*, originally intended by Valéry as his farewell to poetry, inspired him to write other poems. In 1920, "Le Cimetière marin" ("The Graveyard by the Sea") appeared, and 1922 saw the publication of *Charms*, a collection of poems written between 1917 and 1921 (a new edition of *Charms* was published in 1926). Although Valéry continued to compose poetry, these collections contain most of his best work.

The death of Edouard Lebey, in 1922, made Valéry resolve henceforth to earn his living as a freelance intellectual. Valéry's name was everywhere prominent: He became a noted lecturer; produced pamphlets, prefaces, dedications, and new editions of his poems; and wrote the texts of two verse-ballets and a cantata. He was a brilliant essayist whose topics embraced art, philosophy, literature, and social and political criticism. One of his best-known essays, "La Crise de l'esprit" ("The Crisis of the Mind"), published in France in 1919, eloquently warned that the modern world's self-destructive tendencies could condemn it to join the Babylons and Ninevehs of the past; it included one of Valéry's most oft-quoted phrases: "Nous autres, civilisations, nous savons maintenant que nous sommes mortelles" ("We other civilizations, we know now that we are mortal").

His reputation ever-growing, Valéry was elected to the French Academy in 1925; he became a *chevalier* of the Legion of Honor in 1923 and was subsequently promoted to more prestigious ranks. In 1933, he was named administrator of the Centre Universitaire Méditerranéen, at Nice, and he was appointed to a Chair of Poetics at the Collège de France in 1937.

Although his opposition to the Vichy government in World War II and his courageous public eulogy for the

French Jewish philosopher Henri Bergson exposed Valéry to harassment by the German authorities during the occupation of France, it was typical of his generous spirit to speak out after the war in defense of three accused collaborators.

By 1945, Valéry was suffering from cancer; although very ill, he managed to complete the poetry course he had taught every winter since 1937 at the Collège de France. He died on July 20, 1945, at the age of seventy-three. Honored with a state funeral as one of France's greatest men, he was buried in his native Sète, in the cemetery that was the setting for one of his best-known poems, "The Graveyard by the Sea."

ANALYSIS

Paul Valéry's youthful views about poetry, which were anti-Romanticist and somewhat cynical, led him to reject literature as his primary occupation and to lead instead a life of contemplation and study, which he hoped would enable him to understand better the relationships among the phenomena of the world. When he eventually realized that universal knowledge was unattainable and that individual facets of reality could not be frozen or studied in isolation, he began to write poetry again. Where he had earlier rejected the Romantic and Platonic notion of Muse-inspired poetry, he came to grant inspiration its place in the creative process. Perhaps he found in poetry that synthesis of world experience thath he had hoped to find in his studies of scientific phenomena. In any case, the years devoted to such study had produced in Valéry a vigorous and finely honed mind, and he perceived in poetry not only a rewarding exercise of the intellect but also the nearest approach that human beings could make to expressing the ineffable.

Valéry's poetic theories grew out of his strong interest in the workings of human psychology. His model of mental functioning, reflecting the findings of the then relatively new science of psychiatry, portrayed a network of constantly changing interactions of words, feelings, motor impulses, sensations, stimuli, responses, and so on. He thus saw human identity as infinitely varied rather than possessed of an unchanging essence. In Valéry's psychological model, various functions are continually interacting, but only the intellect has a tran-

scendent understanding of them, although it has no control over many of the organism's functions. Moreover, the intellect of a scientist is likely to interpret a given electrical stimulus differently from the way the intellect of a musician or a poet would interpret it. This recognition of the variety among human intellects and of the primal authority of instinctive responses led Valéry to relinquish his earlier faith in calculated technique, a faith that had been influenced in part by Poe's ideas about the ability of a technically skilled poet to manipulate the emotions of his readers and to produce specific predictable effects in all readers.

Valéry connected this model of psychological functioning to a theory of poetry by postulating that the intellect, when stimulated, tends to interpret and classify the information it receives as quickly as possible, in order to return to its habitual state of rest. In terms of this model, prose differs from poetry because the goal of prose is to transmit information; effective prose presents data in such a way that the information is easy to process, is easily extractable from its form, which is relatively unimportant except as a container, a vehicle. The goal of poetry, on the other hand, is to increase internal excitation and awareness and to resist the intellect's attempts to classify and return to a resting state. Valéry therefore sought to create a poetry with "subjects" so fragile and elusive that they would simultaneously charm and mystify the intellect, and that would be presented in forms so compelling to the intellect that they would themselves become part of the message. To summarize Valéry's psychopoetic theory, one could say that rhythm, sound, the use of metaphor and other tropes, and the emotive aspects of language in general serve to increase and sustain the involvement of the subconscious mind and the physical body in the reading process. The interplay of images, memories, ideas, melodies, and sensations prolongs the pleasurable state of internal excitement and delays closure by the intellect, which, captivated by the poem's form, returns to it repeatedly, seeking to prolong or renew its experience.

This view of aesthetic experience has its implications for the poet as well as for the reader. Valéry recognized that the genesis of his poems was usually to be found not in a conscious decision to compose a poem on a particular subject but rather in those verses, couplets, sentence fragments, or insistent rhythmic or sound patterns that came to him as "gifts" from that modern Muse, the unconscious. At the same time, these "inspired" verses needed to be refined by the poet's technical and analytical skills, and integrated with other verses, fashioned more by skill than by inspiration, so as to form a seamless, aesthetic whole. To be successful, Valéry believed, a poem must present difficulties for the poet as well as for the reader; he preferred to work with traditional poetic forms with fixed rhyme schemes and other compositional requirements, because he found that his struggles with these obstacles often produced new and unexpectedly beautiful networks of meaning and sometimes altered the original thrust of the poem.

Valéry was concerned with aesthetic process more than with aesthetic results. In his view, the stimulation and prolongation of aesthetic pleasure which a poem provides is as important for the poet as for the reader. While he is engaged in the creative process, the poet experiences the intellectual growth, spiritual insight, and emotional release that poetic creation stimulates as it keeps the poet's intellect from returning to a state of equilibrium. Because he believed that it was the poetic process and not the end product that provided aesthetic stimulation, Valéry never considered his poems finished, and he was constantly revising his work. He claimed in his essay "Au sujet du *Cimetière marin*" ("On 'The Graveyard by the Sea,'" published in a bilingual edition of "The Graveyard by the Sea" by the University of Texas Press, 1971) that the published form of that poem merely represented its state on the day it was taken away from him by the editor of the *Nouvelle Revue française*.

Although he never felt that poetry could be a product of purely spontaneous composition, Valéry's youthful conception of poetry as a series of calculated effects controlled by the poet was tempered as he matured. He came to believe in the role of inspiration and mystery in the poetic process, as it operated on the intellect of both poet and reader; he believed that the aesthetic experience was so rich and complex that the intellect could never fully contain or understand it.

This aesthetic individualism colored Valéry's attitude toward his readers; he believed that, just as a poet's unique identity marks his poem, so will different readers' identities color their responses to it. He was therefore generous with his critics; although he may have been privately amused by some interpretations, he gave his official blessing to such endeavors, saying, "My poetry has the meaning that people give to it."

Valéry may have been troubled, however, by those critics who sought to reduce his poems to prose summaries. In his own writings, he often stated that a poem cannot be summarized any more than can a melody, that the beauty and power of poetry stem precisely from the fact that it cannot be put into prose without disintegrating. This problem in poetic theory is illustrated by what Valéry and two well-known critical interpreters have said about "The Graveyard by the Sea," a poem characteristic of Valéry's work in terms of its contemplative mood, its philosophical themes, its formal perfection, and its harmonious and evocative language.

"THE GRAVEYARD BY THE SEA"

Perhaps his best-known poem, "The Graveyard by the Sea" was written following Valéry's years of contemplation and study. First published in 1920, it portrays human consciousness becoming aware of itself in relation to time, death, and the expanse of the cosmos. The speaker in the poem ponders this interior vastness of consciousness in an ironic setting: a cemetery overlooking the sea, surrounded by tombstones, under the noon blaze of an apparently motionless sun.

"The Graveyard by the Sea" is composed of twenty-four stanzas of six decasyllabic lines each, with a rhyme scheme of *aabccb*. Valéry resurrected the decasyllabic line, which had been all but abandoned by French poets in favor of the more flowing Alexandrine. Although he welcomed the difficulties posed by the ten-syllable line, he did not consciously choose it. In his essay "On 'The Graveyard by the Sea,'" he states that the poem's genesis took the form of certain unintelligible decasyllabic "murmurings," and he became obsessed with the idea of arranging them into six-line stanzas connected by a network of correspondences and tonal contrasts. The intricate requirements of this form prompted him to seek his subject matter in familiar childhood memories, in the sea and sunlight of his Mediterranean birthplace, Sète. These elemental images led him directly to the contemplation of death.

The composition of "The Graveyard by the Sea" thus resembled the composition of a piece of music, in which the melodic motifs—the ideas—are often the *last* aspects of the composition to take shape. Valéry's essay on this poem stresses his belief that ideas simply do not play the same role in poetry that they do in prose; he conceives of "pure poetry" as a nonreferential network of infinite resonances that profoundly touch the reader's sensibility and cannot be summarized in prose. Elsewhere, however, he acknowledged that this ideal of pure poetry was an impossibility, that actual poems are always combinations of "fragments of pure poetry enclosed in the matter of a discourse," and that readers need some thematic or narrative material to guide them through a poem.

An oft-quoted explication of "The Graveyard by the Sea" that attempts to provide just such a guide is that of Sorbonne professor Gustave Cohen. His *Essai d'explication du "Cimetière marin"* (1933), is largely an elucidation of the poem's thematic development. It regards the poem as the recounting of a philosophical journey, a sort of classical tragedy in four acts, with three characters: Nonbeing, or Nothingness (symbolized by the seeming immobility of the noonday sun); human consciousness (represented by the sea), torn between its desire to unite with Nonbeing and its drive to change and create; and the speaker (whom Cohen calls the author), who is alternately a spectator and a participant in a drama which will irrevocably mark his life.

In Cohen's act 1 (stanzas 1-4), the speaker, transfixed by the sun's unwavering gaze, surveys the sailboats and the sea below him. Seen through the tree branches and tombstones, they resemble a roof covered with doves: "This tranquil roof where doves are walking." All seems motionless, and one feels the speaker's longing to be forever absorbed into the eternal.

The second act (stanzas 5-8) depicts the author's serene acceptance of his inevitable death. Stanza 5 exquisitely describes the loss of corporeal form and the separation of body and soul at death as the slow melting in the mouth of a piece of fruit which then releases a flood of fragrant juices: "As a fruit dissolves into a taste/ changing its absence to deliciousness/ within a palate where its shape must die." The speaker gradually realizes that despite the attraction of eternal changeless-

ness, the essence of human existence is one of constant change. In the finale to this section, Cohen sees the speaker as aware of the vastness of his own consciousness as it exists in that moment of anticipatory emptiness before a poem is born: "Between the void and the pure event,/ I await the echo of my hidden depths."

In the third section (stanzas 9-18), Cohen sees the speaker rejecting the Christian promise of eternal life, and anticipating instead the permanent loss of individuality, sensuality, and awareness that is the fate of the dead, who have forever "melted into a dense absence." He now realizes that his very individuality is what defines him as alive.

Cohen's act 4 (stanzas 19-24) is titled "Triumph of the Momentary, of the Successive, of Change and of Poetic Creation." The speaker recognizes that he cannot deny life; the worm that relentlessly gnaws the living is the worm of consciousness, which will not let him rest: "He lives on life, it's me he never quits!" The speaker is troubled momentarily by Zeno's paradoxes, but a fresh breath of salty air prompts him to brush aside his incertitude. The once-calm sea's curling waves reveal the creative energy constantly boiling beneath its surface; it is likened to the Hydra that swallows its own tail, a symbol of infinity and renewal. The poet's mind also boils with creative fervor; the poem ends with the speaker's vigorous acceptance of life and with a call to the waves to shatter the tranquil sea/roof where the dove/sails had been pecking.

Interpretations such as Cohen's, helpful as they are in understanding the poem, were subsequently faulted for dealing too little with the language and structure of the poem and for providing no basis for an assessment of its aesthetic quality. One such critique of this thematic approach to Valéry was that of Bernard Weinberg, whose well-known study of "The Graveyard by the Sea" in *The Limits of Symbolism* (1966) focuses instead on the poem's structure. Weinberg demonstrates how its principal metaphor develops from an initial state of apparent equilibrium in which sea, cemetery, and spectator seem to be equivalent, through a middle ground in which this balance is threatened and then disrupted, to the end, where the idea of balance is foregone and movement and change are embraced. Paying close attention to the lexical aspects of the poem's language (although neglecting the phonic and rhythmic aspects), Weinberg shows how the repetition and interplay of polyvalent words and images result in a tightly woven unity born out of poetic rather than logical necessity. For example, in his discussion of Valéry's use of Zeno's paradox of infinitely dividing distance (stanza 21), Weinberg shows how Valéry's language simultaneously recalls the poem's opening image of a sun fixed in the sky at high noon and introduces an upcoming allusion to the disparity between substance and shadow. In a later observation, Weinberg demonstrates how the poem's ending is linked to its beginning: The panther skin surface of the sea, spotted with "thousands and thousands of idols of the sun," echoes the "thousand tiles" of the opening sea/roof image; *idole* is a further instance of the recurring religious vocabulary which first appears early in the poem and continues throughout ("temple," *idolâtre*, and so on); the image of the Hydra swallowing its tail recalls the earlier mention of the "forever-recommencing sea" ("The sea, the sea perpetually renewed!").

Concentrating mainly on the poem's diction and the development of its principal metaphor, Weinberg postulates that the presence and placement of every word and image in the poem have a structural justification deriving from and contributing to the poem's unity. Thus, he is able to conclude that "The Graveyard by the Sea" is an excellent poem, because it presents itself to the reader as "a consistent, consecutive, and unified whole."

Decades of critical distance allow one to see not only the complementarity and differences in the interpretations of Cohen and Weinberg, but also certain shared limitations inherent in their approaches. Analyses of "The Graveyard by the Sea" that emphasize resolution (Cohen's) or unity (Weinberg's) or progression (both authors') tend to exclude or de-emphasize references in the poem to circularity and repetition and to those enigmas of existence which forever resist integration into a unified whole.

In the course of this poem, the reader does indeed witness the evolution of the speaker's thought to a point of decision, but the poem's vocabulary and imagery reveal this progression to coexist with references to repetition and circularity. In the poem's twenty-four stan-

zas, there are twenty-three words containing the prefix "re- ." The opening image shows the speaker in a moment of contemplative repose following a previous interval of thought/action and contemplation. Cyclical resonances characterize the poem's major images: The sun suggests the alternation of day and night, the Earth's orbit around the Sun, and also evokes the representation of time as circularity (another critic, Bernard Vannier, sees "The Graveyard by the Sea" as a clock, with its twenty-four hours/stanzas each divided into sixty minutes/feet); the massive solidity of the "forever recommencing sea" is counterbalanced by the oscillation of the waves and the ebb and flow of the tide ("The change of the murmuring shores"); death, too, is portrayed not only as an end but also as the beginning of a cycle ("All goes under the earth, and re-enters the game!").

The image of the Hydra biting its tail (stanza 23) symbolizes a circularity in which endings are contained within beginnings, and vice versa. This same sense of connection and continuity can be seen in the poem's opening and closing stanzas; one has an initial impression of absolute stasis eventually giving way to absolute motion, but each state is linked to and anticipates its opposite. The calm opening stanzas of the poem subtly suggest movement beneath the surface; the sea, seen as a "tranquil roof," "pulses" (*palpite*) in the sunlight, and peace "seems to conceive itself" in this moment of repose. Conversely, coloring the speaker's closing mood of affirmation are hints that he still struggles against the forces of inertia, hesitation, and doubt: "The wind rises! . . . One must attempt to live!/ The immense air opens and closes my book,/ The powdery waves dare to surge over the rocks!") Beginnings in endings also appear in the speaker's closing exhortation to the waves to "break the tranquil roof where the sails were pecking"—a reprise of the poem's opening image. The two notions of circularity and progression are thus fused; insofar as this poem represents the universal experience of every individual who confronts the infinite, the speaker's ultimate decision to embrace life is as much a re-solution (a solving again) as it is a resolution.

But what of those elements that resist resolution or integration into a system, those paradoxes that confound the human mind? The speaker in the poem longs for the oblivion of nonbeing. As long as he is alive and changing, he will never know this peace; finding peace in death, he will also lose it, for he will lose all awareness. The vastness of nonbeing is pure and yet impure; changeless and sufficient unto itself, it needs an imperfect, changing human consciousness ("The flaw in [its] great diamond") to recognize and reflect its perfection. The speaker longs to merge with the absolute but cannot in his present form cross the boundary that separates him from the infinite. The poem abounds in images juxtaposed without being merged: In the cemetery, the living visit the dead, but there is no contact; the sea meets the land but remains forever separate; any substance that reflects the light has a dark half always in shadow. It should be noted, too, that the poem's protagonist does not ever resolve Zeno's paradoxes; in the end, he impetuously allows his vital life-instincts to override the obstacles created by thought and logic.

It seems inappropriate to seek total unity and complete resolution in a poem in which paradox enjoys the status of a theme. According to Zeno's paradoxes, motion cannot exist, and a moving object can never arrive at its destination—yet arrows have been known to pierce their targets. Faced with things beyond comprehension, the living man is afforded a glimpse of infinite vastness; he, like the noonday sun in the poem's opening, "rests above the abyss."

This state of suspension, "between the void and the pure event," brings to mind the similar state that Zen masters seek to produce in their disciples by means of the koan, an enigmatic question that has no answer but the contemplation of which can lead to spiritual enlightenment. In "The Graveyard by the Sea," it is the contemplation of evocative language and poetic enigma that produces a sense of vastness and mystery. Explications that place too great an emphasis on unity and resolution risk stifling other, more elusive echoes that are equally a part of the poem's seductive charms.

OTHER MAJOR WORKS

SHORT FICTION: "La Soirée avec Monsieur Teste," 1896 ("An Evening with Monsieur Teste," 1925).

PLAYS: *Amphion*, pr., pb. 1931 (musical drama; English translation, 1960); *Sémiramis*, pr., pb. 1934 (musical drama; English translation, 1960); *Cantate du Narcisse*, pr. 1939 (musical drama; *The Narcissus Cantata*, 1960); *Mon Faust*, pb. 1946 (*My Faust*, 1960); *The Collected Works of Paul Valéry*, 1956-1975 (15 volumes).

NONFICTION: *Introduction à la méthode de Léonard de Vinci*, 1896 (serial; 1919, book; *Introduction to the Method of Leonardo da Vinci*, 1929); *Eupalinos: Ou, L'Architecte*, 1921 (dialogue; *Eupalinos: Or, The Architect*, 1932); *Variété*, 1924-1944 (5 volumes); *L'Âme et la danse*, 1925 (dialogue; *Dance and the Soul*, 1951); *Analecta*, 1926 (*Analects*, 1970); *Regards sur le monde actuel*, 1931 (*Reflections on the World Today*, 1948); *Degas, danse, dessin*, 1938 (*Degas, Dance, Drawing*, 1960); *Les Cahiers*, 1957-1961.

MISCELLANEOUS: *Selected Writings*, 1950.

BIBLIOGRAPHY

Anderson, Kirsteen. *Paul Valéry and the Voice of Desire*. Oxford, England: Legenda, 2000. An exploration of the power of voice as image and theme throughout Valéry's writing. Anderson highlights the tension between a dominant "masculine" imaginary and the repressed "feminine" dimension that underpins Valéry's work.

Gifford, Paul, and Brian Stimpson, eds. *Reading Paul Valéry: Universe in Mind*. New York: Cambridge University Press, 1998. A collection of essays by internationally recognized scholars offering a comprehensive account of Valéry's work. Perspectives are offered on the immense range of Valéry's experimental and fragmentary writings.

Kluback, William. *Paul Valéry: Illusions of Civilization*. New York: Peter Lang, 1996. A discussion of the meaning of civilization, in particular, Western civilization, as it was investigated in the philosophical works of Valéry. Studies the infrastructure of Valéry's philosophy as it embraced the questions of civilization, history, evil, love, and mortality.

_____. *Paul Valéry: The Realms of the "Analecta."* New York: Peter Lang, 1998. A study of a particular aspect of Valéry's philosophical work, the *Analects*. This is the realm of the imagination, of the image and metaphor. Readers are presented with epigrams that are designed to confuse and challenge their thinking.

Putnam, Walter C. *Paul Valéry Revisited.* New York: Twayne, 1995. An introductory biography and critical study of selected works by Valéry. Includes bibliographical references and index.

Janet L. Solberg

LOPE DE VEGA CARPIO

Born: Madrid, Spain; November 25, 1562
Died: Madrid, Spain; August 27, 1635

PRINCIPAL POETRY

La Dragontea, 1598
El Isidro, 1599
La hermosura de Angélica, 1602
Rimas, 1602
El arte nuevo de hacer comedias en este tiempo,
    1609 (*The New Art of Writing Plays,* 1914)
Jerusalén conquistada, 1609
Rimas sacras, 1614
La Circe, 1621
La filomena, 1621
Triunfos divinos, 1625
La corona trágica, 1627
Laurel de Apolo, 1630
Amarilis, 1633
La gatomaquia, 1634 (*Gatomachia,* 1843)
Rimas humanas y divinas del licenciado Tomé de
    Burguillos, 1634
Filis, 1635
La Vega del Parnaso, 1637
Desire's Experience: A Representative Anthology of
    Lope de Vega's Lyric Poetry, 1991

OTHER LITERARY FORMS

Lope de Vega Carpio (VAY-gah KAHR-pyoh), one of literature's most prolific writers, wrote several prose works, including *La Arcadia* (1598), a pastoral romance; *El peregrino en su patria* (1604; *The Pilgrim: Or, The Stranger in His Own Country,* 1621), a Byzantine romance; *Los pastores de Belén* (1612; the shepherds of Bethlehem), a pastoral romance; *Novelas a*

Marcia Leonarda (1621; stories for Marcia Leonarda, four short novels dedicated to his last love, Marta de Nevares); and *La Dorotea* (1632), a highly autobiographical novel in dialogue. Both his prose and his poetic productions, however, are overshadowed by his plays. Lope de Vega himself claimed to have written about eighteen hundred plays, probably an exaggeration, but even the most conservative estimates place the total at about eight hundred. Some of the better known are *Peribáñez y el comendador de Ocaña* (pb. 1614; *Peribáñez,* 1936); *El villano en su rincón* (pb. 1617; *The King and the Farmer,* 1940); *La dama boba* (pb. 1617; *The Lady Nit-Wit,* 1958); *El perro del hortelano* (pb. 1618; *The Gardener's Dog,* 1903); *Fuenteovejuna* (pb. 1619; *The Sheep-Well,* 1936); *El mejor alcalde, el rey* (pb. 1635; *The King, the Greatest Alcalde,* 1918); and *El caballero de Olmedo* (pb. 1641; *The Knight from Olmedo,* 1961). He also wrote many *autos,* one-act Eucharist plays composed for religious celebrations.

ACHIEVEMENTS

Lope de Vega Carpio lived during the most productive period of Spain's literary history, known as the Golden Age, and shone as its brightest light. He cultivated every literary form—succeeding in each one of them—and quickly gained popularity. A turbulent and charismatic personality, Lope de Vega participated passionately in every aspect of social life, including several scandalous love affairs, all of which he poeticized in one form or another. Writing was so much a part of him that, as some critics have said, his life was literature. He lived for, in, and through literature and was able to afford his carefree lifestyle because of literature; his numerous compositions brought him a steady flow of money. According to his first biographer, Pérez de Montalbán, Lope de Vega composed poems before he even knew how to write, and the author himself claimed that he wrote his first play at twelve. It is known that Lope de Vega was recognized as a good poet and playwright in his early twenties because Miguel de Cervantes praises him very highly in *La Galatea* (1585). Lope de Vega's first collection of lyric poetry appeared in 1602 and, with some alterations and additions was reprinted several times during his lifetime. New collections were published periodically, some of them incorporating long narrative poems that also appeared separately. In 1604, the first volume of his plays was published, and by the time of his death, twenty-two additional volumes (containing twelve dramas each) had appeared. With these plays, Lope de Vega created a new dramatic pattern that, although he felt a need to defend and justify it in *The New Art of Writing Plays*, was accepted and imitated by dramatists for more than a century. Lope de Vega influenced the theater to such an extent that he is considered the founder of the Spanish national drama. Because of this exuberant creativity, coupled with his outgoing personality, he was sought after to promote and to organize literary events when a celebration was in order. Thus, one sees him organizing poetic jousts for any event requiring celebration, from the birth of a prince to the canonization of a saint.

Lope de Vega's literary genius was recognized by all his contemporaries, although some of them resented his immense popularity. In a fitting tribute, Cervantes called him the king of playwrights, a prodigy of nature.

BIOGRAPHY

Lope Félix de Vega Carpio was the third child of Félix de Vega Carpio and Francisca Fernández Flores. Both parents were from Santander and moved first to Valladolid, where their first two children were born. Félix de Vega seems to have had the same passionate traits of character that his son would later show. Infatuated with another woman, Félix de Vega abandoned his family to follow her to Madrid, but Francisca followed her husband and managed to reunite the family. Out of this reconciliation came Lope de Vega, who would later poeticize the event in "Belardo' a Amarilis: Epístola séptima," inserted in *La filomena*, as he did with every aspect of his life.

Lope de Vega was taught Latin and Castilian by Vicente Espinel, a well-known poet and novelist, and soon was recognized as a child prodigy. After a few years at the Jesuit Imperial College—which emphasized the study of grammar and rhetoric—he entered the service of the bishop of Ávila, Don Jerónimo Manrique. Under Manrique's guidance, Lope de Vega studied for the priesthood at the University of Alcalá from 1577 to 1582 but abandoned his studies because of a love affair. It is possible, also, that he studied in

Salamanca the next year before enlisting in the expedition to the Azores Islands. After returning from this expedition, Lope de Vega fell in love with Elena Osorio, thus beginning one of the most turbulent episodes of his life. Following a pattern that soon became a norm, pouring every event of his life into literature, Lope de Vega expressed his love for Elena in passionate verses that told everyone about their love affair. These poetic indiscretions jeopardized the reputation of Elena, a married woman, forcing her to end the relationship. Jealous and hurt, Lope de Vega wrote some compositions highly offensive to Elena and her family and disseminated them throughout Madrid. Elena's family took the case to court, and Lope de Vega was imprisoned while the trial took place and was later sentenced to exile—from the court for eight years and from the kingdom for two.

The court's sentence, not to be broken under penalty of death, did not have a marked effect on Lope de Vega, for soon after, he returned to Madrid and seduced Isabel de Urbina, a young woman from a prominent family. Trying to avoid the scandal, Isabel's father consented to the marriage of the two, and the wedding was done by proxy. A few months later, the poet went to Lisbon to enlist with the Spanish Armada. He was one of the lucky survivors of that disastrous expedition against England, which marked the decline of Spain as a world superpower. After his return, still under banishment from Castile, Lope de Vega went to Valencia with his wife. There, he saw several of his plays staged and seriously began to pursue his career as a playwright. In 1590, when his banishment from Castile was ended, Lope de Vega went to Toledo and entered the service of the marqués de Malpica. Later that year, he moved to Alba de Tormes in the province of Salamanca to work for the famous duke of Alba as one of his secretaries. There, the poet spent some of the most peaceful days of his life, alternating his duties with his literary activity and going frequently to Salamanca, whose university life he portrays so well in his plays. This restful existence ended in 1594 when Isabel died in childbirth, leaving the playwright in great grief.

In 1595, Lope de Vega returned to Madrid, where he was soon involved in another scandalous love affair, this time with a wealthy widow, Antonia Trillo de Armenta. Three years later, the poet married Doña Juana de Guardo, a daughter of a butcher/fishmonger, hoping to better his financial situation with her dowry. At the same time, however, he began another affair with Micaela de Luján, the beautiful wife of actor Diego Díaz de Castro. Lope de Vega spent the next several years sharing his time with the two women, establishing separate homes and families with each.

In 1605, Toledo entrusted him with the organization of a poetic joust to celebrate the birth of Prince Philip, later King Philip IV. Lope de Vega acted as the judge of this contest, contributed verses of his own, and even introduced a "Soneto de Lucinda Serrana" ("Sonnet by Lucinda Serrana"), the pet name of the illiterate Micaela. In 1607, Lope de Vega found yet another love: Jerónima de Burgos, with whom the poet would be involved intermittently for the next ten years. Greatly disappointed, Micaela went back to Madrid and quietly disappeared from his life. Three years later, the playwright returned to the capital, where for a time he led a quiet life dedicated to his family, his writing, and his garden.

Lope de Vega's marriage to Doña Juana marks the most productive period of his life. During that time he published most of his long poems (*La Dragontea, El Isidro, La hermosura de Angélica, Jerusalén conquistada, The New Art of Writing Plays*) and romances (*La Arcadia, The Pilgrim, Los pastores de Belén*), two large collections of *rimas*, and three volumes of his collected plays. It was during this period, also, that the poet became acquainted with the duke of Sessa, starting a long epistolary friendship. Doña Juana died in 1613, leaving Lope de Vega in a state of spiritual crisis that he decided to resolve by becoming a priest. His motivation in taking this step is not completely clear, for the poet continued involving himself with women even when he was preparing for his ordination. Critic Juan Luis Alborg justifies Lope de Vega's actions by saying that he incarnated tragically both the most extreme passions and the most intense religious fervor, but one should not overlook the fact that Lope de Vega was going through financial difficulties and was possibly seeking a more comfortable situation; as a priest, it was easier to obtain some sort of permanent pension. Lope de Vega sought and obtained a chaplaincy in the Church

Lope de Vega Carpio (Library of Congress)

of Saint Segundo in Ávila, with an annual income of 150 ducats.

The ecclesiastical habit did not take Lope de Vega away from women. He was involved with Lucía de Salcedo in 1616 and made a trip to Valencia simply to be with her. The poet soon ended this relationship, however, to attend exclusively to his last love, Marta de Nevares. In her, Lope de Vega found the ideal woman whom he had long been seeking. Marta was married, however, and her enraged husband, Roque Hernández, almost managed to have Lope de Vega killed. Marta began separation procedures, but Roque Hernández died in the midst of the litigation, leaving her free to live with Lope de Vega.

Marta entered Lope de Vega's life in his late years, and she rejuvenated him. She influenced his writing tremendously, and the poet enjoyed another period of intense productivity. In a few short years, he published several volumes of his plays and of his poems, wrote new ones, and, following Marta's encouragement, attempted new literary forms. His private life, however, might have annoyed some people, for he sought the position of royal chronicler but did not obtain it. On the other hand, his living arrangement was not an obstacle when it came to celebrating religious events, such as the 1620 and 1625 poetic contests organized by the city of Madrid to celebrate the beatification and canonization of Saint Isidro. For both occasions, Lope de Vega was in charge of the entire celebration.

The last years of the poet were full of misfortune and disaster. Marta lost her sight and her sanity, becoming extremely violent at times, until she finally died in 1632, leaving Lope de Vega in a state of deep depression. His son Lope drowned two years later while on a pearl-hunting expedition off the coast of the Island of Margarita. Finally, his beloved daughter Antonia Clara was abducted by Cristóbal Tenorio that same year, and Lope de Vega never saw her again. The playwright found himself accompanied by only his memories. Still, he kept poeticizing his emotions and the events of his life. Feeling that death was approaching, Lope de Vega repented daily for his sinful life and finally attained the office of priest. During this time he published *Rimas humanas y divinas del licenciado Tomé de Burguillos* (human and divine verses) under the pseudonym Tomé de Burguillos, as well as *Gatomachia*, a burlesque poem that ridicules the excesses of the Renaissance epic, and his autobiographical novel *La Dorotea*, considered by many as one of the author's best works and one of the most beautiful examples of Spanish prose fiction.

Lope de Vega died in 1635, enjoying the greatest popularity of any living author, and so many people attended his funeral that, as Pérez de Montalbán recounted in *Fama póstuma* (1636), it looked like the funeral of a king.

ANALYSIS

Lope de Vega Carpio reacted poetically to every event of his existence, always leading the true life of an artist. Everything became a poetic pretext for the author, from his passionate love for Elena Osorio to the bitter disappearance of his daughter, Antonia Clara, near the end of his life. As critic José F. Montesinos says, "Lope's biography constitutes the most attractive chapter of our literary history . . . because it shows the existence of the artist in every moment—converting real life facts into poetic creation."

Lope de Vega was conscious of this relationship between life and literature, and he left testimony of it in several of his works. The "Soneto a Lupercio Argensola" ("Sonnet to Lupercio Argensola"), published in the first edition of the *Rimas*, ends with these lines:

> You tell me not to write, or not to live?
> Make sure that my love will not feel,
> Then I will make my pen not to write.

In *La Dorotea*, one of his last works, he writes: "To love and to write verses is all one and the same."

Perhaps because of this intense vitalization of his poetry, Lope de Vega did not write great metaphysical poems, like Francisco Gómez de Quevedo y Villegas, nor did he adapt fully to the new poetic school headed by Luis de Góngora y Argote. He remained a poet of emotions, of feelings, of passions, of love. What is transparent in his poetry, says Dámaso Alonso, is "the life of a man in its turbulent plurality, day after day, in love and in hate, in his picaresque profile and in his periods of true repentance and sincere search for God." In this manner, continues the Spanish critic, Lope de Vega is profoundly original, anticipating the Romantics. Furthermore, these characteristics are not exclusive to his lyric poetry but are present in his objective compositions as well. As Karl Vossler has pointed out, Lope de Vega was able to write with the most lyric and intimate tones when he was poeticizing someone else's love. This does not mean, however, that Lope de Vega was only a poet of natural and simple spontaneity, a poet who cultivated exclusively the popular and traditional meters. He was also a poet full of curiosity who liked to experiment with new forms and poetic conventions. Together with the traditionalist, one finds in Lope de Vega a Petrarchist, a sophisticated poet able to produce very complicated compositions, perfectly assimilating Italian models; a Góngorist, trying to imitate his most vocal enemy in obscure linguistic games; and even a philosophical poet who, unable to imitate Góngora properly, adopts an austere style that is the polar opposite of Góngora's Baroque extravagance.

Lope de Vega published several books of poetry

during his lifetime. Most of them were miscellaneous volumes containing short and long poems and, in some cases, prose works. Unlike Garcilaso de la Vega, Luis de León, and Góngora, Lope de Vega did not cultivate lyric poetry as an independent art. Many of his lyric poems were first incorporated in his plays or prose works, from which they were later taken so as to rescue them from oblivion.

LA DRAGONTEA AND EL ISIDRO

Lope de Vega's first publication was *La Dragontea* (Drake the pirate), an epic poem divided into ten cantos and written in royal octaves. As the title implies, this poetic composition narrates the forays of Sir Francis Drake to the Spanish possessions, concluding with his death in Portobelo at the hands of his own men. Full of patriotic fervor, the poem reveals the common sentiments of the Spaniards toward England in the years after the ill-fated Armada. *La Dragontea* has been criticized by some for its partiality, although it is important to mention that the events are narrated objectively. The poem is also distinguished by the vivid realism of its maritime descriptions, in which Lope de Vega shows his knowledge of nautical vocabulary.

A year later, the ten-thousand-line poem *El Isidro* appeared, written in the popular *quintilla* (five line stanza) and divided into ten books. Of rather mediocre quality, this work was intended to popularize the figure of Saint Isidro the Ploughman, or the Farmer, as a plea for his canonization. A work of great simplicity, *El Isidro* is not an epic poem, but rather a familiar story poeticized with unusual naturalness. In spite of its poetic flaws, there were several editions published during the seventeenth century, certainly the result of the canonization of the saint, which occurred in 1622.

In 1602, the poet published a large volume containing *La hermosura de Angélica* (Angelica's beauty), *Rimas*, and *La Dragontea*. Lope de Vega started writing *La hermosura de Angélica* when he was at sea with the Armada. The poem was probably inspired by the success of Luis Barahona de Soto's *Primera parte de la Angélica* (1586; first part of Angélica), and it clearly shows Lope de Vega's intention of following the steps of Ludovico Ariosto's *Orlando Furioso* (1516, 1521, 1532; English translation, 1591). The poem, divided into twenty cantos and written in royal octaves, presents

such a mixture of adventures and fantastic events that it ends up becoming a kind of Byzantine novel, wild and extravagant. The best parts of the poem are those that are based on Lope de Vega's personal experience, in which the passionate humanity of the poet reveals itself.

JERUSALÉN CONQUISTADA

Lope de Vega's next poetic effort, perhaps the greatest of all, was *Jerusalén conquistada* (Jerusalem regained), a rather long epic poem of six thousand stanzas divided into twenty cantos. He composed this work to emulate Torquato Tasso and also to correct Tasso's omission of the Spaniards in his *Gerusalemme liberata* (1581; *Jerusalem Delivered*, 1600). The poet incorporates here a legend that assumes that Alfonso VIII of Castile participated in the Third Crusade (1187-1192). Furthermore, Alfonso is presented in the foreground of the action after the fourth book, competing with and even overshadowing Richard the Lion-Hearted; thus, a disproportionate part of the poem is dedicated to someone who did not go to Palestine at all. Lope de Vega wrote this poem with unusual care, resulting in many beautiful passages. The author himself esteemed the work highly, as he told the duke of Sessa: ". . . it is something that I have written in my best age and with a different dedication from what I put into the writings of my youth, in which appetite prevailed over reason." In spite of this praise, Lope de Vega did not produce the great masterpiece he set forth to write. His intentions were to give Spain a national epic, doing for his country what Luís de Camões had done for Portugal with *Os Lusíadas* (1572; *The Lusíadas*, 1655). The poet, however, could not accommodate his genius to this enterprise, for, as Alborg says, "he was not able to sustain the solemnity and dignity of intonation that such a composition required." Instead, he assembled an amalgam of adventures, magicians, demons, and angels, much in the manner of a chivalric romance. In addition, he introduced material drawn from his personal life, portraying his mistress, Micaela de Luján, and their illegitimate children.

THE NEW ART OF WRITING PLAYS

In 1609, Lope de Vega published *The New Art of Writing Plays*, a didactic poem in which the playwright presents his formula for success in the theater. He had been writing plays for quite some time by then and had been involved in several controversies regarding his departure from the Aristotelian rules. A mature man of forty-seven, Lope de Vega expresses proudly what he considers to be the correct approach of his trade—that is, to please the common man. He advises playwrights to mix the tragic with the comic, as Nature does; to observe only the unity of action; to avoid an empty stage; to use a language appropriate to the speakers and to adjust the dialogue accordingly; to use different verse forms in accordance to the dramatic situation; to avoid obscure passages; to make the whole appear probable; and to use all the tricks of the trade.

Following the taste of the period, Lope de Vega also wrote several mythological poems, some of which appeared in 1621 with other short compositions. The nightingale in *La filomena* narrates the classical myth of Progne and Philomene in the first part, while the second part, written in *silvas*, portrays the poet, disguised as a nightingale, reciting a diatribe against the crow. "La Andrómeda" tells the fable of Andrómeda and Perseo, showing Gongoristic influences. In *La Circe*, Lope de Vega amplifies that episode of Homer's *Odyssey* (c. 725 B.C.E.; English translation, 1614) with the arrival of Ulysses at the island of Circe, his voyage to Hell, and the love between Polifemo and Galatea.

LA CORONA TRÁGICA AND LAUREL DE APOLO

In 1627, Lope de Vega published *La corona trágica* (the tragic crown), a five-thousand-line poem written in memory of Mary Stuart, Queen of Scots. Here once again, Lope de Vega reflects Spain's hatred for England and Queen Elizabeth, whom the poet addresses with repulsive and offensive names and likens to infamous women from the Bible and from mythology. On the other hand, Mary Stuart is presented as a pure martyr of the Catholic Church. It is a rather dull poem, but, as critic George Ticknor claims, "it savors throughout of its author's sympathy with the religious spirit of his age and country; a spirit, it should be remembered, which made the Inquisition what it was." Lope de Vega dedicated this poem to Pope Urban VIII, who, in turn, gave the poet a degree of doctor of divinity and the Cross of the Order of Saint John.

If his desire to emulate Tasso and Ariosto resulted in the composition of *Jerusalén conquistada* and *La hermosura de Angélica* respectively, the example of

Cervantes' *Viaje del Parnaso* (1614) inspired Lope de Vega to write his *Laurel de Apolo*. A seven-thousand-line poem divided into ten *silvas, Laurel de Apolo* is a catalog of nearly three hundred Spanish poets, as well as some Portuguese, Italian, and French authors and nine Spanish painters. Lope de Vega praises them all very freely, without much artistic discrimination; although he apologizes for possible unintentional omissions, there are some noticeable absences, such as Juan de la Cueva, Saint Teresa de Ávila, and Saint John of the Cross. The poem also presents Lope de Vega's ideas about writing poetry, discussing metrics, Italian influence and innovations, and many other topics. Following his well-established custom, the poet introduces some autobiographical notes.

GATOMACHIA

Near the end of his life, Lope de Vega wrote what is probably his best poetic composition, *Gatomachia*, a burlesque poem divided into seven *silvas* or *cantos*, which he published in 1634 in a miscellaneous volume under the pseudonym of Tomé de Burguillos. The work is a marvelous parody of the pedantic Renaissance epic, a genre that Lope de Vega himself had cultivated. It narrates the love affair of two cats, Micifuf and Zapaquilda, and the pretensions of a third one, Marramaquiz, who tries to seduce Zapaquilda with the help of the magician Garfiñanto. Marramaquiz fails, but during the wedding of the lovers, he kidnaps the bride and takes her to his castle. With the help of his friends, Micifuf captures the fortress, kills Zapaquilda's captor, and is reunited with his beloved; together, they live happily ever after. The tone of the poem is festive and light throughout, particularly the last two *silvas*, where Lope de Vega parodies both epic poets and traditional ballads, always with great success. Lope de Vega dedicated this work to his son, who would die before the book was published.

Lope de Vega used various verse forms in his poetic compositions, but he succeeded especially in two of them: the romance and the sonnet. The romances, or ballads, make up the first important group in Lope de Vega's poetic production. This traditional meter, derived from the epic, had become very popular during the poet's lifetime, as is attested by the publication of the anthology *Romancero general* in 1600 and 1604.

Lope de Vega found the lightness of the romance very much in consonance with his vibrant poetic genius, and he used it to poeticize, for example, his love for Elena Osorio, his libels against her family, and his marriage to Isabel de Urbina. In the fashionable Moorish and pastoral romances, he found a vehicle to express his intimacy, and, disguising his identity under fictional Moorish lovers or shepherds, he wrote some of the best examples of the genre. When the poet suffered a spiritual crisis after the death of his wife Doña Juana de Guardo, he also expressed his most fervent religious sentiments in this poetic form. Lope de Vega's romances became very popular in his own time, a popularity that has endured, for they have a special freshness that makes them readable even today.

Lope de Vega was also a master of the sonnet. He used it frequently in his plays and even jokes about composing one in the well-known "Soneto a Violante" ("Sonnet to Violante"), included in *La niña de plata* (pb. 1617; the stunning beauty). Lope de Vega took many of these sonnets out of his plays and published them in different collections. The first such collection, *Rimas*, contained two hundred sonnets, the majority of which are dedicated to Micaela de Luján; in the refinements and subtleties of *Rimas*, one can clearly see the influence of Petrarch. Lope de Vega's humanity transcends the artificial structure of the form, however, giving these poems a genuine depth of feeling. As Montesinos says, these sonnets "combine literary motifs of two or three generations of poets with Lope's personal experience. In this sense, they are, perhaps, his most characteristic poetic collection." Lope de Vega cultivated the sonnet during his entire life, leaving other collections of different tones, such as those published in *Rimas sacras* (sacred verses), in which the poet fuses his most noble and spiritual feelings with a very refined poetic technique.

OTHER MAJOR WORKS

LONG FICTION: *La Arcadia*, 1598; *El peregrino en su patria*, 1604 (*The Pilgrim: Or, The Stranger in His Own Country*, 1621); *Los pastores de Belén*, 1612; *Novelas a Marcia Leonarda*, 1621; *La Dorotea*, 1632.

PLAYS: *Los comendadores de Córdoba*, pb. 1609 (wr. 1596-1598); *La noche toledana*, pb. 1612 (wr. 1605); *El nuevo mundo descubierto por Cristóbal Colón*, pb. 1614 (wr. 1596-1603; *The Discovery of the New World by Christopher Columbus*, 1950); *Peribáñez y el comendador de Ocaña*, pb. 1614 (wr. 1609-1612; *Peribáñez*, 1936); *El duque de Viseo*, pb. 1615 (wr. 1604-1610); *El anzuelo de Fenisa*, pb. 1617 (wr. 1602-1608); *La dama boba*, pb. 1617 (*The Lady Nit-Wit*, 1958); *Los melindres de Belisa*, pb. 1617 (wr. 1606-1608); *La niña de plata*, pb. 1617 (wr. 1607-1612); *El villano en su rincón*, pb. 1617 (wr. 1611; *The King and the Farmer*, 1940); *El acero de Madrid*, pb. 1618 (wr. 1606-1612; *Madrid Steel*, 1935); *El mayordomo de la duquesa de Amalfi*, pb. 1618 (wr. 1599-1606; *The Majordomo of the Duchess of Amalfi*, 1951); *El perro del hortelano*, pb. 1618 (wr. 1613-1615; *The Gardener's Dog*, 1903); *Las flores de don Juan, y rico y pobre trocados*, pb. 1619 (wr. 1610-1615); *Fuenteovejuna*, pb. 1619 (wr. 1611-1618; *The Sheep Well*, 1936), *La corona merecida*, pb. 1620 (wr. 1603); *El verdadero amante*, pb. 1620 (wr. before 1596); *La buena guarda*, pb. 1621 (wr. 1610); *La hermosa Ester*, pb. 1621 (wr. 1610); *Lo cierto por lo dudoso*, pb. 1625 (wr. 1612-1624; *A Certainty for a Doubt*, 1936); *Amar sin saber a quién*, pb. 1630 (wr. 1620-1622); *El castigo sin venganza*, pb. 1635 (based on Matteo Bandello's novella; *Justice Without Revenge*, 1936); *El mejor alcalde, el rey*, pb. 1635 (wr. 1620-1623; *The King, the Greatest Alcalde*, 1918); *Los Tellos de Meneses I*, pb. 1635 (wr. 1620-1628); *El premio del bien hablar*, pb. 1636 (wr. 1624-1625); *Las bizarrías de Belisa*, pb. 1637; *El guante de doña Blanca*, pb. 1637 (wr. 1627-1635); *El caballero de Olmedo*, pb. 1641 (wr. 1615-1626; *The Knight from Olmedo*, 1961); *La moza de cántaro*, pb. 1646? (wr. 1625-1626); *Castelvines y Monteses*, pb. 1647 (wr. 1606-1612; English translation, 1869); *Four Plays*, 1936; *Five Plays*, 1961.

NONFICTION: *Égloga a Claudio*, 1637.

BIBLIOGRAPHY

Fox, Diane. *Refiguring the Hero: From Peasant to Noble in Lope de Vega and Calderón*. University Park: Pennsylvania State University Press, 1991. Fox examines the image of the hero and class status in the works of Lope de Vega and Pedro Calderón de la Barca. Includes bibliography and index.

Heiple, Daniel L. "Political Posturing on the Jewish Question by Lope de Vega and Faria e Sousa." *Hispanic Review* 62, no. 2 (Spring, 1994): 217. During the Spanish Inquisition, Lope de Vega wrote a poem celebrating the persecution of Jews. Manuel de Faria e Sousa, who shared Vega's anti-Semitic views, also wrote a sonnet in tribute to Vega. Their writings are examined.

McKendrick, Melveena. *Playing the King: Lope de Vega and the Limits of Conformity.* Rochester, N.Y.: Tamesis, 2000. An examination of Lope de Vega's portrayal of the monarchy in his works. Includes bibliography and index.

Samson, Alexander, and Jonathan Thacker, eds. *A Companion to Lope de Vega.* Rochester, N.Y.: Tamesis, 2008. A comprehensive treatment of the life and writings of Lope de Vega.

Wright, Elizabeth R. *Pilgrimage to Patronage: Lope de Vega and the Court of Philip III, 1598-1621.* Lewisburg, Pa.: Bucknell University Press, 2001. This study focuses on the patronage system and the interactions between politics and the life and work of Lope de Vega. Includes bibliography and index.

Juan Fernández Jiménez

VERGIL

Born: Andes, Cisalpine Gaul, near Mantua (now in Italy); October 15, 70 B.C.E.
Died: Brundisium (now Brindisi, Italy); September 21, 19 B.C.E.
Also known as: Virgil

PRINCIPAL POETRY
Eclogues, 43-37 B.C.E., also known as *Bucolics* (English translation, 1575)
Georgics, c. 37-29 B.C.E. (English translation, 1589)
Aeneid, c. 29-19 B.C.E. (English translation, 1553)

OTHER LITERARY FORMS
The greatness of Vergil (VUR-juhl) stems from his poetic works.

ACHIEVEMENTS
Vergil is considered by many to be the greatest poet of ancient Rome, and his influence reaches well into the modern era of Western poetry. Vergil mastered three types of poetry: pastoral (*Eclogues*), didactic (*Georgics*), and national epic (*Aeneid*). This mastery is reflected in the final words of his epitaph, "cecini pascua, rura, duces" ("I sang of shepherds, farmlands, and national leaders"). Vergil's fame was assured even in his own lifetime, as Tibullus, Sextus Propertius, and Horace praised and emulated him. His harshest critic was himself, and it was his dying wish that the unfinished *Aeneid* be destroyed. The emperor Augustus himself intervened, however, and the poem was rescued and edited by Varius and Tucca in 17 B.C.E. The works of Vergil influenced Ovid and Marcus Manilius, and Vergil's epic craft established a tradition that was followed by Lucan, Statius, Silius Italicus, and Valerius Piaccus. Writers of satire, epigram, and history, such as Juvenal, Martial, Livy, and Tacitus, also show the influence of Vergil's thought, language, and prosody. The first critical edition of the *Aeneid*, the work of Probus, appeared in the time of Nero, and the Verona scholia also record interpretations based on editions by Cornutus, Velius Longus, and Asper in the late second century C.E. By this time, the poetry of Vergil had become a school manual, used for teaching grammar, rhetoric, and language.

In the fourth and fifth centuries C.E., Nonius and Ambrosius Theodosius Macrobius discussed and quoted the works of Vergil. The tradition of *centos* soon arose, in which poets employed clever rearrangements of lines of Vergilian poetry to create poems with new meanings. The admiration of Vergil's works eventually approached a kind of worship, with the superstitious practice of consulting random lines of his poetry as one might consult an oracle.

Dante and John Milton both studied Vergil, and their great epics owe much to his works, especially the *Aeneid*. John Dryden called the *Georgics* "the best poems of the best poet"; Alfred, Lord Tennyson, described Vergil's hexameters as "the stateliest measures ever moulded by the lips of man."

Vergil's achievement is therefore enormous. He raised the dactylic hexameter to new levels of grandeur, he elevated the Latin language to new beauty, and he set new standards for three types of poetry. Perhaps his greatest achievement lies in the vision of the imperial grandeur of Rome depicted in the *Aeneid*.

BIOGRAPHY

Publius Vergilius Maro was born on October 15, 70 B.C.E., in Andes, an Italian town located near present-day Mantua. He was not born to Roman citizenship, but the franchise was later granted to his native province. His early education took place at Cremona and at Mediolanum, now called Milan. Like most promising young men of his era, Vergil eventually made his way to Rome, where he studied philosophy, rhetoric, medicine, and mathematics; he also completed preparation for the legal profession, although he spoke only once as an advocate. At this time, he also made the acquaintance of the poets who remained from Catullus's circle and absorbed from them the Alexandrian ideals of poetry. In 41 B.C.E., the farm belonging to Vergil's family was confiscated and given to the soldiers of Marc Antony. According to tradition, this personal catastrophe, referred to in eclogues 1 and 9, was remedied by Octavian himself (after 23 B.C.E., the emperor Augustus) in response to a personal appeal by Vergil, but many scholars believe the loss of the farm was permanent; the references in the *Eclogues* are subject to interpretation. It was during this period, from about 43 to 37 B.C.E., that Vergil wrote the ten *Eclogues*, working first in Northern Italy and later in Rome. The success of the *Eclogues* resulted in an introduction to Maecenas, Octavian's literary adviser, and this personal connection assured financial support for Vergil's literary activities and provided an entrée into the circle of Rome's best writers and poets.

In 38 or 37 B.C.E., Vergil met the great Roman poet Horace and arranged for Horace to meet Maecenas. It was at this time that the two poets and their colleagues, Varius and Tucca, participated in the famous journey to Brundisium described in Horace's *Satires* (35, 30 B.C.E.). From that point on, Vergil lived and wrote in Southern Italy, at a country house near Nola and at Naples. From 37 to 29 B.C.E., he worked slowly on the *Georgics*, a didactic poem in four books that instructs the reader in various aspects of agriculture

Vergil (Library of Congress)

and animal husbandry. Finally, in 29 B.C.E., Vergil began his greatest undertaking, the *Aeneid*, an epic poem that describes the journey of the hero, Aeneas, from the ruins of Troy to the west coast of Italy; in the poem, Aeneas's son Iulus is linked to the Julian clan from which the emperor Augustus claimed descent. The writing of this poem also proceeded laboriously. In 19 B.C.E., Vergil embarked on a journey to Greece and the East, during which he hoped to polish and revise his epic. During his journey, he fell ill at Megara; shortly after reaching Brundisium, the port city on the east coast of Italy that serves as the gateway to Greece, he died. He was buried at Naples, and his dying request for the unrevised *Aeneid* to be destroyed was fortunately countermanded by the orders of Augustus.

Little is known of the character of Vergil, except that he was a shy and reclusive man who never married. He was also of weak physical constitution, often ill. The main source of information about Vergil's life and character is the biography by Aelius Donatus, from the fourth century.

ANALYSIS

To understand more fully the poetry of Vergil, his works should be considered in the light of two relationships: his literary connection with the Greek poetry on which his works are modeled, and his personal and ideological connection with the builders of the Roman Empire. Vergil, like most Roman artists, worked within genres invented by the Greeks, but he also left on his works a uniquely Roman imprint. It was his great genius that he was able to combine both Greek and Roman elements so effectively.

ECLOGUES

Vergil's earliest major work was a group of ten short poems called the *Eclogues*, or the *Bucolics*. The poems are set in an idealized Italian countryside and are populated by shepherds. Vergil has clearly modeled the poems on the thirty idylls of Theocritus, a Greek poet of about 310 to 250 B.C.E. who lived primarily in Sicily. The *Eclogues* are, in fact, the most highly imitative of Vergil's three works, although the Roman element asserts itself clearly. In the first eclogue, which is one of the most Roman, Vergil tells of two shepherds, Tityrus and Meliboeus. Tityrus has retained his farm in the face of confiscation, and he relaxes among his sheep while Meliboeus, ejected from his fields, drives his weary livestock to new pastures. Tityrus expresses his gratitude to the young Octavian, whom he depicts as a god. Here, Vergil uses the Theocritean framework, but the content of the poem reflects Vergil's own private and public Roman experience. Eclogue 2, by contrast, follows Theocritus in both form and substance. Here, the shepherd Corydon bemoans his failure to win Alexis, imitating Polyphemus's lament of the cruelty of Galatea in the *Idylls* (third century B.C.E.). Similarly, the capping contest between shepherds Menalcas and Damon in Eclogue 3 closely follows Idylls 4 and 5.

Eclogue 4 is perhaps the most famous, as well as the most Roman. Here, the shepherd format has been abandoned. The poem honors the consulship of Vergil's early local patron, Asinius Pollio, during which the former governor helped negotiate the Treaty of Brundisium. Welcoming the hope of peace, Vergil predicts the coming of a new Golden Age. His ideas about the cycle of ages are based on a number of sources, including the Sybilline Books and the "ages of man" in

Hesiod. Because the new era of peace is here connected with the birth of a child, scholars of the Middle Ages believed that the poem held a messianic message, predicting the birth of Christ. Present-day scholars disagree about the identity of the young child: Some argue that Vergil refers here to the children of Pollio, who were born around this time, while others believe that the poem expresses hope for the future offspring of Mark Anthony and Octavia, or perhaps of Octavian and his new wife, Scribonia. In any case, the language of the eclogue is sufficiently vague to preclude any clear identification.

Eclogue 5 returns once again to the Theocritean format: Two shepherds, Mopsus and Menalcas, engage in a contest of amoebaean verse (poetry written in the form of a dialogue between two speakers). They sing of the death and deification of Daphnis, also a shepherd, and in so doing they reprise the song of Idyll 1. Eclogue 6 maintains the pastoral theme: Two shepherds catch Silenus (a mythological woodland deity with horses' ears and tail) and induce him to sing of the world's creation and other legends. The preface to this poem, however, deals with more Roman matters: Vergil dedicates the poem to Varus, the man who succeeded Pollio as legate in the region of Vergil's birthplace. Apparently the new legate had urged the poet to write an epic; here the poet demurs. Eclogue 7, like Eclogues 2, 3, and 5, adheres to the Theocritean model: Melliboeus tells of a contest between shepherds Thyrsis and Corydon.

Eclogue 8, like Eclogue 4, is dedicated to Pollio. Two shepherds sing an amoebaeic: Damon grieves over the faithlessness of Nisa, and Alphesiboeus sings of a young woman's attempts to secure the love of Daphnis by magic charms. The latter topic has as its model Idyll 2 of Theocritus, but the ethos is Roman. Eclogue 9 returns to the farm confiscations discussed in Eclogue 1. Shepherd Moeris has been ejected from his farm; shepherd Lycidas expresses surprise, since he had thought that the poetry of Menalcas (Vergil's persona) had secured the safety of all the farms of the region. The collection concludes with Eclogue 10, in which Gallus (a real-life Roman) grieves for the loss of an actress named Lycoris.

Critics agree that these poems, although very artificial, are exercises that show the power of a great poet early in his development. Eclogues 2, 3, 5, and 7, among the first written, follow the Theocritean model rather closely, working within the conventionalized framework of the pastoral genre. Other eclogues introduce matters closer to Vergil's life and times, such as the farm confiscations dealt with in Eclogues 1 and 9 (and alluded to in 6) and the problems of Gallus in Eclogue 10. Eclogue 6 offers the promise of greater works to come, and this promise is redeemed first in the *Georgics* and later in the *Aeneid*.

GEORGICS

The *Georgics* comprise four books of dactylic hexameter verse on the subject of farming and animal husbandry. The basic Greek model is Hesiod's *Works and Days* (c. 700 B.C.E.); however, Vergil's sources for the *Georgics* also include the Alexandrian scientific poets and the Roman Epicurean poet, Lucretius. The *Georgics* are very Italian, and the Hesiodic model provides only a form and an outline: The poet distances himself from his model to a much greater degree than in the *Eclogues*. Vergil's own words suggest that Maecenas, the great Augustan literary patron, suggested the subject matter of this poem. Augustus's vision of the new order, the Pax Romana, had as its cornerstone a revival of "old Roman" virtues, religion, and the simple agrarian life. The *Georgics*, then, aimed to present the simplicity and beauty of Italian country life as an important element of Augustus's new empire. Once again, Vergil is working with a Greek model and Roman ideas, but in the *Georgics*, the model is less intrusive and the Italian element predominates.

Book 1 of the *Georgics* deals with the farming of field crops and the relationship of weather and constellations to this pursuit. Vergil stresses the importance of Jupiter and of Ceres, the goddess of agriculture. Near the end of the book, the discussion of weather phenomena leads the poet to a description of the ominous cosmological omens that accompanied the assassination of Julius Caesar in 44 B.C.E.; Vergil closes the book by expressing his hope that Augustus will save Rome and by expressing his regret that years of civil war have prevented the people of Italy from peacefully farming their lands.

In book 2, Vergil treats the matter of vines and trees, especially the olive tree. He instructs the reader on the propagation, growth, planting, and tending of these plants. Technical discussions of soils, vines, and proper seasons are included, and here the Hesiodic and Alexandrian models are evident, although not predominant. Praise for the agriculture of Italy leads to praise of the country as a whole, and then of its chief, Augustus. The book concludes with a paean to the life of the farmer, especially as contrasted with the life of war. The themes of Augustus's new order find eloquent voice.

Book 3 of the *Georgics* takes up the subject of cattle and their deities. At the beginning of the book, Vergil tells the reader that Maecenas urged the writing of the *Georgics*, and Vergil also promises future works in praise of Augustus and Rome. Following these literary comments, the poet once again turns to technical matters: care of broodmares, calves, and racing foals; the force of love among animals; sheep and goats; and the production of wool, milk, and cheese. A discussion of disease in sheep leads into the very famous and poignant description of the plague, based on similar passages in Lucretius and Thucydides.

In book 4, Vergil turns to the subject of bees and beekeeping. He discusses the location of hives, the social organization of bees, the taking of honey, and the very ancient practice of obtaining a new stock of bees by using the carcass of a dead animal. The book closes with the stories of Aristaeus and Arethusa, and finally of Orpheus.

The matter of sources, then, is much more complex in the *Georgics* than in the *Eclogues*. The *Georgics* reveals a wide variety of sources and a poet who is more confident and thus more willing to depart from his models. Vergil's relationship to Maecenas, Augustus, and the new Roman order manifests itself both in the overall intent of the poem and in specific passages. The artificial landscape of the *Eclogues* yields to the reality and beauty of the Italian countryside.

AENEID

The final and most important work of Vergil's career was the twelve-book hexameter epic called the *Aeneid*. Vergil wished to pay homage to the great Greek epics of Homer—the *Iliad* (c. 750 B.C.E.; English translation, 1611) and the *Odyssey* (c. 725 B.C.E.; English translation, 1614)—and Apollonius Rhodius (the

Argonautica, third century B.C.E.; English translation, 1780), but Vergil also sought to create a work that would supplant the work of Ennius and glorify the Rome of his own day and its leader, Augustus. The solution lay in telling the mythological story of Aeneas, a Trojan hero who fought on the losing side in the great Trojan War. Homer mentions that Aeneas was purposefully rescued by the gods, and a firm post-Homeric tradition told of the hero's subsequent journey to Italy. Vergil, then, would tell the story of Aeneas's travels and of the founding of the Roman race, and in so doing would remain close to the Homeric era; at the same time, prophetic passages could look forward to the Rome of Vergil's lifetime, and the poem overall would stress Roman virtues and ideals. In the figure of Aeneas, Vergil had discovered the perfect transition from the Homeric world in which epic was rooted to the Augustan era of his own day.

The first six books tell of the wandering journey of Aeneas and his men from Troy to the western coast of Italy, a voyage that was impeded by false starts, the anger of the goddess Juno, and Aeneas's own fears, hesitations, and weaknesses. Vergil chose as his basic model for these books Homer's *Odyssey*, also a tale of wandering. Since books 6 through 12 of the *Aeneid* describe the battles between Aeneas and the Italic tribes that opposed him, the poet here emulated the *Iliad*, an epic of war. Indeed, the opening phrase of the *Aeneid*, "I sing of arms and of the man" ("Arma virumque cano"), sets forth this two-part plan very clearly.

Book 1 begins with an introduction in which Vergil states his aim: He will tell of the deeds and sufferings of Aeneas, a man driven by destiny, whose task is to found the city of Rome in the face of strong opposition from Juno, the queen of the gods, whose anger is rooted in past insults (the judgment of Paris, the rape of Ganymede) as well as future offenses (the defeat of Carthage by Rome) of which the gods have advance knowledge. The actual narrative begins not at Troy but in medias res. Aeneas and his Trojan remnant are off the coast of Sicily, about to sail to Italy, when Juno conspires with Aeolus to cause a storm at sea. When the hero finally appears for the first time, he is cold and frightened, wishing that he had died at Troy. It is at once obvious that Aeneas is no courageous Homeric hero, but a man

who must learn through difficulty to understand obedience to destiny and dedication to duty—the very Roman quality of *pietas*, or piety. Indeed, the first six books of the epic demonstrate Aeneas's growing maturity and piety, which increase as he comes to understand fate's grand plan for the future of Rome.

Neptune soon intervenes, calming the wild seas; this act is described in terms of a unique simile—Neptune and the seas are compared to a statesman using words to calm a rebellious mob—which surely is a vague allusion to the great Augustus ushering in an era of peace on the heels of decades of civil war. Aeneas's party finds harbor in North Africa, and the scene quickly changes to Olympus, where Venus complains bitterly to Jupiter about the way her son is being treated. The king of the gods responds with a prophecy: He tells of Aeneas's Italian wars; of the founding of Alba Longa by Aeneas's son Iulus (also called Ascanius); of Romulus and Remus; of the boundless future empire; of Julius Caesar; and, finally, of the new era of peace. Augustus is not explicitly named, but the final lines refer to his Pax Romana, the era of Roman peace. In the short term, Jupiter arranges for Aeneas to receive a warm welcome in Carthage in the person of Queen Dido. Dido's history is related, and it is remarkably similar to that of Aeneas: She, too, is the widowed leader of a group of refugees, from Tyre, and her people have found their new home, which they are building happily, like bees in summer. The leaders meet, and their mutual sympathy is soon deepened through the machinations of Venus and Cupid; Dido falls in love with Aeneas.

Dido arranges a welcoming banquet for her guests, and after dinner Aeneas agrees to tell the story of the fall of Troy, his escape, and his subsequent wanderings in the Mediterranean basin. Books 2 and 3, then, constitute a flashback, the device also used in the *Odyssey*. In these books, Vergil adheres more clearly to his sources than elsewhere in the epic. Book 2, which relates the fall of Troy, relies on the epic cycle, of which only fragments have survived to modern times. Aeneas loses his wife, Creusa, but he escapes carrying his father, Anchises, on his shoulders, bearing the household gods, and holding his son, Ascanius, by the hand. The stories of Laocoön and Cassandra, the death of Priam, and the figure of Helen all derive from the Greek tradition, but Aeneas's ultimate acceptance of destiny and the picture of his devotion to father and son serve to underline ideals and values that are distinctly Roman. Book 3, the narrative of Aeneas's wanderings, contains many episodes based on the *Odyssey* and a few that come from Apollonius. The Trojans make several erroneous attempts to find their new homeland, but omens and progressively clearer prophecies keep them on the track of destiny. Aeneas is warned by Helenus to seek further prophetic information in Italy from the Cumaen Sibyl. The monsters of Greek epic appear, interspersed with more realistic episodes. The book concludes with the most painful incident of all, the death of Anchises. Thus, Aeneas concludes his recollection of the past, a narrative based on the Greek models but heavily laden with Roman ideas of destiny, perseverance, and devotion to duty.

Book 4, perhaps the most famous in the *Aeneid*, tells of the ill-fated love of Dido and Aeneas. Dido's frenzied emotion is pitted against Aeneas's growing *pietas*. Drawing on book 3 of Apollonius's *Argonautica*, Vergil tells the tragic tale. Fire and wound imagery convey Dido's passion in a subjective manner. Through the machinations of the goddesses, the two leaders find themselves driven by a rainstorm, which interrupts a formal hunt, to the same cave. Here they enjoy a sexual union that Vergil surrounds with perverted wedding imagery. Aeneas and Dido live together openly, but only Dido perceives the relationship as a marriage. Aeneas has made no lasting commitment, and worse, the outside world is offended by their conduct. Iarbas, an earlier and unsuccessful suitor of Dido, prays to Jupiter for satisfaction; as a result, Mercury is dispatched to remind Aeneas of his duty. Aeneas at first tries to hide his impending departure, but this fails, and the confrontation that follows does not change the hero's mind. Obeying the call of destiny, Aeneas leaves Carthage. Dido has lost her self-respect and the respect of her people and their neighbors. She commits suicide on a pyre, abandoning her kingdom and her sister Anna. Roman virtue has defeated the passion of the foreign queen, and Aeneas has triumphed over his own weaknesses.

Book 5 describes the funeral games for Anchises and is clearly based on book 23 of the *Iliad*. Like Homer, Vergil uses the games to show his hero in the role of leader and judge. Later in the book, a mutiny of the women in Aeneas's party, incited by Juno, is put down, but most of the ships are burned. A portion of the party elects to remain in Sicily, and Aeneas's father appears in a night vision, urging him to come to the underworld. The book closes with the death of the helmsman Palinurus, which offers a fitting transition to book 6, the narrative of Aeneas's journey to the underworld.

Aeneas arrives at Cumae, meets the Sibyl, and hears a short-term prophecy of events in Italy: He will marry a new wife, but there will be more bloodshed, and Juno will continue to hinder Aeneas's progress. Before Aeneas can descend to the underworld, there are lengthy preliminaries, perhaps aimed at emphasizing the difficulty of a mortal's descent to Hades: Aeneas must obtain the golden bough, a sign of fortune's favor; he must perform the requisite sacrifices; and he must bury his dead comrade Misenus. Finally, Aeneas is permitted to descend to an underworld based largely on book 11 of the *Odyssey*, as well as on folk tradition. After encountering the traditional creatures of the underworld, including the ferryman Charon, Aeneas meets a succession of three figures from his past, beginning with the most recent: First, there is Palinurus the helmsman; next, in the Fields of Mourning, Aeneas finds the silent Dido, who turns away from the hero to the comfort of her first husband, Sychaeus; and, finally, Deiphobus, a Trojan warrior, describes his own death amid the sack of Troy. Through these three encounters, Aeneas makes his peace with the past, an essential preparation for his greeting of the future later in the book. An interlude follows, during which the Sibyl describes Tartarus, the place where the guilty are punished; here again, Vergil relies on Homer and folk tradition.

Aeneas moves on to the Elysian fields and a tearful reunion with Anchises. This portion of the book has many different sources, among them Lucretius's Epicureanism, Pythagorean doctrines of the transmigration of souls, Platonism, and Orphism. Here, mythology yields to history and philosophy. Anchises explains the future to Aeneas, but this prophecy is more detailed than any thus far. Moreover, Anchises is able to illustrate his words by showing Aeneas the souls of the great future Romans as they line up for eventual ascent to the upper world. Here, in the exact center of the epic, a powerful passage reiterates the history of Rome as future prophecy. The Alban kings and Romulus enter the account, and then the chronological order is interrupted for the highly emphatic introduction of Augustus himself: It is predicted that he will renew the Golden Age in Latium, and elaborate phrases describe the new boundaries of the Roman Empire under his rule. Aeneas is reminded that his own courage is needed if all this is to come about.

The history lesson now resumes with the early Roman kings who followed Romulus—Numa, Tullius, Ancus Marcius—and then the Tarquin kings from Etruria. The heroes of the early Republic, such as Brutus and Camillus, follow, and then the chronology is once again interrupted for the introduction of Caesar and Pompey and an admonishment against the evils of civil war. The list of Romans resumes with Mummius, Aemilius Paulus, and other great warriors; the emphasis here is on those whose victories expanded the Empire. Anchises closes with a generalized description of the fields of endeavor in which Romans will achieve greatness—sculpture, oratory, and astronomy—but he isolates leadership and government as the unique responsibility of Rome toward the world. One last shade remains to be named, and that is Marcellus, Augustus's nephew and heir, who showed great promise but died very young. Aeneas then departs from the underworld, through the gate of sleep, taking with him a new and more complete understanding of Roman destiny and his duty to fulfill that destiny; his growth as a man is complete, and in the remaining books he fights an enemy who is purely external.

Book 7 begins the "Iliadic" portion of the *Aeneid*, which describes the war in Latium; Vergil marks the new subject with a second invocation to the Muse and calls his new subject "a greater theme" and "a greater labor." Avoiding Circe's island, the Trojans sail the coast and enter the Tiber River. The mood is tranquil and calm as Vergil introduces the new cast of characters: King Latinus, an older man, who has one child; his daughter Lavinia, much sought after as a wife; Queen Amata; and Turnus, a Rutulian king and relative of Amata, and Amata's preferred choice among Lavinia's

suitors. The omens, however, argue against Turnus and in favor of a heretofore unknown foreign prince. The Trojans, meanwhile, have disembarked on the banks of the Tiber, where a serendipitous omen makes clear that they have, at long last, found their future home. Aeneas and his men are received warmly by Latinus, who offers both alliance and the hand of Lavinia; the Latin king has some understanding of fate and of his own role in Rome's destiny.

The founding of Rome, however, is not so easy a task: Aeneas's relentless enemy, Juno, greets the happy welcome and the new alliance with rage. She searches out Allecto, a gruesome Fury, and sends her to kindle the anger of Amata, using a snake to stir up the queen's emotions. Amata passionately opposes the alliance, the marriage, and the slight to Turnus; she is compared to a top, a madly spinning child's toy, and she passes her fury on to the other matrons of Latium. Allecto moves on to infect Turnus with jealousy, hatred, and lust for war. Once again, Roman piety is opposed by *furor* (passion), here represented by Allecto, Amata, and Turnus; the main symbols of *furor* are snakes and fire—as used earlier in connection with Dido's passion. Still, Allecto's work is not yet complete: She virtually assures the coming of war by inducing Iulus, Aeneas's son, to wound a stag which is the favorite of a girl called Silvia. Silvia summons the men of the region, and the conflict bursts into armed struggle. Latinus withdraws into his palace, and Juno takes the final irrevocable step of forcing open the gates of the temple of Janus, nothing less than formal declaration of war. (Vergil's own times witnessed the closing of those gates, an event that Augustus saw as his greatest achievement.) The book concludes with a catalog of the Latin allies: the impious Mezentius and his son Lausus; Camilla, a female warrior patterned after Penthesilea, the Amazon fighter and Trojan ally described in the epic cycle; and Turnus himself, decked out for war. The catalog, a Homeric device, introduces the characters who will fight in the books that follow, thereby increasing interest in future events. Thus concludes the book which began so differently, on a tranquil note of sunrise, the Tiber, alliance, and betrothal.

Aeneas must also seek allies for the imminent battle, and to that end he sails up the Tiber to Etruria. This journey and the visit with King Evander provide the subject for book 8. En route to Etruria, the omen of the white sow marks for Aeneas the future site of Rome. When the Trojans arrive, they find Evander's people celebrating an ancient feast in honor of the victory of Hercules over the brigand Cacus. Vergil devotes many lines of verse to the retelling of this tale, partly because it conforms to the Augustan theme of civilization overcoming savagery, and partly because Aeneas must learn and assume the customs of Italy as he leaves his Trojan past behind him. Evander offers his guests a brief tour of the area, pointing to future Roman landmarks and discussing the history and lore of central Italy. The Etruscan also provides background information about Mezentius and agrees to an alliance with Aeneas, sending a contingent of warriors led by his own son, Pallas.

In the meantime, Aeneas's mother, Venus, has urged her husband, Vulcan, god of fire and metalworking, to create arms for Aeneas. Vergil follows Homer (in *Iliad*, book 18) in offering a lengthy description of his hero's shield, but whereas the Homeric shield depicted scenes of the human condition, universal in their implication, Aeneas's weapon offers a lesson in Roman history: Ascanius is depicted with his offspring; the wolf suckles Romulus and Remus; the Romans carry off the Sabine women; Romulus and Tatius make peace; Horatius and Manlius perform their heroic exploits; and Rome's enemies are punished in Hades. In the center of the shield is depicted the raging Battle of Actium, the naval conflict of 31 B.C.E. in which Augustus (then Octavian) defeated Mark Anthony while Antony's foreign wife, Cleopatra, fled; the gods of war surrounded the scene. Other panels show Augustus celebrating his triumph and consecrating temples that honor the far-flung boundaries of his empire. Aeneas does not understand everything on the shield, but he lifts it high, signaling his willingness to take on the responsibility of Rome's destiny.

Book 9 is contemporaneous with book 8, describing events in Latium during Aeneas's absence. Iris, Juno's messenger, inflames Turnus to begin the battle: They attack the Trojan fleet. At the urging of Cybele, the mother goddess, the ships are rescued and metamorphosed into sea nymphs. The frightened Rutulians withdraw, ending the day of battle. That night, Nisus and Euryalus, two Trojans bound by special friendship, volunteer to cross enemy lines to reach Aeneas. In a scene based on the *Iliad*, book 10, the night raid ends in catastrophe: Both are killed, although their mutual devotion prevails even in the face of death. Cruel Turnus beheads the two Trojans and impales the heads on pikes as prizes of battle, much to the despair of Euryalus's mother. As the battle continues, Ascanius prevails, killing the insolent Numanus; Turnus, too, enjoys a moment of glory, killing Pandarus, before he escapes by leaping into the Tiber. The book is very reminiscent of the *Iliad* in its gory battle descriptions, but Vergil adds his own imprint with a series of wild animal similes.

Book 10 opens with a council of the gods: Venus and Juno bicker, and Jupiter refuses to take sides. Back in Latium, the weary Trojans are cheered by the return of Aeneas, who brings with him Evander's men and a host of Etruscan allies. The battle resumes, led by Turnus, Mezentius, and Mezentius's son Lausus on the side of Latium, and Aeneas, Pallas, and Iulus on the side of Troy. Turnus kills Pallas and puts on his sword belt, spurring Aeneas to furious deeds of battle; Aeneas's rage at Turnus, however, is frustrated by Juno, who removes Turnus from the battle. In a confrontation with Mezentius, Aeneas kills Lausus and then the repentant Mezentius himself, promising first to bury his enemy. The material of the book is again very Iliadic, but the compassion of Aeneas for friend and foe alike and the emphasis on the father-and-son relationship are very Roman.

Book 11 begins with a truce, during which Evander poignantly receives the corpse of his son, and both sides mourn their dead. The Latins hold a council of war, and it is reported that Diomedes, a Greek hero now living in Italy, will not aid their cause: The years at Troy have made him weary of war, and he respects the renowned piety of Aeneas. A rancorous discussion between Turnus and the Latin Drances is interrupted by the news that Aeneas and his allies are on the march. The battle now resumes, with Turnus guarding the city while the warrior maiden Camilla advances against the cavalry. Camilla excels in battle but is mortally wounded by Arruns; Opis, a nymph attending Diana, avenges Camilla's death, killing Arruns.

In book 12, Turnus, now wounded, speaks with Latinus. He pleads for an opportunity to face Aeneas in single combat. Amata and Lavinia weep, and Latinus favors appeasement, but Turnus and Aeneas agree to a duel. Aeneas prays, divulging his plan for equality of Trojans and Latins and respect for Latin custom. But the compact for single combat is broken when Juturna, a nymph and sister of Turnus, incites the Rutulians and one of them hurls a javelin. Aeneas is wounded as he shouts for both sides to remain calm and respect the truce, but the battle erupts, and Aeneas, now a martyr to the cause of peace and respect for law, is healed by his mother and soon returns to the fray. When the battle reaches the walls, Amata, believing Turnus to be dead, kills herself. As the conflict approaches its climax, Jupiter and Juno reach an agreement: Juno will withdraw from the battle and cease her harassment of the Trojans, and the newly unified nation of Trojans and Latins will be called Latins, using Latin language and Latin dress. Juno will be worshiped and honored by the pious new nation. Juturna, too, withdraws from the conflict, and Aeneas confronts Turnus. The Rutulian is wounded and he surrenders all claim to Lavinia. Aeneas is moved by Turnus's words of acceptance, but a glance at Pallas's sword belt, now worn by Turnus, spurs him to deliver the mortal blow. The epic closes with the flight of Turnus's shade to the world of the dead.

Book 12 completes the portrait of Aeneas as the personification of Roman leadership: He is strong yet compassionate; he obeys and upholds the law; his victory promises to spare the conquered and honor their laws and customs. The confused Trojan fugitive of book 1 has made his peace with his Trojan past and has evolved into a pious, devoted, and progressive leader—a symbol of the glory of Augustan Rome. Turnus, too, commands respect in this book. He possesses all the natural vigor of primitive Italy, which, once harnessed by just government, provides an important component of Roman greatness.

The works of Vergil are thus characterized by a creative tension between deference to Greek models and allegiance to Roman history and values. In the *Eclogues*, Vergil was still striving to find the correct balance, but in the *Georgics* and in the *Aeneid*, he skillfully infused the old Greek forms with the moods and themes of his own day. Augustus's new vision of peace and empire found eloquent expression in the timeless hexameters of Rome's greatest poet.

BIBLIOGRAPHY

Comparetti, Domenico. *Vergil in the Middle Ages*. Translated by E. F. M. Benecke. 1985. Reprint. Princeton, N.J.: Princeton University Press, 1997. This book remains the classic treatment of Vergil's literary legacy showing how it influenced both education and literature for centuries. It is still the best discussion of Vergilian bibliography available. A respected scholarly source.

Hardie, Philip R. *Virgil*. New York: Oxford University Press, 1998. Offers interpretation and criticism of the *Aeneid* and the *Georgics*.

Jenkyns, Richard. *Vergil's Experience, Nature, and History: Times, Names, and Places*. New York: Oxford University Press, 1998. This large-scale work concerns itself with examining Vergil's ideas of nature and historical experience as compared with similar ideas throughout the ancient world. Jenkyns also discusses the influence of Vergil's work on later thought.

Levi, Peter. *Virgil: His Life and Times*. New York: St. Martin's Press, 1999. This notable work by a leading classics scholar places Vergil in the context of his times.

Martindale, Charles, ed. *The Cambridge Companion to Virgil*. New York: Cambridge University Press, 1997. Twenty-one essays (including the editor's introduction) are divided into four sections covering the translation and reception of Vergil's works, his poetic career, historical contexts, and the content of his thought. Includes numerous bibliographies.

Morwood, James. *Virgil: A Poet in Augustan Rome*. New York: Cambridge University Press, 2008. Part of the Classical Civilization series, this work explains the poet through excerpts of his three works.

Otis, Brooks. *Virgil: A Study in Civilized Poetry*. Norman: University of Oklahoma Press, 1995. Excellent work that argues for Vergil as a sophisticated poet who presented mythic, well-known material in a new and meaningful style to his urban readers.

Perkell, Christine, ed. *Reading Vergil's "Aeneid": An Interpretive Guide*. Norman: University of Oklahoma Press, 1999. Contains several essays covering various aspects of the work on a book-by-book basis. The editor also provides an introduction discussing the work's historical background and themes. Several essays on such topics as influences and characters conclude this fine study.

Ross, David O. *Virgil's "Aeneid": A Reader's Guide*. Boston: Blackwell, 2007. An accessible guide to the *Aeneid* that also discusses Vergil's life and times, and Homer's influence on his writing. There are six chapters, an appendix and indexes.

Rossi, Andreola. *Context of War: Manipulation and Genre in Virgilian Battle Narrative*. Ann Arbor: University of Michigan Press, 2004. An excellent study of Vergil's use of allusion to Homer's text in the *Aeneid*. This work points to the classical elements integral to the structure and narrative of the *Aeneid*, while demonstrating the synthesis of these elements into a new form.

Laura M. Stone

ÉMILE VERHAEREN

Born: Saint-Amand, Belgium; May 21, 1855
Died: Rouen, France; November 27, 1916

PRINCIPAL POETRY

Les Flamandes, 1883
Les Moines, 1886
Les Soirs, 1887
Les Débâcles, 1888
Les Flambeaux noirs, 1890
Les Apparus dans mes chemins, 1891
Les Campagnes hallucinées, 1893
Les Villages illusoires, 1895
Les Villes tentaculaires, 1895
Les Heures claires, 1896 (*The Sunlit Hours*, 1916)
Les Visages de la vie, 1899
Petites Légendes, 1900 (*Little Legends*)
Les Forces tumultueuses, 1902
Toute la Flandre, 1904-1911 (includes *Les Tendresses premières*, 1904; *La Guirlande des dunes*, 1907; *Les Héros*, 1908; *Les Villes à Pignons*, 1909; and *Les Plaines*, 1911)
Les Heures d'après-midi, 1905 (*Afternoon*, 1917)
La Multiple Splendeur, 1906
Les Rythmes souverains, 1910
Les Heures du soir, 1911 (*The Evening Hours*, 1918)
Les Blés mouvants, 1912
Poems of Émile Verhaeren, 1915
Les Ailes rouges de la guerre, 1916
The Love Poems of Émile Verhaeren, 1916

OTHER LITERARY FORMS

Émile Verhaeren (vur-HAH-ruhn) wrote several plays, one of which, *Les Aubes* (pb. 1898; *The Dawn*, 1898), was immediately translated into English by Arthur Symons. In the early 1880's, Verhaeren's art criticism, which was published in journals, had a considerable impact, popularizing Impressionism in Belgium. Throughout his life, he continued to produce criticism, treating Low Country painters of the past as well as evaluating artists of his own day. In view of Verhaeren's deep interest in aesthetics and art history, it is no wonder that students of his poems have consistently viewed them in the light of painting and graphics.

ACHIEVEMENTS

Émile Verhaeren's literary reputation has suffered a steady decline since his death. Very popular and highly regarded in his lifetime, commanding both a large readership and respect from such demanding critics as Paul Valéry, he is virtually unread today. Nevertheless, Verhaeren is among Belgium's preeminent poets, and his works, though out of fashion, are of great historical value, reflecting diverse and even contradictory aesthetic trends of his time. A naturalist, a Symbolist, a proto-expressionist, Verhaeren was above all a poet with a passionate faith in humanity.

BIOGRAPHY

Émile Verhaeren was born on May 21, 1855, in Saint-Amand, in the vicinity of Antwerp. During his schooling at the Jesuit College of Sainte-Barbe in Gand

(Ghent), he was to form friendships with three others who were destined to make their mark in Belgian literature: Georges Rodenbach, Maurice Maeterlinck, and Charles van Lerberghe. These men became aware of the Symbolist ferment that was going on in France and was beginning to filter across the borders to Belgium. Verhaeren, in his youth, had been influenced by the works of Alphonse de Lamartine, from whom he gained an appreciation for the purely musical possibilities of poetry, and of Victor Hugo, from whom he learned the skill of arranging poetic collections into architectonic wholes. A reluctant law student at the University of Louvain, Verhaeren gave himself over to a debauched life that was later to contribute crucial motifs to his first important poetic collection. It was also in Louvain that he began to publish poetry. Called to the bar in Brussels in 1881, he came into contact with a group of artists and writers known as Young Belgium. In Brussels, he developed a deep enthusiasm for the visual arts as well as a new political awareness. Under the influence of the Young Belgium group, Verhaeren abandoned the practice of law and devoted himself to art criticism and to the creation of a highly visual style of poetry.

Always extremely sensitive, Verhaeren suffered a nervous breakdown in 1887. His mental illness inspired a series of highly personal poems based on psychological self-revelations. Part of his emotional trauma had stemmed from a confrontation with the urban squalor of fin de siècle London. He was soon to be reconciled, if only in part, to the inextricable combination of good and evil in the technological revolution that was transforming the cities and, by degrees, the European countryside. A series of travels on the Continent gave him a new breadth of vision as well as deepening his interest in social problems. It was during this time, in 1891, that Verhaeren became an active Socialist. He formed a close friendship with the leader of Belgium's Labor Party and gave lectures at the Université Libre at the party's newly established Maison du Peuple at Brussels. Besides actively working for voting and parliamentary reforms, he assisted in the publication of a radical journal, *La Société nouvelle*.

An internationalist in a time of divisive nationalism, Verhaeren formed close friendships with people all over Europe, including Romain Rolland, Jules Romains,

Rainer Maria Rilke, and Stefan Zweig—indeed, the latter was to write an important critical biography of Verhaeren. Verhaeren met the not-so-brave new world of the twentieth century with a refreshing sense of optimism, an optimism that distinguished him from the late Symbolists with whom he is often associated. His happy marriage to Marthe Massin reinforced his positive vision and gave him a desperately needed stability.

Verhaeren's vision was not, as too many critics would have it, a naïve, otherworldly optimism. His was a hard-won hopefulness, tempered by the harsh realities of suffering and exploitation that had inspired his political convictions. Nevertheless, nothing in his experience had prepared him for the horrors of World War I, which destroyed his lifelong faith in humanity. Verhaeren and his wife took refuge in England and Wales, and the poet sought to aid his beleaguered country and exiled compatriots with a flood of verse and of prose, including *Les Ailes rouges de la guerre* (the red wings of war), *La Belgique sanglante* (1915; *Belgium's Agony*, 1915), and *Parmi les cendres* (1916; amid the ashes). During a return to France, he was killed in an accident at the Rouen train station.

ANALYSIS

Émile Verhaeren's first collection of poetry, *Les Flamandes* (the Flemish), was a propitious beginning. While it contained a considerable strain of naturalism, derived from the French novelist Émile Zola and from the Belgian poet Camille Lemonnier, *Les Flamandes* was an unusually accomplished performance for a first work. The collection demonstrates Verhaeren's ability to convey a sense of both the vitality and the brutality of life by means of a harsh diction and a dynamic rhythm; it also reveals his painterly gift for visual imagery.

"THE PEASANTS"

Of this collection of poems, the introductory section to "Les Paysans" ("The Peasants") is the most often anthologized. The poem consists of an introduction followed by three sections, all four parts making a complete statement or picture in itself. Verhaeren's pictorial sense, as well as his interest in art history and its influence on his poetry, is apparent in the first line of "The Peasants," in which Jean-Baptiste Greuze, the eighteenth century genre painter, is mentioned. Greuze is known for his highly sentimentalized vision of the peasants; in the words of Verhaeren, "Ces hommes de labour, que Greuze affadissait/ Dans les molles couleurs de paysanneries" ("These men of labor, which Greuze romanticized/ In pale colors of the rustic scene"). Verhaeren goes on to describe how beautiful these paintings looked amid the rococo decor of a Louis-Quinze salon. With this devastating reference to the leading icon maker of the myth of the happy peasant, Verhaeren constructs in this work the very illusion he seeks to shatter. He concludes the opening lines of this poem with a scathing dismissal of this myth: "Les voici noirs, grossiers, bestiaux—ils sont tels" ("They are dull, coarse, bestial—all that").

In the nineteenth century, the myth of the peasant as revolutionary, which was created in the eighteenth century by the events of the French Revolution, pervaded the political scene, despite the fact that the peasants repeatedly showed themselves to be the mainstay of conservative, even Royalist, governments. Verhaeren observes that ill-educated people are unable to formulate a larger view of history and the world. They know nothing beyond their village, fearing and cheating all strangers. Ironically, it is their sons who provide the soldiers for the nationalistic entities that are beyond their comprehension. The only political reality that can attract their dull sense is "le roi, l'homme en or, fait comme Charlemagne" ("the king, the man in gold, looking like Charlemagne"). A progressive republic is beyond their grasp; if given the vote, they use it to elect glorious anachronisms such as Louis Napoleon. Country people, according to Verhaeren, are completely unable to take up the revolutionary activities that begin in the cities of Europe:

Et s'ils ont entendu rugir, au loin, les villes,
Les révolutions les ont tant effrayés,
Que, dans la lutte humaine, ils restent les serviles,
De peur, s'ils se cabraient, d'être un jour les broyés.

And if they hear the distant roar of urban
Revolutions they are so afraid
That, amid the human struggle, they remain servile
From fear that if they arose they would be brutally
    put down.

The three sections of "The Peasants" present three tableaux of country life among the poor. First, a village is described with its row of thatched cottages. The poet says of the peasants who live there that they are victims of harsh labor and climate. Second, a kitchen is portrayed with the meticulous attention to detail that characterizes Dutch or Flemish still lifes. The third and longer section, bringing the work to a colorful close, is a series of descriptions of the peasants' *kermesses* ("fairs"), where brutal merrymaking prevails. The view of the peasants in the three sections follows the naturalistic theory that peasants are only human beasts. The sections are three concrete pieces of naturalistic documentation, supporting the generalizations of the introduction. The whole is saved from dullness by the rich allusions to paintings by Peter Brueghel and other Dutch masters and by the lively rhythm, which threatens to fracture the confines of the Alexandrine.

"THE MILL"

Verhaeren's mental breakdown resulted in a trilogy of collections: *Les Soirs* (the evenings), *Les Débâcles* (the collapses), and *Les Flambeaux noirs* (the black torches). These are personal psychological confessions of the poet. The poems are, as one might expect, dark and often morbid.

A representative and often excerpted poem from *Les Soirs* is "Le Moulin" ("The Mill"), a poem that again demonstrates Verhaeren's painterly instincts. "The Mill" evokes, in vivid color and sharply delineated details, a winter landscape dominated by a windmill. The purple sail of the mill stands out against the gray sky. A few huts are set before the reader in carefully chosen details such as the following: "Une lampe de cuivre éclaire leur plafond/ Et glisse une lueur aux coins de leur fenêtre" ("A copper lamp illuminates their ceiling/ And slips a gleam to the corners of their windows").

"The Mill" also demonstrates, however, what John Ruskin called the pathetic fallacy, projecting human emotions onto nature. While certainly evocative in its details, "The Mill" is by no means an exercise in purely objective description. The poet has projected his depressed state onto the scene; for example, the daylight is said to be "suffering" and "Les nuages sont las" ("the clouds are tired"). The manic-depressive oscillations of

"The Mill" are typical of many of Verhaeren's mood pieces.

TWO TRILOGIES

Between 1890 and 1910, when Verhaeren's attentions turned to social issues, he produced two trilogies that are breathtaking in their all-encompassing scope. The first includes *Les Campagnes hallucinées* (the deluded countries), *Les Villages illusoires* (the illusory villages), and *Les Villes tentaculaires* (the tentacular cities); the second trilogy consists of *Les Visages de la vie* (the aspects of life), *Les Forces tumultueuses* (tumultuous forces), and *La Multiple Splendeur* (the multiple splendor). These works demonstrate a turning away from a subjective fixation on the self toward a new objectivity in dealing with the world. They are informed by a strong faith in human progress, but this optimism is not unmixed: Verhaeren never forgets the darker side of the new machine age.

Les Villages illusoires is one of Verhaeren's most popular works and one of his most carefully designed collections. The pieces that constitute it alternate between detailed realistic descriptions of various types of workmen going about their activities and quiet mood pieces that describe natural phenomena and that offer interludes between scenes of dynamic, often frenetic, activity.

"THE SNOW"

The most often anthologized poem of this collection is "La Neige" ("The Snow"), one of the atmospheric interludes. This lyric paints a melancholy winter scene not unlike that of "The Mill." The continuous snow is not merely described; its falling is compared in texture to the craft of weaving: "La neige tombe indiscontinûment/ Comme une lente et longue et pauvre laine" ("The snow falls without pause/ Like slow and long and paltry wool"). The monotony of the image is paralleled in the repetitive, almost droning, recurrence of *n*, *m*, and *l* sounds and the redundancy of three adjectives joined by the repeated *et* (and). Repetition, in fact, dominates the poem—lines 2 through 4, for example, all rhyme (*laine*, *plaine*, and *haine*). Words such as *neige*, *tombe*, and *monotone* recur like verbal leitmotifs. The phrase "la morne et longue et pauvre plaine" of the third line is repeated verbatim in the twenty-fifth line. Sometimes rhymes are replaced by a more evocative series of half rhymes or assonances (for example: *des âmes*, *et diaphane*, *sans flamme*, and *les cabanes*).

"The Snow," too easily dismissed as a formalistic virtuoso piece, must be viewed in the larger context of *Les Villages illusoires* if it is to be understood properly; conceived in sweeping designs and rendered with broad strokes, the collection is rather like a single panel from Peter Paul Rubens's great ceilings in the Banqueting House in London or the Jesuit Church in Antwerp. It is this sweeping, Whitmanesque vision that characterizes Verhaeren's verse at its best, rewarding readers who explore his neglected oeuvre.

OTHER MAJOR WORKS

SHORT FICTION: *Five Tales of Émile Verhaeren*, 1924.

PLAYS: *Les Aubes*, pb. 1898 (*Dawn*, 1898); *The Plays of Émile Verhaeren*, pb. 1916.

NONFICTION: *La Belgique sanglante*, 1915 (*Belgium's Agony*, 1915); *Parmi les cendres*, 1916.

MISCELLANEOUS: *Oeuvres d'Émile Verhaeren*, 1914 (includes all of his poetry and prose).

BIBLIOGRAPHY

Friedman, Donald Flanell, ed. *An Anthology of Belgian Symbolist Poets*. New York: Peter Lang, 2003. Contains selections by Verhaeren. Introduction describes Symbolist poetry in Belgium and places Verhaeren in historical context.

Jones, P. Mansell. *Verhaeren*. 1926. Reprint. Cardiff: University of Wales Press, 2000. A short biographical study of Verhaeren's life and work. Includes a bibliography.

Thum, Reinhard H. *The City: Baudelaire, Rimbaud, Verhaeren*. New York: Peter Lang, 1994. A comparative critical study of the works of Verhaeren, Charles Baudelaire, and Arthur Rimbaud. Includes bibliographical references and index.

Zweig, Stefan. *Émile Verhaeren*. 1914. Reprint. Charleston, S.C.: BiblioBazaar, 2008. Zweig worked for Verhaeren as a translator, biographer, and publicist. He had a very high regard for Verhaeren's life-affirming poetry.

Rodney Farnsworth

PAUL VERLAINE

Born: Metz, France; March 30, 1844
Died: Paris, France; January 8, 1896

PRINCIPAL POETRY

Poèmes saturniens, 1866

Fêtes galantes, 1869 (*Gallant Parties*, 1912)

La Bonne Chanson, 1870

Romances sans paroles, 1874 (*Romances Without
    Words*, 1921)

Sagesse, 1881

Jadis et naguère, 1884

Amour, 1888

Parallèlement, 1889, 1894 (English translation,
    1939)

Bonheur, 1891

Chansons pour elle, 1891

Femmes, 1891 (English translation, 1977)

Liturgies intimes, 1892

Élégies, 1893

Odes en son honneur, 1893

Épigrammes, 1894

Dans les limbes, 1894

Chair, dernière poésies, 1896

Invectives, 1896 (English translation, 1939)

Hombres, 1903 (English translation, 1977)

Selected Poems, 1948

Femmes/Hombres, 1977 (includes English
    translation of *Femmes* and *Hombres*)

OTHER LITERARY FORMS

Most of the other published works of Paul Verlaine
(vehr-LEHN) are autobiographical writings and critical articles on contemporary poets. During his lifetime,
he published two plays that were performed—*Les Uns
et les autres* (pr. 1884; the ones and the others) and *Madame Aubin* (pr. 1886)—and one short story, *Louise
Leclercq* (1886). A collection of seven other short stories, *Histories comme ça* (1903; stories like that), was
published posthumously.

The most significant of his critical writings were
published under the title *Poètes maudits* (1884; *The
Cursed Poets*, 2003), which includes articles on Tristan

Corbière, Arthur Rimbaud, Stéphane Mallarmé, Vil-
liers de L'Isle-Adam, and others. Verlaine's *Confessions* (*Confessions of a Poet*, 1950) was published in
1895. Many of his previously unedited writings were
published posthumously in a 1903 edition of his works,
which includes several autobiographical pieces as well
as some original ink drawings. All his prose works
were published in the 1972 Pléiade edition.

ACHIEVEMENTS

Paul Verlaine is universally recognized as one of the
great French poets of the nineteenth century. His name
is associated with those of his contemporaries Charles
Baudelaire, Rimbaud, and Mallarmé. His most famous
and frequently anthologized poems, such as "Chanson
d'automne" ("Song of Autumn"), "Mon rêve familier"
("My Familiar Dream"), "Clair de lune" ("Moonlight"),
and "Il pleure dans mon coeur" ("It Is Crying in My
Heart"), are readily recognized and often recited by
persons with any knowledge of French poetry. Many of
his poems, including those cited, have been set to music
by serious composers.

Verlaine's admirers include both saints and sinners,
for Verlaine is at once the author of one of the most
beautiful collections of religious poetry ever published
and the writer of some explicitly erotic poems. During
his lifetime, Verlaine's poetic genius was recognized
by only a handful of poets and friends. His penchant
for antisocial and occasionally criminal behavior (he
was jailed twice for potentially murderous attacks) undoubtedly contributed to his lack of commercial success or popular recognition during his lifetime. By the
end of his life, he had gained a small measure of recognition and received some income from his royalties and
lecture engagements.

BIOGRAPHY

Paul Marie Verlaine was born in Metz, France, on
March 30, 1844, the only child of Captain Nicolas-
Auguste Verlaine and Elisa Dehée Verlaine. The fam-
ily moved often during Verlaine's first seven years, un-
til Captain Verlaine retired from the army to settle in
Paris. Verlaine attended the Lycée Bonaparte (now
Condorcet) and received his *baccalauréat* in 1862.

Verlaine's adoring mother and equally adoring older

Paul Verlaine (Library of Congress)

cousin Elisa Moncomble, whose death in 1867 affected him profoundly, spoiled the sensitive child, encouraged his demanding capriciousness, and helped him become a selfish, immature, unstable young man.

After his *baccalauréat*, he worked in an insurance office and then found a clerical job in municipal government, which he kept until 1870. In 1863, he published his first poem, "Monsieur Prudhomme." He met Catulle Mendès, an editor of the literary magazine *Le Parnasse contemporain*, in which Verlaine published eight poems. In 1866, he published his first volume of poetry, *Poèmes saturniens*, and in 1869, a second volume, *Gallant Parties*.

Alcoholism began to take its toll on his personal life. Twice in drunken rages, he threatened to kill his mother. His family tried to marry him to a strong-willed cousin, a fate that he avoided by proposing to Mathilde Mauté, whom he married in 1870 and who inspired his third volume of poetry, *La Bonne Chanson*.

Having served as press officer to the Commune of Paris during the 1870 insurrection, Verlaine subsequently fled Paris and lost his government job. He helped to found a new journal, *La Renaissance*, in which he published many of the poems included in his 1874 volume, *Romances Without Words*.

Verlaine's drinking and his friendship with Rimbaud led to violent domestic scenes. Following several fights and reconciliations with Mathilde, Verlaine ran off to Brussels with Rimbaud in July, 1872. During the following year, the two poets lived together in Brussels and London and then returned to Brussels. On July 10, 1873, Verlaine, in a drunken rage, fired a revolver at Rimbaud, who had threatened to leave him. Verlaine was convicted of armed assault and sentenced to two years in prison.

In prison, Verlaine converted to a mystical form of Roman Catholicism and began to write the poems for the volume *Sagesse*, published in 1881. After his release in 1875 and until 1879, he held teaching positions in England and France. He formed a sincere and probably chaste relationship with one of his students, Lucien Létinois. They attempted a joint farming venture, which failed, and then returned to Paris, where Verlaine tried to get back his old government job but was turned down because of his past record. This disappointment, coupled with the sudden death of Létinois in 1883, caused Verlaine to become profoundly discouraged.

After another ill-fated farming venture, Verlaine abandoned himself for a long period to drinking and sordid affairs. A drunken attack on his mother cost him a month in prison in 1885. During his last ten years, his economic distress was somewhat eased by his growing literary reputation. He continued writing and published several more significant volumes of verse.

From 1890 to his death in 1896, Verlaine moved in and out of several hospitals, suffering from a swollen, stiffened leg, the terminal effects of syphilis, diabetes, rheumatism, and heart disease. He lived alternately with two women who cared for him and exploited him. During his last years, he was invited to lecture in Holland, Belgium, and England.

ANALYSIS

In two articles on Baudelaire published in *L'Art* in 1865, Paul Verlaine affirms that the overriding concern of a poet should be the quest for beauty. Without denying the role of inspiration and emotion in the process of poetic creation, Verlaine stresses the need to master them by poetic craftsmanship. Sincerity is not a poetic virtue. Personal emotion must be expressed through the combinations of rhyme, sound, and image that best create a poetic universe in which nothing is the result of chance.

The most obvious result of Verlaine's craftsmanship is the musicality of his verse. Sounds flow together to create a sonorous harmony that repetitions organize and structure as in a musical composition. In his 1882 poem "L'Art poétique," Verlaine gives a poetic recipe that begins with the famous line, "Music above everything else." He goes on to counsel using odd-syllabled lines, imprecise vocabulary and imagery (as if veiled), and nuance rather than color. The poet should avoid wit, eloquence, and forced rhyme. Poetic verse should be light and fugitive, airborne and slightly aromatic. The poem ends with the somber warning, "Anything else is literature."

The subject matter of Verlaine's carefully crafted poetry is frequently his personal experience, certainly dramatic and emotionally charged material. The prologue to *Poèmes saturniens* reveals his consciousness of his miserable destiny. Throughout the rest of his poetry, he narrates the various permutations of his self-fulfilling expectation of unhappiness. "Moonlight," which serves as a prologue to his second volume of verse, presents gallant eighteenth century lovers "who don't appear to believe in their happiness." This skepticism clouds the fugitive moments of happiness throughout Verlaine's poetic pilgrimage. *La Bonne Chanson* is Verlaine's homage to marital bliss. Poem 17, filled with images of love and faithfulness, begins and ends with the question, "Isn't it so?" Poem 13 ends with a similar worry: "A vain hope . . . oh no, isn't it so, isn't it so?" In *Sagesse*, which proposes Roman Catholic mysticism as the ultimate form of happiness, the fear of a return to his old ways haunts the poet's peaceful communion with God.

Because sex, love, God, and wine all fail to provide a safe haven from his saturnine destiny, Verlaine must seek another refuge. What he finds, perhaps not entirely consciously, is sleep. With surprising frequency the final images of Verlaine's poems are images of sleep; many of his musical pieces are thus lullabies whose delicate, soothing images—from which color, laughter, pompousness, loudness, and sharpness have been banished—lead the poet's battered psyche to the unthreatening harbor of sleep. Often, a maternal figure cradles the poet in his sleep or stands by watchfully. In many poems in which the sleep motif is not explicit, the imagery subsides at the end of the poem, leaving an emptiness or absence analogous to the oblivion of sleep.

POÈMES SATURNIENS

Verlaine's first volume of poetry, *Poèmes saturniens*, was published by Lemerre in November, 1866, at the author's expense. It drew very little critical or popular attention. The title refers to the astrological contention, explained in the prologue, that those like Verlaine who are born under the sign of Saturn are doomed to unhappiness, are bilious, have sick, uneasy imaginations, and are destined to suffer.

The volume is the work of a very young poet, some of the poems having been written as early as 1861. They are consequently of uneven quality, but among them is the poem "My Familiar Dream," which is perhaps the most frequently anthologized of all Verlaine's poems and which, according to Verlaine's friend and admirer H. Suquet, the poet preferred to all his others. It is a haunting evocation of an imaginary woman who loves the poet, who understands him, and who is capable of soothing his anguish.

The central section of the volume, titled "Paysages tristes" ("Sad Landscapes"), contains the poems most typical of Verlaine: vague, melancholy landscapes, inspired by his memories of the Artois region, whose fading colors, forms, and sounds reflect the poet's soul and whose ultimate disappearance translates as an innate desire for oblivion.

The first of these poems, "Soleils couchants" ("Setting Suns"), a musical poem of sixteen five-syllable lines, describes a rising sun so weakened that it casts a sunset-like melancholy over the fields, inspiring strange raddish ghosts in the poet's imagination. The short, odd-syllabled lines create a musical effect reinforced by alliteration and repetition—the phrase "setting suns," for example, is repeated four times in a poem about dawn.

"Promenade sentimentale" ("Sentimental Walk")

presents a twilight scene through which the wounded poet passes. The vaguely lit water lilies that glow faintly through the fog in the evening light are swallowed up by the shroudlike darkness in the poem's final image.

"Nuit du Walpurgis classique" ("Classical Walpurgis Night") is full of allusions. Phantoms dance wildly throughout the night in a landscape designed by Johann Wolfgang von Goethe, Richard Wagner, Antoine Watteau, and André Le Nôtre. At dawn's approach, the Wagnerian music fades and the phantoms dissolve, leaving "absolutely" nothing except "a correct, ridiculous, charming Le Nôtre garden." Another noteworthy tone poem, "Song of Autumn," a melodic eighteen-line lyric composed of four- and three-syllable lines, combines *o*'s and nasal sounds to reproduce a melancholy autumn wind that carries off the mournful poet like a dead leaf.

Verlaine's first collection of verse reveals the influence of Baudelaire, Victor Hugo, Charles-Marie Leconte de Lisle, Théodore de Banville, and Théophile Gautier—and of Verlaine's young friends Louis de Ricard and Joseph Glatigny. It is a carefully crafted and original volume, demonstrating that at the age of twenty-four, Verlaine had already mastered the art of poetry and discovered most of the themes of his later works.

GALLANT PARTIES

The mid-nineteenth century's rediscovery of the paintings of Watteau is confirmed by several works dedicated to that artist and to his times, including one by the Edmond de Goncourt and Jules de Goncourt, *L'Art du dix-huitième siècle* (1859-1875; *French Eighteenth Century Painters*, 1948), which undoubtedly had a strong influence on Verlaine's choice of this subject and his interpretation of it. During the composition of the poems of *Gallant Parties*, Verlaine undoubtedly consulted some of the published reproductions of Watteau's works as well as his one painting in the Louvre collection, *Embarkation for Cythère*, a vast work devoted to eighteenth century gallantry, its rites, costumes, myths, poetry, and fashionable devotees. These aristocratic gallants and the characters from *The Italian Comedy*, also painted by Watteau, come alive in Verlaine's second published volume of poetry.

The often-anthologized "Moonlight" opens the volume and sets the mood. This musical evocation of the songs and dances of the masked characters and the relationship between their costumes and their souls insist on the underlying sadness of both. The gallant aristocrats are somewhat sad beneath their fantastic disguises because they do not really believe in the love and life of which they sing. Their dispersed song is absorbed by the moonlight.

These same characters sing, dance, walk, skate, and love through the rest of the volume, sometimes assuming stock character names from commedia del l'arte—Pierrot, Clitandre, Cassandre, Arlequin, Colombine, Scaramouche, and Pulcinella—and sometimes classical names—Tircis, Aminte, Chloris, Eglé, Atys, and Damis.

The landscapes of *Gallant Parties* are very different physically and psychologically from those of the *Poèmes saturniens*. They are sculpted, landscaped, arranged, and peopled. Paths are lined by rows of pruned trees and mossy benches. Fountains and statues are harmoniously placed around well-kept lawns. The relationship between the characters and the landscape is no longer a natural sympathetic mirroring. Nature has been artificially subdued to reflect the characters' forced gaiety and becomes a mocking image of the vanity of their pursuits. One of the obvious formal characteristics of the volume is the presence of dialogue and monologue, couched in the artificial, erotic language of gallantry. There are many allusions to "former ecstasies," "infinite distress," and "mortal languors."

The volume's overriding pessimism is orchestrated by the arrangement of the poems. The latent sadness of the apparently carefree gallants in "Moonlight" becomes the dominant feeling in the second half of the work. While humorous love play and inconsequential erotic exchanges dominate the first half, several disturbing images—such as the statue of a snickering faun who anticipates eventual unhappiness and the sad spectacle of a statue of Cupid overturned by the wind—foreshadow the volume's disastrous conclusion, the poem "Colloque sentimentale" ("Sentimental Colloquium"), in which a ghostly "form" tries to recall a past sentimental adventure. The cold, solitary park, witness to the scarcely heard dialogue, swallows up the desperate efforts to recall a past love as well as the negations of those efforts. One of the lovers tries unsuccessfully to awaken memories of their past love, which the other negates repeatedly: "Do you remember our former ecstasy?" "Why do you want me to remember it?" "Does your heart still beat at the sound of my name?" "No."

ROMANCES WITHOUT WORDS

The Franco-Prussian War of 1870 and the Commune separated Verlaine from his Parnassian friends and led him toward new friendships and a new form of poetry, toward a modernistic vision that replaced the artificiality of Parnassian inspiration with an attempt to capture the essence of contemporary life. During 1872 and 1873, Verlaine wrote the poems of *Romances Without Words*, which was published in 1874. All the poems precede the episode with Rimbaud that resulted in Verlaine's imprisonment. The period was emotionally difficult for Verlaine. Torn between love for Mathilde and dependence on Rimbaud, Verlaine was tormented by his vacillations. *Romances Without Words* fuses his new poetic ideal with his personal struggle.

The sad, lilting songs that make up the first part of the volume, titled "Ariettes oubliées" ("Forgotten Melodies"), include one of the most frequently quoted of Verlaine's poems, "It Is Crying in My Heart," in which the gentle sound of the rain falling on the town echoes the fall of tears within his heart. A more interesting poem, however, is the musical twelve-line poem "Le Piano que baise une main frêle" ("The Piano Kissed by a Fragile Hand"), in which the light, discreet melody rising from the piano corresponds to the faintness in the fading evening light of the visual impression of slight hands on a barely discernible piano. A series of vague, fleeting adjectives seep out of the perfumed boudoir to disappear through a slightly opened window into a small garden. The hushed sonorities of the poem coincide with the diminished intensity of the images. One remarkable phrase in the tenth line embodies both the musical effects and the characteristic tone of Verlaine's verse: "fin refrain incertain" ("delicate, uncertain refrain").

While the influence of music on Verlaine's poetry is certain, the importance of painting is no less significant. *Gallant Parties* is to a great extent a tribute to the painting of Watteau. The "Paysages belges" ("Belgian Landscapes") that Verlaine paints into *Romances Without Words*, are a tribute to the Impressionist school of painting, whose birth corresponds with the date of composition of the collection. Verlaine knew Édouard Manet and Ignace Henri Fantin-Latour and was certainly interested in their technique. The Impressionistic Belgian landscapes that Verlaine has painted are carefree and happy, carrying no reflection of the shadow of Mathilde that haunts the rest of the volume. The first poem in the section, "Walcourt" (a small, industrial town in Belgium), reflects the gaiety of the two vagabond poets (Verlaine and Rimbaud) in a series of brightly colored images that flash by, without help of a verb, in lively four-syllabled lines: tiles and bricks, ivy-covered homes, and beer drinkers in outdoor bars.

The gaiety of the Belgian countryside is interrupted by a bitter poem, "Birds in the Night" (original title in English), which Verlaine had first titled "La Mauvaise Chanson" ("The Bad Song") as an ironic counterpart to his previous book of poems, *La Bonne Chanson*, devoted to marital bliss. "Birds in the Night" accuses Mathilde of a lack of patience and kindness as well as of treachery. The suffering poet offers his forgiveness. The poem suggests a singular lack of understanding of the real causes of their marital discord.

The last section of *Romances Without Words* contains visions of Verlaine's London experience, but the image of Mathilde pierces through the local color with haunting persistence. All six of the poems have English titles. The most interesting is "Green," in which the poet presents to his mistress fruits, flowers, leaves, branches, and then his heart, which he commends to her care. The poem ends with the desire for a restful oblivion on the woman's bosom.

SAGESSE

Only seven of the poems in *Sagesse* were actually composed while Verlaine was in prison. The rest were written between the time of his release in 1875 and the spring of 1880. The title refers to Verlaine's intention to live virtuously according to the principles of his new faith and should perhaps be translated not as "wisdom" but as "good behavior." The volume is divided into three parts, the first of which dwells on the difficulty of converting to a virtuous life, the almost daily battles with overwhelming temptation. The second part narrates the poet's mystic confrontation with God, primarily through a cycle of ten sonnets. The last part describes the poet's return to the world and contains many of the themes and images of his earlier nature poetry. These poems are not overtly religious; the prologue to this part, "Désormais le sage, puni" ("Henceforth, the Virtuous, Punished"), explains the virtuous poet's return to a contemplative love of nature.

Poems 6 and 7 of the first part, both sonnets, are the most poetic of Verlaine's evocations of the contrast between his former and his present preoccupations. Poem 6 presents his former joys as a line of clumsy geese limping off into the distance on a dusty road. Their departure leaves the poet with a welcome emptiness, a peaceful sense of abandonment as his formerly proud heart now burns with divine love. Poem 7 warns of the prevailing appeal of the "false happy days" that have tempted his soul all day. They have glowed in his memory as "long hailstones of flame" that have symbolically ravaged his blue sky. The last line of the poem exhorts the poet's soul to pray against the storm to forestall "the old folly" that threatens to return.

Three of the most moving poems of the third part were written in prison, one on the very day of Verlaine's sentencing: "Un Grand Sommeil noir" ("A Great Black Sleep"). This poem, as well as "Le Ciel est, pardessus le toit" ("The Sky Is, Beyond the Roof") and "Gaspard Hauser chante" ("The Song of Kaspar Hauser"), sings of the poet's despair, plaintively expressing his self-pity, his regrets, and his total sense of shock in the early days of his imprisonment. The third part of *Sagesse* also contains two of Verlaine's most finely crafted sonnets. "L'Espoir luit comme un brin de paille dans l'étable" ("Hope Glistens Like a Blade of Straw in a Stable") is perhaps his most Rimbaudian and most obscure poem. An unidentified protector speaks to the poet reassuringly as he rests in a country inn. The voice is maternal and encourages the poet to sleep, promising to cradle him. The voice shoos away a woman whose presence threatens the poet's rest. The poem opens and closes with a fragile image of glistening hope, which, in the final line, opens up into a hoped-for reflowering of the roses of September.

The sonnet "Le Son du cor" ("The Sound of the Hunting Horn") is perhaps the best example of Ver-laine's poetic art. It was written before his imprisonment, probably in the spring of 1873. This very musical poem blends the sound of the hunting horn, the howling of the wind, and the cry of a wolf into a crescendo that subsides to a mere autumn sigh as the falling snow blots out the last colors of the setting sun. The painful notes of the opening stanza are completely obliterated as day gives way to a cradling, monotonous evening.

Other major works

SHORT FICTION: *Louise Leclercq*, 1886; *Histoires comme ça*, 1903.

PLAYS: *Les Uns et les autres*, pr. 1884; *Madame Aubin*, pr. 1886.

NONFICTION: *Poètes maudits*, 1884 (*The Cursed Poets*, 2003); *Mes hôpitaux*, 1891; *Quinze jours en Hollande*, 1892; *Mes prisons*, 1893; *Confessions*, 1895 (*Confessions of a Poet*, 1950); *Les Mémoires d'un veuf*, 1896; *Charles Baudelaire*, 1903; *Critiques et conférences*, 1903; *Souvenirs et promenades*, 1903; *Voyage en france par un français*, 1903.

Bibliography

Blackmore, A. M., and E. H. Blackmore, eds. *Six French Poets of the Nineteenth Century: Lamartine, Hugo, Baudelaire, Verlaine, Rimbaud, Mallarmé*. New York: Oxford University Press, 2000. This anthology of poetry is preceded by an introduction, notes on text and translations, a select bibliography, and a chronology. Contains poems by and background information on Verlaine.

Ivry, Benjamin. *Arthur Rimbaud*. Bath, Somerset, England: Absolute Press, 1998. A biography of Rimbaud that details his two-year affair with Verlaine. Ivry delves deeply into the relationship, especially its sexual aspects, including possible dalliances with other men, misogynist outbursts, and graphically sexual poems.

Lehmann, John. *Three Literary Friendships: Byron and Shelley, Rimbaud and Verlaine, Robert Frost and Edward Thomas*. New York: Henry Holt, 1984. An examination of the way these friendships influenced each poet's work. Verlaine and Arthur Rimbaud each produced more poetry after their relationship.

Lepelletier, Edmond Adolphe de Bouhelier. *Paul Verlaine: His Life, His Work*. Translated by E. M. Lang. New York: AMS Press, 1970. The only English translation of the hefty 1909 biography.

Nicolson, Harold George. *Paul Verlaine*. 1921. Reprint. New York: AMS Press, 1997. This venerable biography remains useful.

Robb, Graham. *Rimbaud: A Biography*. New York: W. W. Norton, 2001. This biography of Arthur Rimbaud contains discussion of his affair with Verlaine, including the altercation at its end.

Sorrell, Martin. Introduction to *Selected Poems*, by Paul Verlaine. 1999. Reprint. New York: Oxford University Press, 2009. Sorrell's introduction is useful for beginning students in this bilingual edition of 170 newly translated poems by Verlaine.

Whidden, Seth Adam. *Leaving Parnassus: The Lyric Subject in Verlaine and Rimbaud*. Amsterdam: Rodopi, 2007. Notes the influence of Parnassian poetry on Verlaine and Arthur Rimbaud, even as they departed from it. One multichapter section is devoted to various aspects of Verlaine's poetry.

Paul J. Schwartz

ALFRED DE VIGNY

Born: Loches, France; March 27, 1797
Died: Paris, France; September 17, 1863

PRINCIPAL POETRY

Poèmes, 1822
Eloa, 1824
Poèmes antiques et modernes, 1826, 1829, 1837
Les Destinées, 1864

OTHER LITERARY FORMS

Apart from the evidence of the poetry itself, nowhere is there more certain testimony that, as a literary artist, Alfred de Vigny (veen-YEE) considered himself, first and foremost, a poet than in the posthumously published *Le Journal d'un poète* (1867; a poet's diary). Given its well-chosen title by Vigny's friend and literary executor, Louis Ratisbonne, the journal is a kind of mixed personal and literary diary covering the years from 1823 to 1863. Along with entries on personal events and philosophical observations are extensive notes on Vigny's reading and on his literary projects. The latter, many of which are but germs of ideas for works that were never developed or completed, are predominantly concerned with poetry.

In the France of the early nineteenth century, however, it was drama, not poetry or fiction, which was considered the true proving ground of literary merit, and the establishment of the Romantic movement was largely accomplished "on the boards." Vigny played no small part in this task, two of his dramatic works being considered watersheds in the history of the Romantic theater. The first of these was the premiere of Vigny's *Le More de Venise* (1829; the Moor of Venice), a translation of William Shakespeare's *Othello, the Moor of Venice* (pr. 1604), which helped pave the way for the more sensational success of Victor Hugo's *Hernani* (English translation, 1830) at the Comédie-Française in 1830. The second work was the three-act prose drama *Chatterton* (pr., pb. 1835), which developed the popular theme of the poet, the man of genius, persecuted by an uncomprehending, materialistic society. The sensational first performance of *Chatterton* was the greatest public triumph not only in Vigny's career, but also in that of the female lead, the celebrated actress Marie Dorval, who was Vigny's mistress. Vigny's two other works for the stage were composed as display pieces for Dorval: *La Maréchale d'Ancre* (pr. 1831) and the one-act *Quitte pour la peur* (pr. 1833).

Vigny produced one historical novel, *Cinq-Mars: Ou, Une conjuration sous Louis XIII* (1826; *Cinq-Mars: Or, A Conspiracy Under Louis XIII*, 1847); an "experimental" novel, *Stello* (1832); two novel fragments, *L'Alméh* (1831), concerning Napoleon Bonaparte's invasion of Egypt, and *Daphné* (1912), an account of Julian the Apostate; and a work that some consider one of the masterpieces of nineteenth century French fiction, *Servitude et grandeurs militaires* (1835; *The Military Necessity*, 1919), a collection of three stories depicting the soldier's life and exploring the meaning of military experience.

Achievements

Alfred de Vigny's literary output is remarkably small, particularly in comparison with that of most of his contemporaries. Moreover, his reputation in France (he is virtually unknown in the English-speaking world) rests almost exclusively on three works: the drama *Chatterton*, the collection of stories *The Military Necessity*, and the posthumous verse collection *Les Destinées*. Nevertheless, Vigny is ranked by general consensus as one of the four great poets of French Romanticism, along with Alphonse de Lamartine, Alfred de Musset, and Hugo. Vigny consciously set himself apart from these contemporaries to find a distinct, individual style not bound to any literary "school," and the very inclusion of his name in this quartet extends one step further the already misty, indeterminate boundaries of the term "Romantic."

Vigny, by temperament and discipline, stood in dramatic contrast to his contemporaries. He was incapable of the lyric effusion of Lamartine, the confessional tones of Musset, the technical *brio* or the self-proclaimed "voice of the people" attitude of Hugo. Vigny's verse is predominantly sober, dry, and spare; he had no taste for the verbal display that characterized Hugo's collection *Les Orientales*, 1829 (*Les Orientales: Or, Eastern Lyrics*, 1879), and although Vigny had a genius for scene setting, he was rarely sidetracked by the details of the purely picturesque.

Vigny's greatest contribution to the poetry of his time was the introduction of a measure of more profound and more consistent thought than that of any of his major contemporaries. His virtual innovation of the *poème philosophique* provided a new form in an age drunk with delight in the adaptation of forms from the past (such as the epic, and the lyric forms of the elegy and ode). Vigny was the "thinker" among the Romantics (which in no way implies that he was an original or significant philosopher), and it is perhaps not so much for his individual works as for the quality and content of his thinking as a whole that he is remembered. His ideas concerning the role of the person of genius in society, the relationship between humans and God, and the significance of human effort and existence were the inheritance he bequeathed to the artists who followed him, Théophile Gautier, Charles Baudelaire, Charles-

Marie Leconte de Lisle, Stéphane Mallarmé, and Albert Camus among them. Vigny's output was slight, his works of genius even smaller in number, but without Vigny, there would be a tremendous intellectual gap in the flow of modern French letters.

Biography

Alfred Victor, Comte de Vigny, led an essentially quiet, uneventful life in an age noted for the turbulent, sometimes melodramatic lives of its political and artistic figures. He was largely a private man, with a personality of many seeming contradictions. Deeply religious, he subscribed to no single creed or system of belief throughout his adult life, yet on his deathbed he returned to the Roman Catholicism of his upbringing. A man of great literary ambitions, he disdained to publish a single volume for the last twenty-six years of his life. Of a pessimistic and stoic disposition, he possessed an ultimately optimistic belief in the progress of the species.

Vigny's parents were of the old, pre-Revolution, provincial *noblesse*. They had somehow escaped both the guillotine and forced emigration but were required to live under constant government supervision. Of their four children, three died in infancy. The last, Alfred Victor, a rather sickly child, was to be the sole survivor and the family's ultimate scion. Throughout his life, Vigny attached great importance to his noble descent, but he tended to exaggerate the family's degree of nobility, eventually adopting the title of "count" based on some spurious claims of his father. The family moved to Paris when Vigny was not quite two years old, and, not many years later, his mother undertook strict control of her son's education. This instruction was a curious combination of liberal, rationalist philosophy, absorbed by way of Jean-Jacques Rousseau, and an ancien régime adherence to the institutions of the Roman Catholic Church and monarchy. In a youth passed during the turbulence of the Directorate, the Consulate, and the Empire, Vigny was taught to view the Revolution as a hideous reversal of the natural order, to judge Napoleon Bonaparte as a consummate charlatan, and to long for the restoration of the monarchy.

With the fall of Napoleon in 1814 and the restoration of Louis XVIII, opportunities resurfaced for Royalist nobility, and the seventeen-year-old Vigny was enrolled in the elite, ceremonial Gendarmes du Roi as a sublieutenant. Thus, he inaugurated a long and disillusioning military career. During those years, he was transferred from regiment to regiment, always serving honorably, but chafing, like so many young men of his time, at the lack of opportunity for significant advancement and for some chance at glory through action. There was little chance for either, however, in the years immediately succeeding the Napoleonic era; opportunity and stimulation would have to arise in other quarters.

In the early 1820's, when stationed outside Paris, Vigny was introduced into the literary circles of the capital, attending the salons of Madame d'Ancelot and Charles Nodier, where Vigny would eventually meet and befriend the young Hugo. Vigny began to write seriously and, in 1822, published his first volume of poetry, *Poèmes*, followed in 1824 by a miniature epic poem, *Eloa*. In anticipation of war with Spain, his regiment was transferred to various posts in central and southern France, and it was in 1825 in one of these posts that he met and soon married Lydia Bunbury, the daughter of a wealthy and somewhat eccentric lord, Sir Hugh Bunbury. Both Vigny and his mother had cultivated and sealed this alliance, at least partly, in expectation of a sizable inheritance, but Lydia's father was not pleased with the marriage and cut the couple off with a small allowance. After Sir Hugh's death in 1838, Vigny became involved in a lawsuit aimed at claiming an inheritance, an effort that left him and his wife little better off than before. Early in the marriage, Lydia suffered three miscarriages that left her a lifelong invalid. Intellectually, she had little in common with her husband, but neither this nor her physical condition caused Vigny to abandon her, although he had a succession of mistresses throughout the marriage, several of whom could hardly have been unknown to his wife. The marriage held together, however, with Vigny assuming the household duties, managing the slender budget, and, in the end, devotedly attending Lydia in her final sickness.

After numerous successive leaves of absence

from the army, Vigny was placed on permanent and honorable retirement in the spring of 1827. A period of great literary activity ensued, which saw the success of the historical novel *Cinq-Mars*, the republication of *Poèmes antiques et modernes*, and a generally successful series of works for the stage, culminating, in 1835, in the stunning reception of the three-act drama *Chatterton*. In 1831, Vigny had begun a relationship with Dorval, the famous actress who was to play the female lead in *Chatterton*. This liaison, which would last until 1838, proved to be highly unstable, as a result of Dorval's increasingly frequent absences from Paris when on tour and Vigny's violent fits of jealousy. The years with Dorval also saw the publication of the novel *Stello* and a collection of three stories culled from Vigny's experience of army life, collectively titled *The Military Necessity*.

Upon his mother's death in 1837, Vigny inherited the country property of Maine-Giraud, where, in reserved retirement from public life, he and his wife

Alfred de Vigny (Getty Images)

would remain almost exclusively until their deaths. Vigny never published a full-length book after *The Military Necessity*, but he composed a good deal of poetry and puzzled over the ultimate disposition of a selection of poems for a final collection, which was not to be published until after his death by his friend and literary executor, Ratisbonne. Of the eleven poems that constitute this final collection, *Les Destinées*, several were published individually during Vigny's lifetime in the literary review *Revue des deux mondes*, among them "La Mort du loup," "Le Mont des Oliviers," "La Maison du berger," and "La Bouteille à la mer."

In addition to this creative activity, Vigny made five unsuccessful attempts (from 1842 through 1845) to be admitted to the French Academy and was finally elected in 1846. He also stood for election as a Royalist candidate to the National Legislative Assembly in 1848, but he was defeated by his Bonapartist opponent. Vigny's campaigning had been rather too patrician: His political opinions were printed for distribution, but he had disdained to circulate among the constituency he hoped to represent. In any case, the Revolution of 1848 had begun to erode Vigny's loyalties, and he began to question the actual accomplishments of the Bourbon regime. He never again seriously considered a career as an elected official.

In 1860, the health of Vigny's wife began to fail, and for two years, he attended and nursed her faithfully. When she died in December, 1862, Vigny was unable to attend the funeral because he was suffering from the painful stomach cancer that would eventually kill him. Before he died, after years of proudly refusing to submit to a religious creed, Vigny received the last rites and was reconciled with the Roman Catholic Church. He died in Paris on September 17, 1863, and is buried in the cemetery of Montmartre.

ANALYSIS

Traditionally, discussions of Alfred de Vigny's poetry have been characterized by a focus on the ideas that inform individual poems as well as on the quasi-philosophical "system" which informs his oeuvre as a whole. In Vigny studies, technical analysis of how such ideas are expressed (through prosody, form, and so on) has always taken second place to discussion of what is

said. If this is so, it is largely a result of the emphasis the poet himself placed on the concept of the poem as an artistic medium for the exploration of philosophical issues, the concept of the *poème philosophique*. It is certain, from numerous entries in the personal and literary diary *Le Journal d'un poète*, that Vigny conceived of all the technical aspects of poetry as being at the service of underlying philosophical concepts. Discussing poetry in one of his letters, he states, "All of humanity's great problems can be discussed in the form of verse."

Vigny's central themes are few; taken together, they lend one another a resonance that virtually endows them with the coherence of a philosophical system. Humanism is the unvarying foundation of that quasi system; human experience is examined repeatedly in terms of three fundamental relationships: the relationship of the individual person with God, with society, and, in ultimate solitude, with the self. These themes possess a natural kinship, and a Vigny poem may deal with any combination of the three simultaneously. The figure of Christ in the poem "Le Mont des Oliviers" (the Mount of Olives), for example, is seen in relation to God (to whom he prays), in relation to man (for whom he prays), and in relation to his own double identity as God and human. In "La Bouteille à la mer" (the bottle in the sea), humans are seen as purveyors of their own individual knowledge and experience for the benefit of society, but the transmission of knowledge and experience from person to person is a precarious affair in the hands of Divine Will. Vigny's poetry is often obsessed with the special isolation of the poet, the person of genius and vision (a preoccupation finally symbolic of the condition of the species itself). The theme of the particular plight of the poet ran throughout his career, from the youthful "Moïse" (Moses) to the valedictory "L'Esprit pur" (the pure spirit). Religion (the traditional Judeo-Christian ethic, at least) offers little relief for *la condition humaine*, for Vigny conceives of it as the impossible dialogue between a confused creation and a deaf (or at any rate dumb) Creator. In spite of the dark pessimism of this vision, Vigny ultimately asserts the liberating capacity for human dignity in the face of limitations and sustains the idea of progress through human endeavor.

In the early stages of his career, Vigny seized on the

idea of a single, concrete symbol to serve as a dramatic metaphor in each individual poem. The symbol could be a simple object, such as a flute or a bottle cast into the sea; it could be an animal, such as the wolf; or it might be in the form of a person (usually from the Bible), such as Jephthah's daughter, Samson, or Moses. Such symbols frequently attain a mythic dimension appropriate to the scope of the idea expressed, and all Vigny's technical efforts went into their animation.

"MOÏSE"

Some critics have argued that Vigny's most successful realization of the *poème philosophique* came not in the poems of his maturity (collected in *Les Destinées*), but in a work of his youth (written at the age of twenty-five), the masterful "Moïse." Indeed, Moses—lawgiver, leader, prophet—serves as a perfect symbol for Vigny's concept of the poet-prophet, spiritually and intellectually isolated from his fellow humans. Vigny himself stated that his Moses "is not the Moses of the Jews"; he is rather the man of genius in all times, laboring under the weight of the knowledge he attempts to impart to a society that shuns him.

The poem consists of 116 lines in the French heroic meter (Alexandrines in rhyming couplets), a prosodic scheme with an effect of great weight and deliberation. The Alexandrine is a rhetorical and dramatic line that reinforces seriousness of tone and helps create in this Moses a figure of immense and tragic proportions. The poem opens with a vividly descriptive segment (lines 1 through 44) in which the reader views, through the prophet's eyes, the sunlit tents of the Israelite encampment and, farther in the distance, the vast stretches of the Promised Land. Moses is ascending Mount Nebo to speak with the Lord, and his ascent underscores his dual relationship with the people, for he is both superior to them and increasingly excluded from their society. On reaching the summit, Moses is surrounded by a dark cloud, so that his interview with God is cloaked in deepest secrecy, to the confusion of those below. Moses begins his speech, a plaint, with lines that, with some variation, serve as a refrain throughout the course of the poem: "Je vivrai donc toujours puissant et solitaire?/ Laissez-moi m'endormir du sommeil de la terre" ("Must I, then, live always mighty and apart?/ Let me sleep the sleep of the earth").

Moses outlines his accomplishments as leader of his people: He has power over the seas and over nations, and he has conducted the Israelites to the threshold of their salvation. The power he has gained and the control that he exercises, however, come from the knowledge he has acquired as the "elect of God" and that he, in turn, must impart to the uncomprehending masses. The price has been heavy. From the moment of his birth, he has been a stranger to his fellow men, whose "eyes lower before the fire of my eyes." He is literally wearied to death, for this virtual loss of his humanity has created a barrier of fear in his relations with his kind. In the final segment of his plaint, he begs with simple dignity for release from his fate as a man of vision. There is no divine response, at least in words, and as the reader shifts perspective to the Israelite camp below (privileged to return to common humanity as Moses is not), the black cloud of mystery lifts from the mountaintop and the prophet is seen no more. The reaction of the people is simple and somewhat coolly observed: "Il fut pleuré" ("He was mourned"). The actions of Vigny's God are inscrutable and inexplicable. Moses is indeed relieved of his burden, but the reader never learns the answers to Moses's single question: "Why?" As the poem ends and the Israelites take up their journey once more, the mantle of leadership descends on Joshua, who proceeds onward through the wasteland, "pensive and paling."

"LE MONT DES OLIVIERS"

There is something even more ominous about the silence and mystery surrounding God in the poem "Le Mont des Oliviers," from the collection *Les Destinées*, written many years after "Moïse." Drawing once again from Scripture, Vigny dramatizes the scene of Christ's agony in the Garden of Gethsemane prior to his betrayal, arrest, and Crucifixion. Vigny again achieves a heroic scale in his portrayal of Christ, but in the symbol, there is an added poignancy, resulting from Christ's dual nature as both God and man. The mental and physical torment caused by Christ's philosophical dilemma is presented with a vividness never quite achieved in the portrayal of Moses.

The poem (149 lines, again in Alexandrine rhyming couplets) is divided into three unequal sections and a single-stanza postscript. In the first section, the reader becomes acquainted with Christ's peculiar circumstances as partaker in both human and divine natures, as Christ casts a "human thought" over the thirty-three years of his life among humans. The second and longest section is spoken by Christ himself. Unlike Moses, he prays for permission to live and complete his task. In his ministry, he has brought the message of brotherhood, spirit over flesh, and substance for symbol, but he has not yet brought the certitude that alone will deliver humankind from the twin bonds of "Evil and Doubt." He realizes that after his death the message will be perverted, even by his followers, and he fears the uselessness of his sacrifice. He begs to serve as the instrument not only of God's forgiveness of humanity, but also of humanity's pardon of a God who can permit evil and doubt. Only certainty will reopen the paths of communication between Creator and created: "All will be revealed when man finally comprehends/ The place from which he came and that to which he travels." As Jesus finishes his prayer, he catches sight of the approaching torch of Judas through the trees. Is this one flash of light amid the surrounding obscurity the ironic answer to his request? The torchlight is the final image of the scene proper, but the poem itself is formally concluded by a brief postscript, appended some twenty years after the original publication of the piece as a separate poem in *Revue des deux mondes*. It is a single stanza clearly cast in the form of a moral, and its title, "Le Silence," makes a double reference: "The righteous man will counter absence with disdain,/ Responding with only cold silence/ To the everlasting silence of the Divine."

The message (or the moral, at least) is clear: Humankind is forced to establish its own dignity, with or without God. Because this moral was appended, accusations that it is not fully integrated with the dramatic metaphor have some force. Taken as a whole, however, "Le Mont des Oliviers" is a fine example of the poet's habit (in later years) of turning spiritual or intellectual doubt into positive matter.

"LA MORT DU LOUP"

An even finer example, perhaps, of this tendency is found in "La Mort du loup" (the death of the wolf), again from *Les Destinées*. The inspiration for the poem was two lines in Lord Byron's *Childe Harold's Pilgrimage* (1812-1818, 1819): "And the wolf dies in si-lence—not bestow'd/ In vain should such example be." Vigny's poem is praiseworthy from many perspectives: its unity of symbol and idea, its prosodic virtuosity, and its brilliant achievement of scene-setting. It is arranged in three sections of varying length, each of which is characterized by a different point of view. This shifting perspective gives tremendous dramatic scope and roundness; all the characters involved have their moments in the spotlight.

The first and longest section is seen from the hunters' perspective (signaled by the use of first-person plural pronouns). Passing through the murky, almost nightmarish atmosphere of a thick wood, they come upon the tracks of a family of roving wolves (*loups voyageurs*); soon they reach a clearing and are greeted by the flaming eyes of the father wolf. Two wolf cubs are at play, but in silence, for they understand that man, the enemy, is close at hand. The she-wolf, whose dignity is compared to that of the she-wolf who suckled Romulus and Remus, anxiously watches over the cubs. The wolf, realizing that he has been caught unaware, stands his ground. Between his iron jaws, he grabs one dog from the pack of hounds as the hunters open fire and plunge their knives into his body. The wolf calmly regains his former guarding position and dies, steadily watching the hunters, without uttering a cry.

The brief second section gives the viewpoint of a single hunter (signaled by the use of the first-person singular), the narrator of the tale. The wolf's dignity in the face of death unnerves him, and he is unable to pursue the escaping she-wolf and cubs. He realizes that the she-wolf has not abandoned her mate through fear, but to ensure the survival of her cubs. They must be taught resistance. They must avoid at all costs the compromising pact made between man and domesticated animals. They must learn not only the defiance but also the stoic wisdom of her mate, their father. The final section also begins in the voice of the narrator, but it ends with the words ascribed by the narrator to the wolf—that is, from the perspective of the dying wolf himself:

To lament, to weep, to pray, are all equally cowardly.
Actively accomplish your long and weary task
On the path which Fate has chosen for you.
Then, afterwards, like me, suffer and die without a word.

The nobility and optimism of Vigny's anthropomorphic wolf may be subtle, but they are clear. The philosophy promulgated in the wolf's dying words is more than mere stoic resignation. It is, rather, a constructive, ultimately hopeful stratagem for countering the limitations imposed by destiny: "Actively accomplish." The moral of "La Mort du loup" goes one step further than that of "Le Mont des Oliviers" (and is more organically incorporated), for in the former, action supplants restraint and silence. In both poems, the positive thread of Vigny's thought serves to balance the deep pessimism of the scenes depicted. It is this affirmation of human worth, through the symbols of Christ and the wolf, that develops into the faith in human progress which underlies one of the final poems of *Les Destinées*, "La Bouteille à la mer."

"LA BOUTEILLE À LA MER"

"La Bouteille à la mer" is divided into twenty-six (numbered) stanzas, each composed of seven Alexandrine lines. The first stanza serves as a brief prelude, urging the reader to forget the fate of the poets who have gone on before and were prevented by untimely death from completing their work. Indeed, the reader is urged to set aside the personality of the poet altogether and hearken only to the message of the poem. A fable follows, relating the story of the captain of a ship about to founder in perilous seas. He encloses the ship's log, with its scientific records and observations, in a bottle, and he casts the bottle overboard just before the ship goes down, entrusting it to Divine Will, praying that it might reach human hands again. The log is the message of experience, the "sublime testament for future voyagers," and after it undergoes its own hazardous journey, it is eventually retrieved by a simple Breton fisherman. Incapable of reading, the fisherman brings the bottle to the nearest wise man, who recognizes the log as the "treasure of thought and experience" and rejoices in the unceasing, if precarious, triumph of human knowledge.

LES DESTINÉES

The poems collected in *Les Destinées* are undoubtedly Vigny's greatest poetic achievements, and they deserve to be better known in the English-speaking world. In spite of their quality, they have not gone without serious criticism. Vigny has been accused of not fully integrating form and concept, of creating moral messages that are detachable from his dramatic metaphors, of occasional laboriousness and excessive rhetoric, and of becoming enamored of scene-setting while losing the thread of the narrative. Others have vigorously supported his achievement and underscored the integrity of Vigny's self-effacing approach to the difficult task of expressing a personal philosophy in poetic form. As critic Michel Mourre has observed, Vigny, in contrast to the other Romantics, refused to "make a spectacle of himself." He was able to endow his work with his particular sensibility without slipping into solipsism. Moreover, if it is true that Vigny's great legacy to French poetry is the transmission of philosophical concepts, then it may be admitted, at the very least, that his ideas are vividly drawn and, for the most part, have survived any technical weakness.

OTHER MAJOR WORKS

LONG FICTION: *Cinq-Mars: Ou, Une conjuration sous Louis XIII*, 1826 (*Cinq-Mars: Or, A Conspiracy Under Louis XIII*, 1847); *L'Alméh*, 1831; *Stello*, 1832; *Daphné*, 1912.

SHORT FICTION: *Servitude et grandeurs militaires*, 1835 (*The Military Necessity*, 1919).

PLAYS: *Le More de Venise*, pr. 1829 (translation of William Shakespeare's *Othello*); *La Maréchale d'Ancre*, pr. 1831; *Quitte pour la peur*, pr. 1833 (one-act); *Chatterton*, pr., pb. 1835.

NONFICTION: *Le Journal d'un poète*, 1867.

BIBLIOGRAPHY

Bonhomme, Denise. *The Poetic Enigma of Alfred de Vigny: The Rosetta Stone of Esoteric Literature.* Victoria, B.C.: Trafford, 2003. Contains a biography and foreword discussing his works as well as many selections from his poetry, with commentary.

Doolittle, James. *Alfred de Vigny.* New York: Twayne, 1967. This short book is a good introduction in English to Vigny's lyric poetry and to his more famous prose works, including *Cinq-Mars* and *The Military Necessity.* Includes a bibliography.

McGoldrick, Malcolm. "The Setting in Vigny's 'La Mort du loup.'" *Language Quarterly* 29, nos. 1/2 (Winter/Spring, 1991): 104-114. In one of Vigny's best-known poems, the speaker is a hunter who kills a wolf but finally comes to admire the dying wolf's courageous efforts to protect his family. Shows how the setting in a forest isolates the hunter from others and makes him reflect on the consequences of his actions.

McLeman-Carnie, Janette. "Monologue: A Dramatic Strategy in Alfred de Vigny's Rhetoric." *Nineteenth-Century French Studies* 23, nos. 3/4 (Spring/Summer, 1988): 253-265. Some of Vigny's most famous poems are dramatic monologues in which the speaker conveys his understanding of what he sees before him. Vigny was also a dramatist, and this essay examines his skill in making his readers identify with the internal struggles of his speakers.

Wakefield, David. *The French Romantics: Literature and the Visual Arts, 1800-1840*. London: Chaucer Press, 2007. Contains a chapter on Vigny and his importance to the Romantics and a chapter on pictorial imagery in Romantic poetry.

Wren, Keith. *Vigny's "Les Destinées."* London: Grant & Cutler, 1985. A thoughtful study of Vigny's posthumously published book of poetry. This short book describes the artistry and philosophical depth of this work.

Theodore Baroody

FRANÇOIS VILLON

Born: Paris, France; 1431
Died: Unknown; 1463(?)
Also known as: François des Loges; François de Montcorbier

PRINCIPAL POETRY

Le Lais, wr. 1456, pb. 1489 (*The Legacy*, 1878; also known as *Le Petit Testament, The Little Testament*)

Le Grand Testament, wr. 1461, pb. 1489 (*The Great Testament*, 1878)

Ballades en jargon, 1489 (*Poems in Slang*, 1878)

Les Œuvres de Françoys Villon, 1533 (Clément Marot, editor)

The Poems of Master François Villon, 1878
Ballads Done into English from the French of François Villon, 1904
The Testaments of François Villon, 1924
The Complete Works of François Villon, 1928
The Poems of François Villon, 1954, 1977, 1982 (includes *The Legacy, The Great Testament*, and some shorter poems; Galway Kinnell, translator)

OTHER LITERARY FORMS

François Villon (vee-YOHN) indicates in *The Great Testament* that he also wrote a romance titled "Le Rommant du pet au diable" (romance of the devil's fart). This work, apparently about an elaborate student prank, is not extant, and Villon's mention of it is the only evidence that it ever did exist.

ACHIEVEMENTS

Of all the poets of the Middle Ages, perhaps only Dante and Geoffrey Chaucer are better known and more admired than François Villon. He has been widely praised since his own time by voices as diverse as those of Clément Marot in the sixteenth century and Nicolas Boileau-Despréaux in the seventeenth; by Robert Louis Stevenson (whose admiration for Villon's poetic genius was even stronger than his revulsion at the depravity of the poet's life) and Algernon Charles Swinburne; by Dante Gabriel Rossetti, Ezra Pound, and William Carlos Williams. Remarkably enough, Villon has found his way into popular culture as well. He has been the subject of motion pictures (*Beloved Rogue*, with John Barrymore, 1927), novels such as Francis Carco's *Le Roman de François Villon* (1926), and popular songs by George Brassens, Reggiani, and others.

The usual explanation for Villon's extraordinary popularity is exemplified by Pound's contention (in *ABC of Reading*, 1934) that Villon is the most "authentic" of poets and (in *The Spirit of Romance*, 1910) that he is the only poet without illusions. He is, in this view, notable for accepting and admitting his own failures and depravity and speaking of them forthrightly, frequently with regret but always without shame. It is the presumed presence of the poet in his poetry, the fact that when he says "I" he is referring to himself rather than to a disembodied allegorical voice, that readers have found refreshing and appealing. Nor is the world around the poet an abstract or idealized place. His poetry is more firmly rooted in his own historical and geographical context (Paris at the end of the Middle Ages, a place and time of social and intellectual turmoil) than is that of any other medieval poet. His city, its students and thieves and judges, its priests and prostitutes, are both his dramatis personae and his subject.

The personal element in Villon's poetry—his honesty, sincerity, and authenticity—is related, according to the usual view, to his apparent lack of poetic artifice. Pound insisted that "Villon is destitute of imagination; he is almost destitute of art." He is considered to be without affectation, personal or literary. It is presumably the voice of a fallible, ordinary man and not the calculated utterance of a poet that the reader hears. Such is the reaction of many students, casual readers, poets, and critics alike. Such an assessment must represent, however, something of a misreading if it is intended literally. The Villon to whom readers are drawn is clearly a persona that he has crafted with great care and subtlety, and while that persona has much in common with the historical Villon, one is nevertheless the creature of the other. Villon is far from "destitute of art": While a very great poet and a very bad one might appear to be destitute of art, only the former is likely to be remembered. Perhaps one should say instead that Villon is destitute of obvious art: The impression of artlessness is his most artful illusion.

Although many generations have read and admired Villon, they have seen entirely different things in him— hero or coward, criminal or degenerate or tortured soul. This multiplicity of readings suggests that Villon is a great and complex poet, whose themes have universal appeal and whose command of his poetic resources is equal to the demands that his vision places on them.

BIOGRAPHY

François Villon was born François de Montcorbier (or perhaps des Loges) and later took as his own the name of his benefactor, Guillaume de Villon. He was a native of Paris, born there the year Joan of Arc died, and presumably reared there. He received his baccalaureate in 1449 and became a master of arts three years later.

François Villon (Library of Congress)

Much of the fragmentary information that is available concerning Villon's life comes from legal documents dating back to 1455. In that year, he was involved in a brawl and killed a priest named Phillippe Chermoye or Sermoise, but he was later pardoned for justifiable homicide. The following Christmas season, he and others committed a burglary at the College of Navarre, after which he apparently fled Paris.

In 1461, Villon was in a dungeon at Meung. Incarcerated there for reasons unknown, he was (as he says in *The Great Testament*) cruelly mistreated by Bishop Thibault d'Aussigny, but along with other prisoners, he was released when the newly crowned King Louis XI passed through the town. Evidently unable to stay out of trouble, Villon was before long imprisoned once again, this time at the Châtelet in Paris. He was soon released again, but he had been incriminated in the College of Navarre burglary by a talkative accomplice, Guy Tabary, and had to agree to repay his share of the loot. Very soon, Villon was arrested yet again, following a brawl. This time, he was sentenced to be hanged; the sentence was commuted, however, and he was exiled instead. At that point, the trail ends, and further references to him (in François Rabelais's works, for example) are probably pure fictions. He died during or after 1463.

At some time, perhaps after he first fled from Paris, Villon spent a while at Blois, at the court of Charles d'Orléans, and a poem is preserved (titled "Je meurs de seuf auprès de la fontaine"/ "I Am Dying of Thirst near the Fountain") which he composed for a poetry contest held by Charles. His first long poem, *The Legacy*, was composed shortly after the 1456 Christmas burglary, while *The Great Testament* was written following his release from the Meung prison.

ANALYSIS

François Villon's poetry offers a depiction of his narrator so vivid and effective that readers have traditionally inferred that the narrator is the poet himself, assuming that Villon is dispensing with poetic mediation in order to express directly the thoughts and fears of a fifteenth century Parisian. That readers find themselves fascinated with Villon the man, even to the point of ignoring his poetry, is a testimony to the mastery of Villon the artist. The methods by which he creates and presents his narrator thus provide one of the most accessible keys to an analysis of his poetry. Foremost among his methods is the thematic inconsistency and apparent formlessness that one would expect to characterize not literary activity, but the thoughts of a complex human being.

Although Villon generally deals with sober and important themes (injustice and intolerance; disease, decrepitude, and death), the tone of his poetry is not always as heavy as these subjects would suggest. Villon can be lighthearted and playful one instant, sober and bitter the next. Throughout his work, he shows himself to be a master of irony. In many cases, that irony is directed at his enemies, whom he may characterize either as magnanimous friends or as needy and worthy citizens. (In a number of such cases, Villon's ironic intent was revealed to posterity only in the last century or the present one, when historical research permitted the identification of most of the people mentioned by the poet.) He also, however, directs his irony at himself; for example, he may present himself as love's martyr, the

victim of an unhappy affair, when in fact it is clear that his "broken heart" is a thinly veiled reference to his criminal activity.

At times, Villon's irony and humor fall away, and he launches into a direct and abusive attack on his enemies. This invective, all the more striking because it brusquely interrupts a lighter tone and sometimes interrupts another thought, has convinced readers that this, at least, is the "real" Villon, yet such "outbursts" can also be regarded as carefully planned poetic effects designed to add realism to his persona. Similarly, Villon often suspends banter and invective alike to offer a simple, plaintive statement of regret or a plea for forgiveness—although he is likely to cancel such a statement in turn by a joke or another attack. His work is thus built on contrast and digression, on a systematic rejection of consistency. His poetry is carefully composed so as not to appear to have been carefully composed, and it is certainly as dynamic as any ever written.

THE LEGACY

Villon's first long poem, *The Legacy*, is a work of 320 octosyllabic lines arranged in eight-line stanzas. It was probably composed around the end of 1456, after the burglary at the College of Navarre, when Villon had fled from Paris or was preparing to do so. Characteristically, Villon uses events from his own life, and the premise for *The Legacy* is the necessity that he leave the city. The work is thus a *congé* (leave taking), a traditional genre describing one's reasons and preparations for a departure. Critics have sometimes interpreted *The Legacy* as an alibi intended to provide evidence that Villon was away from Paris when the Christmas robbery took place. It is more likely that his fictional absence was an "inside joke" for the benefit of his friends or accomplices who knew of his involvement in the burglary.

In any case, the robbery itself is not mentioned in the poem. Instead, the narrator tells us that he is leaving because a love affair has ended painfully. His discussion of the relationship and its end is replete with mock allegorical imagery drawn from the traditional vocabulary of courtly love. He thus speaks of the "prison of love," the "pain of love," and "sweet glances." He concludes that his only recourse is to flee, but his poetic intent quickly becomes clear when the reader notes that the word he uses, *fouïr*, means not only to "flee" but also to "copulate," and his double meaning is obvious when he insists, for example, that he must "plant in other fields." Specifically, he announces that his destination is Angers, but, as David Kuhn has pointed out, "going to Angers" was a slang reference to orgasm.

Following this introduction is a series of bequests, in which Villon, by antiphrasis, leaves to others fictitious possessions or exaggerated assets (his money, tents, and fame—the first two nonexistent, the third undesirable), makes obscene puns (his *branc*, which he bequeaths to Ythier Marchant, means either "sword" or "excrement"), and bestows otherwise ironic gifts (as when he leaves money to "three poor orphans"—who, research has revealed, were actually three rich merchants and usurers).

The third and final section of *The Legacy* offers a closure that is an elaborate parody of Scholastic language; typically, however, Villon's lines constitute not only an indictment of Scholasticism but also a system of sexual, specifically masturbatory, imagery. Thus, Villon closes the circle of his poem—although he does so in an unexpected way. He has told us that he is leaving a woman and that he is leaving Paris. He announces his destination (Angers), which indicates also his sexual intention, and that intention is enacted in the "Scholastic" section and achieved when, at the end, Villon's senses clear and, his "candle extinguished" and his "ink frozen," he is unable to continue writing. While some scholars have interpreted these details as realistic images of Villon's miserable existence, they are rather the burlesque conclusion of his sexual situation: He is spent. *The Legacy* thus relates travel, courtly and Scholastic thought, and poetic effort in a complex progression that ends in mock-pathetic autoerotic exhaustion.

THE GREAT TESTAMENT

The Great Testament, written five days after *The Legacy*, is longer (2,023 lines), generally less comical, and far more complex. It is considered to be a mature and serious recasting of *The Legacy*, and indeed many of the same persons and images recur in it. While this view can claim some justification, however, it would be unjust to the earlier poem to see in it nothing more than a prefiguration of Villon's mature work. *The Legacy* is a comic masterpiece in its own right; *The Great Testament* uses some of the same methods and materials to produce a masterpiece of an entirely different sort. Indeed, the two works have relatively little in common other than certain characters and the fact that each of them offers a series of ironic or burlesque bequests. Even the irony varies. That of *The Legacy* appears for the most part good-natured. In *The Great Testament*, the irony is most often bitterly vituperative, and at times, Villon suspends his ironic detachment altogether, as when, at the very beginning of the poem, he launches into a vicious attack on Bishop Thibault, who mistreated Villon in prison.

The subject of *The Great Testament* is no longer the loss of Villon's love, but the loss of his youth and the impending loss of his life. He is, he suggests, an aging and weak man who regrets his wasted youth and must put his life in order. However, there is another side of him, a side that has no desire to waste even a precious hour of life preparing for death: He has too much to do, perhaps too many friends to see and pranks to play, but especially he has too many scores to settle and too many enemies to malign. Thus the poet presents, developed in sharp relief, the two sides of his character: the heart and the flesh, the conscience and the appetites, the contrite sinner preoccupied with the hereafter and the mortal desperately clinging to life, preoccupied with the present. Much of the artistic tension of the work derives from the conflict of these opposing impulses, intercutting each other ever more quickly and more frantically as the poem progresses.

The form of *The Great Testament* could be described with a fair degree of accuracy as a structure of digression. The pattern is set when Villon interrupts his very first sentence to launch into the lengthy attack on Thibault, then soon after to offer elaborate praise of King Louis XI, before finally returning to the ostensible subject of the work. Although the ultimate destination of the poem (the narrator's death) is clear from the beginning, the path to it is circuitous, as the poet digresses repeatedly to offer details of his past, his associates, his fears, and his regrets.

The work incorporates a number of lyric pieces (ballades and rondeaux) which represent in most cases the illustration or crystallization of a thematic development. These lyric poems are thought by some scholars to have been composed earlier and chosen for use in

The Great Testament (a contention that has not been proved and that is of no great consequence in any case, because whether they were written early or late, their inclusion indicates that they satisfactorily served Villon's purposes). The best known of these pieces is the "Ballade des dames du temps jadis" ("Ballad of Dead Ladies"), which, along with two accompanying poems, the "Ballade des seigneurs du temps jadis" ("Ballad of Men from the Past") and the "Ballade en vieil langage françoys" ("Ballad in Old French"), develops the *ubi sunt* motif in regard to illustrious persons from the past. While the "Ballad of Dead Ladies" is justly praised, its meaning has been distorted in English by the traditional translation of its famous refrain as "Where are the snows of yesteryear?" *Antan*, the last word of the refrain, means simply "last year," and the correct rendering of the line, while robbing it of a rather romantic poignancy, restores its effectiveness in another way: Villon is, after all, contrasting the passing of a fragile and rather commonplace phenomenon with the loss of remarkable, famous, and (by implication) equally fragile women from history.

It is in fact typical of Villon not to reach for the extravagant image or the elaborate paraphrase; often his most effective passages are, as here, impressive for their directness and simplicity. He also has a tendency to move from the distant to the immediate, from the abstract to the concrete. Thus, for example, while these early *ballades* effectively suggest the loss of life and fame, that theme is far more strikingly developed when he later refers simply to "skulls stacked up in cemeteries" or when he presents the lament of Belle Hëaulmiere, an aging prostitute who recalls the firm, attractive body she once had and contrasts it with the shriveled and repulsive form it has now, to her horror, become. Her contemplation is followed by a *ballade* in which she urges a group of prostitutes to seize the day.

These lyric poems are inserted irregularly, but with increasing frequency toward the end. The subject matter, moreover, follows a general evolution toward the realistic, direct, and sometimes coarse. From the three *ballades* treating illustrious people from the past (and from another early one, a masterful prayer to Notre Dame intended to be offered by Villon's simple and naïve mother), he goes on to present Hëaulmiere and,

later, la Grosse Margot (Fat Margot, a prostitute whose consort Villon is, and the subject of a poem by Stevenson, who describes her as "grimy" and as "gross and ghastly"). Villon's themes—misery, aging, and death—are hardly subjects to be developed abstractly in pretty ballads, and indeed the appeal of his poetry for many is precisely that he is willing to suspend obvious poetic musing and present death in all its ugliness and pain—and himself as a man whose flesh is weak and whose spirit is only sporadically willing.

Even though *The Great Testament* is bitter, vituperative, and often uncompromisingly realistic, and even though its predominant tone is sober, it is by no means devoid of comedy, although the humor of *The Great Testament* is humor with a sharp edge. The "three poor orphans" reappear here, as do a number of other characters from *The Legacy*; in this case, however, Villon's banter only thinly covers a venomous attitude. He jokes about his legatees, but the jokes are mostly intimations of sexual and other disorders on the part of his adversaries. Nor does he spare himself: He indicates (as he did in his earlier poem) that he is a martyr to love, but the specific details he offers in support of that suggestion have led some scholars to theorize that his martyrdom took the form of advanced syphilis.

Throughout the poem, the reader hears Villon's two voices (sinner and penitent) clearly, but the work is also structured around a variety of other voices, and in some cases other narrators appear as well. The interplay of voices in *The Great Testament* is in fact very complex, and toward the end, as the tempo quickens and the realism intensifies, these complexities multiply. In the fiction of the poem, Villon presents himself as aging, becoming increasingly infirm, and approaching death. Indeed, at the end, he composes his own epitaph, and his fiction even includes looking back from beyond the grave to describe his death. In this section, some passages are not only in the past but also in the third person, as though another narrator were taking over. At one point, Villon comments in the first person on his third-person character: "Et je croy bien que pas n'en ment" ("And *I* do not think *he* is lying"; emphasis added). This is the culmination of a movement that has developed throughout the work, whereby Villon creates two entities, a persona and a character, who periodically merge and separate and who are finally established as entirely distinct from each other. The interplay of voices confirms the poet as partially independent of the character he creates; the latter follows the fictional course set for him (lamenting his age, preparing his will, and dying), while the poet uses him and the text to indulge in an examination of, and commentary on, life, death, sexuality, the judicial system, his friends, enemies, and accomplices—and above all, Villon himself.

The Great Testament is thus a remarkable portrait of its narrator, of Paris, of the life led by a medieval "student, poet, and housebreaker" (according to Stevenson's characterization), but it is also a remarkable poem, a masterpiece of verbal wit, of structural complexity, of poetic voice and virtuosity. *The Legacy* is in many ways a remarkable work of undeniable merit, but it is lighter not only in tone but also in literary weight. *The Great Testament* is the complex and mature masterpiece of a consummate poet.

POEMS IN SLANG

Whether *Poems in Slang* is also a masterpiece remains open to question: The poems included are virtually incomprehensible to modern readers. Many of the words and expressions, drawn from underworld slang, have been identified through documents that preserve them; the meaning of others can be deduced from their context. Still, enough mysteries remain to frustrate critical efforts. Scholar Pierre Guiraud has offered one of the more elaborate and controversial attempts to deal with these poems, proposing three distinct levels of meaning and consequently three translations for each. The first level deals with criminal activity, the second with cheating at cards, the third with sodomy. Whether Guiraud has successfully deciphered Villon's system—and a good number of scholars remain unconvinced—the fact remains that the *Poems in Slang* are still largely inaccessible. Modern scholars cannot adequately assess the poetic value of the volume because their attention is still on its meaning, in the most basic sense: the definition of words. For the present, these poems must remain an enigma, a closed system constructed in a language that is largely foreign even to the best specialists in Villon's Middle French.

His remaining miscellaneous poems are extremely varied in subject matter, style, date of composition, and literary value, and the very authorship of some of them is disputed. Certain of them are no more than playthings or poetic pastimes. Others, however, are very interesting, and two deserve brief comment here. "L'Épitaphe Villon" ("Villon's Epitaph") offers a horrible portrait of corpses on the gallows—swinging in the breeze, flesh rotting, eyes pecked out by birds—and asks for compassion and absolution. "Le Débat du cuer et du corps de Villon" ("The Dialogue of Villon's Heart and Body") provides a confrontation of basic human impulses, as the personified heart attempts to persuade the body to abandon its dissolute ways. Both poems are reminiscent in certain ways of *The Great Testament*, the former in the realistic images of death, the latter in the dramatization of the fundamental conflicts within Villon and within all of us, and both of them in the impressive poetic sensibility that informs them.

For Swinburne, Villon was "our sad bad glad mad brother." That is indeed what Villon has been for most readers. What is conspicuously absent from such assessments (except perhaps by implication) is precisely Villon's artistic status, his success in creating the persona that many readers mistake for the poet. When one looks directly at his poetry—stripping away the veneer of romantic imagery, bypassing Victorian revulsion at his manners and character, going beyond popular distortions and fanciful interpretations—it becomes clear that Villon is, quite simply, the finest French poet of the Middle Ages and an enduring artist for any age.

BIBLIOGRAPHY

Burl, Aubrey. *Danse Macabre: François Villon, Poetry, and Murder in Medieval France*. Stroud, Gloucestershire, England: Sutton, 2000. Biography studies Villon within the context of fifteenth century Paris, seeking out the truth behind the poet's crimes as well as the surpassing depth and beauty of his poetry.

Daniel, Robert R. *The Poetry of Villon and Baudelaire: Two Worlds, One Human Condition*. New York: Peter Lang, 1997. Daniel traces many themes that Villon shared with Charles Baudelaire, such as mortality and the *danse macabre*, or dance of death. The result is an illumination of the poetry of a modern and a medieval poet that highlights Villon's medieval and modern characteristics.

Fein, David A. *François Villon Revisited*. New York: Twayne, 1997. A basic biography of Villon that also examines his poetry.

Freeman, Michael. *François Villon in His Works: The Villain's Tale*. Atlanta: Rodopi, 2000. Arguing that no analysis of Villon is complete without taking into account the Paris in which he lived, this book describes that rough place and also tells how Villon consciously fashioned his own image.

Peckham, Robert D. *François Villon: A Bibliography*. New York: Garland, 1990. This comprehensive text is the starting place for anyone wishing to understand Villon's poetry, his influence, and his times. Peckham lists all the manuscripts containing Villon's poetry and translations of it, and he includes the critical texts relating to the poetry, even works inspired by Villon's poetry, up to 1985.

Simpson, Louis. Preface to *François Villon's "The Legacy" and "The Testament."* Ashland, Oreg.: Story Line, 2000. Simpson's preface provides a useful introduction to Villon's life and times, and the notes provide commentary on Villon's language and clarify the many obscure allusions that enrich Villon's poetry.

Taylor, Jane H. M. *The Poetry of François Villon: Text and Context*. New York: Cambridge University Press, 2001. Study highlights the flair and originality of Villon's poetry, showing how it appealed to his contemporary readers.

Norris J. Lacy

MIHÁLY VÖRÖSMARTY

Born: Kápolnásnyék, Hungary; December 1, 1800
Died: Pest, Hungary; November 19, 1855

PRINCIPAL POETRY

Zalán futása, 1825
Minden munkái, 1864 (12 volumes)
Összes munkái, 1884-1885 (8 volumes)
Összes művei, 1960-1979 (18 volumes)

OTHER LITERARY FORMS

Although best known for his lyric and epic poetry, which constitutes six of the eighteen volumes of the critical edition of his works published in 1979, Mihály Vörösmarty (VUH-ruhsh-mor-tee) was also an important dramatist during the formative years of the Hungarian theater. His Romantic historical dramas are seldom performed today, but they still present enjoyable reading for students of the period. On the other hand, his *Csongor és Tünde* (pr. 1830; Csongor and Tünde), a fairy play having strong philosophical overtones and bearing the influence of William Shakespeare's *A Midsummer Night's Dream* (pr. c. 1595-1596), is regularly staged and has been translated into several languages. In order to nurture the fledgling Hungarian National Theater, Vörösmarty ably translated the classics: His Hungarian renderings of Shakespeare's *King Lear* (pr. c. 1605-1606) in 1856 and *Julius Caesar* (pr. c. 1599-1600) in 1848 are unsurpassed to this day.

Through his theoretical and critical writings, Vörösmarty was influential in defining the aesthetic issues of his times and in encouraging the emerging trends of Romanticism and populism. As an editor or associate of several of the period's most important journals, he introduced and encouraged the talents of young artists, including the twenty-one-year-old Sándor Petőfi, thus greatly enriching the literature of Hungary. He also authored and compiled a number of dictionaries, grammars, and handbooks for the Hungarian Academy of Sciences. His extensive correspondence provides invaluable documentation of the period's political and cultural life.

ACHIEVEMENTS

Born into what is considered one of the most exciting and eventful periods in the political and cultural development of Hungary, Mihály Vörösmarty made a significant contribution to nearly every aspect of his nation's intellectual life. Vörösmarty began his literary career fully committed to classical ideals, and he never lost his admiration for the craftsmanship of the Greek and Latin poets, but he soon fell under the influence of the prevailing literary trend, Romanticism. Calls for national revival were sounding all over the Continent, and in Hungary such calls were perhaps louder and more impatient than elsewhere. Vörösmarty became one of the most enthusiastic and effective of the reformers, and he served their cause with his literary as well as his political activities.

Two specific characteristics of his oeuvre distinguish him from his contemporaries: As a descendant of the nobility, he remained bewildered and somewhat repulsed by the idea of mass movements. This background made him a reluctant and pessimistic advocate of radical democratic transformation and somewhat colored the sincerity of his social proclamations. However, he was able to progress beyond the limitations of his nationalistic contemporaries at a surprisingly young age, and by the 1830's, he was able to view the fate of Hungary in a more inclusive context. In his best philosophical poems (few of which have been translated into English), he speaks with total conviction and determination about the future of humankind. Vörösmarty's mature poetry is remarkably free of the feelings of inferiority and ethnocentricity that had often characterized the works of earlier Hungarian poets.

Biography

As the oldest of nine children in a noble but impoverished Roman Catholic family in western Hungary, Mihály Vörösmarty could obtain a higher education only with the help of wealthy patrons. After attending the gymnasium at Székesfehérvár and Pest, and losing his father when he was seventeen, he had to accept the post of private tutor with the aristocratic Perczel family. At the same time, he continued his studies toward a law degree. These years of servitude and the hopeless love he felt for his employer's daughter left marks of sensitivity, wariness, and pessimism on his character.

In 1823, Vörösmarty obtained a position as a law clerk while maintaining his post with the Perczel family. He had been writing poetry and drama since he was fifteen, and the lively company of his peers contributed to the further development of his talent, making him conscious of the importance of patriotic literature. During this time, he also made contact with the restless noblemen of the countryside who were conducting a determined campaign of resistance in the face of the absolutist Viennese government. Under their influence, Vörösmarty wrote the first of his anti-Habsburg poems

and a number of expressive, complex historical dramas. The memory of unhappy love and the realization of limitations placed on him by a rigidly structured society continued to haunt him, and in 1826, he left the Perczel household. His goal to "become an independent man and a writer" was instrumental in his decision to settle in Buda, which was emerging as the cultural center of Hungary. Faced with squalor and the indifference of the reading public, he was on the verge of giving up his literary activities and setting up a law practice when he was offered the editorship of the *Tudományos Gyüjtemény*, one of the most prestigious journals in Hungary. He edited this publication and its supplement, the *Koszorú*, from 1828 to 1832. While this provided him with a steady income, the drudgery of the work and disheartening political developments occurring at the time made his voice somber and pessimistic.

During the early years of the 1830's, the Reform movement gained new momentum, and the cultural life of Hungary was also invigorated by the publication of *Aurora*, the first genuine literary monthly, edited by József Bajza, Ferenc Toldy, and Vörösmarty. The poet's financial situation had improved. His works were regularly published, he won several literary prizes, and in 1830, he became an elected (and paid) member of the Hungarian Academy of Sciences. He contributed significantly to the linguistic, orthographic, and lexicographic publications of the academy, was instrumental in the democratization of its bylaws, and remained active in public life, largely through the journals *Athenaeum* and *Figyelmező*, which became the arbiters of Hungarian cultural and literary affairs. His cautious stand on political reforms notwithstanding, he attracted the suspicion of the Habsburg police.

When the first permanent Hungarian theatrical company became active in Buda in 1833, there was an urgent need for original Hungarian dramas. Vörösmarty enthusiastically supported this company and contributed five successful plays in as many years. His activities as a dramatist and critic were instrumental in the development of the Hungarian theater.

In 1836, Vörösmarty and a small circle of intellectuals founded the Kisfaludy Társaság, named after the recently deceased Károly Kisfaludy, the first professional writer-poet of Hungary, who had played a significant role in making the twin communities of Buda and Pest, the cultural center of the country.

The 1830's witnessed the full development of political lyricism in Vörösmarty's work. Among other writings, he produced more than 150 incisive epigrams which demonstrated his commitment to a course of sensible reforms and revealed his acute sensitivity to the public and aesthetic issues of the times.

The 1840's were the most eventful years in Vörösmarty's life. In 1842, to the consternation of his friends, he married the eighteen-year-old Laura Csajághy. Theirs was a successful and happy marriage, and they had four children. The livelier political atmosphere and the liberalizing tendencies of the decade encouraged and motivated him, while the impending specter of a revolution occasionally filled him with doubt and foreboding. Lajos Kossuth, Ferenc Deák, and Miklós Wesselényi, the leaders of the Hungarian independence struggle, were among his friends, and he was elected president of the National Circle, one of the centers of political activity. His participation in aesthetic debates was reduced somewhat, but his prestige and influence enabled him to help the younger generation of poets and writers to gain recognition; for example, he was first to publish the works of the young Petőfi, the foremost Hungarian lyric poet.

After the revolution of March 15, 1848, Vörösmarty took an active part in political activities, wholeheartedly supporting the policies of Kossuth. He obtained a seat in the Chamber of Deputies, and later, during the months of armed struggle, was appointed judge by the independent Hungarian government. Hungary's defeat in the War of Independence crushed Vörösmarty; after several months in hiding, he reported to the imperial authorities, who, after an investigation, cleared him in 1850. Disappointed and disillusioned, Vörösmarty concentrated on providing a livelihood for his family. Since he was only marginally successful as a landowner, he was often forced to accept the charity of his supporters. Finding himself unable to resume fully his literary activities, he produced only a few bitter, tragically prophetic laments and elegies and turned more and more to alcohol for consolation. In 1855, his deteriorating health forced him to move to Pest, where he

died two days after his arrival. The Habsburg authorities took every measure to quell any popular outpouring of sympathy; in spite of this, Vörösmarty's funeral turned into the first mass demonstration against Austrian rule since 1849. His friends, through private correspondence, were able to collect a sizable amount to provide for the widow and children of the poet.

ANALYSIS

Mihály Vörösmarty experimented with versification as a teenager, and he was amazed and overjoyed when he discovered that the Hungarian language was readily adaptable to the requirements of metrical poetry. Because the early decades of the nineteenth century were considered the golden age of literary classicism in Hungary, and because Vörösmarty's education at the gymnasium was also heavily classical, it is not surprising that he produced a great number of odes, epigrams, and other verse forms patterned after the poets of antiquity. The other important influence in his early youth was an all-pervasive patriotism, which obliged him to produce a number of historical epics. In these, he demonstrated a naïve view of Hungarian nobility and its relationship to the king, attributing any conflicts between the two to personal rivalries and the divisive intrigue of (usually foreign) courtiers.

ZALÁN FUTÁSA

The work that stands out among his early creations and that made him a nationally known poet was *Zalán futása* (the flight of Zalán), a heroic epic in ten cantos, completed in 1825. Vörösmarty successfully combined the treatment of a major Hungarian literary motif with the use of polished classical hexameters, while putting into practice his conviction that the depiction of epochal events from the nation's history was an excellent way to reawaken a national consciousness in nineteenth century Hungarians. He also revived the genre of the heroic epic in Hungarian literature, paralleling the activities of Miklós Zrínyi (1620-1664). Vörösmarty's work is a patriotic epic, notwithstanding its many interpolated lyrics, which relate episodes of love, fulfilled or unrequited—recounting how the chieftain Árpád and his Hungarians (Magyars) achieved victory in 896 over the Slavic settlers of the Danubian basin. Medieval chronicles discovered in the eighteenth century provided much of Vörösmarty's source material; he also drew on the Ossianic ballads and nationalistic literature of the time.

For nineteenth century Hungarians, *Zalán futása* derived its significance from an insistent tone that ran throughout its descriptions of battle scenes, war councils, and military preparations. Vörösmarty urged his generation of "indolent, soft, and lethargic" Hungarians to emulate Árpád and his heroic warriors. The epic is not, however, a call to arms, but rather a summons to patriotism. Indeed, what makes it enjoyable reading today is that its message, although outdated, is expressed not in strident, ethnocentric proclamations, but in a personal, elegiac voice, gently chiding rather than criticizing the weak descendants of mighty forefathers. Vörösmarty's deeply felt convictions are given full expression through the magic of language (a reformed and rejuvenated Hungarian) and style (a seductively personal blend of classical forms and pre-Romantic turns). Even in this, his best-known epic creation, Vörösmarty was essentially a lyric rather than an epic poet.

The classical influence always remained discernible in Vörösmarty's works: He continued to reject the effusive rhetoric of fashionable poetry, to defend pure sentiment from the inroads of mere sentimentality, and to seek an ultimate rationale behind humankind's existence and the course of human history. At the same time, he could not resist Romanticism, especially since it emphasized the role of the individual, the power of the supernatural, and the incomprehensible and erratic nature of human events—traits that made Romanticism especially attractive to Hungarians. Even in his early works, Vörösmarty had exhibited an exalted manner of expression and an unusual breadth of vision; these are elements of his natural pre-Romantic disposition. In *Zalán futása*, however, he reveals even more of his Romanticism, in the frequency of intimate episodes, the role of Titans and fairies, and the depiction of earthy love affairs, while in form, structure, and the presentation of his central characters, he strictly conforms to classical requirements.

USE OF FOLK TRADITIONS

Around the end of the 1820's, the liberal intelligentsia of Hungary began to turn toward the commoners in their search for allies against Habsburg oppression. The clearest thinkers among them also realized that the cultural regeneration of the country could not be accomplished without the adoption and utilization of folk traditions, especially folk literature. The wave of literary populism, so eloquently promoted by Johann G. Herder and the Grimm brothers in Germany, made rapid gains in Hungary. From the first decades of the nineteenth century, the poets made it one of their goals to be able to write in the manner of folk songs or, indeed, to write "folk songs." Vörösmarty's works in this genre resembled the genuine article more closely than did those of his contemporaries. He was intimately familiar with life in rural Hungary and was able to use the expressions of the villagers with ease. His folk songs include didactic lyrics placed in the mouths of his populist heroes, as well as lyrical passages that express his own feelings. An excellent example of the latter is "Haj, száj, szem" ("Hair, Lips, Eyes"), a flirty outpouring of infatuation that imaginatively mirrors the sentiments expressed in one of the popular songs of the time. In adapting the direct and unaffected voice of the Hungarian people to formal literature, Vörösmarty was the direct forerunner of the most brilliant Hungarian populist poet, Petőfi.

CSONGOR ÉS TÜNDE

Csongor és Tünde, a fairy play in five acts, completed in 1830, profited greatly from Vörösmarty's use of populist elements. It tells the story of two lovers who, after becoming separated, overcome a number of earthly and mythical temptations and obstacles in order to be reunited. Beyond this, however, the play is a dramatic tale with philosophical and allegorical overtones. Csongor seeks not only his own happiness but the fulfillment of humankind as well. The setting of his sojourn is the entire earth; the three wanderers whom he meets represent the worst of negative human traits, while the monologue of Night reveals the course of human history. The story has a moral: Greed, conquest, and the desire for abstract knowledge do not necessarily bring happiness; on the contrary, they can be destructive.

Vörösmarty based *Csongor és Tünde* on a sixteenth century epic, the *Story of Prince Argirus*, which had survived as cheap popular entertainment. Nevertheless, the play has remained enjoyable and worthy of the stage. This may be because it presents a romantic panorama of the world, with everyday figures, conspiracy, jealousy, evil, and the drunkenness of lust. It is presented in harmonic unity and speaks in a popular, expressive language. The formal elements of classicism are present: The humorous passages are set in rhymed or unrhymed trochaic tetrameters, while the words of wisdom are spoken in iambic pentameters and hexameters. At the same time, Vörösmarty made judicious use of folkloric elements by introducing witches, fairies, trees with golden apples, the realms of Dawn and Night, and even the sons of the Devil fighting over their inheritance. The two heroes have their earthly counterparts in their escorts, whose realism provides a sober counterpoint to the idealism of Csongor.

SOMBER OUTLOOK

Crises and disillusionments were not infrequent in Vörösmarty's life. For more than ten years, he carried the memory of a youthful love doomed to failure by the values of a society based on titles and wealth. The poet never became a revolutionary, but his belief in rational, deliberate progress under the leadership of his class, the liberal nobility, was severely shaken. Much of his pessimism and sense of inferiority resulted from this early failure. Although he later successfully courted and married a woman twenty-four years his junior, dark thoughts and doubts continued to surface in his poems. Vörösmarty was also sensitive to the events of public life, which are reflected in the violently alternating emotions of his poems. He glowed with energy and optimism when the dynamism of the political scene and the liberalization of public discussions seemed to justify his faith in progress. At other times, such as when the assembly of Hungarian noblemen had disbanded without solving the problems entrusted to their care or when the cause of Polish independence was dealt a serious blow by the Austrian-inspired Galician peasant rebellion, his outlook became somber, and he wrote dark poems about the hopelessness of the human condition. "Az emberek" ("Mankind") posits malevolent intellect and the misguided anger of the masses as the two greatest obstacles to the fulfillment of humanity's dreams.

"THE SUMMONS"

In 1836, Vörösmarty wrote his best-known political poem, "Szózat" ("The Summons"). It appeared at a time when the outcome of the sharpening struggle between Vienna and the Hungarian reformers was undecided and when the Habsburg counteroffensive against the Hungarian independence movement was discouraging many of the more cautious liberals. Vörösmarty wrote what could be considered an affirmation of faith in the future of Hungary, but his scope was no longer narrowly nationalistic. With an enlarged and refined historical consciousness, he placed the fate of his country in the context of world history. The best and most promising characters of Hungary's history are invoked and made part of the new Hungarian course of action, in which the possibility of compromise is not mentioned. This is not a call to the weak, shiftless descendants of long-dead heroes; in the meticulously rhymed lines of this Romantic ode, which became the second national anthem of Hungary, the historical consciousness of a small but unbroken nation is proclaimed before the world.

SOCIOPOLITICAL CONTENT

Throughout the 1830's, the voice of Vörösmarty's lyricism steadily grew stronger, though at the expense of his epic output. In more than a hundred epigrams, he demonstrated that there was no aspect of national life that escaped his attention. After 1835, he turned to the women of Hungary, a hitherto largely ignored segment of the population, and encouraged them to become active participants in the nation's cultural life. In the 1840's, the course of political events accelerated, adding new depth to the social content of Vörösmarty's poems. Inexperienced Hungarian leaders were thwarted by indecisiveness and internal squabbles. Vörösmarty seldom participated in these destructive recriminations, but his poems reveal the acute struggle raging within him.

"Gutenberg Albumba" ("For the Gutenberg Album") greets the decade on an accusatory note; according to Vörösmarty, the world is not deserving of the great heritage of Johann Gutenberg, inventor of the printing press. In "Liszt Ferenchez" ("To Ferenc Liszt"), he continues to broaden his concept of progress, striking the tones of a proud citizen of the world. His 1843 poem "Honszeretet" ("Patriotism") proposes the elimination of noble privileges and the cultivation of a strong bourgeoisie, with special stress on the full political and social equality of the common people.

"Gondolatok a könyvtárban" ("Thoughts in the Library") recapitulates Vörösmarty's ideas and states his political creed. It may also be considered the greatest document of the struggle with conscience experienced by nearly all nineteenth century Hungarian liberals. The poem starts with a passionate accusation aimed at humanity, pointing to a "horrible lesson": While millions are born into misery, only a few thousand enjoy the good life. Vörösmarty asks: "Where is the happiness of the majority?" In answer, the poet advocates the universal solidarity of humankind and continuous striving for a better future.

POET OF NATIONAL TRAGEDY

The bloodless and relatively nonviolent revolution of 1848 filled Vörösmarty with hope for the future; he greeted the freedom of the press, the institution of an accountable national government, and the abolition of serfdom with joyous and inspiring poems. As the reactionary circles of Austria planned to take stern measures against the Hungarian reformers, the poet began to have forebodings of tragedy and advised against rash, immoderate action. The counsel of confident Hungarian radicals, however, prevailed; there was a desperate armed struggle between the imperial forces and the small army of independent Hungary. By the autumn of 1849, the Hungarians were defeated, with the help of sizable Russian forces, and the worst forebodings of Vörösmarty were realized.

Because he had actively supported the cause of "rebels," Vörösmarty was forced into hiding to avoid the vengeance of the imperial military authorities. By 1850, he thought it advisable to turn himself in to the authorities, who dismissed his case after a brief investigation. The man was free, but the poet was fatally wounded, not only by the military defeat and the subsequent humiliation of his nation, but also by the loss of his friends (some of whom died on the battlefield, some of whom were imprisoned, and some of whom chose exile) and by the shattering of his hopes and beliefs. In the sterile atmosphere of absolutist control, there was hardly a trace left of Hungarian cultural life: Publications ceased, institutions were disbanded, and even the reading public lost its disposition to support Hungarian literature. Vörösmarty encountered serious problems supporting his family, and his literary activities suffered.

Vörösmarty became "the poet of national tragedy," reduced to expressions of hopelessness and grief over the fate of a nation that was being destroyed in full view of an "uncaring, indifferent world." The obsessive power of this erstwhile lyric voice, however, reached new heights in "A vén cigány" ("The Old Gypsy"); completed about a year before the poet's death, it became one of Vörösmarty's most-recited poems. It was befitting that Vörösmarty chose the figure of an aged musician-entertainer to symbolize the fate of the Hungarian poet of the times. The poet looks toward the future of humankind even while examining its present predicament and arrives at a mood of faint hopefulness only after having traversed the whirlpools of despair. In the process, the language and the association of the images have become almost demented, and the poet expresses with near-biblical intensity his exaltation and pain. Hope is not dead; in his swan song, the fatally broken poet calls for a "cleansing storm" to bring a better world and a genuine occasion for universal rejoicing.

OTHER MAJOR WORKS

PLAYS: *Csongor és Tünde*, pr. 1830; *A kincskeresök*, pr. 1833; *Vérnász*, pb. 1833; *A fátyol titkai*, pr. 1834; *Árpád ébredése*, pr. 1837; *Marót Bán*, pb. 1838; *Julius Caesar*, pr. 1848 (translation of William Shakespeare's play); *Lear király*, pr. 1856 (translation of Shakespeare's play).

BIBLIOGRAPHY

Basa, Eniko Molnár, ed. *Hungarian Literature*. New York: Griffon House, 1993. A historical and critical analysis of Hungarian literature. Includes bibliographic references. Provides context for understanding Vörösmarty.

Czigány, Lóránt, ed. *The Oxford History of Hungarian Literature from the Earliest Times to the Present*. Rev. ed. New York: Oxford University Press, 1986. Overview of Hungarian literature sheds light on Vörösmarty and Hungarian poetry.

Jones, David Mervyn. *Five Hungarian Writers*. Oxford, England: Clarendon Press, 1966. Jones looks extensively at five prominent writers, including Vörösmarty, and their works' significance both within and outside Hungarian literature.

Makkai, Adam, ed. *In Quest of the "Miracle Stag": The Poetry of Hungary*. Rev. ed. Chicago: Atlantis-Centaur, 2000. This anthology of Hungarian poetry contains a short biography of Vörösmarty and a number of his selected poems in translation.

Mark, Thomas R. "The First Hungarian Translation of Shakespeare's Complete Works." *Shakespeare Quarterly* 16, no. 1 (Winter, 1965): 105-115. To fill what they saw as a void in Hungarian literature, Hungarian writers, including Vörösmarty, began translating William Shakespeare's plays into the Hungarian language. Mark discusses a variety of results, such as the thirteen plays somewhat unsuccessfully translated by an eighteen-year-old woman, and Vörösmarty's eloquent translation of *Julius Caesar* and *King Lear*.

Murray, John Christopher, ed. *Encyclopedia of the Romantic Era, 1760-1850*. Vol. 2. New York: Fitzroy Dearborn, 2004. Contains a short analysis of *Zalán futása*.

András Boros-Kazai

W

WALTHER VON DER VOGELWEIDE

Born: Probably in lower Austria; c. 1170
Died: Near Würzburg, Bavaria, Holy Roman Empire
(now in Germany); c. 1230

PRINCIPAL POETRY
Songs and Sayings of Walther von der Vogelweide,
1917
Poems, 1952
Die Gedichte, 1959 (Lachmann-Kraus edition)
*Walther von der Vogelweide: The Single-Stanza
Lyrics*, 2002 (bilingual text; translated and
edited by Frederick Goldin)

OTHER LITERARY FORMS
Walther von der Vogelweide (VOL-tur fawn dur
FOH guhl-vi-duh) was exclusively a lyric poet.

ACHIEVEMENTS
Walther von der Vogelweide is recognized as the
single most important Middle High German lyric poet.
According to Peter Wapnewski, he made two pioneering contributions to literary history. First, he moved
German courtly love poetry from the sterile artificiality
of conventional literature to a fresh personal expression, even inventing a corresponding lyric genre, the
Mädchenlieder (songs to a common-class girl, sometimes also misleadingly called songs of "lower love").
Second, he gave a new nobility to didactic and political
poetry. Kuno Francke goes so far as to see in Walther's
love songs "the struggle for the emancipation of the individual" that eventually led to the overthrow of "the
whole system of medieval hierarchy" and "an anticipation of this great emancipation movement, a protest of
the individual against the dictates of society." Scholar
Peter Rühmkorf deromanticizes the ultrapatriotic German image of Walther and sees him primarily in indi-
vidualistic terms as a "self" struggling for personal

identity and recognition in a time of social crisis.

This much is certain: Whether addressing an emperor, a pope, or a high nobleman or lady, Walther
speaks with courage, authority, and clarity; he is not in-
timidated by any class distinctions. In his love poetry,
he is not satisfied with a one-sided platonic relationship
or an adulation of mere external beauty or high social
status; for him, love is a shared affection, a reciprocal
meeting of hearts and minds, an inner attitude, an important ennobling force in the lives of men and women.
The scope of Walther's themes and the tone and manner of their treatment make it unmistakably clear that
his office as a lyric poet went beyond courtly entertainment and included functions of political propaganda
and ethical critique, functions that are performed today
by the communications media. However, Walther, like
other medieval lyric poets, composed and sang his own
songs, and he was more highly praised by his contemporaries for his singing than for his lyrics.

BIOGRAPHY
Walther von der Vogelweide was born about 1170,
possibly of the lower nobility. Because the term *Vogelweide* was a common word meaning bird sanctuary,
numerous places have claimed to be the poet's birthplace, most conspicuously Vogelweidhof, near Bozen,
South Tyrol, where an impressive monument in his
honor has been erected; since this region did not belong
to Austria at the time and the Austrian dialect was not
spoken there, however, scholars speculate that Walther
probably was born in lower Austria. Wherever his
birthplace, the poet "learned to sing and recite in Austria," appearing at the court of Duke Frederick in Vienna about 1190 and probably learning his craft from
Reinmar von Hagenau.

In 1198, Walther's patron died; Walther was forced
to leave Vienna to begin the uncertain life of a wandering minstrel. The only extant historical document concerning him is a receipt showing that Wolfger, bishop
of Passau, had given "to the singer Walther de Vogelweide five solidi for a fur coat on Saint Martin's Day in
the year 1203." Among his many other patrons was
Count Hermann of Thuringia, at whose court he met
Wolfram von Eschenbach, author of *Parzival* (c. 1200-
1210; English translation, 1894), and other lyric poets.

Walther wrote songs for three emperors; after Philip of Swabia was murdered and his successor Otto IV allegedly did not pay the poet enough, Walther shifted his allegiance to Friedrick II, who eventually rewarded him with a small property near Würzburg in about 1220. Presumably, Walther did not participate in the Crusade of 1228 and died about 1230 near Würzburg, where his grave could still be seen in the cathedral garden half a century later. Another minstrel, Hugo von Trimberg, grieved over Walther's death with the words, "Ah Sir Walther von der Vogelweide, I would feel sorry for whomever forgot you."

ANALYSIS

In only one generation, from 1180 to 1210, the great flowering of Middle High German courtly culture under the Hohenstaufen Dynasty produced—in addition to four great epic writers, Hartmann von Aue, Gottfried von Strassburg, Wolfram von Eschenbach, and the anonymous author of the *Nibelungenlied* (c. 1200; English translation, 1848)—numerous lyric poets, the most renowned of them being Walther von der Vogelweide. Even princes and emperors ranked among the courtly love poets. The roots of this German medieval poetry are multiple: Provençal and northern French courtly love poetry, indigenous songs and Goliardic verse such as that collected in *Carmina burana* (1847), and a variety of Latin secular and religious genres (eulogies, sequences), some dating back to antiquity. Medieval German poetry features a great variety of meters and melodies, since the minstrel was expected to compose a new meter and melody for each song.

Courtly love poetry (*Minnesäng*) was symptomatic of a new secular culture that rejected the "contempt of the world" preached for centuries by the monastic orders and that sought instead to harmonize eternal salvation with earthly happiness. The role of women in the courts and castles was to elevate and dignify life and to convey a certain *hoher muot* (joy of life), which was the crowning virtue in the knightly code. Although the love songs sometimes have a trace of the occasional in them—they often are addressed to a particular woman and reflect specific circumstances—such love poetry was not a stylized proposal for a literal love relationship, but an artistic achievement, a fictional, public musical presentation on the theme of love for the amusement and edification of the entire court (estimated as usually comprising between thirty and seventy persons). Since the idolized woman was supposed to be of high rank, married and virtuous, no erotic reciprocation was expected but, at most, a greeting or token of appreciation. Praise of the woman was not a means to an end but an ennobling activity in itself, for the lady represented the humane ideal of beauty and dignity for which this secular knightly society was striving. Her being not only was physically beautiful and charming but also encompassed a catalog of virtues such as honor, self-discipline, constancy, moderation, and loyalty—traits of a proud, aristocratic society.

Walther von der Vogelweide (©Bettmann/CORBIS)

MÄDCHENLIEDER

Walther regarded highly his function as a courtly love poet who could express for the men and women of his society the emotions of body and soul. Under Walther's predecessor and teacher, Reinmar, *Minnelyrik* (love poetry) had degenerated into a genre that was obsessed with the monotonous theme of the unrequited lover. Walther broke with this tradition—and from Reinmar—and introduced many new dimensions into the thematics of courtly love poetry. His *Mädchenlieder* scandalized society by directing love and the title *Frouwe* (noble lady) to a common-class girl. He also introduced into courtly poetry a mature, reciprocally fulfilled marital love, contrary to the tradition of unrequitedness. Late in life, he rejected the ribaldry and crudity that was brought into courtly love poetry under the influence of peasant dances by a new generation of minstrels, including Neidhart von Reuenthal. Finally, he turned away from "Lady World" and his "many errors" as a *Minnesänger* and addressed God himself as "you sweet true Love." Underlying this broad span of the love concept in Walther's poems is the medieval idea of "gradualism," which sees all reality as an ascending ladder of being, each rung different in degree but analogous to the ones above and below—from the various levels of earthly reality, through a person, who is both body and soul, to the heights of spirit in God.

Paul Stapf divides the love lyrics chronologically into six periods: early love songs, songs from 1198 to 1203, high courtly love, *Mädchenlieder*, new high courtly love, and late songs.

Walther's early love songs, written before leaving the Viennese court in 1198, though still quite within the conventions of the genre, already display the sharp tension created by the ambiguity of traditional love poetry. On one hand, it was supposed to represent an approved public relationship involving "conversation" with and "instruction" as well as "praise" of the woman by the poet, who was rewarded with a "greeting" or token of esteem, all strictly on a platonic level; on the other, by the very nature of love between man and woman, it sometimes involved an implicit erotic attraction that threatened to erupt into socially unacceptable amorous fulfillment. In these early poems, the poet's love is rejected; the woman is unapproachable and on the defen-

sive; she has maintained her dignity as a woman and will hold him accountable for any violation of proper decorum. In some poems, she would like to grant his desire for a love affair, but social pressure prevents it; she has a duty to maintain her honor. With a touch of resignation, she submits to the dictates of society: "Mir tuot einer slahte wille" ("Can She Alone Be Happy When All Others Are Sad?"). Sometimes the concept of honor is deepened to a personal ethical code. She wants "to have a woman's proper qualities . . . since a beautiful body is worthless without understanding," that is, without moral responsibility.

Perhaps the very ambiguity and wide range of meaning of courtly love is what invites some poems to be highly rational and analytical: "Whoever says that love is a sin, should first reflect well, for love contains many a distinction which one can rightly enjoy, and its consequence is constancy and great happiness. . . . I am not speaking of false love, which would better be called non-love: I will always oppose it." However, the same poem also speaks from living experience: "No one knows what true joy is who did not receive it from a woman." Walther leaves no doubt as to the edifying and positive nature of love: "Love is the source of all good qualities; without love no heart can be truly happy."

MINSTREL YEARS

Walther's departure from the court at Vienna marks a sharp break in his life and poetry and begins a second stage of his creative activity, his early years as a wandering minstrel, from 1198 to 1203. His songs now show the direct influence of the vagabond poets of the *Carmina burana*. One single theme runs through them all: how summer follows winter and love chases away sadness. Their execution is smoother and the nature imagery is brighter, used economically like a kind of symbolic shorthand: In winter, the frost hurts the little birds so much that they no longer sing; in summer, the girls will be playing ball in the street again (a rare glimpse of medieval everyday life). The poet celebrates the great power of May over humans and nature. Perhaps May is a magician, he suggests; wherever his delight goes, no one is old. The winter of 1198 must have been particularly severe; the poet believed he would "never again pick red flowers in the green meadows." His death, he muses, would have been "a loss to all good men who long for joy and who like to sing and dance."

HIGH COURTLY LOVE POEMS

The poet's third period, from 1203 to 1205, was characterized by poems of "high courtly love" which were traditional, rational, and sophisticated. Most of the poems of this period are united by a single theme: constancy and reciprocity. These are two sides of the same coin: The lady demands fidelity on the poet's part and rebukes him for praising other women; the poet replies that he cannot continue praising only her if she refuses to reciprocate his love.

A highly optimistic poem called "Ir Sult sprechen" ("Speak a Welcome") illustrates the poet's praise of other women: He has seen many countries, and German ways please him the best. German men are handsome, and German women are like angels; whoever scolds any of them is mistaken (probably an allusion to the Provençal poet Peire Vidal's castigations of German manners). Whoever seeks virtue and pure love should come to Germany. "From the Elbe to the Rhein and back again as far as Hungary live the best people I have ever known in the world. If I can judge good upbringing and beauty, by God, the women are nobler here than anywhere else." Now a harsh note is struck: His lady reproaches him for praising other women and thus being guilty of inconstancy. As if enraged at the lady's rebuke, he retaliates in the song "Staet ist ein Angest und ein Nôt" ("Constancy Is Fear and Torment"), harping ironically on constancy, naming it twelve times in two short stanzas, and finally exclaiming "Lady Constancy, set me free!"

Poem after poem reflects a period of strife, for example, "Saget mir ieman, waz ist Minne?" ("What Is Loving?"), "Daz ich dich sô selten grüeze" ("That I So Seldom Praise You Is No Misdeed of Mine"), and "Mîn Frowe ist ein ungenaedic Wîp" ("My Lady Is a Cruel Woman"). Finally, in "What Is Loving?," the poet hammers out the principle that will lead to the end of his relationship with this "lady" and to his abandonment of one-sided courtly love: "Love is the joy of two hearts. If they share equally, then love is there; if this is not so, then one heart cannot receive it." The poet, however, does not conceal a sour, unchivalric remark: "If I have grown old in her service, she's not gotten any younger

either." Finally, he exhorts his young rival: "Avenge me and whip her old skin with fresh switches."

LOWER LOVE SONGS

The fourth group of songs (written after 1203 and therefore somewhat overlapping the previous group) overcomes this discord and enters a new phase of fulfillment with a woman of equal or lower rank. In "Herzeliebez Frowelîn" ("Little Maid So Dear"), whatever joy the poet experienced in this world was caused "by her beauty, her goodness, and her red mouth that laughs so lovingly." He responds to those who criticize him for directing his love songs to a person of lower rank, claiming that "they don't have any idea what love is, they have never experienced true love, since they love only for wealth or external beauty. What kind of love is that?" He reiterates his reason for having changed from "high courtly love" to this more satisfying relationship: "A Lover's affection is nothing if it goes unrequited. One-sided love is worthless; it must be shared, permeating two hearts and none besides."

The most famous of Walther's songs of "lower love" is "Unter der Linden" ("Under the Linden-Tree"), in which a naïve, common-class girl rejoices in her love experience under the linden tree, the crushed flowers still showing the place where the couple had lain. What he did with her no one will ever know except he and she and the little bird that sang the refrain "Tandaradei!" Equally masterful is the poem "Die welt was gelf, rôt unde blâ" ("The World in Red and Blue Was Gay"), also called the "vowel poem" since, in German, each stanza rhymes with one of the vowels *a, e, i, o,* and *u;* it is a highly graphic poem calling for the end of winter. One wryly humorous poem, "Wer kan nû ze danke singen?" ("Who Can Please Everyone with His Song?"), lauds the poet's broad range of experience, which makes it possible for him to sing a wide variety of songs, but observes that people still are dissatisfied.

NEW HIGH LOVE

In his fifth period, that of "new high love" (from 1205 to about 1220), Walther's songs show more depth, maturity, and formal perfection. The "lady" seems to be of very high social rank, and the relationship is a conventional one. There is sadness at court, the times are unsuited for song, true love has died, and the whole world is beset with troubles. Song is tempted to wait for better times, as in "Die zwîvelaere Sprechent" ("The Doubters"). The exuberance of youth is over, and the poet articulates a positive attitude even toward the unequal relationship represented by conventional courtly love, as long as there is some reciprocation: "He is certainly also fortunate who observes her virtues precisely so that it moves his heart. An understanding woman should respond with affection." This kind of love can motivate poetry: "Just a loving look from a woman gives joy to the heart. . . . But what is like the happiness where a beloved heart is faithful, beautiful, chaste, and of good morals? The lucky man who has won this does nothing wrong to praise it before strangers." The importance of moderation is explained in "Ich hoere iu sô vil tugende jehen" ("I Hear You Speak of So Many Virtues") and "Allerwerde keit ein Füegerinne" ("Co-ordinator of All Values, Lady Moderation"). One of Walther's very best poems and the crown jewel of this period is "Sô die Bluomen ûz dem Grase dringent" ("When the Flowers Spring Out of the Grass"), which compares a beautiful May day with a beautiful noblewoman in all her finery. If the poet had to choose between the two, the outcome would be: "Sir May, you would have to become March before I gave up my lady."

LATE SONGS

Three poems can adequately represent the late songs (from 1220 to 1230). "Ir reinen Wîp" ("Ye Women Pure") is a sort of literary testament: "For forty years or more I have sung of love and of how one should live" (note the educational function of the poet). In "Frô Welt" ("Lady World"), he renounces the world because, while her beauty is lovely to look at from the front, from behind she is so horridly shameful that he wishes to spurn her forever. In "Ein Meister las" ("A Wise Man"), he meditates on the transitory quality of life and says, "It is high time for penance, since I, a sick man, now fear grim death." The poem ends in a vein of religious repentance, an emphasis found in several poems, including the long *Leich*.

SPRUCH GENRE

About half of Walther's poems belong to the broad genre of *Spruch* (political or didactic) poetry. Walther's type of *Spruch* was formerly believed to have been a single-stanza spoken poem, but the melodies of some of them have been recovered, and it is now known

that they were not recited but sung. Friedrich Maurer's "song-theory" brought together in a single poem stanzas of the same "tone" or melody that had been variously scattered in the manuscripts. In Maurer's view, each "tone" of a political song was invented in its own separate period, and thus stanzas belonging to one "tone" could be dated far apart in Walther's time, although some of them were written over a period of a few years. "Each tone," Maurer asserts, "has its briefly extended time of origin, but especially its own theme and subject matter." Poems with different melodies, even though thematically similar, are not contemporaneous. The advantages of Maurer's theory are that it facilitates study of the gradual evolution of Walther's stanzaic art; it enriches interpretation by retrieving the overarching meaning connecting the stanzas of one "tone"; and it elucidates stanza-internal meaning by contrast and comparison. Maurer's theory, however, has not been unanimously accepted by scholars. Stapf, editor of a fine annotated edition and modern German translation of Walther's poems, rejects Maurer's theory in favor of more accurate dating of the individual stanzas. Annette Georgi, in her study of the Latin and German *Preislied*, seems to follow Maurer.

The major controversy discussed in Walther's political poems is the struggle between the empire and the papacy during the period of turmoil following the election of two pretenders to the imperial throne in 1198. After the death of Henry VI, son of Frederick Barbarossa, the Hohenstaufen faction elected Henry's brother, Philip of Swabia, to succeed him, while the opposing Guelphs elected Otto IV of Brunswick. When Philip was murdered, Otto succeeded him with the approval of Pope Innocent III, who later shifted his support to the Hohenstaufen Frederick II. During this time, the petty princes tried to stake their own areas of power at the expense of the Crown. In these controversies, Walther supported first Philip, then Otto, and finally Frederick II, probably reflecting the successive allegiances of his princely patrons. In "Diu Krône ist elter danne der Künec Philippes sî" ("The Crown Is Older than King Philip"), Walther argues for Philip—his legitimacy based on the preestablished condition that the crown, which is older than he, fits him so well, a poetic allusion to the Hohenstaufen's possession of the real Imperial crown (while his opponent Otto IV was crowned in the proper place, Aachen, and by the right ecclesiastic, the bishop of Cologne). Another poem in the "Philip tone" parallels, with some doctoring of historical facts, a procession of Philip at Magdeburg with the birth of Christ; Philip's wife Irene (later renamed Mary), daughter of the Byzantine Emperor, is compared with the Virgin Mary, "rose without thorn, dove without gall." Again the possession of the right insignia is stressed, but an even stronger title, the link with the great Hohenstaufen predecessors, is compared with the Trinity: "There walked an Emperor's brother and an Emperor's son in one garment, though the names are three" (Frederick, Henry, and Philip). To medieval man, accustomed to thinking in terms of the "analogy of being," the impact of this poem confirming divine appointment must have been grat.

"I WAS SITTING UPON A ROCK"

Written in the "imperial tone," the most famous of Walther's poems, "Ich saz ûf eine Steine" ("I Was Sitting upon a Rock"), depicts Walther in the pose in which he is illustrated in the *Manessische Handschrift*: sitting on a large rock with his legs crossed and his chin and one cheek supported by the palm of one hand. He was pondering very anxiously on "how one should live in the world." He could give no advice on "how one could acquire three things," so that none of the three would be ruined. The first two are honor and property, "which often are harmful to one another"; the third is God's grace, "which is worth more than the other two." The poet would like to have all three in one chest, but unfortunately it is impossible for property, worldly honor, and God's grace ever to dwell in one heart. "Paths and roads are blocked to them: Treachery lies in ambush, violence moves on the street; peace and justice are very sorely wounded. The three have no safe convoy, until these two recover." The subject of the stanza is how to order one's life correctly in this world.

The main components of the poem are seven abstract nouns; the main structuring device is a system of mathematical vectors that creates an ethical topography and conveys an impression of objective moral certainty. There are three goals that one should attempt to attain in life: honor (a), property (b), and God's favor (c), which is more valuable than property and honor

and is also eternal. There are two instrumental goods: peace (d) and justice (e). Because a and b are incompatible and together endanger c, one cannot hope to attain them all. At this point, an extended metaphor is inserted: The streets are insecure for a, b, and c, since two negative abstractions, treachery (f) and violence (g), threaten. The two ancillary values d and e are sorely wounded. The solution to a, b, and c's predicament would be an extension and reversal of the metaphor "unsafe roads." This solution cannot be achieved until the two ancillary values d and e have the "remedy" that corresponds to their "ailment." A secondary rhetorical figure occurs twice, an *apo koinu* (the relation of one grammatical component to two others, one before and one after it); the clause "I could give no advice" can relate to the "how" clause before and the "how" clause after it. Similarly, "unfortunately this cannot be" negates both "I wanted to put them in one chest" and the possibility that honor, property, and God's favor might come together in one heart.

"OTTO TONE"

Of the six poems in the "Otto tone," the first in Maurer's sequence welcomes Otto IV and announces the submission of the princes, specifically of Walther s patron Dietrich von Meissen; the second alludes to the eagle and lion on Otto's coat of arms and calls on him to establish peace in Germany with "generosity" and "power" and to direct his country's power against the pagans. The third, "Hêr Keiser" ("Sir Emperor"), calls even more emphatically for a crusade: "Sir Emperor, I am an official messenger and I bring you a message from God: you govern the earth, he governs the kingdom of heaven: he has ordered me to complain to you (you are his regent) that in his Son's land the Pagans are exulting to the disgrace of you both. You should protect His rights." The fourth Otto poem, "Hêr Bâbest" ("Sir Pope"), refers to the contradiction created when the pope first endorsed Otto and then switched to support his opponent: "We heard you command Christendom as to which Emperor they were to obey. . . . You should not forget that you said: 'Whoever blesses you let him be blessed; whoever curses you, let him be cursed with a complete curse.' For God's sake, think that over, if the honor of the clergy means anything to you." The fifth Otto poem applies the same complaint to the clergy at large: "We laymen are puzzled by the clergy's instructions. What they taught us till a few short days ago, they now want to contradict. . . . One of the two instructions is false." The sixth Otto poem retells the story of Jesus with the coin, and the conclusion gains cogency because the Middle High German words for "Caesar" and "Emperor" are identical: "Render to the Emperor what is the Emperor's and to God what is God's."

ANTIPAPAL POEMS

The thread of unity in Walther's political stance is his advocacy of a strong, united empire. This explains why in a good number of his poems he opposed the papacy, blaming papal interference in the affairs of the *Reich* for the widespread disorder in Germany. In "Künc Constantin der gap sô vil" ("King Constantine Gave So Much"), an angel cries "Alas, alas, three times alas" because of Constantine's famous (forged) donation of temporal power to the papacy, which poisoned all Christendom by striking at its civil head: "All princes now live in honor except that the highest one is weakened. . . . The clergy want to pervert secular law." From the first, Walther had blamed the pope for appointing two Germans to one throne "so that they would destroy and devastate the realm" and had identified cupidity as the motive: "Their German silver flows into my Italian coffers." Elsewhere Walther minces no words about the negative influence of the clergy: "You bishops and noble clergy are misled. See how the Pope ties you with the devil's ropes. If you tell us he has St. Peter's keys, then tell us why he scrapes his words out of the Bible." He then accuses the clergy of simony and of being the devil's spokesmen. Certain lines most clearly identify the evil as seen by Walther: "If [the pope] is greedy, then all are greedy with him; if he lies, all lie with him; and if he deceives, they deceive with the same deception." Walther's viewpoint is clear: Christendom is ailing because its highest religious authority, the pope, undermines the chief secular authority, the emperor; moreover, by the pope's high authority, the evil at the top contaminates all the parts.

PATRONAGE POEMS

An astonishing number of Walther's poems deal with complaints about inadequate financial support or a lack of respect from one patron or another, including the Emperor Otto, whose stinginess Walther blames for

his change of allegiance to Frederick. At first, the modern reader may be repelled by an impression of crass venality, but in time, he perceives the need of a poet struggling in a marginal, insecure existence for a basic livelihood and for minimal social acceptance in the feudal class system. Two poems treat of a misunderstanding with a noble patron because a subordinate official had failed to give Walther the promised clothing. Two others describe a lawsuit against a certain Gerhart Atze for shooting Walther's horse on the grounds that its "relative" had bitten off Atze's finger. Apparently, Walther's class status was at stake, but, whatever the outcome, Walther avenged himself on Atze by poetic mockery. Other poems testify to the difficulties of being a dependent, wandering, unpropertied poet. One poem summarizes Walther's weariness with the wanderer's life: "Tonight here and tomorrow there, what a juggler's life that is." The reader rejoices with Walther when he finally receives from Frederick the small property that gives him a home of his own: "I have my fief, all the world, I have my fief! Now I do not fear the frost on my toes."

"ELEGIE"

One of the most poignant poems Walther wrote is the famous "Elegie," consisting of three stanzas all beginning with "Alas." The second stanza deals with the sad state of the empire and the "ungentle letters" from Rome (excommunicating Frederick II in 1227); the third is a call for a crusade and contains a primitive but striking image of fallen earthly reality: "The world is beautiful on the outside, white, green and red, and within black in color, dark as death." In the first stanza, Walther looks back on his life with elegiac poignancy like a reawakening Rip van Winkle: "Alas, where have all my years vanished? Did I dream my life, or is it true? Was all I dreamed existed really nothing? . . . My former playmates are tired and old. The meadow has been plowed, the forest has been cleared: If the river didn't flow as it once did, truly my sorrow would be great."

BIBLIOGRAPHY

Berleth, Richard J. *The Orphan Stone: The Minnesinger Dream of Reich*. New York: Greenwood Press, 1990. Berleth uses Walther's lyrics in this study of the relationship of the German political scene and

German lyric poetry. Mixes biographical, literary, and the broader political elements of Walther's career and output.

Garland, Henry, and Mary Garland. *Oxford Companion to German Literature*. 3d ed. New York: Oxford University Press, 1997. Encyclopedic reference work with a brief but informative section on Walther. Contains several important bibliographic references.

Gibbs, Marion E., and Sidney Johnson. *Medieval German Literature: A Companion*. 1997. Reprint. New York: Routledge, 2004. Contains an overview of Walther's life and works, with a few translated passages and bibliography.

Heinen, Hubert. "Lofty and Base Love in Walther von der Vogelweide's 'So die bluomen' and 'Aller werdekeit.'" *German Quarterly* 51 (1978): 465-475. Treats Walther's concept of love; includes quotations in German and English, notes, and bibliography.

Jones, George. *Walther Von der Vogelweide*. 1968. Reprint. New York: Twayne, 1970. A brief but comprehensive study of Walther's life and major works. The first monographic treatment of Walther in English.

Kaplowitt, Stephen J. *The Ennobling Power of Love in the Medieval German Lyric*. Chapel Hill: University of North Carolina Press, 1986. Studies the theme for twenty-one minnesingers in twenty-one short chapters, of which Walther's is the longest at forty-five pages. Poems are discussed and described, but only briefly quoted.

McFarland, Timothy, and Silvia Ranawake, eds. *Walther von der Vogelweide: Twelve Studies*. Oxford, England: Meeuws, 1982. A collection of essays that covers a wide range of issues regarding influences on Walther, his influences on the genre, and his works' forms and content.

Sayce, Olive. *The Medieval German Lyric, 1150-1230: The Development of Its Theme and Forms in Their European Context*. Oxford, England: Clarendon Press, 1982. A widely ranging and very readable study that places Walther and his works in both the German and broader European streams of lyric development.

Scheibe, Fred Karl. *Walther von der Vogelweide: Troubadour of the Middle Ages*. New York: Vantage Press, 1969. A good brief introduction to Walther's life and poetry that also surveys the reception of his works and lists English translations. Contains a bibliography.

Sullivan, Robert G. *Justice and the Social Context of Early Middle High German Literature*. New York: Routledge, 2001. A history of the Holy Roman Empire hinging on an examination of High German literature and its authors' focus on social, political, and spiritual issues during a time of transformation. Bibliographical references, index.

David J. Parent

ADAM WAŻYK

Born: Warsaw, Poland; November 17, 1905
Died: Warsaw, Poland; August 13, 1982

PRINCIPAL POETRY
Semafory, 1924
Oczy i usta, 1926
Wiersze zebrane, 1934
Serce granatu, 1943
Wiersze wybrane, 1947
Nowy wybór wierszy, 1950
Widzialem Kraine Środka, 1953
Wiersze, 1940-1953, 1953
Poemat dla doroslych i inne wiersze, 1956
Wiersze i poematy, 1957
Piosenka na rok 1949, 1959
Labirynt, 1961
Wagon, 1963
Wybór poezji, 1967
Zdarzenia, 1977
Wiersze wybrane, 1978

OTHER LITERARY FORMS
A cursory glance at the output of Adam Ważyk (VAH-zeek) would suggest that he was a versatile writer who practiced all principal literary forms and

pursued various interests. All his major works, however, refer in one way or another to his poetry, his poetic program, or his biography as a poet. Among his novels, for example, the most important one, *Epizod* (1961), is an autobiographical account of his participation in Polish avant-garde movements before World War II. His insightful essays, which cover a wide range of problems from Polish versification through the history of Romanticism to French Surrealism, seem to have one common denominator: They are various versions of Ważyk's continuous quest for his own poetic roots. His plays are a somewhat irrelevant part of his output. He attached greater importance to his numerous translations of poetry from French, Russian, and Latin into Polish, and indeed he ranks among the most outstanding Polish representatives of the art of translation. The broad scope of his interests in this field (at various times, he translated such disparate poets as Alexander Pushkin, Arthur Rimbaud, Aleksandr Blok, Guillaume Apollinaire, Max Jacob, Vladimir Mayakovsky, Paul Éluard, and Horace) reflects his constant search for a tradition and his changing conception of the role of poetry.

ACHIEVEMENTS

Adam Ważyk's literary career falls very distinctly into three phases, which stand in sharp contrast as far as both their specific character and their later appreciation are concerned. His first two collections were acclaimed and still are regarded as highly original contributions to Polish avant-garde poetry of the 1920's. After those promising beginnings, Ważyk lapsed into silence as a poet, to resurface only in the 1940's. His volume *Serce granatu* opened the second phase of his career, during which he appeared to be one of the staunchest promoters and supporters of Socialist Realism in poetry. This period, undoubtedly Ważyk's worst, came to an abrupt end in 1955 with the publication of his famous "Poemat dla dorosłych" ("Poem for Adults"), a harbinger of the antidogmatist renewal of Polish culture in the mid-1950's. "Poem for Adults" remains Ważyk's best-known work, although it has been artistically surpassed by his later work. It is the last phase of his development that has come to be viewed as the most valuable. In his poems published in the 1960's and 1970's, Ważyk in a

certain sense returned to his poetic beginnings, but he also enriched his cubist method with a new significance resulting from his reflection on twentieth century history. His poetry can by no means be considered a relic of the past; on the contrary, its impact on contemporary Polish literature is increasingly appreciated.

BIOGRAPHY

Adam Ważyk was born into a middle-class family of Jewish descent. After having been graduated from a Warsaw high school in 1924, he began to study mathematics at Warsaw University but soon found himself engrossed in the vigorous literary life of the 1920's. He made his literary debut very early by publishing a poem in the monthly *Skamander* in 1922. He entered into closer contact, however, not with the influential and popular poetic group called Skamander but with its opponents, who formed various avant-garde groups. Ważyk associated first with the Futurists (he was a coeditor of their publication, *Almanach Nowej Sztuki*) and later with the so-called Kraków Vanguard. His own position within those groups remained rather individual, however, and not fully consistent with their programs. In his two books of poems published in 1924 and 1926, he appeared as a Polish adherent to French cubism and Surrealism. In the 1930's, he stopped writing poetry altogether and shifted to fiction, the most interesting example of which was his autobiographical novel *Mity rodzinne* (1938).

The outbreak of World War II prompted a dramatic change both in Ważyk's life and in his art. In September, 1939, he arrived with other refugees at the city of Lvov, which soon fell prey to the Soviet invasion. Ważyk joined those Polish intellectuals who decided to collaborate with Soviet authorities. In the early 1940's, he lived in Saratov and Kuibyshev, where he was made an officer in the Polish army formed under Soviet auspices. In this capacity, he was in charge of cultural activities of the army, controlling its theater's repertory and its radio programs as well as writing popular military songs. In 1944, he returned to Poland with the rank of captain, with the Soviet-controlled Kościuszko Division.

In Stalinist Poland, Ważyk was entrusted with various official functions: Among others, he served as secretary general of the Polish Writers' Union; worked as an editor of the chief organ of Socialist Realism, the weekly *Kuźnica*; and between 1950 and 1954 served as editor in chief of the monthly *Twórczość*. In 1953, he was awarded a State Literary Prize for his poetry and translations.

On August 19, 1955, the weekly *Nowa Kultura* published Ważyk's long "Poem for Adults," which immediately became the object of perhaps the fiercest political controversy in postwar Polish literature. Praised by advocates of the political and ideological "thaw," the poem provoked, on the other hand, violent accusations from the Communist Party hard-liners and a number of officially sponsored public protests and condemnations; the editor in chief of *Nowa Kultura* lost his position in the wake of the Communist Party's outrage. The poem, however, gained enormous popularity; it was under its influence that the new wave of "settling accounts" with Stalinist ideology soon emerged to dominate Polish literary life for the next several years.

The last decades of the poet's life were spent mostly in Warsaw, where in the 1960's and 1970's Ważyk wrote and published numerous collections of poems, essays, and poetic translations as well as his only postwar novel, *Epizod*. His gradual withdrawal from public life was counterpoised by his growing recognition as a writer.

ANALYSIS

In Adam Ważyk's poetic career, there were two dramatic turnabouts, the first of which can be described as vehement acceptance of the doctrine of Socialist Realism and the other as its equally vehement rejection. Thus, the middle segment of his work forms a strictly demarcated enclave that does not seem to have anything in common either with Ważyk's avant-garde beginnings or with his last phase. There is an apparent discontinuity, then, and only a closer look allows the reader to discern a hidden logic in Ważyk's development.

As a young poet, Ważyk was obsessed with one of the central problems of twentieth century psychology: the problem of the discontinuity of perception. Under the influence of the art and poetry of the French cubists, he discovered that the overall perception of an object is, in fact, twofold: The final impression of a whole is pre-

ceded by the act of perceiving its separate elements. Accordingly, his early poetry focused on that first stage of the act of perception by showing the world as a mosaic of stray fragments of everyday reality, put together by the means of syntactic juxtaposition. Such a perception of reality as a discrete sequence of its elements was a major source of lyrical illumination.

It was, however, a source of growing doubt and increasing anxiety as well. Discontinuity meant also disorder, lack of hierarchy, and the absence of any system of values. It is deeply significant that the young Ważyk was not able to identify fully either with the Futurists (whose anarchism he repudiated) or with the Kraków Vanguard (whose program of constructivism he considered naïve and overly optimistic). The twentieth century seemed to have brought liberation from oppressive rationalism, but what in the 1920's had appeared as a refreshing sense of freedom was, in the 1930's, already acquiring a threatening suggestion of chaos. Therefore, in Ważyk's prewar poetry the technique of loose juxtapositions paradoxically coincides with an explicit craving for some undefined "order" that only the future might bring. In the 1930's, apparently unable to reconcile those two opposite tendencies, he discarded poetry altogether.

It was only Ważyk's acceptance of Communist ideology that, a decade later, allowed him to resume writing poetry. Communism offered him a new, seemingly consistent and comprehensive vision of his dreamed-of "order." He could not, however, return to his previous stylistic manner: The new belief could be expressed only by the means of utterly regular, classical forms. Such a marriage of Communism and classicism was, incidentally, not quite unprecedented in Polish poetry, to mention only the work of Lucjan Szenwald. Ważyk pushed that tendency to its extremes: He not only, to use the words of Mayakovsky, "stepped on the throat of his song," but also assumed, as it were, a totally new artistic identity. The former avant-garde experimenter changed into a classicist; the turbulent youth became a poet official and member of the establishment; the cubist turned into a Socialist Realist. In the 1940's and early 1950's, Ważyk's painstaking efforts to create his own version of Stalinist classicism yielded, however, rather uneven results. A few of the poems written in that period achieve an uneasy marriage of stylistic allusions to Horace with propaganda slogans, but the majority of them appear today as embarrassing examples of downright didacticism and blatant whitewash, made even worse by Ważyk's propensity for using journalistic clichés and monotonous rhythms.

"POEM FOR ADULTS"

The literary audience of the 1950's, which knew Ważyk as an official poet of Stalinism and a relentless exterminator of "bourgeois" tendencies in Polish culture, was, therefore, completely astounded by the 1955 publication of his "Poem for Adults." In this long poetic manifesto, Ważyk not only returned to his prewar methods of discontinuous presentation, juxtaposition, and free verse, but also gave vent to his bitter political disillusionment and moral perplexity. Instead of prophesying the rosy future, he again—as in his early phase—focused his attention on particulars of everyday reality. This time, however, such a perspective led to more disquieting conclusions: The scrupulous, unflinching observation of reality was used not for its own sake but to confront the empty promises and hypocritical slogans of official ideology.

To twenty-first century readers, "Poem for Adults" seems to be slightly naïve and content with half measures. Its speaker still sincerely believes in the mirages of Communist ideology; it is not ideology but reality that does not measure up to lofty principles. Accordingly, he resents not his own short-sightedness but some mysterious manipulators who duped him and his generation. The poem stopped halfway, then, but it nevertheless had a galvanizing impact on Polish literature. In Ważyk's own career, it also marked the beginning of his return to his previous artistic integrity.

RETURN TO CUBIST ROOTS

This return was particularly noticeable in the 1960's and 1970's, when Ważyk's poetry underwent a remarkable evolution while remaining faithful to his philosophical and psychological obsessions. The problem of discontinuity of perception acquired new significance, set against the background of twentieth century history and the poet's own experiences. Ważyk's most ambitious poems from that period can be interpreted as attempts to reconstruct the effort of human consciousness, memory, and logic, trying to put reality in order

despite its apparently chaotic character. The long poem *Labirynt*, for example, is a paradoxical attempt to revive the old genre of the descriptive poem in order to prove its futility; seemingly a quasi-epic story taking place in a middle-class milieu in prewar Poland, it is actually a poem about the shortcomings of human memory, which can visualize the past only as a "labyrinth that leads no one knows where." In another long poem, *Wagon*, the speaker's observation post is a train compartment; his indiscriminate registration of juxtaposed objects, minute facts, and the travelers' insignificant behavior proves to be another fruitless effort of the human mind faced with the chaos of external reality.

In poems such as these, and particularly in his 1977 volume, *Zdarzenia*, Ważyk's evident return to his cubist beginnings has, however, some new implications. The familiar method of juxtaposition of images serves more complex purposes. The world smashed into pieces is no longer a source of innocent illumination, nor is it a reason for yearning for some "order" imposed by history. On the contrary, the world's disarray appears to be an irreversible process started by the twentieth century disintegration of stable systems of values. Although Ważyk in his final phase was far from moralizing, his poetry can be read as an indirect comment on the immorality of the present epoch.

OTHER MAJOR WORKS

LONG FICTION: *Człowiek w burym ubraniu*, 1930; *Latarnie świeca w Karpowie*, 1933; *Mity rodzinne*, 1938; *Epizod*, 1961.

NONFICTION: *W strone humanizmu*, 1949; *Mickiewicz i wersyfikacja narodowa*, 1951; *Przemiany Slowackiego*, 1955; *Esej o wierszu*, 1964; *Od Rimbauda do Éluarda*, 1964; *Kwestia gustu*, 1966; *Surrealizm*, 1973; *Gra i doświadczenie*, 1974; *Dziwna historia awangardy*, 1976; *Cudowny kantorek*, 1980.

BIBLIOGRAPHY

Gillon, Adam, and Ludwik Krzyzanowski, eds. *Introduction to Modern Polish Literature*. Rev. ed. New York: Hippocrene Books, 1982. An anthology of translations of Polish literature with some commentary. Contains works by Ważyk.

Miłosz, Czesław. *The History of Polish Literature*. 2d

ed. Berkeley: University of California Press, 1983. A critical study of the history of Polish literature that provides information on Ważyk as well as a historical and cultural background to his works. Includes bibliographical references.

Sandauer, Artur. *On the Situation of the Polish Writer of Jewish Descent in the Twentieth Century: It Is Not I Who Should Have Written this Study—*. Jerusalem: Hebrew University Magnes Press, 2005. Examines Jewish writers in Poland in the twentieth century, including Ważyk and his problematic relationship with the Communists.

Segel, Harold B. *The Columbia Literary History of Eastern Europe Since 1945*. New York: Columbia University Press, 2008. Discusses Ważyk briefly in a chapter on Communism and its effect on writing in Eastern Europe. Provides perspective and background to understanding Ważyk.

Shore, Marci. *Caviar and Ashes: A Warsaw Generation's Life and Death in Marxism, 1918-1968*. New Haven, Conn.: Yale University Press, 2006. Examines how the avant-garde of the 1920's in Poland became Communists and then fell away from Marxism. Ważyk's role is discussed.

Stanisław Barańczak

WOLFRAM VON ESCHENBACH

Born: Probably Eschenbach bei Ansbach, Franconia (now in Germany); c. 1170

Died: Probably Eschenbach bei Ansbach, Franconia (now in Germany); c. 1217

PRINCIPAL POETRY

Lieder, c. 1200

Parzival, c. 1200-1210 (English translation, 1894)

Willehalm, c. 1212-1217 (English translation, 1977)

Titurel, c. 1217 (*Schionatulander and Sigune*, 1960)

OTHER LITERARY FORMS

All surviving manuscripts of works attributed to Wolfram von Eschenbach (VAWL-from fawn EHSH-uhn-bok) lead to the conclusion that he was exclusively a poet. His masterpiece, *Parzival*, is considered the founder of the bildungsroman, or novel of development. This paternity is extremely tenuous, however, resting on affinities of characterization rather than of genre; the first recognizable novel did not appear until some 450 years after *Parzival*.

ACHIEVEMENTS

Although Wolfram von Eschenbach was roundly criticized by his contemporary Gottfried von Strassburg as a "fabricator of wild tales," other poets and especially Wolfram's audience were more appreciative. The extraordinarily large number of extant manuscripts—eighty-four separate manuscripts or fragments of *Parzival* and seventy-six of *Willehalm*—attests his popularity. In comparison, other major works of the High Middle Ages would seem to have been in less demand; the *Nibelungenlied* (c. 1200; English translation, 1848) exists in thirty-four versions, Gottfried von Strassburg's *Tristan und Isolde* (c. 1210; *Tristan and Isolde*, 1899) in only twenty-three. Many modern critics also proclaim Wolfram to have been a careless poet, unrefined and unlearned; however, Wolfram's works sparkle with his own vital personality in an era of subdued conventionality. In contrast to the sophisticated stylists Gottfried and Hartmann von Aue, Wolfram wrote with color, depicting exotic scenes and exciting adventures in vibrant tones. His language is uniquely robust, studded with heroic (rather than courtly) terminology, Franconian dialect, and French loanwords, as well as a number of neologisms. Often chosen for resonance and acoustical effect, his language lends additional energy to his rhetorically crafted tales. His style is serious and humorous, insightful and charmingly frivolous. In short, Wolfram was a thoroughly delightful storyteller who constantly manipulated his audience as well as his characters.

Wolfram has not attained immortality as a result of his personality or style, however. Because of his inferior social status as a layman, Wolfram was able to view courtly society from both within and without, to question assumptions and conventions with unusual detachment, often with humor. He fused disparate sources and traditions to form new and challenging visions of people and society which remain viable to this day. In *Parzival*, for example, he created a poem monumental in size and scope that illuminates timeless concepts such as ignorance and wisdom, grief and courage, guilt and salvation. This tale of the Holy Grail, of King Arthur's Round Table and attendant knights and ladies, transcends the realm of the courtly romance; indeed, the Arthurian circle is shown to be less than the ideal so often propagated by lesser poets. Of greater import is the development of an individual who ultimately attains the highest position on earth, a worldly king who represents the highest of spiritual values as well—a noble goal for all humankind. Wolfram's works all exhibit this critical yet hopeful attitude. Wolfram invested his poetry with vitality, humor, mystery, and a lofty purpose. These same qualities engage the reader, now as then, and will continue to command thoughtful consideration.

BIOGRAPHY

To possess factual information pertaining to the life of any courtly poet is a rare occurrence; the poet as professional writer and public figure is, after all, a relatively recent phenomenon. In the case of Wolfram von Eschenbach, few documented details exist. Fortunately, Wolfram was a personable poet who could not refrain from injecting his experiences and opinions into his works. From his utterances, scholars have been able to reconstruct a plausible, if sketchy, vita.

Drawing on literary references, dialect evidence, and geographical speculation, scholars have concluded that Wolfram's home was probably in Eschenbach bei Ansbach, Franconia (now in Germany). There is no record of his family, of his formative years, or of his schooling. In fact, Wolfram's innocent pronouncement in *Parzival*, "I don't know a single letter of the alphabet," has become enigmatic: Does he intend to admit his unlearned background, to boast of his literary accomplishment despite his inability to read and write, or to twit his educated principal critic, Gottfried? In any event, it is clear that he was not formally educated, for influences of classical Latin writers (a staple in the

Wolfram von Eschenbach (©Bettmann/CORBIS)

monastery schools) are absent in his poems. Significantly, Wolfram himself never mentioned having "read" from his literary sources; his frequent references to having "heard" information leads scholars to presume that source material was actually dictated to him by a succession of literate scribes. One assumes today that Wolfram was an autodidact who learned those things necessary for the background of his tales; he was certainly familiar with French literature of the day and well acquainted with the works of contemporary German authors.

Despite his fame as a poet, Wolfram considered himself to be first and foremost a knight, though it is unlikely that he ever wielded a sword. As a layman and member of the petty nobility, he was unpropertied and poor his entire life, at the mercy of his patrons and audience. One of Wolfram's patrons, at least for a time, was the fabled Landgrave Herrmann of Thuringia; the legendary *Sängerkrieg*, or troubadours' competition, at Hermann's castle, however, appears to be only that: a legend.

A definitive chronology of Wolfram's works cannot be established. His lyric poetry, of which only nine songs still exist, consists primarily of *Tagelieder*, or morning songs—some of the finest in German poetry. Since there are so few, and they are of a conventional nature, most scholars presume that they were created before Wolfram's greater epic poems. From historical references included in the work, it appears that *Parzival* was begun about the beginning of the thirteenth century and, with interruption, finally completed approximately ten years later. *Willehalm* would appear to be the most mature of Wolfram's writings in style and content, while the other fragment, *Schionatulander and Sigune*, contains a historical note that suggests that it originated well after the completion of *Parzival*. The details of Wolfram's death remain a mystery. He is thought to have died in Eschenbach bei Ansbach about 1217; one contemporary insists that he died while writing the manuscript of *Schionatulander and Sigune*.

ANALYSIS

The small corpus of nine songs that can be safely attributed to Wolfram von Eschenbach were presumably composed early in his literary career. More than half of these can be categorized as *Tagelieder*, or morning songs, a type of courtly poem that Wolfram refined for his German audience. The typical situation depicts daybreak and the call of the watchman, announcing the day's arrival to a pair of young lovers. Obviously, the man must leave, for if he were seen, his honor and the lady's reputation would be ruined. There is a tearful farewell, a last embrace, and the man departs. Wolfram's songs develop this theme artistically, allowing each of the three figures—watchman, man, and woman—to present in turn the episode from his (or her) individual point of view. Wolfram employed rhythmic crescendos to accentuate the dramatic moments of daybreak and farewell in a sensual atmosphere.

One noteworthy variation among Wolfram's lyrics is the antimorning song. Here, the poet speaks directly to the watchman, reprimanding him for warning the waking lovers. In praise of connubial bliss, the poet extols the security of matrimony, which requires no secrecy and no painful farewells at dawn. Although this song is not one of Wolfram's finer creations, it does highlight his witty and often mocking temperament, a trait that can be traced throughout his later works. The same parodistic tone is evident in the remaining songs. The common theme in these poems is courting the favor of a lady. Conventional and even second-rank in appearance, these works display qualities that parody the entire established tradition of courtly love poetry. By pirating famous lines from other poems and including trite love phrases, Wolfram created fanciful songs that attest the superficiality of courtly conventions.

PARZIVAL

Wolfram's greatest achievement is clearly *Parzival*. This epic romance is enormous in scope, portraying literally dozens of legendary characters who span Europe and Asia over an extended period of time. The number of questions surrounding its creation are enormous as well: Which source or sources inspired Wolfram? Is *Parzival* indebted to Chrêtien de Troyes and Robert de Boron, to a combination of various related tales, or to the mysterious "Kyot," as Wolfram insists? Was the work interrupted by war or by Wolfram's changing mood? Was it written under the auspices of one or more patrons? Was the work composed in the same chronological order in which it appears today? Were the first two books—that is, the prologue—written only after the completion of the entire manuscript and then added to the beginning of Parzival's story? These are a few of the nagging questions surrounding Wolfram's classic tale. It is certain only that *Parzival* was not written in one uninterrupted effort and that publication of separate episodes preceded the final edition of almost twenty-five thousand lines.

Though *Parzival* is an Arthurian romance, it is clearly differentiated from earlier versions by its non-Celtic preoccupation with Christianity and the Holy Grail. Artificially divided into sixteen books by the philologist Karl Lachmann, the work traces the life and development of Parzival and his Arthurian counterpart, Gawan. In a prologue, the audience learns that Parzival's father, Gahmuret, was an exemplary knight. Through a series of adventures, Gahmuret wins and marries first a heathen queen and then a Christian queen, finally to die in chivalric pursuit of further love and fame. Upon the birth of her son, Parzival, the Christian queen fears that he will end like his father; therefore, she rears the boy in complete ignorance of courtly society. One day, young Parzival encounters several knights and immediately decides that he, too, must partake of this splendid life. For his protection, his mother sends him off in fool's garb and gives misleading advice, hoping that he will soon return unharmed and chastened. After his departure, she dies of a broken heart, but young Parzival perseveres, soon joining King Arthur's knights at the Round Table. He then discovers the Grail Castle and its king, Anfortas, who suffers from a most painful affliction. Failing to "ask the question"—that is, to show compassion and inquire as to the origins of the wound and the condition of the king—Parzival is expelled from the castle for his uncharitable silence. Because of his ignorance, inexperience, and overwhelming desire to become a knight, he commits numerous sins of omission and commission. Guided only by his heart and the wise counsel of the hermit, Trevrezent, Parzival matures through years of lonely struggle, proving that he is worthy of his responsibilities as a knight and as a Christian.

As Parzival wanders off into the wilderness in search of himself, Wolfram introduces Gawan, a member in good standing of Arthur's Round Table. Gawan is the epitome of the medieval knight, at once adept in chivalric combat and skillful in the conventional graces required of all nobility. He is ever willing to fight on behalf of a worthy cause or a beautiful lady, and he fulfills his Christian duties with similar ease. During the course of the tale, Wolfram clearly distinguishes Gawan from Parzival on one crucial issue: Gawan's Christianity is the fulfillment of a chivalric vow, an obligation to which he is committed, while Parzival's spiritual quest derives from inner motivation. Whereas Gawan accepts his religion unquestioningly, Parzival must struggle with doubt, at one point even renouncing God for his apparent injustice. This difference is finally decisive; it is the reason that Parzival and not Gawan will ultimately become Grail King—that is, the personification of the highest values both in worldly society (as

king) and in the spiritual realm (of the Grail). At the conclusion of the epic, Parzival is crowned King of the Grail, reunited with his wife and friends, and introduced to a stranger from India; this speckled man is his half brother, Feirefiz, the child of Gahmuret's heathen queen. Together, from Europe to India (that being the extent of the known world in Wolfram's day), the sons of Gahmuret will uphold courtly and Christian values, to the benefit of all humankind.

It is clear, then, that *Parzival* is not the shallow, disorganized composition described by Wolfram's critics. The epic can and should be considered on various levels: as a historical depiction of the encounter between East and West, evidenced by the Crusades and the Christian mission to baptize non-Christians; as an Arthurian romance in which the knight's achievements are judged by this exemplary courtly society; as a "double novel" concerning the separate exploits of both Parzival and Gawan; and, finally, as an account of the spiritual development of a worthy soul from simpleton to sage, from sin to redemption and the attainment of humility and purity.

SCHIONATULANDER AND SIGUNE

Schionatulander and Sigune, like *Willehalm*, is an epic fragment composed at the end of Wolfram's life. The 164 stanzas of the original were later expanded by an anonymous poet who added more than six thousand stanzas to form *Der jüngere Titurel* (c. 1272)—though this final version does not seem to correspond to Wolfram's intentions. In any event, most scholars believe that the work is nearly complete as it now stands. There are few possibilities for diversion; the inevitable conclusion (Schionatulander's death) clearly limits the narrative's chronological scope.

Though there is an indication that *Schionatulander and Sigune* was Wolfram's final work, most scholars would prefer to place *Willehalm* in that position, based primarily on sentimental reasons. The latter deals with major ethical and philosophical questions concerning world peace and interdenominational coexistence, while the former is a tale revolving around two minor characters from *Parzival*. The German title *Titurel* is, in fact, a misnomer, corrected in the English translation (according to medieval custom, the title was taken from the name of the first character to appear). Thus, in a prologue, old King Titurel reflects on his long and eventful life before surrendering his kingdom and the Holy Grail to his son. Years later, one of Titurel's grandchildren marries a knight, only to die in childbirth; her surviving offspring is Sigune. Already the attentive listener will recall from *Parzival* this fateful name; Sigune is shown mourning the death of her beloved Schionatulander, who died at the hand of Orilus. This fragment, then, accounts for the earlier years of their relationship and clarifies their tragic fate. In short, the two youths fall in love and must abide by courtly convention—that is, they must restrain their passion. While on a walk in the forest one day, they discover a dog wearing a jeweled collar; the collar itself is inscribed with the love story of a similar couple. Before Sigune can finish reading the story, the dog dashes off. She then declares that she will not grant her love to Schionatulander until he brings back the collar. Here the fragment ends. From episodes appearing in *Parzival*, the listener knows that this pure, youthful love can never be fulfilled and that Sigune will spend the rest of her days mourning her lost lover until they are reunited in Heaven.

The theme here is tragic, the atmosphere filled with the poet's realization that life's brief happiness must be purchased at a fearful price. Sigune does not criticize the courtly conventions by which she must act (although some critics note that her trivial demand leads to her lover's death); as mentioned above, several other couples in Wolfram's works suffer similar losses. Sigune must learn to live with her fate and accept the fact that she was destined to love Schionatulander chastely, in sublimation of their great passion for each other. Loyalty, constancy, and God's grace will ultimately purify their love.

WILLEHALM

It is generally agreed that even had Wolfram not written his *Parzival*, he would deserve lasting fame for his *Schionatulander and Sigune* and for *Willehalm*. While *Schionatulander and Sigune* depicts the beauties and sorrows of courtly love, *Willehalm* is strikingly innovative in its treatment of timeless values. Wolfram's primary source, *Bataille d'Aliscans* (late twelfth century), was provided by Landgrave Herrmann of Thuringia for a commission, though the epic Wolfram

created went far beyond the original, in scope and significance. The historical Willehalm (Guillaume d'Orange) contributed to the defeat of invading Arabs with his valiant efforts in combat, yet scarcely ten years later he renounced worldly ambitions and entered a monastery. Although Wolfram does not specifically emphasize this aspect of Willehalm's spiritual development, it becomes obvious that his story is intended as a sort of *Legende*, or life of a saint.

As one would assume from the French source, war is a major theme in *Willehalm*. Willehalm, the son of Count Henry of Narbonne, is sent into the world to seek his fortune at the court of Charlemagne. After numerous adventures, Willehalm marries Gyburg, the daughter of a heathen king who then invades Willehalm's realm to reclaim his daughter. Willehalm gathers his army and engages in fierce battles with the enemy. In spite of his ferocity, Willehalm's heroic exploits are not to be misconstrued; his immediate desire is simply to protect his wife. The increasingly murderous battle scenes are twice interrupted by carefully placed interludes; in both instances, Willehalm is able to rejoin Gyburg, and the couple enjoy a brief respite from the war in each other's arms. Here, Wolfram presents conjugal love as an extension of God's love, as a means to offset the brutal reality of life and as a form of *unio mystica* through which God's grace can be anticipated. Gradually, Willehalm and Gyburg come to the realization that both heathen and Christian are children of God, that it is a great loss when so many must die. Wolfram's is the first depiction in German literature of a loving, merciful God who would protect all his children, regardless of their faith. Following the conclusive victory over the heathen army, Willehalm's newly gained tolerance is very much in evidence; he frees his prisoners, allowing the vanquished to collect their dead and transport them to their homeland, there to be honored and buried according to their own religious customs.

Knights of the Middle Ages were deeply imbued with an Augustinian worldview: Heathens were servants of the Devil, and it was the duty of all Christians to destroy the infidel, thereby achieving more quickly the Kingdom of God on Earth. If one killed a heathen, honor and fame were the reward; if one were killed fighting heathens, so much the better, for the knight was guaranteed eternal life in Heaven. The Crusades were conducted in this spirit. Willehalm, too, pronounces his support for this credo at the outset, but as the story progresses and the slaughter mounts on both sides, Willehalm undergoes a dramatic change of heart. His initial missionary zeal, reminiscent of the Crusades, is replaced by understanding and tolerance. Thus does Wolfram combine his two major themes of war and love in a strikingly innovative presentation that proved extremely popular with its audiences.

Wolfram depicts two contending armies, heathen and Christian, which nevertheless are governed by similar conventions: knights on both sides fighting on behalf of their ladies in courtly service. Though the heathens are influenced by an almost carnal love, which is raised to a religious fervor, the Christians are motivated by courtly love and spiritual devotion to God. Wolfram's critical insight here is that both sides represent poles of one great love that originates in God. This sophisticated concept of love is Wolfram's contribution to eternal respect, love, and peace.

Willehalm could have concluded with a happy ending reminiscent of fairy tales, but the older Wolfram sought a more realistic solution, one which recognized that life's brief joys are often outweighed by horrendous tragedy and sadness. Despite obvious similarities, the significant differences between *Parzival* and *Willehalm* concern the appearance of this new reality, akin to the modern concept of existential angst. These differences are partly the result of the differences in the two distinct literary forms, the romance, which calls for a reliable reassuring order, and the battle epic, which draws attention to the fragility of human existence. In *Willehalm*, Wolfram demonstrates that courtly convention is precisely that: a formality that does not protect the individual from the vicissitudes of life. Here it becomes evident how far Wolfram has strayed from the Augustinian attitude. His literary creation, Willehalm, is no missionary zealot, possessed with exterminating the heathens. He is a defender of Christian values as embodied in the Holy Roman Empire, though his martial duties are as painful to him as his enforced separation from his wife, Gyburg. However, she, too, plays an important role in this new vision of Christian tolerance,

for in this character Wolfram has created perhaps the most vivid portrait of a woman in all medieval literature. Though Gyburg, as a woman, has no recourse to such knightly philosophy, she represents in her person the admirable traits of humanity, piety, mercy, and love, which are a reflection of God's grace. Like Willehalm, Gyburg is proclaimed a saint at the story's conclusion.

Out of a desire for symmetry or the aforementioned sentimentality, most scholars would find it especially fitting if *Willehalm*—this mature, noble, and modern work—were Wolfram's last testament. His *Parzival* will continue to inspire readers with its idealism, but it is *Willehalm* which offers the most hope to humankind through its thoughtful and realistic portrayal of tolerance and universal love as antidotes to the eternal curses of prejudice, hate, and aggression.

BIBLIOGRAPHY

Gibbs, Marion E., and Sidney M. Johnson. "Wolfram von Eschenbach." In *German Literature of the High Middle Ages*, edited by Will Hasty. Rochester, N.Y.: Camden House, 2006. Briefly discusses what is known about Wolfram and contains sections on his best-known writings, as well as his songs.

Groos, Arthur. *Romancing the Grail: Genre, Science, and Quest in Wolfram's "Parzival."* Ithaca, N.Y.: Cornell University Press, 1995. With roots in the critical theory of Russian scholar Mikhail Bakhtin, this study examines the narrative discourse of one of Wolfram's major poems. Unfortunately, Groos is not especially successful in applying a critical theory that was designed to interpret modern novels to this major work of medieval poetry. Moreover, he does not pay enough attention to Wolfram's other major works.

Hasty, Will, ed. *A Companion to Wolfram's "Parzival."* Columbia, S.C.: Camden House, 1999. Essays provide analysis of the popular vernacular work as well as social and cultural context.

Hughes, Jolyon Timothy. *Wolfram von Eschenbach's Criticism of "Minnedienst" in His Narrative Works.* Lanham, Md.: University Press of America, 2009. Examines *Parzival* and *Schionatulander and Sigune* for *Minnedienst* ("love service") and how it negatively affects female characters.

Jones, Martin, and Timothy McFarland, eds. *Wolfram's "Willehalm": Fifteen Essays*. New York: Camden House, 2001. Jones and McFarland provide fifteen essays on Wolfram's epic of the Christian-Muslim conflict, placing it in historical and literary context and elucidating the epic's main themes, characters, and techniques.

Murphy, G. Ronald. *Gemstone of Paradise: The Holy Grail in Wolfram's "Parzival."* New York: Oxford University Press, 2006. Murphy examines the Holy Grail, which Chrétien de Troyes had described as a golden serving dish set with jewels, large enough for a fish, and linked to Celtic traditions, and which Robert de Boron had described as a chalice and associated with Christianity. Wolfram instead asserts that the grail is a green stone, with special powers.

Poag, James F. *Wolfram von Eschenbach*. New York: Twayne, 1972. A useful introduction with quotations in both English and German. Contains index and bibliography.

Sivertson, Randal. *Loyalty and Riches in Wolfram's "Parzifal."* New York: Peter Lang, 1999. A reinterpretation of *Parzival* as the presentation of a conflict in medieval knighthood between the fight for abstract ideals and service for material gain. The author argues that Wolfram's epic defends feudal values that were in a state of decline. Compares works by Chrétien de Troyes and others.

Starkey, Kathryn. *Reading the Medieval Book: Word, Image, and Performance in Wolfram von Eschenbach's "Willehalm."* Notre Dame, Ind.: University of Notre Dame Press, 2004. Starkey relates the image and performance of *Willehalm* to the written word in an attempt to further understanding of the work.

Wynn, Marianne. *Wolfram's "Parzival": On the Genesis of Its Poetry*. 2d ed. New York: Peter Lang, 2002. Examines *Parzival* as poetry, examining Wolfram's creative process.

Todd C. Hanlin

Z

Adam Zagajewski

Born: Lwów, Poland (now in Ukraine); April 21, 1945

Principal poetry
Komunikat, 1972
Sklepy mięsne, 1975
List, 1978
Oda do wielości, 1983
Jechać do Lwówa, 1985
Tremor: Selected Poems in English, 1985
Płótno, 1990 (*Canvas*, 1991)
Dzikie czereśnie: Wybór wierszy, 1992
Ziemia Ognista, 1994
Mysticism for Beginners, 1997
Trzej Aniołowie = Three Angels, 1997 (bilingual selection)
Późne Święta, 1998
Pragnienie, 1999
Without End: New and Selected Poems, 2002
Powrót, 2003
Anteny, 2005
Eternal Enemies, 2008

Other literary forms

Although poetry constitutes the most important part of the oeuvre of Adam Zagajewski (zah-gah-YEW-skee), he also has written three novels: *Ciełpo zimno* (1975; it's cold, it's warm), *Das absolute Gehör* (1982; absolute pitch), and *Cienka kreska* (1983; thin line). Zagajewski's fiction, patterned on the traditional bildungsroman, is an ironic reworking of this nineteenth century genre.

Zagajewski also published a number of important essays and essay collections. His *Świat nie przedstawiony* (1974; the world not represented), coauthored by Julian Kornhauser, played a seminal role in shaping the literary consciousness of the decade. *Drugi Oddech* (1978; second wind) and *Solidarność i samotność* (1986; *Solidarity, Solitude: Essays*, 1990), continue probing the question of literature's ethical and social responsibility. *Dwa miasta* (1991; *Two Cities: On Exile, History, and the Imagination*, 1995) and *W cudzym pięknie* (1998; *Another Beauty*, 2000) explore the richness and variety of Europe, as found in the author's memories, readings, and travels. Zagajewski is also the author of *Polen: Staat im Schatten der Sowjetunion* (1981; Poland: a state in the shackles of the Soviet Union), an analysis of the Polish state under Soviet rule.

Achievements

The literary debut of Adam Zagajewski took place in a country oppressed by Soviet domination. This historical circumstance led the poet and other writers of his generation (known as the Generation of '68, or the New Wave) to take upon themselves the duty of opposing both political oppression and the conformist attitudes found among Polish intellectuals, thus turning around the Communist slogan, "Writers are the conscience of the nation." Although in his later writings Zagajewski abandoned the earlier political agenda, his poetry never ceased to defend the human right to individual perception and sensitivity. Zagajewski's poems have been translated into English, French, German, Greek, Hebrew, Italian, and Swedish.

Zagajewski received a number of prestigious fellowships and awards, including the Jurzykowski Foundation Award, a fellowship from the Berliner Kunstlerprogram, a Guggenheim Fellowship, the Prix de la Liberté, the International Vilenica Award, the Kurt Tucholsky Prize, the Tranströmer Prize, and the Neustadt Prize. His *Without End* was nominated for a National Book Critics Circle Award.

Biography

Adam Zagajewski was born in Lwów in 1945 to a family of Polish intelligentsia. When he was four months old, his family was forced to abandon the city of his birth and to move westward, reflecting the newly reshuffled Polish borders. The Zagajewskis settled in the Silesian town of Gliwice, where Adam spent his childhood and adolescence. Throughout these early years, his family kept alive the memory of their hometown: "I spent my childhood in an ugly industrial city; I was brought there when I was barely four months old, and then for many years afterward I was told about an extraordinarily beautiful city that my family had to leave." Nevertheless, Zagajewski's sensitivity allowed him to find enchantment even in the unattractive town of his youth.

At the age of eighteen, Zagajewski left Gliwice to pursue a university education in the historic town of Kraków. After receiving degrees in philosophy and psychology at the Jagiellonian University, he worked as an assistant professor at the Akademia Górniczo-Hutnicza (University of Mining and Metallurgy). It was during this period that he became the cofounder of the poetic group Teraz (Now) as well as the coauthor of its literary program. The poets of Teraz emphasized the social importance of poetry and its role in reclaiming a language devalued by the rhetorical manipulations of a bureaucratic, totalitarian state. In 1972, Zagajewski became one of the editors of *Student*. He was also involved in editorial work at such prestigious literary

Adam Zagajewski (©Sophie Bassouls/Sygma/CORBIS)

journals as *Odra* and *Znak*. After signing a letter of protest concerning amendments to the Polish constitution in 1976, Zagajewski suffered the fate of many Polish writers of the time: The government placed a ban on his publications, effectively ending the official circulation of his works.

In 1979, Zagajewski won a scholarship from the Berlin Kunstlerprogram and went to Berlin. After a brief return to Poland, he emigrated to Paris in 1982. Unlike many Polish artists, Zagajewski chose to leave his homeland for personal, not political, reasons. In Paris, he became involved in editing *Zeszyty Literackie* (literary review), a seminal émigré literary journal. In 1989, Zagajewski began teaching creative writing at the University of Houston, Texas, spending four months there out of each year. He has also taught at Chicago University.

Having moved from Lwów to Gliwice to Kraków to Berlin to Paris to Houston, then to Kraków again in 2002, in the course of his life Zagajewski became a wanderer and a citizen of the world. The poet described his own cosmopolitan status:

> I am now like a passenger of a small submarine, which has not one, but four periscopes. The first, and major, one points to my native tradition. The second opens up toward the literature of Germany, its poetry, its—one-time—desire of the infinite. The third—toward the landscape of French culture, with its penetrating intelligence and Jansenist morality. The fourth—toward [William] Shakespeare, [John] Keats and Robert Lowell, the literature of the concrete, of passion and conversation.

ANALYSIS

Critics frequently divide the poetry of Adam Zagajewski into two major periods: one "political," focused on the problems of the human community, the other "philosophical," concerned with the individual. The poet's first three collections, published during the 1970's, followed the poetic program of the Generation of '68, with its emphasis on the social responsibilities of the artist in a totalitarian state. Beginning with the fourth collection, *Oda do wielości* (ode to plurality), published after his emigration to Paris, Zagajewski turned to a poetry of philosophical reflection, rich in complex metaphors and sophisticated symbolism. A number of his contemporaries had commented on the poet's passage from one period to the other. However, it is also important to emphasize the continuity of themes and methods in Zagajewski's work. Even in the most political poems, he deals with the oppression of the individual. Even the most private lyrical reflections are situated within the broader context of European, or world, culture.

KOMUNIKAT, SKLEPY MIĘSNE, AND LIST

When Zagajewski and other poets of his generation, such as Stanisław Barańczak, Julian Kornhauser, Ryszard Krynicki, and Ewa Lipska, set out to wage poetic war on the Communist state, they focused their efforts on laying bare the "falsified language" of state propaganda and bureaucracy. The newspeak favored by the government and disseminated by the mass media had become, according to the young poets, a tool of totalitarian oppression. Rather than representing reality, such language falsified it. In contrast, the poetry of the Generation of '68 was to be plain, clear, and direct. It aimed at a sincere realism, a reclamation of the concrete. This goal is illustrated in Zagajewski's poem "Sklepy Mięsne" (meat shops). The poem describes the change from the older, straightforward term "butcher," to the new, sanitized "meat shop," a name that conceals rather than reveals the true nature of the establishment.

Another feature of Generation of '68 poetry is an interest in the problems of its time, adequately reflected in the name of the poetic group Teraz (Now), of which Zagajewski was a cocreator. His early poetry collections, *Komunikat* (communiqué), *Sklepy mięsne*, and, to a lesser extent, *List* (a letter), realized the ideals of contemporaneity and simplicity. These poems spoke of Communist Poland in a language verging on the prosaic. They were characterized by a frequent use of the present tense (conveying a sense of immediacy), a scarcity of conjunctions and adverbs, and a disciplined syntax. Syntactic simplicity is particularly apparent in the first collection and gives way to slightly more sophisticated structures, such as inversion, in the later volumes. This simple, almost conversational form revealed a deep distrust of inflated or manipulative language. The goal of Zagajewski's early poetry was to defend the individual against the obscure manipulations, linguistic and otherwise, of the regime. Like other members of his generation, Zagajewski strongly believed in the ethical dimension of a poetic calling.

ODA DO WIELOŚCI

The title poem of Zagajewski's fourth collection, *Oda do wielości*, introduced a theme that would become central to the poet's subsequent writing: a fascinated affirmation of the world's multiplicity and richness:

> I don't understand it all and I am
> even glad that the world like a restless
> ocean exceeds my ability
> to understand . . .
> You, singular soul, stand before
> This abundance. Two eyes, two hands,
> Ten inventive fingers, and
> Only one ego, the wedge of an orange,
> the youngest of sisters. . . .

While a number of poems in this 1982 collection still address painful political issues, such as "Petit," "Zwycięstwo" (victory), and "Ogień" (fire), others point in a new direction. Tadeusz Nyczek, in 1988, described this ideological shift in Zagajewski's writing as a turn from "no" to "yes," from negation (negating the totalitarian state) to affirmation (affirming the world, its richness, and its sensual existence). With the expansion of themes came an expansion of form: The syntax became more intricate; the metaphors became increasingly sophisticated and abundant. Zagajewski's later poetry is characterized by complex metaphorical structures of great intensity and beauty. Czesław Miłosz in 1985 described the artistic development of his fellow Pole and poet: "His poems have been acquiring a more and more sumptuous texture, and now he appears to me as a skillful weaver whose work is not unlike Gobelin tapestries where trees, flowers, and human figures coexist in the same pattern."

JECHAI DO LWÓWA, CANVAS, AND ZIEMIA OGNISTA

Jechai do Lwówa (to go to Lwów), *Canvas*, and *Ziemia Ognista* (Tierra del Fuego), the collections published from the mid-1980's to the mid-1990's, offer sophisticated meditations on the nature of memory, history, art, culture, and the spiritual quest of humankind at the end of the twentieth century.

The poem "Jechai do Lwówa" ("To Go to Lwów") is an imaginary journey to the place of the poet's birth, conjuring up both the magic of the "lost" city, with its "white napkins and a bucket/ full of raspberries standing on the floor" and the ruthless political "scissors" that brought about destruction and exile. The poem "W obcych miastach" (in strange cities, from *Canvas*) captures the delight of journeys to unknown places: "In strange cities, there's an unexpected joy/ the cool pleasure of a new regard." Cities, visited in person or in the imagination, become an important theme in Zagajewski's poetry. "Widok Krakowa" (the view of Kraków, from *Jechai do Lwówa*) is a tender and eclectic portrait of the former Polish capital. "Widok Delf" (the view of Delf) from the same collection honors both the place and its painter.

These are poems deeply embedded in the European cultural tradition. Zagajewski pays poetic homage not only to Europe's metropolises but also to its artists and thinkers. The poet invokes the composers Franz Schubert and Wolfgang Amadeus Mozart, the painters Jan Vermeer and Rembrandt, the poet C. K. Norwid, the philosopher Friedrich Nietzsche, and many others.

While delighting in the richness of art and culture, Zagajewski remains aware of the reverse side of civilization—wars, genocide, cruelty. His poems present a world in a state of paradox. An acute awareness of the paradoxical nature of reality is expressed in the poem "Lawa" (lava) from *Canvas*:

> And what if Heraclitus and Parmenides
> are both right
> and two worlds exist side by side,
> one serene, the other insane; one arrow
> thoughtlessly hurtles, another, indulgent,
> looks on; the selfsame wave moves and stands still. . . .

The proper response to a paradoxical reality is perhaps a stance of permanent inquiry, constant alertness and distrust. Such a mind-set has always been part of Zagajewski's poetics. One of his preferred characters is the wanderer—homeless, always journeying toward a yet unknown goal. The collection *Ziemia Ognista* is dominated by traveling and homelessness, as in the poem "Szukaj" (search):

> I returned to the town
> where I was a child
> and a teenager and an old man of thirty.
> The town greeted me indifferently . . .
> Find another place.
> Search for it.
> Search for your true homeland.

Zagajewski's mature poetry has become a poetry of spiritual inquiry. Agnostic and mystical, it seeks the "nameless, unseen, silent." In "Gotyk" ("The Gothic," from *Jechai do Lwówa*), the speaker asks: "Who am I here in this cool cathedral and who/ is speaking to me so obscurely?" Another poem from the same collection brings the lament: "So many errors, with an incorporeal/ ruler governing a tangible reality." The title poem of *Ziemia Ognista* ends with the prayer: "Nameless, unseen, silent,/ save me from anesthesia,/take me to Tierra del Fuego. . . ."

PRAGNIENIE

The contrast between the "anesthetized" late twentieth century with its bored, sate conformity, and the desire for a genuine spiritual experience is the theme of *Pragnienie* (desire). This fin de siècle collection opens with childhood memories and ends with a self-portrait of a mature artist, "between the computer, a pencil, and a typewriter," living in "strange cities," listening to "Bach, Mahler, Chopin, Shostakovich," reading "poets, living and dead." This artist is no longer young and knows it. His voice has grown quiet, reflective. At this stage of his life, he has many dead to mourn. The collection contains a number of elegies dedicated to other poets (Joseph Brodsky, Zbigniew Herbert) and artists (Krzysztof Kieślowski, Józef Czapski). The theme of death and loss pervades this nostalgic volume.

Pragnienie is both a very private reflection on the poet's life and, as Zagajewski's former translator Renata Gorczyńska has it, a report on the conditions of the human community at the end of the twentieth century. Zagajewski portrays a Western culture devoid of genuine spiritual values, atrophied, sedated, paralyzed with boredom. Always sensitive to the ethical role of literature, the poet has diagnosed a new threat to the human spirit: Like a totalitarian regime, mass culture blunts sensitivity and chokes metaphysical inquiry. Can poetry kindle a new flame? Awaken a new desire?

These are the questions Zagajewski poses at the end of a troubled century.

OTHER MAJOR WORKS

LONG FICTION: *Ciełpo zimno*, 1975; *Das absolute Gehör*, 1982; *Cienka kreska*, 1983.

NONFICTION: *Świat nie przedstawiony*, 1974 (with Julian Kornhauser); *Drugi Oddech*, 1978; *Polen: Staat im Schatten der Sowjetunion*, 1981; *Solidarność i samotność*, 1986 (*Solidarity, Solitude: Essays*, 1990); *Dwa miasta*, 1991 (*Two Cities: On Exile, History, and the Imagination*, 1995); *W cudzym pięknie*, 1998 (*Another Beauty*, 2000); *Obrona żarliwości*, 2002 (*A Defense of Ardor*, 2004).

TRANSLATIONS: *Świat i uczestnik*, 1981 (of Raymond Aron); *Religia, literatura, i komunizm: Dziennik emigranta*, 1990 (of Mircea Eliade).

EDITED TEXT: *Polish Writers on Writing*, 2007.

BIBLIOGRAPHY

Bieńkowski, Zbigniew. "The New Wave: A Non-Objective View." In *The Mature Laurel: Essays on Modern Polish Poetry*, edited by Adam Czerniawski. Chester Springs, Pa.: Seren Books, Dufour Editions, 1991. A sensitive and balanced overview of New Wave (Generation of '68) poetry in the context of several earlier postwar poetic generations. Includes translations of poems by Zagajewski, Ewa Lipska, Julian Kornhauser, and Stanisław Barańczak.

Carpenter, Bogdana. "A Tribute to Adam Zagajewski." *World Literature Today* 79, no. 2 (May-August, 2005): 14-16. A brief profile of Zagajewski on his winning of the Neustadt Prize. Describes the polarities in his life and writing.

Corn, Alfred. "Poetry and Dialectic." Review of *Eternal Enemies*. *Hudson Review* 61, no. 4 (Winter, 2009): 801-809. Corn uses the review as an opportunity to profile Zagajewski, discussing his life, his exile, his poetry, and the difficulty of translation.

Karpowicz, Tymoteusz. "Naked Poetry: A Discourse About the Newest Polish Poetry." *Polish Review* 1/2 (1976): 59-70. An insightful report on the state of Polish poetry, from the time Zagajewski was publishing his first collections. Written by a well-known Polish poet.

Shallcross, Bożena. "The Divining Moment: Adam Zagajewski's Aesthetic Epiphany." *Slavic and East European Journal* 44, no. 2 (2000): 234-252. An analysis of epiphany and its importance to the artistic sensitivity of Zagajewski; looks at Zagajewski's responses to works of art, such as Jan Vermeer's painting *Girl Interrupted in Her Music* and Carlos Saura's film *Flamenco*.

_____. *Through the Poet's Eye: The Travels of Zagajewski, Herbert, and Brodsky*. Evanston, Ill.: Northwestern University Press, 2002. This biographical work looks at the travels of Zagajewski, Zbigniew Herbert, and Joseph Brodsky. Examines the effect on their writings.

Witkowski, Tadeusz. "The Poets of the New Wave in Exile." *Slavic and East European Journal* 33, no. 2 (1989): 204-216. An account of the émigré works by poets once belonging to the New Wave; addresses the problem of poetry's ethical responsibility and presents the poetic and ideological debate between Zagajewski and another poet of his generation, Ryszard Krynicki.

Magdalena Mączyńska

STEFAN ZWEIG

Born: Vienna, Austria; November 28, 1881
Died: Petropolis, Brazil; February 22, 1942

PRINCIPAL POETRY

Silberne Saiten, 1901
Die frühen Kränze, 1906
Gesammelten Gedichte, 1924
Ausgewählte Gedichte, 1932
Silberne Saiten: Gedichte und Nachdichtungen, 1966

OTHER LITERARY FORMS

Stefan Zweig (tsvik), one of the most prolific and, in his time, most widely read authors of the twentieth century, began his literary career as a poet, but his lyric poetry is not among his most important or most enduring achievements. His reputation rests largely on his short fiction, his biographies, his essays, and one of his plays. Zweig the storyteller is noted for his vivid, virtuosic style and his skillful psychological penetration of his characters. His work in the novella form ranges from *Die Liebe der Erika Ewald* (1904; Erika Ewald's love) to his last completed work, *Schachnovelle* (1942; *The Royal Game*, 1944), which poignantly foreshadows a time of increasing specialization, mechanization, and dehumanization in which men of mind are doomed to be checkmated by brutish technocrats. The collection *Erstes Erlebnis* (1911; first experience) contains sensitive stories of childhood and adolescence; the stories in *Verwirrung der Gefühle* (1927; *Conflicts*, 1927) and *Amok* (1922; English translation, 1931) deal with adult passions and problems. Zweig's only completed novel, *Ungeduld des Herzens* (1938; *Beware of Pity*, 1939), is a haunting portrayal of a crippled girl and her love. Recently discovered and published in 1982, *Rausch der Verwandlung* (*The Post-Office Girl*, 2008) is a fragmentary novel about a lowly Austrian post-office clerk whose penurious life is transformed when she gets a taste of opulent living and again when she is drawn into the vortex of big-city crime.

Another literary form in which Zweig achieved great success and an international readership in more than thirty languages was the *vie romancée* (biographical novel). As a biographer, Zweig favored the cyclical form, attempting to present a "typology of the spirit." *Drei Meister* (1920; *Three Masters*, 1930) contains biographical studies of Honoré de Balzac, Charles Dickens, and Fyodor Dostoevski; *Der Kampf mit dem Dämon* (1925; *The Struggle with the Demon*, 1928-1930, 1939) examines Friedrich Hölderlin, Heinrich von Kleist, and Friedrich Nietzsche, poets and thinkers who went insane or committed suicide; and *Drei Dichter ihres Lebens* (1928; *Adepts in Self-Portraiture*, 1928) presents the great autobiographers Casanova, Stendhal, and Leo Tolstoy. In 1935, these biographical studies appeared in one volume as *Baumeister der Welt*, appearing in English translation in 1939 as *Master Builders*. Another biographical trilogy, *Die Heilung durch den Geist* (1931; *Mental Healers*, 1932), explores the lives and influences of Franz Anton Mesmer, Mary Baker Eddy (who is debunked), and Sigmund

Freud (to whom Zweig felt close intellectually and personally). Other biographical volumes include *Joseph Fouché* (1929; English translation, 1930), *Marie Antoinette* (1932; English translation, 1933), *Maria Stuart* (1935; *Mary, Queen of Scotland and the Isles*, 1935), *Magellan* (1938; *Magellan, Pioneer of the Pacific*, 1938), and *Balzac* (1946; English translation, 1946). *Triumph und Tragik des Erasmus von Rotterdam* (1934; *Erasmus of Rotterdam*, 1934) is a very personal book, for Zweig regarded the Dutch Humanist, who disdained political action in a turbulent age, as his spiritual ancestor and mentor. Zweig's collaboration with Richard Strauss on the comic opera *Die schweigsame Frau* (the silent woman), based on a work by Ben Jonson, became a cause célèbre in 1935 because of the composer's refusal to renounce his Jewish collaborator in Nazi Germany. Most notable among Zweig's several dramas is the powerful pacifist play *Jeremias* (1917; *Jeremiah*, 1922), which premiered in Switzerland. In his universally admired autobiography, *Die Welt von Gestern* (1941; *The World of Yesterday*, 1943), Zweig self-effacingly keeps his own life and work in the background as he presents a brilliant, poignant panorama of European life, thought, and culture in the first half of the twentieth century.

ACHIEVEMENTS

In both his life and his work, Stefan Zweig was a cultural mediator. All his life, he was a translator in an elevated sense, attempting to inform, to educate, to inspire, and to arouse appreciation and enthusiasm across literary, cultural, national, and personal boundaries. He once wrote that it was his aim

> to understand even what is most alien to us, always to evaluate peoples and periods, figures and works only in their positive and creative sense, and to let this desire to understand and convey this understanding to others serve humbly and faithfully our indestructible ideal: humane communication among individuals, mentalities, cultures, and nations.

For fifteen years, Zweig's impressive home on the picturesque Kapuzinerberg in Salzburg was a shrine to his central idea, the intellectual unification of Europe, and the mecca of a cultural elite, many of whom Zweig numbered among his friends. His world travels as well as his bibliophilic pursuits, particularly his legendary collection of literary and musical holograph manuscripts, nurtured his art and aided his wide-ranging cultural and humanitarian activities. Zweig's correspondence with Martin Buber during World War I as well as other documents indicates that he prized the Diaspora and interpreted his Jewishness rather willfully as offering him an opportunity to be a citizen of the world: "Perhaps it is the purpose of Judaism to show over the centuries that community is possible without country, only through blood and intellect, only through the word and faith."

At an early age, Zweig became aware of the crisis facing his era, and for many years, he was bedeviled by the growing antinomy between a bourgeois humanism whose position had become undermined by the failure of its adherents to commit themselves to positive action and the ever-rising current of political and social activism which was compelling individuals to commit themselves to some form of action. While Zweig's knowledge of history and the typology of human motivations and personalities could not have left him blind to the need for change, he consciously adopted and maintained an eminently apolitical stance.

Displaying a becoming awareness of the dignity and spiritual superiority of the dispossessed and the vanquished, Zweig repeatedly and movingly portrayed apolitical individuals (such as that "bibliosaurus," the transplanted Eastern European Jew Jakob Mendel, called Book Mendel) caught up in the impersonal, unfeeling machinery of world politics and conflicts. Zweig's biographical study of Joseph Fouché, Napoleon's minister of police, is a great moral condemnation of *homo politicus*; teaching an object lesson in unprincipled behavior, the author warned the peoples of Europe against falling for politicians of that stripe. In an essay written in 1922, "Ist die Geschichte gerecht?" (Is there justice in history?), Zweig tried to supply a humanistic antidote and alternative to the cult of power, warning the masses against glorifying their oppressors and worshiping their chains. He pointed out that, all too often, history has been rewritten in favor of those who have prevailed by virtue of brute strength and that there

is a tendency to create myths about the strong and the heroic, while the infinitely worthier heroes of everyday life remain unsung. Might and morality must be clearly sundered; it behooves people not to be bedazzled by the seductive glamour of success and to reexamine history from a humanistic point of view.

In *The World of Yesterday*, Zweig said about himself that as an Austrian, a Jew, a writer, a humanist, and a pacifist, he had always stood at the exact point where the global clashes and cataclysms of the century were at their most violent. His response to these blows of fate was an excessive objectivity and feckless neutrality, a reluctance to become involved in political action, and an increasing contempt for merely political adjustments. Zweig's frequently naïve stance is reminiscent of the inaction and near-paralysis of Viennese intellectuals at the turn of the century; he came to regard Europe as his "sacred homeland," and his Europeanism ultimately led him to view the tragedy of the Jews as only part of the larger and presumably more important tragedy of Europe.

While Zweig was a physician who could not heal himself, his undogmatic and nonideological humanism is eminently relevant to the present age. While his brand of liberalism is old-fashioned, his contribution to pan-European thought must be regarded as an enduring one. His was one of the first voices to call for a cosmopolitan community of the youth of Europe, and he proposed the establishment of an international university that would function interchangeably in several capital cities. In a lecture delivered in 1932, "Die moralische Entgiftung Europas" (the moral decontamination of Europe), Zweig called for well-organized student exchanges to reduce political tensions and collective animosities. He felt that the history of culture and of the human spirit rather than military or political history should be taught in the schools of the world. Some causes for which Zweig worked tirelessly and that seemed utopian during his lifetime, such as Franco-German understanding, are actualities today. Zweig's apotheosis of Brazil, his last refuge, shows that his interest was not limited to Europe and that he was alive to both the problems and the potentialities of what has been called the Third World. "Our greatest debt of gratitude," wrote Zweig in his unfinished last work, a study of Michel Eyquem de Montaigne, "is to those who in these inhuman times confirm the human in us, who encourage us not to abandon our unique and imperishable possession: our innermost self." These words also sum up Zweig's quest and his achievement.

Biography

The second son of a wealthy industrialist, Stefan Zweig had an early and auspicious start in literature in what he later described as a "world of security," taking "flight into the intellectual" from his father's stultifying business mentality and his mother's overbearing snobbishness. Having an essay accepted by Theodor Herzl, the influential editor of the prestigious Vienna daily *Neue Freie Presse*, was an important boost to the career of the fledgling writer, who soon became an outstanding member of the literary group *Jung Wien* (Young Vienna). His first book was published when he was still in his teens.

In 1904, Zweig earned a doctorate from the University of Vienna with a dissertation on Hippolyte Taine. Early trips to Germany, France, Belgium, Holland, England, Italy, Spain, India, and North America served to broaden the horizons of the young man, but what most decisively shaped Zweig's evolution from an aesthetically oriented man of letters to a "great European" was his encounter with the Flemish poet Émile Verhaeren. Zweig regarded Verhaeren's intense, vibrantly contemporary, and life-affirming poetry as a lyrical encyclopedia of his age. Zweig tirelessly served Verhaeren as a translator, biographer, and publicist. Zweig's European education was continued through his friendship with the French writer Romain Rolland, whose exemplary pacifist and humanist activities in wartime were a great inspiration to Zweig. While working at the Austrian War Archives in Vienna, Zweig was able to write his pacifist drama *Jeremiah*. He went to Zurich to join a group of intellectuals who, like himself, rejected nationalism and worked toward the restoration of the community of European men of mind.

In 1919, Zweig moved to Salzburg and was soon able to solemnize his union with the writer Friderike Maria Burger von Winternitz. The years in Salzburg, where he lived with his wife and two stepdaughters, were his most productive ones. In addition to having his

works published by the prestigious Insel Verlag of Leipzig, he became a trusted adviser to that publishing house, ever ready to help other writers and artists by introducing and championing their work. His readings and lectures took him all over the world. One of the most notable of these journeys was his trip to Russia in 1928 on the occasion of the Tolstoy centennial.

After 1933, the centrally located Salzburg became an inhospitable and dangerously exposed place, and an almost paranoid uneasiness took hold of the apolitical Zweig. His move to England in 1934 marked the beginning of years of insecurity, restless globe-trotting, and mounting despair. The breakup of his marriage was but one of many symptomatic events and situations that bedeviled the man who had acquired the coveted British citizenship and was materially far better off than most emigrants. Profoundly depressed by the fate of his spiritual homeland, Europe, and fearing that the humanist spirit was crushed forever, Zweig committed suicide in 1942 in a country that he had celebrated in a book as "a land of the future." He was joined in death by his second wife, Elisabeth Charlotte Altmann, whom he had married at Bath in 1939.

Analysis

The poetry that Stefan Zweig began writing at an early age, published in *Die Gesellschaft*, *Die Zukunft*, *Die Welt*, *Deutsche Dichtung*, and other newspapers, periodicals, and almanacs, was informed by the zeitgeist of fin de siècle Vienna. The last decades of the moribund Habsburg empire, governed by a six-hundred-year-old dynasty, were characterized by a latter-day *Weltschmerz*, by overrefinement and an aesthetic cult of beauty expressive of an aloofness from the world's pursuits, and by surface smiles masking a world-weary abandonment of political solutions. Zweig himself described these early efforts, Impressionistic poems marked by preciosity, as "verses of vague premonition and instinctive feeling, not created out of my own experience, but rather born of a passion for language." The same may be said of the astonishingly precocious poems of Hugo von Hofmannsthal, who published his verse as a schoolboy under the pseudonym Loris and for whom Zweig always had admiration and affection, though it turned out to be a case of unrequited love. While Zweig's early poems, however, are eminently lyrical and display great musicality as well as a certain mastery of form, they lack the psychological penetration, the poetic intuition, and the linguistic magic of Hofmannsthal's poetry.

In 1900, Zweig wrote in a letter to Karl Emil Franzos: "I have published to date 150 or 200 poems, written double that number, and now have put together a volume under the title *Silberne Saiten* which contains 50, that is, a most stringent selection." That volume appeared in February of 1901 with a dedication "to my dear parents." It was well received, even by such established poets as Detlev von Liliencron, Richard Dehmel, and Rainer Maria Rilke. The *Revue allemande* noted that "a quiet, solemn beauty pervades the lines of this Young Vienna poet, a translucence rarely to be found in first works . . . Zweig is a virtuoso in technique; each single poem gives us fresh opportunity to enjoy the fineness of his diction, of immeasurable harmony and wealth of imagery." A severe judgment, however, was rendered by Erich Mühsam, who rejected "a book that, with its obtrusive sickly sweetness and insipid exaggeration, would hardly be worth mentioning were it not typical of the pretentious manner which is spreading ever more widely through the Young Vienna movement and which seeks to impress by mere playing with form." Even though Zweig had the satisfaction of seeing the eminent composer Max Reger set to music two of the poems from *Silberne Saiten*, "Neue Fülle" and "Ein Drängen ist in meinem Herzen," he soon disowned this early poetry and refused to have it reprinted in later collections.

DIE FRÜHEN KRÄNZE

Some of the young Zweig's characteristic feelings, themes, and stances (dreaming, longing, youthful ardor aiming at interpersonal relationships, evanescence, delicate autumnal and nocturnal moods, subtle transitions) are also in evidence in the poetry written in the early years of the twentieth century and published in Zweig's second collection, *Die frühen Kränze* (the early wreaths), issued in 1906. This volume is notable, among other reasons, for marking Zweig's first collaboration with the celebrated Insel Verlag. Here, Zweig presented his more mature, though still rather unoriginal poetry, with its cyclical form adumbrating the later

Stefan Zweig (Hulton Archive/Getty Images)

grouping of a number of his prose works. Thus, the series "Fahrten" (journeys) includes poetic evocations of a sunrise in Venice ("Sonnenaufgang in Venedig"), nights on Lake Como ("Nächte am Comersee"), and the city of Constance ("Stadt am See"). The sequence "Lieder des Abends" (songs of evening) contains the euphoric "Lied des Einsiedels" (hermit's song); the cycle "Frauen" (women) includes "Das fremde Lächeln" (a female stranger's smile), "Die Zärtlichkeiten" (the caresses), and "Terzinen an ein Mädchen" (terze rima for a girl); and the cycle "Bilder" (images, or portraits) includes one of Zweig's longest poems, "Der Verführer" (the seducer).

GESAMMELTEN GEDICHTE

Many of these and other groupings are included in the more ambitious collection of his poems that Zweig published in 1924, *Gesammelten Gedichte*. Its first section, "Musik der Jugend" (music of youth), presents a selection from the early poems. The cycle "Die Herren des Lebens" (the masters of life), placed toward the end of the volume, gathers eleven of what may be described as lyric statues. Notable among these is the only poem (or work of any kind) of which Zweig is known to have made a recording: "Der Bildner" (the sculptor). This poem memorializes Zweig's visit to Maison Rodin at Meudon in 1913. He depicts the aged sculptor surrounded by his timeless and changeless works, those "frozen crystals of infinity," and describes his astonishment in the petrified forest of his studio as he prayerfully comes to realize what his true mission is: to represent, shape, and complete something more permanent than he is, to create life beyond his own life. "Der Kaiser" is a poetic evocation of Emperor Franz Joseph, and "Der Dirigent" (the conductor) was written in memory of Gustav Mahler.

Two of the most powerful poems in this collection were born of Zweig's vibrant pacifism. "Der Krüppel" (the cripple) is a sensitive poetic depiction of a war-injured man on crutches, and "Polyphem" evokes the mythical monster Polyphemus, the cannibalistic giant who comes under attack as the demon or bringer of war. The long "Ballade von einem Traum" (ballad of a dream), written after World War I, which concludes the *Gesammelten Gedichte*, may be read as a highly personal allegory. In a nightmare, the poet feels that his vaunted private sphere has been invaded and his most secret self exposed. He reads the fiery handwriting on the wall: "Du bist erkannt!" (You are known!). Tormented by this revealing refrain, he finally awakes, grateful that his innermost thoughts have not, in fact, been betrayed and that his deepest self remains inviolate.

TRANSLATIONS

Zweig's activities as a cultural mediator, and in particular as a translator of poetry, significantly shaped his own creativity as a poet. His first great idol was Verhaeren, and Zweig's initial lack of self-sufficiency may have made him respond all the more strongly to certain antithetical traits that he found in the Belgian poet: a hymnal spirit, a prodigious strength, universal love, enthusiasm, and a feeling of exaltation. What others regarded as a barren field for poetry—the machines, the big cities, the industrial life, the masses of people, the entire ferment of modern civilization—Verhaeren

considered eminently fertile material for poetic expression. His example purged Zweig's own poetry of the last vestiges of fin de siècle Decadence. After the decisive caesura of World War I, however, Zweig did not attempt to emulate Verhaeren's poetic style. The three-volume edition of Verhaeren's writings that Zweig translated and edited for the Insel Verlag in 1910 included a volume containing his translations (from the French) of fifty-one of Verhaeren's poems; another volume had preceded it in 1904. Other French poets for whom Zweig served as a sensitive translator and commentator are Paul Verlaine, Charles Baudelaire, and Marceline Desbordes-Valmore. His translations from Verhaeren, Baudelaire, and Verlaine are rightly reprinted in the edition of Zweig's collected poetry issued in 1966.

"DER SECHZIGJÄHRIGE DANKT"

After the appearance of *Gesammelten Gedichte* in the mid-1920's, Zweig concentrated on his fiction and biographies, writing poetry only occasionally. Particular poignance attaches to his last poem, "Der Sechzigjährige dankt" (the sixty-year-old gives thanks), which Zweig sent a few months before his death to close friends who had congratulated him on his birthday. This widely admired poem has been set to music by Henry Jolles and by Felix Wolfes. It bespeaks serenity despite the poet's presentiment of death, expresses calm detachment and resignation as "farewell's blazing gloss" opens up new vistas, and says that what remains of life can be enjoyed *sub specie aeternitatis*, for the approach of old age frees one from the constraints, burdens, and goads of desire, ambition, and self-recrimination.

OTHER MAJOR WORKS

LONG FICTION: *Die Liebe der Erika Ewald*, 1904 (novella); *Brennendes Geheimnis*, 1913 (*Burning Secret*, 2008); *Angst*, 1920; *Der Zwang*, 1920; *Ungeduld des Herzens*, 1938 (*Beware of Pity*, 1939); *Schachnovelle*, 1942 (novella; *The Royal Game*, 1944); *Rausch der Verwandlung*, 1982 (*The Post-Office Girl*, 2008).

SHORT FICTION: *Erstes Erlebnis*, 1911; *Amok*, 1922 (English translation, 1931); *Verwirrung der Gefühle*, 1927 (*Conflicts*, 1927).

PLAYS: *Tersites*, 1907; *Der Haus am Meer*, 1912; *Jeremias*, 1917 (*Jeremiah*, 1922); *Volpone*, 1926 (translation); *Das Lamm des Armen*, 1929; *Die schweigsame Frau*, 1935 (libretto).

NONFICTION: *Émile Verhaeren*, 1910 (English translation, 1914); *Das Herz Europas*, 1918; *Drei Meister*, 1920 (*Three Masters*, 1930); *Der Kampf mit dem Dämon*, 1925 (*The Struggle with the Demon*, 1928-1930, 1939); *Sternstunden der Menschheit*, 1927 (*The Tide of Fortune*, 1940); *Drei Dichter ihres Lebens*, 1928 (*Adepts in Self-Portraiture*, 1928); *Joseph Fouché*, 1929 (English translation, 1930); *Die Heilung durch den Geist*, 1931 (*Mental Healers*, 1932); *Marie Antoinette*, 1932 (English translation, 1933); *Triumph und Tragik des Erasmus von Rotterdam*, 1934 (*Erasmus of Rotterdam*, 1934); *Maria Stuart*, 1935 (*Mary, Queen of Scotland and the Isles*, 1935); *Castellio gegen Calvin*, 1936 (*The Right to Heresy*, 1936); *Magellan*, 1938 (*Magellan, Pioneer of the Pacific*, 1938); *Brasilien, ein Land der Zukunft*, 1941 (*Brazil: A Land of the Future*, 1941); *Die Welt von Gestern*, 1941 (*The World of Yesterday*, 1943); *Balzac*, 1946 (English translation, 1946); *Stefan und Friderike Zweig: Ein Briefwechsel 1912-1942*, 1954 (*Stefan and Friderike Zweig: Their Correspondence*, 1954); *Richard Strauss und Stefan Zweig: Briefwechsel*, 1957 (*A Confidential Matter: The Letters of Richard Strauss and Stefan Zweig, 1931-1935*, 1977).

BIBLIOGRAPHY

Arens, Hanns, ed. *Stefan Zweig: A Tribute to His Life and Work*. Translated by Christobel Fowler. London: W. H. Allen, 1951. A short biographical and critical study of Zweig's oeuvre.

Gelber, Mark H., ed. *Stefan Zweig Reconsidered: New Perspectives on His Literary and Biographical Writings*. Tübingen, Germany: Niemeyer, 2007. Contains proceedings from a conference in 2004, six of which are in English.

Klawiter, Randolph J. *Stefan Zweig: An International Bibliography*. Riverside, Calif.: Ariadne Press, 1999. A valuable reference catalog of publications by and about Zweig.

Spitzer, Leo. *Lives in Between: The Experience of Marginality in a Century of Emancipation*. New York: Hill and Wang, 1999. A study of three broadly different yet compellingly similar human stories that range from the late nineteenth century to the mid-twentieth century. This important work focuses on three marginal groups—Jews in Austria, mulattoes in Brazil, and freed slaves in Sierra Leone—and their tragic quest for assimilation. Within the study of the experiences of Jews in Austria, Spitzer examines the historical, sociological, and psychological aspects of Zweig's life.

Wright, Patrick. "Enemy Alien: Lives and Letters." Review of *The World of Yesterday*. *The Guardian*, February 2, 2008. Notes that though Zweig was a successful poet and novelist, his life was overturned by war, as best understood through this autobiography.

Zweig, Stefan. *Stefan Zweig, Joseph Gregor: Correspondence, 1921-1938*. Edited by Kenneth Birkin. Dunedin, New Zealand: University of Otago Press, 1992. A collection of letters that provides invaluable insight into Zweig's life and work. Includes bibliographical references and indexes.

Harry Zohn

RESOURCES

EXPLICATING POETRY

Explicating poetry begins with a process of distinguishing the poem's factual and technical elements from the readers' emotional ones. Readers respond to poems in a variety of ways that may initially have little to do with the poetry itself but that result from the events in their own lives, their expectations of art, and their philosophical/theological/psychological complexion.

All serious readers hope to find poems that can blend with the elements of their personal backgrounds in such a way that for a moment or a lifetime their relationship to life and the cosmos becomes more meaningful. This is the ultimate goal of poetry, and when it happens—when meaning, rhythm, and sound fuse with the readers' emotions to create a unified experience—it can only be called the magic of poetry, for something has happened between reader and poet that is inexplicable in rational terms.

When a poem creates such an emotional response in readers, then it is at least a partial success. To be considered excellent, however, a poem must also be able to pass a critical analysis to determine whether it is mechanically superior. Although twenty-first century criticism has tended to judge poetic works solely on their individual content and has treated them as independent of historical influences, such a technique often makes a full explication difficult. The best modern readers realize that good poetry analysis observes all aspects of a poem: its technical success, its historical importance and intellectual force, and its effect on readers' emotions.

Students of poetry will find it useful to begin an explication by analyzing the elements that poets have at their disposal as they create their art: dramatic situation, point of view, imagery, metaphor, symbol, meter, form, and allusion. The outline headed "Checklist for Explicating a Poem" (see page 1152) will help guide the reader through the necessary steps to a detailed explication.

Although explication is not a science, and a variety of observations may be equally valid, these step-by-step procedures can be applied systematically to make the reading of most poems a richer experience for the reader. To illustrate, these steps are applied below to a difficult poem by Edwin Arlington Robinson.

Luke Havergal

Go to the western gate, Luke Havergal,
There where the vines cling crimson on the wall,
And in the twilight wait for what will come.
The leaves will whisper there of her, and some, 4
Like flying words, will strike you as they fall;
But go, and if you listen, she will call.
Go to the western gate, Luke Havergal—
Luke Havergal.   8

No, there is not a dawn in eastern skies
To rift the fiery night that's in your eyes;
But there, where western glooms are gathering,
The dark will end the dark, if anything: 12
God slays Himself with every leaf that flies,
And hell is more than half of paradise.
No, there is not a dawn in eastern skies—
In eastern skies.   16

Out of a grave I come to tell you this,
Out of a grave I come to quench the kiss
That flames upon your forehead with a glow
That blinds you to the way that you must go.   20
Yes, there is yet one way to where she is,
Bitter, but one that faith may never miss.
Out of a grave I come to tell you this—
To tell you this.   24

There is the western gate, Luke Havergal
There are the crimson leaves upon the wall.
Go, for the winds are tearing them away,—
Nor think to riddle the dead words they say,   28
Nor any more to feel them as they fall;
But go, and if you trust her she will call.
There is the western gate, Luke Havergal—
Luke Havergal.

E. A. Robinson, 1897

STEP I-A: *Before reading*

1. "Luke Havergal" is a strophic poem composed of four equally lengthened stanzas. Each stanza is long enough to contain a narrative, an involved description or situation, or a problem and resolution.

2. The title raises several possibilities: Luke Havergal

CHECKLIST FOR EXPLICATING A POEM

I. THE INITIAL READINGS
  A. Before reading the poem, the reader should:
    1. Notice its form and length.
    2. Consider the title, determining, if possible, whether it might function as an allusion, symbol, or poetic image.
    3. Notice the date of composition or publication, and identify the general era of the poet.
  B. The poem should be read intuitively and emotionally and be allowed to "happen" as much as possible.
  C. In order to establish the rhythmic flow, the poem should be re-read. A note should be made as to where the irregular spots (if any) are located.
II. EXPLICATING THE POEM
  A. *Dramatic situation.* Studying the poem line by line helps the reader discover the dramatic situation. All elements of the dramatic situation are interrelated and should be viewed as reflecting and affecting one another. The dramatic situation serves a particular function in the poem, adding realism, surrealism, or absurdity; drawing attention to certain parts of the poem; and changing to reinforce other aspects of the poem. All points should be considered. The following questions are particularly helpful to ask in determining dramatic situation:
    1. What, if any, is the narrative action in the poem?
    2. How many personae appear in the poem? What part do they take in the action?
    3. What is the relationship between characters?
    4. What is the setting (time and location) of the poem?
  B. *Point of view.* An understanding of the poem's point of view is a major step toward comprehending the poet's intended meaning. The reader should ask:
    1. Who is the speaker? Is he or she addressing someone else or the reader?
    2. Is the narrator able to understand or see everything happening to him or her, or does the reader know things that the narrator does not?
    3. Is the narrator reliable?
    4. Do point of view and dramatic situation seem consistent? If not, the inconsistencies may provide clues to the poem's meaning.
  C. *Images and metaphors.* Images and metaphors are often the most intricately crafted vehicles of the poem for relaying the poet's message. Realizing that the images and metaphors work in harmony with the dramatic situation and point of view will help the reader to see the poem as a whole, rather than as disassociated elements.
    1. The reader should identify the concrete images (that is, those that are formed from objects that can be touched, smelled, seen, felt, or tasted). Is the image projected by the poet consistent with the physical object?
    2. If the image is abstract, or so different from natural imagery that it cannot be associated with a real object, then what are the properties of the image?
    3. To what extent is the reader asked to form his or her own images?

  4. Is any image repeated in the poem? If so, how has it been changed? Is there a controlling image?
  5. Are any images compared to each other? Do they reinforce one another?
  6. Is there any difference between the way the reader perceives the image and the way the narrator sees it?
  7. What seems to be the narrator's or persona's attitude toward the image?
  D. *Words.* Every substantial word in a poem may have more than one intended meaning, as used by the author. Because of this, the reader should look up many of these words in the dictionary and:
    1. Note all definitions that have the slightest connection with the poem.
    2. Note any changes in syntactical patterns in the poem.
    3. In particular, note those words that could possibly function as symbols or allusions, and refer to any appropriate sources for further information.
  E. *Meter, rhyme, structure, and tone.* In scanning the poem, all elements of prosody should be noted by the reader. These elements are often used by a poet to manipulate the reader's emotions, and therefore they should be examined closely to arrive at the poet's specific intention.
    1. Does the basic meter follow a traditional pattern such as those found in nursery rhymes or folk songs?
    2. Are there any variations in the base meter? Such changes or substitutions are important thematically and should be identified.
    3. Are the rhyme schemes traditional or innovative, and what might their form mean to the poem?
    4. What devices has the poet used to create sound patterns (such as assonance and alliteration)?
    5. Is the stanza form a traditional or innovative one?
    6. If the poem is composed of verse paragraphs rather than stanzas, how do they affect the progression of the poem?
    7. After examining the above elements, is the resultant tone of the poem casual or formal, pleasant, harsh, emotional, authoritative?
  F. *Historical context.* The reader should attempt to place the poem into historical context, checking on events at the time of composition. Archaic language, expressions, images, or symbols should also be looked up.
  G. *Themes and motifs.* By seeing the poem as a composite of emotion, intellect, craftsmanship, and tradition, the reader should be able to determine the themes and motifs (smaller recurring ideas) presented in the work. He or she should ask the following questions to help pinpoint these main ideas:
    1. Is the poet trying to advocate social, moral, or religious change?
    2. Does the poet seem sure of his or her position?
    3. Does the poem appeal primarily to the emotions, to the intellect, or to both?
    4. Is the poem relying on any particular devices for effect (such as imagery, allusion, paradox, hyperbole, or irony)?

could be a specific person; Luke Havergal could represent a type of person; the name might have symbolic or allusive qualities. Thus, "Luke" may refer to Luke of the Bible or "Luke-warm," meaning indifferent or showing little or no zeal. "Havergal" could be a play on words. "Haver" is a Scotch and Northern English word meaning to talk foolishly. It is clear from the rhyme words that the "gal" of Havergal is pronounced as if it had two "l's," but it is spelled with one "l" for no apparent reason unless it is to play on the word "gal," meaning girl. Because it is pronounced "gall," meaning something bitter or severe, a sore or state of irritation, or an impudent self-assurance, this must also be considered as a possibility. Finally, the "haver" of "Havergal" might be a perversion of "have a."

3. Published in 1897, the poem probably does not contain archaic language unless it is deliberately used. The period of writing is known as the Victorian Age. Historical events that may have influenced the poem may be checked for later.

STEP I-B: *The poem should be read*

STEP I-C: *Rereading the poem*

The frequent use of internal caesuras in stanzas 1 and 2 contrast with the lack of caesuras in stanzas 3 and 4. There are end-stopped lines and much repetition. The poem reads smoothly except for line 28 and the feminine ending on lines 11 and 12.

STEP II-A: *Dramatic situation*

In line 1 of "Luke Havergal," an unidentified speaker is addressing Luke. Because the speaker calls him by his full name, there is a sense that the speaker has assumed a superior (or at least a formal) attitude toward Luke and that the talk that they are having is not a casual conversation.

In addition to knowing something about the relationship in line 1, the reader is led to think, because of the words "go to the western gate," that the personae must be near some sort of enclosed house or city. Perhaps Luke and the speaker are at some "other" gate, since the western gate is specifically pointed out.

Line 2 suggests that the situation at the western gate is different from that elsewhere—there "vines cling crimson on the wall," hinting at some possibilities

about the dramatic situation. (Because flowers and colors are always promising symbols, they must be carefully considered later.)

The vines in line 2 could provide valuable information about the dramatic situation, except that in line 2 the clues are ambiguous. Are the vines perennial? If so, their crimson color suggests that the season is late summer or autumn. Crimson might also be their natural color when in full bloom. Further, are they grape vines (grapes carry numerous connotations and symbolic values), and are the vines desirable? All of this in line 2 is ambiguous. The only certainty is that there is a wall—a barrier that closes something in and something out.

In lines 1-3, the speaker again commands Luke to go and wait. Since Luke is to wait in the twilight, it is probably now daylight. All Luke must do is be passive because whatever is to come will happen without any action on his part.

In line 4, the speaker begins to tell Luke what will happen at the western gate, and the reader now knows that Luke is waiting for something with feminine characteristics, possibly a woman. This line also mentions that the vines have leaves, implying that crimson denotes their waning stage.

In line 5, the speaker continues to describe what will happen at the western gate: The leaves will whisper about "her," and as they fall, some of them will strike Luke "like flying words." The reader, however, must question whether Luke will actually be "struck" by the leaves, or whether the leaves are being personified or being used as an image or symbol. In line 6, the speaker stops his prophecy and tells Luke to leave. If Luke listens, "she" will call, but if he does not, it is unclear what will happen. The reader might ask the questions, to whom is "she" calling, and from where?

In summarizing the dramatic situation in stanza 1, one can say that the speaker is addressing Luke, but it is not yet possible to determine whether he or she is present or whether Luke is thinking to himself (interior monologue). The time is before twilight; the place is near a wall with a gate. Luke is directed to go to the gate and listen for a female voice to call.

From reading the first line in the second stanza, it is apparent that Luke has posed some kind of question, probably concerned with what will be found at the western gate. The answer given is clearly not a direct answer to whatever question was asked, especially as the directions "east" and "west" are probably symbolic. The reader can expect, however, that the silent persona's response will affect the poem's progress.

Stanza 3 discloses who the speaker is and what his relationship is to Luke. After the mysterious discourse in stanza 2, Luke has probably asked "Who are you?" The equally mysterious reply in stanza 3 raises the issue of whether the voice speaking is a person or a spirit or whether it is Luke's imagination or conscience.

Because the voice says that it comes out of the grave, the reader cannot know who or what it is. It may be a person, a ghost, or only Luke's imagination or conscience. Obviously the answer will affect the dramatic situation.

In line 18, the reader learns that the speaker is on a particular mission: "to quench the kiss," and the reader can assume that when the mission is complete he or she will return to the grave. This information is sudden and shocking, and because of this sharp jolt, the reader tends to believe the speaker and credit him or her with supernatural knowledge.

In stanza 4, it becomes apparent that Luke and the speaker have not been stationary during the course of the poem because the western gate is now visible; the speaker can see the leaves upon the wall (line 26).

The wind is blowing (line 27), creating a sense of urgency, because if all the leaves are blown away they cannot whisper about "her." The speaker gives Luke final instructions, and the poem ends with the speaker again pointing toward the place where Luke will find the female persona.

In summary, one can say that the dramatic situation establishes a set of mysterious circumstances that are not explained or resolved on the dramatic level. Luke has been told to go to the western gate by someone who identifies himself or herself as having come from the grave in order to quench Luke's desire, which seems to be connected with the estranged woman, who is, perhaps, dead. The dramatic situation does not tell whether the commanding voice is an emissary from the woman or from the devil, or is merely Luke's conscience; nor does it suggest that something evil will happen to Luke at the western gate, although other elements in the poem make the reader afraid for him.

The poet, then, is using the dramatic situation to draw the reader into questions which will be answered by other means; at this point, the poem is mysterious, obscure, ambiguous, and deliberately misleading.

STEP II-B: *Point of view*

There are a number of questions that immediately come to mind about the point of view. Is the speaker an evil seducer, or is he or she a friend telling Luke about death? Why is the poem told from his or her point of view?

From a generalized study, readers know that the first-person singular point of view takes the reader deep into the mind of the narrator in order to show what he or she knows or to show a personal reaction to an event.

In "Luke Havergal," the narrator gives the following details about himself and the situation: a sense of direction (lines 1 and 9); the general type and color of the vegetation, but not enough to make a detailed analysis of it (line 2); a pantheistic view of nature (line 4); a feeling of communication with the leaves and "her" (lines 5 and 6); a philosophic view of the universe (stanza 2); the power to "quench the kiss," a sense of mission, and a home—the grave (line 18); special vision (line 20); a sense of destiny (lines 21 and 22); and a sense of time and eternity (lines 27 through 29).

Apparently, the narrator can speak with confidence about the western gate, and can look objectively at Luke to see the kiss on his forehead. Such a vantage point suggests that the speaker might represent some aspect of death. He also knows the "one way to where she is," leaving it reasonable to infer that "she" is dead.

There is another possibility in regard to the role of the speaker. He might be part of Luke himself—the voice of his thoughts, of his unconscious mind—or of part of his past. This role might possibly be combined with that of some sort of spirit of death.

The poem, then, is an internal dialogue in which Luke is attempting to cope with "she," who is probably dead and who might well have been his lover, though neither is certain. He speaks to another persona, which is probably Luke's own spirit which has been deadened by the loss of his lover.

Once it is suggested that Luke is a man who is at the depth of despair, the dramatic situation becomes very important because of the possibility that Luke may be driving himself toward self-destruction.

The dramatic situation, therefore, may not be as it originally seemed; perhaps there is only one person, not two. Luke's psychological condition permits him to look at himself as another person, and this other self is pushing Luke toward the western gate, a place that the reader senses is evil.

If the voice is Luke's, then much of the mystery is clarified. Luke would have known what the western gate looked like, whereas a stranger would have needed supernatural powers to know it; furthermore, Luke had probably heard the leaves whispering before, and in his derangement he could believe that someone would call to him if he would only listen.

Establishing point of view has cleared up most of the inconsistencies in this poem's dramatic situation, but there is still confusion about the grave and the kiss. It is easy to make the grave symbolically consistent with point of view, but the reader should look for other possibilities before settling on this explanation.

In stanzas 1 and 2, there is no problem; the dramatic situation is simple and point of view can be reconciled since there is no evidence to prove that another person is present. If, however, the voice is that of Luke's other self, then why has it come from the grave, and where did the kiss come from? At this point, it is not possible to account for these inconsistencies, but by noting them now, the reader can be on the alert for the answers later. Quite possibly accounting for the inconsistencies will provide the key for the explication.

STEP II-C: *Images and metaphors*

Finding images in poems is usually not a difficult task, although seeing their relation to the theme often is. "Luke Havergal" is imagistically difficult because the images are introduced, then reused as the theme develops.

In stanza 1, the reader is allowed to form his or her own image of the setting and mood at the western gate; most readers will probably imagine some sort of mysterious or supernatural situation related to death or the dead. The colors, the sound of the words, and the particular images (vines, wall, whispering leaves) establish the relationship between the living and the dead as the controlling image of the entire poem.

Within the controlling death-in-life image, the metaphors and conceits are more difficult to handle. Vines clinging crimson on the wall (line 2) and waiting in the twilight for something to come (line 3) are images requiring no particular treatment at this point, but in lines 4 and 5 the reader is forced to contend directly with whispering leaves that are like flying words, and there are several metaphorical possibilities for this image.

First, there is the common image of leaves rustling in a breeze, and in a mysterious or enchanted atmosphere it would be very easy to imagine that they are whispering. Such a whisper, however, would ordinarily require a moderate breeze, as a fierce wind would overpower the rustling sound of leaves; but there is more ambiguity in the image: "The leaves will whisper there for her, and some,/ Like flying words, will strike you as they fall."

Because of the syntactical ambiguity of "some,/ Like flying words, will strike," the reader cannot be sure how close or literal is the similarity or identity of "leaves" and "words." The reader cannot be completely sure whether it is leaves or words or both that will strike Luke, or whether the sight of falling leaves might be forcing him to recall words he has heard in the past. There is a distinct metaphoric connection between leaves and words, however, and these in some way strike Luke, perhaps suggesting that the words are those of an argument (an argument in the past between Luke and "her" before her death) or perhaps meant to suggest random words which somehow recall "her" but do not actually say anything specific.

In stanza 2, the poet forces the reader to acknowledge the light and dark images, but they are as obscure as the falling leaves in stanza 1. The dawn that the reader is asked to visualize (line 9) is clear, but it is immediately contrasted with "the fiery night that's in your eyes"; Luke's smoldering, almost diabolic eyes are imagistically opposed to the dawn.

Line 11 returns to the western gate, or at least to the "west," where twilight is falling. The "western glooms" become imagistic as the twilight falls and depicts Luke's despair. Twilight is not "falling," but dark is "gathering" around him, and glooms not only denotes darkness but also connotes Luke's emotional state.

The paradox in line 12, "The dark will end the dark," beckons the reader to explore it imagistically, but it is not easy to understand how darkness relieves darkness, unless one of the two "darknesses" is symbolic of death or of Luke's gloom. With this beckoning image, the poet has created emphasis on the line and teases with images which may really be symbols or paradoxes. The same thing is true for lines 13 and 14, which tempt the reader to imagine how "God slays Himself" with leaves, and how "hell is more than half of paradise."

The beginning of stanza 3 does not demand an image so much as it serves to tell where the narrator comes from, and to present the narrator's method for quenching the kiss. Line 19, however, presents an image that is as forceful as it is ambiguous. The kiss, which may be the kiss of the estranged woman, or "the kiss of death," or both, flames with a glow, which is also paradoxical. The paradox, however, forms an image which conveys the intensity of Luke's passion.

Stanza 4 returns to the imagery of stanza 1, but now the whispering leaves take on a metaphorical extension. If the leaves are whispering words from the dead, and if the leaves are "her" words, then once the wind tears all the leaves away, there will no longer be any medium for communication between the living and the dead. This adds a sense of urgency for Luke to go to the western gate and do there what must be done.

In summary, the images in "Luke Havergal" do more than set the mood; they also serve an important thematic function because of their ambiguities and paradoxical qualities.

STEP II-D: *Words*

Because the poem is not too old, the reader will find that most of the words have not changed much. It is still important, however, for the reader to look up words as they may have several diverse meanings. Even more important to consider in individual words or phrases, however, is the possibility that they might be symbolic or allusive.

"Luke Havergal" is probably not as symbolic as it at first appears, although poems that use paradox and allusion are often very symbolic. Clearly the western gate is symbolic, but to what degree is questionable. No doubt it represents the last light in Luke's life, and once he passes beyond it he moves into another type of existence. The west and the twilight are points of embarka-

tion; the sun is setting in the west, but even though the sun sets, there will not be a dawn in the east to dispel Luke's dark gloom. Traditionally the dark, which is gathering in the west, is symbolic of death (the west is also traditionally associated with death), and only the dark will end Luke's gloom in life, if anything at all can do it.

There is one important allusion in the poem, which comes in stanza 3; the kiss which the speaker is going to quench may be the "kiss of death," the force that can destroy Luke.

In both concept and language, stanza 3 is reminiscent of the dagger scene and killing of Duncan (act 2, scene 1) in William Shakespeare's *Macbeth* (pr. 1606). Just before the murder, Macbeth has visions of the dagger:

> Art thou not, fatal vision, sensible
> To feeling as to sight? or art thou but
> A dagger of the mind, a false creation,
> Proceeding from the heat-oppressed brain?
> I see thee yet, in form as palpable
> As this which now I draw.
> Thou marshall'st me the way that I was going

And a few lines later (act 2, scene 2) Lady Macbeth says:

> That which hath made them drunk hath made me bold;
> What hath quench'd them hath given me fire.

The reversal in point of view in "Luke Havergal" gives the poem added depth, which is especially enhanced by the comparison with Macbeth. The line, "That blinds you to the way that you must go" is almost a word-for-word equivalent of "Thou marshall'st me the way that I was going," except that in "Luke Havergal" whoever is with Luke is talking, while Macbeth himself is talking to the dagger.

The result of the allusion is that it is almost possible to imagine that it is the dagger that is talking to Luke, and the whole story of Macbeth becomes relevant to the poem because the reader suspects that Luke's end will be similar to Macbeth's.

The words of Lady Macbeth strengthen the allusion's power and suggest a male-female relationship that is leading Luke to his death, especially since, in the resolution of *Macbeth*, Lady Macbeth goes crazy and whispers to the spirits.

If the reader accepts the allusion as a part of the poem, the imagery is enhanced by the vivid descriptions in *Macbeth*. Most critics and writers agree that if a careful reader finds something that fits consistently into a poem, then it is "there" for all readers who see the same thing, whether the poet consciously put it there or not. Robinson undoubtedly read and knew Shakespeare, but it does not matter whether he deliberately alluded to *Macbeth* if the reader can show that it is important to the poem.

There is a basic problem with allusion and symbol that every explicator must resolve for himself: Did the poet intend a symbol or an allusion to be taken in the way that a particular reader has interpreted it? The New Critics answered this question by coining the term "intentional fallacy," meaning that the poet's *intention* is ultimately unimportant when considering the finished poem. It is possible that stanza 3 was not intended to allude to *Macbeth*, and it was simply by accident that Robinson used language similar to Shakespeare's. Perhaps Robinson never read *Macbeth*, or perhaps he read it once and those lines remained in his subconscious. In either case, the reader must decide whether the allusion is important to the meaning of the poem.

STEP II-F: *Meter, rhyme, structure, and tone*

Because "Luke Havergal" is a poem that depends so heavily on all the elements of prosody, it should be scanned carefully. Here is an example of scansion using the second stanza of the poem:

> Nŏ, thĕre/ ĭs nŏt/ ă dáwn/ ĭn eás/tĕrn skíes
> Tŏ rĭft/ thĕ fíe/rў níght/ thăt's ĭn/ yŏur eyes;
> Bŭt thĕre,/ whĕre wĕs/tĕrn glóoms/ ăre gáth/ĕrĭng,
> Thĕ dárk/ wĭll énd/ thĕ dárk,/ ĭf ăn/ўthĭng:
> Gŏd sláys/ Hĭmsélf/ wĭth éve/rў léaf/ thăt flíes,
> Ănd héll/ ĭs móre/ thăn hálf/ ŏf pár/ădĭse.
> Nŏ, thĕre/ ĭs nŏt/ ă dáwn/ ĭn eást/ĕrn skíes—
> Ĭn eás/tĕrn skíes.

The basic meter of the poem is iambic pentameter, with frequent substitutions, but every line except the last in each stanza contains ten syllables.

The stanza form in "Luke Havergal" is very intri-

cate and delicate. It is only because of the structure that the heavy *a* rhyme (*aabbaaaa*) does not become monotonous; yet it is because of the *a* rhyme that the structure works so well.

The pattern for the first stanza works as follows:

Line	Rhyme	Function
1	a	Sets up ideas and images for the stanza.
2	a	Describes or complements line 1.
3	b	Lines 3, 4, and 5 constitute the central part of the mood and the fears. The return to the *a* rhyme unifies lines 1-5.
4	b	
5	a	
6	a	Reflects on what has been said in lines 1-5; it serves to make the reader stop, and it adds a mysterious suggestion.
7	a	Continues the deceleration and reflection.
8	a	The repetition and dimeter line stop the stanza completely, and the effect is to prepare for a shift in thought, just as Luke's mind jumps from thought to thought.

Stanza 2 works in a similar manner, except for lines 13 and 14, which tie the stanza together as a couplet. Thus, lines 13 and 14 both unify and reflect, while lines 15 and 16 in the final couplet continue to reflect while slowing down.

Lines	Rhyme	Function
9 and 10	a	Opening couplet.
11 and 12	b	Couplet in lines 11-12 contains the central idea and image.
13 and 14	a	Couplet in 13-14 reflects on that in 11-12, but the autonomy of this third couplet is especially strong. Whereas in stanza 1, only line 5 reflects on the beginning of the stanza to create unity, this entire couplet is now strongly associated with the first, with the effect of nearly equating Luke with God.
15 and 16	a	Final couplet reflects on the first and completes the stanza.

Stanza 3 works in the same manner as stanza 2, while stanza 4 follows the pattern of stanza 1.

Each stanza is autonomous and does not need the others for continuation or progression in plot; each stanza appears to represent a different thought as Luke's mind jumps about.

The overall structure focuses on stanza 3, which is crucial to the theme. Stanzas 1 and 2 clearly present the problem: Luke knows that if he goes he will find "her," and the worst that can happen is that the darkness will remain. With stanza 3, however, there is a break in point of view as the narrator calls attention to himself.

With stanza 4 there is a return to the beginning, reinforced by the repetition of rhyme words; the difference between stanzas 4 and 1 is that the reader has felt the impact of stanza 3; structurally, whatever resolution there is will evolve out of the third stanza, or because of it.

The stanza form of "Luke Havergal" achieves tremendous unity and emphasis; the central image or idea presented in the *b* lines is reinforced in the remainder of the stanza by a tight-knit rhyme structure. There are several types of rhymes being used in the poem, all of which follow the traditional functions of their type. Stanza 1 contains full masculine end rhyme, with a full masculine internal rhyme in line 2 (*There where*). Lines 2 and 3 contain alliteration (*c* in line 2, *t* in line 3) also binding the lines more tightly.

With "go" occurring near the end of stanza 1 and "No" appearing as the first word in stanza 2, this rhyme becomes important in forming associations between lines. Lines 9, 10, 15, 16, and 18 form full masculine end rhyme, with line 14 "paradise" assonating with a full rhyme. Lines 11 and 12 are half falling rhymes; these lines also contain a full internal rhyme ("there," "where") and alliteration (*g* and *w* in line 11). "Dark" in line 12 is an exact internal rhyme. The *l* and *s* in "slays" and "flies" (line 14) create an effect similar to assonance; there is also an *h* alliteration in line 15.

In stanza 3, the plosive consonants *c* and *q* make an alliterative sound in line 18, binding "come" and "quench" together; there is also an *f* alliteration in line 19. All the end rhymes are full masculine in stanza 3 except line 21, which assonates. Stanza 4 contains full masculine end rhyme, with one internal rhyme ("they

say") in line 28, one alliteration in line 29, and consonance ("will call") in line 30.

In addition to its function in developing the stanza, rhyme in "Luke Havergal" has important influence on sound, and in associating particular words and lines.

In lines 1 and 2 of "Luke Havergal," there are a number of plosive consonants and long vowels, in addition to the internal rhyme and *c* alliteration. The cadence of these lines is slow, and they reverberate with "cling" and "crimson." The tone of these lines is haunting (which is consistent with the situation), and the rhythm and sound of the poem as a whole suggest an incantation; the speaker's voice is seductive and evil, which is important to the theme, because if Luke goes to the gate he may be persuaded to die, which is what the voice demands.

Through its seductive sound, the poem seems to be having the same effect on the reader that it does on Luke; that is, the reader feels, as Luke does, that there is an urgency in going to the gate before all the leaves are blown away, and that by hearing "her" call, his discomfort will be relieved. The reader, unable to see the evil forces at work in the last stanza, sympathizes with Luke, and thinks that the voice is benevolent.

Whereas sound can be heard and analyzed, tone is a composite of a number of things that the reader can feel only after coming to know the poem. The poet's attitude or tone may be noncommittal or it may be dogmatic (as in allegory); sometimes the tone will affect the theme, while at other times it comes as an aside to the theme.

Poems that attempt to initiate reform frequently have a more readily discernible tone than poems that make observations without judging too harshly, although this is not always true. "Luke Havergal" is, among other things, about how the presence of evil leads toward death, but the poet has not directly included his feelings about that theme. If there is an attitude, it is the poet's acceptance of the inevitability of death and the pain that accompanies it for the living.

Perhaps the poet is angry at how effectively death can seduce life; it is obvious that Robinson wants the poem to haunt and torment the reader, and in doing so make him or her conscious of the hold death has on humanity.

Luke must meet death part way; he must first go to

the gate before he can hear the dead words, which makes him partly responsible for death's hold over him. The tone of "Luke Havergal" is haunting and provocative.

STEP II-F: *Historical context*

Finished in December, 1895, "Luke Havergal" was in Robinson's estimation a Symbolist poem. It is essential, then, that the explicator learn something about the Symbolist movement. If his or her explication is not in accord with the philosophy of the period, the reader must account for the discrepancy.

In a study of other Robinson poems, there are themes parallel to that of "Luke Havergal." One, for example, is that of the alienated self. If Robinson believes in the alienated self, then it is possible that the voice speaking in "Luke Havergal" is Luke's own, but in an alienated state. This view may add credence to an argument that the speaker is Luke's past or subconscious, though it by no means proves it. Although parallelisms may be good support for the explication, the reader must be careful not to misconstrue them.

STEP II-G: *Themes and motifs, or correlating the parts*

Once the poem has been placed in context, the prosodic devices analyzed, and the function of the poetical techniques understood, they should be correlated, and any discrepancies should be studied for possible errors in explication. By this time, every line should be understood, so that stating what the poem is about is merely a matter of explaining the common points of all the area, supporting it with specific items from the poem, secondary sources, other poems, other critics, and history. The reader may use the specific questions given in the outline to help detail the major themes.

BIBLIOGRAPHY

Coleman, Kathleen. *Guide to French Poetry Explication*. New York: G. K. Hall, 1993.

Gioia, Dana, David Mason, and Meg Schoerke, eds. *Twentieth-Century American Poetics: Poets on the Art of Poetry*. Boston: McGraw-Hill, 2003.

Hirsch, Edward. *How to Read a Poem and Fall in Love with Poetry*. New York: Harcourt Brace, 1999.

Kohl, Herbert R. *A Grain of Poetry: How to Read Contemporary Poems and Make Them a Part of Your Life*. New York: HarperFlamingo, 1999.

Lennard, John. *The Poetry Handbook: A Guide to Reading Poetry for Pleasure and Practical Criticism*. 2d ed. New York: Oxford University Press, 2006.

Martínez, Nancy C., and Joseph G. R. Martínez. *Guide to British Poetry Explication*. 4 vols. Boston: G. K. Hall, 1991-1995.

Oliver, Mary. *A Poetry Handbook*. San Diego, Calif.: Harcourt Brace, 1994.

Preminger, Alex, et al., eds. *The New Princeton Encyclopedia of Poetry and Poetics*. 3d rev. ed. Princeton, N.J.: Princeton University Press, 1993.

Ryan, Michael. *A Difficult Grace: On Poets, Poetry, and Writing*. Athens: University of Georgia Press, 2000.

Statman, Mark. *Listener in the Snow: The Practice and Teaching of Poetry*. New York: Teachers & Writers Collaborative, 2000.

Steinman, Lisa M. *Invitation to Poetry: The Pleasures of Studying Poetry and Poetics*. Walden, Mass.: Wiley-Blackwell, 2008.

Strand, Mark, and Eavan Boland, eds. *The Making of a Poem: A Norton Anthology of Poetic Forms*. New York: W. W. Norton, 2000.

Wolosky, Shira. *The Art of Poetry: How to Read a Poem*. New York: Oxford University Press, 2001.

Walton Beacham

LANGUAGE AND LINGUISTICS

Most humans past the infant stage have a spoken language and use it regularly for understanding and speaking, although much of the world's population is still illiterate and cannot read or write. Language is such a natural part of life that people tend to overlook it until they are presented with some special problem: They lose their sight or hearing, have a stroke, or are required to learn a foreign language. Of course, people may also study their own language, but seldom do they stand aside and view language for what it is—a complex human phenomenon with a history reaching back to humankind's beginnings. A study of the development of one language will often reveal intertwinings with other languages. Sometimes such knowledge enables linguists to construct family groups; just as often, the divergences among languages or language families are so great that separate typological variations are established.

True language is characterized by its systematic nature, its arbitrariness of vocabulary and structure, its vocality, and its basis in symbolism. Most linguists believe that language and thought are separate entities. Although language may be necessary to give foundation to thought, it is not, in itself, thinking. Many psychologists, however, contend that language is thought. An examination of language on the basis of these assertions reveals that each language is a purely arbitrary code or set of rules. There is no intrinsic necessity for any word to sound like or mean what it does. Language is essentially speech, and symbolism is somehow the philosophical undergirding of the whole linguistic process. The French author Madame de Staël (1766-1817) once wrote, in describing her native language, that language is even more: "It is not only a means of communicating thoughts, feeling and acts, but an instrument that one loves to play upon, and that stimulates the mental faculties much as music does for some people and strong drink for others."

ORIGIN OF LANGUAGE

How did language originate? First, the evidence for the origin of language is so deeply buried in the past that it is unlikely that people shall ever be able to do more than speculate about the matter. If people had direct knowledge of humankind's immediate ancestors, they should be able to develop some evolutionary theory and be able to say, among other things, how speech production and changes in the brain are related. Some linguists maintain that language ability is innate, but this assertion, true though it may be, rests on the assumption of a monogenetic theory of humanity's origin. Few scholars today are content with the notion that the human race began with Adam and Eve.

According to the Bible, Adam is responsible for human speech. Genesis reports:

> And out of the ground the Lord God formed every beast of the field, and every fowl of the air, and brought them unto Adam to see what he would call them; and whatsoever Adam called every creature, that was the name thereof. And Adam gave names to all cattle, and to the fowl of the air, and to every beast of the field.

If the story of Adam and Eve is taken literally, one might conclude that their language was the original one. Unfortunately, not even the Bible identifies what this language was. Some people have claimed that Hebrew was the first language and that all the other languages of the world are derived from it; Hebrew, however, bears no discernible relationship to any language outside the Hamito-Semitic group. Besides, any so-called original language would have changed so drastically in the intervening millennia before the onset of writing that it would not bear any resemblance to ancient Hebrew. Whatever the "original" language was—and there is every reason to believe that many languages sprang up independently over a very long span of time—it could not sound at all like any language that has been documented.

Many theories of the origin of language have been advanced, but three have been mentioned in textbooks more frequently than others. One, the "bow-wow" or echoic theory, insists that the earliest forms of language were exclusively onomatopoeic—that is, imitative of the sounds of animals and nature, despite the fact that the so-called primitive languages are not largely composed of onomatopoeic words. Furthermore, some measure of conventionalization must take place before echoisms become real "words"; individual young children do not call a dog a "bow-wow" until they hear an older child or adult use the term. Another theory, called the "pooh-pooh" or interjectional theory, maintains that language must have begun with primitive grunts and groans—that is, very loose and disjointed utterances. Many have held that such a theory fits animals better than humans; indeed, this kind of exclamatory speech probably separates humans quite clearly from the animals. Still another theory, dubbed the "ding-dong" theory, claims that language arose as a response to natural stimuli. None of these theories has any strong substantiation. Some linguists have suggested that speech and song may have once been the same. The presence of tones and pitch accent in many older languages lends some plausibility to the idea; it is likely that language, gestures, and song, as forms of communication, were all intertwined at the earliest stages.

Is it a hopeless task to try to discover the origin of language? Linguists have continued to look into the question again, but there is little chance that more than a priori notions can be established. It has been suggested, for example, that prehumans may have gradually developed a kind of grammar by occasionally fitting together unstructured vocal signals in patterns that were repeated and then eventually understood, accepted, and passed on. This process is called compounding, and some forms of it are found in present-day gibbon calls.

THE HISTORY OF LANGUAGE STUDY

In the history of language study, a number of signposts can be erected to mark the path. The simplest outline consists of two major parts: a prescientific and a scientific period. The first can be dispensed with in short order.

The earliest formal grammar of any language is a detailed analysis of classical Sanskrit, written by the Indian scholar Pānini in the fourth century B.C.E. He called it the Sutras (instructions), and in it, he codified the rules for the use of proper Sanskrit. It is still an authoritative work. Independently of Pānini, the ancient Greeks established many grammatical concepts that strongly influenced linguistic thinking for hundreds of years. Platonic realism, although by today's standards severely misguided in many respects, offered a number of useful insights into language, among them the basic division of the sentence into subject and predicate, the recognition of word stress, and the twofold classification of sounds into consonants and vowels. In the third century B.C.E., Aristotle defined the various parts of speech. In the next century, Dionysius Thrax produced a grammar that not only improved understanding of the sound system of Greek but also classified even more clearly the basic parts of speech and commented at length on such properties of language as gender, number, case, mood, voice, tense, and person. At no time, though, did the Hindu and Greek scholars break away from a focus on their own language to make a comparison with other languages. This fault was also largely one of the Romans, who merely adapted Greek scholarship to their own needs. If they did any comparing of languages, it was not of the languages in the Roman world, but only of Latin as a "corrupt" descendant of Greek. In sum, the Romans introduced no new concepts; they were, instead, content to synthesize or reorganize their legacy from ancient Greece. Only two grammarians come to mind from the fourth and fifth centuries of the Roman Empire—Priscian and Donatus, whose works served for centuries as basic texts for the teaching of Latin.

The scientific period of language study began with a British Sanskrit scholar, Sir William Jones, who headed a society organized in Calcutta for the exploration of Asia. In 1786, he delivered a paper in which he stated that

> the Sanskrit language . . . [was] more perfect than the Greek, more copious than the Latin, and more exquisitely refined than either; yet [bore] to both of them a stronger affinity . . . than could possibly have been produced by accident; so strong, indeed, that no philologer could examine them all three without believing them to have sprung from some common source, which, perhaps, no longer exists.

He went on to say that Germanic and Celtic probably had the same origin. His revolutionary assertion that Sanskrit and most of the languages of Europe had descended from a single language no longer spoken and never recorded first produced considerable scholarly opposition, but shortly thereafter set the stage for comparative analysis. He insisted that a close examination of the "inner structures" of this family of languages would reveal heretofore unsuspected relationships.

Franz Bopp, a German born in 1791 and a student of Oriental languages, including Sanskrit, was the founder of comparative grammar. In his epochmaking book *Über das Conjugationssystem der Sanskritsprache in Vergleichung mit jenem der griechischen, lateinischen, persischen und germanischen Sprache* (1816), he demonstrated for all time what Jones and Friedrich von Schlegel and other researchers had only surmised. A young Danish contemporary named Rasmus Rask corroborated his results and established that Armenian and Lithuanian belong to the same language group, the Indo-European. The tool to establish these relationships was the "comparative method," one of the greatest achievements of nineteenth century linguistics. In applying this method, linguists searched in the various languages under investigation for cognates—words with similar spelling, similar sound, and similar meaning. They then set up sound correspondences among the cognates, much like looking for the lowest common denominator in a mathematical construction, from which the original linguistic forms could be constructed.

The German linguist Jakob Grimm (one of the Brothers Grimm known for books of fairy tales) took Rask's work one step further and, in a four-volume work published between 1819 and 1822, showed conclusively the systematic correspondences and differences between Sanskrit, Greek, and Latin, on one hand, and the Germanic languages, on the other hand. The formulation of this system of sound changes came to be known as Grimm's law, or the First Sound Shift, and the changes involved can be diagramed as follows:

Proto-Indo-European: *bh dh gh b d g p t k*
Proto-Germanic: *b   d   g   p t k f Θ h*

Where the Indo-European, as transmitted through Latin or Greek, had a *p* sound (as in *piscis* and *pēd*), the German-based English word has an *f* ("fish" and "foot");

the Latinate *trēs* becomes the English "three." In addition to the changes described above, another important change took place in the Germanic languages. If the *f Θ h* resulting from the change of *p t k* stood after an unaccented vowel but before another vowel, they became voiced fricatives, later voiced stops, as in the pair *seethe : sodden*. This change also affected *s*, yielding *z*, which later became *r* (Rhotacism) and explains, for example, the alternations in *was : were*. It was described by Karl Verner, a Danish linguist, and is known appropriately as Verner's law. There are one or two other "laws" that explain apparent exceptions to Grimm's law, illustrating the basic regularity of Grimm's formulations. At the very end of the nineteenth century, the neo-Grammarians, led by Karl Brugmann, insisted that all exceptions could be explained—that, in fact, "phonetic laws are natural laws and have no exceptions." Even those studying the natural sciences do not make such a strong assertion, but the war cry of the neo-Grammarians did inspire scholars to search for regularity in language.

The German language itself underwent a profound change beginning probably in the far south of the German-speaking lands sometime during the fifth century, causing a restructuring of the sounds of all of the southern and many of the midland dialects. These became known, for geographical reasons, as High German, while those dialects in the north came to be known as Low German. Six consonants in various positions were affected, but the most consistently shifted sounds were the Indo-European *b*, which in English became *p* and in German *pf*, and the *d* to *t* and *ts*. For example, the Latin *decim* became the English "ten" and the German *zehn*.

In the course of the nineteenth century, all such changes were recognized, and scholars were enabled to identify and diagram the reflex languages of Indo-European into five subgroups known as *satem* languages and four known as *centum* languages. This division is significant both geographically—the *satem* languages are located clearly to the east of where the original home of the Indo-Europeans probably was—and linguistically—the *satem* languages have, among other characteristics, *s* sounds where the *centum* languages have *k* sounds (the word *centum* is pronounced

---

THE *SATEM* LANGUAGES

Indo-Iranian	Earliest attested form, Sanskrit; modern languages include Hindi, Bengali, and Persian.
Albanian	Spoken by a small number of Balkan people.
Armenian	Spoken by a small number of people in that country.
Slavic	Divided into East Slavic (Great Russian, the standard language; Little Russian or Ukrainian; White Russian, spoken in the region adjacent to and partly in modern-day Poland); West Slavic (Czech, Slovak, Polish); South Slavic (Slovenian and Serbo-Croatian; Bulgarian).
Baltic	Lithuanian and Lettic, spoken in the Baltic states.

---

with an initial hard *c*). The very words *satem* and *centum*, meaning "hundred" in Avestan (an Indo-Iranian language) and Latin, respectively, illustrate the sound divergence.

INDO-EUROPEAN LANGUAGES

The original home of the Indo-Europeans is not known for certain, but it is safe to say that it was in Europe, and probably close to present-day Lithuania. For one thing, the Lithuanians have resided in a single area since the Neolithic Age (2500-2000 B.C.E.) and speak a language of great complexity. Furthermore, Lithuania is situated on the dividing line between *centum* and *satem* languages. One would also assume that the original home was somewhere close to the area where the reflex languages are to be found today and not, for example, in Africa, Australia, or North or South America. For historical and archaeological reasons, scholars have ruled out the British Isles and the peninsulas of southern Europe. Last, there are indications that the Indo-Europeans entered India from the northwest, for there is no evidence of their early acquaintanceship with the Ganges River, but only with the Indus (hence "Indo-"). Certain common words for weather conditions, geography, and flora and fauna militate in favor of a European homeland.

Scholars have classified the Indo-European languages as a family apart from certain other languages on the basis of two principal features: their common word stock and their inflectional structure. This type of classification, called genetic, is one of three. Another, called geographical, is usually employed initially. For example, if nothing whatsoever was known about American Indian languages, one might divide them into North American and South American, Eastern North American and Western North American, and perhaps some other geographical categories. A third variety of classification, called typological, is possible only when a good deal is

---

THE *CENTUM* LANGUAGES

Greek (Hellenic)	Attic, Ionic, and Doric, formerly spoken throughout the eastern areas around the Mediterranean; modern Greek.
Italic	Latin; modern Italian, French, Spanish, Portuguese, Catalan, Sardinian, Romanian, and Rhaeto-Romanic.
Celtic	Modern Welsh, Cornish, Breton, Irish, and Scots Gaelic.
Germanic (Teutonic)	East Germanic (Gothic, now extinct); North Germanic (Danish, Norwegian, Swedish, Icelandic); West Germanic (Low German: English, Dutch, Frisian, Plattdeutsch; High German: standard German).
In addition	Several extinct Indo-European languages, such as Tocharian and the Anatolian languages, especially Hittite.

---

known about the structure of a language. The four main types of languages arrived at through such classification are inflectional, meaning that such syntactic distinctions as gender, number, case, tense, and so forth are usually communicated by altering the form of a word, as in English when -*s* added to a noun indicates plurality but, when added to a verb, singularity; agglutinative, meaning that suffixes are piled onto word bases in a definite order and without change in phonetic shape (for example, Turkish *evlerimden*, "house-s-my-from"); isolating, meaning that invariable word forms, mostly monosyllabic, are employed in variable word order (for example, Chinese *wŏ*, meaning, according to its position in the utterance, "I," "me," "to me," or "my"); and incorporating or polysynthetic, meaning that a sentence, with its various syntactic features, may be "incorporated" as a single word (for example, Eskimo /a: wlisa-utiss?ar-siniarpu-na/, "I am looking for something suitable for a fish-line").

OTHER LANGUAGES

Although the Indo-European languages have been studied in more detail than other language families, it is possible to classify and describe many of the remaining language families of the world, the total comprising more than twenty-seven hundred separate languages. In Europe and Asia, relatively few languages are spoken by very large numbers of people; elsewhere many distinct languages are spoken by small communities. In Europe, all languages are Indo-European except for Finnish, Estonian, Hungarian, and Basque. The last-named is something of a mystery; it appears to predate Indo-European by such a long period that it could conceivably be descended from a prehistoric language. The first three belong to the same family, the Finno-Urgic. Sometimes Turkish is added to the group, and the four are called the Ural-Altaic family. All are agglutinative.

The most extensive language family in eastern Asia is the Sino-Tibetan. It consists of two branches, the Tibeto-Burman and Chinese. Mandarin is the language of the northern half of China, although there are three different varieties—northern, southwestern, and southern. In the south, there is a range of mutually unintelligible dialects. All are isolating in structure.

In other parts of Asia are found the Kadai family, consisting of Thai, Laotian, and the Shan languages of Burma, and in southern Asia, the Munda languages and Vietnamese. The latter has a considerable number of speakers.

Japanese and Korean are separate families, even though cultural relationships between the two countries have produced some borrowing over the years. Japanese is essentially agglutinative.

On the continent of Africa, the linguistic family of prime importance is the Hamito-Semitic family. Hebrew, Arabic, and some of the languages of Ethiopia make up the Semitic side. There are four Hamitic languages: Egyptian, Berber, Cushitic, and Chad. All exhibit some inflectional characteristics. In addition to these languages, Hausa, an important trade language, is used throughout the northern part of the continent.

In central and southern Africa, the Niger-Congo language family is dominant. The largest subgroup of this family is Bantu, which includes Swahili in central and eastern Africa, Kikuyu in Kenya, and Zulu in the south. Most appear to be either agglutinative or polysynthetic.

The Malayo-Polynesian languages are spoken as original tongues all the way from Madagascar to the Malay Peninsula, the East Indies, and, across the Pacific, to Hawaii. Many seem to be isolating with traces of earlier inflections.

The Indian languages of the Americas are all polysynthetic. Until recently, these Indian languages were classified geographically. Many of the North American languages have been investigated, and linguists group them into distinct families, such as Algonquian, Athabaskan, Natchez-Muskogean, Uto-Aztecan, Penutian, and Hokan.

MODERN LANGUAGES

In addition to the distinction between prescientific and scientific periods of language study, there are other divisions that can help clarify the various approaches to this vast topic. For example, the entire period from earliest times until the late nineteenth century was largely historical, comparative at best, but scarcely truly scientific in terms of rigor. Beginning with the neo-Grammarians Brugmann and Delbrück, the stage was set for what may be called a period of general or descriptive linguistics. Languages were examined not only diachronically—that is, historically—but also synchronically, where a segment or feature of language was scrutinized without regard to an earlier stage. The most important names associated with this descriptive school are those of N. S. Trubetzkoy and Roman Jakobson. Strongly influenced by the theories of the Swiss linguist Ferdinand de Saussure, they examined each detail of language as a part of a system. In other words, they were ultimately more interested in the system and the way it hung together than in each individual detail. These scholars were members of the European school of linguistic thought that had its origin in Jakobson's Prague circle. Across the Atlantic, their most important counterpart was Leonard Bloomfield, who, in 1933, published his classic linguistics text, *Language.* Like his contemporary, Edward Sapir, Bloomfield began as a comparativist in Germanic linguistics, then studied American Indian languages, and finally became an expert in the general principles of language. Bloomfield's theory of structuralism has been criticized for its resemblance to the psychological theory of behaviorism, which restricts itself to the observable and rejects the concept of mind.

Since the 1930's, there has been a steady procession of American linguists studying and reporting on the sounds and grammatical features of many different languages, in some sense all derivative from the foundation laid by the phonemicists beginning with Saussure and Bloomfield. Kenneth Pike's tagmemics, in part an attempt to present language behavior empirically through a description at each level of grammatical form, evolved directly out of descriptive linguistics. In 1957, Noam Chomsky launched transformational-generative grammar, concerned at first only with syntax, but later also with phonology. Considerable tension has developed between structuralists and transformational-generative grammarians, concerning not only syntactic analysis but also the representation of sounds. For some, stratificational grammar provides a connection, through strata or levels of description, among descriptive, tagmemic, and computational analyses.

THE TECHNICAL SIDE OF LANGUAGE

A language is made up of its sound system, grammar, and vocabulary. The former two may differ considerably from language family to language family, but there is a workable range in the extent and type of sounds and grammatical functions. The inventory of significant sounds in a given language, called phonemes, extends from about twenty to about sixty. English has forty-six, including phonemes of pitch, stress, and juncture. If the grammatical facts of a complicated language can be written out on one or two sheets of paper, the grammar of English can be laid out on the back of an envelope. In short, some languages are simpler phonologically or grammatically than others, but none is so complicated in either respect that every child cannot learn his or her language in about the same time.

The study of the sounds of which speech is made up became scientific in method by the end of the nineteenth century, when Paul Passy founded the International Phonetic Association. Down to the present day, articulatory phonetics has borne a close relationship to physiology in the description of the sounds of speech according to the organs producing them and the position of these organs in relation to surrounding structures.

By the mid-1920's, phoneticians realized that the unit of description of the phonology of a language had to be a concept rather than some physical entity. The term phoneme was chosen; it designates a minimally significant sound unit, an abstraction around which cluster all the phonetic realizations of that generalized sound. Thus, the English phoneme /p/ represents all recognizably similar pronunciations of [p], with more or less or no aspiration depending on position within a word or the speech habits of a given speaker. In other words, it designates a class of sounds distinct from others in the language. It carries no meaning as such, but it serves to distinguish one sound from another and, together with other phonemes, produces morphemic, or meaning, differences. Thus /p/, /i/, and /n/ are separate phonemes, but, taken together, make up a morpheme—the word *pin*—which is distinct, by virtue of a single phoneme, from, say, /bin/, "bin," or /tin/ "tin." Sometimes, morphemes show relations between words, as when -*s* is added to a noun to indicate plurality or possession or to a verb to indicate singularity.

The sound system and grammar of a language are thus closely related. Grammar, at least for Indo-European languages and many others, can be defined as consisting of a morphology and syntax, where, expressed simply, the former refers to the words and their endings and the latter to the order of words. Accompanying the words are, however, other features of language that can alter meaning. It matters, for example, whether the stress occurs on the first or second syllable of the word *pervert* or *permit.* If the stress falls on the first syllable, the word is a noun; if on the second, it is a verb. It matters whether the last few sounds of an utterance convey an upturn or a downturn and trail-off, for a question or a statement may result. It matters also what the pitch level is and whether juncture is present. These features, too, are phonemic.

To function in a language, one must have control of close to 100 percent of the phonology and 75 percent or more of the grammar, but a mere 1 percent of the vocabulary will enable the speaker to function in many situations. For a speaker of a language the size of English, a vocabulary of six thousand words will suffice. Possessing a vocabulary implies an unconscious knowledge of the semantic relationship to the phonology and grammar of the language. One theory of the word regards the word as a compound formed of two components: a physical element, the sequence of sounds of speech; and a semantic element, the amount of meaning expressed by the segment of speech. The first is called the formant, the second the morpheme. The word "cook" /kuk/ is one morpheme expressed by one formant—the formant consisting of one syllable, a sequence of three phonemes. In the plural of "cook," -*s* is a formant that is not even a syllable. In fact, a formant is not even necessarily a phoneme, but can be the use of one form instead of another, as in "her" instead of "she." There is no reason that the same formant, such as -*s*, cannot express more than one morpheme: "cooks" (noun) versus "cook's" versus "cooks" (verb). The same morpheme can also be expressed by more than one formant; there are, for example, many different formants for the plural, such as basis/bases, curriculum/curricula, datum/data, ox/oxen, child/children, man/men, woman/women, cherub/cherubim, monsignore/monsignori.

The distinction in morphology made above between words and their endings needs further amplification. An examination of a stanza from Lewis Carroll's "Jabberwocky" (from *Alice's Adventures in Wonderland*, 1865) illustrates the manner in which the poet uses formants with no evident meaning to the average speaker:

> 'Twas brilling, and the slithy toves
> Did gyre and gimble in the wabe;
> All mimsy were the borogoves,
> And the mome raths outgrabe.

Alice herself remarks that the words fill her head with ideas, but she does not know what they are. There is a rightness about the way the poem sounds because the endings, the structural morphemes, are correctly placed. When the message is of primary importance and the speaker knows the language only imperfectly, the structural morphemes may be incorrect or missing and a string of pure message morphemes may be the result: Her give man bag money.

Message morphemes have their own peculiar properties, limiting their use to certain contexts, regardless of the accuracy of the combined structural morphemes. To illustrate this principle, Chomsky composed the sentence "Colorless green ideas sleep furiously." The subject is "colorless green ideas"; the predicate, "sleep furiously." This sentence has the same structure as any sentence of the shape: adjective/adjective/noun/intransitive verb/adverb. However, there is something semantically troubling. How can one describe something green as colorless? Can ideas be green? How can an intransitive verb that describes such a passive activity be furiously involved in an action?

Chomsky's example was designed to combine structural familiarity with semantic impossibility. It is possible to devise similar sentences that, though semantically improbable, could conceivably be used by an actual speaker. The sentence "Virtue swims home every night" attributes to an abstract noun an action performed by animate beings, and poses other difficulties as well (in what setting can one swim home?), yet such strange semantic violations, given a meaningful context, are the stuff of poetry.

Indeed, semantic change actually occurs with a

measure of frequency in the history of a language. It is usually of two types. Words that are rather specific in meaning sometimes become generalized; for example, Latin *molīna* (gristmill) originally meant "mill" but expanded to cover "sawmill," "steel mill," even "diploma mill." Many words in English of very broad meanings, such as "do," "make," "go," and "things," derive from words of more specific notions. At the same time, the opposite often happens. Words that once were very general in meaning have become specific. Examples include *deer*, which formerly meant merely "animal" (compare German *Tier*), and *hound*, "dog," now a particular kind of dog. Sometimes, words undergo melioration, as in the change in *knight*, meaning originally a "servant," to "king's servant," or pejoration, as in the change in *knave*, meaning "boy" (compare German *Knabe*), to "rascal."

Perhaps the most significant force for change in language is analogy. It is occasioned by mental associations arising because of similarity or contrast of meaning and may affect the meaning or the form of words or even create new words. Most verbs in English are regular and form their preterit and past participles by the addition of *-ed* (or *-t*), as "dream, dreamed, dreamt," and not by vowel change, as in "drink, drank, drunk." New words taken into the language, as well as some of the irregular ones already in use, will usually become regular. It is by no means unusual to hear a child use analogy in forming the past of, say, "teach" or "see" as "teached" and "see'd" instead of "taught" and "saw." Since most English nouns form their plural by the addition of *-s*, it is to be expected that unfamiliar words or words with little-used, learned plural forms will be pluralized in the same way: for example, "memorandums" (or "memos") for *memoranda*, "stadiums" for *stadia*, "gymnasiums" for *gymnasia*, "prima donnas" for *prime donne*, and "formulas" for *formulae*. Sometimes a resemblance in the form of a word may suggest a relationship that causes a further assimilation in form. This process is known as folk etymology and often occurs when an unfamiliar or foreign word or phrase is altered to give it a more meaningful form. There are many examples: "crayfish" comes from Old French *crevisse* (crab), but *-visse* meant nothing and thus was changed to the phonetically similar *-fish*; a hangnail is not a (fin-

ger)nail that hangs, but one that hurts (from Old English *ang*); the second element of "titmouse" has nothing to do with a mouse, but comes from Middle English *mose*, the name for several species of birds.

There are many other processes in language by which changes are brought about. Among them are several of great importance: assimilation, dissimilation, conversion, back formation, blending, and the creation of euphemisms and slang.

Assimilation causes a sound to change in conformance with a neighboring sound, as in the plural of "kit" with [-s] (/kits/), as opposed to the plural of "limb" with [-z] (/limz/), or in the preterit and participial forms of regular verbs: "grazed" [greyzd], but "choked" [čowkt].

Dissimilation is the opposite process, whereby neighboring sounds are made unlike, as in "pilgrim" from Latin *peregrīnus*, where the first *r* dissimilates.

Conversion is the change of one part of speech or form class into another, as the change from noun to verb: The nouns "bridge," "color," and "shoulder" are converted to verbs in "to bridge a gap," "to color a book," and "to shoulder a load."

A back formation occurs when a word is mistakenly assumed to be the base form from which a new word is formed, as in "edit" from "editor," "beg" from "beggar," "peddle" from "pedlar."

Some words are blends: "flash" + "blush" = "flush"; "slight" (slim) + "tender" = "slender"; "twist" + "whirl" = "twirl"; "breakfast" + "lunch" = "brunch."

Euphemisms are words and expressions with new, better-sounding connotations—for example, to "pass away" or "breathe one's last" or "cross the river" for "to die"; "lingerie" or "intimate wear" for "underwear"; "acute indigestion" for "bellyache."

Slang consists of informal, often ephemeral expressions and coinages, such as "turkey" for "stupid person," "blow away" for "to kill," and "kook," meaning "odd or eccentric person," from "cuckoo."

All three constituents of language change over a long period of time—sounds, structure, and vocabulary—but each language or dialect retains its distinctiveness. The most durable and unchanging aspect of language is writing, of which there are two major varieties: picture writing, also called ideographic writing, and alphabetic writing. The former kind of writing began as actual pictures and developed gradually into ideograms linked directly to the objects or concepts and having no connection with the sounds of the language. The latter variety began as symbols for syllables, until each symbol was taken to represent a single spoken sound. Although alphabetic writing is much more widespread and easier to learn and use, ideographic writing has the advantage of maintaining cultural unity among speakers of dialects and languages not mutually intelligible. An alphabetic writing system can, over time, act as a conservative influence on the spoken language as well as provide valuable etymological clues. Ideographic writing can be, and often is, seen as art capable of conveying messages separate from speech. Both systems are vehicles for the transmission of history and literature without which civilization would falter and perish.

THE SOCIAL SIDE OF LANGUAGE

The social side of language is inextricably linked to behavior. It is concerned with the use of language to create attitudes and responses toward language, objects, and people. For example, certain overt behaviors toward language and its users can create unusual political pressures. The insistence by the Québecois on French as the primary, if not sole, language of their province of Canada has led to near secession and to bitter interprovincial feelings. The creation of modern Hebrew has helped to create and sustain the state of Israel. The Irish are striving to make Irish the first language of that part of the British Isles. The Flemish urge full status for their variety of Dutch in the Brussels area. African Americans sometimes advocate clearer recognition of black English. Frisians, Bretons, Basques, Catalans, and Provençals are all insisting on greater acceptance of their mother tongues.

Within a language or dialect, there can be specialized vocabulary and pronunciation not generally understood. The term "dialect" is commonly taken to mean a regional variety of language or one spoken by the undereducated, but, strictly speaking, it is differentiated from language as such, being largely what people actually speak. Some dialects differ so substantially from standard, national tongues that, to all intents and

purposes, they are languages in their own right. The term "vernacular" is similar in that it designates everyday speech as opposed to learned discourse. "Lingo" designates, somewhat contemptuously, any dialect or language not readily comprehended. "Jargon" is specialized or professional language, often of a technical nature; in this context, the term "cant," as in "thieves' cant," is virtually synonymous with "jargon." Closely related to these two terms is the term "argot," referring to the idiom of a closely knit group, as in "criminal argot." Finally, "slang," discussed above, refers to the colorful, innovative, often short-lived popular vocabulary drawn from many levels of language use, both specialized and nonspecialized.

Words, like music, can produce moods. They can raise one's spirits or lower them. They can stir up discontent or soothe human anger. They can inspire and console, ingratiate and manipulate, mislead and ridicule. They can create enough hatred to destroy but also enough trust to overcome obstacles. While a mood may originate in physical well-being or physical discomfort and pain, language can express that mood, intensify it, or deny it. Language can be informative (emotionally neutral), biased (emotionally charged), or propagandistic (informatively neutral).

Language is informative when it states indisputable facts or asks questions dealing with such facts, even though those facts are very broad and general. One can also inform with misstatements, half-truths, or outright lies. It does not matter whether the statement is actually true or false, only that the question can be posed.

Language often reflects bias by distorting facts. Frequently, the substitution of a single derogatory term is sufficient to load the atmosphere. Admittedly, some words are favorably charged for some people, unfavorably for others. Much depends on the context, word and sentence stress, gestures, and former relationship.

Language can be propagandistic when the speaker desires to promote some activity or cause. The load that propaganda carries is directly proportional to the receiver's enthusiasm, bias, or readiness to be deceived. Almost invariably, propaganda terms arise out of the specialized language of religion, art, commerce, education, finance, government, and so forth. Propaganda is a kind of name calling, using words from a stock of esoteric and exclusive terms. Not many people are thoroughly familiar with the exact meanings of words such as "totalitarian," "fascist," "proletarian," and "bourgeois," but they think they know whether these words are good or bad, words of approval or disapproval. The effect is to call forth emotions as strong as those prompted by invectives.

The language of advertising achieves its effectiveness by conveniently combining information, bias, and propaganda. A good advertisement must gain immediate attention, make the reader or listener receptive to the message, ensure its retention, create a desire, and cause the person to buy the product without setting up resistance. Advertising must, moreover, link the product to "pleasant" or "healthy" things. In advertising circles, there is no widespread agreement as to which is more important: the avoidance of all associations that can create resistance or the creation of desire for a particular object. Even if the latter is regarded as the prime objective, it is still important to avoid resistance. The most powerful tools of the advertiser are exaggeration and cliché. The words generally used in ads deal with the basic component and qualities of a product, while the qualifiers are hackneyed and overblown: lather (rich, creamy, full-bodied); toothpaste (fights cavities three ways, ten ways, tastes zesty); cleanser (all-purpose, powerful, one-step); coffee (full of flavor buds, brewed to perfection, marvelous bouquet). The danger of advertising is evident when its pathology carries over into other areas of life. Every culture must be on guard against the effect of advertising on the health of its citizenry and the shaping of its national image. Even foreign policy can be the victim of advertising that stresses youth over maturity, beauty of body over soundness of mind, physical health over mental serenity, or the power of sex appeal over everything else.

In the latter part of the twentieth century, language began to be closely examined by certain groups aiming to rid it of inherent prejudice. Of all of these groups, perhaps feminists have had the greatest effect on the vocabulary, and even the structure, of languages that differentiate along sex lines. A vociferous contingent of women contend that the symbols of perception—words—give both meaning and value to the objects they define and that many of these words are loaded with a male-chauvinist aspect. For example, words with the affix *-man* are being avoided or paired with *-woman* or *-person:* "congressman"/"congresswoman," "chairman"/"chairwoman"/"chairperson." In some instances, gender is eliminated altogether: "humankind" for "mankind," "chair" for "chairman" or "chairwoman." There are many more techniques employed to desexualize English; some even involve tampering with personal pronouns, a much less likely area for success. Nevertheless, any language can cope with any pressing linguistic problem. The impetus for a solution begins with the individual or a small group, but the community as a whole often applies brakes to change that is too rapid or drastic, dramatizing the fact that language exists not for the individual alone but for the community as a whole.

APPLICATIONS

Almost everybody is intimately acquainted with at least one language. Everybody can produce the sounds and sound combinations of his or her language and understand the meanings of the sounds produced by other speakers. Everybody knows which sounds and sound combinations are allowable and which do not fit the language. Sentences that are grammatically or semantically unacceptable or strange are easily recognized. Despite this intuitive or unconscious knowledge of one's language, the average native speaker cannot comment authoritatively on the sound system or the structure of his or her language. Furthermore, there are no books containing the complete language of English or Arabic or Mandarin Chinese in which all possible sentences and sound combinations are listed. Instead, people must rely largely on dictionaries for a list of words and on grammars and linguistic texts for a statement of rules dealing with sounds, morphology, and syntax. To study one's language as an object or phenomenon is to raise one's consciousness of how language functions.

Some people have a professional need to know a lot about a language as opposed to simply being able to use it. Some of the more obvious examples include language teachers, speech therapists, advertising writers, communications engineers, and computer programmers. Others, such as the anthropologist or the historian, who often work with documents, employ their knowledge as an ancillary tool. The missionary may have to learn about some very esoteric language for which there is no grammar book and perhaps even no writing. The psychologist studies language as a part of human behavior. The philosopher is often primarily interested in the "logical" side of language. Students of foreign languages can benefit greatly from linguistic knowledge; they can often learn more efficiently and make helpful comparisons of sounds and structures between their own and the target language.

Translation and interpretation are two activities requiring considerable knowledge about language. Strictly speaking, the terms are not interchangeable; translation refers to the activity of rendering, in writing, one language text into another, whereas interpretation is oral translation. Translation is of two kinds, scientific and literary, and can be accomplished by people or machines. In general, machine translation has been a disappointment because of the grave difficulties involved in programming the many complexities of natural language. Interpretation is also of two kinds: legal and diplomatic. Whereas the legal interpreter requires a precise knowledge of the terminology of the court and must tread a thin line between literal and free interpretation, the diplomatic interpreter has the even more difficult task of adding, or subtracting, as circumstances dictate, allusions, innuendos, insinuations, and implications. Interpretation is accomplished in two ways: simultaneously with the speaker, or consecutively after a given segment of speech.

One of the important questions before linguistics is: Does linguistics aid in the study and appreciation of literature? Many would automatically assume that the answer is an unqualified yes, since the material of which literature is made is language. There are others, however, who find linguistic techniques of analysis too mechanical and lacking in the very feeling that literature tries to communicate. Probably most thoughtful people would agree that linguistics can make a contribution in tandem with more traditional analytical approaches, but that alone it cannot yet, if ever, disclose the intrinsic qualities of great literary works.

By one definition at least, literature consists of texts constructed according to certain phonological, morpho-logical, and syntactic restrictions, where the result is the creation of excellence of form and expression. For poetry in the Western tradition, for example, the restriction most frequently imposed is that of rhythm based on stress or vowel quantity. In other cultures, syntactic and semantic prescriptions can produce the same effect.

For both poetic and prose texts, the discovery and description of the author's style are essential to analysis. In contrast to the methods of traditional literary criticism, linguistics offers the possibility of quantitative stylistic analysis. Computer-aided analysis yields textual statistics based on an examination of various features of phonology and grammar. The results will often place an author within a literary period, confirm his region or dialect, explain the foreign-vocabulary influences, describe syllabication in terms of vowel and consonant count, list euphemisms and metaphors, and delineate sentence structure with regard to subordinating elements, to mention some of the possibilities. All of these applications are based on the taxemes of selection employed by an individual author.

Of all literary endeavors, literary translation seems to stand in the closest possible relationship to linguistics. The translator must perform his task within the framework of an awareness, be it conscious or intuitive, of the phonology, syntax, and morphology of both the source language and the target language. Like the linguist, he should also be acquainted in at least a rudimentary fashion with the society that has produced the text he is attempting to translate. His work involves much more than the mechanical or one-to-one exchange of word for word, phrase for phrase, or even concept for concept. The practice of translation makes possible the scope and breadth of knowledge encompassed in the ideal of liberal arts, and without translation relatively few scholars could claim knowledge and understanding of many of the world's great thinkers and literary artists.

BIBLIOGRAPHY

Akmajian, Adrian, et al. *Linguistics: An Introduction to Language and Communication.* Cambridge, Mass.: MIT Press, 2001. The first part of this work deals with the structural and interpretive parts of language, and the second part is cognitively oriented and includes chapters on pragmatics, psychology of language, language acquisition, and language and the brain.

Beekes, Robert S. P. *Comparative Indo-European Linguistics: An Introduction*. Philadelphia: John Benjamins, 1996. Examines the history of Indo-European languages and explores comparative grammar and linguistics.

Cavalli-Sforza, L. L. *Genes, Peoples, and Languages*. Berkeley: University of California Press, 2001. Cavalli-Sforza was among the first to ask whether the genes of modern populations contain a historical record of the human species. This collection comprises five lectures that serve as a summation of the author's work over several decades, the goal of which has been nothing less than tracking the past hundred thousand years of human evolution.

Chomsky, Noam. *Language and Thought*. Wakefield, R.I.: Moyer Bell, 1998. Presents an analysis of human language and its influence on other disciplines.

Lycan, William G. *Philosophy of Language: A Contemporary Introduction*. 2d ed. New York: Routledge, 2008. Introduces nonspecialists to the main issues and theories in the philosophy of language, focusing specifically on linguistic phenomena.

Pinker, Stephen. *The Language Instinct: How the Mind Creates Language*. New York: HarperPerennial Modern Classics, 2009. Explores how humans learn to talk, how the study of language can provide insight into the way genes interact with experience to create behavior and thought, and how the arbitrary sounds people call language evoke emotion and meaning.

Ruhlen, Merritt. *The Origin of Language: Tracing the Evolution of the Mother Tongue*. New York: John Wiley & Sons, 1996. Provides an accessible examination of nearly 100,000 years of human history and prehistory to uncover the roots of the language from which all modern tongues derive.

Trudgill, Peter. *Sociolinguistics: An Introduction to Language and Society*. 4th ed. New York: Penguin Books, 2007. Examines how speech is deeply influenced by class, gender, and ethnic background and explores the implications of language for social and educational policy.

Vygotsky, Lev S. *Thought and Language*. Edited by Alex Kozulin. Rev. ed. Cambridge, Mass.: MIT Press, 1986. A classic foundational work of cognitive science. Vygotsky analyzes the relationship between words and consciousness, arguing that speech is social in its origins and that only as a child develops does it become internalized verbal thought. Revised edition offers an introductory essay by editor Kozulin that offers new insight into the author's life, intellectual milieu, and research methods.

Yule, George. *The Study of Language*. 4th ed. New York: Cambridge University Press, 2010. Revised edition includes a new chapter on pragmatics and an expanded chapter on semantics; incorporates many changes that reflect developments in language study in the twenty-first century.

Donald D. Hook

GLOSSARY OF POETICAL TERMS

Accentual meter: A base meter in which the occurrence of a syllable marked by a stress determines the basic unit, regardless of the number of unstressed syllables. It is one of four base meters used in English (accentual, accentual-syllabic, syllabic, and quantitative). An example from modern poetry is "Blue Moles" by Sylvia Plath, the first line of which scans: "They're out of the dark's ragbag, these two." Because there are five stressed syllables in this accentually based poem, the reader can expect that many of the other lines will also contain five stresses. See also *Scansion.*

Accentual-syllabic meter: A base meter that measures the pattern of stressed syllables relative to the unstressed ones. It is the most common base meter for English poetry. In the first line of William Shakespeare's sonnet 130, "My mistress' eyes are nothing like the sun," there is a pattern of alternating unstressed with stressed syllables, although there is a substitution of an unstressed syllable for a stressed syllable at the word "like." In the accentual-syllabic system, stressed and unstressed syllables are grouped together into feet.

Allegory: A literary mode in which a second level of meaning—wherein characters, events, and settings represent abstractions—is encoded within the surface narrative. The allegorical mode may dominate the entire work, in which case the encoded message is the work's primary excuse for being, or it may be an element in a work otherwise interesting and meaningful for its surface story alone.

Alliteration: The repetition of consonants at the beginning of syllables; for example, "Large mannered motions of his mythy mind." Alliteration is used when the poet wishes to focus on the details of a sequence of words and to show relationships between words within a line. Because a reader cannot easily skim over an alliterative line, it is conspicuous and demands emphasis.

Allusion: A reference to a historical or literary event whose story or outcome adds dimension to the poem. "Fire and Ice" by Robert Frost, for example, alludes to the biblical account of the flood and the prophecy that the next destruction will come by fire, not water. Without recognizing the allusion and understanding the bib-

lical reference to Noah and the surrounding associations of hate and desire, the reader cannot fully appreciate the poem.

Anacrusis: The addition of an extra unstressed syllable to the beginning or end of a line; the opposite of truncation. For example, anacrusis occurs in the line: "their shoul/ders held the sky/suspended." This line is described as iambic tetrameter with terminal anacrusis. Anacrusis is used to change a rising meter to falling and vice versa to alter the reader's emotional response to the subject.

Anapest: A foot in which two unstressed syllables are associated with one stressed syllable, as in the line, "With the sift/ed, harmon/ious pause." The anapestic foot is one of the three most common in English poetry and is used to create a highly rhythmical, usually emotional, line.

Anaphora: The use of the same word or words to begin successive phrases or lines. Timothy Steele's "Sapphics Against Anger" uses anaphora in the repetition of the phrase "May I."

Approximate rhyme: Assonance and half rhyme (or slant rhyme). Assonance occurs when words with identical vowel sounds but different consonants are associated. "Stars," "arms," and "park" all contain identical *a* (and *ar*) sounds, but because the consonants are different the words are not full rhymes. Half rhyme or slant rhymes contain identical consonants but different vowels, as in "fall" and "well." "Table" and "bauble" constitute half rhymes; "law," "cough," and "fawn" assonate.

Archetype: 1) Primordial image from the collective unconscious of humankind, according to psychologist Carl Jung, who believed that works of art, including poetry, derive much of their power from the unconscious appeal of these images to ancestral memories. 2) A symbol, usually an image, that recurs so frequently in literature that it becomes an element of the literary experience, according to Northrop Frye in his extremely influential *Anatomy of Criticism* (1957).

Assonance: See *Approximate rhyme*

Aubade: A type of poem welcoming or decrying the arrival of the dawn. Often the dawn symbolizes the separation of two lovers. An example is William Empson's "Aubade" (1937).

Ballad: A poem composed of four-line stanzas that alternate rhyme schemes of *abab* or *abcb*. If all four lines contain four feet each (tetrameter), the stanza is called a long ballad; if one or more of the lines contain only three feet (trimeter), it is called a short ballad. Ballad stanzas, which are highly mnemonic, originated with verse adapted to singing. For this reason, the poetic ballad is well suited for presenting stories. Popular ballads are songs or verse that tell tales, usually impersonal, and they usually impart folk wisdom. Supernatural events, courage, and love are frequent themes, but any experience that appeals to people is acceptable material. A famous use of the ballad form is *The Rime of the Ancient Mariner* (1798), by Samuel Taylor Coleridge.

Ballade: A popular and sophisticated French form, commonly (but not necessarily) composed of an eight-line stanza rhyming *ababbcbc*. Early ballades usually contained three stanzas and an envoy, commonly addressed to a nobleman, priest, or the poet's patron, but no consistent syllable count. Another common characteristic of the ballade is a refrain that occurs at the end of each stanza.

Base meter: Also called metrical base. The primary meter employed in poems in English and in most European languages that are not free verse. Based on the number, pattern, or duration of the syllables within a line or stanza, base meters fall into four types: accentual, accentual-syllabic, syllabic, or quantitative. Rhythm in verse occurs because of meter, and the use of meter depends on the type of base into which it is placed.

Blank verse: A type of poem having a base meter of iambic pentameter and with unrhymed lines usually arranged in stichic form (that is, not in stanzas). Most of William Shakespeare's plays are written in blank verse; in poetry it is often used for subject matter that requires much narration or reflection. In both poetry and drama, blank verse elevates emotion and gives a dramatic sense of importance. Although the base meter of blank verse is iambic pentameter, the form is very flexible, and substitution, enjambment, feminine rhyme, and extra syllables can relax the rigidity of the base. The flexi-

bility of blank verse gives the poet an opportunity to use a formal structure without seeming unnecessarily decorous. T. S. Eliot's "Burnt Norton," written in the 1930's, is a modern blank-verse poem.

Cadence: The rhythmic speed or tempo with which a line is read. All language has cadence, but when the cadence of words is forced into some pattern, it becomes meter, thus distinguishing poetry from prose. A prose poem may possess strong cadence, combined with poetic uses of imagery, symbolism, and other poetic devices.

Caesura: A pause or break in a poem, created with or without punctuation marks. The comma, question mark, colon, and dash are the most common signals for pausing, and these are properly termed caesuras; pauses may also be achieved through syntax, lines, meter, rhyme, and the sound of words. The type of punctuation determines the length of the pause. Periods and question marks demand full stops, colons take almost a full stop, semicolons take a long pause, and commas take a short pause. The end of a line usually demands some pause even if there is no punctuation.

Cinquain: Any five-line stanza, including the madsong and the limerick. Cinquains are most often composed of a ballad stanza with an extra line added to the middle.

Classicism: A literary stance or value system consciously based on the example of classical Greek and Roman literature. Although the term is applied to an enormous diversity of artists in many different periods and in many different national literatures, classicism generally denotes a cluster of values including formal discipline, restrained expression, reverence for tradition, and an objective rather than a subjective orientation. As a literary tendency, classicism is often opposed to Romanticism, although many writers combine classical and romantic elements.

Conceit: A type of metaphor that uses a highly intellectualized comparison; an extended, elaborate, or complex metaphor. The term is frequently applied to the work of the Metaphysical poets, notably John Donne.

Connotation: An additional meaning for a word other than its denotative, formal definition. The word "mercenary," for example, simply means a soldier who is paid to fight in an army not of his own region, but connotatively a mercenary is an unprincipled scoundrel who kills for money and pleasure, not for honor and patriotism. Connotation is one of the most important devices for achieving irony, and readers may be fooled into believing a poem has one meaning because they have missed connotations that reverse the poem's apparent theme.

Consonance: Repetition or recurrence of the final consonants of stressed syllables without the correspondence of the preceding vowels. "Chair/star" is an example of consonance, since both words end with *r* preceded by different vowels. Terminal consonance creates half or slant rhyme (see *Approximate rhyme*). Consonance differs from alliteration in that the final consonants are repeated rather than the initial consonants. In the twentieth century, consonance became one of the principal rhyming devices, used to achieve formality without seeming stilted or old-fashioned.

Consonants: All letters except the vowels, *a*, *e*, *i*, *o*, *u*, and sometimes *y*; one of the most important sound-producing devices in poetry. There are five basic effects that certain consonants will produce: resonance, harshness, plosiveness, exhaustiveness, and liquidity. Resonance, exhaustiveness, and liquidity tend to give words—and consequently the whole line if several of these consonants are used—a soft effect. Plosiveness and harshness, on the other hand, tend to create tension. Resonance is the property of long duration produced by nasals, such as *n* and *m*, and by voiced fricating consonants such as *z*, *v*, and the voiced *th*, as in "them." Exhaustiveness is created by the voiceless fricating consonants and consonant combinations, such as *h*, *f*, and the voiceless *th* and *s*. Liquidity results from using the liquids and semivowels *l*, *r*, *w*, and *y*, as in the word "silken." Plosiveness occurs when certain consonants create a stoppage of breath before releasing it, especially *b*, *p*, *t*, *d*, *g*, *k*, *ch*, and *j*.

Controlling image/controlling metaphor: Just as a poem may include as structural devices form, theme, action, or dramatic situation, it may also use imagery for structure. When an image runs throughout a poem, giving unity to lesser images or ideas, it is called a controlling image. Usually the poet establishes a single idea and then expands and complicates it; in Edward

Taylor's "Huswifery," for example, the image of the spinning wheel is expanded into images of weaving until the reader begins to see life as a tapestry. Robert Frost's "The Silken Tent" is a fine example of a controlling image and extended metaphor.

Couplet: Any two succeeding lines that rhyme. Because the couplet has been used in so many different ways and because of its long tradition in English poetry, various names and functions have been given to types of couplets. One of the most common is the decasyllabic (ten-syllable) couplet. When there is an end-stop on the second line of a couplet, it is said to be closed; an enjambed couplet is open. An end-stopped decasyllabic couplet is called a heroic couplet, because the form has often been used to sing the praise of heroes. The heroic couplet was widely used by the neoclassical poets of the eighteenth century. Because it is so stately and sometimes pompous, the heroic couplet invites satire, and many poems have been written in "mock-heroic verse," such as Alexander Pope's *The Rape of the Lock* (1712, 1714). Another commonly used couplet is the octasyllabic (eight-syllable) couplet, formed from two lines of iambic tetrameter, as in "L'Allegro" by John Milton: "Come, and trip as we go/ On the light fantastic toe." The light, singsong tone of the octasyllabic couplet also invited satire, and Samuel Butler wrote one of the most famous of all satires, *Hudibras* (1663, 1664, 1678), in this couplet. When a couplet is used to break another rhyme scheme, it generally produces a summing-up effect and has an air of profundity. William Shakespeare found this characteristic particularly useful when he needed to give his newly invented Shakespearean sonnet a final note of authority and purpose.

Dactyl: A foot formed of a stress followed by two unstressed syllables ($\prime\ \smile\ \smile$). It is fairly common in isolated words, but when this pattern is included in a line of poetry, it tends to break down and rearrange itself into components of other types of feet. Isolated, the word "meaningless" is a dactyl, but in the line "Polite/ meaning/less words," the last syllable becomes attached to the stressed "words" and creates a split foot, forming a trochee and an iamb. Nevertheless, a few dactylic poems do exist. "After the/pangs of a / desperate/lover" is a dactyllic line.

Deconstruction: An extremely influential contemporary school of criticism based on the works of the French philosopher Jacques Derrida. Deconstruction treats literary works as unconscious reflections of the reigning myths of Western culture. The primary myth is that there is a meaningful world that language signifies or represents. The deconstructionist critic is most often concerned with showing how a literary text tacitly subverts the very assumptions or myths on which it ostensibly rests.

Denotation: The explicit formal definition of a word, exclusive of its implications and emotional associations (see *Connotation*).

Depressed foot: A foot in which two syllables occur in a pattern in such a way as to be taken as one syllable without actually being an elision. In the line: "To each/ he boul/ders (that have)/fallen/to each," the base meter consists of five iambic feet, but in the third foot, there is an extra syllable that disrupts the meter but does not break it, so that "that have" functions as the second half of the iambic foot.

Diction: The poet's "choice of words," according to John Dryden. In Dryden's time, and for most of the history of English verse, the diction of poetry was elevated, sharply distinct from everyday speech. Since the early twentieth century, however, the diction of poetry has ranged from the banal and the conversational to the highly formal, and from obscenity and slang to technical vocabulary, sometimes in the same poem. The diction of a poem often reveals its persona's values and attitudes.

Dieresis: Caesuras that come after the foot (see *Split foot* for a discussion of caesuras that break feet). They can be used to create long pauses in the line and are often used to prepare the line for enjambment.

Dramatic dialogue: An exchange between two or more personas in a poem or a play. Unlike a dramatic monologue, both characters speak, and in the best dramatic dialogues, their conversation leads to a final resolution in which both characters and the reader come to the same realization at the same time.

Dramatic irony: See *Irony*

Dramatic monologue: An address to a silent person by a narrator; the words of the narrator are greatly influenced by the persona's presence. The principal reason for writing in dramatic monologue form is to control the speech of the major persona through the implied reaction of the silent one. The effect is one of continuing change and often surprise. In Robert Browning's "My Last Duchess," for example, the duke believes that he is in control of the situation, when in fact he has provided the emissary with terrible insights about the way he treated his former duchess. The emissary, who is the silent persona, has asked questions that the duke has answered; in doing so he has given away secrets. Dramatic monologue is somewhat like hearing one side of a telephone conversation in which the reader learns much about both participants.

Duration: The length of the syllables, which is the measure of quantitative meter. Duration can alter the tone and the relative stress of a line and influence meaning as much as the foot can.

Elegy: Usually a long, rhymed, strophic poem whose subject is meditation on death or a lamentable theme. The pastoral elegy uses the natural setting of a pastoral scene to sing of death or love. Within the pastoral setting the simplicity of the characters and the scene lends a peaceful air despite the grief the narrator feels.

Elision: The joining of two vowels into a single vowel (synaeresis) or omitting of a vowel altogether (syncope), usually to maintain a regular base meter. Synaeresis can be seen in the line "Of man's first disobedience, and the fruit," in which the "ie" in "disobedience" is pronounced as a "y" ("ye") so that the word reads dis/o/bed/yence, thereby making a five-syllable word into a four-syllable word. An example of syncope is when "natural" becomes "nat'ral" and "hastening" becomes "hast'ning." Less frequent uses of elision are to change the sound of a word, to spell words as they are pronounced, and to indicate dialect.

Emphasis: The highlighting of or calling attention to a phrase or line or a poem by altering its meter. A number of techniques, such as caesura, relative stress, counterpointing, and substitution can be used.

End rhyme: See *Rhyme*

End-stop: A punctuated pause at the end of a line in a poem. The function of end-stops is to show the relationship between lines and to emphasize particular words or lines. End-stopping in rhymed poems creates more emphasis on the rhyme words, which already carry a great deal of emphasis by virtue of their rhymes. Enjambment is the opposite of end-stopping.

Enjambment: When a line is not end-stopped—that is, when it carries over to the following line—the line is said to be "enjambed," as in John Milton's: "Avenge, O Lord, thy slaughtered saints, whose bones/ Lie scattered on the Alpine mountains cold." Enjambment is used to change the natural emphasis of the line, to strengthen or weaken the effect of rhyme, or to alter meter.

Envoy: Any short poem or stanza addressed to the reader as a beginning or end to a longer work. Specifically, the envoy is the final stanza of a sestina or a ballade in which all the rhyme words are repeated or echoed.

Epic: A long narrative poem that presents the exploits of a central figure of high position.

Extended metaphor: Metaphors added to one another so that they run in a series. Robert Frost's poem "The Silken Tent" uses an extended metaphor; it compares the "she" of the poem to the freedom and bondage of a silken tent. See also *Controlling image/controlling metaphor.*

Eye rhyme: Words that appear to be identical because of their spelling but that sound different. "Bough/ enough/cough" and "ballet/pallet" are examples. Because of changes in pronunciation, many older poems appear to use eye rhymes but do not. For example, "wind" (meaning moving air) once rhymed with "find." Eye rhymes that are intentional and do not result from a change in pronunciation may be used to create a disconcerting effect.

Fabliau: A bawdy medieval verse, such as many found in Geoffrey Chaucer's *The Canterbury Tales* (1387-1400).

Falling rhyme: Rhyme in which the correspondence of sound comes only in the final unstressed syllable, which is preceded by another unstressed syllable. T. S. Eliot rhymes "me-tic-u-lous" with "ri-dic-u-lous" and creates a falling rhyme. See also *Feminine rhyme; Masculine rhyme.*

Falling rhythm: A line in which feet move from stressed to unstressed syllables (trochaic or dactyllic). An example can be seen in this line from "The Naming of Parts," by Henry Reed: "Glistens/like cor'al in/all of the/neighboring/gardens." Because English and other Germanic-based languages naturally rise, imposing a falling rhythm on a rising base meter creates counterpointing.

Feminine rhyme: A rhyme pattern in which a line's final accented syllable is followed by a single unaccented syllable and the accented syllables rhyme, while the unaccented syllables are phonetically identical, as with "flick-er/snick-er" and "fin-gers/ma-lin-gers." Feminine rhymes are often used for lightness in tone and delicacy in movement.

Feminist criticism: A criticism advocating equal rights for women in a political, economic, social, psychological, personal, and aesthetic sense. On the thematic level, the feminist reader should identify with female characters and their concerns. The object is to provide a critique of phallocentric assumptions and an analysis of patriarchal ideologies inscribed in male-centered and male-dominated literature. On the ideological level, feminist critics see gender, as well as the stereotypes that go along with it, as a cultural construct. They strive to define a particularly feminine content and to extend the canon so that it might include works by lesbians, feminists, women of color, and women writers in general.

First person: The use of linguistic forms that present a poem from the point of view of the speaker. It is particularly useful in short lyrical poems, which tend to be highly subjective, taking the reader deep into the narrator's thoughts. First-person poems normally, though not necessarily, signal the use of the first person through the pronoun "I," allowing the reader direct access to the narrator's thoughts or providing a character who can convey a personal reaction to an event. See also *Third person.*

Foot/feet: Rhythmic unit in which syllables are grouped together; this is the natural speech pattern in English and other Germanic-based languages. In English, the most common of these rhythmic units is composed of one unstressed syllable attached to one stressed syllable (an iamb). When these family groups are forced into a line of poetry, they are called feet in the accentual-syllabic metrical system. In the line "My mis/tress' eyes/are noth/ing like/the sun" there are four iambic feet (◡′) and one pyrrhic foot (◡◡), but in the line "Thére whére/the vĭnes/clĭng crím/sŏn ŏn/thĕ wáll," there are three substitutions for the iamb—in the first, third, and fourth feet. The six basic feet in English poetry are the iamb (◡′), trochee (′◡), anapest (◡◡′), dactyl (′◡◡), spondee (′′), and pyrrhus (◡◡).

Form: The arrangement of the lines of a poem on the page, its base meter, its rhyme scheme, and occasionally its subject matter. Poems that are arranged into stanzas are called strophic, and because the strophic tradition is so old, a large number of commonly used stanzas have evolved particular uses and characteristics. Poems that run from beginning to end without a break are called stichic. The form of pattern poetry is determined by its visual appearance rather than by lines and stanzas, while the definition of free verse is that it has no discernible form. Some poem types, such as the sestina, sonnet, and ode, are written in particular forms and frequently are restricted to particular subject matter.

Formalism, Russian: A twentieth century Russian school of criticism that employed the conventional devices used in literature to defamiliarize that which habit has made familiar. The most extreme formalists treated literary works as artifacts or constructs divorced from their biographical and social contexts.

Found poetry: Poems created from language that is "found" in print in nonliterary settings. They can use any language that is already constructed, but usually use language that appears on cultural artifacts, such as cereal boxes. The rules for writing a found poem vary, but generally the found language is used intact or altered only slightly.

Free verse: A poem that does not conform to any traditional convention, such as meter, rhyme, or form, and that does not establish any pattern within itself. There is, however, great dispute over whether "free" verse actually exists. T. S. Eliot said that by definition poetry must establish some kind of pattern, and Robert Frost said that "writing free verse is like playing tennis with the net down." However, some would agree with Carl Sandburg, who insisted that "you can play a better game with the net down." Free verse depends more on cadence than on meter.

Ghazal: A poetic form based on a type of Persian poetry. It is composed of couplets, often unrhymed,

that function as individual images or observations but that also interrelate in sometimes subtle ways.

Gnomic verse: Poetry that typically includes many proverbs or maxims.

Haiku: A Japanese form that appeared in the sixteenth century and is still practiced in Japan. A haiku consists of three lines of five, seven, and five syllables each; in Japanese there are other conventions regarding content that are not observed in Western haiku. The traditional haiku took virtually all of its images from nature, using the natural world as a metaphor for the spiritual.

Half rhyme: See *Approximate rhyme*
Heroic couplet: See *Couplet*
Historical criticism: A school of criticism that emphasizes the historical context of literature. Ernst Robert Curtius's *European Literature and the Latin Middle Ages* (1940) is a prominent example of historical criticism.

Hymn stanza: See *Ballad*
Hyperbole: A deliberate overstatement made in order to heighten the reader's awareness. As with irony, hyperbole works because the reader can perceive the difference between the importance of the dramatic situation and the manner in which it is described.

Iamb: A foot consisting of one unstressed and one stressed syllable (◡′). The line "Sŏ lóng/ăs mén/căn bréathe/ŏr éyĕs/căn sée" is composed of five iambs. In the line "Ăcóld/cómĭng/wĕ hád/ŏf ĭt," a trochaic foot (a trochee) has been substituted for the expected iamb in the second foot, thus emphasizing that this is a "coming" rather than a "going," an important distinction in T. S. Eliot's "The Journey of the Magi."

Iambic pentameter: A very common poetic line consisting of five iambic feet. The following two lines by Thomas Wyatt are in iambic pentameter: "I find no peace and all my war is done,/ I fear and hope, I burn and freeze like ice." See also *Foot/feet*; *iamb*.

Identical rhyme: A rhyme in which the entire final stressed syllables contain exactly the same sounds, such as "break/brake," or "bear" (noun), "bear" (verb), "bare" (adjective), "bare" (verb).

Imagery: The verbal simulation of sensory perception. Like so many critical terms, imagery betrays a visual bias: It suggests that a poetic image is necessarily visual, a picture in words. In fact, however, imagery calls on all five senses, although the visual is predominant in many poets. In its simplest form, an image recreates a physical sensation in a clear, literal manner, as in Robert Lowell's lines, "A sweetish smell of shavings, wax and oil/ blows through the redone bedroom newly aged" ("Marriage"). Imagery becomes more complex when the poet employs metaphor and other figures of speech to re-create experience, as in Seamus Heaney's lines, "Right along the lough shore/ A smoke of flies/ Drifts thick in the sunset" ("At Ardboe Point"), substituting a fresh metaphor ("A smoke of flies") for a trite one (a cloud of flies) to help the reader visualize the scene more clearly.

Interior monologue: A first-person representation of a persona's or character's thoughts or feelings. It differs from a dramatic monologue in that it deals with thoughts rather than spoken words or conversation.

Internal rhyme: See *Rhyme*

Irony: A figure of speech in which the speaker's real meaning is different from (and often exactly opposite to) the apparent meaning. Irony is among the three or four most important concepts in modern literary criticism. Although the term originated in classical Greece and has been in the vocabulary of criticism since that time, only in the nineteenth and twentieth centuries did it assume central importance. In Andrew Marvell's lines, "The Grave's a fine and private place,/ But none I think do there embrace" ("To His Coy Mistress"), the speaker's literal meaning—in praise of the grave—is quite different from his real meaning. This kind of irony is often called verbal irony. Another kind of irony is found in narrative and dramatic poetry. In the *Iliad* (c. 750 B.C.E.; English translation, 1611), for example, the reader is made privy to the counsels of the gods, which greatly affect the course of action in the epic, while the human characters are kept in ignorance. This discrepancy between the knowledge of the reader and that of the character (or characters) is called dramatic irony. Beyond these narrow, well-defined varieties of irony are many wider applications.

Limerick: A comic five-line poem rhyming *aabba* in which the third and fourth lines are shorter (usually five syllables each) than the first, second, and last lines, which are usually eight syllables each. The limerick's anapestic base makes the verse sound silly; modern limericks are almost invariably associated with bizarre indecency or with ethnic or anticlerical jokes.

Line: A poetical unit characterized by the presence of meter; lines are categorized according to the number of feet (see *Foot/feet*) they contain. A pentameter line, for example, contains five feet. This definition does not apply to a great deal of modern poetry, however, which is written in free verse. Ultimately, then, a line must be defined as a typographical unit on the page that performs various functions in different kinds of poetry.

Lyric poetry: Short poems, adaptable to metrical variation, and usually personal rather than having a cultural function. Lyric poetry developed when music was accompanied by words, and although the lyrics were later separated from the music, the characteristics of lyric poetry have been shaped by the constraints of music. Lyric poetry sings of the self, exploring deeply personal feelings about life.

Mad-song: Verse uttered by someone presumed to have a severe mental illness that manifests in a happy, harmless, inventive way. The typical rhyme scheme of the mad-song is *abccb*, and the unrhymed first line helps to set a tone of oddity and unpredictability, since it controverts the expectation that there will be a rhyme for it. The standard mad-song has short lines.

Marxist criticism: A school of criticism based on the nineteenth century writings of Karl Marx and Friedrich Engels that views literature as a product of ideological forces determined by the dominant class However, many Marxists believe that literature operates according to its own autonomous standards of production and reception: It is both a product of ideology and able to determine ideology. As such, literature may overcome the dominant paradigms of its age and play a revolutionary role in society.

Masculine rhyme: A rhyme pattern in which rhyme exists in the stressed syllables. "Men/then" constitute masculine rhyme, but so do "af-ter-noons/spoons." Masculine rhyme is generally considered more forceful than feminine rhyme, and while it has a variety of uses, it generally gives authority and assurance to the line, especially when the final syllables are of short duration.

Metaphor: A figure of speech in which two strikingly different things are identified with each other, as in "the waves were soldiers moving" (Wallace Stevens). Metaphor is one of a handful of key concepts in modern literary criticism. A metaphor contains a "tenor" and a "vehicle." The tenor is the subject of the metaphor, and the vehicle is the imagery by which the subject is presented. In D. H. Lawrence's lines, "Reach me a gentian, give me a torch/ let me guide myself with the blue, forked torch of this flower" ("Bavarian Gentians"), the tenor is the gentian and the vehicle is the torch. This relatively restricted definition of metaphor by no means covers the usage of the word in modern criticism. Some critics argue that metaphorical perception underlies all figures of speech. Others dispute the distinction between literal and metaphorical description, saying that language is essentially metaphorical. Metaphor has become widely used to identify analogies of all kinds in literature, painting, film, and even music. See also *Simile.*

Meter: The pattern that language takes when it is forced into a line of poetry. All language has rhythm; when that rhythm is organized and regulated in the line so as to affect the meaning and emotional response to the words, then the rhythm has been refined into meter. Because the lines of most poems maintain a similar meter throughout, poems are said to have a base meter. The meter is determined by the number of syllables in a line and by the relationship between them.

Metrical base. See *Base meter*

Metonymy: Using an object that is closely related to an idea stand for the idea itself, such as saying "the crown" to mean the king. Used to emphasize a particular part of the whole or one particular aspect of it. See also *Synecdoche.*

Mnemonic verse: Poetry in which rhythmic patterns aid memorization but are not crucial to meaning. Ancient bards were able to remember long poems partly through the use of stock phrases and other mnemonic devices.

Mock-heroic: See *Couplet*

Modernism: An international movement in the arts that began in the early years of the twentieth century. Although the term is used to describe artists of widely varying persuasions, modernism in general was characterized by its international idiom, by its interest in cultures distant in space or time, by its emphasis on formal experimentation, and by its sense of dislocation and radical change.

Multiculturalism: The tendency to recognize the perspectives of works by authors (particularly women and non-European writers) who, until the latter part of the twentieth century, were excluded from the canon of Western art and literature. To promote multiculturalism, publishers and educators have revised textbooks and school curricula to incorporate material by and about women, ethnic and racial minorities, non-Western cultures, gays, and lesbians.

Myth: Anonymous traditional stories dealing with basic human concepts and antinomies. Claude Lévi-Strauss says that myth is that part of language where the "formula *tradutore, traditore* reaches its lowest truth value. . . . Its substance does not lie in its style, its original music, or its syntax, but in the story which it tells."

Myth criticism: A school of criticism concerned with the basic structural principles of literature. Myth criticism is not to be confused with mythological criticism, which is primarily concerned with finding mythological parallels in the surface action of a narrative.

Narrator: The person who is doing the talking—or observing or thinking—in a poem. Roughly synonymous with persona and speaker. Lyric poetry most often consists of the poet expressing his or her own personal feelings directly. Other poems, however, may involve the poet adopting the point of view of another person entirely. In some poems—notably in a dramatic monologue—it is relatively easy to determine that the narrative is being related by a fictional (or perhaps historical) character, but in others it may be more difficult to identify the "I."

New Criticism: A formalist movement whose members held that literary criticism is a description and evaluation of its object and that the primary concern of the critic is with the work's unity. At their most extreme, these critics treated literary works as artifacts or constructs divorced from their biographical and social contexts.

Occasional verse: Any poem written for a specific occasion, such as a wedding, a birthday, a death, or a public event. Edmund Spenser's *Epithalamion* (1595), which was written for his marriage, and John Milton's "Lycidas," which commemorated the death of his schoolmate Edward King, are examples of occasional verse, as are W. H. Auden's "September 1, 1939" and Frank O'Hara's "The Day Lady Died."

Octave: A poem in eight lines. Octaves may have many different variations of meter, such as ottava rima.

Ode: A lyric poem that treats a unified subject with elevated emotion, usually ending with a satisfactory resolution. There is no set form for the ode, but it must be long enough to build intense emotional response. Often the ode will address itself to some omnipotent source and will take on a spiritual hue. When explicating an ode, readers should look for the relationship between the narrator and some transcendental power to which the narrator must submit to find contentment. Modern poets have used the ode to treat subjects that are not religious in the theological sense but that have become innate beliefs of society.

Ottava rima: An eight-line stanza of iambic pentameter, rhyming *abababcc*. Probably the most famous English poem written in ottava rima is Lord Byron's *Don Juan* (1819-1824), and because the poem was so successful as a spoof, the form has come to be associated with poetic high jinks. However, the stanza has also been used brilliantly for just the opposite effect, to reflect seriousness and meditation.

Oxymoron: The juxtaposition of two paradoxical words, such as "wise fool" or "devilish angel."

Pantoum: A French form of poetry consisting of four quatrains in which entire lines are repeated in a strict pattern of 1234, 2546, 5768, 7183. Peter Meinke's "Atomic Pantoum" is an example.

Paradox: A statement that contains an inherent contradiction. It may be a statement that at first seems true but is in reality contradictory. It may also be a statement that appears contradictory but is actually true or that contains an element of truth that reconciles the contradiction.

Pentameter: A type of rhythmic pattern in which each line consists of five poetic feet. See also *Accentual-syllabic meter*; *Foot/feet*; *Iamb*; *Iambic pentameter*; *Line*.

Periphrasis: The use of a wordy phrase to describe something that could be described simply in one word.

Persona: See *Narrator*

Phenomenological criticism: A school of criticism that examines literature as an act and focuses less on individual works and genres. The work is not seen as an object, but rather as part of a strand of latent impulses in the work of a single author or an epoch. Proponents include Georges Poulet in Europe and J. Hillis Miller in the United States.

Point of view: The mental position through which readers experience the situation of a poem. As with fiction, poems may be related in the first person, second person (unusual), or third person. (The presence of the words "I" or "we" indicates singular or plural first-person narration.) Point of view may be limited or omniscient. A limited point of view means that the narrator can see only what the poet wants him or her to see, while from an omniscient point of view the narrator can know everything, including the thoughts and motives of others.

Postcolonialism: The literature that emerged in the mid-twentieth century when colonies in Asia, Africa, and the Caribbean began gaining their independence from the European nations that had long controlled them. Postcolonial authors, such as Salman Rushdie, V. S. Naipaul, and Derek Walcott, tend to focus on both the freedom and the conflict inherent in living in a postcolonial state.

Postmodernism: A ubiquitous but elusive term in contemporary criticism that is loosely applied to the various artistic movements that followed the era of so-called high modernism, represented by such giants as writer James Joyce and painter and sculptor Pablo Picasso. In critical discussions of contemporary fiction, postmodernism is frequently applied to the works of writers such as Thomas Pynchon, John Barth, and Donald Barthelme, who exhibit a self-conscious awareness of their modernist predecessors as well as a reflexive treatment of fictional form. Such reflexive treatments can extend to poetry as well.

Prose poem: A poem that looks like prose on the page, with no line breaks. There are no formal characteristics by which a prose poem can be distinguished from a piece of prose. Many prose poems employ rhythmic repetition and other poetic devices not normally found in prose, but others use such devices sparingly if at all. Prose poems range in length from a few lines to three or four pages; most prose poems occupy a page or less.

Psychological criticism: A school of criticism that places a strong emphasis on a causal relation between the writer's psychological state, variously interpreted, and his or her works. A notable example of psychological criticism is Norman Fruman's *Coleridge, the Damaged Archangel* (1971).

Pun: The use of words that have similar pronunciations but entirely different meanings to establish a connection between two meanings or contexts that the reader would not ordinarily make. The result may be a surprise recognition of an unusual or striking connection, or, more often, a humorously accidental connection.

Pyrrhus: A poetic foot consisting of two unstressed syllables, as in the line "Appear/and dis/appear/in the/ blue depth/of the sky," in which foot four is a pyrrhus.

Quatrain: Any four-line stanza. Aside from the couplet, it is the most common stanza type. The quatrain's popularity among both sophisticated and unsophisticated readers suggests that there is something inherently pleasing about the form. For many readers, poetry and quatrains are almost synonymous. Balance and antithesis, contrast and comparison not possible in other stanza types are indigenous to the quatrain.

Realism: A literary technique in which the primary convention is to render an illusion of fidelity to external reality. Realism is often identified as the primary method of the novel form: It focuses on surface details, maintains a fidelity to the everyday experiences of middle-class society, and strives for a one-to-one relationship between the fiction and the action imitated. The realist movement in the late nineteenth century coincides with the full development of the novel form.

Regular meter: A line of poetry that contains only one type of foot. Only the dullest of poems maintain a regular meter throughout, however; skillful poets create interest and emphasis through substitution.

Relative stress: The degree to which a syllable in pattern receives more or less emphasis than other syllables in the pattern. Once the dominant stress in the line has been determined, every other syllable can be assigned a stress factor relative to the dominant syllable. The stress factor is created by several aspects of prosody: the position of the syllable in the line, the position of the syllable in its word, the surrounding syllables, the type of vowels and consonants that constitute the syllable, and the syllable's relation to the foot, base meter, and caesura. Because every syllable will have a different stress factor, there could be as many values as there are syllables, although most prosodists scan poems using primary, secondary, and unstressed notations. In the line "I am there like the dead, or the beast," the anapestic base meter will not permit "I" to take a full stress, but it is a more forceful syllable than the unstressed ones, so it is assigned a secondary stress. Relative to "dead" and "beast," it takes less pressure; relative to the articles in the line, it takes much more.

Resolution: Any natural conclusion to a poem, especially to a short lyric poem that establishes some sort of dilemma or conflict that the narrator must solve. Specifically, the resolution is the octave stanza of a Petrarchan sonnet or the couplet of a Shakespearean sonnet in which the first part of the poem presents a situation that must find balance in the resolution.

Rhyme: A correspondence of sound between syllables within a line or between lines whose proximity to each other allows the sounds to be sustained. Rhyme may be classified in a number of ways: according to the sound relationship between rhyming words, the position of the rhyming words in the line, and the number and position of the syllables in the rhyming words. Sound classifications include full rhyme and approximate rhyme. Full rhyme is defined as words that have the same vowel sound, followed by the same consonants in their last stressed syllables, and in which all succeeding syllables are phonetically identical. "Hat/ cat" and "laughter/after" are full rhymes. Categories of approximate rhyme are assonance, slant rhyme, alliteration, eye rhyme, and identical rhyme.

Rhyme classified by its position in the line includes end, internal, and initial rhyme. End rhyme occurs when the last words of lines rhyme. Internal rhyme occurs when two words within the same line or within various lines recall the same sound, as in "Wet, below the snow line, smelling of vegetation" in which "below" and "snow" rhyme. Initial rhyme occurs when the first syllables of two or more lines rhyme. See also *Masculine rhyme*; *Feminine rhyme*.

Rhyme scheme: A pattern of rhyme in a poem, designated by lowercase (and often italicized) letters. The letters stand for the pattern of rhyming sounds of the last word in each line. For example, the following A. E. Housman quatrain has an *abab* rhyme scheme.

> Into my heart an air that kills
> From yon far country blows:
> What are those blue remembered hills,
> What spires, what farms are those?

As another example, the rhyme scheme of the poetic form known as ottava rima is *abababcc*. Traditional stanza forms are categorized by their rhyme scheme and base meter.

Rime royal: A seven-line stanza in English prosody consisting of iambic pentameter lines rhyming *ababbcc*. William Shakespeare's *The Rape of Lucrece* (1594) is written in this form. The only variation permitted is to make the last line hexameter.

Romanticism: A widespread cultural movement in the late eighteenth and early nineteenth centuries, the influence of which is still felt. As a general literary tendency, Romanticism is frequently contrasted with classicism or neoclassicism. Although there were many varieties of Romanticism indigenous to various national literatures, the term generally suggests an assertion of the preeminence of the imagination. Other values associated with various schools of Romanticism include primitivism, an interest in folklore, a reverence for nature, and a fascination with the demoniac and the macabre.

Rondeau: One of three standard French forms assimilated by English prosody; generally contains thirteen lines divided into three groups. A common stanzaic grouping rhymes *aabba*, *aabR*, *aabbaR*, where the *a* and *b* lines are tetrameter and the *R* (refrain) lines are dimeter. The rondel, another French form, contains fourteen lines of trimeter with alternating rhyme (*ababab bababab*) and is divided into two stanzas. The rondeau and rondel forms are always light and playful.

Rondel: See *Rondeau*

Rubaiyat stanza: An iambic pentameter quatrain that has a rhyme scheme of *aaba*.

Scansion: The assigning of relative stresses and meter to a line of poetry, usually for the purpose of determining where variations, and thus emphasis, in the base meter occur. Scansion can help explain how a poem

generates tension and offer clues as to the key words. E. E. Cummings's "singing each morning out of each night" could be scanned in two ways: (1) singing/each morn/ing out/of each night or (2) sing/ing each/ morning/out of/each night. Scansion will not only affect the way the line is read aloud but also influences the meaning of the line.

Secondary stress: See *Relative stress*

Seguidilla: An imagistic or mood poem in Spanish, which, like a haiku, creates emotional recognition or spiritual insight in the reader. Although there is no agreement as to what form the English seguidilla should take, most of the successful ones are either four or seven lines with an alternating rhyme scheme of *ababcbc*. Lines 1, 3, and 6 are trimeter; lines 2, 4, 5, and 7 dimeter.

Semiotics: The science of signs and sign systems in communication. Literary critic Roman Jakobson says that semiotics deals with the principles that underlie the structure of signs, their use in language of all kinds, and the specific nature of various sign systems.

Sestet: A six-line stanza. A Petrarchan or Italian sonnet is composed of an octave followed by a sestet.

Sestina: Six six-line stanzas followed by a three-line envoy. The words ending the lines in the first stanza are repeated in different order at the ends of lines in the following stanzas as well as in the middle and end of each line of the envoy. Elizabeth Bishop's "Sestina" is a good example.

Shakespearean sonnet: See *Sonnet*

Simile: A type of metaphor that signals a comparison by the use of the words "like" or "as." William Shakespeare's line "My mistress' eyes are nothing like the sun" is a simile that establishes a comparison between the woman's eyes and the sun. See also *Metaphor*.

Slant rhyme: See *Approximate rhyme*

Sonnet: A poem consisting of fourteen lines of iambic pentameter with some form of alternating rhyme and a turning point that divides the poem into two parts. The sonnet is the most important and widely used of traditional poem types. The two major sonnet types are the Petrarchan (or Italian) sonnet and the Shakespearean sonnet. The original sonnet form, the Petrarchan (adopted from the poetry of Petrarch), presents a problem or situation in the first eight lines, the octave, then resolves it in the last six, the sestet. The octave is composed of two quatrains (*abbaabba*), the second of which complicates the first and gradually defines and heightens the problem. The sestet then diminishes the problem slowly until a satisfying resolution is achieved.

During the fifteenth century, the Italian sonnet became an integral part of the courtship ritual, and most sonnets during that time consisted of a young man's description of his perfect lover. Because so many unpoetic young men had generated a nation full of bad sonnets by the end of the century, the form became an object of ridicule, and the English sonnet developed as a reaction against all the bad verse being turned out in the Italian tradition. When Shakespeare wrote "My mistress' eyes are nothing like the sun," he was deliberately negating the Petrarchan conceit, rejoicing in the fact that his loved one was much more interesting and unpredictable than nature. Shakespeare also altered the sonnet's formal balance. Instead of an octave, the Shakespearean sonnet has three quatrains of alternating rhyme and is resolved in a final couplet. During the sixteenth century, long stories were told in sonnet form, one sonnet after the next, to produce sonnet sequences. Although most sonnets contain fourteen lines, some contain as few as ten (the curtal sonnet) or as many as seventeen.

Speaker: See *Narrator*

Split foot: The alteration of the natural division of a word as a result of being forced into a metrical base. For example, the words "point/ed," "lad/der," and "stick/ing" have a natural falling rhythm, but in the line "My long/two-point/ed lad/der's stick/ing through/a tree" the syllables are rearranged so as to turn the falling rhythm into a rising meter. The result of splitting feet is to create an uncertainty and delicate imbalance in the line.

Spondee: When two relatively stressed syllables occur together in a foot, the unit is called a spondee or spondaic foot, as in the line "Appear/and dis/appear/in the/blue depth/of the sky."

Sprung rhythm: An unpredictable pattern of stresses in a line, first described near the end of the nineteenth century by Gerard Manley Hopkins, that results from taking accentual meter is to its extreme. According to Hopkins, in sprung rhythm "any two stresses may either follow one another running, or be divided by one, two, or three slack syllables."

Stanza: A certain number of lines meant to be taken

as a unit, or that unit. Although a stanza is traditionally considered a unit that contains rhyme and recurs predictably throughout a poem, the term is also sometimes applied to nonrhyming and even irregular units. Poems that are divided into fairly regular and patterned stanzas are called strophic; poems that appear as a single unit, whether rhymed or unrhymed, or that have no predictable stanzas, are called stichic. Both strophic and stichic units represent logical divisions within the poem, and the difference between them lies in the formality and strength of the interwoven unit. Stanza breaks are commonly indicated by a line of space.

Stichic verse: See *Stanza*

Stress: See *Relative stress*

Strophic verse: See *Stanza*

Structuralism: A movement based on the idea of intrinsic, self-sufficient structures that do not require reference to external elements. A structure is a system of transformations that involves the interplay of laws inherent in the system itself. The study of language is the primary model for contemporary structuralism. The structuralist literary critic attempts to define structural principles that operate intertextually throughout the whole of literature as well as principles that operate in genres and in individual works. The most accessible survey of structuralism and literature is Jonathan Culler's *Structuralist Poetics* (1975).

Substitution: The replacement of one type of foot by another within a base meter. One of the most common and effective methods by which the poet can emphasize a foot. For example, in the line "Thy life/a long/dead calm/of fixed/repose," a spondaic foot (′′) has been substituted for an iambic foot (‿′). Before substitution is possible, the reader's expectations must have been established by a base meter so that a change in those expectations will have an effect. See also *Foot/feet*; *iamb*; *spondee*.

Syllabic meter: The system of meter that measures only the number of syllables per line, without regard to stressed and unstressed syllables.

Symbol: Any sign that a number of people agree stands for something else. Poetic symbols cannot be rigidly defined; a symbol often evokes a cluster of meanings rather than a single specific meaning. For example, the rose, which suggests fragile beauty, gentleness, softness, and sweet aroma, has come to symbolize love, eternal beauty, or virginity. The tide traditionally symbolizes, among other things, time and eternity. Modern poets may use personal symbols; these take on significance in the context of the poem or of a poet's body of work, particularly if they are reinforced throughout. For example, through constant reinforcement, swans in William Butler Yeats's poetry come to mean as much to the reader as they do to the narrator.

Synaeresis: See *Elision*

Synecdoche: The use of a part of an object to stand for the entire object, such as using "heart" to mean a person. Used to emphasize a particular part of the whole or one particular aspect of it. See also *Metonymy*.

Tenor: See *Metaphor*

Tercet: Any form of a rhyming triplet. Examples are *aaa bbb*, as used in Thomas Hardy's "Convergence of the Twain"; *aba cdc*, in which *b* and *d* do not rhyme; *aba bcb*, also known as terza rima.

Terza rima: A three-line stanzaic form in which the middle line of one stanza rhymes with the first line of the following stanza, and whose rhyme scheme is *aba bcb cdc*, and so on. Since the rhyme scheme of one stanza can be completed only by adding the next stanza, terza rima tends to propel itself forward, and as a result of this strong forward motion it is well suited to long narration.

Theme: Recurring elements in a poem that give it meaning; sometimes used interchangeably with motif. A motif is any recurring pattern of images, symbols, ideas, or language, and is usually restricted to the internal workings of the poem. Thus, one might say that there is an animal motif in William Butler Yeats's poem "Sailing to Byzantium." Theme, however, is usually more general and philosophical, so that the theme of "Sailing to Byzantium" might be interpreted as the failure of human attempts to isolate oneself within the world of art.

Third person: The use of linguistic forms that present a poem from the point of view of a narrator, or speaker, who has not been part of the events described and is not probing his or her own relationship to them; rather, the speaker is describing what happened without the use of the word "I" (which would indicate first-person narration). A poet may use a third-person point of view, either limited or omniscient, to establish a distance between the reader and the subject, to give credi-

bility to a large expanse of narration, or to allow the poem to include a number of characters who can be commented on by the narrator.

Tone: The expression of a poet's attitude toward the subject and persona of the poem as well as about himself or herself, society, and the poem's readers. If the ultimate aim of art is to express and control emotions and attitudes, then tone is one of the most important elements of poetry. Tone is created through the denotative and connotative meanings of words and through the sound of language (principally rhyme, consonants, and diction). Adjectives such as "satirical," "compassionate," "empathetic," "ironic," and "sarcastic" are used to describe tone.

Trochee: A foot with one stressed syllable and one unstressed syllable (´˘), as in the line: "Double/double toil and/trouble." Trochaic lines are frequently substituted in an iambic base meter in order to create counterpointing. See also *Foot/feet*; *iamb*.

Truncation: The omission of the last, unstressed syllable of a falling line, as in the line: "Tyger,/tyger/ burning/bright," where the "ly" has been dropped from bright.

Vehicle: See *Metaphor*

Verse: A generic term for poetry, as in *The Oxford Book of English Verse* (1939); poetry that is humorous or superficial, as in light verse or greeting-card verse; and a stanza or line.

Verse drama: Drama that is written in poetic rather than ordinary language and characterized and delivered by the line. Verse drama flourished during the eighteenth century, when the couplet became a standard literary form.

Verse paragraph: A division created within a stichic poem (see *Stanza*) by logic or syntax, rather than by form. Such divisions are important for determining the movement of a poem and the logical association between ideas.

Villanelle: A French verse form that has been assimilated by English prosody, usually composed of nineteen lines divided into five tercets and a quatrain, rhyming *aba*, *bba*, *aba*, *aba*, *abaa*. The third line is repeated in the ninth and fifteenth lines. Dylan Thomas's "Do Not Go Gentle into That Good Night" is a modern English example of a villanelle.

BIBLIOGRAPHY

CONTENTS

ABOUT THIS BIBLIOGRAPHY

This bibliography contains three main sections. The first, "General Reference Sources," lists books that treat poetry of all time periods and countries, including European poets. The section "History of European Poetry" covers sources primarily relevant to poetry from these countries written in five different eras. The final section, "Poets by Country," divides poets and poetry geographically (using current place-names), with added subdivisions for France, Germany, Italy, and Spain.

GENERAL REFERENCE SOURCES

BIOGRAPHICAL SOURCES

Colby, Vineta, ed. *World Authors, 1975-1980*. Wilson Authors Series. New York: H. W. Wilson, 1985.

_____. *World Authors, 1980-1985*. Wilson Authors Series. New York: H. W. Wilson, 1991.

_____. *World Authors, 1985-1990*. Wilson Authors Series. New York: H. W. Wilson, 1995.

Cyclopedia of World Authors. 4th rev. ed. 5 vols. Pasadena, Calif.: Salem Press, 2003.

Dictionary of Literary Biography. 254 vols. Detroit: Gale Research, 1978-   .

International Who's Who in Poetry and Poets' Encyclopaedia. Cambridge, England: International Biographical Centre, 1993.

Jackson, William T. H., ed. *European Writers*. 14 vols. New York: Scribner, 1983-1991.

Kunitz, Stanley, and Vineta Colby, eds. *European Authors, 1000-1900: A Biographical Dictionary of European Literature*. New York: Wilson, 1967.

Serafin, Steven, ed. *Encyclopedia of World Literature in the Twentieth Century*. 3d ed. 4 vols. Detroit: St. James Press, 1999.

_____. *Twentieth-Century Eastern European Writers: First Series*. Dictionary of Literary Biography 215. Detroit: Gale Group, 1999.

_____. *Twentieth-Century Eastern European Writers: Second Series*. Dictionary of Literary Biography 220. Detroit: Gale Group, 2000.

_____. *Twentieth-Century Eastern European Writers: Third Series*. Dictionary of Literary Biography 232. Detroit: Gale Group, 2001.

Seymour-Smith, Martin, and Andrew C. Kimmens, eds. *World Authors, 1900-1950*. 4 vols. Wilson Authors Series. New York: H. W. Wilson, 1996.

Thompson, Clifford, ed. *World Authors, 1990-1995*. Wilson Authors Series. New York: H. W. Wilson, 1999.

Wakeman, John, ed. *World Authors, 1950-1970*. New York: H. W. Wilson, 1975.

_____. *World Authors, 1970-1975*. Wilson Authors Series. New York: H. W. Wilson, 1991.

Willhardt, Mark, and Alan Michael Parker, eds. *Who's Who in Twentieth Century World Poetry*. New York: Routledge, 2000.

CRITICISM

Brooks, Cleanth, and Robert Penn Warren. *Understanding Poetry*. 4th ed. Reprint. Fort Worth, Tex.: Heinle & Heinle, 2003.

Classical and Medieval Literature Criticism. Detroit: Gale Research, 1988-   .

Coleman, Arthur. *A Checklist of Interpretation, 1940-1973, of Classical and Continental Epics and Metrical Romances*. Vol. 2 in *Epic and Romance Criticism*. New York: Watermill, 1974.

Contemporary Literary Criticism. Detroit: Gale Research, 1973-   .

Day, Gary. *Literary Criticism: A New History*. Edinburgh, Scotland: Edinburgh University Press, 2008.

Draper, James P., ed. *World Literature Criticism 1500 to the Present: A Selection of Major Authors from Gale's Literary Criticism Series*. 6 vols. Detroit: Gale Research, 1992.

Habib, M. A. R. *A History of Literary Criticism: From Plato to the Present*. Malden, Mass.: Wiley-Blackwell, 2005.

Jason, Philip K., ed. *Masterplots II: Poetry Series, Revised Edition*. 8 vols. Pasadena, Calif.: Salem Press, 2002.

Krstovic, Jelena, ed. *Hispanic Literature Criticism*. Detroit: Gale Research, 1994.

Literature Criticism from 1400 to 1800. Detroit: Gale Research, 1984-   .

Lodge, David, and Nigel Wood. *Modern Criticism and Theory*. 3d ed. New York: Longman, 2008.

Magill, Frank N., ed. *Magill's Bibliography of Literary Criticism*. 4 vols. Englewood Cliffs, N.J.: Salem Press, 1979.

MLA International Bibliography. New York: Modern Language Association of America, 1922-   .

Nineteenth-Century Literature Criticism. Detroit: Gale Research, 1981-   .

Twentieth-Century Literary Criticism. Detroit: Gale Research, 1978-   .

Vedder, Polly, ed. *World Literature Criticism Supplement: A Selection of Major Authors from Gale's Literary Criticism Series*. 2 vols. Detroit: Gale Research, 1997.

The Year's Work in Modern Language Studies. London: Oxford University Press, 1931.

Young, Robyn V., ed. *Poetry Criticism: Excerpts from Criticism of the Works of the Most Significant and Widely Studied Poets of World Literature*. 29 vols. Detroit: Gale Research, 1991.

DICTIONARIES, HISTORIES, AND HANDBOOKS

Auty, Robert, et al. *Traditions of Heroic and Epic Poetry*. 2 vols. Vol. 1, *The Traditions*; Vol. 2, *Characteristics and Techniques*. Publications of the Modern Humanities Research Association 9, 13. London: Modern Humanities Research Association, 1980, 1989.

Bede, Jean-Albert, and William B. Edgerton, eds. *Columbia Dictionary of Modern European Literature*. 2d ed. New York: Columbia University Press, 1980.

Carey, Gary, and Mary Ellen Snodgrass. *A Multicul-*

tural Dictionary of Literary Terms. Jefferson, N.C.: McFarland, 1999.

Deutsch, Babette. *Poetry Handbook: A Dictionary of Terms*. 4th ed. New York: Funk & Wagnalls, 1974.

Drury, John. *The Poetry Dictionary*. Cincinnati, Ohio: Story Press, 1995.

France, Peter, ed. *The Oxford Guide to Literature in English Translation*. New York: Oxford University Press, 2000.

Henderson, Lesley, ed. *Reference Guide to World Literature*. 2d ed. 2 vols. New York: St. James Press, 1995.

Kinzie, Mary. *A Poet's Guide to Poetry*. Chicago: University of Chicago Press, 1999.

Lennard, John. *The Poetry Handbook: A Guide to Reading Poetry for Pleasure and Practical Criticism*. New York: Oxford University Press, 1996.

Matterson, Stephen, and Darryl Jones. *Studying Poetry*. New York: Oxford University Press, 2000.

Oinas, Felix, ed. *Heroic Epic and Saga: An Introduction to the World's Great Folk Epics*. Bloomington: Indiana University Press, 1978.

Packard, William. *The Poet's Dictionary: A Handbook of Prosody and Poetic Devices*. New York: Harper & Row, 1989.

Preminger, Alex, et al., eds. *The New Princeton Encyclopedia of Poetry and Poetics*. 3d rev. ed. Princeton, N.J.: Princeton University Press, 1993.

Pynsent, Robert B., ed. *Reader's Encyclopedia of Eastern European Literature*. New York: HarperCollins, 1993.

Shipley, Joseph Twadell, ed. *Dictionary of World Literary Terms, Forms, Technique, Criticism*. Rev. ed. Boston: George Allen and Unwin, 1979.

Weber, Harry B., George Gutsche, and P. Rollberg, eds. *The Modern Encyclopedia of East Slavic, Baltic, and Eurasian Literatures*. 10 vols. Gulf Breeze, Fla.: Academic International Press, 1977.

INDEXES OF PRIMARY WORKS

Frankovich, Nicholas, ed. *The Columbia Granger's Index to Poetry in Anthologies*. 11th ed. New York: Columbia University Press, 1997.

_____. *The Columbia Granger's Index to Poetry in Collected and Selected Works*. New York: Columbia University Press, 1997.

Guy, Patricia. *A Women's Poetry Index*. Phoenix, Ariz.: Oryx Press, 1985.

Hazen, Edith P., ed. *Columbia Granger's Index to Poetry*. 10th ed. New York: Columbia University Press, 1994.

Hoffman, Herbert H. *Hoffman's Index to Poetry: European and Latin American Poetry in Anthologies*. Metuchen, N.J.: Scarecrow Press, 1985.

Hoffman, Herbert H., and Rita Ludwig Hoffman, comps. *International Index to Recorded Poetry*. New York: H. W. Wilson, 1983.

Kline, Victoria. *Last Lines: An Index to the Last Lines of Poetry*. 2 vols. Vol. 1, *Last Line Index, Title Index*; Vol. 2, *Author Index, Keyword Index*. New York: Facts On File, 1991.

Marcan, Peter. *Poetry Themes: A Bibliographical Index to Subject Anthologies and Related Criticisms in the English Language, 1875-1975*. Hamden, Conn.: Linnet Books, 1977.

Poem Finder. Great Neck, N.Y.: Roth, 2000.

POETICS, POETIC FORMS, AND GENRES

Attridge, Derek. *Poetic Rhythm: An Introduction*. New York: Cambridge University Press, 1995.

Brogan, T. V. F. *Verseform: A Comparative Bibliography*. Baltimore: Johns Hopkins University Press, 1989.

Fussell, Paul. *Poetic Meter and Poetic Form*. Rev. ed. New York: McGraw-Hill, 1979.

Gasparov, M. L. *A History of European Versification*. Translated by G. S. Smith and Marina Tarlinskaja. New York: Oxford University Press, 1996.

Hollander, John. *Rhyme's Reason*. 3d ed. New Haven,: Yale University Press, 2001.

Jackson, Guida M. *Traditional Epics: A Literary Companion*. New York: Oxford University Press, 1995.

Padgett, Ron, ed. *The Teachers and Writers Handbook of Poetic Forms*. 2d ed. New York: Teachers & Writers Collaborative, 2000.

Pinsky, Robert. *The Sounds of Poetry: A Brief Guide*. New York: Farrar, Straus and Giroux, 1998.

Preminger, Alex, and T. V. F. Brogan, ed. *New Princeton Encyclopedia of Poetry and Poetics*. 3d ed. Princeton, N.J.: Princeton University Press, 1993.

Spiller, Michael R. G. *The Sonnet Sequence: A Study of*

Its Strategies. Studies in Literary Themes and Genres 13. New York: Twayne, 1997.

Turco, Lewis. *The New Book of Forms: A Handbook of Poetics.* Hanover: University Press of New England, 1986.

Williams, Miller. *Patterns of Poetry: An Encyclopedia*

of Forms. Baton Rouge: Louisiana State University Press, 1986.

Wimsatt, William K., ed. *Versification: Major Language Types: Sixteen Essays.* New York: Modern Language Association, 1972.

HISTORY OF EUROPEAN POETRY

ANCIENT AND MEDIEVAL

Briggs, Ward W. *Ancient Greek Authors.* Dictionary of Literary Biography 176. Detroit: Gale Research, 1997.

_____. *Ancient Roman Writers.* Dictionary of Literary Biography 211. Detroit: Gale Group, 1999.

Classen, Albrecht, ed. and trans. *Late-Medieval German Women's Poetry: Secular and Religious Songs.* Rochester, N.Y.: D. S. Brewer, 2004.

Cyzevkyj, Dmytro. *A History of Ukrainian Literature: From the Eleventh to the End of the Nineteenth Century.* Translated by Dolly Ferguson, Doreen Gorsline, and Ulana Petyk, edited by George S. N. Luckyi. 2d ed. New York: Ukrainian Academic Press, 1997.

Gaunt, Simon, and Sarah Key, eds. *The Cambridge Companion to Medieval French Literature.* New York: Cambridge University Press, 2008.

Kleinhenz, Christopher. *The Early Italian Sonnet: The First Century, 1220-1321.* Collezione di Studi e Testi n.s. 2. Lecce, Italy: Milella, 1986.

McTurk, Rory, ed. *A Companion to Old Norse-Icelandic Literature and Culture.* Malden, Mass.: Blackwell, 2005.

Makkai, Adam, ed. *In Quest of the "Miracle Stag": The Poetry of Hungary, an Anthology of Hungarian Poetry in English Translation from the Thirteenth Century to the Present.* Foreword by Árpád Göncz. Urbana: University of Illinois Press, 1996.

Pagis, Dan. *Hebrew Poetry of the Middle Ages and the Renaissance.* Berkeley: University of California Press, 1991.

Palmer, R. Barton, ed. and trans. *Medieval Epic and Romance: An Anthology of English and French*

Narrative. Glen Allen, Va.: College Publishing, 2007.

Sinnreich-Levi, Deborah, and Ian S. Laurie, eds. *Literature of the French and Occitan Middle Ages: Eleventh to Fifteenth Centuries.* Dictionary of Literary Biography 208. Detroit: Gale Group, 1999.

Switten, Margaret Louise. *Music and Poetry in the Middle Ages: A Guide to Research on French and Occitan Song, 1100-1400.* New York: Garland, 1995.

Weevers, Theodoor. *Poetry of the Netherlands in Its European Context, 1170-1930.* London: University of London-Athlone Press, 1960.

RENAISSANCE

Cyzevkyj, Dmytro. *A History of Ukrainian Literature: From the Eleventh to the End of the Nineteenth Century.* Translated by Dolly Ferguson, Doreen Gorsline, and Ulana Petyk, edited by George S. N. Luckyi. 2d ed. New York: Ukrainian Academic Press, 1997.

Makkai, Adam, ed. *In Quest of the "Miracle Stag": The Poetry of Hungary, an Anthology of Hungarian Poetry in English Translation from the Thirteenth Century to the Present.* Foreword by Árpád Göncz. Urbana: University of Illinois Press, 1996.

Moss, Ann. *Poetry and Fable: Studies in Mythological Narrative in Sixteenth-Century France.* New York: Cambridge University Press, 2009.

Pagis, Dan. *Hebrew Poetry of the Middle Ages and the Renaissance.* Berkeley: University of California Press, 1991.

Stortoni, Laura A., and Mary P. Lillie, eds. *Women Poets of the Italian Renaissance: Courtly Ladies and Courtesans.* New York: Italica, 1997.

Weevers, Theodoor. *Poetry of the Netherlands in Its European Context, 1170-1930*. London: University of London-Athlone Press, 1960.

SEVENTEENTH AND EIGHTEENTH CENTURIES

Browning, Robert M. *German Poetry from 1750 to 1900*. New York: Continuum, 1984.

Cyzevkyj, Dmytro. *A History of Ukrainian Literature: From the Eleventh to the End of the Nineteenth Century*. Translated by Dolly Ferguson, Doreen Gorsline, and Ulana Petyk, edited by George S. N. Luckyj. 2d ed. New York: Ukrainian Academic Press, 1997.

Foster, David Williams, Daniel Altamiranda, and Carmen de Urioste, eds. *Spanish Literature: 1700 to the Present*. Spanish Literature 3. New York: Garland, 2000.

Harper, Anthony, and Margaret C. Ives. *Sappho in the Shadows: Essays on the Work of German Women Poets of the Age of Goethe, 1749-1832*. New York: Peter Lang, 2000.

Makkai, Adam, ed. *In Quest of the "Miracle Stag": The Poetry of Hungary, an Anthology of Hungarian Poetry in English Translation from the Thirteenth Century to the Present*. Foreword by Árpád Göncz. Urbana: University of Illinois Press, 1996.

Weevers, Theodoor. *Poetry of the Netherlands in Its European Context, 1170-1930*. London: University of London-Athlone Press, 1960.

NINETEENTH CENTURY

Beck, Richard. *History of Icelandic Poets, 1800-1940*. Ithaca, N.Y.: Cornell University Press, 1950.

Beum, Robert, ed. *Nineteenth-Century French Poets*. Dictionary of Literary Biography 217. Detroit: Gale Group, 2000.

Bishop, Michael. *Nineteenth-Century French Poetry*. Twayne's Critical History of Poetry Series. New York: Twayne, 1993.

Browning, Robert M. *German Poetry from 1750 to 1900*. New York: Continuum, 1984.

Cyzevkyj, Dmytro. *A History of Ukrainian Literature: From the Eleventh to the End of the Nineteenth Century*. Translated by Dolly Ferguson, Doreen Gorsline, and Ulana Petyk, edited by George S. N.

Luckyj. 2d ed. New York: Ukrainian Academic Press, 1997.

Forsås-Scott, Helena. *Swedish Women's Writing, 1850-1995*. Atlantic Highlands, N.J.: Athlone, 1997.

Foster, David Williams, Daniel Altamiranda, and Carmen de Urioste, eds. *Spanish Literature: 1700 to the Present*. Spanish Literature 3. New York: Garland, 2000.

Harper, Anthony, and Margaret C. Ives. *Sappho in the Shadows: Essays on the Work of German Women Poets of the Age of Goethe, 1749-1832*. New York: Peter Lang, 2000.

Makkai, Adam, ed. *In Quest of the "Miracle Stag": The Poetry of Hungary, an Anthology of Hungarian Poetry in English Translation from the Thirteenth Century to the Present*. Foreword by Árpád Göncz. Urbana: University of Illinois Press, 1996.

Poggioli, Renato. *The Poets of Russia, 1890-1930*. Cambridge, Mass.: Harvard University Press, 1960.

Tschizewskij, Dmitrij. *History of Nineteenth-Century Russian Literature*. Translated by Richard Noel Porter, edited by Serge A. Zenkovsky. Nashville, Tenn.: Greenwood Press, 1974.

Weevers, Theodoor. *Poetry of the Netherlands in Its European Context, 1170-1930*. London: University of London-Athlone Press, 1960.

Wiener, Leo. *The History of Yiddish Literature in the Nineteenth Century*. 2d ed. New York: Hermon Press, 1972.

TWENTIETH CENTURY AND CONTEMPORARY

Barkan, Stanley H., ed. *Four Postwar Catalan Poets*. Rev. ed. Translated by David H. Rosenthal. Merrick, N.Y.: Cross-Cultural Communications, 1994.

Beck, Richard. *History of Icelandic Poets, 1800-1940*. Ithaca, N.Y.: Cornell University Press, 1950.

Bellver, Catherine G. *Absence and Presence: Spanish Women Poets of the Twenties and Thirties*. Lewisburg, Pa.: Bucknell University Press, 2001.

Bien, Peter, et al., eds. *A Century of Greek Poetry, 1900-2000*. Bilingual edition. Westwood, N.J.: Cosmos, 2004.

Boland, Eavan, ed. and trans. *After Every War: Twenti-*

eth-Century Women Poets. Princeton, N.J.: Princeton University Press, 2004.

Caws, Mary Ann, ed. *The Yale Anthology of Twentieth-Century French Poetry*. New Haven, Conn.: Yale University Press, 2004.

Crowe, Anna, ed. *Light off Water: Twenty-five Catalan Poems, 1978-2002*. Translated by Iolanda Pelegri. Manchester, England: Carcanet Press, 2007.

Dombroski, Robert S. *Italy: Fiction, Theater, Poetry, Film Since 1950*. Middle Village, N.Y.: Council on National Literatures, 2000.

Forsås-Scott, Helena. *Swedish Women's Writing, 1850-1995*. Atlantic Highlands, N.J.: Athlone, 1997.

Foster, David Williams, Daniel Altamiranda, and Carmen de Urioste, eds. *Spanish Literature: 1700 to the Present*. Spanish Literature 3. New York: Garland, 2000.

French, Alfred. *The Poets of Prague: Czech Poetry Between the Wars*. New York: Oxford University Press, 1969.

Hofmann, Michael, ed. *Twentieth-Century German Poetry: An Anthology*. New York: Farrar, Straus and Giroux, 2008.

Kolumban, Nicholas, ed. and trans. *Turmoil in Hungary: An Anthology of Twentieth Century Hungarian Poetry*. St. Paul, Minn.: New Rivers Press, 1996.

Leeder, Karen J. *Breaking Boundaries: A New Generation of Poets in the GDR, 1979-1989*. New York: Oxford University Press, 1996.

Makkai, Adam, ed. *In Quest of the "Miracle Stag": The Poetry of Hungary, an Anthology of Hungarian Poetry in English Translation from the Thirteenth Century to the Present*. Foreword by Árpád Göncz. Urbana: University of Illinois Press, 1996.

Mudrovic, W. Michael. *Mirror, Mirror on the Page: Identity and Subjectivity in Spanish Women's Poetry, 1975-2000*. Bethlehem, Pa.: Lehigh University Press, 2009.

Nader, Andrés José, ed. *Traumatic Verses: On Poetry in German from the Concentration Camps, 1933-1945*. Rochester, N.Y.: Camden House, 2007.

Poggioli, Renato. *The Poets of Russia, 1890-1930*. Cambridge, Mass.: Harvard University Press, 1960.

Rosenthal, David H. *Postwar Catalan Poetry*. Lewisburg, Pa.: Bucknell University Press, 1991.

St. Martin, Hardie, ed. *Roots and Wings: Poetry from Spain, 1900-1975*. Buffalo, N.Y.: White Pine Press, 2004.

Stecher-Hansen, Marianne, ed. *Twentieth-Century Danish Writers*. Dictionary of Literary Biography 214. Detroit: Gale Group, 1999.

Van Dyck, Karen. *Kassandra and the Censors: Greek Poetry Since 1967*. Ithaca, N.Y.: Cornell University Press, 1998.

Volkova, Bronislava, and Clarice Cloutier, eds. and trans. *Up the Devil's Back: A Bilingual Anthology of Twentieth-Century Czech Poetry*. Bloomington, Ind.: Slavica, 2008.

Weevers, Theodoor. *Poetry of the Netherlands in Its European Context, 1170-1930*. London: University of London-Athlone Press, 1960.

Zawacki, Andrew, ed. *Afterwards: Slovenian Writing, 1945-1995*. Buffalo, N.Y.: White Pine Press, 1999.

POETS BY COUNTRY

ALBANIA

Elsie, Robert. *Dictionary of Albanian Literature*. Westport, Conn.: Greenwood Press, 1986.

_____. *Studies in Modern Albanian Literature and Culture*. East European Monographs 455. New York: Distributed by Columbia University Press, 1996.

Jakobson, Roman, C. H. van Schooneveld, and Dean S. Worth, eds. *Slavic Poetics: Essays in Honor of Kiril Taranovsky*. Slavistic Printings and Reprintings 267. The Hague: Mouton, 1973.

Mihailovich, Vasa D., comp. and ed. *Modern Slavic Literatures*. New York: F. Ungar, 1972.

Pipa, Arshi. *Contemporary Albanian Literature*. East

European Monographs 305. New York: Distributed by Columbia University Press, 1991.

Ressuli, Namik. *Albanian Literature*. Edited by Eduard Lico. Boston: Pan-Albanian Federation of America Vatra, 1987.

Tschizewskij, Dmitrij. *Comparative History of Slavic Literatures*. Translated by Richard Noel Porter and Martin P. Rice, edited by Serge A. Zenkovsky. Nashville, Tenn.: Vanderbilt University Press, 1971.

ANCIENT GREECE AND ROME (*see also* GREECE)

Albrecht, Michael von. *Roman Epic: An Interpretive Introduction*. Boston: Brill, 1999.

Braund, Susanna Morton. *Latin Literature*. New York: Routledge, 2002.

Briggs, Ward W. *Ancient Greek Authors*. Dictionary of Literary Biography 176. Detroit: Gale Research, 1997.

_____. *Ancient Roman Writers*. Dictionary of Literary Biography 211. Detroit: Gale Group, 1999.

Budelmann, Felix, ed. *The Cambridge Companion to Greek Lyric*. New York: Cambridge University Press, 2009.

Constantine, Peter, et al., eds. *The Greek Poets: Homer to the Present*. New York: W. W. Norton, 2009.

David, A. P. *The Dance of the Muses: Choral Theory and Ancient Greek Poetics*. New York: Oxford University Press, 2006.

Dihle, Albrecht, and Clare Krojzl, trans. *A History of Greek Literature: From Homer to the Hellenistic Period*. New York: Routledge, 1994.

Green, Ellen, ed. *Women Poets in Ancient Greece and Rome*. Norman: University of Oklahoma Press, 2005.

Harrison, Stephen, ed. *A Companion to Latin Literature*. Malden, Mass.: Blackwell, 2004.

Kessels, A. H. M., and W. J. Verdenius, comps. *A Concise Bibliography of Ancient Greek Literature*. 2d ed. Apeldoorn, Netherlands: Administratief Centrum, 1982.

King, Katherine Callen. *Ancient Epic*. Hoboken, N.J.: Wiley-Blackwell, 2009.

Lefkowitz, Mary R. *The Lives of the Greek Poets*. Baltimore: The Johns Hopkins University Press, 1981.

Lyne, R. O. *Collected Papers on Latin Poetry*. Edited by S. J. Harrison. New York: Oxford University Press, 2007.

Raffel, Burton, trans. *Pure Pagan: Seven Centuries of Greek Poems and Fragments*. New York: Random House, 2004.

West, M. L., trans. *Greek Lyric Poetry*. 1993. Reprint. New York: Oxford University Press, 2008.

BULGARIA

Jakobson, Roman, C. H. van Schooneveld, and Dean S. Worth, eds. *Slavic Poetics: Essays in Honor of Kiril Taranovsky*. Slavistic Printings and Reprintings 267. The Hague: Mouton, 1973.

Matejic, Mateja, et al. *A Biobibliographical Handbook of Bulgarian Authors*. Translated by Predrag Matejic, edited by Karen L. Black. Columbus, Ohio: Slavica, 1981.

Mihailovich, Vasa D., comp. and ed. *Modern Slavic Literatures*. New York: F. Ungar, 1972.

Tschizewskij, Dmitrij. *Comparative History of Slavic Literatures*. Translated by Richard Noel Porter and Martin P. Rice, edited by Serge A. Zenkovsky. Nashville, Tenn.: Vanderbilt University Press, 1971.

CROATIA

Jakobson, Roman, C. H. van Schooneveld, and Dean S. Worth, eds. *Slavic Poetics: Essays in Honor of Kiril Taranovsky*. Slavistic Printings and Reprintings 267. The Hague: Mouton, 1973.

Mihailovich, Vasa D., comp. and ed. *Modern Slavic Literatures*. New York: F. Ungar, 1972.

Miletich, John S. *Love Lyric and Other Poems of the Croatian Renaissance: A Bilingual Anthology*. Bloomington, Ind.: Slavica, 2009.

Tschizewskij, Dmitrij. *Comparative History of Slavic Literatures*. Translated by Richard Noel Porter and Martin P. Rice, edited by Serge A. Zenkovsky. Nashville, Tenn.: Vanderbilt University Press, 1971.

CZECH REPUBLIC

French, Alfred. *The Poets of Prague: Czech Poetry Between the Wars*. New York: Oxford University Press, 1969.

Jakobson, Roman, C. H. van Schooneveld, and Dean S. Worth, eds. *Slavic Poetics: Essays in Honor of Kiril*

Taranovsky. Slavistic Printings and Reprintings 267. The Hague: Mouton, 1973.

Kovtun, George J. *Czech and Slovak Literature in English: A Bibliography*. 2d ed. Washington, D.C.: Library of Congress, 1988.

Lodge, Kirsten, ed. and trans. *Solitude, Vanity, Night: An Anthology of Czech Decadent Poetry*. Prague: Charles University, 2007.

Mihailovich, Vasa D., comp. and ed. *Modern Slavic Literatures*. New York: F. Ungar, 1972.

Novák, Arne. *Czech Literature*. Translated by Peter Kussi, edited by William E. Harkins. Joint Committee on Eastern Europe Publication Series 4. Ann Arbor: Michigan Slavic Publications, 1976.

Tschizewskij, Dmitrij. *Comparative History of Slavic Literatures*. Translated by Richard Noel Porter and Martin P. Rice, edited by Serge A. Zenkovsky. Nashville, Tenn.: Vanderbilt University Press, 1971.

Volkova, Bronislava, and Clarice Cloutier, eds. and trans. *Up the Devil's Back: A Bilingual Anthology of Twentieth-Century Czech Poetry*. Bloomington, Ind.: Slavica, 2008.

DENMARK

Borum, Poul. *Danish Literature: A Short Critical Survey*. Copenhagen: Det Danske Selskab, 1979.

Rossel, Sven H., ed. *A History of Danish Literature*. Lincoln: University of Nebraska Press, 1992.

Sjåvik, Jan. *Historical Dictionary of Scandinavian Literature and Theater*. Lanham, Md.: Scarecrow Press, 2006.

Stecher-Hansen, Marianne, ed. *Twentieth-Century Danish Writers*. Dictionary of Literary Biography 214. Detroit: Gale Group, 1999.

Sumari, Anni, and Nicolaj Stochholm, eds. *The Other Side of Landscape: An Anthology of Contemporary Nordic Poetry*. New York: Slope Editions, 2006.

Zuck, Virpi, ed. *Dictionary of Scandinavian Literature*. New York: Greenwood Press, 1990.

FRANCE

Bibliography

Kempton, Richard. *French Literature: An Annotated Guide to Selected Bibliographies*. New York: Modern Language Association of America, 1981.

Biographical sources

Beum, Robert, ed. *Nineteenth-Century French Poets*. Dictionary of Literary Biography 217. Detroit: Gale Group, 2000.

Sinnreich-Levi, Deborah, and Ian S. Laurie, eds. *Literature of the French and Occitan Middle Ages: Eleventh to Fifteenth Centuries*. Dictionary of Literary Biography 208. Detroit: Gale Group, 1999.

Criticism

Coleman, Kathleen. *Guide to French Poetry Explication*. New York: G. K. Hall, 1993.

Dictionaries, histories, and handbooks

Acquisto, Joseph. *French Symbolist Poetry and the Idea of Music*. Burlington, Vt.: Ashgate, 2006.

Aulestia, Gorka. *The Basque Poetic Tradition*. Translated by Linda White. Reno: University of Nevada Press, 2000.

Banks, Kathryn. *Cosmos and Image in the Renaissance: French Love Lyric and Natural-Philosophical Poetry*. London: Legenda, 2008.

Bishop, Michael. *Nineteenth-Century French Poetry*. Twayne's Critical History of Poetry Series. New York: Twayne, 1993.

Brereton, Geoffrey. *An Introduction to the French Poets, Villon to the Present Day*. 2d rev. ed. London: Methuen, 1973.

Caws, Mary Ann, ed. *The Yale Anthology of Twentieth-Century French Poetry*. New Haven, Conn.: Yale University Press, 2004.

Dolbow, Sandra W. *Dictionary of Modern French Literature: From the Age of Reason Through Realism*. New York: Greenwood Press, 1986.

France, Peter, ed. *The New Oxford Companion to Literature in French*. New York: Clarendon Press, 1995.

Gaunt, Simon, and Sarah Key, eds. *The Cambridge Companion to Medieval French Literature*. New York: Cambridge University Press, 2008.

_____. *The Troubadours: An Introduction*. New York: Cambridge University Press, 1999.

Levi, Anthony. *Guide to French Literature*. 2 vols. Chicago: St. James Press, 1992-1994.

Moss, Ann. *Poetry and Fable: Studies in Mythological Narrative in Sixteenth-Century France*. New York: Cambridge University Press, 2009.

Palmer, R. Barton, ed. and trans. *Medieval Epic and*

Romance: An Anthology of English and French Narrative. Glen Allen, Va.: College Publishing, 2007.

Shaw, Mary Lewis. *The Cambridge Introduction to French Poetry*. New York: Cambridge University Press, 2003.

Switten, Margaret Louise. *Music and Poetry in the Middle Ages: A Guide to Research on French and Occitan Song, 1100-1400*. New York: Garland, 1995.

Thomas, Jean-Jacques, and Steven Winspur. *Poeticized Language: The Foundations of Contemporary French Poetry*. University Park: Pennsylvania State University Press, 1999.

Willett, Laura, trans. *Poetry and Language in Sixteenth Century France: Du Bellay, Ronsard, Sébillet*. Toronto: Centre for Reformation and Renaissance Studies, Victoria University, 2004.

Women writers

Sartori, Eva Martin, and Dorothy Wynne Zimmerman. *French Women Writers: A Bio-bibliographical Source Book*. New York: Greenwood Press, 1991.

Shapiro, Norman R., ed. and trans. *French Women Poets of Nine Centuries: The Distaff and the Pen*. Baltimore: Johns Hopkins University Press, 2008.

GERMANY

Biographical sources

Hardin, James, ed. *German Baroque Writers, 1580-1660*. Dictionary of Literary Biography 164. Detroit: Gale Research, 1996.

_____. *German Baroque Writers, 1661-1730*. Dictionary of Literary Biography 168. Detroit: Gale Research, 1996.

Hardin, James, and Will Hasty, eds. *German Writers and Works of the Early Middle Ages, 800-1170*. Dictionary of Literary Biography 148. Detroit: Gale Research, 1995.

_____. *German Writers and Works of the High Middle Ages, 1170-1280*. Dictionary of Literary Biography 138. Detroit: Gale Research, 1994.

Hardin, James, and Siegfried Mews, eds. *Nineteenth-Century German Writers to 1840*. Dictionary of Literary Biography 133. Detroit: Gale Research, 1993.

_____. *Nineteenth-Century German Writers, 1841-1900*. Dictionary of Literary Biography 129. Detroit: Gale Research, 1993.

Hardin, James, and Max Reinhart eds. *German Writers of the Renaissance and Reformation, 1280-1580*. Dictionary of Literary Biography 179. Detroit: Gale Group, 1997.

Hardin, James, and Christoph E. Schweitzer, eds. *German Writers from the Enlightment to Sturm und Drang, 1720-1764*. Dictionary of Literary Biography 97. Detroit: Gale Research, 1990.

_____. *German Writers in the Age of Goethe, 1789-1832*. Dictionary of Literary Biography 90. Detroit: Gale Research, 1989.

_____. *German Writers in the Age of Goethe: Sturm und Drang to Classicism*. Dictionary of Literary Biography 94. Detroit: Gale Research, 1990.

Dictionaries, histories, and handbooks

Appleby, Carol. *German Romantic Poetry: Goethe, Novalis, Heine, Hölderlin*. Maidstone, Kent, England: Crescent Moon, 2008.

Baird, Jay W. *Hitler's War Poets: Literature and Politics in the Third Reich*. New York: Cambridge University Press, 2008.

Browning, Robert M. *German Poetry from 1750 to 1900*. New York: Continuum, 1984.

_____. *German Poetry in the Age of the Enlightenment: From Brockes to Klopstock*. University Park: Pennsylvania State University Press, 1978.

Dobozy, Maria. *Re-membering the Present: The Medieval German Poet-Minstrel in Cultural Context*. Turnhout, Belgium: Brepois, 2005.

Faulhaber, Uwe K., and Penrith B. Goff. *German Literature: An Annotated Reference Guide*. New York: Garland, 1979.

Hanak, Miroslav John. *A Guide to Romantic Poetry in Germany*. New York: Peter Lang, 1987.

Hofmann, Michael, ed. *Twentieth-Century German Poetry: An Anthology*. New York: Farrar, Straus and Giroux, 2008.

Hutchinson, Peter, ed. *Landmarks in German Poetry*. New York: Peter Lang, 2000.

Leeder, Karen J. *Breaking Boundaries: A New Generation of Poets in the GDR, 1979-1989*. New York: Oxford University Press, 1996.

Mathieu, Gustave, and Guy Stern, eds. *Introduction to*

German Poetry. New York: Dover Publications, 1991.

Nader, Andrés José, ed. *Traumatic Verses: On Poetry in German from the Concentration Camps, 1933-1945*. Rochester, N.Y.: Camden House, 2007.

Owen, Ruth J. *The Poet's Role: Lyric Responses to German Unification by Poets from the GDR*. Amsterdam: Rodopi, 2001.

Women writers

Boland, Eavan, ed. and trans. *After Every War: Twentieth-Century Women Poets*. Princeton, N.J.: Princeton University Press, 2004.

Classen, Albrecht, ed. and trans. *Late-Medieval German Women's Poetry: Secular and Religious Songs*. Rochester, N.Y.: D. S. Brewer, 2004.

Harper, Anthony, and Margaret C. Ives. *Sappho in the Shadows: Essays on the Work of German Women Poets of the Age of Goethe, 1749-1832*. New York: Peter Lang, 2000.

GREECE (*see also* ANCIENT GREECE AND ROME)

Bien, Peter, et al., eds. *A Century of Greek Poetry, 1900-2000*. Bilingual ed. Westwood, N.J.: Cosmos, 2004.

Constantine, Peter, et al., eds. *The Greek Poets: Homer to the Present*. New York: W. W. Norton, 2009.

Demaras, Konstantinos. *A History of Modern Greek Literature*. Translated by Mary P. Gianos. Albany: State University of New York Press, 1972.

Saïd, Suzanne, and Monique Trédé. *A Short History of Greek Literature*. Translated by Trista Selous et al. New York: Routledge, 1999.

Valaoritis, Nanos, and Thanasis Maskaleris, eds. *An Anthology of Modern Greek Poetry*. Jersey City, N.J.: Talisman House, 2003.

Van Dyck, Karen. *Kassandra and the Censors: Greek Poetry Since 1967*. Ithaca, N.Y.: Cornell University Press, 1998.

HUNGARY

Gömöri, George, and George Szirtes, eds. *The Colonnade of Teeth: Modern Hungarian Poetry*. Chester Springs, Pa.: Dufour Editions, 1996.

Kolumban, Nicholas, ed. and trans. *Turmoil in Hungary: An Anthology of Twentieth Century Hungar-*

ian Poetry. St. Paul, Minn.: New Rivers Press, 1996.

Makkai, Adam, ed. *In Quest of the "Miracle Stag": The Poetry of Hungary, an Anthology of Hungarian Poetry in English Translation from the Thirteenth Century to the Present*. Foreword by Árpád Göncz. Urbana: University of Illinois Press, 1996.

Suleiman, Susan Rubin, and Éva Forgács, eds. *Contemporary Jewish Writing in Hungary: An Anthology*. Lincoln: University of Nebraska Press, 2003.

Szirtes, George, ed. *Leopard V: An Island of Sound—Poetry and Fiction Before and Beyond the Iron Curtain*. New York: Random House, 2004.

ICELAND

Beck, Richard. *History of Icelandic Poets, 1800-1940*. Ithaca, N.Y.: Cornell University Press, 1950.

McTurk, Rory, ed. *A Companion to Old Norse-Icelandic Literature and Culture*. Malden, Mass.: Blackwell, 2005.

Neijman, Daisy, ed. *A History of Icelandic Literature*. Vol. 5 in *A History of Scandinavian Literatures*, edited by Sven H. Rossel. Lincoln: University of Nebraska Press, 2006.

Sjåvik, Jan. *Historical Dictionary of Scandinavian Literature and Theater*. Lanham, Md.: Scarecrow Press, 2006.

Sumari, Anni, and Nicolaj Stochholm, eds. *The Other Side of Landscape: An Anthology of Contemporary Nordic Poetry*. New York: Slope Editions, 2006.

Zuck, Virpi, ed. *Dictionary of Scandinavian Literature*. New York: Greenwood Press, 1990.

ISRAEL

Alonso Schokel, Luis. *A Manual of Hebrew Poetics*. Subsidia Biblica 11. Rome: Editrice Pontificio Istituto Biblico, 1988.

Alter, Robert. *The Art of Biblical Poetry*. New York: Basic Books, 1985.

Burnshaw, Stanley, T. Carmi, and Ezra Spicehandler, eds. *The Modern Hebrew Poem Itself: From the Beginnings to the Present, Sixty-nine Poems in a New Presentation*. With new afterword, "Hebrew Poetry from 1965 to 1988." Cambridge, Mass.: Harvard University Press, 1989.

Gevirtz, Stanley. *Patterns in the Early Poetry of Israel.* Chicago: University of Chicago Press, 1963.

Kugel, James L. *The Great Poems of the Bible: A Reader's Companion with New Translations.* New York: Free Press, 1999.

Liptzin, Solomon. *A History of Yiddish Literature.* Middle Village, N.Y.: Jonathan David, 1985.

Madison, Charles Allan. *Yiddish Literature: Its Scope and Major Writers.* New York: F. Ungar, 1968.

O'Connor, M. *Hebrew Verse Structure.* Winona Lake, Ind.: Eisenbrauns, 1980.

Pagis, Dan. *Hebrew Poetry of the Middle Ages and the Renaissance.* Berkeley: University of California Press, 1991.

Petersen, David L., and Kent Harold Richards. *Interpreting Hebrew Poetry.* Minneapolis: Fortress Press, 1992.

Watson, Wilfred G. E. *Classical Hebrew Poetry: A Guide to Its Techniques.* 2d ed. Sheffield, England: JSOT Press, 1986.

Wiener, Leo. *The History of Yiddish Literature in the Nineteenth Century.* 2d ed. New York: Hermon Press, 1972.

Zinberg, Israel. *Old Yiddish Literature from Its Origins to the Haskalah Period.* Translated and edited by Bernard Martin. Cincinnati: Hebrew Union College Press, 1975.

ITALY

Biographical sources

De Stasio, Giovanna Wedel, Glauco Cambon, and Antonio Illiano, eds. *Twentieth-Century Italian Poets: First Series.* Dictionary of Literary Biography 114. Detroit: Gale Research, 1992.

_____. *Twentieth-Century Italian Poets: Second Series.* Dictionary of Literary Biography 128. Detroit: Gale Research, 1993.

Dictionaries, histories, and handbooks

Bohn, Willard, ed. and trans. *Italian Futurist Poetry.* Toronto: University of Toronto Press, 2005.

Bondanella, Peter, and Julia Conaway Bondanella, eds. *Dictionary of Italian Literature.* Rev. ed. Westport, Conn.: Greenwood Press, 1996.

Cavallo, Jo Ann. *The Romance Epics of Boiardo, Ariosto, and Tasso: From Public Duty to Private Pleasure.* Toronto: University of Toronto Press, 2004.

Condini, Ned, ed. and trans. *An Anthology of Modern Italian Poetry in English Translation, with Italian Text.* New York: Modern Language Association of America, 2009.

Dombroski, Robert S. *Italy: Fiction, Theater, Poetry, Film Since 1950.* Middle Village, N.Y.: Council on National Literatures, 2000.

Holmes, Olivia. *Assembling the Lyric Self: Authorship from Troubador Song to Italian Poetry Book.* Minneapolis: University of Minnesota Press, 2000.

Italian Poets of the Twentieth Century. Florence, Italy: Casalini Libri, 1997.

Kleinhenz, Christopher. *The Early Italian Sonnet: The First Century, 1220-1321.* Collezione di Studi e Testi n.s. 2. Lecce, Italy: Milella, 1986.

Payne, Roberta L., ed. *Selection of Modern Italian Poetry in Translation.* Montreal: McGill-Queen's University Press, 2004.

Zatti, Sergio. *The Quest for Epic: From Ariosto to Tasso.* Translated by Sally Hill with Dennis Looney, edited by Looney. Toronto: University of Toronto Press, 2006.

Women writers

Blum, Cinzia Sartini, and Lara Trubowitz, eds. and trans. *Contemporary Italian Women Poets: A Bilingual Anthology.* New York: Italica Press, 2001.

Frabotta, Biancamaria, ed. *Italian Women Poets.* Translated by Corrado Federici. Toronto: Guernica Editions, 2002.

Stortoni, Laura A., and Mary P. Lillie, eds. *Women Poets of the Italian Renaissance: Courtly Ladies and Courtesans.* New York: Italica, 1997.

MACEDONIA

Jakobson, Roman, C. H. van Schooneveld, and Dean S. Worth, eds. *Slavic Poetics: Essays in Honor of Kiril Taranovsky.* Slavistic Printings and Reprintings 267. The Hague: Mouton, 1973.

Mihailovich, Vasa D., comp. and ed. *Modern Slavic Literatures.* New York: F. Ungar, 1972.

Osers, Ewald, ed. *Contemporary Macedonian Poetry.* Translated by Eward Osers. London: Kultura/Forest Books, 1991.

Tschizewskij, Dmitrij. *Comparative History of Slavic Literatures*. Translated by Richard Noel Porter and Martin P. Rice, edited by Serge A. Zenkovsky. Nashville, Tenn.: Vanderbilt University Press, 1971.

NETHERLANDS AND BELGIUM

Meijer, Reinder P. *Literature of the Low Countries: A Short History of Dutch Literature in the Netherlands and Belgium*. New ed. Boston: Nijhoff, 1978.

Nieuwenhuys, Robert. *Mirror of the Indies: A History of Dutch Colonial Literature*. Translated by Frans van Rosevelt, edited by E. M. Beekman. Library of the Indies. Amherst: University of Massachusetts Press, 1982.

Vermij, Lucie, and Martje Breedt Bruyn. *Women Writers from the Netherlands and Flanders*. Amsterdam: International Feminist Book Fair Press/ Dekker, 1992.

Weevers, Theodoor. *Poetry of the Netherlands in Its European Context, 1170-1930*. London: University of London-Athlone Press, 1960.

NORWAY

McTurk, Rory, ed. *A Companion to Old Norse-Icelandic Literature and Culture*. Malden, Mass.: Blackwell, 2005.

Naess, Harald S. *A History of Norwegian Literature*. Lincoln: University of Nebraska Press, 1993.

Neijman, Daisy, ed. *A History of Icelandic Literature*. Vol. 5 in *A History of Scandinavian Literatures*, edited by Sven H. Rossel. Lincoln: University of Nebraska Press, 2006.

Sjåvik, Jan. *Historical Dictionary of Scandinavian Literature and Theater*. Lanham, Md.: Scarecrow Press, 2006.

Sumari, Anni, and Nicolaj Stochholm, eds. *The Other Side of Landscape: An Anthology of Contemporary Nordic Poetry*. New York: Slope Editions, 2006.

Zuck, Virpi, ed. *Dictionary of Scandinavian Literature*. New York: Greenwood Press, 1990.

POLAND

Barańczak, Stanisław, and Clare Cavanagh, eds. and trans. *Polish Poetry of the Last Two Decades of Communist Rule: Spoiling Cannibals' Fun*. Fore-word by Helen Vendler. Evanston, Ill.: Northwestern University Press, 1991.

Carpenter, Bogdana, ed. *Monumenta Polonica: The First Four Centuries of Polish Poetry, a Bilingual Anthology*. Ann Arbor: Michigan Slavic Publications, 1989.

Czerniawski, Adam, ed. *The Mature Laurel: Essays on Modern Polish Poetry*. Chester Springs, Pa.: Dufour Editions, 1991.

Czerwinski, E. J., ed. *Dictionary of Polish Literature*. Westport, Conn.: Greenwood Press, 1994.

Grol, Regina, ed. *Ambers Aglow: An Anthology of Contemporary Polish Women's Poetry*. Austin, Tex.: Host, 1996.

Jakobson, Roman, C. H. van Schooneveld, and Dean S. Worth, eds. *Slavic Poetics: Essays in Honor of Kiril Taranovsky*. Slavistic Printings and Reprintings 267. The Hague: Mouton, 1973.

Mengham, Rod, et al., trans. *Altered State: The New Polish Poetry*. Ottawa, Ont.: Arc, 2003.

Mihailovich, Vasa D., comp. and ed. *Modern Slavic Literatures*. New York: F. Ungar, 1972.

Miłosz, Czesław, ed. *Postwar Polish Poetry: An Anthology*. 3d ed. Berkeley: University of California Press, 1983.

Tschizewskij, Dmitrij. *Comparative History of Slavic Literatures*. Translated by Richard Noel Porter and Martin P. Rice, edited by Serge A. Zenkovsky. Nashville, Tenn.: Vanderbilt University Press, 1971.

SERBIA

Holton, Milne, and Vasa D. Mihailovich, eds. and trans. *Serbian Poetry from the Beginnings to the Present*. New Haven, Conn.: Yale Center for International and Area Studies, 1988.

Jakobson, Roman, C. H. van Schooneveld, and Dean S. Worth, eds. *Slavic Poetics: Essays in Honor of Kiril Taranovsky*. Slavistic Printings and Reprintings 267. The Hague: Mouton, 1973.

Mihailovich, Vasa D., comp. and ed. *Modern Slavic Literatures*. New York: F. Ungar, 1972.

Simic, Charles, ed. and trans. *The Horse Has Six Legs: An Anthology of Serbian Poetry*. St. Paul, Minn.: Graywolf Press, 1992.

Tschizewskij, Dmitrij. *Comparative History of Slavic*

Literatures. Translated by Richard Noel Porter and Martin P. Rice, edited by Serge A. Zenkovsky. Nashville, Tenn.: Vanderbilt University Press, 1971.

SLOVAKIA

Jakobson, Roman, C. H. van Schooneveld, and Dean S. Worth, eds. *Slavic Poetics: Essays in Honor of Kiril Taranovsky*. Slavistic Printings and Reprintings 267. The Hague: Mouton, 1973.

Kovtun, George J. *Czech and Slovak Literature in English: A Bibliography*. 2d ed. Washington, D.C.: Library of Congress, 1988.

Kramoris, Ivan Joseph, ed. *An Anthology of Slovak Poetry: A Selection of Lyric and Narrative Poems and Folk Ballads in Slovak and English*. Scranton, Pa.: Obrana Press, 1947.

Mihailovich, Vasa D., comp. and ed. *Modern Slavic Literatures*. New York: F. Ungar, 1972.

Petro, Peter. *A History of Slovak Literature*. Montreal: McGill-Queen's University Press, 1995.

Smith, James Sutherland, Pavol Hudik, and Jan Bajanek, eds. *In Search of Beauty: An Anthology of Contemporary Slovak Poetry in English*. Translated by Jan Bajanek. Mundelein, Ill.: Bolchazy-Carducci, 2004.

Tschizewskij, Dmitrij. *Comparative History of Slavic Literatures*. Translated by Richard Noel Porter and Martin P. Rice, edited by Serge A. Zenkovsky. Nashville, Tenn.: Vanderbilt University Press, 1971.

SLOVENIA

Cooper, Henry R., ed. *A Bilingual Anthology of Slovene Literature*. Bloomington, Ind.: Slavica, 2003.

Jakobson, Roman, C. H. van Schooneveld, and Dean S. Worth, eds. *Slavic Poetics: Essays in Honor of Kiril Taranovsky*. Slavistic Printings and Reprintings 267. The Hague: Mouton, 1973.

Jurkovič, Tina, ed. *Contemporary Slovenian Literature in Translation*. Translated by Lili Potpara. Llubjana, Slovenia: Študentska založba, 2002.

Mihailovich, Vasa D., comp. and ed. *Modern Slavic Literatures*. New York: F. Ungar, 1972.

Mokrin-Pauer, Vida. *Six Slovenian Poets*. Translated by Ana Jeinika, edited by Brane Mozetič. Todmorden, Lancashire, England: Arc, 2006.

Tschizewskij, Dmitrij. *Comparative History of Slavic*

Literatures. Translated by Richard Noel Porter and Martin P. Rice, edited by Serge A. Zenkovsky. Nashville, Tenn.: Vanderbilt University Press, 1971.

Zawacki, Andrew, ed. *Afterwards: Slovenian Writing, 1945-1995*. Buffalo, N.Y.: White Pine Press, 1999.

SPAIN

Bibliography

Sefami, Jacobo, comp. *Contemporary Spanish American Poets: A Bibliography of Primary and Secondary Sources*. Bibliographies and Indexes in World Literature 33. Westport, Conn.: Greenwood Press, 1992.

Biographical sources

Perna, Michael L., ed. *Twentieth-Century Spanish Poets: First Series*. Dictionary of Literary Biography 108. Detroit: Gale Research, 1991.

Winfield, Jerry Phillips. *Twentieth-Century Spanish Poets: Second Series*. Dictionary of Literary Biography 134. Detroit: Gale Research, 1994.

Dictionaries, histories, and handbooks

Bellver, Catherine G. *Dictionary of the Literature of the Iberian Peninsula*. Cranbury, N.J.: Associated University Presses, 2001.

Florit, Eugenio, ed. *Introduction to Spanish Poetry*. New York: Dover Publications, 1991.

Foster, David Williams, Daniel Altamiranda, and Carmen de Urioste, eds. *Spanish Literature: 1700 to the Present*. Spanish Literature 3. New York: Garland, 2000.

Merwin, W. S., ed. and trans. *Spanish Ballads*. Port Townsend, Wash.: Copper Canyon Press, 2008.

Newmark, Maxim. *Dictionary of Spanish Literature*. Westport, Conn.: Greenwood Press, 1972.

St. Martin, Hardie, ed. *Roots and Wings: Poetry from Spain, 1900-1975*. Buffalo, N.Y.: White Pine Press, 2004.

Walters, Gareth. *The Cambridge Introduction to Spanish Poetry*. New York: Cambridge University Press, 2003.

West-Settle, Cecile, and Sylvia Sherno, eds. *Contemporary Spanish Poetry: The Word and the World*. Madison, N.J.: Fairleigh Dickinson University Press, 2005.

Woodbridge, Hensley Charles. *Guide to Reference Works for the Study of the Spanish Language and Literature and Spanish American Literature*. 2d ed. New York: Modern Language Association of America, 1997.

Women writers

Bellver, Catherine G. *Absence and Presence: Spanish Women Poets of the Twenties and Thirties*. Lewisburg, Pa.: Bucknell University Press, 2001.

Fox, Gwyn. *Subtle Subversions: Reading Golden Age Sonnets by Iberian Women*. Washington, D.C.: Catholic University of America Press, 2008.

McNerny, Kathleen, and Cristina Enriques de Salamanca, eds. *Double Minorities of Spain: A Biobibliographic Guide to Women Writers of the Catalan, Galician, and Basque Countries*. New York: Modern Language Association of America, 1994.

Mudrovic, W. Michael. *Mirror, Mirror on the Page: Identity and Subjectivity in Spanish Women's Poetry, 1975-2000*. Bethlehem, Pa.: Lehigh University Press, 2009.

Pérez, Janet. *Modern and Contemporary Spanish Women Poets*. New York: Prentice Hall International, 1996.

Wilcox, John. *Women Poets of Spain, 1860-1990: Toward a Gynocentric Vision*. Urbana: University of Illinois Press, 1997.

Catalonia

Barkan, Stanley H., ed. *Four Postwar Catalan Poets.* Rev. ed. Translated by David H. Rosenthal. Merrick, N.Y.: Cross-Cultural Communications, 1994.

Crowe, Anna, ed. *Light off Water: Twenty-five Catalan Poems, 1978-2002*. Translated by Iolanda Pelegri. Manchester, England: Carcanet Press, 2007.

Rosenthal, David H. *Postwar Catalan Poetry*. Lewisburg, Pa.: Bucknell University Press, 1991.

SWEDEN

Scobbie, Irene. *Aspects of Modern Swedish Literature*. 2d ed. Norwich, England: Norvik Press, 1999.

Forsås-Scott, Helena. *Swedish Women's Writing, 1850-1995*. Atlantic Highlands, N.J.: Athlone, 1997.

Page, Edita, ed. *The Baltic Quintet: Poems from Estonia, Finland, Latvia, Lithuania, and Sweden*. Hamilton, Ont.: Wolsak and Wynn, 2008.

Sjåvik, Jan. *Historical Dictionary of Scandinavian Literature and Theater*. Lanham, Md.: Scarecrow Press, 2006.

Sumari, Anni, and Nicolaj Stochholm, eds. *The Other Side of Landscape: An Anthology of Contemporary Nordic Poetry*. New York: Slope Editions, 2006.

Warme, Lars G., ed. *A History of Swedish Literature*. Vol. 3 in *A History of Scandinavian Literatures*, edited by Sven H. Rossel. Lincoln: University of Nebraska Press, 1996.

Zuck, Virpi, ed. *Dictionary of Scandinavian Literature*. New York: Greenwood Press, 1990.

Maura Ives; updated by Tracy Irons-Georges

GUIDE TO ONLINE RESOURCES

WEB SITES

The following sites were visited by the editors of Salem Press in 2010. Because URLs change frequently, the accuracy of these addresses cannot be guaranteed; however, long-standing sites, such as those of colleges and universities, national organizations, and government agencies, generally maintain links when their sites are moved.

A Celebration of Women Writers

http://digital.library.upenn.edu/women

This site is an extensive compendium on the contributions of women writers throughout history. The "Local Editions by Authors" and "Local Editions by Category" pages include access to electronic texts of the works of numerous writers. Users can also access biographical and bibliographical information by browsing lists arranged by writers' names, countries of origin, ethnicities, and the centuries in which they lived.

LitWeb

http://litweb.net

LitWeb provides biographies of hundreds of world authors throughout history that can be accessed through an alphabetical listing. The pages about each writer contain a list of his or her works, suggestions for further reading, and illustrations. The site also offers information about past and present winners of major literary prizes.

The Modern Word: Authors of the Libyrinth

http://www.themodernword.com/authors.html

The Modern Word site, although somewhat haphazard in its organization, provides a great deal of critical information about writers. The "Authors of the Libyrinth" page is very useful, linking author's names to essays about them and other resources. The section of the page headed "The Scriptorium" presents "an index of pages featuring writers who have pushed the edges of their medium, combining literary talent with a sense of experimentation to produce some remarkable works of modern literature."

Poetry in Translation

http://poetryintranslation.com

This independent resource provides modern translations of classic texts by famous poets and also provides original poetry and critical works. Visitors can choose from several languages, including English, Spanish, Chinese, Russian, Italian, and Greek. Original text is available as well. Also includes links to further literary resources.

Poetry International Web

http://international.poetryinternationalweb.org

Poetry International Web features information on poets from countries such as Indonesia, Zimbabwe, Iceland, India, Slovenia, Morocco, Albania, Afghanistan, Russia, and Brazil. The site offers news, essays, interviews and discussion, and hundreds of poems, both in their original languages and in English translation.

Poet's Corner

http://theotherpages.org/poems

The Poet's Corner, one of the oldest text resources on the Web, provides access to about seven thousand works of poetry by several hundred different poets from around the world. Indexes are arranged and searchable by title, name of poet, or subject. The site also offers its own resources, including "Faces of the Poets"—a gallery of portraits—and "Lives of the Poets"—a growing collection of biographies.

Voices from the Gaps

http://voices.cla.umn.edu/

Voices from the Gaps is a site of the English Department at the University of Minnesota, dedicated to providing resources on the study of women artists of color, including writers. The site features a comprehensive index searchable by name, and it provides biographical information on each writer or artist and other resources for further study.

Western European Studies

http://wess.lib.byu.edu

The Western European Studies Section of the Association of College and Research Libraries maintains this collection of resources useful to students of Western European history and culture. It also is a good place to find information about non-English-language literature. The site includes separate pages about the literatures and languages of the Netherlands, France, Germany, Iberia, Italy, and Scandinavia, in which users can find links to electronic texts, association Web sites, journals, and other materials, the majority of which are written in the languages of the respective countries.

ELECTRONIC DATABASES

Electronic databases usually do not have their own URLs. Instead, public, college, and university libraries subscribe to these databases, provide links to them on their Web sites, and make them available to library card holders or other specified patrons. Readers can visit library Web sites or ask reference librarians to check on availability.

Bloom's Literary Reference Online

Facts On File publishes this database of thousands of articles by renowned scholar Harold Bloom and other literary critics, examining the lives and works of great writers worldwide. The database also includes information on more than forty-two thousand literary characters, literary topics, themes, movements, and genres, plus video segments about literature. Users can retrieve information by browsing writers' names, titles of works, time periods, genres, or writers' nationalities.

Literary Reference Center

EBSCO's Literary Reference Center (LRC) is a comprehensive full-text database designed primarily to help high school and undergraduate students in English and the humanities with homework and research assignments about literature. The database contains massive amounts of information from reference works, books, literary journals, and other materials, including more than 31,000 plot summaries, synopses, and overviews of literary works; almost 100,000 essays and articles of literary criticism; about 140,000 author biog-

raphies; more than 605,000 book reviews; and more than 5,200 author interviews. It contains the entire contents of Salem Press's MagillOnLiterature Plus. Users can retrieve information by browsing a list of authors' names or titles of literary works; they can also use an advanced search engine to access information by numerous categories, including author name, gender, cultural identity, national identity, and the years in which he or she lived, or by literary title, character, locale, genre, and publication date. The Literary Reference Center also features a literary-historical time line, an encyclopedia of literature, and a glossary of literary terms.

Literary Resource Center

Published by Gale, this comprehensive literary database contains information on the lives and works of more than 130,000 authors in all genres, in all time periods, and throughout the world. In addition, the database offers more than 70,000 full-text critical essays and reviews from some of Gale's reference publications, including *Contemporary Literary Criticism*, *Literature Criticism from 1400-1800*, *Nineteenth-Century Literature Criticism*, and *Twentieth-Century Literary Criticism*; more than 7,000 overviews of frequently studied works; more than 650,000 full-text articles, critical essays, and reviews from about three hundred scholarly journals and literary magazines; more than 4,500 interviews; and about five hundred links to selected Web sites. Users can retrieve information by browsing author name, ethnicity, nationality, and years of birth and death; titles of literary works; genres; selected literary movements or time periods; keywords; and themes of literary works. Literary Resource Center also features a literary-historical time line and an encyclopedia of literature.

MagillOnLiterature Plus

MagillOnLiterature Plus is a comprehensive, integrated literature database produced by Salem Press and available on the EBSCOhost platform. The database contains the full text of essays in Salem's many literature-related reference works, including *Masterplots*, *Cyclopedia of World Authors*, *Cyclopedia of Literary Characters*, *Cyclopedia of Literary Places*, *Critical*

Survey of Poetry, Critical Survey of Long Fiction, Critical Survey of Short Fiction, World Philosophers and Their Works, Magill's Literary Annual, and *Magill's Book Reviews.* Among its contents are articles on more than 35,000 literary works and more than 8,500 poets, writers, dramatists, essayists, and philosophers; more than 1,000 images; and a glossary of more than 1,300 literary terms. The biographical essays include lists of authors' works and secondary bibliographies, and hundreds of overview essays examine and discuss literary genres, time periods, and national literatures.

Rebecca Kuzins; updated by Desiree Dreeuws

TIME LINE

c. 750 B.C.E.	Homer composes the *Iliad* (English translation, 1611), a Greek epic poem that recounts the fall of Troy. This work and Homer's subsequent poem the *Odyssey* (c. 725 B.C.E.; English translation, 1614) will establish the epic poem as a genre in Western literature and will influence European literature and culture for centuries.
c. 700 B.C.E.	The Greek poet Hesiod writes *Erga kai Emerai* (*Works and Days*, 1618), in which the poet instructs his wastrel brother Perses about the virtues of hard work and provides advice about farming techniques.
c. 630 B.C.E.	Sappho, one of the most admired poets of the ancient world, is born on the Greek island of Lesbos.
c. 498-446 B.C.E.	Pindar produces *Epinikia* (*Odes*, 1656), a collection of odes celebrating the victories of athletes in the Panhellenic festival games.
c. 334-323 B.C.E.	Aristotle writes *De poetica* (*Poetics*, 1705), an early work of literary criticism in which he analyzes the essence of poetry and distinguishes its various forms, including the epic, comic, and tragic.
October 15, 70 B.C.E.	Vergil, whom many consider the greatest poet of ancient Rome, is born in Andes, Cisalpine Gaul, near Mantua (now in Italy).
c. 17 B.C.E.	Horace, the premier Roman lyric poet, analyzes the poetic genre in *Ars poetica* (*The Art of Poetry*, 1567), which is included in *Epistles* (c. 20-15 B.C.E., English translation, 1567). Among his literary theories, Horace praises consistency as the highest virtue of poetry and advises poets to carefully choose each word and incident, as well as the meter of their compositions.
c. 8 C.E.	The Roman poet Ovid composes *Metamorphoses* (English translation, 1567), an epic recounting more than two hundred stories from Greek and Roman mythology, legend, and history.
c. 103 C.E.	Martial, the Roman writer who perfected the genre of epigrammatic poetry, dies in Hispania (now in Spain).
ninth-twelfth centuries	Anonymous writers compose the Old Norse poems that are collected in the *Poetic Edda*. These poems are primarily preserved in the Icelandic *Codex Regius*, a manuscript written in the thirteenth century. The *Poetic Edda* is the most important source of information on Norse mythology and Germanic heroic legends.
twelfth century	*Chanson de Roland* (*The Song of Roland*, 1880), the oldest surviving French medieval epic poem, is written. This epic, recounting the defeat of Count Roland, Charlemagne's nephew, by a Saracen army in 877, is one of about one hundred surviving French *chansons de geste* (songs of heroic action).
c. 1200	*Nibelungenlied* (English translation, 1848) is written in Middle High German by an unknown Austrian monk. This epic poem explores Germanic conceptions of the true values of knighthood.
early thirteenth century	The oldest surviving Spanish epic poem, *Cantar de mío Cid* (*Chronicle of the Cid*, 1846), is composed. This work describes the exploits of the Spanish hero El Cid.

July 20, 1304	Petrarch is born in Arezzo, Tuscany (now in Italy). His work will include vernacular poems in which he celebrates his everlasting love for a woman named Laura.
c. 1320	Dante creates his masterpiece, the three-volume *La divina commedia* (*The Divine Comedy*, 1802). This work describes the poet's journey through the three realms of the Christian otherworld—Hell, Purgatory, and Paradise.
1572	*Os Lusíadas* (*The Lusiads*, 1655), Luís de Camões's epic poem about Portugal's expansion, is published.
1770	Johann Wolfgang von Goethe publishes *Neue Lieder* (*New Poems*, 1853), his first volume of poetry. In his lyric poetry, Goethe mastered the use of diverse meters, techniques, and styles as had no other German writer before him.
1800	German writer Friedrich Schiller composes his best-known poem, "Das Lied von der Glocke" ("The Song of the Bell"), a philosophical ballad in which he projects humankind's mortal existence against the background of the bell's creation.
1820	*Méditations poétiques* (*Poetical Meditations*, 1839), by Alphonse de Lamartine, hailed as the first masterpiece of French Romantic poetry, is published.
1827	*Buch der Lieder* (*Book of Songs*, 1856), by the German poet Heinrich Heine, is published. The most controversial poet of his time, Heine is renowned for his love poetry.
1831	French Romantic poet Victor Hugo attains lyrical maturity with the publication of *Les Feuilles d'automne*, in which he treats themes of childhood, nature, and love.
1857	The first edition of French poet Charles Baudelaire's *Les Fleurs du mal* (*Flowers of Evil*, 1931) is published. The poems in this collection are characterized by their bold metaphors and bizarre juxtapositions of beauty and ugliness.
1873	*Une Saison en enfer* (*A Season in Hell*, 1932), by Arthur Rimbaud, is published. Rimbaud will become one of the most influential of the French Symbolist poets.
1876	*L'Après-midi d'un faune* (*The Afternoon of a Faun*, 1936), by French Symbolist poet Stéphane Mallarmé, is published. Mallarmé's work influenced younger poets, who hailed him as an exemplar of Symbolism.
1877	Jacint Verdaguer publishes *La Atlántida*, written in the Catalan language. Verdaguer's works exemplify the religious, patriotic, and epic characteristics of the nineteenth century Renaixença, a period of rebirth for Catalan literature and art.
1913	*Alcools: Poèmes, 1898-1913* (*Alcools: Poems, 1898-1913*, 1964), by Guilluame Apollinaire, is published. Apollinaire was one of the first French poets to describe the discontinuity and disorientation of modern society.
August 19, 1936	Federico García Lorca is executed by members of the Spanish fascist party during the Spanish Civil War. His poetry is characterized by startling images and metaphors drawn from traditional Spanish culture.
1951	Gottfried Benn receives the Georg Büchner Prize, the most important literary prize in Germany.
1956	Spanish poet Juan Ramón Jiménez is awarded the Nobel Prize in Literature.
1963	Hans Magnus Enzensberger receives the Georg Büchner Prize, the most important literary prize in Germany.

1966	German-born poet Nelly Sachs is awarded the Nobel Prize in Literature.
1976	Jorge Guillén receives the Miguel de Cervantes Prize, which honors the lifetime achievement of an outstanding writer in the Spanish language.
1980	Polish writer Czesław Miłosz is awarded the Nobel Prize in Literature.
1986	Yves Bonnefoy is awarded the Goncourt Prize in Poetry by the Goncourt Literary Society of France.

Rebecca Kuzins

Major Awards

Adonais Prize for Poetry

The Adonais Prize for Poetry, or Premio Adonáis de Poesía, is awarded annually in Spain to an unpublished Spanish-language poem from any country. Created in 1943 by the publishing house Biblioteca Hispánica, the prize was placed in the hands of Ediciones RIALP in 1946.

1943: José Suárez Carreño (Spain)—"Edad del hombre"; Vicente Gaos (Spain)—"Arcángel de mi noche"; Alfonso Moreno (Spain)—"El vuelo de la carne"

1944: no award

1945: no award

1946: no award

1947: José Hierro (Spain)—"Alegría"

1948: no award

1949: Ricardo Molina (Spain)—"Corimbo"

1950: José García Nieto (Spain)—"Dama de soledad"

1951: Lorenzo Gomis (Spain)—"El caballo"

1952: Antonio Fernández Spencer (Dominican Republic)—"Bajo la luz del día"

1953: Claudio Rodríguez (Spain)—"Don de la ebriedad"

1954: José Angel Valente (Spain)—"A modo de esperanza"

1955: Javier de Bengoechea (Spain)—"Hombre en forma de elegía"

1956: María Elvira Lacaci (Spain)—"Humana voz"

1957: Carlos Sahagún (Spain)—"Profecías del agua"

1958: Rafael Soto Verges (Spain)—"La agorera"

1959: Francisco Brines (Spain)—"Las brasas"

1960: Mariano Roldán (Spain)—"Hombre nuevo"

1961: Luis Feria (Spain)—"Conciencia"

1962: Jesús Hilario Tundidor (Spain)—"Junto a mi silencio"

1963: Félix Grande (Spain)—"Las piedras"

1964: Diego Jesús Jiménez (Spain)—"La ciudad"

1965: Joaquín Caro Romero (Spain)—"El tiempo en el espejo"

1966: Miguel Fernández (Spain)—"Sagrada materia"

1967: Joaquín Benito de Lucas (Spain)—"Materia de olvido"

1968: Roberto Sosa (Honduras)—"Los pobres"

1969: Angel García López (Spain)—"A flor de piel"

1970: Pureza Canelo (Spain)—"Lugar común"

1971: José Infante (Spain)—"Elegía y no"

1972: José Luis Alegre Cudos (Spain)—"Abstracción de Mío Cid con Cid Mío"

1973: José Antonio Moreno Jurado (Spain)—"Ditirambos para mi propia burla"

1974: Julia Castillo (Spain)—"Urgencias de un río interior"

1975: Angel Sánchez Pascual (Spain)—"Ceremonia de la inocencia"

1976: Jorge G. Aranguren (Spain)—"De fuegos, tigres, ríos"

1977: Eloy Sánchez Rosillo (Spain)—"Maneras de estar solo"

1978: Arcadio López-Casanova (Spain)—"La oscura potestad"

1979: Laureano Albán (Costa Rica)—"Herencia del otoño"

1980: Blanca Andreu (Spain)—"De una niña de provincias que vino a vivir en un Chagal"

1981: Miguel Velasco (Spain)—"Las berlinas del sueño"

1982: Luis García Montero (Spain)—"El jardín extranjero"

1983: Javier Peñas Navarro (Spain)—"Adjetivos sin agua, adjetivos con agua"

1984: Amalia Iglesias Serna (Spain)—"Un lugar para el fuego"

1985: Juan Carlos Mestre (Spain)—"Antífona de otoño en el valle del Bierzo"

1986: Juan María Calles (Spain)—"Silencio celeste"

1987: Francisco Serradilla (Spain)—"El bosque insobornable"

1988: Miguel Sánchez Gatell (Spain)—"La soledad absoluta de la tierra"

1989: Juan Carlos Marset (Spain)—"Puer profeta"

1990: Diego Doncel (Spain)—"El único umbral"

1991: Jesús Javier Lázaro Puebla (Spain)—"Canción para una amazona dormida"

1992: Juan Antonio Marín Alba (Spain)—"El horizonte de la noche"

1993: María Luisa Mora Alameda (Spain)—"Busca y captura"

1994: Ana Merino (Spain)—"Preparativos para un viaje"

1995: Eduardo Moga (Spain)—"La luz oída"

1996: Rosario Neira (Spain)—"No somos ángeles"

1997: Luis Martínez-Falero (Spain)—"Plenitud de la materia"

1998: Luis Enrique Belmonte (Venezuela)—"Inútil registro"

1999: Irene Sánchez Carrón (Spain)—"Escenas principales de actor secundario"

2000: Joaquín Pérez Azaústre (Spain)—"Una interpretación"

2001: José Antonio Gómez-Coronado (Spain)—"El triunfo de los días"

2002: Adrián González da Costa (Spain)—"Rua dos douradores"

2003: Javier Vela (Spain)—"La hora del crepúsculo"

2004: José Martínez Ros (Spain)—"La enfermedad"

2005: Carlos Vaquerizo (Spain)—"Fiera venganza del tiempo"

2006: Jorge Galán (pseudonym of George Alexander Portillo; El Salvador)—"Breve historia del Alba"

2007: Teresa Soto González (Spain)—"Un poemario (Imitación de Wislawa)"

2008: Rogelio Guedea (Mexico)—"Kora"

2009: Rubén Martín Díaz (Spain)—"El minuto interior"

GEORG BÜCHNER PRIZE

Given yearly by the Deutsche Akademie für Sprache und Dichtung to German-language authors, the Georg Büchner Prize is the most important literary prize in Germany. Created in 1923 to be given to visual artists, poets, actors, and singers, in 1951 it became a general literary prize. The list below includes only poets who have received the award.

1929: Carl Zuckmayer

1932: Albert H. Rausch

1945: Hans Schiebelhuth

1946: Fritz Usinger

1948: Hermann Heiss

1950: Elisabeth Langgässer

1951: Gottfried Benn

1954: Martin Kessel

1955: Marie Luise Kaschnitz

1956: Karl Krolow

1957: Erich Kästner

1959: Günter Eich

1960: Paul Celan

1963: Hans Magnus Enzensberger

1964: Ingeborg Bachmann

1965: Günter Grass

1969: Helmut Heissenbüttel

1970: Thomas Bernhard

1976: Heinz Piontek

1977: Reiner Kunze

1979: Ernst Meister (posthumous)

1984: Ernst Jandl

1985: Heiner Müller

1987: Erich Fried

1991: Wolf Biermann

1993: Peter Rühmkorf

1995: Durs Grünbein

1996: Sarah Kirsch

1997: Hans Carl Artmann

2000: Volker Braun

2001: Friederike Mayröcker

2002: Wolfgang Hilbig

2006: Oskar Pastior (posthumous)

MIGUEL DE CERVANTES PRIZE

Spain's ministry of culture awards its prize to honor the lifetime achievement of an outstanding writer in the Spanish language. Recipients, nominated by the language academies of Spanish-speaking countries, can be of any nationality. The list below includes only poets who have received the award.

1976: Jorge Guillén (Spain)
1978: Dámaso Alonso (Spain)
1979: Jorge Luis Borges (Argentina) and Gerardo Diego (Spain)
1981: Octavio Paz (Mexico)
1982: Luis Rosales (Spain)
1983: Rafael Alberti (Spain)
1990: Adolfo Bioy Casares (Argentina)
1992: Dulce María Loynaz (Cuba)

1996: José García Nieto (Spain)
1998: José Hierro (Spain)
2001: Álvaro Mutis (Colombia)
2002: José Jiménez Lozano (Spain)
2003: Gonzalo Rojas (Chile)
2005: Sergio Pitol (Mexico)
2006: Antonio Gamoneda (Spain)
2007: Juan Gelman (Argentina)
2009: José Emilio Pacheco (Mexico)

FLAIANO PRIZE

The Flaiano Prize (Premio Flaiano) is an Italian international award recognizing achievement in the fields of theater, cinema, television, and literature (novels, poetry, and literary criticism). Below are the winners of the Poetry Prize.

1986: Maria Luisa Spaziani
1987: Luciano Luisi
1988: Elio Filippo Accrocca
1989: Pietro Cimatti, Vivian Lamarque, Benito Sablone
1990: Edoardo Albinati, Dario Bellezza, Vico Faggi
1991: Renzo Barsacchi, Isabella Scalfaro, Massimo Scrignòli
1992: Marco Guzzi, Luciano Roncalli, Mario Trufelli
1993: Attilio Bertolucci, Cesare Vivaldi

1994: Piero Bigongiari
1995: Seamus Heaney
1996: Yves Bonnefoy
1997: Miroslav Holub
1998: Lawrence Ferlinghetti
1999: Yang Lian
2000: Derek Walcott
2001: Charles Tomlinson
2002: Adonis

GOLDEN WREATH AWARD

Struga Poetry Evenings, a major international poetry festival in Macedonia, presents its award to living poets for lifetime achievement.

1966: Robert Rozhdestvensky (Soviet Union)
1967: Bulat Okudzhava (Soviet Union)
1968: László Nagy (Hungary)
1969: Mak Dizdar (Bosnia and Herzegovina)
1970: Miodrag Pavlović (Serbia)
1971: W. H. Auden (United States)
1972: Pablo Neruda (Chile)

1973: Eugenio Montale (Italy)
1974: Fazıl Hüsnü Dağlarca (Turkey)
1975: Léopold Senghor (Senegal)
1976: Eugène Guillevic (France)
1977: Artur Lundkvist (Sweden)
1978: Rafael Alberti (Spain)
1979: Miroslav Krleža (Croatia)

1980: Hans Magnus Enzensberger (Germany)
1981: Blaže Koneski (Macedonia)
1982: Nichita Stănescu (Romania)
1983: Sachchidananda Hirananda Vatsyayan Agyey
    (India)
1984: Andrey Voznesensky (Soviet Union)
1985: Yannis Ritsos (Greece)
1986: Allen Ginsberg (United States)
1987: Tadeusz Różewicz (Poland)
1988: Desanka Maksimović (Serbia)
1989: Thomas W. Shapcott (Australia)
1990: Justo Jorge Padrón (Spain)
1991: Joseph Brodsky (United States)
1992: Ferenc Juhász (Hungary)
1993: Gennadiy Aygi (Chuvash Republic)
1994: Ted Hughes (England)

1995: Yehuda Amichai (Israel)
1996: Makoto Ooka (Japan)
1997: Adunis (Syria)
1998: Lu Yuan (China)
1999: Yves Bonnefoy (France)
2000: Edoardo Sanguineti (Italy)
2001: Seamus Heaney (Northern Ireland)
2002: Slavko Mihalić (Croatia)
2003: Tomas Tranströmer (Sweden)
2004: Vasco Graça Moura (Portugal)
2005: W. S. Merwin (United States)
2006: Nancy Morejón (Cuba)
2007: Mahmoud Darwish (Palestine)
2008: Fatos Arapi (Albania)
2009: Tomaž Šalamun (Slovenia)
2010: Ljabomir Levčev (Bulgaria)

GONCOURT PRIZE IN POETRY

The Goncourt Literary Society of France, also known as the Goncourt Academy, has awarded its prize in poetry since 1985.

1985: Claude Roy
1986: Yves Bonnefoy
1987: no award
1988: Eugène Guillevic
1989: Alain Bosquet
1990: Charles Le Quintrec
1991: Jean-Claude Renard
1992: Georges-Emmanuel Clancier
1993: no award
1994: no award
1995: Lionel Ray
1996: André Velter
1997: Maurice Chappaz

1998: Lorand Gaspar
1999: Jacques Réda
2000: Liliane Wouters
2001: Claude Esteban
2002: Andrée Chedid
2003: Philippe Jaccottet
2004: Jacques Chessex
2005: Charles Dobzynski
2006: Alain Jouffroy
2007: Marc Alyn
2008: Claude Vigée
2009: Abdellatif Laabi

NEUSTADT INTERNATIONAL PRIZE FOR LITERATURE

Awarded biennially since 1970, this award sponsored by the University of Oklahoma honors writers for a body of work. The list below includes only poets who have received the award.

1970: Giuseppe Ungaretti (Italy)
1974: Francis Ponge (France)
1976: Elizabeth Bishop (United States)

1978: Czesław Miłosz (Poland)
1980: Josef Škvorecky (Czechoslovakia/Canada)
1982: Octavio Paz (Mexico)

1984: Paavo Haavikko (Finland)
1990: Tomas Tranströmer (Sweden)
1992: João Cabral de Melo Neto (Brazil)
1994: Edward Kamau Brathwaite (Barbados)
2000: David Malouf (Australia)

2002: Alvaro Mutis (Colombia)
2004: Adam Zagajewski (Poland)
2006: Claribel Alegría (Nicaragua/El Salvador)
2010: Duo Duo (China)

NIKE AWARD

Established in 1997 and sponsored by the Polish newspaper Gazeta Wyborcza *and the consulting company NICOM, the NIKE Literary Award (Nagroda Literacka NIKE) is given to the best book by a single living author writing in Polish published the previous year. It is open to works in all literary genres. Only poetry collections that have received the jury award are listed below:*

1998: Czesław Miłosz—*Piesek przydrożny* (*Road-side Dog*)
1999: Stanisław Barańczak—*Chirurgiczna precyzja* (surgical precision)
2000: Tadeusz Różewicz—*Matka odchodzi* (mother is leaving)

2003: Jarosław Marek Rymkiewicz—*Zachód słonca w Milanówku* (sunset in Milanówek)
2009: Eugeniusz Tkaczyszyn—*Dycki for Piosenka o zaleznosciach i uzaleznieniach* (song of dependency and addiction)

NOBEL PRIZE IN LITERATURE

Awarded annually since 1901, this prize is given to an author for his or her entire body of literary work. The list below includes only the poets who have been so honored.

1901: Sully Prudhomme
1906: Giosuè Carducci
1907: Rudyard Kipling
1913: Rabindranath Tagore
1923: William Butler Yeats
1945: Gabriela Mistral
1946: Hermann Hesse
1948: T. S. Eliot
1956: Juan Ramón Jiménez
1958: Boris Pasternak
1959: Salvatore Quasimodo
1960: Saint-John Perse
1963: George Seferis
1966: Nelly Sachs
1969: Samuel Beckett

1971: Pablo Neruda
1974: Harry Martinson
1975: Eugenio Montale
1977: Vicente Aleixandre
1979: Odysseus Elytis
1980: Czesław Miłosz
1984: Jaroslav Seifert
1986: Wole Soyinka
1987: Joseph Brodsky
1990: Octavio Paz
1992: Derek Walcott
1995: Seamus Heaney
1996: Wisława Szymborska
2005: Harold Pinter
2009: Herta Müller

TIN UJEVIĆ AWARD

The Tin Ujević Award is an award given for contributions to Croatian poetry. Founded in 1980 and awarded by the Croatian Writers' Society, it is considered the most prestigious such award in Croatia.

1981: Nikica Petrak—"Tiha knjiga"
1982: Slavko Mihalić—"Pohvala praznom džepu"
1983: Irena Vrkljan—"U koži moje sestre"
1984: Nikola Milićević—"Nepovrat"
1985: Branimir Bošnjak—"Semanti ka gladovanja"
1986: Igor Zidić—"Strijela od stakla"
1987: Dragutin Tadijanović—"Kruh svagdanji"
1988: Tonko Maroević—"Trag roga ne bez vraga"
1989: Tonći Petrasov Marović—"Moći ne govoriti"
1990: Luko Paljetak—"Snižena vrata"
1991: Vlado Gotovac—"Crna kazaljka"
1992: Zvonimir Golob—"Rana"
1993: Mate Ganza—"Knjiga bdjenja"
1994: Dražen Katunarić—"Nebo/Zemlja"
1995: Vladimir Pavlović—"Gral"

1996: Dubravko Horvatić—"Ratnoa noć"
1997: Boris Domagoj Biletić—"Radovi na nekropoli"
1998: Gordana Benić—"Laterna magica"
1999: Andrijana Škunca—"Novaljski svjetlopis"
2000: Mario Suško—"Versus axsul"
2001: Ivan Slamnig—"Ranjeni tenk" (posthumous)
2002: Petar Gudelj—"Po zraku i po vodi"
2003: Vesna Parun—"Suze putuju"
2004: Alojzije Majetić—"Odmicanje pau ine"
2005: Borben Vladović—"Tijat"
2006: Željko Knežević—"Kopito trajnoga konja"
2007: Ante Stamać—"Vrijeme, vrijeme"
2008: Miroslav Slavko Mađer—"Stihovi dugih naziva"
2009: Tomislav Marijan Bilosnić—"Molitve"

Chronological List of Poets

This chronology of the poets covered in these volumes serves as a time line for students interested in the development of poetry in Europe from the eighth century B.C.E. to modern times. The arrangement is chronological on the basis of birth years, and the proximity of writers provides students with some insights into potential influences and contemporaneous developments.

Born before 1000

Homer (c. early eighth century B.C.E.)
Hesiod (fl. c. 700 B.C.E.)
Theognis (c. seventh century B.C.E.)
Archilochus (c. 680 B.C.E.)
Sappho (c. 630 B.C.E.)
Anacreon (c. 571 B.C.E.)
Pindar (c. 518 B.C.E.)
Theocritus (c. 308 B.C.E.)
Leonidas of Tarentum (fl. early third century B.C.E.)
Apollonius Rhodius (between 295 and 260 B.C.E.)
Meleager (c. 140 B.C.E.)
Lucretius (c. 98 B.C.E.)
Catullus (c. 85 B.C.E.)
Vergil (October 15, 70 B.C.E.)
Horace (December 8, 65 B.C.E.)
Propertius, Sextus (c. 57-48 B.C.E.)
Ovid (March 20, 43 B.C.E.)
Persius (December 4, 34 C.E.)
Martial (March 1, c. 38-41 C.E.)
Lucan (November 3, 39 C.E.)
Statius (between 40 and 45 C.E.)
Juvenal (c. 60 C.E.)
Callimachus (c. 305)

Born 1001-1400

Judah ha-Levi (c. 1075)
Marie de France (c. 1150)
Hartmann von Aue (c. 1160- 1165)
Walther von der Vogelweide (c. 1170)
Wolfram von Eschenbach (c. 1170)
Gottfried von Strassburg (flourished c. 1210)
Guillaume de Lorris (c. 1215)
Cavalcanti, Guido (c. 1259)
Dante (May or June, 1265)
Petrarch (July 20, 1304)

Boccaccio, Giovanni (June or July, 1313)
Christine de Pizan (c. 1365)
Chartier, Alain (c. 1385)
Charles d'Orléans (November 24, 1394)

Born 1401-1700

Villon, François (1431)
Manrique, Jorge (c. 1440)
Boiardo, Matteo Maria (May, 1440 or 1441)
Poliziano (July 14, 1454)
Bembo, Pietro (May 20, 1470)
Ariosto, Ludovico (September 8, 1474)
Michelangelo (March 6, 1475)
Fracastoro, Girolamo (c. 1478)
Garcilaso de la Vega (1501)
Du Bellay, Joachim (c. 1522)
Stampa, Gaspara (c. 1523)
Camões, Luís de (c. 1524)
Ronsard, Pierre de (September 11, 1524)
León, Luis de (1527)
John of the Cross, Saint (June 24, 1542)
Tasso, Torquato (March 11, 1544)
Malherbe, François de (1555)
Góngora y Argote, Luis de (July 11, 1561)
Vega Carpio, Lope de (November 25, 1562)
Marino, Giambattista (October 18, 1569)
Calderón de la Barca, Pedro (January 17, 1600)
La Fontaine, Jean de (July 8, 1621)
Boileau-Despréaux, Nicolas (November 11, 1636)

Born 1701-1800

Goethe, Johann Wolfgang von (August 28, 1749)
Schiller, Friedrich (November 10, 1759)
Hölderlin, Friedrich (March 20, 1770)
Novalis (May 2, 1772)
Foscolo, Ugo (February 6, 1778)

Tegnér, Esaias (November 13, 1782)
Manzoni, Alessandro (March 7, 1785)
Eichendorff, Joseph von (March 10, 1788)
Lamartine, Alphonse de (October 21, 1790)
Vigny, Alfred de (March 27, 1797)
Heine, Heinrich (December 13, 1797)
Solomos, Dionysios (April 8, 1798)
Leopardi, Giacomo (June 29, 1798)
Mickiewicz, Adam (December 24, 1798)
Vörösmarty, Mihály (December 1, 1800)

BORN 1801-1850

Hugo, Victor (February 26, 1802)
Lönnrot, Elias (April 9, 1802)
Mörike, Eduard (September 8, 1804)
Nerval, Gérard de (May 22, 1808)
Giusti, Giuseppe (May 12, 1809)
Słowacki, Juliusz (September 4, 1809)
Musset, Alfred de (December 11, 1810)
Gautier, Théophile (August 30, 1811)
Arany, János (March 2, 1817)
Baudelaire, Charles (April 9, 1821)
Petőfi, Sándor (January 1, 1823)
Gezelle, Guido (May 1, 1830)
Carducci, Giosuè (July 27, 1835)
Bécquer, Gustavo Adolfo (February 17, 1836)
Castro, Rosalía de (February 24, 1837)
Mallarmé, Stéphane (March 18, 1842)
Verlaine, Paul (March 30, 1844)
Corbière, Tristan (July 18, 1845)

BORN 1851-1875

Rimbaud, Arthur (October 20, 1854)
Verhaeren, Émile (May 21, 1855)
Pascoli, Giovanni (December 31, 1855)
Laforgue, Jules (August 16, 1860)
D'Annunzio, Gabriele (March 12, 1863)
Cavafy, Constantine P. (April 17, 1863)
Holz, Arno (April 26, 1863)
Unamuno y Jugo, Miguel de (September 29, 1864)
George, Stefan (July 12, 1868)
Claudel, Paul (August 6, 1868)
Dučić, Jovan (February 5, 1871)
Morgenstern, Christian (May 6, 1871)
Valéry, Paul (October 30, 1871)

Péguy, Charles-Pierre (January 7, 1873)
Hofmannsthal, Hugo von (February 1, 1874)
Kraus, Karl (April 28, 1874)
Machado, Antonio (July 26, 1875)
Rilke, Rainer Maria (December 4, 1875)

BORN 1876-1900

Hesse, Hermann (July 2, 1877)
Ady, Endre (November 22, 1877)
Apollinaire, Guillaume (August 26, 1880)
Zweig, Stefan (November 28, 1881)
Jiménez, Juan Ramón (December 23, 1881)
Kazantzakis, Nikos (February 18, 1883)
Saba, Umberto (March 9, 1883)
Babits, Mihály (November 26, 1883)
Benn, Gottfried (May 2, 1886)
Trakl, Georg (February 3, 1887)
Perse, Saint-John (May 31, 1887)
Arp, Hans (September 16, 1887)
Ungaretti, Giuseppe (February 8, 1888)
Pessoa, Fernando (June 13, 1888)
Cocteau, Jean (July 5, 1889)
Reverdy, Pierre (September 13, 1889)
Salinas, Pedro (November 27, 1891)
Sachs, Nelly (December 10, 1891)
Södergran, Edith (April 4, 1892)
Guillén, Jorge (January 18, 1893)
Foix, J. V. (January 28, 1893)
Słonimski, Antoni (November 15, 1895)
Éluard, Paul (December 14, 1895)
Breton, André (February 19, 1896)
Tzara, Tristan (April 4, 1896)
Montale, Eugenio (October 12, 1896)
Aragon, Louis (October 3, 1897)
Brecht, Bertolt (February 10, 1898)
Aleixandre, Vicente (April 26, 1898)
García Lorca, Federico (June 5, 1898)
Ponge, Francis (March 27, 1899)
Michaux, Henri (May 24, 1899)
Seferis, George (March 13, 1900)
Prévert, Jacques (February 4, 1900)

BORN 1901-1920

Manger, Itzik (May 28, 1901)
Quasimodo, Salvatore (August 20, 1901)

Seifert, Jaroslav (September 23, 1901)

Cernuda, Luis (September 21, 1902)

Illyés, Gyula (November 2, 1902)

Alberti, Rafael (December 16, 1902)

Follain, Jean (August 29, 1903)

Martinson, Harry (May 6, 1904)

Ważyk, Adam (November 17, 1905)

Hein, Piet (December 16, 1905)

Beckett, Samuel (April 13, 1906)

Char, René (June 14, 1907)

Ekelöf, Gunnar (September 15, 1907)

Pavese, Cesare (September 9, 1908)

Pentzikis, Nikos (October 30, 1908)

Swir, Anna (February 7, 1909)

Radnóti, Miklós (May 5, 1909)

Ritsos, Yannis (May 14, 1909)

Miłosz, Czesław (June 30, 1911)

Elytis, Odysseus (November 2, 1911)

Otero, Blas de (March 15, 1916)

Bobrowski, Johannes (April 9, 1917)

Celan, Paul (November 23, 1920)

BORN 1921 AND AFTER

Różewicz, Tadeusz (October 9, 1921)

Pasolini, Pier Paolo (March 5, 1922)

Popa, Vasko (July 29, 1922)

Bonnefoy, Yves (June 24, 1923)

Szymborska, Wisława (July 2, 1923)

Holub, Miroslav (September 13, 1923)

Herbert, Zbigniew (October 29, 1924)

Gomringer, Eugen (January 20, 1925)

Bachmann, Ingeborg (June 25, 1926)

Grass, Günter (October 16, 1927)

Pavlović, Miodrag (November 28, 1928)

Enzensberger, Hans Magnus (November 11, 1929)

Haavikko, Paavo (January 25, 1931)

Bernhard, Thomas (February 10, 1931)

Tranströmer, Tomas (April 15, 1931)

Kunze, Reiner (August 16, 1933)

Biermann, Wolf (November 15, 1936)

Breytenbach, Breyten (September 16, 1939)

Zagajewski, Adam (April 21, 1945)

Barańczak, Stanisław (November 13, 1946)

INDEXES

GEOGRAPHICAL INDEX OF POETS

CATEGORIZED INDEX OF POETS

The Categorized Index of Poets covers three primary subject areas: Culture/Group Identities, Historical Periods/Literary Movements, and Poetic Forms and Themes.

Cultural/Group Identities

Historical Periods/Literary Movements

Poetic Forms and Themes

AESTHETIC POETS

Baudelaire, Charles, 80
Gautier, Théophile, 368
George, Stefan, 377
Goethe, Johann Wolfgang von, 396
Schiller, Friedrich, 949

AGE OF GOETHE. *See* GOETHE, AGE OF

ALEXANDRIAN POETS

Apollonius Rhodius, 30
Callimachus, 175
Leonidas of Tarentum, 602
Theocritus, 1023

AUGUSTAN AGE, ROMAN

Horace, 510
Ovid, 763
Propertius, Sextus, 866
Vergil, 1080

AVANT-GARDE POETS

Apollinaire, Guillaume, 22
Aragon, Louis, 35
Breton, André, 157
Celan, Paul, 214
Cocteau, Jean, 253
Ekelöf, Gunnar, 306
Foix, J. V., 329

Herbert, Zbigniew, 458
Laforgue, Jules, 584
Mallarmé, Stéphane, 644
Reverdy, Pierre, 883
Seifert, Jaroslav, 961
Tzara, Tristan, 1044
Ważyk, Adam, 1126

BALLADS

Arany, János, 42
Biermann, Wolf, 119
Cavalcanti, Guido, 210
García Lorca, Federico, 355
Goethe, Johann Wolfgang von, 396
Jiménez, Juan Ramón, 533
Manger, Itzik, 650
Schiller, Friedrich, 949
Słonimski, Antoni, 968
Tasso, Torquato, 1014
Villon, François, 1106

CHILDREN'S/YOUNG ADULT POETRY

La Fontaine, Jean de, 577
Seifert, Jaroslav, 961

CLASSICISM: SEVENTEENTH AND EIGHTEENTH CENTURIES

La Fontaine, Jean de, 577

CLASSICISM: NINETEENTH CENTURY

Carducci, Giosuè, 185
Hölderlin, Friedrich, 485
Mickiewicz, Adam, 702
Musset, Alfred de, 736
Vörösmarty, Mihály, 1112

CLASSICISM: TWENTIETH CENTURY

Martinson, Harry, 681

CONCRETE POETRY

Apollinaire, Guillaume, 22
Gomringer, Eugen, 405

CUBISM

Apollinaire, Guillaume, 22
Cocteau, Jean, 253
Reverdy, Pierre, 883
Ważyk, Adam, 1126

DADAISM

Aragon, Louis, 35
Arp, Hans, 62

Critical Survey of Poetry Series: Master List of Contents

The *Critical Survey of Poetry, Fourth Edition, profiles more than eight hundred poets in four subsets:* American Poets; *British, Irish, and Commonwealth Poets;* European Poets; *and* World Poets. *Although some individuals could have been included in more than one subset, each poet appears in only one subset. A fifth subset,* Topical Essays, *includes more than seventy overviews covering geographical areas, historical periods, movements, and critical approaches.*

AMERICAN POETS

BRITISH, IRISH, AND COMMONWEALTH POETS

EUROPEAN POETS

WORLD POETS

TOPICAL ESSAYS

CUMULATIVE INDEXES

SUBJECT INDEX

All personages whose names appear in **boldface type** in this index are the subject of articles in *Critical Survey of Poetry, Fourth Edition.*